INTERIORS

AN INTRODUCTION

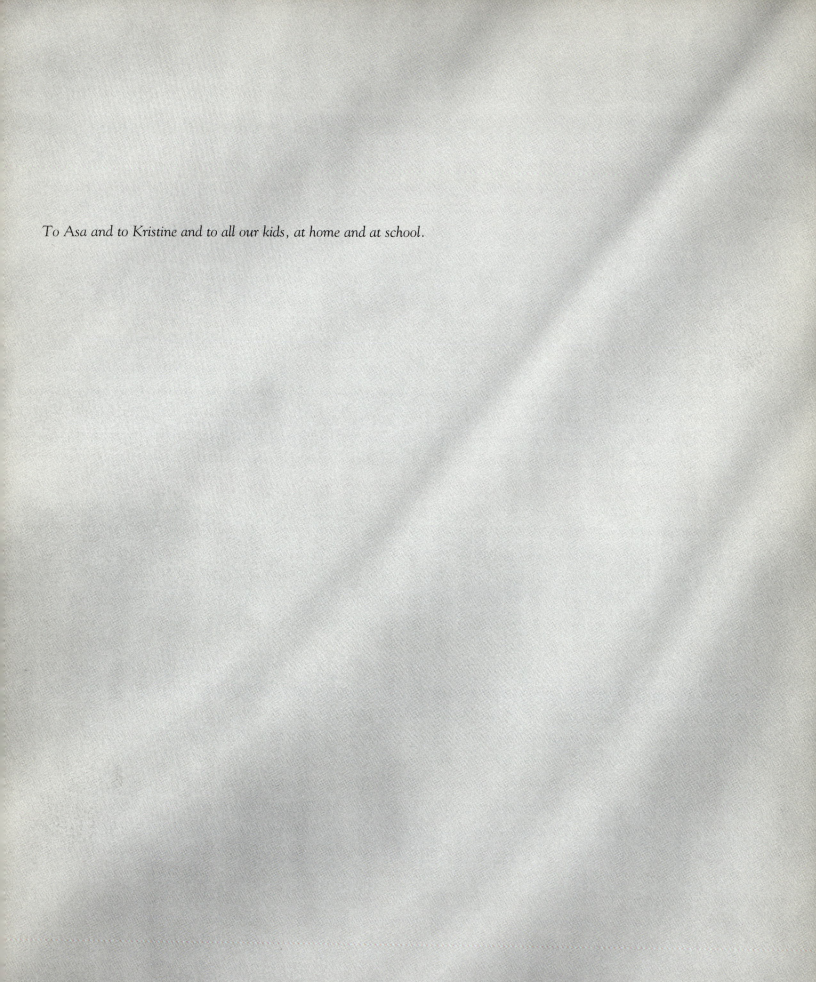

To Asa and to Kristine and to all our kids, at home and at school.

second edition

INTERIORS

AN INTRODUCTION

Karla J. Nielson
BRIGHAM YOUNG UNIVERSITY

David A. Taylor
BRIGHAM YOUNG UNIVERSITY

Boston, Massachusetts   Burr Ridge, Illinios   Dubuque, Iowa
Madison, Wisconsin   New York, New York   San Francisco, California   St. Louis, Missouri

McGraw·Hill

A Division of The **McGraw·Hill** *Companies*

Book Team

Associate Publisher *Rosemary Bradley*
Developmental Editor *Deborah Reinbold*
Production Editor *Ann Fuerste*
Designer *Christopher E. Reese*
Art Editor *Carla Goldhammer*
Photo Editor *Shirley M. Lanners*
Visuals/Design Developmental Consultant *Marilyn A. Phelps*
Visuals/Design Freelance Specialist *Mary L. Christianson*
Marketing Manager *Elizabeth Haefele*
Advertising Coordinator *Colleen Howes*

Executive Vice President/General Manager *Thomas E. Doran*
Vice President/Editor in Chief *Edgar J. Laube*
Vice President/Sales and Marketing *Eric Ziegler*
Director of Production *Vickie Putman Caughron*
Director of Custom and Electronic Publishing *Chris Rogers*

President and Chief Executive Officer *G. Franklin Lewis*
Corporate Senior Vice President and Chief Financial Officer *Robert Chesterman*
Corporate Senior Vice President and President of Manufacturing *Roger Meyer*

Cover photos © Jessie Walker

Copyedited by Moria Urich

Library of Congress Catalog Card Number: 93-74636

ISBN 0-697-12543-2

Printed in the United States of America

10 9 8 7 6

C O N T E N T S

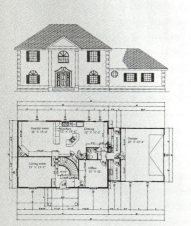

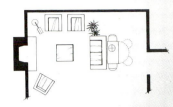

CONTENTS

CHAPTER 9

ARCHITECTURAL DETAIL 171

CHAPTER 10

WALL, CEILING, AND WINDOW TREATMENTS 189

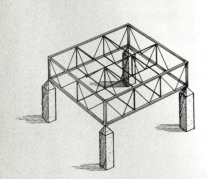

CHAPTER 15

HISTORIC DESIGN 309

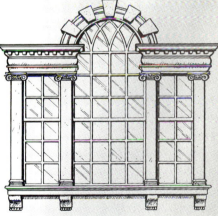

CHAPTER 16

THE PROFESSION 369

Interiors: An Introduction is a beginning point for a lifetime of design education, appreciation, and enjoyment. The fact that you now hold this book in your hand indicates that to some degree, interior design is a value to you. That value is like a seed that needs to be nourished and cultivated with knowledge, training, and experience. As design awareness grows and matures, we see our world with fresh new eyes. Life can be richer and better for this effort, and that is the real value of studying interior design. From this book, a deeper appreciation and understanding of interior design may be obtained. It is a complex and intriguing subject, yet one in which personal satisfaction and enrichment are available to all who seek and study.

Interiors is a book for the beginning college or university student of interior design and for all who wish to acquaint themselves with the foundation of the major aspects of interior design. As such, the goals of this book are threefold:

1. To introduce a philosophy of and encourage an appreciation of fine design wherever and whenever it is found
2. To present the timeless design principles and elements and their application to interiors
3. To make the student aware of the numerous choices of materials, furnishings, and components that are used in interior design

Because the main emphasis of introductory courses in interior design is the home, this book presents all topics as they relate to residential interiors. Home is the most important interior in our personal lives. Individual expression and the greatest satisfaction in design can be found there. At the end of each chapter is a section entitled "Nonresidential Considerations," which relates the information to interiors we visit, where we do business, or where we obtain services beyond the home. This organized, twofold approach will be a starting point for those who will become interior designers.

Many people are finding rewarding careers in interior design. For these, studying and learning are necessary prerequisites to professional practice. Their study of interior design must be thorough and detailed because they are responsible to all of us for the development of interiors that are safe and functional as well as beautiful. Interior design is an exciting discipline that makes life better through effective solutions to problems. The satisfaction and pride that come with a well-designed interior are worth the effort it takes to learn, study, and assimilate the vast body of knowledge in this field.

For those who do not pursue interior design as a career, this book will form a basis for judging and understanding good design in both the home and nonresidential public spaces. Indeed, most of us will spend a great deal of time in places where we work or do business. The person who can appreciate good design wherever it is found and who can evaluate why poor design is not pleasing will find life more rewarding and interesting. With the understanding gleaned from *Interiors*, we can seek to personalize our homes and work spaces with greater skill and sensitivity to beauty.

Interiors is planned for flexibility. Because beginning interior design courses are so different in approach, every chapter of the text may not be applicable to every course. Some chapters may be eliminated for a given course if desired. Much technical data has been incorporated into charts that may be utilized according to the teacher's preference. Some may continue to use the data as a reference for years to come. A glossary is provided at the conclusion of the book for understanding and clarity. The illustration program is also planned for understanding fine design and the processes that bring design to reality. The quality line drawings help the student understand the numerous terms that are so important to the comprehension of interior design.

Unique features brought to this first revision of *Interiors* include Design for Special Populations—such as the elderly, physically handicapped, or visually impaired. As the demographics of today's Western world shift, there are more people living alone, and family situations vary with different stages of life. Flexible interior design caters to all living situations—families with small children in the home, grown children who are reluctant to leave, adult children moving back home and bringing their children with them, elderly parents and grandparents who need in-home care, and even grandparents who simply like to indulge grandchildren.

America is now experiencing a new baby boom parented by a health- and fashion-conscious generation. If we plan for each stage of life as we plan space, select furnishings, adhere to personal style, and consider upkeep, we will make wiser and better informed decisions and better meet our own evolving program. We can also select "universal design"—objects (e.g., from sofas to appliances) that can cross boundaries and be useful to young and old, healthy and handicapped. This, too, is part of making wise choices.

Another vital issue facing us at the end of the twentieth century is the impact of the environment on interiors, and vice versa. Not only should we select quality materials that will not require frequent replacement so as to conserve resources and not add to landfills, we also need to be aware of the source of those materials. The quality of our interior environment is likewise crucial to our personal well-being. This means clean air, judicious use of lighting, and safe and comfortable interiors. This revised edition of *Interiors* has addressed this issue with an Environmental Considerations section at the end of each applicable chapter.

Another new aspect to the second edition of *Interiors* is the discussion of remodeling—a major trend as new housing costs have soared. In addition, there is discussion of the "total sound/media environment" so desired in today's interior. Seasonal Affective Disorder (SAD) is a new concept in the lighting chapter.

A new chapter in this edition of *Interiors* is dedicated to the historic information so important to today's informed and well-rounded student of interior design. This satisfies the requests of professors and will increase ease and continuity in those courses where historic overview is integral to the course. It can also serve as a springboard and introduction to more in-depth study of our treasured architectural and design heritage. It is interesting to note that awareness of historic preservation, as well as new architecture and interiors reflecting historic styles, is more prevalent now than at any time since the 1940s, when the Beaux Arts era ended. At the end of a century, it may be natural to look back fondly and appreciate more deeply the designs and dignity of the past. The focus now is to keep the best of each era. Our spaces should not be just museums but must function viably for those who occupy them. Understanding the complete package of each era will guide us toward the fine design of today and tomorrow.

As technological advancement increases and as people deal with concern about crime, the environment, and personal safety, the accompanying stress has driven people deeper into the "cocooning" phenomenon. Nothing is more intriguing than creating secure, personalized interiors; nothing in the 1990s is as important as our homes. Interest in and money spent on remodeling and redecorating, in purchasing new and restoring old furnishings for the home, is at an all-time high. We are seeing this phenomenon in the advent of "home theater"—entertainment systems furniture featuring a big-screen television as its focal point.[1] And since the home is the most expensive personal investment we will make in our lifetime, it makes sense to us as authors that the more we know about our interior design options, the better our choices will be. Let this book be not simply enjoyable reading, but the beginning of *your* lifetime of involvement in *Interiors*.

ACKNOWLEDGMENTS

This book is the result of the efforts of many talented and supportive people. We would like to express our thanks to our spouses, Asa S. Nielson and Kristine B. Taylor, and to our children, extended families, and our professional peers for their moral and thoughtful support.

We appreciate those who contributed illustrations: Jim Park for his high-quality pen-and-ink work, and the many photographers whose creativity is manifest. Also thanks to individuals and corporations whose designs and products appear in this book, contributing to the state of the art in design excellence.

We are also grateful for the comments of the reviewers for this edition of *Interiors:* Joyce Eileen Butts, Florida Community College at Jacksonville; Maribeth Christensen, Ricks College; Karlene E. Morris, Mt. San Antonio College; Stella F. Underwood, Sinclair Community College; and Eileen Ward, Northern Virginia Community College.

Finally, our appreciation goes to the many fine people at Brown & Benchmark who have worked on this text. These people include Developmental Editor Deborah Reinbold, Art Editor Carla Goldhammer, Photo Editor Shirley Lanners, Designer Chris Reese, Production Editor Ann Fuerste, and Copyeditor Moira Urich for their expertise and commitment in bringing this new edition to reality.

Karla J. Nielson
Orem, Utah
David A. Taylor
Provo, Utah

---

1. Robert Marks, "Home Theater in an Emerging Market," *Home Furnishings Daily* 66, no. 41 (12 October 1992): 31.

C · H · A · P · T · E · R

1

THE PROCESS OF DESIGN

© 1990 Ted Spiegel.

SOLVING PROBLEMS

Design is the process of solving problems, and good solutions have the power to make us feel positive and happy about our surroundings and ourselves. When we buy designer products or hire designers, we are buying solutions to problems we either cannot or do not want to solve ourselves. We are also buying the good feelings that come from beauty. We are literally surrounded by the work of trained and untrained designers; the result of their efforts is often good but sometimes misses the mark. All the things surrounding us—buildings, interiors, clothing, electronics, automobiles, furniture, signage, books, magazines, covers for compact discs, even mechanical pencils—all have been touched by the hand of a designer. The success of each design depends on how well the designer has solved various problems.

In a sense, each of us is a designer and we often solve problems by design, even subconsciously. We gather and analyze information, consider options, study and invent variations, make selections and choices, and plan and build solutions to all kinds of problems. We may even have dabbled in areas of design that are considered the domain of trained professionals. We all have made posters without consulting a graphic designer, we may have customized a bicycle without the aid of a product designer, we may have designed and built tool sheds without the help of an architect, and more people have decorated their own homes than have hired a professional interior designer.

DESIGN DISCIPLINES

There are many design disciplines. Every designer in each design field—from graphic design to product design, and from architectural design to interior design—must solve very different kinds of problems. Graphic designers select photos and illustrations and combine them with typography in printed form to communicate a message. They create identities—logos, stationery, business cards, reports, brochures, posters, menus, and advertising—for businesses, governments, and every imaginable kind of endeavor. Graphic designers also create magazine layouts, book designs, package designs, compact disc covers, and signage to help us find our way through environments and buildings.

Products are designed or redesigned to meet an increasing demand for better devices that make life more efficient or pleasurable. Product designers create automobiles, planes, motorcycles, and other kinds of transportation, as well as copiers, computers, stereo systems, and the whole range of electronic equipment. They design furniture, household appliances, plumbing fixtures, lighting fixtures, tools, and specialized equipment for offices, hospitals, and restaurants. They even design tiny things like mechanical pencils and paper clips.

Architectural designers plan every conceivable kind of building, from stadiums and arenas to shopping malls and houses. Designing a building that is beautiful to look at is not enough. Solutions to architectural problems lie not only in an aesthetic design (pleasing to the senses), but also in function. If the needs of those who use the building have not been met, if people with special problems such as impaired motion cannot adequately use the building, then the problem has not been completely solved.

Civil and structural engineers, city planners, landscape architects, fashion designers, textile designers, and lighting designers solve different kinds of problems, and their work is also everywhere around us. Yet, we often take their work and the work of all designers for granted unless the design does *not* work. We then become frustrated. When design needs are well planned and carefully researched, life is easier. Successful interior design makes life better and makes us feel good about our surroundings and ourselves.

INTERIORS AND WELL-BEING

The great British Prime Minister Winston Churchill said that we build our buildings and then they shape us. This is certainly true of anyplace we spend time, but nowhere is it more true than in the home. The home is a refuge from the elements and the pressures of everyday life. It is the place where children are nurtured. Here they can be taught the value of work and cleanliness and the satisfaction that comes from a job well done. They can learn honesty, integrity, dependability, and service to others by taking appropriate responsibility for the home, its maintenance, and the quality of life it provides. The home is where we come for entertainment and relaxation. It is a place where we seek physical rest and sleep—no bed feels as good as the one at home. Here we can cook in order to feed and fortify ourselves for the onslaught of daily living. Home should be a place of refreshment and support, and it should be important to us as a place where the finest values can be espoused and reinforced.

Interior design is the means to making homes pleasant and functional. In our fast-paced society, life is often filled with stress, and sometimes unhappiness. Poorly planned interiors can add to this emotional burden and can be an unnecessary source of frustration. Well-planned and lovely homes are no guarantee of happiness, but a well-designed interior certainly helps smooth the rough edges of life. It is also significant to note that there is no relationship between the size and luxury of a home and its ability to function. A tiny but well-planned apartment may make a better home than an enormous mansion. Likewise, a modest cottage, if it meets the needs of those who call it home, can be a pleasant and lovely place to live. It is up to us to create the kind of interior that best meets our needs and our expectations of what will take place there.

HOMES OF CHARACTER

Our homes represent what we are or what we want people to think we are. Louis XIV of France built the Palace of Versailles not because he needed a home but as a symbol of his power and a monument to a unified France. To a lesser degree, our interiors also say who we are. It is this principle, when fol-

Figure 1.1 *Interesting pieces of personal value give this room great individuality and character.*
© 1988 Norman McGrath.

Each morning we reach into the closet and select clothes that were chosen basically to cover our bodies. However, some dress with great style and verve, whereas others merely get dressed. So, too, every interior can be planned with great concern and sensitivity, or with capriciousness and lack of care. Because the investment required to furnish an interior is not trivial, it makes sense to do it well. If well planned, the design not only will be appealing to the senses but will also meet the needs of those who use it and will create a safe and satisfying environment.

WHEN DO WE NEED INTERIOR DESIGN

If you haven't already done so, at some point you will come face to face with your own interior design project. You will eventually have some kind of home of your own. It could be an apartment or an existing home, or you might plan and build a new customized home. The reasons for getting involved in an interior design project are varied.

lowed honestly, that results in the most charming and appealing interiors. When interiors are designed purely as an expression of wealth and status, they will often be pretentious and unsatisfying.

Homes filled with objects and materials of personal value will be unlike any other home anywhere. It is pleasant to sit in the home of a musician or theater professional, for example, and sense their interests and experiences merely by looking around. When homes have the good fortune of growing and evolving with their occupants over a number of years, the charm will likely be even greater. This is the reason model homes often lack the emotional warmth of real home environments. Even though they may be designed and furnished with great sensitivity and filled with exciting objects and ideas, they may still lack the sense of ownership and distinction that comes to a home that is lived in with love and care over a period of years.

WHY STUDY INTERIOR DESIGN

There are many reasons why you may choose to study interior design. Some may want to be professional interior designers. However, most of us study design because we find it interesting and we know that someday we will have an apartment, home, or office that will require some measure of interior design.

- New homes require complete designs. A new home must be completely planned—from the arrangement and allocation of space to the selection of new materials and furnishings. The extent of the purchase of new furnishings will often depend on whether one is moving from an existing home or starting a new home from scratch. Those starting fresh will have to select every item, whereas those who move from a more settled situation may be able to use existing furnishings if they are in character with the new home.

- Interiors need refurbishing. With time, materials and furnishings become worn and are no longer suitable. The average life span for better-than-average soft goods (upholstery, draperies, and floor coverings), paint, and wall coverings is six to twelve years; when they wear out, they will need to be replaced.

- The program changes. As the composition of a household changes, a home may need remodeling or refurnishing. For example, as children are born into a family, more bedroom space may be required. As the children grow and move on to college and out of the home, their rooms may be given to younger brothers and sisters, or they may become long-desired personal spaces for Mom or Dad, requiring some design alterations. Environments that are created in response to change are satisfying because they function better and are suited to real needs.

Fashions change. No matter how carefully our interiors are designed, we may find ourselves longing for a change. As exciting new materials and furnishings become available, we can see expanded possibilities for change that will bring freshness to our homes. This is an area that requires careful balance. The interior furnishings industry thrives on changes in fashion, and new directions in design are frequently exciting. Yet if durable furnishings are carefully chosen with an eye to classic styling, they will not date and will not need replacing. If furnishings are well chosen, then updating with a new paint color, fabric, piece of furniture, or accessory may satisfy the craving for new fashion.

INTERIOR DESIGN IS WHERE YOU FIND IT

Although the focus of our interest in interior design is often personal, it certainly need not be limited to our personal home environment. Life-styles today often dictate that we spend many of our waking hours in working situations, shopping, and dealing with various types of business services. We also spend time eating out, traveling, and staying in hotels. These nonresidential environments should be as well planned as the home environment.

It is exciting to apply what we learn about interior design to the places where we shop, eat, stay, or receive public or professional services. After studying interior design, we will view all these places with new eyes. When they function well and are creatively developed, we will feel good about being there. Armed with a new awareness of design, we become amateur critics. Even though no one may take our critique seriously, we find our appreciation and enjoyment increasing with each fresh exposure to design.

LEARNING TO SPEAK THE LANGUAGE OF DESIGN

Interior design is an exciting career, and it is also a marvelous avocation, providing a lifetime of personal aesthetic and intellectual fulfillment. A recent survey in a cutting edge residential design magazine demonstrated that even those who do not practice interior design as a profession often create interiors worthy of recognition and publication. The colored pages featured the work of architects and designers, along with the designs of an illustrator, an account executive, an inventor, a hotel owner, a clothing fabricator, a law student, a housewares retailer, a writer, a contractor, and others. Anyone with a keen interest can become knowledgeable about design and can even create interiors of charm and style.

The great design educator Sherrill Whiton compared studying interior design to learning a foreign language. If the vocabulary and the grammar of a language are mastered, we can adequately express ourselves. Interior design has a vocabulary of materials, styles, forms, details, light, colors, patterns, textures, lines, and mass. The grammar can be compared to design principles of balance, rhythm, emphasis, scale, proportion, unity, variety, and harmony. And in the same way that we select words to form sentences according to rules of grammar, we use elements of design to create interiors according to established principles. And like master writers who manipulate the language in interesting new ways, inspired design often breaks with established rules and expectations to create new trends and tastes.

Being involved in interior design is an exciting and rewarding pursuit that broadens intellectual horizons and deepens aesthetic sensitivity. Interior design is vital, vibrant, and dynamic; it is never static. As the world changes, life also changes and design keeps pace. An interior design will never really be "finished," because as life changes, so do we. Styles evolve, our outlook changes, the composition of our families and households alters, careers shift, and our designs adjust to life's ebb and flow. What an exciting thing it is to be fluent in the language of design, to know the historic roots of the design language and to understand the new expressions of the language all around us. It is even more exciting to be able, at times, to speak the language of design by creating our own interiors. It is truly a rewarding lifelong avocation that is within the reach of any who are willing to invest the time and effort.

Figure 1.2 *Even nonresidential interiors can possess a sense of intimacy and comfort.*
© Bill Crofton/Nawrocki Stock Photo, Inc.

PULLING THE INTERIOR DESIGN TOGETHER

Interiors come to life through a series of selections. Sometimes the selections are carefully planned, researched, and related to important influencing factors; sometimes selections are arbitrary. The results can be good, indifferent, or disastrous, as most of us know from personal experience.

An interior design begins with the selection of a home or building. It is the building that provides the shell for the interior. The building may already exist or it may be custom designed for a particular person, group, or function. We choose the building that best meets the criteria we have established: location, site, cost, style, aesthetics, size, and other considerations.

When we have selected a building, we make space selections that meet our needs. These may already be established in an accompanying floor plan, although room sizes and shape can be adjusted and adapted to existing spaces. If we like the exterior style but are not satisfied with the interior space plan, we can remodel. If we are building from scratch, we can select room size and placement right from the beginning, or blueprint stage.

Interior design also involves selecting materials and finishes for floors, walls, and ceilings from among thousands of possibilities. Decisions about cabinetry, plumbing fixtures, and lighting fixtures are also part of the selection process. In an existing building some of the materials, finishes, cabinets, and fixtures may be acceptable, but in new construction, all must be selected, ordered, and installed.

Existing buildings will have their own architectural details such as doors, windows, and stairs. If they are not desirable they can be changed as part of the remodeling process. In new construction these details must also be selected when the building is planned.

Because furniture is a major component of an interior design, determining what has to be purchased new and what can be used from present furnishings is important. Perusing catalogs, furniture showrooms, antique stores, or even garage sales to find the right pieces of furniture is important. Selecting furniture also involves choosing textiles for upholstered pieces, which in turn requires looking through swatch books in furniture showrooms, examining swatches with a designer, or visiting fabric showrooms in design centers.

Selecting window treatments can be a delightful experience, but one that requires choosing from the numerous options available. The best selection may be a hard treatment such as shutters or blinds, a soft drapery treatment, or a combination of both. The use of soft treatments again requires selecting the fabrics

Figure 1.3 *The comfortable upholstered pieces with loose-fitting slipcovers lessen the formality of this room.*
Courtesy of Laura Ashley.

best suited to the desired treatment. Wall coverings are usually selected concurrently with window treatments.

Choosing accessories, the finishing touches in an interior, is also part of the selection process. The choice of artwork, lamps, plants and flowers, bed/bath/table linens, and even tableware gives the interior a strong signature. These selections make the interior personal and different from any other space.

All of these choices can be made with great style and taste, regardless of the amount of money spent; even a small student apartment can be appealing. On the other hand, you have likely seen interiors where the selections have created a visual nightmare. With the knowledge we gain as we examine the components of interior design, we can make our interiors not only personal and unique, but beautiful and pleasurable. That is what pulling a design together means: understanding what interior design is, how it is accomplished, making wise choices, ordering materials and furnishings, installing and arranging, then living with, evaluating, and enjoying the finished product.

THEMATIC INTERIOR DESIGN

Thematic design is based on historic, regional, ethnic, environmental, and even emotional influences and relationships. Themes such as Victorian Romantic, Nautical, Cowboy/Wild West, Santa Fe, Country French, English Country House, and Bauhaus Modern all provide direction and focus for a design. Some themes will rise and fall in popularity, while others seem to hold on year after year. Fall from public favor does not necessarily indicate bad design, just changes in taste. For example, the Scandinavian Modern that was so popular in the 1950s was good design, and when seen in the context of a 1950s designer house, it still looks well designed even though it is not popular today. On the other hand, the primitive styles of Colonial America have remained consistently popular since their introduction in the seventeenth century.

Often, a theme is adopted by manufacturers of interior design products who interpret and reinterpret the theme or style until it is no longer recognizable. Such is the fate of "Early American," which lost its hand-crafted, primitive qualities and was drowned in a sea of ruffled lamp shades. Fortunately, one can still find wonderful ladder-back chairs with rush seats and other pieces of value that clearly convey the original theme.

In order to effectively create thematic designs, we must understand the stylistic elements of the theme. This requires an understanding of what makes each period, culture, or influence unique. Armed with this new awareness, we can begin to choose a direction for our design and select the most appropriate furnishings.

The following represent only a sampling of popular themes.

Historic Themes

An interior design can be based on historic or "period" interiors such as French Rococo, or Early Georgian/Queen Anne. Styles such as these can be selected as part of an exact recreation or preservation of historic interiors from a certain period. Accuracy and authenticity are an important part of the preparation of museum rooms and houses. These help us to value the craftsmanship of each period, and even to relate the interior and its historic setting to the great people of the time. Historic interiors bring history to life and make it real. Preservation of our history is also important because we can appreciate how people lived and see the harmony of authentic furniture, textiles, architectural elements, and even accessories. These then can be interpreted in the way we live today.

Traditional Themes

Museum-quality rooms do not always offer enough of the comfort and convenience we have come to expect from our homes, so it is more common to simply borrow the theme or capture the feeling of a period. Traditional themes are based on elements of the finest historic design periods such as Rococo, Neoclassic, Georgian, and the Empire. These were not the designs of the common people; they were used in the finest craftsmanship and styling that the cultures of the time had to offer. We often see elements from these periods in today's homes. Because

Figure 1.4 *Fine architectural detail and a historic mix of furnishings create a lovely traditional setting.*
Courtesy of Focal Point, Inc., Atlanta, Georgia.

we are not creating museums, we may freely mix fine pieces of more than one period with comfortable contemporary pieces. It would not be unusual to see a traditional room designed with a nondescript but comfortable Lawson or tuxedo sofa mixed with beautiful Louis XV fauteuils, or Chippendale and Queen Anne wing chairs together with Oriental rugs over wooden floors, sumptuous fabrics, and wonderful brass accessories. Walls and window treatments, too, are inspired by sophisticated contemporary or historic designs. Traditional design unifies today's comfort and the finest pieces from history.

Classic Modern Themes

Sophisticated and formal, the classic modern harmony incorporates furniture pieces designed by the great masters of modern design combined with hard surfaces and clean architectural lines. The sleek lines, innovative use of new technologies such as bent tubular steel, and rich materials like polished plaster, chrome, fine leather, and thick glass table tops, give distinction to the designs of the early twentieth century. Classic modern pieces may be combined with comfortable, nondescript, transitional contemporary seating pieces to add livability to modern design. With modern-styled tables, chairs, lighting fixtures, and other pieces by the world's best designers, modern interiors are more exciting than ever. Post-modern use of simplified classical elements and rich woods—together with high-tech components of black metal and extraordinarily creative new lighting fixtures—are also finding their way into today's modern theme.

Figure 1.5 *Historic pieces are mixed with comfortable contemporary seating to create the traditional theme of this room.*
© Jessie Walker.

Organic/Environmental Themes

Our awareness of the importance of our relationship to the environment has not only highlighted the need to preserve our fragile ecosystem, it has also given us renewed appreciation for the beauty of nature's materials, patterns, and textures. Be they wood, stone, and tile in our floors and walls, or textiles of natural cotton, wool, linen, and silk, we find these materials both easy to care for and easy to live with—which is important to today's busy life-styles. Expanses of glass to bring nature indoors, frankly exposed wooden ceiling beams, and an emphasis on structural elements are characteristic of this uncluttered theme. There is much of this theme in the primitive log cabin, the provincial home, the innovative organic designs of Frank Lloyd Wright, and the "woodsy modern" homes of the 1970s. The intrinsic qualities of the natural materials give this theme dignity and character.

Eclectic Themes

Eclectic design utilizes elements from many sources. Most eclectic interiors today try to achieve the comfort discussed above, or they reflect furnishing collected over time without a specific design harmony in mind. The result might be charming, but it could also be chaotic. True eclectic design is chosen with the principle of harmony in mind: different design sources or styles provide the variety, but we must also be able to sense the unity. Often the harmony may be surprising and even beyond logic. For example, logically a Louis XV fauteuil, or a primitive Windsor chair, would not seem to have anything in common with a clean modern chrome and glass table. Yet in the right setting, that kind of selection is not only right, it makes the design far more exciting than "appropriate" matching pieces would. Good eclectic design is challenging, but successful combinations are exciting.

English Country House Theme

Great country houses are the pride of England. They are often palatial in scale and quite different from what we associate with cottagelike country homes in America. The theme is much the same as traditional, but with an eccentric twist. The main seating pieces (sofas and chairs) are large-scaled, overstuffed, rumpled, and frequently covered with floral chintz, plain cotton, or wool slip-covers to create a lived-in look. The other furniture is fine historic English or French pieces. The floors are wooden (even parquet) with Oriental or French-style rugs. The walls are paneled or covered with rich textiles, and the windows are hung with floral prints or damasks. The rooms often feature wonderful large-scale paintings, porcelain pieces, books, and informal displays of fresh-cut flowers from prolific English gardens. This look is elegant, yet lived-in, well worn, and loved.

Vernacular/Country Themes

Vernacular design, often called "country," comes to us from the common people of many cultures and regions. The simple handcrafted furnishings of colonial times, the charm of interiors seen in the French or English countryside, the unaffected furnishings of nineteenth-century pioneers who pushed westward across America—all are examples of the country theme.

Figure 1.6 *Country French chairs, plank floors, beamed ceiling, and a French baker's rack reinforce the Country French theme of this room.*
© Jessie Walker.

Each influence has its own distinctive features but all are characterized by simple, handcrafted, and homespun quality. Wooden or stone floors with braided or woven rag rugs (or well-worn Oriental rugs), beamed ceilings, and simple draperies with wooden or wrought-iron rods add typical charm to country interiors. Walls of simple plaster, or those covered with tongue-and-groove or board-and-batten panels, are consistent with the theme.

Country furniture is charming but unsophisticated. Because wood turning was a simple technology, vernacular furniture will generally feature wooden turnings in the legs, backs, and cross-pieces rather than carving. Rush and cane seats, too, are common to country seating pieces. Upholstered goods are not usual vernacular pieces, but comfortable, well-scaled contemporary sofas and lounge chairs mix well with true country pieces for today's life-style; the typical country setee makes an excellent accent. Accessories are of wood, pewter, wrought iron, and brass. Collections of ceramics such as fine porcelain, bundles of fresh or dried herbs, and flowers from the garden—together with utilitarian objects such as baskets and quilts—add great charm and personality to country interiors.

Ethnic Themes

Ethnic African themes reflect the native designs of the true African people (and no longer reflect the "great white hunter" look with safari elements of animal trophies and mosquito nets). The African theme is expressed with native patterns, textiles, textural materials, and architecture.

Native American design figures prominently into both the Wild West/Cowboy and the Santa Fe themes. The Santa Fe-style furniture is a modification of Spanish colonial types, and the Cowboy style incorporates mission-style pieces as well as twig furniture. The Cowboy theme also makes use of Navajo weavings and rugs, as well as Pendleton blanket-patterned textiles. The Pendleton blankets, originally produced for use by Native Americans, are still widely sold in trading posts throughout the Southwest. Utilitarian objects such as kerosene lamps or cast iron pots combine with decorative Native American folk art to complete this look.

Romantic Victorian Theme

The look of Victorian and Edwardian times, popularized by Laura Ashley and others, is filled with nostalgic comfort. Slip covers, big overstuffed lounge chairs, button-tufted ottomans, butler's tables with fat turned legs, floral chintz, and lamp shades with tassled fringe all add to this theme. These rooms feature antique silver and porcelain, tea sets on cut lace doilies, and antique graphic botanical prints with beautiful frames. Wood floors are covered with Oriental or Portuguese needlepoint rugs. Windows are shuttered, draped with fine lace, or generously hung with cabbage rose and other florals. The theme is lavish, decorative, and cluttered—filled with treasured objects and collections that provide comfort and stability in today's hectic world.

Other Themes

As we observe design in the world around us, we will see countless other themes that appeal to us in different ways. It is particularly interesting to observe the use of thematic design in the places where we shop. For example, Banana Republic—which built its reputation on a "safari" theme with plank floors, grass roofs, rusty tin, and corrugated steel—has changed to a more up-scale traditional theme with contemporary overtones. Ralph Lauren helped popularize the exclusive "club" theme with fine wood panels and moldings, wooden floors with Oriental rugs, overstuffed leather furniture, and chandeliers with small shades on each candle. In addition, the closely associated "hunting lodge" theme includes Scottish tartan plaids, as well as antlers or other hunting trophies.

Figure 1.7 *Pendleton blanket patterns and Native American accessories enhance the Western theme of this comfortable space.*

© Timothy Street-Porter, courtesy of Rogers & Associates.

Thematic design is not intended to provide recipes for interior style, but rather to give insight into how harmony can be achieved by closely observing the way certain elements fit quite naturally together. Observation with fresh eyes will lead to new understanding and personal creativity. Then the interior design will not only fulfill the all important functional needs of the users, it will also provide visual stimulation and the sensory response we call *aesthetics*.

THOSE WHO PULL IT TOGETHER

An interior design is almost always a team effort on the part of design professionals, craftspeople, and laypeople. There is no set combination of participants; the variations could be infinite. The scope of interior design projects varies from something as simple as new window coverings or carpet to a complete new building. What needs to be done will determine how many people are involved. Those most commonly involved with interior design projects are interior designers, architects, contractors, subcontractors, cabinet makers, retailers, fabricators, craftspeople, installers, and laypeople. Other specialists such as lighting designers or kitchen planners are called in as needed.

Interior designers interview clients to establish desire, function, and emotional needs. They inventory present furnishings and prepare a master plan that itemizes materials and furnishings for the home or building, where those will be obtained, and who will fabricate, build, manufacture, and install the goods. Interior designers place orders for materials and furnishings (or in some cases help the customer to place the order). They also supervise or oversee installation and placement of an interior's components.

Interior designers often foster expertise by focusing on specific types of design. Residential designers create interiors for homes. They may be involved in planning the space, designing or selecting furniture and cabinetry, specifying materials and finishes, designing and specifying floor coverings and window treatments, and even selecting accessories. The same is true for *nonresidential designers*. For example, firms that deal with health care design plan interiors for hospitals, clinics, hospices, and care centers. Others, involved with hospitality design, create interiors for hotels and restaurants. Some even design prisons, jails, and courthouses—a specialty called justice design. Still others are generalists who tackle all kinds of design problems.

Designers may work in design firms or as freelance professionals. Design firms have in-house samples and catalogs of materials and furnishings, and they may also utilize the services of sales representatives and design centers. In several U.S. states, interior designers are licensed and allowed to use that title only if they meet strict requirements and are able to pass a qualifying examination (the National Council for Interior Design Qualification exam).

Interiors, particularly nonresidential interiors, are often designed by architects and their firms. Each year when the list of the top 100 interior design firms is published, many of those are architectural firms with design departments. The same is true of many of the interiors published in magazines that feature both residential and nonresidential design; they were designed by architects. Many architectural firms have interior design departments, giving them the ability to handle every aspect of the design. (Architects are licensed and legally responsible for the outcome of their design.)

Even though their training may not be in design, it is common for contractors and builders to design buildings and interiors. The design may even include the selection of all the interior details as well as the materials and finishes. Builders, developers, and contractors who want to appeal to an upscale clientele will often hire architects, landscape planners, and interior designers to give their developments the proper amenities. Regardless of who plans a design, it is usually the licensed contractor who builds it.

Subcontractors are specialists who handle specific aspects of a project such as plumbing, electrical, concrete, drywall or plaster, siding, painting, and even finish carpentry. These subcontractors rarely branch out beyond their specialty.

Furniture stores, paint and wall covering stores, lighting showrooms, window-covering professionals, and floor-covering dealers often provide interior design services with or without trained and/or licensed interior designers. These kinds of businesses usually sell at retail prices to the public but often will provide discounts to builders, contractors, or interior designers.

Craftspeople and artists provide resources that add unique touches to the creation of interior designs. Stained glass artisans, stone carvers, custom furniture and cabinet makers, restoration specialists, stencilers, and fine artists provide important services and design elements that are invaluable to certain design projects.

Fabricators and upholsterers turn the textiles and materials of the design into window coverings or upholstered pieces, which are an indispensable part of an interior design.

Installers lay carpet, tile, and vinyl; hang wallpaper; mount drapery rods, blinds, and shades; and hang draperies. Installers may also be involved in measuring and estimating when the design is being planned. Finished interiors will reflect the level of quality provided by subcontractors, craftspeople, fabricators, and installers.

Laypeople also do interior design. Houses have been designed and furnished by people with no design training, sometimes to save money and sometimes for the sheer pleasure of doing it. Building one's own house isn't as common as it was in the last century, but designing the interior certainly is. Many people make all the design decisions in their homes without the help of professionals. They may rely on the same resources the professionals do, but they make decisions and selections themselves. Some stores cater to the do-it-yourself market. Even nonresidential design is done by the layperson. Doctors' offices designed by the doctor or spouse dot the country, and retail stores designed by the proprietor or owner are common.

The variety of relationships and exchange among these designers, craftspeople, resources, and laypeople is unlimited. There is no one set way to accomplish an interior design. Inspired design is not the sole domain of one group or another; it may show up in the work of a world-class designer or in a small country cottage created by someone with no professional training. That is because good design is both functional and aesthetic. Aesthetics can be taught and developed, but they are also in-nate. A great benefit of training, even for the layperson, is the awareness of what can and should be done to make interiors functional. Professional designers use research and programming to help them create the very best possible design within a given set of circumstances.

UNDERSTANDING THE PROGRAM

To truly make an interior functional and successful, design must solve problems. Problem solving entails goals, requirements, and restrictions. The first step in the *design process* is identifying goals, defining objectives and requirements, and clarifying restrictions that affect the way the design must be conceived and executed. A clear understanding of the problem will lead to a better design solution. In the interior design profession, the goals, requirements, and restrictions associated with a design problem are often called the *program*. The program is the total of all the factors that must be considered for a successful design solution. The process of gathering the information necessary to understand the program and solve the problem is called *programming*. When all of the information gathered in the programming process has been analyzed and verified, it is often compiled in a document also called a *program*. This is used formally in non-residential design, but it can be used formally or informally in residential design.

CHART 1.1   THE DESIGN PROCESS

LETTER OF AGREEMENT (CONTRACT)

PROBLEM STATEMENT

RESEARCH AND PROGRAMMING
Identifies and asks questions about:
- Users
- Life-style and function
- Relationships
- Space requirements
- Environmental factors
- Mechanical considerations
- Psychological and sociological considerations
- Economic factors
- Codes and restrictions

WRITING A PROGRAM
Includes:
- Analysis of research data
- Organizing the data into a written program

DESIGN DEVELOPMENT
The program is implemented through:
- Initial concept development
- Working drawings and specifications
- Execution

POST-OCCUPANCY EVALUATION

THE PROBLEM STATEMENT

Initial identification of the problem might begin with some kind of *problem statement* indicating the basic nature of the project—as a primary residence, vacation house, office, clinic, retirement center, restaurant, hotel, or clothing store. Such a statement might also include the location of the project and even a specific address. The person or group commissioning the project could also be named in a design statement.

RESEARCH AND PROGRAMMING

There are times when the program for a project will be provided by those commissioning the design, but it will probably still be necessary to collect additional data to complete the program. When the designer is responsible for the program, it will be necessary to conduct research, surveys, interviews, studies, and inventories as part of the programming process. The following are typical factors that might be considered in research and programming.

Users

The research process begins with identification of each of the *users*. The users, as the name implies, are those who will use the design directly or indirectly, from principal occupants to service people to guests and friends.

In a residential design, a *profile* is developed for each of the principal residents who will live in the home. The profile should include such things as age, sex, background, culture, values, temperament, personality, personal habits, need for privacy, style preferences, responses to color, and an inventory of possessions and furnishings that need to be accommodated.

Profiles reveal household *demographics*, which is statistical information about numbers and kinds of residents. This would include traditional families with two parents, as well as nontraditional families such as those in combined households, single-parent households, and special populations such as the elderly or handicapped. Household demographics can be determined through interviews of the principal users, or by means of a questionnaire developed by the designer.

Life-Style and Function

The profile helps the designer understand the *life-style* of the principal users. Life-style is a term frequently used in residential design to describe part of the program for a home. It represents the constantly changing way a person or group of people live and how they use their time. It includes such considerations as whether they like to read, write, or use a computer; whether they have special hobbies such as sewing, crafts, or woodworking; or to what extent they enjoy and participate in sports. The way people choose to entertain; how they prepare, serve, and eat meals; whether or not a grandparent lives with them; the way they use their leisure time; the type of instruments they play; the routine they use for dressing

Figure 1.8 *The user of this loft is an artist whose special profile has led to the creation of a very individual environment.*
Courtesy of Laura Ashley.

and their personal toilette; the amount and type of interaction they want with their children—all are examples of life-style considerations. As the composition of families or groups changes and as people grow older, interests, needs, and life-styles also change. Consequently, flexibility in planning for potential modifications is very important in order to meet changes without major upheaval.

Since life-styles are in a constant state of flux as household demographics change, it is important to be aware of the effect such changes will have. For example, many families with small children may find a playroom well suited to their needs. Tiny children can use the space for toys and for play. As children begin to bring friends into the home, the room will provide space for playing games with peers. As children become teenagers and young adults, the playroom can accommodate music and entertainment, and even parties and dancing. When the young adults leave home, the room may start the cycle all over again with space for grandchildren.

Another example of accommodating a changing life-style might be the evolution of a bedroom from nursery into child's room and then into a teenager's or young adult's room. When the young adult leaves home, the room could be used for hobbies, study, television, a home office, a guest room, or a combination of uses.

Figure 1.9 *This delightful space was created expressly for the enjoyment of grandchildren who visit this home.*

Interior design by MEA designs, M. Enid Arckless, ASID/Photos by Reed Kaestner.

Figure 1.10 *A dining area in a greenhouse is far from a standard solution to space usage, but the result is both charming and functional.*
© 1988 Norman McGrath.

The foresight to project changes in life-style is an important asset in the programming process.[1]

Many kinds of design solutions have come to be accepted as standard. However, the life-style of the users will often dictate solutions to design problems that go beyond standard. Individual needs should be assessed in terms of the kinds of functions a user envisions for a space, as well as the kinds of furnishings and equipment required. For example, questions one might ask in planning a kitchen space are:

- How many of the users will be cooking at once?
- What kinds of equipment will be needed?
- Will there be minimal or gourmet cooking?
- What kind of supplies must be accommodated?
- How should supplies be stored?
- What kind of dining, if any, should be planned?

In a bedroom we might ask:

- Do the users like to read in bed?
- Will the bedroom be used for studying?
- Is an area for seating desirable?
- Will there be television or other forms of electronic entertainment?
- What are the storage needs?

In living areas we might want to know:

- Is the space used by company, family, or both?
- Will there be a piano or other musical instruments?
- Will television and entertainment be included here?
- Should books and reading be part of the planning?
- Will conversation be an important function?
- Will the space be used to display art?

Determinations should be made regarding every space and its use. For example, a bedroom could accommodate study or sewing space as well as sleeping. The family room could be used for dining, television, and stereo, as well as conversation and games. The laundry and sewing could be planned in the same space. The dining room or guest room could double as a library or hobby room. This kind of flexibility is crucial because the cost of space is high, and infrequently used rooms

Figure 1.11 *Because of careful inventory and planning, this very small room is able to accommodate a computer work space as well as storage for several slide carousels.*
© 1983 Norman McGrath.

need to be made more useful by planning for several functions. Every life-style will dictate different kinds of functions for each area; thorough inquiry will determine precisely what the functions are. With this exact data, planning can be effective and accurate, and life-style differences can be well accommodated.

Relationships

When the functions for each space have been assessed, the relationships of each function must be determined. Important lines of communication and the need for proximity must be identified. For example, it might be convenient to plan sewing and ironing near the laundry. The laundry needs to be close to the kitchen for daytime convenience, or it could be near the bedrooms and bathrooms where soiled clothes are removed. Bedrooms should be planned in relationship to bathrooms. Easy access from the nursery to the master bedroom may be ideal for some, but other parents might want children's rooms and activities isolated from their own. Kitchens and dining areas where food will be served should have logical and convenient relationships. A home office might most appropriately be located near the front door and close to a seating area such as a living room, for the convenience of those who visit the office.

The consideration of relationships should even extend to the location of areas outside the building. For example, the convenient relationship of garbage containers to the kitchen or of kitchen to patio or garden is important. When bringing in groceries, the relationship of the garage or parking spaces to the kitchen or pantry is significant. Identifying these types of relationships facilitates efficient use of space and makes the design more effective because of its convenience. Well-planned relationships also smooth lines of communication, cut building costs, and make traffic patterns more efficient.

Space Requirements

When the designer actually puts pencil to paper, it is important to know exactly how to divide the space. Consequently, during the programming step, it is necessary to estimate the amount of space each function will demand. This requires some understanding of standard amounts of space allowed for traffic, as well as standard dimensions for furnishings. Programming space requirements includes establishing inventories of furnishings, clothing, and special equipment belonging to the users. In most cases programming even includes taking actual measurements of those items. Life-style profiles will also help in estimating space requirements. A sample checklist might include the following kinds of questions:

- How is entertaining handled, and how much space does that require?
- How many people might need to be seated for formal dining?
- What is the maximum number of guests that might stay at one time?
- What pieces of equipment will be used in the kitchen?
- How much food will be stored in the pantry?
- What kind of vacuums, mops, brooms, and other cleaning supplies are there?
- Are there collections of slides, videos, or movies that require space?
- Do card tables and folding chairs need to be stored?
- How many books, records, or tapes does the user have?
- How much sporting equipment needs storage?
- How many shirts, sweaters, etc. does the user own?
- How many pairs of shoes need to be stored?
- Are there seasonal decorations that require storage?

The old saying, "A place for everything, and everything in its place," neatly summarizes an important aspect of a well-designed space: Most interior environments need not be of any particular size to be well designed. If a space accommodates possessions and activities in a logical and orderly fashion, life will be more pleasant. However, it is also important to remember that design is problem solving. Some programs may have requirements that go beyond the realm of adequate

Figure 1.12 *A mild climate allowed the designer to create a space that is completely open to the outdoors.*
Interior design by John Saladino. Photo © 1989 Norman McGrath.

function to creating spaces of impressive size for visual im-pact. That is probably why Louis XIV built the Palace of Versailles. The program was not just for a house—he already had several—but for a building that would also be a symbol of power. Only a building as grand, spacious, and opulent as Versailles could fulfill his program.

One last consideration of space again extends beyond the functional measurement of actual space needs to the psycho-logical realm of perception. Not only should there be adequate space for movement and circulation within a space, but the designer should also consider how the mind moves through a space. Inadequate space, or spaces without windows where the eye and mind cannot expand, is unpleasant for many and even claustrophobic for some. Psychological space perception is as important as actual space.

Environmental Factors

Our relationship with and responsibility toward the environment has become a very important issue. As the developed nations in particular gobble resources, pollute, and destroy the environment at an alarming rate, the preservation of the environment has be-come not only a moral issue, but a political one as well.

Because all of us have a responsibility to be wise stewards of the environment, you will find a section at the end of each applicable chapter called Environmental Considerations. These sections will list some of the things that responsible designers can do to preserve the environment. An awareness of these is-sues can lead to action that will affect the quality of life for us and future generations.

Environmental considerations—such as climate, weather, and physical location—must be examined as part of the pro-gramming process. Some aesthetically pleasing designs are fail-ures because they ignore important environmental questions. Environmental concerns cannot be subordinated to aesthetics; there must be a synthesis of the two.

Climate and Weather

Problems of climate and weather are generally straightforward. Climates with extremes of heat and/or cold will require ample insulation, as well as adequate heating and/or cooling systems. Climate and weather also influence the placement of a building to take advantage of favorable climate conditions or to avoid unpleasant conditions. In fact, weather and climate should be keys to determining the type of structure to be built. Building materials should be suitable to the climate so they will not be subject to excessive deterioration.

Physical Location

Physical location involves factors such as site, view, prevailing winds, solar exposure, noise, and environmental hazards.

Site

The site of a building should influence its design. The building should be compatible with its neighbors, though the style need not be the same, merely harmonious. Where conservation and preservation of the environment are important, the design should be well suited to, and harmonious with, the natural surroundings. Plans should be developed to do the least possible damage to nature and to integrate the building with existing natural features.

In other cases, the design may be created to stand out in contrast with its environment; the environment may even be altered and reworked by the designer. Good and responsible judgment is paramount in such situations. Building and development are the natural results of growth and change and should be planned so that in years to come they will have improved with age.

View

Delightful daytime or nighttime views are a valuable asset to an interior and should be featured in the design of the building. They should not be hidden by excessively ornate window treatments. Where views are unpleasant or nonexistent, attention should be focused inward, and treatments should be selected to hide unpleasant views.

Prevailing Winds

Prevailing winds can be a positive or negative feature of a location. They can provide cooling breezes or cold disturbing winter winds. When pleasant breezes prevail, buildings should be oriented to use them for natural cooling. When winds are icy cold, the building and its landscaping should provide shelter and protection. *Berms* (small hills) or trees planted in a *windbreak* can help minimize the effect of cold winter winds.

Solar Exposure

Like the wind, the sun can be both a positive and negative factor. In the winter, the sun streaming through south windows may be warm and comforting, but without adequate protection from the sun, an interior may become too hot and difficult to cool, and ultraviolet rays and heat can damage furnishings. Chapter 14, Building Systems, contains a thorough discussion of solar factors.

Noise

Some types of noise are pleasant. The tumbling of a small creek or brook, the sound of waves breaking at the seashore, the crackle of a warm fire in the fireplace, or a breeze rustling leaves can be comforting and pleasant sounds. Most people enjoy an environment free from loud, annoying noise. However, it is amazing how humans can adapt to noise. Those who sleep in rooms facing busy city streets may soon find it difficult to sleep in a completely quiet environment.

Noise from the outside and noise through interior walls can be controlled with extra insulation, adequate construction, and insulated glass. Noise within an environment can be controlled by the use of materials that *refract* (bend) or absorb sound waves. Textile applications (upholstery and floor, wall, and window coverings) refract and absorb sound waves and can largely eliminate echo noise, or *reverberation*.

Environmental Hazards

When planning, it is important to be aware of hazardous conditions, some serious enough to warrant selection of a new site. Fault lines, slide areas, eroding waterfronts, areas subject to flooding, high-power lines, railroad lines, heavy industries, areas of extreme pollution, and even former pollution sites—all are examples of potential hazards. Streets with heavy traffic may be hazards for families with small children.

Mechanical Considerations

Mechanical considerations include heating, ventilation, air-conditioning (HVAC), plumbing, lighting, and telephone. A basic knowledge of the way these systems function will be helpful in understanding how they must integrate with the completed interior. Such understanding will also lead to a smoother and more productive working relationship with the skilled technicians who install these systems. Mechanical systems are also discussed in chapter 5, Lighting, and chapter 14, Building Systems.

Psychological and Sociological Considerations

Psychological and sociological needs also must carefully be considered because the design of an interior has tremendous power to make people feel good about their environments and can even affect the way they feel about each other. Most people recognize the effect that an interior environment can have (for both good and ill) on our well-being and even on some aspects of our character. The use of space, color, texture, pattern, scale, balance, furnishings, and all the other design elements and principles that constitute our interiors make us feel and act in certain ways. Knowledgeable use of these elements can lead to the creation of environments that make us feel emotional responses such as cool, warm, happy, romantic, nostalgic, awed, compassionate, hungry, full, restless, soothed, stimulated, or relaxed. That is why an interior design must carefully consider subtle manipulations that affect us so strongly.

Other sociological and psychological considerations include the need for privacy and interaction, cultural relationships, security and safety, and familiarity and stability.

Privacy and Interaction

Some people are rather private by nature, whereas others are more gregarious. Regardless of our basic social nature, we all have times when we need to be alone and times when we need to interact with others. Spaces such as living rooms, family rooms, game rooms, dining rooms, and even kitchens should be planned for interaction. In many homes the kitchen is the heart. Even when homes are provided with areas for individual study, many times the family will end up studying around the kitchen table. When guests arrive for parties, they frequently gravitate to the kitchen. It is this tendency that has led to the popularity of *great rooms* which are large kitchen/dining/family room spaces where most of the day-to-day living is centered.

It is equally important to plan spaces where members of the household can be alone. Libraries, studies, workrooms, or bedrooms are logical places for privacy. When children share a room, some means of division or separation should be planned so that a degree of privacy can be achieved when needed. A desire for solitude and introspection is a basic human need that must be planned for and respected.

Cultural Relationships

Distinctive aspects of local culture or family history can enhance the quality of an interior. For example, the Pueblo Indian design of New Mexico with its adobe construction has been adapted into a local style that is charming and well suited to its environment. It is also closely tied into the history and culture of the

Figure 1.13 *These adobe-style buildings in Santa Fe have strong ties to local culture and are well suited to the New Mexican climate.*

Photo by Markus Fant.

area and provides an emotional link with the prevailing culture. Some families may have strong ties to foreign cultures that should be considered in the design of the home. Displaying art or collections of crafts from those cultures makes the home an extension of personal history and experience.

Security and Safety

The physical safety of the occupants and possessions can affect the psychological well-being of a home. There are few things that compare with the feeling of terror and despair associated with a fire or other disaster. To help prevent accidents and fire danger, government agencies have established guidelines and rules (codes) for safety and fire prevention. Smoke detectors and fire extinguishers offer even greater security, both physical and emotional.

The need for protection is one of the most basic reasons for seeking the shelter of a home. Home security has become a multimillion dollar industry providing alarm systems and other means of securing homes. These security systems may utilize complex equipment and sophisticated electronic surveillance, while others are as basic as well-engineered locking mechanisms. For many, these kinds of measures provide a sense of calm and well-being that makes a home the center of security that it should be.

Familiarity and Stability

The design of an interior can include items that create stability and reassurance through their familiarity. For example, space might be designated for family photographs and other personal mementos. Art, accessories, and furnishings collected while traveling also have the same effect of tying us to our personal experiences. Such belongings are often reminders of events or people and are part of an emotional support system. The use or display of cherished collections, objects, or furnishings should be included as part of the planning process. Because of their familiarity and warm associations, our environments can support better mental and emotional health (see also chapter 13, Art and Accessories).

Economic Factors

The last consideration is one of the most important because it has such an impact on the extent of the design. Without proper funding, a design can remain forever on paper. Economic considerations will govern all aspects of the interior design—from the time allotted to research, develop, and execute the design to the quality of materials and furnishings.

There are some considerations that will make designs more economical. For example, building materials that are plentiful or indigenous to an area will usually be economical. This means that brick is less costly near the factory because shipping costs are generally less. Where brick has to be transported many hundreds of miles, the cost will escalate. Wood is a natural choice in wooded areas and adds the economical quality of good insulation as well. Building and finish materials that require the least upkeep and give the greatest length of service or durability for the climate and location are also economical choices, a justification for selecting brick or siding instead of wood.

Exterior and interior building components that are standard sizes are more economical than those special ordered or custom manufactured. Examples include doors, windows, and ceiling heights, and standard "in stock" items such as appliances and plumbing fixtures.

The cost of replacement when materials wear out is also an important factor in planning for economy. It is sad when a home that has been mortgaged for fifteen, twenty, or even thirty years is outfitted with materials that need replacing in as few as five years. For example, a lower grade vinyl flooring or carpet will likely wear out and cost more to replace than a better quality, durable flooring would have cost in the beginning. Hardwood, tile, or even stone floors, which are initially expensive, will seldom wear out or need replacing. In the long run, cheap may cost more than expensive because poor quality goods wear out before replacement is economically feasible, then those who use the design must live with shabby goods. The credo "buy once and buy good quality" will serve well all choices for design materials and furnishings.

The cost of maintenance or upkeep of materials is another factor in planning for economy. If a finish or material requires constant dusting, cleaning, polishing, waxing, or other maintenance, it may not be the best choice. The cost is counted in two ways—the money for repair or hired cleaning help and the time and effort spent in maintaining it yourself.

Economy may also include planning ahead for future changes or additions. Plumbing and wiring can be installed for central vacuum systems, intercom units, or for entertainment and sound systems that will be added later. Planning ahead saves costly remodeling, with its accompanying inconvenience and frustration. The list of projected changes and additions should include any item that is built-in and must be planned for in advance.

Codes

Codes and restrictions are laws established by federal, state, and local governments and their agencies for the health, safety, and welfare of the consumer. They are exacting, often complex, and tie the designer to a considerable amount of liability. Codes provide requirements for mechanical systems that will function both safely and properly and for fire and occupational safety with certain types of materials, equipment, and structures.

WRITING A PROGRAM

This list of considerations may seem lengthy, yet raising and answering as many questions as possible establishes a clear understanding or mastery of the problem. Such mastery becomes the basis for a good design solution. The only limiting factor in asking questions is the time limitation. At some point the design must move forward. When each of these aspects has been completely explored and the data have been confirmed by the users, then the data can be analyzed and compiled into the written program mentioned earlier.

Since the program is a constantly changing set of circumstances, the gathered data will only reveal the program at a given point in time. The program gives the direction the design solution must take, and in this way it is like a road map that helps the design stay on course. The length of the written program will vary according to the size of the project.

The finished design will only be as good as the quality of research and articulation of the data. A fine design is the result of spending adequate time to analyze and organize before beginning to create.

DESIGN DEVELOPMENT: SOLVING THE PROBLEM

The creative mind will be generating ideas for design solutions all the way through the research phase of the design process. However, only after the research data have been analyzed and clearly articulated in the written program can the development of the ideas, or *concepts*, be formulated with accuracy.

Initial Concept Development

Concept development usually begins with *brainstorming*, freely generating many ideas without stopping to judge their quality. The ideas can be verbal, sketched, or written. Some very good design solutions have been scrawled on table napkins and scraps of building lumber. The important part of brainstorming is the flow of ideas as one idea often triggers another and the two may suggest a third or a combination idea. When the best ideas emerge, they are put on paper as the basis for the design solution.

The ideas take the form of quick drawings called *schematics*, which are used to help visualize space plans, traffic patterns, details, or even possible color schemes. These can be modified as the process continues until the parts begin to form the whole. As the design starts to come together, the brainstorming process continues as one scheme generates variations. These ideas must be examined, and at some point decisions must be made. Some ideas must be rejected and those that survive can be accepted, altered, or expanded. This process continues until the pile of drawings reaches the ceiling or until time runs out. The ideation stage could go on indefinitely since solutions are limited only by imagination.

At some point, the best ideas are brought to a degree of completion and the design concept begins to emerge. A commitment is then made to the ideas, and they are refined to a level where they can be presented for analysis. The presentation of the proposed interior design is generally made with a series of boards (mat board, foam-core, or illustration board) displaying:

- *Conceptual drawings*, which quickly demonstrate the ideas for the plan of the design without the time-consuming precision of finished drawings. These include scaled drawings showing furniture placement.

- *Materials and finishes boards*, which are mounted with actual materials suggesting color schemes and other selections.

- *Renderings*, colored perspective drawings of the space, which help to visualize how the finished design will appear.

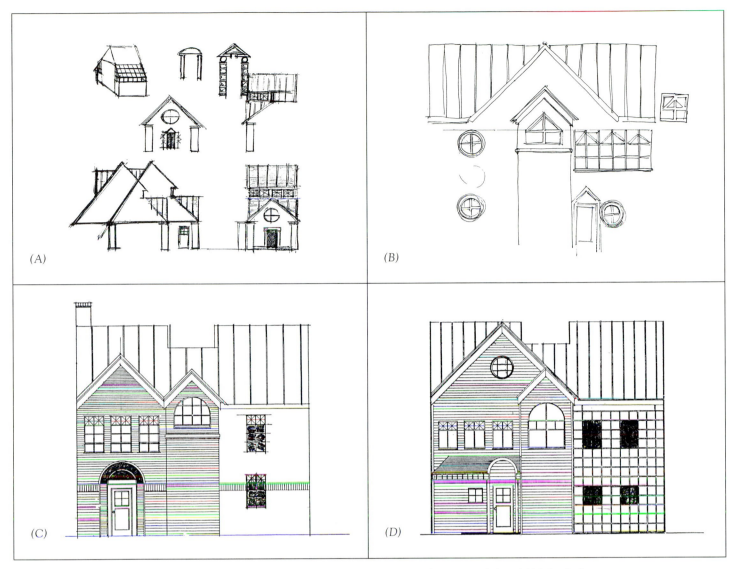

Figure 1.14 *These drawings show the evolution of a small house, from (A) and (B) schematics to (C) and (D) finished concept.*
Drawings by Carl Blake and Doug Beaudoin.

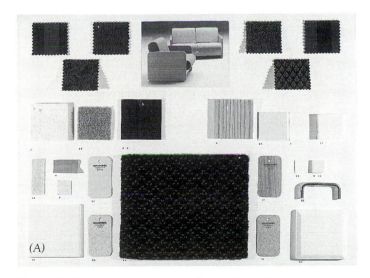

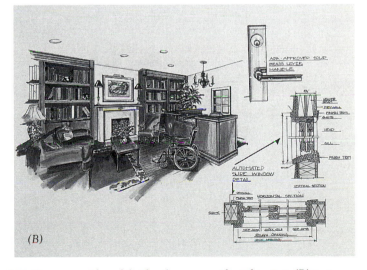

Figure 1.15 *Presentation boards help the client understand design concepts. (A) shows materials and finishes for a nonresidential project. (B) is a rendering of a reception area in a small home office, together with details for a window.*

(B) Rendering by Jonna Robison.

Based on the presentation, the client may approve the concept. If it is not agreeable, the design must go back to the drawing board and the process begins again with additional client input. When the concept is approved, the design work may proceed.

Working Drawings and Specifications

With the approval of the concept, final design development begins with working drawings and written specifications. When approved and signed, these may become part of the agreement or legal document between the client and the designer. The working drawings are the finished mechanical drawings or plans prepared for use by the contractors in making bids and completing the construction of the design. The working drawings are often prepared in blueprint form showing the details as they are to be executed. The complete set of working drawings (also called construction drawings) might include a title sheet, an index, perspective drawings, site plans, floor plans, electrical plans, reflected ceiling plans (showing lighting, ventilation, and other ceiling fixtures), sections (a view sliced through the building), elevations (straight-on views), detailed drawings of architectural elements, fixtures, or cabinetwork, and schedules (listing types and finishes of architectural and design elements).

The furnishings and materials to be used in the design must be itemized and documented in lists called *specifications*. The specifications include:

- Identification of the item
- Its manufacturer
- Pricing per unit and extended total; labor costs
- Quantities and types of materials
- Standards of durability or fire resistance
- Types of finishes
- Special instructions for construction or installation
- Dimensions (sizes) and shipping weights
- Any other necessary data

If these are not carefully and completely spelled out, the item or construction may not turn out as intended because it was subject to interpretation. Bids may also be inaccurate and inconsistent. When the working drawings and specifications are complete and approved and the contract arrangements have been made, the design process moves into its final phase.

Execution

The *execution* is the implementation of the design. During the execution, the actual construction begins, and the materials and furnishings orders are finalized. Ordering can be time consuming, yet like each step in the design process, it must be done with great care and accuracy. When working to meet a deadline, nothing is more frustrating than receiving fewer materials or different furnishings than expected.

During this phase of the design process, the work of the contractors should be inspected to ensure that the plans are being carried out properly. This might entail working with builders who do the actual construction and with electricians and plumbers to make sure the electrical, lighting, and plumbing systems are installed as planned and specified. It usually includes meeting with the carpenters and cabinetmakers who construct and install custom woodwork to verify style, dimensions, and quality. It is necessary to check with window treatment fabricators and installers as well as wall-covering and flooring installers to assure that the goods are correctly fabricated and installed. All of this supervision is a sort of a juggling act, but it is a crucial part of the process that will help guarantee success. This process is discussed further in chapter 14, Building Systems, where scheduling, critical path, and punch lists are explained and illustrated.

During installation, furnishings must be inspected for damage. Unfortunately, damage or flaws are somewhat common. In this case any necessary insurance claims with shipping firms and manufacturers must be processed without delay.

Although there are inevitable frustrations during the execution phase, it can also be the most gratifying part of the design process. There is great satisfaction when the research and design development finally come together into a completed design. It is exciting to witness what was once a few scrawls on a scrap of paper emerging into something very real, innovative, beautiful, and functional.

POST-OCCUPANCY EVALUATION

After a period of time when users have lived with and tested the effectiveness of the design, the *post-occupancy evaluation (POE)* reveals how well the design functions. The evaluation can be accomplished by on-location interviews and open-ended questionnaires. It might seem that the information from such evaluations would be too late to be of any value. The value lies in future improvements and in the benefit of information that can be implemented in other projects. The evaluation is a tool that helps the designer perform better because of the added insight provided.[2]

NONRESIDENTIAL CONSIDERATIONS

The design process for nonresidential interiors is largely the same as for a residence with the exception of the following.

- Nonresidential design has a greater emphasis on the preparation of contracts and agreements between the client and designer. This is the reason nonresidential design is often referred to as contract design. However, contracts for residential projects are not uncommon today.

- Preparation of bids is a more common procedure in nonresidential design. The designer develops a concept and prepares an estimate of how much the

Figure 1.16 *Hospitality design is a specialty that focuses on the creation of restaurants and hotels such as this.*

Photo courtesy of Victor Huff Partnership/Karl Francetic, photographer.

implementation of the concept will cost. This information is presented to the client, who can compare the concept and its cost with similar presentations by other designers.

- The specialties in nonresidential design are diverse, including health care, hospitality (hotels and restaurants), commercial (stores and businesses), and office planning. Specialization allows the designer to stay current on issues within his or her area of focus. However, any designer willing to invest the time in research might be able to develop a suitable design solution for any area of specialty.

- The profile for a nonresidential design may be more generic. Because customers, employees, and guests are transient, the design of a nonresidential space may not be for a specific person but rather for any person who performs a certain task or uses a certain space. Consequently, it is more important to identify most nonresidential users in terms of numbers and functions, which are generic considerations. However, for others—such as a president, a chairman of the board, or the senior partner of a law firm—personal preferences will have to be assessed as they would for a residential user. Their offices might be furnished with more personal and costly items.

- Nonresidential designs are often larger in scope, size, and budget, so their planning may be more complex. For example, on large projects, such as hotels or hospitals that require several years for completion, it is usually necessary to substitute for items that may have been discontinued by the manufacturer in the interim. The designer will select substitutes that maintain the integrity of the original design.

- Codes and restrictions also force the designer to be aware of the needs of the handicapped. Today, all areas of a public building must be easily accessible to those with physical limitations (see chapter 2, Design for Special Populations). Codes are contained in documents available from state building boards, from health, safety, and welfare departments, and from agencies such as the American National Standards Institute, which have prepared specifications for making buildings accessible to the physically handicapped. The International Conference of Building Officials has prepared a document called the Uniform Building Code (UBC). This is a set of guidelines for construction that is accepted nationwide.[3]

NOTES

1. For a more complete set of life-style considerations: June Curran, *Profile Your Lifestyle* (Los Altos: Brooks, 1979).

2. *ASID Report*, vol. XII, no. 4, 13–16.

3. The UBC is available from International Conference of Building Officials, 5360 South Workman Road, Whittier, Cal. 90601.

C H A P T E R

2

DESIGN FOR SPECIAL POPULATIONS

Bradley Slade, photographer.

THE ADA AND UNIVERSAL DESIGN

In January 1992, the Americans with Disabilities Act of 1990 (the ADA) became law. This landmark civil rights legislation represents one of the most significant steps in eliminating widespread discrimination caused by the imposition of barriers restricting those with disabilities. It is no longer satisfactory to provide separate facilities for people with disabilities; they must be integrated into facilities planned for the general public. The law recognizes that they *are* the general public and that they are entitled to the same treatment received by the public at large. Those who have difficulty or limitations with life activities such as walking, hearing, seeing, or using their hands are protected by the ADA. Designers have responded to the challenge with the concept of *universal design*.[1]

Universal design implies that well-planned designs will meet the needs of every user without drawing attention to those with disabilities. For example, older buildings with many steps are not accessible to regular wheelchair users. Ramps can be installed to make the building accessible. But the ramp is a special addition, and while it is functional, it draws attention to the wheelchair user who must use a different method of entry. New facilities designed on level grade, where all can enter in the same manner, are examples of universal design—everyone is accommodated without drawing attention to distinctions of ability.

The universal design concept raises philosophical questions about whether the goal is obtainable or even desirable in some cases. The ADA allows that it is not necessary to tear down existing structures with steps; they need to be modified, not destroyed. It is doubtful that our world will ever be completely *accessible* without isolating, to some degree, those with disabilities. New planning and design will certainly be universal, but older facilities will always be a reminder of a time when little thought was given to making life "normal" for those with limited ability. In Europe, where many buildings and much of the infrastructure are older, strategies for accessibility include the design of new wheelchairs capable of climbing stairs. Universal design is the ideal that has been mandated for today and the future, and where universal design is impossible, accessibility is imperative.

Given the fact that we may all encounter some form of impairment at some point in our lives, it is remarkable that our home designs rarely are planned accordingly. The experiences of one woman, who spent many years caring for her wheelchair-bound mother, are not uncommon. Her experience included dealing with the enormous difficulty created by barriers. Her mother's home was never planned to accommodate such limited mobility, and it was necessary to construct an inconvenient makeshift wooden ramp up the steep front steps. The kitchen and bathroom designs made the situation even more difficult.

After the death of her mother, the woman planned and built a home for herself that was based on universal design principles. According to her *barrier-free design*, all of the entrances were on the level or accessed by gentle slopes, and the garage was level with the utility entrance. All doorways were wide enough to accommodate passage of a wheelchair, bathrooms were large enough to maneuver a wheelchair, and wall frames were reinforced to allow later addition of grab bars. She commented that had it not been for the experience with her mother's disability, she would never have planned as she did. Visitors to the home are unaware of the subtle differences, and the costs in planning and building were slight. The home is beautiful and functions perfectly for her, even if she may never need the features she has built in.

Few of us have the foresight to imagine that such planning will be of benefit to us or a family member at some point in our lives. Whether impaired or not, universal design works well for everyone.

SPECIAL POPULATIONS

Those with distinctive but similar design needs constitute special populations. Such populations include those with limited motion, hearing, or vision, as well as the elderly who may have some form of impairment in one or more of those areas. Our bias seems to be to lump people into tidy groups, but it is important to note that impairments need not be measured by fixed standards and that the population in general is prone to some type of limitation, whether temporary or chronic. For example, many of us wear glasses for impaired vision, some of us find ourselves with broken limbs, and those of us who have spent too much time listening to loud music will find that we have mild or significant hearing losses. Impairments are relative and affect almost everyone at some point. The designation of special populations is helpful only because it makes us aware of needs.

DESIGN FOR MOTION IMPAIRMENTS

Those with impaired motion may be "ambulant-disabled," meaning that difficulty in walking may require the use of crutches, a cane, or a walker. The "chairbound-disabled" depend on a wheelchair for mobility. The motion-impaired may also have some loss of ability to use the hands. Most of the considerations for those with impaired motion center around physical barriers such as level changes introduced by curbs, multiple stories, steps, and paving or flooring materials of varying thicknesses. Doors, either by their narrow width or their weight, also form barriers. Standard bathroom and kitchen designs present a number of challenges for those with impaired motion, particularly for those confined to wheelchairs.

Figure 2.1 *A ramp added near steps, together with an automatic door, make this entrance barrier-free.*
Bradley Slade, photographer.

The following is a list of design considerations for those with motion impairment. These considerations, while not all-inclusive, are representative and intended to create awareness. (The complete requirements of the ADA are not included here.)[2]

Steps and Ramps

‣ Many ambulant-disabled find stairs easier to negotiate than ramps (which are necessary for the chairbound). Consequently, a minimum slope for ramps is best, with a rise of one foot for every twelve feet of length (1:12).

‣ Steps should not have protruding nosing which will catch the toes of those with stiff legs, braces, or other leg problems.

‣ All ramps and steps should be well lit, with focus lighting directed at walking hazards. Whenever possible, they should be covered to remain dry and free from ice.

‣ The top of a *handrail* should be thirty-four to thirty-eight inches above the ramp or steps.

‣ Handrails should be oval or round, with 1 1/2-inch hand clearance between the rails and the wall. This will provide ease of grip but will prevent the hand or wrist from slipping between the handrail and the wall if the person loses balance.

‣ The handrail should have a gripping surface of 1 1/4 to 1 1/2 inches, and should not be interrupted by newel posts or other elements.

Handrail diagram.

Passage and Turning

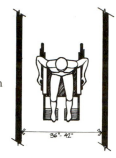

- For a single wheelchair, thirty-two inches is minimum clearance at a point such as a door (thirty-six inches is better), and thirty-six inches is minimum clearance in a continuous passage (forty-two to forty-eight inches is better). Minimum clearance for two chairs to pass each other is sixty inches.

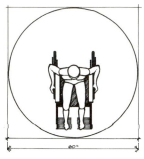

- The space required by a wheelchair to make a 180-degree turn is a clear space of sixty inches.
- The clear floor space required for a wheelchair is thirty by forty-eight inches.
- The force needed to push a door open should not exceed eight pounds of pressure.

- Lever-type door handles are easier to operate than round doorknobs, which are slippery and hard to operate with limited strength. Thumb-latch fixtures are equally hard to operate with limited strength or motion.
- A kickplate at the bottom of a door protects the door from the impact of a wheelchair's footrest.
- Floors should have a flat, nonskid surface. If carpet is used, then it should be securely attached, without a cushion or pad. Pile depth should not be more than one-half inch, since anything with a deeper pile makes passage difficult.
- Flooring materials should be flush, since a change in depth greater than one-half inch forms a barrier.

Kitchens

- All areas of a kitchen should be accessible to a frontal approach as well as a parallel approach by a wheelchair. This means an access space of no less than thirty by forty-eight inches, or a minimum distance of forty-eight inches between opposing elements. In a U-shaped kitchen, the distance should be increased to sixty inches.

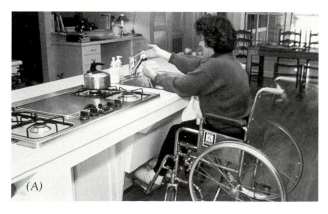

- Varying countertop heights are recommended. A low counter near the sink for food preparation is helpful. Heights of twenty-eight, thirty-two, and thirty-six inches are good, with a maximum depth of twenty-four inches so items on the countertop can be easily reached.

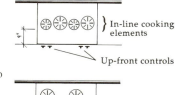

- Upper cabinets should be adjustable to several heights. Eight inches above the counter is the minimum for very small users.
- Handles on upper cabinets should be mounted a maximum of forty-eight inches from the floor, with those on lower cabinets a minimum of twenty-seven inches from the floor.
- Leaving space under the counter, especially at the sink, allows a wheelchair to approach. Hot water pipes should be insulated so the wheelchair user will not be burned.
- The sink controls should be mounted on the side or no more than eighteen inches from the front of the counter for easy reach.
- The toe-kick space under cabinets should be twelve inches high and eight inches deep to accommodate a wheelchair footrest.
- Pull-out trays allow better access than standard drawers and shelves.

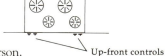

- Wall-mounted ovens and microwaves allow wheelchair access.
- Cook tops should have staggered burners so the users do not have to reach over a hot front burner to access a back burner.
- Cook-top controls should be front mounted for easy reach by a seated person.

In-line cooking elements
Up-front controls
Up-front controls

(A) Both the height of the countertop and the cutouts below the sink allow the user complete access. (B) Eye-level window placement in this barrier-free kitchen creates a pleasant environment.

© Barrier-Free Environments, Inc., Raleigh, NC.

Bathrooms

- Doors should be at least thirty-six inches wide (preferably thirty-nine inches). Pocket doors keep the space clear and make access easier.
- No cabinet under the sink makes the vanity accessible.
- Toilets should be wall mounted nineteen inches off the floor for easy approach by a wheelchair. The toilet is most easily accessed from the side or with a diagonal approach.

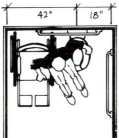

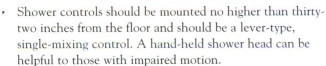
Diagonal approach

- Grab bars must be anchored in wood so they will support at least 250 pounds. There should be a twenty-four to thirty-six-inch horizontal grab bar located behind, and three inches above, the back of the toilet, as well as a thirty-inch horizontal bar mounted twelve inches from the back wall on the wall beside the toilet.

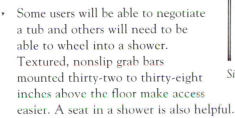
Side approach

- Some users will be able to negotiate a tub and others will need to be able to wheel into a shower. Textured, nonslip grab bars mounted thirty-two to thirty-eight inches above the floor make access easier. A seat in a shower is also helpful.
- Shower controls should be mounted no higher than thirty-two inches from the floor and should be a lever-type, single-mixing control. A hand-held shower head can be helpful to those with impaired motion.
- Faucets at the sink should also be lever controlled as well as side mounted. Water temperature should be set down to prevent scalding.
- Medicine cabinets should be mounted lower in a side wall so they can be easily accessed.
- Vanity mirrors should be installed low enough to be used by someone seated in a wheelchair. The mirror should be at least sixteen by twenty inches and may need to be tilted for complete visibility.
- Nonslip flooring is imperative, as is good ventilation to prevent condensation that might cause slipping.

Bedrooms

- The height of the mattress should be equal to the height of the wheelchair. The nightstand should be the height of the bed.
- To accommodate a wheelchair, there must be a sixty-by sixty-inch clear space, usually between the bedroom door and the bed, or between the storage space and the bed. A minimum of thirty-six inches at the foot and far side of the bed will facilitate making the bed and cleaning.

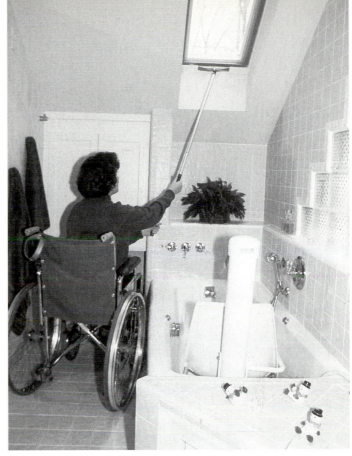

Ample space allows mobility in this bathroom, and the window can be controlled with the use of a hand-held extension. Also note the lift in the bathtub.
© Barrier-Free Environments, Inc., Raleigh, NC.

- A footboard and headboard will often help in getting in and out, and a slatted headboard may be helpful in turning over or moving in bed.

Closets

- Bifold or sliding doors are best.
- Rods should be mounted forty-five to fifty-four inches for access from a wheelchair.
- Shelves higher than fifty inches are not accessible from a seated position.
- Slide-out shelves are more accessible.

General Consideration Around the House

- Electrical outlets should be twenty-seven to twenty-eight inches above the floor. Switches should be thirty-six inches above the floor.
- At least one sixty-inch-diameter turning space is required in each room of the house.
- Drawer pulls throughout the house should be D-shaped for better gripping.
- Windowsills set at a maximum of thirty-six inches make windows accessible to wheelchair users.
- Crank-operated casement windows are ideal for those with impaired motion.

DESIGN FOR HEARING IMPAIRMENT

Over eight million people in the United States have extreme hearing loss. These people want to live normal and productive lives. Design can help make the quality of their lives better by alleviating some of the problems inherent in the interior environment. Many of the problems associated with hearing loss center around noise and sound reverberation, as well as adequate light to use manual communication (signing and lip reading).

- Carpet and fabric wall coverings reduce noise reverberation and improve the acoustics for the hearing impaired.

- Good lighting is imperative for adequate decoding of manual communication and lip reading.

- Good natural light helps visually and also creates the psychological feeling of openness and well-being.

- Furniture arranged in a semicircle or U-shape facilitates signing and lip reading by providing clear sight lines from speaker to listener.

- A round dining table is better than a rectangular table because it also provides clear sight lines.

- Visual signals such as flashing lights can provide important visual cues. The lights are activated by the telephone, doorbell, alarm clock, fire alarm/smoke detector, or a crying baby. The lights can be placed in panels at strategic locations throughout the house.

- Special phone systems are available for the hearing impaired. These systems are called TDD, an acronym for telecommunication device for the deaf. The TDD includes a screen and keyboard and will require a specially planned space.

- Because of the addition of extra electronic devices, adequate outlets should be planned to avoid the unnecessary use of extension cords.

DESIGN FOR VISUAL IMPAIRMENT

Different kinds of physical impairments may require conflicting considerations. For example, curbs that are cut away for the wheelchair bound do not signal the blind that they have reached the street. The person in the wheelchair prefers spaces that are open and larger than normal, while the blind person is more comfortable in a smaller space where many things are within reach. The hearing impaired need a space with little sound reverberation, while the blind need an acoustically "live" space to help find their way.

- The blind need tactile warning of danger. Door handles may be textured to indicate a dangerous area beyond the door, and landings and curbs can be textured to indicate steps or changes of grade.

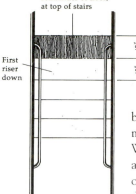

Identifiable texture change, or texture strip—same color as remainder of floor, at top of stairs

First riser down

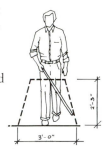

- Outdoors, hanging or projecting objects (even plants and tree branches) that extend into the path of the blind person are dangerous because they cannot be detected with a cane.

- Handrails should extend one foot beyond the end of a stairway, even if it means extending it around a corner. Where there is more than one story, a handrail should extend continuously from floor to floor, rather than stopping at the landing.

- Signage is important. Small groups of letters and numbers can be easily read with the fingers, but larger groups of letters and long texts are difficult for the blind to read.

- Persons born blind learn braille, while most persons blinded later in life do not. Signage should include both letters/numbers and braille symbols.

- To be useful, tactile signals and signage should be uniform throughout a building.

- Audible signals for the blind are helpful at crosswalks, in elevators, and for emergency systems such as smoke detectors/fire alarms.

Raised numerals and letters are legible to those with visual impairment.
Bradley Slade, *photographer.*

- Gas cook tops tend to be better for the blind because they can hear the gas. In addition, electric elements retain heat that can be dangerous for them. Controls should be mounted where the blind will not have to reach over the flame or coils to operate the cook top. Elements, too, should be arranged to avoid reaching over one to get to the other.

- A lip on the counter may be helpful in preventing objects from being pushed off the edge.

- Furniture should have rounded corners and edges, and some padding of table edges may be advisable.

- A hook next to electrical outlets might be desirable to hang a plug where it can be found easily.

Hook for plug may be convenient

- Changes of grade in flooring materials are obstacles for the blind and should be avoided.

DESIGN FOR THE ELDERLY

People are living longer today than ever before. As a result, the elderly population is growing rapidly and becoming an important political and social force. The concerns of the elderly include limited mobility, loss of hearing, and loss of visual acuity. Consequently, all of the considerations listed above apply to the elderly. There may also be loss of memory or other mental powers that makes some tasks more difficult. In addition to the considerations listed above, the following are also important:

- Visual contrast is important in judging space and distance. For example, a countertop should be light or dark in value to contrast with the floor. This helps with depth perception and makes the edges more obvious. The same is true for a tabletop, where depth perception is important.

- In some public spaces and facilities designed for the elderly, wayfinding is important. In a long hallway the location of doors can be indicated with a slight recess in the wall surrounding the doors. Distinctive pieces of furniture and art can be visual reminders of location. Color coding of areas or floors may also prove helpful.

- With age, there may be a tendency in some for the cornea of the eye to yellow. This causes a distortion of color perception and may make a color scheme appear drab and ugly to some. The designer can use a yellow lens to evaluate color schemes for the elderly, making selections that maintain their appeal.

- Loss of control over certain bodily functions may make it desirable to select textiles for upholstery that have been specially treated to resist moisture, or laminated with a thin layer of plastic. The lamination process is almost undetectable.

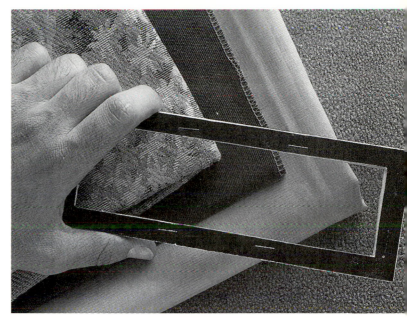

The yellow acetate lens framed in black allows the designer to see colors as older users might.
Bradley Slade, photographer.

OTHER SPECIAL POPULATIONS

This chapter has focused on design for the elderly and those with impaired motion, hearing, and vision. But these represent just a fraction of those with special needs. Other special populations include children, the homeless, the abused, the chemically dependent, religious groups, ethnic and cultural groups, convicted criminals, the poor, the rich, the mentally ill, the sick, the terminally ill, and many others. Again, in most cases these are not fixed groups, but rather situations through which the general population moves. Unlike the design needs of those with physical impairments, the design needs of these groups do not always lend themselves to universal design. For example, public toilets are not scaled to children because the population at large cannot use the small-scaled facilities comfortably. The kind of security demanded by law for convicted criminals is unnecessary for everyone. The considerations associated with these groups are important and worthy of the designer's attention, but they are not always applicable to the needs of people in general.

NONRESIDENTIAL CONSIDERATIONS

We can never be sure if or when a disability will become a reality for us, a friend, an associate, or a member of our family. Until that happens, we often ignore the kind of design that makes life better for those with impairments. But with the passage of the ADA, many of these considerations are law; they can no longer be ignored. The law has pushed us from a perspective of sympathy into a mode of action. In our homes the choice is still ours, but in public, there is no choice.

Figure 2.2 *A hospice for the terminally ill incorporates the reassuring qualities of home.*
Courtesy of Brunschwig & Fils.

Sympathy is one matter and empathy is another. If we all tried spending a day or two with a self-imposed handicap, we would see how frustrating design can be, and we would quickly come to understand the need for the law. We can become aware of how special needs are being met in public spaces, but even more importantly, we can become advocates of good design for special populations.

NOTES

1. The August 1992 issue of *Interior Design* is dedicated to the topic of universal design.

2. For a complete set of information regarding the ADA, contact the U.S. Department of Justice, P.O. Box 66118, Washington, D.C. 20530-6118, (202) 514-0301.

DESIGN PRINCIPLES AND ELEMENTS

Courtesy of Victor Huff Partnership, Karl Francetic, photographer.

THE PRINCIPLES OF DESIGN

The *principles of design—scale* and *proportion, balance, rhythm, emphasis,* and *harmony (variety* and *unity)*—are somewhat abstract concepts that have been in existence and important to great architecture, art, furnishings, textiles, and hard materials for many centuries. The principles form the theory of *design*. Ideally, the theory of design implies that truly fine interior design incorporates appropriate scale and good proportion, carefully achieved and harmony of all the elements, which is achieved through sensitive balance of variety and unity. These design principles are the bylaws that are universally accepted as the philosophy or rules that should govern the use of the elements of design. Furthermore each element can be judged right or wrong in its use and placement through an evaluation of the principles of design.

For example, the use of color, an important and emotive element of design, can be judged or evaluated in this way according to each principle of design.

- Scale: Is the size or amount of the color appropriate for the decorative scheme, or is it used in too large or too small a quantity or an area?

- Proportion: Do colors complement each other, or is one ill-proportioned by too much or too little intensity or quantity?

- Balance: Is the color balanced with other colors in terms of size and intensity, and is the color distributed throughout the interior to create a balanced effect?

- Rhythm: Does the color carry the eye along with rhythmic smoothness, or is it too punctuated and abrupt in its use?

- Emphasis: Does the color create or support a focal point, or does it detract from the area of emphasis?

- Harmony: Does the use of color yield harmony through the adherence to a unified theme (unity) with enough subtle or dramatic difference to maintain interest in the scheme (variety)? Or does the interior lack harmony because the colors are too weak or competitive?

CHART 3.1   PRINCIPLES OF DESIGN

DESIGN PRINCIPLES

The principles constitute the design theory, bylaws, or governing concepts that work together to make a design composition successful.

Scale: The size of a space or an object, such as the overall dimensions or the largeness or smallness of a room, an object, or a pattern.

Proportion: The size relationship or ratio of parts to the whole, such as the size and placement of the arm compared to the chair.

Balance: The state of equilibrium achieved by arranging architectural components, furnishings, or patterns either symmetrically (exactly the same on each side of a center point), asymmetrically (different on each side), or radially (spokes or concentric circles).

Rhythm: The smooth flow of elements that carries the eye around the room. Types include repetition and alternation, progression or gradation, transition, opposition or contrast, and radiation.

Emphasis: An enhanced point of interest, or a focal point. A room may contain more than one and in varying degrees of dominance.

Harmony (variety and unity): The selection of compatible elements and furnishings that create a pleasing whole.

Scale

Scale deals with actual and relative size and visual weight. Scale is generally categorized as small or light, medium, large or heavy, or grand (extra large). One of the goals of pleasing interior design is to select furnishings that are in scale with one another. This implies a similarity of objects in overall dimensions or in mass (density), in pattern, or in other forms of visual weight. When objects are out of scale with one another, they are not appropriate or harmonious selections. To evaluate the compatibility of objects in relation to scale is of paramount importance in interior design.

Figure 3.1 *Large-scale screens, furniture, patterns, and accessories atop a large-grid floor.*
Courtesy of Brunschwig & Fils.

Although the actual dimensions of two objects may be similar, one may be of a visually heavier scale than the other because of its weight or mass and the selection of material. For example, a glass table on legs will appear smaller scaled than a solid wooden chest table. While the overall dimensions might be exactly the same, the glass-topped table allows us to see through the piece, which visually scales it down and makes it appear smaller than the wooden piece.

Pattern and ornament also visually determine scale. A pattern with large motifs may appear visually heavy or massive, while a pattern of the same overall dimensions filled with small motifs and empty areas will appear smaller scaled overall. Likewise, color will affect our impression of scale. Bright, bold colors will appear larger than light, pastel ones.

The scale, or size, of the architecture will often determine the scale of furnishings; small-scale furnishings are used in small interiors and large-scale furnishings are used in large or lofty interiors. This rule can be broken to provide drama or excitement, such as a large-scale pattern in a small area (which will also make the space seem much smaller). Conversely, small scale in a large interior might look tailored and may visually expand the space even further. Floor plans are drawn to scale, with 1/4, 1/8, or 1/16 inch usually equaling one foot.

In choosing or judging scale, perhaps the most important consideration is human scale. Very large and very small scale often feel awkward to people. Although grand scale is impressive and dramatic in public architecture, and small scale is wonderful for children, for the majority of adults, scale is most appropriate when it complements and easily accommodates the average human form. Because we are most comfortable with these dimensions, the standard ceiling height in homes is eight feet, and chairs and sofas generally have a standard seating height and depth.

Often we need to determine if the scale is right for the setting. This is done by comparing the scale of the object to other objects and to the architecture where it is found. This comparison tells us if the scale is well chosen. When parts of the object are compared to other parts of itself, the comparison forms the basis for proportion and is the reason the two principles—scale and proportion—are frequently discussed together; they are interdependent.

Proportion

Proportion is closely related to scale and is usually expressed in terms of the size relationship of parts to one another and to the whole. Proportion also deals with shapes and forms and their dimensions. It is, for example, the relationship of a chair seat or back to its base or arms, or of the size and scale of the tabletop to its legs. When the relationship or ratio is

---

CHART 3.2   ELEMENTS OF DESIGN

DESIGN ELEMENTS

The elements are the components that can be manipulated to give form to the principles of design. The elements are seen in the arrangement of architectural structure and details and in the compositions of materials, furnishings, and accessory items.

Space: The defining of open and closed areas and positive (filled) space versus negative (empty) space to create a building, interior, or furnishings composition.

Shape or form: Shape is the two-dimensional outline often seen as a geometric figure, such as a rectangle, triangle, or circle. Form is three-dimensional, as seen in cubes, cones, and spheres.

Mass: The actual or visual weight, density, or relative solidity of a form.

Line: The connection of two points that gives direction: vertical, horizontal, angular, or curved. Each has a psychological impact.

Texture: The relative smoothness or roughness of a surface; texture is read physically (by touch) or visually. Very small pattern is often read as texture.

Pattern: The arrangement of motifs to create a unified design, such as a pattern seen in an area rug or upholstery textile.

Light: Natural sunlight and artificial light (lamps, bulbs) that affect the appearance of all other elements of design.

Color: Hues such as red, yellow, and blue that can vary from light to dark and from intense to dull, can be mixed with other colors, and can be combined in color schemes or hue combinations to create a psychological impression within interior design.

Figure 3.2 *Small-scale chair, balusters, and wood work are charming and intimate in this seaside cottage.*

Window shades by and photo courtesy of Hunter Douglas Corp.

pleasing, the furniture is well proportioned. The evaluation of proportion is based on ratios, or the comparison of sizes. For example, a table that is well proportioned has side dimensions (width and length) that relate well to each other, creating a nicely shaped rectangle—neither too wide nor too narrow for the function of the piece. Another example might be a sofa table (placed behind the back of the sofa and the same height as the back), which must be relatively narrow or it will be cumbersome and ill proportioned. Likewise, a family dining table that is wider than three and one-half feet may be too wide for food to be comfortably passed across it. Tables for other uses should have sizes evaluated according to their use or function.

Throughout the centuries that humans have worked toward pleasing proportions, many theories of what is good and acceptable have been espoused. One of the best known is that of the ancient Egyptians and, later, the classical Greeks. They stated that pleasing proportions were termed golden. The *golden mean* is a line of division that visually divides an object, a wall, a tieback drapery treatment, or other furnishings into two unequal but harmonious parts; that line falls somewhere between one-half and one-third (vertically or horizontally). For example, the placement of a chair rail or dado molding creates pleasing proportions above and below the molding when it is placed not in the middle of the wall or one-third of the way up the wall, but somewhere in between. Tieback draperies or curtains are also divided into pleasing proportions somewhere between one-third to one-half way up from the bottom or down from the top of the treatment.

The *golden section* refers to proportions of parts to one another and to the whole. The progressions—3 to 5 to 8 to 13 to 21 and so on—are considered pleasing ratios or proportions as they relate to one another and roughly equate the theory of the golden mean. Further, these increments can be translated into sides of rectangles, called golden rectangles, which form the basis for a study of good proportions. For example, a table or art piece three feet by five feet is a pleasing proportion, as are multiples (or divisions) of those dimensions: twelve by twenty (four times three and four times five) or fifteen by twenty-five (five times three and five times five). A room with golden rectangle dimensions will theoretically be the easiest in which to arrange furnishings, and a golden rectangle window should pose few aesthetic window treatment problems. The golden mean, golden section, and golden rectangle are examples of how harmonious proportions can be calculated.

Figure 3.3 *This historic chest on chest is divided according to the golden section, just below the halfway mark.*

Many other philosophies of good proportion exist, but the bottom line is the "sense of rightness" that we feel or recognize when good proportion is evident. Recognizing good proportion is an intuitive ability for some people, and for others, it may take time and deliberate study to learn to recognize and to sense pleasing proportion. Much of what we learn about good proportion comes from studying classic architectural exteriors, interior detail, classic furniture, great works of art, and the beautiful application of finish materials and other furnishings—the design of these has been recognized for years or even centuries as good, or of pleasing proportions.

Balance

Balance is *equilibrium*, or the arrangement of objects physically or visually to reach a state of stability and poise. Balance is an important concept because of the human need for balance in our lives. Balance is not only necessary for physical confidence in our actions and movements, it is a guidepost in achieving satisfaction and fulfillment in life itself, and so we naturally seek it in our interiors. This state of equilibrium is achieved in one of three ways: through *symmetrical* or *formal balance*, through *asymmetrical* or *informal balance*, or by *radial balance*.

Symmetrical Balance

Symmetrical balance is also known as *bisymmetrical*, *formal*, or *passive balance*. Symmetrical balance creates a mirror image by the placement of items that are exactly the same on both sides of a central point. This might be a matching pair

Figure 3.4 *Formal symmetrical balance (mirror image) is dignified and restrained.*

Courtesy of Focal Point, Inc., Atlanta, GA.

Figure 3.5 *Studied symmetry is found in the matching bookcases, chairs, and accessories. The asymmetrical placement of the plants, art, and door relieves the exactness.*

of mantel vases on each side of a painting or mirror. Or formal balance can be seen as matching nightstands or end tables with matching lamps placed on them. It could be a formal dining table where the chairs are placed exactly across from each other. Symmetrical balance suggests restraint, refinement, orderliness, and formality. Bisymmetrical balance is passive because it requires no judgment; we know exactly what to expect. Because formal balance is predictable, it adds a type of steadiness and durability to interior design. Much classical design—from the Greeks and Romans to the Renaissance, Baroque, and subsequent periods—was symmetrical. The symmetry created a sense of power and grandeur.

However, because of its unchanging nature, symmetrical balance can become stale and boring. In fact, it has been said that a really good symmetrical composition always contains elements of asymmetry. The symmetrical nature of historic designs was broken by asymmetric placement of figures in a frieze or by inclusion of dissimilar sculptural pieces in symmetrical niches. Rigid symmetry is less suitable to today's less formal and more relaxed life-style.

Asymmetrical Balance

Asymmetrical balance is also known as *informal*, *active*, *optical*, or *occult balance*. Asymmetrical balance can be accomplished in two ways:

1. Dissimilar objects can be placed at varying distances from the center point.

2. Objects of similar visual weight or form may be balanced at equal distance from an imaginary central dividing line.

Asymmetrical balance is often difficult to accomplish. It requires finding objects that are compatible yet varied enough to be interesting, then arranging the objects, judging the arrangement, and often rearranging them over and over until the sense of equilibrium is judged to "feel right." This effort justifies the nickname active, because it requires active participation to accomplish. The term optical balance is derived from the necessity of judging the composition with the eye, or the optic sense. Achieving asymmetrical balance demands patience and sensi-

Figure 3.6 *Asymmetrical or informal balance is seen in the arrangement of furniture and accessories. Courtesy of Better Homes and Gardens, member of Home Furnishings Council.*

tivity and certainly comes easier to some people than to others. Yet the results are definitely worth the efforts because asymmetrical balance can be deeply pleasing and does not readily become tiresome.

Although informal balance is the most common of the alternative names of asymmetrical balance, it is also known as occult balance because it has no set rules of what is right and is, therefore, somewhat elusive or mysterious. The Western world has learned much of asymmetrical balance from the strong Japanese influence in architecture and design. Oriental philosophies are based on the intrinsic, harmonious, and asymmetrical arrangement seen in nature, then translated through careful study and application to interior design compositions.

Radial Balance

Radial balance is a state of equilibrium that is based on the circle. It is seen as chairs surrounding a round table or as concentric circles in a chandelier or lighting fixture. On a small scale, it is seen on the round dial of a clock; on a larger scale, as circular furniture arrangements of comfortable chairs for a group gathering. Radial balance can also be seen as spokes extending from a wheel, pedestal table, or chair base. A form of radial balance can be seen in the grain of a dining table where the veneer (top layer) is laid in quarter sections that meet in the center. Historic wooden pieces frequently incorporated radial balance with inlaid pieces of wood. Spiraling forms can also create a type of radial balance.

Rhythm

Rhythm is a concept familiar in music as the beat that continually carries along the melody. In interior design, rhythm carries the eye along a path at a pace determined by the elements that illustrate it. For example, rhythm might be found in the repetitive use of a color, pattern, texture, line, or furniture piece or style. Architectural detail such as stairs, window panes, and moldings illustrate rhythm. Rhythm is also a matter of expectation and anticipation and is a major part in the concept of emphasis or surprise. There are five types of rhythm:

1. Repetition and alternation
2. Progression or gradation
3. Transition
4. Opposition or contrast
5. Radiation

Repetition establishes rhythm through the repetitive use of an element of design, as previously suggested. Repetition not only establishes a continuity and flow of rhythm, it also provides unity, or sameness, which is a part of the principle of harmony. For example, a color repeated throughout an interior can establish rhythm if the eye can smoothly connect rather than jumping or leaping from colored object to colored object. Repetition is seen in rows of seats in a church or theater, in a set of books bound to match, or in the same style of lighting fixture

Figure 3.7 *Repetitive rhythm is seen in the floor pattern, cabinetry detail, and even the rabbits on the soffit near the ceiling.* © Jessie Walker.

used many times in a public space. In architectural detail, repetition may be seen in the same window in classic architecture such as the elegant Georgian home (see chapter 15) or in moldings such as dentil trim or in the classic egg-and-dart sequence (see chapter 15). The egg-and-dart motif repeats two shapes symbolizing birth and death, and they are used in alternation, where every other design is the same.

Alternation is the sequence of two or more components by which the eye can follow a rhythmic pattern. It is also seen in historic buildings with coffered ceilings, where a wafflelike pattern has both high and low areas.

Progression, or *gradation*, is seen in shapes progressing from large to small or small to large, such as the front steps leading to the *piano nobile* (raised entrance) in classic architecture, or a set of nesting tables, where each smaller table fits beneath its next larger counterpart. A collection of different-sized boxes or a candelabrum (descending branched candlestick) are accessory items that can create rhythm by progression, or gradation.

Progressive rhythm (rhythm by gradation) can also be seen in the value of color, where a color scheme contains shades that vary from very light values (perhaps on the ceiling) to medium values (on the wall) to dark values (on the floor) and where the values are further expanded in the furnishings. This light-to-medium-to-dark progressive sequence is also discussed in chapter 4, Color, as the concept of value distribution.

Figure 3.8 Rhythm by gradation is seen in the decreasing sizes of the nesting tables. Angular lines juxtaposed by the chair's curved arm suggest rhythm by opposition.
Photo by Gordon Lonsdale.

Transition is a rhythm that leads the eye without interruption from one point to another. Rhythm by transition can be established by a continuous line, usually an architectural element such as a crown or dado molding or an arched doorway. A stenciled or wallpaper border or a painted graphic or a long carpet runner are methods of creating an uninterrupted visual, rhythmically flowing line.

Opposition, or *contrast*, is an abrupt change that forms interesting, repetitive rhythm and is seen in three ways. First, as repetitive 90-degree angles—such as window frames or grids, as built-in units (such as cabinetry and luminous ceilings), and as the corners of angular furniture or framed artwork. Second, opposition or contrast can be seen in patterns: open and closed, busy and plain, light and dark combinations of fabric, area rugs, or other textiles or wall coverings. Third, forms can be placed to contrast in a pleasing rhythm. Angular shapes placed next to rounded shapes not only create rhythm by contrast or opposition, they also give relief and a type of asymmetrical balance.

Figure 3.9 Rhythm by opposition is seen in the right angles of this window fenestration, chest, and screen.

Radiation, which is essentially the same as radial balance, is the final type of rhythm. The type of rhythm that is established by radiating concentric or spokelike lines or forms can be dramatic and impressive. It is sometimes employed as designs in large, custom floor coverings in places such as lobbies and ballrooms or in grand ceilings where architectural carving or cast plaster creates a radial effect. As such, it can be very

Figure 3.10 Rhythm by radiation is seen in concentric circles in the steps and as spokelike lines in the glass arch of the winter garden at the World Financial Center in New York City. See also chapter opening photo.

© Rafael Macia/Photo Researchers, Inc.

beautiful and give the room a circular, sweeping, rhythmic movement. On a smaller scale, radiation can be seen in place settings at a round or oval table or as furniture forms in a circular grouping.

Emphasis

Emphasis is the creation of a *focal point*—an area visually important enough to draw and hold attention. Examples of dramatic, demanding focal points include a beautiful fireplace, a view from a window (or even an art glass window), a wall of dramatic art, or an impressive piece or grouping of furniture. A rhythmic progression—a many-doored hallway, for example, ending in a vista such as a fine furniture piece or artwork—is the principle of emphasis.

Some interiors may have multiple focal points, each one with a different level of emphasis, progressing from the most to the least dominant in order to avoid conflict. Logically, smaller areas can handle fewer focal points than larger areas. An exception might be an art gallery, where each piece of art is given equal opportunity to be a point of interest and emphasis.

Where varying levels of emphasis are planned, the dominant focal point could migrate. For example, in the winter the fireplace is a logically comforting focal point that dominates interest. In warmer seasons, through rearrangement of the furnishings, the dominant focal point might become a large window with a view. Where no focal point exists, one can be created in the guise of bookcases, china cabinets, artwork (displayed individually or in group arrangements), tapestries, rugs, quilts or other art fabrics, and mirrors.

The elements of design can be manipulated to give greater emphasis to a focal point. Arranging furniture shapes to face the focal point, directing lines toward the focal point, grouping or massing objects to give visual weight to the focal point, or using more dramatic color at the area of the focal point are ways to increase emphasis.

Figure 3.11 *The rustic fireplace grouping is the focal point in this Western setting.*
Courtesy of Waverly.

Harmony: Variety and Unity

Harmony is the combination of design elements, architecture, and furnishings into a pleasing or orderly whole—a state of agreement or a feeling of rightness. Harmony is the result of a delicate balance of two subprinciples: variety and unity.

Variety is the absence of monotony or sameness, yet it is much more. Variety is a healthy, positive influence that brings about vitality, interest, and diversity. It can be seen through a selection of differing colors, textures, furniture and accessory styles, through the contrast of hard materials with soft materials, and through the combination of seemingly divergent old (historic) and new (modern) architecture and furnishings. Yet variety without some order or a master plan can become confusing and dissonant.

Unity, the other component of harmony, complements and balances variety. Unity suggests a oneness and uniformity—an identity that establishes a master plan. Unity is the goal that is being sought and, hopefully, achieved when all the various elements and furnishings are brought together.

Unity can be achieved by carrying out a cohesive color scheme or by keeping the character and style of the furniture consistent. Unity dictates selecting background materials, fabrics, and accessories that all have a similar feeling. This means that the use of pattern or ornament, color and value, surface textures (smooth or rough), and even the grain of the wood (coarse or fine) is consistent in character with the master plan.

Unity is often thematic, as discussed in chapter 1. At the outset, every planned interior should have goals of identity and oneness. This design statement, master plan, or set of goals should be organized and set forth on paper in written and graphic form, so that every furnishing item, whether purchased at once or over a period of years, will be selected to

Figure 3.12 *Harmony is made of two subprinciples: unity and variety. Here, colors and textures unify, while form and accessories provide variety.*
© Jessie Walker.

Figure 3.13 *A Soho, New York, loft with expansive space made livable by furniture groupings.*
© Rafael Macia/Photo Researchers, Inc.

complement all other furnishings specified. It is wise and thoughtful planning that sets apart fine design from interiors that lack harmony. True harmony is within the reach of everyone who studies, plans, and directs their efforts toward design of the highest caliber.

THE ELEMENTS OF DESIGN

The *elements of design—space, shape* or *form, mass, line, texture, pattern, light,* and *color*—are used by every designer in every discipline, from interior design to fashion design to landscape design to architecture to community planning. These elements were not invented but discovered and skillfully incorporated and balanced by artisans and designers over the course of history. Because of the basic and crucial nature of the elements of design, they are discussed in nearly every fine art textbook and wherever the education or evaluation of a designed work takes place.

Keep in mind that every element of design can be used effectively or ineffectively and that many compositions exist that are not perfect in their use of the elements. For example, an interior may have dramatic space, perfectly balanced light, well-proportioned form or mass, and appropriate line but may be filled with poorly selected pattern, texture, or color. Or perhaps the pattern, texture, and color are well chosen, yet some of the other elements are used ineffectively. As students of design, we seek to recognize and to perfect the skillful use of the elements of design in interiors.

Space

Although the elements of design are equally important, space is perhaps the cornerstone of interior design elements, because space exists as a diffuse, endless entity until it is defined. The definition of space occurs with building construction, resulting in exterior and interior spacial allotments. Space-restricting devices within the building—walls, floors, ceilings, and furnishings—create a series of spaces with individual dimensions and qualities. These qualities can only be discovered as a person moves through spaces and perceives them one at a time: one space flowing into another or one abruptly ending and another beginning. When the space/time movement is complete, the perceptions are mentally assembled to give a true picture and judgment of the space.

The divisions and restrictions of space form the foundation of architectural planning. Interior designers often create unequal space allotments within buildings not only for aesthetic reasons but to answer human needs, as well. Treating spaces of different sizes addresses two basic human needs. First is the need to be protected, enclosed, and comforted. Small spaces give a sense of security from intruders and from the buffeting of the outside world. Small spaces establish territory; they give a sense of pride, of ownership, and offer opportunity to personalize our own space. Conversely, small spaces can be restricting or confining and can spawn restlessness and frustration. Small spaces that are inadequate for functions that are performed there may visually be expanded through the use of light colors, wall-to-wall neutral floor coverings, small-scaled furnishings, mirrors, and smoothly textured surfaces or textures with little pattern. Generous light from more than one source can also give the impression of more space than actually exists.

Large space fills a second basic human need as an outgrowth of the confinement of small space. This is the need to be free, to mentally soar into a space devoid of restrictions, to be stimulated by the immensity of space as compared to the insignificance of human scale. After a while, however, the lack of restriction can create feelings of insecurity and inadequacy and a desire to return to the safe, secure quarters of small spaces. Large interior spaces can be difficult to handle; often there is a need to make the space seem smaller than it is. Effective ways of creating more intimacy in large spaces include using medium- to large-scale patterns and dark or vivid colors that visually advance, furniture that is heavy or solid looking, area rugs (particularly patterned or colored ones that visually break the floor space), large-scale artwork, and multiple furniture groupings (see also chapter 7, Furniture Arrangement).

Many well-planned interiors incorporate both small and large spaces. We see this in homes where a living area or solarium has a high ceiling, where a family room or great room has generous square footage, or where several rooms open onto a solarium, deck, or covered patio. In nonresidential interiors, such as business and professional centers, shopping malls, or hotels, the small, enclosed quarters are offices, boutiques, shops, or hotel rooms, and these are often grouped around a courtyard, atrium, ballroom, or multistoried open lobby area. To emerge from small spaces into large or tall spaces can be exhilarating and satisfying, yet the return to the small areas can bring about a needed sense of personal belonging, security, and safety.

Interior designers create interesting areas of *positive* and *negative* space. Positive space is space that is filled with color, texture, form, or mass. This could be walls, furnishings, art, area rugs, or even graphics or scenes painted on walls. Negative space is the empty space surrounding the positive space—the windows between walls, the floor around the area rug, the wall around and between works of art, the space between furniture pieces or even the cubic footage. In a successful interior, the positive and negative spaces should be balanced in terms of both amount and placement. Some areas may be primarily positive space, others primarily negative, and still others equally distributed between the two. For example, the proportion of negative (empty wall) space between works of art hanging on walls may remain relatively even, or it may be unevenly distributed.

Figure 3.14 *The shape and form of new modern design. (A) The Tric-Trac table lamp imported from Italy makes a bold Art Deco statement. (B) The Piccolo chair—with leather-upholstered seat, arm, and back is adaptable to both residential and nonresidential seating. (C) The Flou-Flou sofa is a plump sumptuous cover draping fluidly over a puffy upholstered base.*

(A) *Courtesy of Calger Lighting, Inc.* (B) *Courtesy of Cy Mann International.*
(C) *Courtesy of Ligne Roset.*

Shape or Form

While we sometimes think of shape as only a two-dimensional outline, form (which is an extension of shape) is the three-dimensional configuration of the objects within the interior. For example, furniture seen in silhouette has shape that can be perceived, and as we move around the furniture, the silhouette changes and we begin to comprehend the three-dimensional quality of the form.

Often an interior is successful because the forms that fill it are beautifully shaped and well proportioned one to another. There are several kinds of shapes: two-dimensional outline shapes or planes—such as rectangles, squares, triangles, circles, and other geometric shapes—or meandering, curved, or angular shapes that do not fit neatly into geometry. When these geometric planes are given a third dimension, they become forms such as cubes, cones, spheres, or forms that are sinuous or curving.

For example, a rectangular table can be an appreciated form and shape that is simple and pleasing, yet if the entire room were filled with similar shapes and forms, the room would become boring and repetitious. Certainly there needs to be a balance of form—a curved chair, perhaps with upholstery covering, to soften the straight lines of the table form. The forms that are placed next to each other will have considerable effect on each other. Sometimes the juxtaposition of unlikely elements, such as the tandem placements of a vintage piece of furniture with a thoroughly modern piece, can create a delightful and charming surprise. On the other hand, certain forms destroy the integrity of each other and prove disastrous to both objects. This might be the placement of a delicate and lacy plant next to the abstract lines of a modern painting where the incongruity is jolting and disturbing. Perhaps a sculptural, abstract plant form, such as a cactus, would be better suited to the shapes in the painting.

The key to selecting forms is to balance them against the proportion and scale of the architecture for the desired psychological effect or feeling and to select each form to complement other nearby forms.

The sensitive and careful selection and arrangement of forms is crucial in an interior because forms have great power to persuade us to feel certain ways, such as alert and attentive or relaxed and secure. Shapes and forms appeal to the senses and can have amazing impact on the person who enters the room. For example, a person entering a room filled with cubes will probably perceive the interior as a no-nonsense one where, perhaps, business takes place. Curved forms are gracious, may make people feel more relaxed, and are commonly used in residential living rooms and bedrooms.

Being sensitive to sculptural forms can increase our appreciation for classical beauty and modern abstract expression. Classic furniture pieces (as discussed in chapter 8) are sculptural forms that are so important that the character of an interior can become impressive with their added presence. Furniture pieces that have endured decades or centuries are revered and appreciated today as fine decorative art largely because of their timeless and appealing forms.

Mass

Mass is the solidity, matter, or density that is defined by shape or form. In furniture, mass is *actual density* when the material is filled in, such as a solid block of wood. Mass can also be *optical density* where the material may not be solid. Heavier or more solid mass will make furniture pieces look larger than furniture with the same overall dimensions but with empty areas instead of solid areas. Examples of furniture with solid or heavy mass include sofas, chairs, and *ottomans* (oversized footstools) with skirts to the floor and/or with oversized cushions; end tables and nightstands supported with bracket feet or no feet or with doors or solid fronts; dining room tables with heavy solid legs or pedestals; and bookcases filled with books (as compared to bookcases with empty areas or areas of art or sculpture).

Figure 3.15 *These ottomans illustrate heavy mass—density or solidity. The upholstery covers the seats to the floor. The dense mass is accentuated by massing, or grouping, three ottomans.*
Courtesy of Brunschwig & Fils.

Heavy mass is desirable where the room is large and furnishings need to visually take up as much space as possible or where furniture needs to appear dignified or commanding.

Massing means grouping together components such as accessories, furniture, or blocks of architecture to create a unified "group mass." Massing will give a weighted, more solid, or

Figure 3.16 *Massing can be seen even on a small scale in this collection of folk art accessories.*
© Bill Crofton/Nawrocki Stock Photo, Inc.

imposing appearance. For example, several framed art pieces on a wall will create an important, heavier looking arrangement than just one or two isolated small pieces. On the coffee table, a book, potted plant, and objects of art grouped into an interesting composition will draw more attention than would the book alone. And, certainly, two sofas placed in an L shape or parallel to each other will look more impressive than a single sofa.

Furniture, accessories, and artwork can be massed together to balance other larger pieces or architectural components such as

windows or fireplaces or to fit into the scale of a room. For example, a low chest with a table lamp could be massed together with a framed art piece to become a visual unit. This unit could then balance a larger case piece such as a breakfront or secretary-type cabinet. Massing can be instrumental in giving richness and completeness to the other components that otherwise might look empty or unfinished when used alone. Certainly a framed artwork by itself on the wall may float awkwardly without something (a table, chair, or chest) to visually anchor it; this is the role of massing.

Architects use massing as a tool to create emphasis or to draw attention. For example, when an exterior is analyzed, it is often clear that the architect has manipulated window openings, wings, or shapes of the roof in such a way as to create areas of emphasis and balance.

Line

Line is the connection of two or more points. The eye also perceives line when two planes meet and when shape is seen in silhouette as an outline. Lines may be *straight* (*horizontal* or *vertical*), *angular* (*diagonal* or *zigzag*), and *curved* (circular, *flowing*, or tightly curved). Lines are used by interior designers to create effects such as increased height, width, or the impression of movement. The psychology of line is important to creating ambience or a particular mood in interior design. The types of line are listed in Chart 3.3, along with the psychological effect of each.

Combining Lines

Lines are used in combination in every interior, yet often one line will be planned to dominate in order to accomplish a desired effect, such as the vertical lines that produce awe and lift the eye heavenward in a church. Furthermore, vertical and horizontal lines generally form the structural foundation for a building in the form of perpendicular floors, walls, and ceilings. Angular and curved lines are utilized for reinforcement, strength, interest, movement, and relief, as seen in triangular roof truss systems and angled ceilings or walls and in dignified archways and domed ceilings.

Figure 3.17 *Stair and window arrangements provide excellent studies in linear composition.*
Left: © Janis Schwartz/International Stock Photo. Center and right: © 1988 Norman McGrath.

CHART 3.3 PSYCHOLOGICAL EFFECTS OF LINE

STRAIGHT LINES:

Horizontal Lines: Weighty, Secure, Restful, Repose.

Horizontal lines suggest a solid, harmonious relationship with the earth; earth's gravity has no further pull. Long horizontal lines can visually expand space, making rooms appear wider or longer. When found in a connecting architectural detail such as a molding, horizontal lines provide a smooth transition between rooms or areas. If they lead to a focal point, they help to emphasize it; when they stop at a window, the eye is guided to the exterior view. Too many horizontal lines in an interior may become boring and lack interest.

Horizontal lines

Vertical Lines: Imposing, Lofty, Solid, Formal, Restrained.

Vertical lines lift the eye upward. They have the ability to lift the mind and the spirit as well. As such, vertical lines are a purposeful tool for architects and designers of churches and public buildings because they inspire awe and tend to diminish the significance of human scale. The use of vertical lines can make an interior seem higher, apparently increasing vertical space. Vertical lines are stable because they represent a perpendicular resistance to earth's gravity. They convey a feeling of strength and dignity and are quite appropriate in formal dining rooms, entry-ways, and formal living areas. This formality can bring a stiffness or commanding feeling to the interior. Too many vertical lines can cause a feeling of uneasiness, of too much confinement and predictability.

ANGULAR LINES:

Diagonal Lines: Action, Movement, Interest, Angular Stability.

Diagonal lines are flexible because their exact direction may vary from shallow to steep angles. Diagonal lines generally suggest movement, action, or dynamism, perhaps because diagonal lines are associated with going places: up or down a diagonal staircase or an escalator, the taking off or landing of an airplane. Interest is usually sustained longer with diagonal lines than with horizontal or vertical lines, possibly because the angles appear to defy gravity and the eye and mind are stimulated. Yet diagonal lines can also be secure, such as the reinforcing diagonals of an angled roof truss system. Too many diagonal lines, particularly on the wall, can be overstimulating and perhaps tiresome.

Vertical and diagonal lines

Zigzag Lines: Exciting, Lively, Rhythmic Movement.

Zigzag lines are short diagonal lines that reverse upon themselves and form a regular or irregular pattern. A zigzag line can be one single line or several in a set. A set of regular zigzag lines is called a chevron or herringbone pattern, and irregular zigzag lines are called a flamestitch pattern. Angular zigzag lines can add energy and life to an interior. If too many zigzag lines are incorporated, however, the effect can be frenzied and agitating.

CURVED LINES:

Curved or Circular Lines: Soft, Humanizing, Repetitive Tempo, Gracefulness.

Curved or circular lines provide relief and softness to straight and angular lines and balance the harshness of too many straight lines. Curved lines give a human quality to interiors; they can be easy on the eyes and pleasant to view. A series of curved lines, such as in an arcade (a procession of arches), gives a rhythmic cadence to the room, suggesting graceful movement. In architectural components, round or elliptic segments (sections of circles or ovals) such as archways provide graceful dignity to interiors. Generously curved lines are viewed as feminine. An excess of curved lines may become too decorative and, consequently, visually disturbing.

Flowing Lines: Gentle Movement, Growth, Linear Development.

Flowing lines are irregularly curved lines that move gently in a random or spiraling manner. Flowing lines may be seen in large, live interior trees, in spiral or curved staircases, or in the lines of fine, Oriental rugs, for example. Inspiration may be taken from the graceful curved lines of growing and changing plant forms. Because we are never certain where the line will end, flowing lines can provide a great deal of interest.

Gently curved to flowing to tightly curved lines

Tightly Curved or Busy Lines: Playful Activity, Zest, Lively Visual Stimulation.

Tightly curved or busy lines are most often seen in textiles and in wall and floor coverings as complicated patterns that are lively, busy, or active. Tightly curved lines can add frivolity and fun to interiors and can make up a pattern that conceals so and visually closes in space. Complicated tightly curved compositions, such as those in vivid floral fabric patterns or in area rugs, add life and may be visually stimulating and even aesthetically satisfying. As such, busy lines may save interiors from becoming dull or boring, yet control over the quality of the design is imperative. Colors and contrast that are bold or feature too much obvious pattern might prove displeasing and detract from the harmony of the interior.

Texture

Texture is the surface characteristics and appearance inherent in every element and component of interior design. As the relative smoothness or roughness of a surface, texture is determined in two ways: by touching the physical texture or by visually reading the surface, which may appear quite different to the eye than it actually is to the touch. Some textures that read as rough are painted or printed tiny patterns that give the impression of a texture when it does not actually exist. An example is the painting of surfaces to look like rock, brick, or tile.

Smooth textures generally are associated with more formal, high-style interiors, while rough textures are often thought to be more casual. Textures generally need to be handled in

Figure 3.18   *Smooth textures abound in this New York penthouse.*
Courtesy of Noel Jeffrey, Inc.

a unified manner, with a compatible feeling to every other texture selected for the interior. However, some contrast in texture is vital for relief and for emphasis. If every texture reads as smooth and glassy, for example, the interior would seem cold and unwelcoming. If every texture is rough, the interior may become harsh and irritating. A balance or a variety of textures is necessary within the unified theme or ambience in order to achieve harmony.

Thus, texture can be used by different individuals to express different preferences.

Upkeep is also a consideration in selecting texture. Light-colored, rough textures will show very little dirt because the relief (high and low areas that produce highlight and shadow) will conceal soil. Smooth surfaces, such as flat walls, glass, or dark, polished wood, will reveal dust and fingerprints.

Pattern

Pattern is the arrangement of forms or designs to create an orderly whole. Pattern often consists of a number of motifs, or single-design units, arranged into a larger design composition. Pattern is seen in printed and woven textiles such as upholstery and drapery fabric, floor rugs, and carpeting. Pattern is also seen in wall coverings and in carved or inlaid furniture designs. Pattern that is too small to distinguish may read as texture.

Figure 3.19   *Rustic elements and rough textures establish a western theme.*
Courtesy of Waverly.

Figure 3.20 *Striped, floral, and chevron designs are handsomely combined in this vignette.*
Courtesy of Waverly.

The Character of the Pattern

When two or more patterns are used in the same interior, the characters or styles must be compatible. For example, a dignified Georgian damask or brocade fabric will not be compatible with a country Victorian printed cotton one. They will have an entirely different look or character.

The Color Scheme

Generally, a closely related color scheme will foster harmony. If one pattern contains blues and yellows, for example, then other patterns should also contain exact, similar, or compatible hues, values, and intensities. If the colors are close but "off," then the patterns will not combine successfully.

The Scale of the Pattern

Pattern scale or size can be similar if the style and the color are compatible. However, when the scale is the same, multiple patterns often seem to conflict. Varying the size or scale of the patterns by using, for example, a large pattern, a small pattern, a tiny pattern, a finely blended stripe or a compatible geometric shape, along with appropriate textures, can be a good means of achieving success in combining pattern.

Light

Light in interior design has two sources: natural light and artificial light. Although natural light admitted in a large quantity through expanses of glass windows may need some means of screening to prevent glare (too much bright light) or heat buildup, natural light is a desirable and an appreciated element of design. The quality, quantity, and color of light affects the way we see our surroundings and, as such, needs direction, control, and perhaps supplemental sources of light.

When natural light cannot fully meet the needs of the interior design, artificial lighting can make up the difference. Artificial light generally comprises incandescent (the common light bulb with a tungsten element that glows to produce heat) and fluorescent (luminous lamps) light. Both natural and artificial light are discussed in further detail in chapter 5.

Light as an element of design affects all other elements. Light can make space appear large or small, friendly or cold. Areas well lit with clear, bright light will make spaces appear larger, whereas dim lights and shadows cast upon walls will seem to close in space.

Combining Patterns

Patterns are frequently combined in interior design. While some combinations are very successful, we often sense incompatibility in other combined pattern schemes. To achieve a feeling of rightness, four things need to be evaluated: (1) the placement of emphasis, (2) the character of the pattern, (3) the color scheme, and (4) the scale of the patterns to be combined.

The Placement of Emphasis

Emphasis is giving importance to one pattern over another so that conflict is minimized. Emphasis is established by using a greater amount of one pattern or a larger scale of one pattern than another.

Figure 3.21 _Natural light illuminates the lobby of International Business Machines (IBM) in Purchase, New York._

© Steve Rosenthal. Courtesy of Pei, Cobb, Freed & Partners, Architects.

Light can alter the apparent form or shape of furnishings. By lighting portions and leaving other areas in darkness, the form can appear much different than it actually is. Low-wattage light sources or backlighting (throwing light behind an object) can affect mass by making objects appear heavier than they really are.

Light affects the way we interpret texture when it highlights textural relief (surface irregularities), and light affects pattern by clarifying or by submerging details. For example, a rough texture can appear even rougher when a light is cast on it at a parallel angle. Light directed onto a surface at a low, nearly parallel angle will emphasize the relief through highlight and shadow. A smooth texture will appear smoother with a directional band of light, such as a spotlight or a smooth wash of light. Likewise, clear light shining directly on a pattern will emphasize the pattern details, and low light casting shadows on a pattern will minimize the details.

Light can change the apparent identity of a color through the color and type of light that hits the surface. Further, different materials may reflect light and color in different ways, affecting the relationship of the colors to each other.

Color

Color, the last element of design, is the most emotional and personal of all the elements. Although everyone has individual preferences toward, and prejudices against, certain colors, humans generally respond similarly to color combinations within each culture. Here the psychology of color is based on the reaction of people in the United States and similar cultures in regard to color hue, value, and intensity.

Hues, or colors, such as reds, oranges, and yellows are stimulating; blues, greens, and violets are calming. Hues as seen on the standard color wheel can be divided into equal groups where one-half of the wheel consists of warm colors that are stimulating, friendly, cozy, and inviting, and the other half consists of calming cool colors that suggest restraint, dignity, and formality.

Color values are the relative lightness or darkness of the hues; for example, a high-value, light red is a pink; a low value, dark red is a burgundy. Lighter colors seem to recede, making space appear larger and giving a more airy look to the interior, whereas darker values do the opposite—close in and give a cavelike coziness. Distribution of value is sought after in most fine interior design, where some values of light, medium, and dark hues are carefully placed to achieve the desired effect. When placed next to each other, light and dark values (*high contrast*) can be dramatic, whereas hues close in value (*low contrast*) create a subtly blended, calming environment.

Color intensity is the brightness versus the dullness of a hue. Pure colors can be lowered in intensity by adding a neighboring or a contrasting color or by adding white, black, gray, or any combination of these. Bright, bold, pure colors are exciting and happy. These need careful handling so as not to become overbearing through overuse or indiscriminate placement. Dull colors can be dark, medium, or light in value but are generally easy to live with because they are undemanding. Often a good balance is found in rooms that utilize the law of chromatic distribution: The larger areas are dulled and neutralized, and the smallest areas are brightest, with the intensity becoming brighter as the areas become smaller.

Color is examined in greater depth in chapter 4, which covers the theory, guidelines, and psychology of color.

Figure 3.22 *In the apartment of the late artist Andy Warhol, unusual furnishings provide an opportunity to evaluate design.*
© 1987 Norman McGrath.

EVALUATING DESIGN

The principles and elements of design are the foundation of every design discipline; they form the basis for judging design quality and integrity. All around us there is design that can be appreciated—from the intrinsically beautiful scenes of nature at any season and climate to great public and private architecture and their finely designed interiors. Learning to evaluate design will help us be more objective about the way we feel in the interiors where we live, work, and obtain services.

The evaluation process begins with an understanding of the theory of design or, in other words, implementing the principles by asking questions such as, How do I feel in this room? and What principles of design cause me to feel this way? If the reaction is less than positive, then an evaluation of the application of the elements of design can enable us to see what changes could be made to improve the interior.

Further, there are four general considerations that serve to clarify and simplify design evaluation: function, cultural context, appropriateness, and criteria for good structural and decorative design. These form a basis for understanding whether or not architecture or furnishings are well designed and how well objects interrelate with other objects and with the interior and exterior design. Looking at the overall effect is important because no interior can fully be separated from the permanent features of its architecture.

Function

Function is the way the elements perform in an interior—whether they are durable, operable, or serve the purpose for which they are intended. Each choice made in interior design—from the arrangement of the structural members (floors, walls, windows, ceilings) to the selection of furnishings, art, and accessories—must fulfill the needs and purposes for which it is intended, or the design is ineffective.

The process of design is one of problem solving. Therefore the evaluation of how well the finished design works as intended is of paramount importance. As was mentioned, this is known as post-occupancy evaluation (POE), which is a thorough critique of how well the design fulfilled the needs of the program. In homes as well, good design can be aesthetically pleasing only if the goals of the design statement and program have been completely satisfied.

Cultural Context

When an object is evaluated, it must first be viewed according to its original context. Context is defined as the whole situation, background, or environment relevant to a particular object. This means, for example, that to begin to truly appreciate Chippendale furniture, we need to see it in its original context in a Late Georgian setting. Then fine Chippendale furniture can be incorporated into more contemporary settings where it is appropriate and contributes beauty. Likewise, to fully appreciate modern Scandinavian or Italian furnishings, we need to internalize the concept that "form follows function."

Many accessory items that come from ethnic or primitive cultures can be genuinely appreciated for their beauty when we understand the society of their origin, its aesthetic views, and its cultural traditions of decorative design. An example is the symbolic nature of the patterns and colors in rugs from ethnic cultures such as the Navajo.

Figure 3.23 *The late champion of common Americana, artist Andy Warhol, brought to our attention the value of cherishing the reality of our past, however tacky it might seem to the modern discriminating eye. Here an array of ceramic dinnerware and cookie jars brings back warm nostalgia to almost everyone who remembers a grandmother.*
© 1987 Norman McGrath.

When these authentic sources are misused or misrepresented, or when the object is mass-produced in a material that is not suited for the purpose, the item is poorly designed. For example, the classic Thonet bentwood rocker is attractive because of the beauty of the wood that is curved under heat and pressure to its well-known shape. When the curvature is duplicated in metal or plastic, it is out of its authentic context and loses much of its original design integrity (honesty and sincerity). Not only must the materials be suited for the design, but the colors, lines, patterns, and textures must also be appropriate and harmonious.

Thematic Interior Design

Much of interior design that is produced today is *thematic*— based on a theme. Often the selected theme forms the unity; a necessary ingredient in an interior's harmony. The theme may be a mood, such as romantic or South Seas, or more often it is based on a historic style, described under Traditional Design, chapter 1.

In order to accomplish thematic interior design, we must have a sound understanding of the authentic period from which a theme is derived. Chapter 15 has an overview, although this text can provide only an introduction of thematic interiors. All the historic elements—architecture, furnishings, textiles, and accessories—should be a part of this study.

When we recreate exact period interiors, it is termed "historic restoration or adaptation." Thematic interior design, however, does not need to be this exact. It most often captures the look and spirit of the time in a contemporary setting. The finished interior should adhere to the time-honored principles and elements of design. Thematic interior design will be successful when we respect the cultural context and when we use skill and creativity in putting it together.

For example, a thematic Late Georgian interior may include Chippendale furniture, dog-ear mantelpieces, classic

Figure 3.24 *A Western theme guided the selection of all these authentic and adaptation furnishings.*

Window shades by and photo courtesy of Hunter Douglas.

Figure 3.25 *A thematic Late Georgian interior at Filoli, near San Francisco.*

Textiles by and photo courtesy of Brunschwig & Fils/Peter Vitale, photographer.

moldings and details, raised panel dados painted white, dark wood trim, banisters with white balusters, beautiful chandeliers, elegant window treatments, damask fabrics, painted or mural-covered walls, and wood floors with Oriental rugs. Overall this theme is rich, formal, traditional, and elegant.

A Country French thematic interior typically has ceramic tile or wood floors, stucco or papered walls, wooden Rococo-shaped mantelpieces, simplified Rococo furniture, and fabrics such as plaid, toile de Jouy, ticking, and printed florals. The look is sophisticated yet earthy.

A Western theme uses natural textures, hard materials, primitive accessories, Navajo rugs, and fabrics and items that relate to or are inspired by the Wild West days. This look is masculine, romantic in a rustic sense, and in harmony with the desert or Rocky Mountain environment.

Appropriateness

Appropriateness means suitability, fitness, or rightness of components for a specific purpose. Every element in interior design can be used appropriately or inappropriately. It is often said, for example, that there is no such thing as an ugly color, only colors that are not used correctly. This means that we need to look at not only the hue itself but also at intensity (brightness versus dullness), value (lightness versus darkness), placement (where is it located), and quantity (area to be covered). Color is but one of the elements we scrutinize in terms of appropriateness.

Each selection, from wall and floor materials to accessory items, needs to be a suitable choice for the particular interior if that design is to succeed.

Often the architecture determines which style of furnishing elements are appropriate or suitable. For example, certain combinations—sheers and tied-back layers of elegant fabric topped with swags and fringe that are placed over a wide expanse of a modern picture window—are simply not appropriate. It will cause both the window architecture and the window treatment to seem ill chosen and out of place. On the other hand, where an older, historic interior forms the background, it is often most appropriate to complement the existing interior architecture with colors, textiles, and furnishings that add to the richness of the period. This is not to say that furnishings should look antiquated, for fresh new design is always welcome when it is suitable and appropriate. It is only when the selections are poor that the design loses integrity and becomes either shocking or banal and distasteful.

Selecting items that are appropriate often takes study and consideration, and a scanning of what is available on the market is essential to selecting suitable components. We should observe interiors in magazines, public spaces, homes, and models open to the public and continually ask, Is this appropriate? Do these furnishings and elements really feel right together and with the architecture? We often will sense the rightness of good design and feel fulfilled and satisfied when it is experienced.

Structural and Decorative Design

Structural and decorative or ornamentive design are two basic divisions of design that are not generally considered with the principles and elements, yet they are important in evaluating the success of a design.

Structural Design

Structural design is seen in any element of interiors where the design is intrinsic to the structure and the form indicates the function of the piece. The concept of "form follows function" is a credo followed by architects and designers who have created modern classic works that are simple yet exactingly well thought out and executed. To say that form follows function means that the first priority in a design is its function, and the parameters of that purpose or function will dictate the shape or form of the design. For example, many modern chairs are designed primarily for the comfort and physical support of their users. The study of ergonomics or "ergofit" means that a chair (or even the entire range of furnishings and the building itself) is best suited for specific functions that will take place there. A chair designed to follow the dictum form follows function will be stripped of embellishment and will fulfill only the needs of its function, with an eye to fine, sleek, and simplified design.

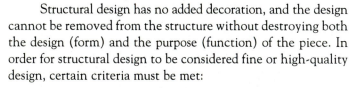

Figure 3.26 *A structurally designed kitchen*

Structural design has no added decoration, and the design cannot be removed from the structure without destroying both the design (form) and the purpose (function) of the piece. In order for structural design to be considered fine or high-quality design, certain criteria must be met:

- *Structural design must be simple.* The form and materials will never be complicated or arbitrary. Ironically, however, simplicity is often much more difficult to design and execute than ornate design. Every curve, angle, and part of the design is absolutely necessary to the form and the function of the design.
- *Structural design is unadorned.* There will be no carving, decals, unnecessary color changes, or extras of any sort. The design is found in the form and the materials used—wood grain, for example, or stainless steel or plastic—all frankly exposed to reveal their real worth.
- *The function of the piece must be apparent.* For example, a well-designed structural clock will look exactly like a clock and not like anything else.
- *A structural piece must be well proportioned to be good design.* This is particularly true since there is no decoration to cover up the dimensions, the scale, and the relationship of parts.

Much of today's designs from Italy and Scandinavia are structural design.

Decorative Design

Decorative design is also called applied or ornamentive design and refers to the ornamentation, or embellishment, of the object or structure. Some objects are in themselves decorative because of the way they are formed, whereas others may be structural pieces with decorative design added. Added decoration can be painted, inlaid, fired, engraved, or carved. There are four types or categories of decorative design.

1. **Naturalistic design** looks so real we could mistake it for a photo or the real plant, animal, or object from nature.
2. **Conventional design** uses designs from nature in a simplified, stylized, or adapted way. The design is "inspired" by nature but does not copy it accurately.
3. **Geometric design** is based on geometry: circles, diamonds, squares, rectilinear shapes, and patterns.
4. **Abstract design** is pattern or shape where the source or inspiration is not clear; it could be a combination, for example, of conventional and geometric designs.

When decorative architecture, interior architectural detail, or applied design on furnishings is well done, it will have the following characteristics:

- *There must be a sympathetic relationship between the style and method of decoration and the object,* such as precise etching or engraving of glass or carving or inlaying of wood.
- *The decoration must be suitable for the function and/or style of the piece.* If the object is a French Rococo form, for example, then the decoration should not reflect unrelated Victorian motifs. Also, truly fine decorative design will complement the function. The decoration of a clock face, for example, should not obscure the ability to read the time but should enhance the clock's design richness.

Figure 3.27 *Decorative design seen as French Rococo furniture and ornament.*

- *The proportion of the decoration must be right for the size of the object.* This means two things: (1) the scale of the decoration should be right for the scale of the object (not too large or too small in proportion) and (2) the amount of decoration should be in accordance with the size of the object. A piece too heavily ornamented will likely be considered poor design.
- *The ornamentation should embrace the form and not interfere with its function.*

Figure 3.28 *This Boston loft shows examples of naturalistic, conventional, geometric, and abstract design.*
Fabrics and furniture by and photo courtesy of Brunschwig & Fils.

DISCERNMENT AND DESIGN EXCELLENCE

When we evaluate an object, we often quantify its design. We may say the design of the object is excellent or fine; it may be good, fair, mediocre, or poor; or it may be pretentious and in bad taste, sometimes called kitsch. These labels are useful because they help us see that many aesthetic levels of design do indeed exist, and it clarifies our responsibility to select only design that will stand the test of time—that is, to select items of furnishing that will not only be appealing today but will seem just as beautiful many years later. Items that are beautifully, artistically, and sensitively designed will not become dated. Rather, they will endear themselves to us because of the timelessness of their beauty, their classic lines, their excellence of forms, and their sensitive use of textures and colors. This is just as true in well-designed structural objects as it is in well-designed objects that are decorative.

The Power of Discernment

The ability to recognize and appreciate fine design wherever it is found is known as the power of discernment. Discernment is the conscious effort required to make good choices and is of paramount importance in today's world of mass production, mass media, and instant information. We are barraged with choices that demand decisions. We must choose from a vast array of furnishing products and art pieces to furnish our environments. Since much average and poor design exists, it becomes necessary that everything we choose should be selected only after evaluation with a discriminating eye. We can also evaluate selections that are beyond our control, as we see them in retail stores, business offices, medical facilities, hotels, public buildings, and churches. In short, we can become discerning by evaluating everything we see.

The key to developing discernment is to studiously look and expose ourselves to design at every opportunity, and then to critically evaluate the level of design we see. Visit museums and art galleries, great public and church architecture, quality furniture stores, and even fine gift shops. Most cities have groups that support museum homes and sponsor home shows, and model homes exist in almost every community. It has been said that good design is there for the finding, which is to say that almost every place we look we will find good design in some form.

One of the easiest ways to develop the power of discernment or discrimination is to look through design periodicals—the magazines that appear monthly and tell us what is fashionable. However, not all that is fashionable will necessarily be good design, and the discriminating eye will be able to see through the fads and promotion to what is truly timeless and beautiful.

Another key to developing discernment is to observe, study, and value what nature has given to us. The majesty of nature was created through time, wearing away, and evolution of the landscape. Nature possesses a patina, or mellow, warm, old glow, that speaks not only to our senses but to our souls.

Great interior design often parallels this. It is based on a commitment to time spent in research, programming, and deliberate effort, time in seeking until just the right furnishing elements are discovered, and time in putting the elements together so that it appears as though they have fallen into place. Good design is based not only on the selection of individual items, but on the composition or grouping that gives to each a significance and a rightness. Like a thrilling scene in nature, fine interior design can be uplifting and rewarding.

A final key to understanding discernment is to establish the relationship of cost to design. Whereas many items that are very costly are good design, it is just as true that expense often gets in the way of good design, because wealth can lead to ostentation.[1] Often the more expensive of two alternatives is less acceptable to those who are visually aware.[2] It reveals greater discrimination when a simple interior design reflects good taste and true sophistication. Items that are simple and even roughly made can be just as beautiful as the most elegant and expensive furnishings. It is through the evaluation of the principles and elements of good design, and of the careful balance of beauty and craftsmanship, that we discover real and individual worth.

DEVELOPING SENSITIVITY AND THE ABILITY TO DISCRIMINATE

Merely surrounding oneself with things of personal value will not guarantee an aesthetically pleasing environment. Such environments may be quite personal, but they may also be rather unattractive. Beauty is most certainly in the eye of the beholder. However, knowledgeable people with a trained and an experienced eye can appreciate a good design even if it is not what they would personally choose. Developing this ability to discriminate and sensitively evaluate is one of the most important reasons for studying interior design. Some people do seem to be gifted with an innate sense of style, but like an appreciation for fine art or music, it is cultivated and developed through education, exposure, and effort. Developing the ability to discriminate is a lifetime pursuit.

The art and music/design analogy is apt. To decide to study and learn about art or music, the discipline must be of value to us. When well-designed interiors become important to us, we will take the time to study and observe. The more we are exposed to design and its principles, the better we can sense the rightness or wrongness of a design. This exposure comes through the deliberate study of design, by taking classes, reading books, and visiting design showrooms to observe style options and quality levels.

It is also important to study historical exteriors and interiors to gain an appreciation for designs that have passed the test of time and become classics that are still loved and appreciated. Museums and historic homes and buildings can provide such a laboratory. As we travel we should be aware of opportunities to learn and to observe, since study and exposure will sharpen the senses and increase the ability to make educated judgments about architecture and its furnishings.

Education is the key to developing the ability to discriminate. Interior design is a very complex discipline that goes far beyond the selection of beautiful fabrics and well-designed pieces of furniture. These decorative aspects are certainly an important part of the process of interior design, but interior design is also founded in the knowledge of a wide range of technical information and in the creative capacity to solve design problems.

Good Taste and Style

The development of sensitivity and the ability to discriminate will eventually lead to what we call good taste or style. When we say that certain people have good taste, we mean that they exhibit sound aesthetic judgment and thoroughly understand the needs of their individual life-style. It appears that people with good taste always make good choices and that perhaps it comes easy to them. However, anyone can develop good taste and can make good choices once they realize that it requires a conscious effort in every detail of our lives. From the clothes we wear to the books we read, the films we see, and the food we eat—all are aspects of living that are governed by taste.[3]

Figure 3.29 *As a result of the unusual, yet discriminating selection of furnishings, this room shows great personal style. © Jessie Walker.*

Although many of us are uncertain about our tastes, we can be educated, we can elevate our tastes, and we can learn to judge good design. To begin with, we need to understand our life-style, the needs of our surroundings, and what choices are available in terms of style and material for every element that goes into the interior. This requires careful attention to detail and means that everything we choose serves to create harmony.

People with great style sometimes do things that are totally unexpected and out of the ordinary, perhaps ahead of their time. But although they may seem to abandon all trends in favor of their own good choices, their choices are never made to shock, amaze, or impress anyone. True style is tuning into and following what is naturally right. It has little to do with what is in fashion, although an awareness of fashion is always evident in people with taste. Fashion passes, style remains. Style abhors cliché, cuteness, and conformity in favor of an uncompromising approach to first-class design quality and individuality. Truly great design is innovative yet demanding of the best.

People with style seem to know when to stop just short of excess. They often intuitively know that "less is more," or that, as Plato said, "beauty of style depends on simplicity." Perhaps the first step toward evolving a personal style is to pare back to the essentials before piling on any extras.

Style is most importantly an individual matter. You cannot copy another's style any more than you can copy another's personality. To create or copy an interior for the sake of correctness often falls short of style and appropriateness. In today's instant society, we are often impatient to have style developed immediately, but this is often not the way real beauty is made. As with nature, who took time to create her masterpieces, it is worth waiting to find just the right accessory, fabric, or piece of furniture to fit your style. And in the process of looking, we develop a distinctive personal style. Certainly there are many nonresidential interiors that reflect good taste and great style, but it is in the home where these are most personally evident.

Of all the objectives we may choose to incorporate in life, the dedication to creating a warm, welcoming, attractive, and individual home is one of the most worthwhile and precious. It is upon the theory (principles) and application (elements) that tasteful selections are blended with style and cherished for years to come.

NONRESIDENTIAL CONSIDERATIONS

The principles and elements of design are evident not only in homes but in public spaces as well. Those who have traveled abroad and visited castles and palaces have experienced the transcendence of exquisitely decorated large spaces, along with the feelings of awe and grandeur that they inspire. Although many of the castles and palaces that are open to the public were intended as private residences, they are today often used not only for tours but as gathering places for civic events. In such places we can experience the large-scale handling of the design principles and elements, along with an evaluation of design in spaces that have carefully been preserved over decades or even hundreds of years. Similarly, museums are often grand examples of architecture and contain glimpses of past eras that educate us in traditional and folk uses of the design principles and elements.

The typically lofty spaces of church architecture—with their predominance of vertical lines, often curving upward—give us a feeling of insignificance and lead thoughts to higher planes. This is particularly true in cathedrals, mosques, synagogues, and larger churches and temples.

There are many public spaces where we may have the opportunity to evaluate the levels of good design. The principles and elements are used for better or for worse in retail spaces, restaurants, offices, banks, and medical facilities. We see design that bridges the gap between residential and nonresidential design when we stay in hotels and resorts where both small spaces and large spaces play important parts in the rest and recreation procedure. Time spent in theaters before and after the entertainment allows us to ponder the level and integrity of interior design there. The theatrical or stage "set" can exemplify good design or form the basis for critique.

There is drama implicit in the lofty interiors of some civic or government buildings and in large-scale office or corporate buildings. In large spaces meant to impress, we often see fascinating uses of natural hard materials (such as stone) that give texture, pattern, and color to the interior.

The working environment is perhaps the place where we are best able to scrutinize design. At work stations we can see how the principles and elements make our working interiors more pleasant. We may also be able to detect how improvements can be made to increase job efficiency, working or spacial relationships (proxemics), and job satisfaction.

The manipulation of the design principles and elements to create beautiful environments can even go beyond our homes and nonresidential interiors to the limitless variety of nature scenes where we escape the pressures and confines of civilization. In nature we view structural design at its finest, and through the careful orchestration of the elements, we see every principle of design illustrated in one form or another. Indeed, the beauty of nature has been accomplished over a long period of time, and through observation of this careful, deliberate effort, we view beauty that is not simply voguish or stylish but, rather, beauty that endures. From nature we can learn, as a final lesson in the use of design principles and elements, that beautiful interiors do take planning, thought, effort, and time, and that when great interiors are created they will stay pleasing for many years to come.

ENVIRONMENTAL CONSIDERATIONS

The principles and elements of design form a basis with which to judge the selection and application of products and materials in an interior. When we choose wisely and arrange furnishings to create fine design, those materials will not need to be replaced often because they will visually stand the test of time. This is one of the wisest things we can learn from our study of interior design—that to select with beauty, durability, and livability in mind will yield interiors that do not become trite, trendy, or boring. Good, well-chosen design will protect the environment by accomplishing the goals identified during programming. When we utilize the principles and elements and develop good taste and style, we increase our ability to ensure the longevity of our interior design.

Further, we need to become aware that resources are consumed and money is spent to both install and remove, and that discarded materials and furnishings usually become part of the landfill when replaced with new furnishings. Only then will we become more careful in designing, selecting, and arranging of materials and furnishings. Designing to accomplish individual needs—and to accommodate inevitable changes in program and demographics—helps us to choose products that are universally designed, lasting beyond the immediate needs to serve future needs as well.

We examined how we can evaluate design by examining its function, cultural context, appropriateness, and adherence to good structural or decorative design. But we can also judge an interior design's environmental appropriateness by our sensitivity to the source and use of materials, and by our awareness of whether the interior conserves natural resources through lighting/electrical usage and recycling. This is an ongoing challenge. It should not be just an evaluation of the initial design concept; rather, it should be a continual evaluation of how the interior functions and how conserving we are in our actions. As we live and work in our interiors, we should be continually aware of how we can protect our world resources and enhance the healthfulness of our interior environment.

NOTES

1. Sherrill Whiton, *Interior Design and Decoration* (New York: Lippincott, 1976), 749-56.

2. David Hicks, *On Living—With Taste* (London: Leslie Frewin, 1968), 10-11.

3. Ibid.

COLOR

COLOR THEORY

A good understanding of color theory leads to sound expertise in interior design. This basic information is as valuable to people in home or working environments as it is to professionals.

For centuries, artists, scientists, and observers of nature have theorized about color. They have studied how it is made; what it is made of (pigment and light, for example); how nature uses color; how people use color; how colors affect one another; and how colors affect people both emotionally and physiologically. They observed what lightness, darkness, and intensity do to color; how colors may be combined, blended, broken up, or otherwise manipulated to achieve specific results; and what colors make pleasing harmonies or schemes. Of the many who theorized about color, a few have made significant observations that still guide our understanding and use of color in interiors. *M.E. Chevreul* (1786–1889), a French chemist and head of dyestuffs at the Gobelin Tapestry Works near Paris, published a book in 1825 that has been translated into English and is still in use today: *The Principles of Harmony and Contrast of Colors.* This book is considered one of the best ever written on color; in it are found the roots of all our present theories.[1]

The Standard Color Wheel Theory

The Standard Color Wheel theory, or system, is also known as the *Palette theory,* the *Prang theory,* and the *David Brewster Color theory.* This theory is based on a conventional color circle or wheel where three *primary hues*—red, yellow, and blue—are placed equidistant. *Secondary hues* are placed between these primaries and are a result of mixing any two of them: red plus yellow yields orange; yellow plus blue yields green; blue plus red yields violet. Hence, the secondary colors are orange, green, and violet and are placed in their proper places between the primaries. By mixing a primary and a secondary color on the color wheel, an *intermediate* or *tertiary hue* emerges—for example, yellow plus orange yields yellow-orange. These colors are yellow-orange, yellow-green, blue-green, blue-violet, red-violet, and red-orange. (Note that the primary color is written first.)

These twelve primary, secondary, and intermediate colors, placed in a circle, constitute the conventional color wheel. However, variously mixing the colors on the wheel—along with black and white—yields an unlimited number of colors (hence the name Palette theory). This method can be used to mix paint in literally any hue, value, and intensity, to match or blend with any wall covering or fabric, or to achieve any artistic result. We have only to observe the overwhelming number of choices of paint-chip colors on the market to see that this is so.

When a color wheel is divided between red-violet and violet and across to green and yellow-green, some of the colors are considered *warm colors*—red-violet, red, red-orange, orange, yellow-orange, yellow, and yellow-green. The other colors are considered *cool colors*—green, blue-green, blue, blue-violet, and violet. The warmth or coolness of a color is also relative to the amount of white or black added. For example, very light yellow may be rendered

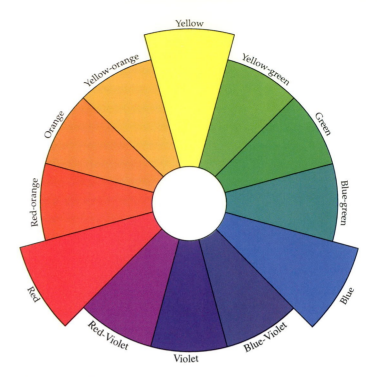

Figure 4.1   *The standard color wheel.*

Figure 4.2   *Warm colors dominate this fabric-indulged interior.*
Courtesy of Robert Allen, Inc.

CHART 4.1   COLOR WHEEL THEORY / COLOR SCHEMES

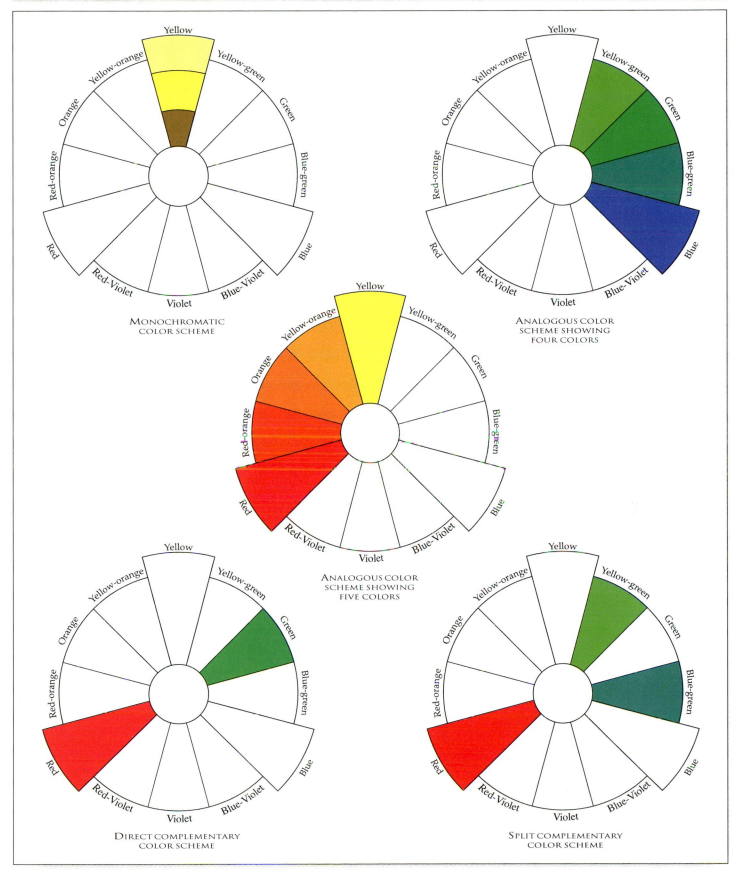

MONOCHROMATIC
COLOR SCHEME

ANALOGOUS COLOR
SCHEME SHOWING
FOUR COLORS

ANALOGOUS COLOR
SCHEME SHOWING
FIVE COLORS

DIRECT COMPLEMENTARY
COLOR SCHEME

SPLIT COMPLEMENTARY
COLOR SCHEME

Figure 4.3   *Cool colors are dreamy in this little girl's room.*
Photo by Gordon Lonsdale.

Figure 4.4   *Dramatic and rich, this red interior is an example of a*
monochromatic color scheme.
Courtesy of Waverly.

cool because it recedes away from the viewer and gives feelings of
light and space. The visual temperature is also dependent on the
strength or intensity of the color and by the placement of colors
next to each other. The psychology of these warm and cool hues
will be considered later in this chapter.

Chevreul discovered through his studies that color combinations could be divided into "analogous and contrasting harmonies." Today we have expanded this concept by the use of
color schemes based on the standard color wheel.

Monochromatic color schemes are based on one color. Successful monochromatic schemes often utilize light, medium, and
dark values, varieties of the color in intensity and dullness, and
the addition of other hues such as a complement to neutralize
or to vary the hue slightly. Ample amounts of white or off-white,
or small amounts of black or the complement hue can be added
to a monochromatic interior to balance the color distribution
or relieve a potentially overwhelming use of color.

Analogous harmonies or schemes are colors adjacent to
each other on the color wheel. Generally, three to six colors
are used in analogous harmonies, with one color predominat-
ing, another secondary in importance, and a third (up to the
sixth) used as accents. Here, a key to success often lies in the
variety of the lightness, darkness, intensity or clarity, dullness,
and exactness of the hue and in the uneven use of the different colors. For example, in a scheme of orange, yellow-orange,
yellow, and yellow-green, perhaps a softened or neutralized
yellow would dominate, with yellow-orange used in smaller
proportions and more neutralized tones and the orange and
yellow-green as accent colors.

Figure 4.5   *An analogous scheme: neutralized orange, yellow, and green.*
© Ted Spiegel.

Figure 4.6 *Complementary colors form a livable personal color scheme.*
© *Lisl Dennis.*

Complementary colors are those opposite on the color wheel.

- *Direct complement* colors are pairs exactly opposite—red and green; yellow and violet; blue and orange. Or they may be intermediate colors such as blue-green and red-orange, for example, that when lightened and/or dulled are a lovely combination.

- *Split complements* contain a base hue and the two colors on each side of its direct complement—yellow, red-violet, and blue-violet, for example.

- *Triadic complements* are three colors that are equidistant on the color wheel. Examples include the primary colors, (red, yellow, and blue) or the secondary colors (green, orange, and violet) or a set of intermediate hues (yellow-green, blue-violet, and red-orange).

- *Double complements* are two pairs of direct complements that are adjacent or next to each other, such as yellow and violet and yellow-orange and blue-violet.

- *Tetrad complements* are four colors that are equidistant on the color wheel, such as yellow-orange, green, blue-violet, and red.

- *Alternate complements* are triad schemes with a direct complement of one of the hues.

Chevreul noted that colors that are far apart on the wheel enhance the intensity of one another. In other words, the greater the difference, the more apparent or obvious the difference. He deemed complementary combinations more beautiful than analogous ones. Both analogous and complementary harmonies are generally more aesthetically pleasing when the colors are used in unequal proportions with one color clearly dominating. When the colors in the scheme vary in intensity and value, there are no equal amounts of equal intensities and values to compete for attention.

Chevreul also did considerable research into afterimages, a concept that had a profound impact on modern art. Afterimages will be discussed later in this chapter under Color Psychology.

The Munsell Theory

The *Munsell theory* is a major color theory in general use for interior design today. *Albert H. Munsell* (1858–1918), an American colorist, published his studies in several books. One study published in 1905 and still in use today is his *Color Notation*. His basic theory is widely used today in industry, manufacturing, interior design, and other fields such as science and medicine. Munsell "packets" are available today from Munsell Color for color study and implementation of exact color needs.[2]

The Munsell theory is a precise, formula-based system for notating specific colors. Munsell formulated a color wheel, then expanded it to a three-dimensional globe with leaves or pages of color variations. The system is based on three attributes that determine the exact color identity:

1. *Hue*—the color name; for example, the hue red.
2. *Value*—the lightness or darkness of the hue (the amount of white or black added to the hue). Hues with white added are called tints, and hues with black added are called shades.
3. *Chroma* or *intensity*—the amount of pure chroma in a given hue; the relative brightness versus the dullness or neutralization of the hue.

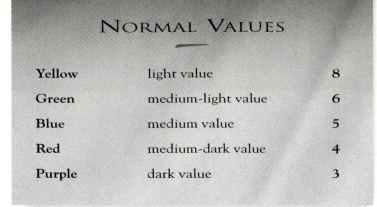

NORMAL VALUES

Yellow	light value	8
Green	medium-light value	6
Blue	medium value	5
Red	medium-dark value	4
Purple	dark value	3

The Munsell system is based on five hues: red, yellow, green, blue, and purple (not violet). The colors between these are red-yellow, yellow-green, blue-green, blue-purple, and red-purple. Hue families are given a letter and a numerical notation, 2.5, 5, 7.5, and 10, where 5 is the pure hue. Pure red (R), for example, without any of its neighbors to the left (purple hues) or to the right (yellow hues) is assigned a 5, hence 5R. If the red page or palette had some yellow in it, the hue page would be assigned 7.5R. This is essentially red-orange. If the red hue were slightly red-purple, the page is 2.5R. Therefore, the numerical designation is based on the pureness of the hue. Yellow without any yellow-red or green added is 5Y, 5B is blue without any green or purple influence, and so on.

Value, the lightness or darkness, is geared to a central column of value. White, at the top, is designated as 10; black, at the bottom, is designated as 0; in between is a step series of grays going from dark gray, or 1 (next to black at the bottom), to light gray, or 9 (next to white at the top). Every color has what is termed a normal value. This means that every hue has a certain value level as it occurs naturally or in its most natural-appearing state. Yellow is naturally very light and has the lightest *natural saturation point*. Violet is the darkest.

Figure 4.7 *A horizontal cross section of the Munsell system of color notation "tree" showing hue symbols and their relation to one another. There are five primary hues and five intermediate hues.*

Courtesy of Macbeth, New Windsor, NY.

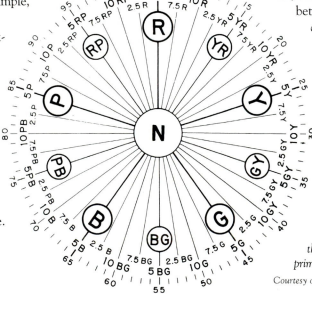

Figure 4.8 *A center cutaway revealing the core of neutrals at the 5/ value level is a comparison of how many hues extend to the greatest chroma, or brightness.*

Courtesy of Macbeth, New Windsor, NY.

Figure 4.9 *A cutaway illustration of the Munsell color notation system in three-dimensional form.*

Courtesy of Macbeth, New Windsor, NY.

At the natural saturation point, more color chips will be found on the Munsell page. For example, more light yellows exist than dark yellows, and more darker purple than light purple.

Chroma or intensity, the brightness or purity of a hue, is also designated with a number that follows the value number and a slash. The numbers range from 1 to 16, with the lower numbers meaning neutralized or dulled colors. A color is dulled or lessened in intensity by adding its color-wheel complement. The higher numbers indicate less of that complementary color, so the color becomes clearer and purer, and sometimes brighter, as the numbers increase.

Figure 4.10 *Color harmony is the sensitive bringing together of colors that are then blended by the eye.*
© Janis Schwartz/International Stock Photo.

Johannes Itten (1888–1967) was a teacher at the Bauhaus in Germany between the world wars who did comprehensive work in color theory. He became a great color teacher at Yale University and published two important works: *The Art of Color* and *The Elements of Color*.[4]

Josef Albers (1888–1976), who also taught at the Bauhaus and at Yale University, has become famous for his studies in simultaneous and successive contrast. He experimented with the optic of color. As author of the text *Interaction of Color*, he is considered one of the most influential teachers of this century.[5]

A sample of the Munsell notation for a pure, light, clear yellow would be 5Y 8/12; a clear, naturally occurring red would be 5R 4/14. A dull, medium-value purple would be 5P 5/2. A less pure red, one with some purple added and found in a light value and dull intensity, would be 2.5R 7/4. The advantage to this system is that it states clearly the attributes of a color. The precision of the system is also a boon to color use where exactness is paramount.

Other Color Theories

Many others have contributed to our knowledge of color. Some of the outstanding colorists who have strongly influenced interior design include *Wilhelm Ostwald, Johannes Itten,* and *Josef Albers.*

The *Ostwald theory* has some similarities to Munsell's but is plotted as triangular pages with hues varied not by chroma but by the amount of black and white. The formula bases pure hue or color (C) at one angle, white (W) at the second angle, and black (B) at the third. Harmonious colors are those that have the same content or amount of hue, white, and black—(C + W + B = 1). Further, harmonies can be established in parallels, where colors with the same whiteness work nicely with colors of the same content of black. Harmonies of verticals and of step values (called shadow series) are also harmonious. Complex ring-star and elliptic path harmonies were also plotted by Ostwald. Wilhelm Ostwald (1853–1932) was a physicist who won the Nobel Prize in 1909 for chemistry. He turned his research to color and produced a book *Die Farbenfibel,* which was translated into English as *The Color Primer.*[3]

Color Harmony

Color harmony is the arrangement of colors so that they are pleasing to the eye and to the senses. Color harmonizing is a skill that comes naturally to some people, and only after significant struggle and effort for others. People generally see colors in the same way unless they have color blindness or are losing their eyesight and cannot adequately see the less intense colors. Color blindness to some degree affects roughly 1.5 percent of the population and is found more often in men than in women.

It has been said that there is no such thing as an ugly color; a color becomes displeasing only if it is used incorrectly. Using colors correctly requires an understanding of how colors change identity and character as they are literally blended with other hues, and how colors are affected visually when placed next to other hues.

First, the hue identity itself must be examined closely to determine what its character really is. A blue, for example, is rarely just a blue. It may be a blue with black added (called navy); a blue with green added (called teal); a light and cool blue (called baby blue); a pure and deep blue (American blue); a blue leaning toward violet and darker in value (called royal blue); or blues with varying amounts of green, red, yellow, white, black, orange, or violet added. Blue is often considered the most difficult of colors to work with since it is so easily swayed by other hues or by the white or black that has been mixed into it.

All colors are influenced by other colors; other colors inherent in mixed hues are called *undertones.* Undertones can be evaluated according to whether the basic hue has become lighter or darker, warmer or cooler, more or less pure, or if the hue leans toward another identity or hue. Once the undertones have been discovered, then other colors with similar tendencies can be more successfully blended with or placed near to create color harmonies. Generally speaking, colors that are neutralized or grayed will harmonize as a family, colors that are browned will harmonize as a group, and pure colors (or their tints and/or shades) will harmonize well together. Undertones can also render a color warm or cool. Warm colors—yellow, orange, and red—become cooler when blues, greens, and violets are mixed into them, and vice versa.

An important fact in color harmony is that colors placed next to each other will be blended by the eye and will be influenced by the type and relative warmth or coolness of the light striking the combination. In small quantities, colors will actually blend into different colors from a distance. If the colored surface is a large area and if the colors surrounding it are not related via undertones, warmth, or clarity, then dissonance will likely result.

Small samples may make it difficult to select colors for a large area. A tiny paint chip is rarely the color of the entire wall when it is painted because of the large quantity of paint or color on the surface and because of the way the light affects the color. It may appear darker or lighter than the paint chip, often more intense,

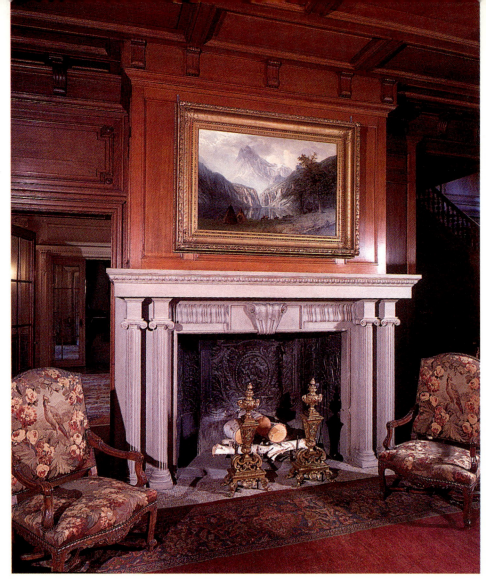

Figure 4.11 *Neutralized colors, deep and rich, are called tones and are seen here at historic Mills Mansion: Hudson Valley, New York.*
© Stan Ries/International Stock Photo.

and the undertones will become more obvious. Likewise, floor coverings, textiles, and wall coverings sometimes produce a shock when the color installed looks different from the sample. Working with large samples is not always possible. However, a quart of paint applied to a portion of the wall in situ (on the site), where the effects of natural and artificial lighting can be evaluated, is a small price to pay compared to dissatisfaction. Fabric can be tested out as well; with only a yard or two placed next to a portion of painted wall, surprising results may emerge that could save anguish as well as money.

Color harmony can also apply to the completed interior as a whole. The Japanese concept of Shibusa states that all elements and colors must interrelate to be subtly harmonious, so that nothing offends the eye. Contrary to this is the concept of color harmony, espoused by some designers, that colors should be bold, high contrast, or even shocking to be most effective.

Either philosophy should be used only after evaluating the needs of the people who will occupy the space, the amount of time spent there, and what activities will be performed. For example, a peaceful shibui scheme would be a wise choice in a bedroom suite, whereas the bold, stimulating types of colors in a shopping plaza may be selected to encourage spending and to produce a feeling of euphoria.

NEUTRALIZED COLORS

True color harmony cannot be achieved without understanding the roles that both neutralized colors and neutrals play in interior design. *Neutralized colors* are those that are made less pure, are dulled in intensity or grayed, and are influenced by other colors. Neutralized colors, or *tones*, are achieved in a number of ways:

Figure 4.12   *The Law of Chromatic Distribution: the largest areas are colored in the most neutral (grayed) hues. As the area becomes smaller, chroma proportionately increases. Only smallest areas are very bright color.*
© Jessie Walker.

1. By mixing any two hues on the color wheel, the resultant hue is less pure than either original color. By mixing colors that are far apart, such as complementary hues, these tones are rich and deep. A small amount of the complement will effectively neutralize in degrees, where the hue becomes less and less pure and finally becomes a deep tone that still maintains its identity. More of the complement renders it a murky, nondescript color, then the mixture progressively becomes tones of the complement.

2. By adding black to a hue, a shade is created, effectively neutralizing the hue. Adding only white to a hue yields tints, which are also less pure than the hue but still rather intense.

3. By adding gray or brown, a color becomes neutralized. Grays, browns, or blacks with colored undertones will neutralize the color differently than will pure neutrals.

4. Adding one or more other hues will neutralize a color. Adding yellow and violet to blue, for example, will neutralize the blue and produce undertones. Some very interesting tones, shades, pastels, and tints can be achieved this way.

5. Adding white to neutralized tones yields beautiful soft or grayed pastels in medium to very light neutralized colors. These often make beautiful and livable wall colors.

The value of neutralization lies in the easy-to-live-with, nonassertive colors that can be effective in businesses, offices, medical facilities, hotels, restaurants, and, most especially, the home.

The *law of chromatic distribution* effectively utilizes neutralized colors. It states: The more neutralized colors of the scheme are found in the largest areas, and the smaller the area, the brighter or more intense the chroma becomes. This means that backgrounds such as floors, walls, ceilings, and draperies use less intense colors or tones and pastels; smaller areas use brighter, intense colors.

Figure 4.13 *An interior done in neutrals: whites and off-whites, grays, blacks and off-blacks, browns and beiges.*
Courtesy of Del Mar Window Coverings.

NEUTRALS

Neutrals are the families of whites and off-whites, grays, and blacks and off-blacks. Browns and beiges are also often considered neutrals, even though they are actually neutralized colored hues.

Whites and off-whites give interiors increased visual space. Whitened floors, ceilings, and walls look light, spacious, and farther away than they are. Furnishings that are hues seem cleaner and crisper surrounded with whites. Off-whites are produced by adding other neutrals (gray, black, brown) to white or by mixing color and neutrals into white. These undertones produce off-whites that may be warm or cool, clean or dirty, more neutralized or more colored. Thousands of different off-whites are used in today's interiors. These are seen in paints, wall coverings, textiles, floor coverings, and accessories. It is usually wise to avoid using off-whites that are not similar in undertone. For example, a clear yellowish off-white and a dirty neutralized pinkish off-white will be disturbing; one will appear as the wrong color. However, off-whites with similar warmth, clarity, and color undertones will blend harmoniously.

Grays are achieved by mixing various amounts of black and white, which makes true achromatic (no color) grays. As such, gray is often an ideal background color against which to show other colors. Grays are easily colored with other hues to produce a wide variety of pinkish grays, yellowish grays, greenish grays, brownish grays, and so on. Colored grays need to be carefully matched or blended to be harmonious and, like off-white, gray may be rendered cool or warm, depending on the undertones. Warm grays can be welcoming and comforting; cool grays tend to be cold and uninviting.

Figure 4.14 *Metamerism is the apparent changing of color under different light sources.*
© Ted Spiegel in cooperation with the Lightolier Company.

Blacks and off-blacks give deep, dark value to the set off neutrals. Black sharpens and adds richness to other colors placed next to it. Black used generously may create a dramatic and theatrical setting, although it might produce feelings of depression in some people. Accents of black give richness to interiors. Off-blacks may be very dark grays or tinted blacks where the hue is barely discernible and can effectively tie into color schemes.

Browns and beiges are often favored because of the warm qualities that they bring to an interior. Browns are achieved by mixing several colors on the color wheel or by neutralizing orange. Often browns are introduced into an interior through stained woods, which do not need to match as long as they harmonize. Used in large amounts, browns can produce either a cavelike coziness or a feeling of oppression. Browns are often at their peak when good value distribution is employed, utilizing many steps of lightness from beige to very dark brown.

Designing rooms entirely in neutrals is not a new idea, nor will it readily be a dated one. Interiors of true neutrals—whites, grays, and blacks—are termed *achromatic*, or without color. Many beautiful interiors are created using achromatic whites, grays, and blacks, along with the brown/beige group. These environments make fine backgrounds for colorful artwork and accessories. One major advantage of selecting neutrals for interiors is the flexibility to change color schemes without being locked into a set color. Interiors employing neutrals in every room also allow furnishings to be moved from one room to another.

COLOR-INFLUENCING FACTORS

Many factors influence the way we see color in interior design. Perhaps the most important are light, texture and material, color placement, and value distribution and contrast.

Light

Light contains color. A light shown through a prism is simple proof of the rays of the color spectrum seen in light. The colors of the rainbow found in nature are arranged similarly to the color wheel, except that light rays are seen from the longest to the shortest: red, orange, yellow, green, blue, and violet. Since color exists in light, all light is colored. The degree of color, or the warmth or coolness of the light, is a variable in each interior design installation and will affect the background and furnishing colors. Light influences color more, perhaps, than any single factor or element.

We perceive color in paint, materials, and furnishings because of the physics of light. When light strikes an item that has been colored with pigment or dye, then all the light rays are absorbed except those that are reflected by that pigment. We are therefore able to identify the material by color or hue.[6]

Natural light affects color according to: (1) the *orientation*, or direction, of light (east light is clear and bright, north light is cool, south light is constant and warm, west light is hazy and hot),

(2) the season of the year, and (3) other environmental factors, such as humidity, and clarity versus fog, smog, or overcast conditions.

Interior *artificial lighting* also affects the way we see color. *Incandescent light* is usually warm and flattering; luminescent or *fluorescent light* can be warm or cool but is always clear and virtually shadowless.

Candlelight and firelight, used on occasion in homes and in contract settings such as restaurants and some hotel lobbies, is lighting by *combustion*. It is similar to incandescent lighting in that it is warm and flattering. It is, however, a darker light source, and because it flickers, colors will appear darker and less defined or precise.

The placement of the lighting, the direction from which it hits the color, and even the time of the day can each give a different look or personality to color. *Metamerism* is the characteristic of color to appear as one color in one light and another color in another light (considering all the lighting factors). Testing color on the site and under every lighting condition is always the best avenue for success.

Figure 4.15 *Medium-to-light values make this interior "high key".*

Texture and Material

Texture and materials affect color because of the different ways light is caught and absorbed or because of the degree of reflection on the surface. Smooth surfaces will reflect more light, which makes colors appear lighter and more intense than normal. Materials that are grained, such as wood, or those textured in any way will absorb or refract (break up) the light, causing colors to appear somewhat darker than normal. Because of this, the exact match in colored samples will not appear as the same colors when installed. Paint, draperies, carpeting, upholstery, and laminates will never be exactly the same color, and the attempt to match may cause frustration and dissonance in the finished interior. It is wiser to blend color, purposefully selecting various values or harmonious undertones and allowing the inherent differences that come from the texturizing of materials to enhance the entire color scheme.

Wood furniture sets, groups, or suites have been produced in single-colored stains for many years. This has sometimes led people to believe that all wood furniture and backgrounds should match. Today we have come to realize that beautiful interiors often feature many different woods in varying stains and values. When the grain is similar and the undertones are compatible, then different woods can often be successfully used together in an interior.

Color Placement

Color placement of hues in *juxtaposition*, or close together, will cause colors to affect one another. A color placed near green, for example, may take on a greenish cast or bring out a greenish undertone. When a color is selected alone and then installed in combination with other hues, it may take on undertones that give a different character to that color. Sometimes the result is pleasing, and at other times the color combination is disharmonious. Coordinating colored samples under similar lighting conditions or on the site before actual installation can avoid unpleasant surprises when the colors become permanent in the interior.

Value Distribution and Contrast

Similarly, the placement within the interior can yield surprising results. Traditionally, darkest colors were used on the floors, lighter colors on the walls, and lightest colors on the ceiling—imitative of the natural color placement in nature. However, dark value on the wall will visually close in the space and render the room more cozy. Dark values on the ceilings will visually lower the ceiling, which may be useful when the ceiling is very high and the volume of space is not welcoming. Conversely, lighter colors on the floor will visually expand space and may effectively unify the color schemes between rooms. Again, trying out an unusual placement of color where it is to be used will help to ensure success of the completed work.

Value distribution and contrast refer to the degree of lightness of the hue (white added) versus the degree of darkness (or black). Light or *high values* are tints, and dark or *low values*

Figure 4.16 *Dark values in this "low-key" value sitting area create an atmosphere of traditional dignity.*
© Jessie Walker.

Figure 4.17 *An example of high contrast is seen in the crisp contrast of black and white, creating a clean, high-tech looking kitchen.*
© *Bill Crofton/Nawrocki Stock Photo, Inc.*

are shades. When an interior is filled with a variety of values, from very light to very dark as well as in between, then the room is said to have good *value distribution*. However, various types of *value contrast* can also be put to good use. Values that are similar—all light values (*high key*) or all middle values or all darker values (*low key*), for example—are termed *low-contrast values*. These interiors are generally soothing and calming. Light values produce an airy, somewhat carefree feeling. Middle-range values give a sense of normality and calm, and dark values give a stable or anchored mood to the interior. Very light and very dark values (no middle values) used in a single interior are termed *high-contrast values*. High-contrast schemes are dramatic, theatrical, or intense. They can look sophisticated, professional, and stimulating, but rarely are they comforting or relaxing.

It is important to note that not only can colors be manipulated to achieve value distribution and contrast, but the same can be done with achromatics (blacks, whites, grays) beiges, and browns as well.

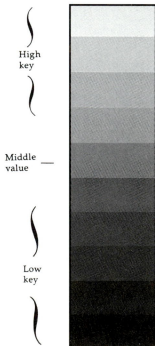

Figure 4.18 *Value scale indicating high key (light values), middle values, and low key (low values).*

COLOR PSYCHOLOGY

Although nearly everyone perceives color the same way, the way we interpret or feel about color can vary because of our experiences with color, our education of color, and our cultural associations with color.

The psychology of color is a valuable tool the interior designer can use to fulfill the needs of the users. In homes as well as public buildings, a knowledge of how colors are generally viewed and understood by humans can help create effective and efficient interiors.

Common color associations or *symbolisms* are based on the response people have to hues in general. Based on intensities and values, some common associations in Western societies include those listed in chart 4.2.

Color group moods can also be determined based on research. Philip Thiel, in his book *Visual Awareness and Design*, has discovered that groups of colors may produce emotional responses:

1. Light-value colors that are high in chroma (light and bright) produce feelings of spontaneity and happiness.

2. Colors light or high in value and dark or deep in chroma (light and dull or neutralized) produce feelings of calmness and relaxation.

3. Colors with deep values and dull chroma (dark and dull or neutralized) are serious and profound.

4. Colors dark in value and bright in chroma (jewel tones) suggest richness and strength.[7]

Warm and cool colors have traditionally been used to determine the psychological effects of color. Warm colors will visually and psychologically warm the temperature of an interior to a remarkable degree. Warm colors are inviting, homey, optimistic, encouraging, stimulating to the appetite, and they blend objects, patterns, and textures. Warm colors also tend to

CHART 4.2 COMMON COLOR ASSOCIATIONS

RED

Pure, intense: Danger, passion, love, excitement, stimulus, conspicuousness.

Dark, neutralized: Wealth, power, sometimes evil.

Pure chroma pink: Cheerfulness, youth, festivity.

Light or pastel pink: Femininity, innocence, relaxation, delicacy.

ORANGE

Pure, intense: Friendliness, warmth, celebration, clarity.

Dark, neutralized: Wealth, success, fame, rich depth.

Light or pastel: Stimulation (to the appetites), security, relaxed euphoria (sense of well-being).

YELLOW

Pure, bright: Cheerful optimism, sunshine, springtime, renewal, intensity, demanding, revealing, warmth (too much is hot), intellect, stimulation.

Dark, neutralized golden yellow: Wealth, affluence, status, distinction, high esteem. Too much is brash, garish, or ostentatious.

Middle to light value: Intelligence, wisdom, compassion, freshness, cheerfulness, optimism, goodness, clarity, cleanliness.

GREEN

Pure, bright: Nature, calmness, friendliness, integrity, practicality, frankness.

Dark, neutralized: Solidity, wealth, anchored tenacity, security.

Blue-green: Sea and sky, cleanliness, nostalgia, calmness.

Yellow-green: Youthfulness, freshness, happiness.

BLUE

Pure, intense: Loyalty, honesty, integrity, royalty, stimulation, restlessness. These also apply to deep or neutralized blues.

Deep, neutralized: Sincerity, conservatism, safety, peacefulness, kindness, compassion. These also apply to pure or intense blues.

Light or pastel: Tentativeness, cleanliness, calm, expanded time and space, lack of security.

PURPLE OR VIOLET

Pure, intense: Optimism, imagination, royalty, dignity, poise, renewal, commitment, drama.

Dark, neutralized: Depth, richness, security, sternness, soberness, sobriety, dullness.

Light or pastel: Freshness, springtime, flowers, imaginativeness, femininity, kindness, sensitivity.

---

reduce space and create more intimate interiors. Keep in mind that these are generalities. Depending on the value and the intensity of the chroma, colors can be very warm (high chroma, which intensifies these attributes), warm, or only slightly warm (middle to low chroma, which deemphasizes the qualities listed).

Cool colors generally calm and relax the mind and body, giving the impression of lack of pressure and plenty of time to wait or to accomplish tasks. Cool colors often suggest more formality and precision of detail, pattern, and color. These visually expand space, making them effective tools in small, cramped quarters. Cool colors subdue the appetite and emotions. Very cool colors are intense, cool colors are middle chroma, and slightly cool colors are low in chroma (neutralized).

Humans are sensitive to complementary pairs of colors, directly across from each other on the color wheel. (It is to pairs of colors that people may become colorblind—not just to red but to green as well, for example.) When the eye focuses on an intense color for as few as thirty seconds, then focuses on a neutral area, the complementary color appears in the same pattern as an *afterimage*. Pairs of intense, high-chroma complementary colors of equal value placed in juxtaposition will create a vibrating afterimage where they border, which can cause problems with eye focusing and be responsible for irritation or headaches after a period of time.

Afterimages, therefore, can affect anyone and potentially create a disturbing visual and, hence, emotional state of being. Afterimages can be reduced by varying the intensity of colors placed together, by separating them in distance, or by carefully handling strong graphics and patterns. A stark white background is far more likely to create an afterimage than a neutralized color or a gray. A strong chroma of a hue will bring the complement into the visual area, which will be seen in the neutrals. Varying the value of colors will also reduce visual discomfort.

Figure 4.19 *A cheerful, stimulating conversation area is drenched in pastel yellow and natural sunshine.*
Courtesy of Laura Ashley.

COLOR IN RESIDENTIAL INTERIORS

Perhaps the most important application of color in interior design to most people is in the home, for it is there that we are free to select colors that are the most personally appealing to us. There we have control over the selection of color in the major background elements and the application of color in the more flexible aspects of the design. When color schemes are neutral, children and extended-family members can express themselves with art and accessories without disturbing the general color scheme of the rest of the house. Because neutrals or neutralized color schemes convey a sense of rest and repose, a home in which they are used can become a calming, peaceful sanctuary.

Color is a good way to change a home's look, mood, or formality without spending a lot of money. Although reupholstering furniture, replacing carpeting, and selecting custom window coverings often are costly, many other colored items are usually not. Paint, for example, is relatively inexpensive considering the square footage it covers. Bed, bath, and kitchen linens can change the look entirely when backgrounds are suitably neutralized. Likewise, art and accessories may be changed with the seasons or moods. Smaller colored areas that are bright and cheerful might be preferred by younger children who can benefit from them intellectually. Tailored for their needs, these same areas may provide a source of identity and individuality for teens and young adults, may be soothing and relaxing for working adults, and may be comforting and reminiscent for senior citizens.

Color in homes can be tailor-made to individual needs beyond age. Those who are housebound or prone to depression can be cheered with warm, encouraging colors. People with poor eyesight may benefit from light, clear color and value. Those who need reassuring environments in which to work at home can select colors that are calming or stable. Various task or hobby areas within the home can also be outfitted for individuality. However, living areas where people congregate or are entertained should be neutralized enough to be generally appealing to everyone.

(A)

(B)

Figure 4.20 *Neutralized colors create a peaceful, easy-to-live-with residence shown here as (A) entry-staircase and (B) adjoining living-dining area.*

Photo by Gordon Lonsdale.

THE COLOR TREND MARKET

Today color trends or palettes are established by color forecasting organizations. These changes are most evident in fashion apparel, yet they do permeate the interior design marketplace as well. There are a number of explanations for the rapid change:

1. The public responds to new colors introduced by the mass media. When fashion changes and a new look is introduced, people are generally quite receptive in order to stay in style or to stay on the forefront of fashion change.

2. Our fast-paced society leads us to not only accept change but expect and even be impatient for it.

3. High technology—instant access to pools of computer or media-based information—has made us a change-oriented society.

4. Economic growth paves the way for expansion of the interior design profession. Consequently, further research into organizational and individual behavior based on color response is also possible.

There are associations that research color direction and forecast color trends with remarkable accuracy. These forecasts aid manufacturers who are anxious to keep products selling well in the marketplace, where appealing and popular color is of primary importance in item selection. Color trends for each year are established by professional groups. Three of the best known and most influential are the Color Marketing Group (CMG), the Color Association of the United States (CAUS), and the International Colour Authority (ICA).[8] As these groups trace the advance and recession of color popularity, they select new hues while also freshening hues currently on the market. In addition, they look at and decide which hues the public is most likely to accept. These decisions are based on the following:

1. An awareness of color trend evolutions, and past and present trends

2. An awareness of the constant demand by consumers for change in color preference

3. The input from national and international companies that produce the colors and from association members who market these colors

4. An understanding of human response or psychological reaction to specific hues, and an intuition for color based on this understanding

5. National or international events that affect color trends, as they have in the past

6. Creative designers and artists, whose well-known works influence decisions

7. Public personalities, such as political leaders, royalty, media personalities, and other high-profile people with charisma or controversial status; these people set a trend through their personal style

These three groups are the organizations that establish color trends and forecasting. In addition, other organizations and corporations provide specific consulting services for groups or manufacturers. These companies may provide color swatches for marketing a specific product, they may perform color trend consulting, or they may help companies improve their public relations as they market the rapidly changing colors.

Color Organizations

Color Marketing Group (CMG), 4001 North Ninth Street, Suite 102, Arlington, VA 22203, is a nonprofit organization whose membership is involved in the process of color selection or specification. The association selected colors for the marketing services and products. Members pay an association fee and attend meetings—regional and semiannual national meetings. At the spring meeting, colors are chosen, and at the fall meeting, they are presented to the members. Members are sent resourceful newsletters and have access to workshops and educational seminars.

Color Association of the United States (CAUS), 24 East 48th Street, New York, NY 10016, issues color charts for home and contract furnishings each September and apparel swatches each March and September, intended to be eighteen to twenty months ahead of the actual selling season. Members receive the charts and monthly color newsletters and may attend New York-based seminars. Colors each year are selected by a rotating panel of eight to ten members recognized for their color expertise and professionalism.

Members of the International Colour Authority (ICA), c/o Benjamin Dent & Company, 33 Bedford Place, London WC1B 5JX, England, meet in the spring and fall in London where forecasts emerge from international members' panels on both home furnishings and apparel. Members receive a continuous printout of ICA data that indicates colors to be promoted worldwide. Monthly reports from subscribers are tabulated and divided into specific areas. The information is then sent back to the subscribers and is followed up with a written report that evaluates and documents trend development and forecasted color use.

Munsell Color, 2441 N. Calvert Street, Baltimore, MD 21218, is a resource for designers and educators. Munsell Color can provide many tools and educational materials for use in defining, identifying, and recording or matching colors through the Munsell color notation system.

Nonresidential Considerations

Color in public and in work spaces is a complex topic. For example, color in medical facilities will often be handled differently than in hospitality interiors, office interiors, retail businesses, or production or assembly-line facilities. The differences lie in the specialized needs of the users of these various environments. Designers must be sensitive to these needs that govern emotional responses, since they can affect behavior, attitude, productivity, or patronization. Often considerable research will be conducted to determine how to best serve the psychological responses of the users.

Medical facilities include hospitals, doctors' offices, outpatient facilities, and geriatric facilities. Here the philosophy of color has changed significantly in the past several years. Medical facilities used to be white or pale tints and cool looking, full of hard surfaces, an echo of the sterile environment. Today we have found that soft or neutralized colors in a variety of values, from dark to light, are relaxing and can promote healthfulness. Also, colored background elements are no longer always hard. Often medical facilities will incorporate carpet, warm wood textures, and fireproof fabric or wall coverings on the partitions and walls. This offers a more human, caring atmosphere to those in sometimes frightening and bewildering circumstances.

Hospitality interiors include hotels and motels, resorts and spas, and restaurants. These are areas where color and design are dictated by the culture and the climate. Often more lavish colors and patterns will dominate reception areas and rooms and suites. In restaurants, red- and orange-related hues are found to be the most stimulating to the appetite, although colors that complement the food color enhance the visual appeal and flavor of the food. Where climates are very warm, cooler colors are often used, and in colder climates, warmer colors are often more welcoming.

Office interiors in the past several years have become increasingly more sophisticated in terms of equipment and furniture systems and the use of computers to simplify procedures, storage, and retrieval systems. The whole complexion of office interiors has changed. Although color trends will always be reflected in contemporary office design, the major shift has been away from clear, obvious hues toward grayed tones and grays accented or coordinated with either pure chroma or neutralized hues. These types of colors reflect an attitude of increased professionalism in the business world.

The objective of retail businesses is to entice customers to purchase goods and services. Two major color trends in recent years have developed to meet these goals. One is the use of stimulating, warm, cheerful, and advancing colors, a technique often utilized in large stores and shopping malls where the bright colors help customers locate departments and services. To an extent, glitter or neon-bright color have been incorporated into retail businesses that appeal to youth.

The other retail business color trend reflects the hues in office interiors. It is the use of more subtle, deep-value tones and neutralized pastels, accented with jewel tones or pure chroma. The addition of polished wood or classic brass or chrome gives retail businesses an exclusive or rich appearance. This method does not necessarily limit the clientele to those with money. Rather, it is aimed toward making customers feel that they deserve quality merchandise and can afford it.

Production plants have requirements of psychological comfort, productivity, and safety. Light pastel colors that reflect light are generally more pleasing than stark whites, intense colors, or dark values. Cheerful colors influence workers to be cheerful.

Figure 4.21 *A pleasing scheme is presented in the lobby of the Marriott Suites at Symphony Towers, San Diego, California.*
Courtesy of Victor Huff Partnership/Karl Francetic, photographer.

Productivity can be increased by eliminating eye fatigue caused by afterimages, intense chroma, stark whites, very dark values, or shiny or glossy surfaces at the workstation. Matte or dull surfaces that provide a pleasing contrast to the material or object being worked on will aid production and add some color and texture contrast also necessary for both comfort and productivity. Primary colors used to identify controls or parts of machinery will increase efficiency. Warm colors in cool environments and cool colors in warm environments will help workers feel more comfortable.

Safety can be enhanced by using bold or intense colors on dangerous parts of machinery or in areas of potential hazard. The use of color to reduce eye fatigue will help workers be more alert and help prevent accidents.

ENVIRONMENTAL CONSIDERATIONS

One of the real challenges in interior design is to find the "right color" to coordinate with our furnishings. If we select a color scheme based on trendy colors, we may not find those same colors available in furnishings in just a few years. Consumers are offered a new color palette every year, and though some colors stay popular for a few years and some change or evolve slightly in hue or value, none exist in mass merchandising for very long. This can result in a throw-away-and-replace attitude: "If I can't find my color, I'll just have to start over again with new products in a new color scheme."

Part of the solution to this wasteful dilemma is to select colors for our interiors that will be attractive to us for a long time. Never let your choices be influenced merely by fashion. Remember that next year they may be out of style. Choose colors for your home that you love to live with. The exact value and intensity you prefer at any given point in your life may vary, but chances are you will love the same colors ten years later.

Of course you may need to compromise when you live with others. A good rule is to keep common areas neutral and to let the private areas such as bedrooms reflect personal color preference.

Colors that are somewhat neutralized rather than pure or intense are generally considered easy to live with and maintain their lasting appeal. Colors with an old look—with a mellow quality or patina—are now in vogue. These colors, inspired by nature, are seen in "natural" finishes for walls, floors, ceilings, fabrics, woods, faux stones, and real metals. The patterning, texturing, and shading of colors we see today lend a natural look to interiors. This, in turn, can increase our sensitivity and appreciation for nature and the environment. We are appreciating that nature gives us beautiful, livable, and enduring color.

Figure 4.22 *Natural, environmental colors and materials are at home in the Marriott Hotel, Colorado Springs.*
Courtesy of Victor Huff Partnership/Karl Francetic, photographer.

Colors not only have to "live" well; they also must physically wear well. One cliché states that the best carpeting choice is the "nicest dirty color you can find." Dull or neutralized colors can conceal dirt, require less cleaning, and conceal wear better. This increases the life of the product, whether it be carpet, hard flooring, wall or window treatments, furniture, or other fabric items. Patterned and textured products also wear well, provided there is long-term appeal. Ask yourself, "Will I still love this pattern-texture-color combination in ten years?" If you sincerely think you will, it is probably a good color choice.

NOTES

1. M.E. Chevreul, *The Principles of Harmony and Contrast of Colors and Their Applications* (New York: Van Nostrand Reinhold, 1981), 63–70.

2. Munsell Color. Macbeth. A division of Kollmorgen Corporation, 2441 North Calvert Street, Baltimore, MD 21218.

3. Faber Birren, *Color and the Human Response* (New York: Van Nostrand Reinhold, 1978), 64–65.

4. Johannes Itten, *The Art of Color: The Subjective Experience and Objective Rationale of Color* (New York: Van Nostrand Reinhold, 1973), 11–17.

5. Josef Albers, *Interaction of Color* (New Haven: Yale University Press, 1963), 1–74.

6. Arnold Friedman, John F. Pile, and Forrest Wilson, *Interior Design: An Introduction to Architectural Interiors* (New York: American Elsevier, 1970), 52.

7. Philip Thiel, *Visual Awareness and Design* (Seattle: University of Washington Press, 1981), 189.

8. Darlene Kinning, "How Color Connects" *Draperies and Window Coverings Magazine* 2, no. 27 (February 1985): 18–21.

LIGHTING

Photo courtesy of Victor Huff Partnership/Karl Francetic, photographer.

LIGHTING IN INTERIOR DESIGN

Light, as an element of design, is so important that an entire chapter is dedicated here to its aesthetic, practical, and technical aspects. It is through light that we see color, and by light we discern all the elements and components of an interior. In this chapter we will examine the ways lighting is handled, what effects it has in an interior, the types of lighting and lamps (bulbs), and lighting's effects on our minds. We will also examine technical terms and information to help us make wise, informed choices.

LIGHT CONTROL

The goals of lighting an interior should include the following:

1. To make lighting effective and practical for the activities or purposes of the interior
2. To make the interior more aesthetically pleasing
3. To make the interior psychologically useful
4. To wisely select lighting and to use it economically in terms of both product and power

These goals are accomplished by the appropriate selection, placement, and control of lighting fixtures.

CATEGORIES OF LIGHTING EFFECTS

In order to accomplish the goals of lighting, categories are useful in directing the design. In homes, these categories of lighting include: *general, ambient, task, accent* and *mood lighting,* and *lighting as art*. These are discussed here, and other categories of lighting are found at the end of the chapter under Nonresidential Considerations.

General and Ambient Lighting

General lighting is usually planned into the blueprints of the home (see Wiring Plans later in the chapter). General lighting provides a uniform or even, broad plane of light for general use. It may be accomplished with *direct lighting* such as ceiling fixtures that shine downward, illuminating the general area. Direct general lighting often takes the form of fluorescent or other utilitarian incandescent ceiling fixtures. These fixtures, particularly the fluorescent type, may provide good general lighting for kitchens, offices, workrooms, and classrooms, where tasks are performed throughout the space. However, one of the drawbacks of this type of lighting is that it may be bland or monotonous, making it unsuited for areas such as living rooms and bedrooms where aesthetics are an important part of the lighting plan.

Figure 5.1   *Freestanding "torcheres" cast light upward onto the wall and ceiling to provide indirect ambient light.*
Window shades by and photo courtesy of Hunter Douglas.

Ambient lighting generally comes from an indirect source that throws background light against a surface such as a wall or ceiling, reflecting the light back into the room. One popular *indirect lighting* ambient fixture is the *uplighter* that casts light onto the ceiling, where it is reflected back and creates a soft general illumination of the room or space. Another method of achieving ambient lighting is the use of fixtures recessed into the ceiling around the perimeter of a room that "wash" the walls with light. This type of lighting creates a pleasant quality of illumination but may not provide enough light for specific tasks. For this reason ambient lighting is often combined with other types of task or accent lighting.

Task Lighting

Task lighting directs a pool of light where it is needed to perform tasks requiring hand-eye coordination. Some of these tasks are reading, typing or word processing, writing, drawing, assembling parts, working with tools, cooking, dining, sewing, and personal grooming. Task lighting should not constitute dramatic, high-contrast areas of light and dark. If the pool of light abruptly ends and darkness begins, unnecessary eyestrain and fatigue will result. It is wise to combine task lighting with general, ambient, or natural lighting whenever possible. In the kitchen, for example, the *luminous ceiling* (general lighting) is typically accompanied by task lighting built into the ceiling, over the soffit, or under the cupboard (which may be a portable light). Task lighting in the kitchen is desirable for the sink, range, and food preparation areas.

Task lighting may also be seen as strip lights placed around a mirror or above a work area. *Track lighting* and *spotlights* are also favorite ways to focus light onto a task area.

Task lighting can also be accomplished with *portable luminaires*, such as *table lamps*, that can be moved from one area to another. These include *floor* and *table lamps*, plug-in wall sconces, and under-the-counter strips.

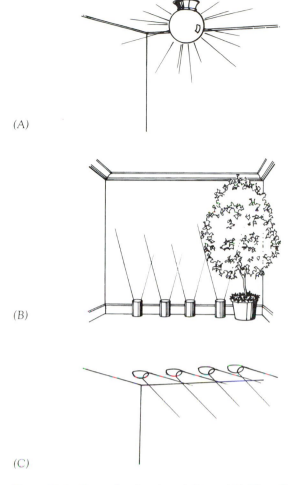

(A)

(B)

(C)

Figure 5.2 *General and ambient lighting.* (A) *The ceiling luminaire lights an area from above eye level.* (B) *Uplighters wash this wall with light, illuminating the ceiling and the area nearby. Light-colored walls will reflect and increase footlamberts.* (C) *Eyeball spotlights wash the wall from ceiling level.*

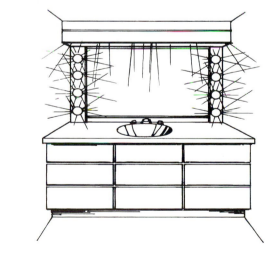

(A)

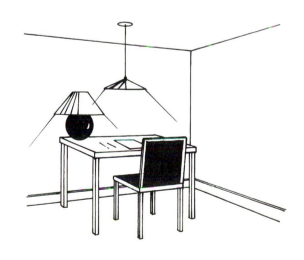

(B)

Figure 5.3 *Task lighting for specific purposes:* (A) *personal grooming;* (B) *reading, writing, or studying.*

Accent and Mood Lighting

Accent lighting is sometimes referred to as *artistic lighting*. Accent lighting may focus on a piece of art or an accessory item, giving that object greater importance in the room. Accent lighting can create interest and drama through shadows created with small spots of light or by casting light in small areas against a dark background. This *high contrast* of dark and light areas gives interest and life to an interior through the patterns of light and dark. It is stimulating and may appear as a play of *brilliants*—a myriad of pinpoints of light.

Mood lighting creates a sense of inviting coziness. The contrast of soft, low, or even glittering light against a dark background (where the ambient or general lighting has been lowered) adds sparkle and excitement to interior design. In this sense, lighting from a fireplace is an effective method of mood lighting. It emotionally draws people near for not only visual interest and comfort but for warmth as well. The heart of the home has long been its hearth, where meals were prepared and served for centuries. Today a seating area around a flickering fireplace is still inviting. It can become even more effective and beautiful with the addition of spotlights or directed low-voltage lighting.

General lighting, ambient lighting, task lighting, and accent lighting are frequently combined, since each type of lighting fulfills different purposes. Lighting may overlap to fit the time of day or night and the particular activities that are taking place within the interior. For example, on an overcast day general lighting may be needed as backup for natural lighting. General lighting is mandatory in interiors where no windows exist and for general nighttime occupation. Task lighting may supplement general lighting for specific work projects during the day or night; accent lighting is used primarily at night and in windowless interiors during the day. Because these types of lighting are often used concurrently, there needs to be some control of their usage for the sake of the life of the bulb and the energy each consumes.

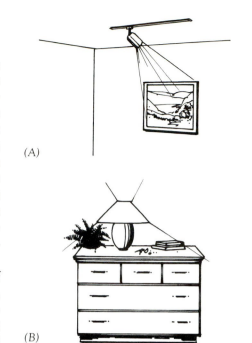

(A)

(B)

Figure 5.4 *Accent or mood lighting. (A) Track spotlight accentuates artwork. (B) Low lighting from a small luminaire (table lamp) creates a mellow mood.*

Lighting as Art

There are new frontiers in planned lighting, and one of the most exciting is lighting as art—where the light fixture and method of lighting become art itself. Besides traditional *decorative luminaire* lamps, there are several ways that lighting can become artistic:

‣ The fixture or luminaire itself may be the emphasized point of vision, as in a neon sign or artistic lighting fixture. Innovative artists are working with not only light but with other materials and textures and combining them for intriguing artistic effects.

‣ Colored light and patterns of light and dark from one or many sources can turn lighting into art.

‣ Lighted, etched *acrylic sheets* allow light to shine through the etched areas, giving unlimited design possibilities to art, floors, walls, and other areas.

‣ *Light pipes* made of acrylic can conduct a variety of lights in artistic ways: by sunlight and by a selection of lamps that produce intense light up to 1,000 watts. Subtle and/or changing color can be inserted into the pipe. When the pipe is formed into shapes such as prisms, the effect can be multiplied, giving the interior designer phenomenal freedom in creating color impressions.

‣ *Laser* lights, commonly used in light shows, can be made stationary or changeable and can project images of art, furniture, people, or even the illusion of more interior space.

‣ Already research and experimentation have shown that the *hologram* can produce amazing effects, even creating three-dimensional images in midair.[1]

Figure 5.5
The connecting concourse of the United Airlines terminal at O'Hare Airport in Chicago, with its dazzling light show, is an engaging art lighting experience.
© Ted Spiegel.

LIGHTING EFFECTS IN THE INTERIOR

Lighting effects can be handled many ways in an interior; this aspect is perhaps the most enjoyable of all the aspects of interior lighting. Lighting can change the apparent shape, color, and texture of the interior by highlighting certain objects or areas and leaving others in shadow.

- An ambient *bank* or *plane of light* is a large, well-lit area. Although it may not encompass the entire interior, it can designate smaller areas within a large space.

- An even *wash* is a soft plane of light from spotlights or track lights aimed at a wall or ceiling that can illuminate artwork, for example.

- A light shining at a steep angle or very close to the object or to a surface *grazes* it with luminescence—an effective way of emphasizing texture.

- A *pool of light* is a round circle of light thrown by a downlighter or spotlight, for example, or it may be thrown onto the wall or the ceiling. Spotlighting from more than one direction can *balance light* and emphasize detail by eliminating harsh shadows.

- *Perimeter lighting,* around the outside of a room or an area, will visually expand the space.

- *Point or pinpoint* lighting spotlights a tiny area. Pinpoint lighting can emphasize or create shiny, glittery accents if it strikes a reflective surface.

- *Line or outline lighting* can emphasize a shape or light an area such as a dressing table and mirror. This may be done with a line of incandescent lamps or with fluorescent or neon tubes.

- Lights shining directly downward will cause shadows beneath and around the object. Downward light on people casts unflattering shadows.

- Silhouette lighting is accomplished by shining a light directly on an object so that the shadow behind it echoes its shape.

- Lights that shine upward behind objects such as plants and art will "model" that shape, thereby creating patterns on the wall or ceiling.

Figure 5.6 *Perimeter spotlights shine downward on the food preparation area, producing an even wash at the countertop. Pendant lighting casts pools of light on the dining area.*

Courtesy of American Lighting Association.

Figure 5.7 *At the Sign of the Dove restaurant in New York City, (A) natural light filtered through a draped material at lunchtime creates an ambient bank or plane of light. (B) In the evening, track lighting washes the wall with a soft plane of light.*

Both © Ted Spiegel.

Figure 5.8 *Welcome sunlight floods the Spa Cafe at the Cliff Lodge, Snowbird, Utah.*
© Ricke–Hults/Photo Researchers, Inc.

NATURAL LIGHT

Natural light, or light from the sun, has a *full spectrum* of colors. Natural light makes colors appear rich and vibrant and is a healthful, cheerful light necessary for living. A balance of natural light evenly distributed from two or more directions is desirable since it helps reduce shadows in the interior and consequent visual and physical fatigue.

Yet even natural light can lean toward one color, depending on factors such as the time of day, season, weather conditions, orientation, climate, and location. The color of light at morning, noon, and evening will vary from one another and individually, according to the season and weather conditions. The morning sun in the summer is brighter and warmer than the morning winter sun, and it is more brilliant and yellow on clear days than on overcast days.

Orientation refers to the direction of the light. For example, southern-exposure light will be warmer and northern light will be cooler. Orientation also takes into account reflected surfaces. If that northern exposure faces a large orange building, then certainly that color will be reflected into the north-facing interior, rendering the light warmer than it would otherwise be. Light reflecting a deep blue sea or an azure sky will bring bluish light into the interior.

Natural light is not completely predictable. When there is no cloud cover or screening at the window, natural light can become too bright and intense, resulting in *glare,* excessive *luminance* in the visual field that can cause irritation and fatigue. Glare is a problem that requires interior shading or screening window treatments. (Artificial glare will be discussed later on.) There are also times when overcast conditions or the size and orientation of the window cause natural light to be inadequate. Too little natural light for activities such as reading, writing, or other detailed tasks can cause eyestrain and fatigue. When natural light is too dim for the occupants to function well, it must be combined with an artificial light source to become fully effective. Most people turn on lights during the day when cloud cover, fog, or smog reduces the luminance of natural light.

Combustion Lighting

Firelight, candlelight, and lanterns are another natural source of lighting called combustion lighting. For centuries, combustion lighting was the only way to supplement daylight in the interior; at night it was the only source of light. Light from fires and candles flickers, as do lanterns when they are moved about. This inconsistency can be charming and create a cozy feeling.

The warmth from a combustion source can also be an asset. A fireplace draws people near it for warmth and comfort as much as for the light. Drawbacks to combustion lighting, however, include the mess of making fires or monitoring the melting candle wax. Many homes have "gas logs" installed that burn natural gas with a flickering flame imitative of a real fire but without the work and mess. Likewise, *luminaires* (lighting fixtures) may incorporate flame-shaped bulbs that flicker to copy the light of real candles.

UNDERSTANDING ARTIFICIAL LIGHTING

In artificial lighting, we select *lamps* (light *bulbs*) that contain color characteristics that will enhance or diminish the colors specified for an interior. It is necessary to match colors under both the natural light and artificial lamps in the actual setting. If this is impossible because, say, the actual installation is not finished or is in another city, then the hard and soft materials (floor, wall, window, ceiling, and furnishing materials) should be matched under at least two kinds of light. By doing this, we can prevent a *metameric shift*, or the appearance of an object or textile as one color in one light and another color in another light. The metameric shift is caused by the *spectral energy distribution*, or color characteristics of the material or object, that will absorb or reflect the light. This is the reason colors that match perfectly in the store may not match when they are installed at home.

It is always important to bring samples of paint, carpeting, and so on, to the interior where they will be installed. Look at the colors during different times of the day and at night. Lighting can affect the way a paint chip appears compared to the actual painted surface. Applying a quart of paint to a section of the wall is an inexpensive way to determine if the color is a good choice under all types of light in that interior. It can then be more realistically matched or harmoniously blended with samples under that lighting.

Artificial lighting can create moods, add sparkle and emphasis, and be directed and manipulated to meet the needs of the interior. Although artificial lighting is often considered a stable source of light, it is interesting to note that over the life of the lamp, the lumen output (level of brightness) is reduced. There is also a color shift when dimming the lamp and a gradual color change over the life of the lamp.

Figure 5.9 *Candlelight is a warm and intriguing form of combustion lighting.* Photo by David A. Taylor.

Although many kinds of artificial lighting sources exist today, the most commonly used are incandescent (common filament light bulbs), *fluorescent* (tubes for general, luminous lighting), *HID* (high-intensity discharge) *lighting*, and *cold cathode lighting*. HID lighting and cold cathode lighting are discussed under Nonresidential Considerations at the end of this chapter.

Incandescent Lighting

Incandescent light is light produced by heating a high-resistance *tungsten filament* with an electric current until it glows intensely.[2] Incandescent light contains a continuous, warm, mellow color spectrum. However, incandescent lighting does produce heat and is costly. Bulbs, or lamps, wear out quickly and are discarded (or recycled into other materials such as ceramic tiles). Long-life bulbs cost more, but they last longer and more wisely use natural resources.

We use incandescent lighting in most ceiling and portable fixtures, such as table lamps. This lighting is flattering and is the best for warm mood lighting.

Figure 5.10 *Warm, mellow light is cast on the ceiling and cabinetry from the incandescent chandelier.*

Wood blinds by and photo courtesy of Del Mar Window Coverings.

Colored incandescent lighting can be achieved by using colored glass on the lamps or by placing a colored screen over the light. The most familiar are the colored Christmas bulbs that light our homes and spirits during the holidays.

Tungsten Halogen Lighting

Another type of incandescent light is the *tungsten halogen lamp.* The filament of the small lamp is surrounded with halogen gas. As the tungsten burns off, the halogen reacts with the tungsten, creating a bright light. This type of light enables one to direct light to a certain area and to intensify the light by placing the bulb inside a reflective (PAR) lamp. Tungsten halogen lights cost more than common incandescent lighting but will usually last longer.

Tungsten halogen bulbs are now available as standard lamps that look similar to the arbitrary bulbs and screw into any in-candescent socket. In bulbs of standard wattage, halogens last three times longer, burn 10 percent brighter, and are closer to the natural sunlight spectrum.[3]

Low-Voltage Lighting

Low-voltage lighting uses a type of bulb or lamp that controls the beam spread. The lamp typically has a built-in reflector with a tungsten halogen bulb that produces superior accent lighting. It also incorporates transformers to reduce voltage to the source. *Low-voltage lamps* come in various sizes, depending on whether they are for indoor (small) or outdoor (large) use. Indoor low-voltage lighting is often used inside recessed or track fixtures.

These lights are particularly useful in retail stores to highlight specific merchandise such as jewelry, which sparkles under a low-voltage halogen beam. We also see low voltage in art galleries or other places where artwork is displayed.

CHART 5.1 **TYPES OF INCANDESCENT LAMPS**

Types of incandescent lamps (bulbs) vary according to shape and purpose. Commonly used lamps, available in a wide range of wattage, are listed in this chart. The numerical system that indicates the size of the lamp uses numbers such as *R-20, R-30, R-40* and indicates the diameter of the lamp in inches divided by one-eighth of an inch. For example, R-20 is a lamp 2 1/2 inches wide.

LAMP SHAPES

A lamp: Arbitrary-shaped bulb; the most common lamp shape.	B lamp: Candelabra lamp—a smooth torpedo-shaped (oval or ovoid) bulb.	C lamp: Cone-shaped bulb.	F lamp: Flame-shaped bulb.

G lamp: Globe-shaped (spherical or round) bulb.	T lamp: Tubular lamp, also a designation for tungsten halogen lamps.	PS lamp: Pear-shaped lamp—a rounded, longer shape.	R lamp: Common cone-shaped reflector is brighter and shaped to spread the beam wider.

OTHER REFLECTIVE LAMPS

ER-lamp: Elliptic-shaped reflector lamps focus the light beam to two inches in front of the lamp, thereby saving energy with increased light in one spot.

PAR lamp: Parabolic aluminized reflector lamps have heavy, protective glass that makes them suitable for both interior and exterior (outdoor) use. Silvering is used to establish the beam spread and the reflective quality of the lamp, and to determine whether the beam will spread out into a *floodlight* or will be used for a spotlight. Silvering also creates *glare-free* lamps. The lamp face (the nonsilvered portion) also affects the beam spread.

HID lamps: Mercury vapor and high-pressure sodium are two of the most common high-intensity discharge lamps. Commonly used outdoors.

PL lamp: Compact twin fluorescent lamp bulb.

Figure 5.11 *Low-voltage halogen lighting spotlights Utah geological photography at the Salt Lake International Airport.*
Andrew Arnone and Darlene Langford, photographers.

Figure 5.12 *Fluorescent lighting is even and shadowless, seen here above this vanity and bathtub in luminous ceiling fixtures.*
© Jessie Walker.

Fluorescent Lighting

Fluorescent light is produced by an arc between two electrodes inside a glass tube filled with very low-pressure mercury vapor. The arc or discharge produces ultraviolet (invisible) radiation in wavelengths that excite or activate the white powder (phosphorus crystals) lining the lamp. The phosphor *fluoresces* (glows), converting the ultraviolet energy into visible light energy.[4]

Fluorescent light is a relatively shadowless, even light, making it ideal for general lighting (discussed earlier in this chapter) of environments where tasks are performed but where task lighting would be impractical or undesirable. In homes, fluorescent lighting is most commonly used in luminous ceiling panels, recessed into a dropped ceiling and covered with textured, translucent panels. Fluorescent lights are also commonly used in under-the-cabinet lighting over counters, in bathroom lighting, and over work surfaces in hobby rooms or offices. This type of even, clear light provides an environment where work can take place for a long period of time without lighting-caused fatigue.

Traditionally, fluorescent lamps have been available in straight, circular, or U- or V-shaped tubes. Now, with the development of compact fluorescents, fluorescent lamps come in many shapes. Although they initially cost more than incandescent bulbs, they require far less energy to run and last far longer than incandescent lamps. The exact difference in cost, energy saved, and longevity varies according to the type of fluorescent lamp and the type of incandescent lamp it is compared with. Fluorescent tubes become less effective as they age because they lose lumens and may hum or flicker prior to burning out. *Rapid-start fluorescent lamps* have eliminated the problem of blinking when the lights are switched on.

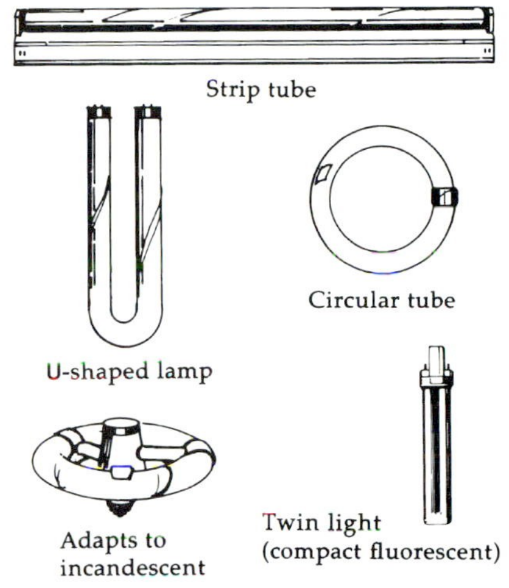

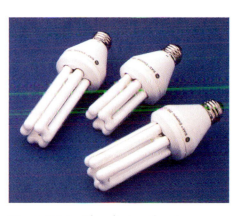

Figure 5.13 *Shapes of fluorescent lamps.*

Strip tube

Circular tube

U-shaped lamp

Adapts to incandescent

Twin light (compact fluorescent)

Fluorescent lighting is available in both warm and cool color spectrums. The fluorescent lamps that are cold and unflattering are the cheaper lamps, and although they are cold, the lumens per watt are high and the light is cost efficient. *Cool white deluxe* and *warm white deluxe* lamps have a balanced spectrum and are more flattering. However, they also cost more than standard fluorescent lamps. Fluorescent lamps are available in a wide range of styles and types; each dealer will have a chart with all the kinds of fluorescent lamps listed. When shopping for fluorescent lamps, it is wise to consult with the lighting personnel for help in selecting lamps that will be most appropriate.

Compact Fluorescent Lamps

Greater availability of energy-efficient *compact fluorescent (CF) lamps* has led to their increased acceptance and popularity. Although they are initially more expensive, CF lamps consume as little as one-fifth of the power and last up to thirteen times longer than incandescent lamps. CF lamps also offer a choice of colors and degrees of "warmth." Some can even be dimmed. The choices are not just in the lamps, but also in the ballasts that connect the lamp to the fixture and can convert an incandescent fixture into a fluorescent one. Ballasts can be classified as standard electromagnetic, energy-efficient electromagnetic, or electronic, with novel options such as radio interference suppression or power factor correction.[5]

Colored Fluorescent Lighting

Colored fluorescent light is cold cathode, commonly called *neon lamps*. These use different gases or vapors to produce colors. Neon lighting has traditionally been used to light exterior signs in business districts, but today, creative uses of neon lighting have brought this type of light to residential interiors. Lighting as art frequently incorporates neon lighting in homes with surprising and intriguing effects.

Figure 5.14 *The selection of compact fluorescents is seeing explosive growth because of the demand for economically and ecologically sound lighting.*

Courtesy of GE Lighting.

Figure 5.15 *Sunlight pours deeply into this interior. Bringing natural light into the interior helps relieve Seasonal Affective Disorder, or SAD.*
© Bob Daemmrich/The Image Works.

LIGHT AND THE MIND AND BODY

The psychological and physical effects of lighting, or the way light can affect the mind and body, is a fascinating and complex study. For example, nearly everyone has experienced a light-hearted, cheerful outlook on sunny days and a gloomy attitude on dark, dreary days when clear, natural light is lacking.

Seasonal Affective Disorder (SAD)

The diagnosis of *seasonal affective disorder (SAD)* was a medical breakthrough in understanding how light affects the mind and body. This condition occurs in some people who are deprived of natural light during the long winter season. SAD is considered to be a disruption in the circadian entrainment rhythms—meaning that the process by which we "set" our biological clocks through regular exposure to light has been interrupted. SAD symptoms include depression and fatigue.

Research has shown that light is needed by eye exposure based on the amount of brightness, measured in lux. Minimum lux for reading is 100. Bright light in an interior is about 500 lux. Exposure to natural sunlight outside on a cloudless day is 10,000 lux, and standing by a window on a sunny day exposes us to 2,500 lux. Treatment for SAD includes phototherapy, which directly exposes the patient to approximately 2,500 lux from special lights at a distance of three feet. The patient is required to sit in front of a specially designed phototherapy light box for one-hour sessions, glancing at the light for ten to fifteen seconds out of every minute.

Phototherapy lights can be purchased for home use as well. The best known brand name is Vita-Light, which has a color index (balance of pure white light) of ninety-one, compared to 100 for natural full-spectrum light. Many people have been dramatically helped to overcome SAD through the home use of these lights. The caution here is *not* to install phototherapy lights for general lighting in the home or office, since the exposure can be overstimulating; rather, those requiring therapy should seek professional medical guidance.[6]

Figure 5.16 *Lighting sets the mood in the lounge of the Colorado Springs Marriott Hotel.*
Courtesy of Victor Huff Partnership/Karl Francetic, photographer.

A less formal approach favored by many people today is to plan or remodel homes with large expanses of glass to admit natural light. Basking by a sunny window is considered by most of us to be therapeutic. The solarium or greenhouse, discussed in chapter 14, also exemplifies how we can bring full-spectrum sunlight into our homes. We often feel more rested, cheerful, or optimistic when sunlight is a part of our daily regime.

Manipulating Mood With Interior Lighting

Interior lighting can also affect our outlook and physical state. Factors that determine the psychosocial, physical, or physiological effects of lighting include the light's size and source, direction, color, and the color and texture of the objects being lit. For example, the plane or bank of light minimizes form and bulk, reducing the importance of objects and even people. It can fill a person with a sense of space and freedom and can be restful and reassuring. This type of general lighting is effective in open areas of public buildings, offices, hotels, and retail businesses. In homes, it is often used in rooms such as kitchens, bathrooms, workrooms, or hobby rooms, where moderately bright light (whether from incandescent or fluorescent lighting) produces a general feeling of well-being.

Large areas of bright light are thought to stimulate a temporary psychological and physical surge of energy, which may cause undue fatigue after periods of prolonged exposure. In addition, the mind will become bored or dulled after a barrage of continuous bright lights. If the light becomes too brilliant, it can cause malaise or a feeling of illness. This is one reason why phototherapy lights for treating SAD should not be installed as general lighting.

Moderate to low levels of indirect lighting are sometimes called mood lighting, meaning that the area is inviting, cozy, and intimate. This type of lighting is used in restaurants where the clientele come not only for good food but for a relaxed, private, and unhurried conversation. Mood lighting is also favored in the home in areas such as the formal living or dining room and the master bedroom. Mood lighting can also be accomplished with backlighting (placing lights behind furnishings) and from *flickering light* emitted from candles, fireplaces, or electric flame lamps. Flickering light is usually warm in color, casting a healthy glow.

Low lighting can give an impression of intrigue and intimacy. It is usually employed in lounges and nightclubs. In the home, low lighting can enhance the feeling of relaxation and privacy in a bed-

CHART 5.2   TYPES OF GLARE

Direct glare is bright light or insufficiently shielded light sources in the field of view. Placement of lighting sources is very important; light in the center of a room can produce direct glare, as can some accent lighting. Direct glare is a problem in offices where the desk faces the window. This may be corrected by turning the desk so that the light is coming from the side rather than the front. (Note that light from behind a seated person will cause shadows on the work surface and will be equally unacceptable.)

Reflecting glare is something shiny reflecting in the area of the task, such as reflection of a light on a computer terminal screen. Fatigue is augmented when reflecting glare is present.

Veiling glare prevents us from seeing a task clearly. It is caused by light reflecting off a surface, causing a blind spot. What we see are the reflected images of the light source rather than the task at hand. Veiling glare can make seeing extremely difficult and cause eyestrain; it is due to incorrect placement of the lighting source or an inadequate baffle (screening device) of the light fixture.

---

room, for example. In media/presentation rooms (for television, slides, or films), low lighting diminishes eye strain. It helps establish the perimeter of the room and produces a sense of security.

Colored light also has profound effect on the mind and body. Warm white light and soft warm colored light generally are welcoming and uplifting. However, intensely colored light, such as bright red, orange, and yellow, produce considerable eye strain. This may lead to an eventual feeling of physical exhaustion as the mind struggles to avoid coping with the intensity.

Cool white light and cool-colored lights (blue, cool green, and violet) produce calm, restful environments but can eventually become unfriendly, cold, or depressing.

Glare

Glare means excessive light that causes irritation or fatigue. Heat buildup from excessive natural or incandescent lighting, as well as too much brightness, will cause discomfort and irritation. Dark areas surrounding lighted areas cause eyestrain, fatigue, and even depression as peripheral vision constantly has to deal with the dark-bright contrast.[7]

Natural daylighting often requires shading window treatments. Glare from artificial light can be controlled by lowering the wattage, using a *cool-beam lamp*, or adjusting the direction of the lighting source. Another means of diverting or diffusing glare is through *baffles*. Baffles come in many forms:

1. A length of wood placed in front of lights directs the light upward or downward.

2. Louvers or grooves on or inside a luminaire or fixture act as baffles.

3. A metal or wooden grid diffuses the light and produces more even distribution.

4. The lens or glass covering can be textured or coated to diffuse glare.

5. Reflectors inside the bulb itself can further control the light and glare.

The most common types of glare are listed in chart 5.2. These are *direct glare*, *reflecting glare*, and *veiling glare*.

CHART 5.3   UNITS OF MEASUREMENT

Volts or voltage means the units for measuring electric potential, defining the force or pressure of electricity in the power line.

Ampere or amp is the measurement of the current that is taken from the main line and fed into a building as a *circuit*. A typical residence, for example, has a fifteen-amp circuit.

Watt or wattage is the unit for measuring electric power that defines the energy consumed by a lamp or electric fixture.

Footcandle is the amount of direct light thrown by one candle on a square foot of flat surface.

Lumen refers to the flow of light. Lumens are listed on the package of a *fixture* or *luminaire*. Lumens per watt is the measure of *efficacy*, or efficiency, or how much energy is expended per watt.

Footlambert (fl) measures the light reflected off a surface. We actually see by footlamberts. Reflectance is the amount of light that reflects, or bounces off, an object and can increase the apparent brightness of the light. A white wall reflects 80 percent of the light, whereas a black wall reflects only 2 percent of the light.[8]

POWER TERMINOLOGY AND UNITS OF MEASUREMENT

To understand how incandescent and fluorescent lighting is measured, it is necessary to understand basic power terminology and units of measurement.

Incandescent and fluorescent lighting is measured in *footcandles, footlamberts*, and *lumens* (see chart 5.3) These terms allow lighting engineers and designers to create and evaluate lamps for specific purposes. These terms are a part of the general body of interior design knowledge.

Incandescent lamps, or light bulbs, typically vary in wattage—15, 25, 60, 75, 100, 120, 150, and 175. In a luminaire that contains two or more lamps, there is often a limitation on the wattage so that the fixture will not be overheated and risk catching fire. The wattage of fluorescent lamps is 18, 20, 32, 40, 60, or 80; they deliver greater brightness per watt than incandescent lighting, making fluorescent lamps more energy efficient.

CHART 5.4   SUGGESTIONS FOR
LIGHTING ECONOMY

- Turn out lights when not in use.
- Put light only where it is needed, keeping in mind that a high contrast (a pool of light surrounded by dark) can cause fatigue and even distress.
- Use dimmer switches to control and lower the wattage.
- Use photoelectric cells or timers to turn outdoor lights on and off automatically.
- Open window treatments to allow natural light in, supplementing with artificial light only when needed.
- Use light-colored surfaces to reflect and thereby increase light, and use textures that will not absorb much light.
- Use only some of the lights in an interior (use one, rather than two, table lamps).
- Switch on portable luminaires with fewer lamps or lower wattage to illuminate local tasks rather than using ambient or general overhead lighting.
- Use one higher wattage bulb rather than multiple lower wattage bulbs. For example, one 100-watt bulb will use less energy than two 60-watt bulbs.
- Install extra light switches so that at each doorway the light can be turned off without inconvenience.
- Use low-voltage or lower wattage lamps.
- Use new materials (such as acrylic) that conduct and reflect light but use a fraction of the electricity required for traditional incandescent lighting.
- Use energy-saving fluorescent lighting in place of incandescent lighting where aesthetically practical. It is estimated that fluorescent lighting uses only one-fifth to one-third as much electricity as incandescent lighting with comparable lumen ratings. Warm white deluxe fluorescent lamps are suggested as replacements for incandescent lighting in the home.
- Replace incandescent lamps with CF lamps that can be screwed in their place, using only about 18 watts in place of a 75-watt incandescent lamp. These fluorescent lamps, when properly installed and ventilated, last as long as ten average incandescent lamps. There is no humming of the ballast or interference with radio or television reception.
- Line new or retrofitted older light fixtures with reflective material, which dramatically reduces the number of lamps required and the amount of electricity used to produce the same number of lumens.
- Use motion sensors to turn lights on when the room is occupied and off when unoccupied.

Ordinary incandescent lamps (bulbs) last from 750 to 2,500 hours, and long-life bulbs (which cost more initially and deliver less light for the electricity used) last from 2,500 to 3,500 hours. Low-voltage incandescent lamps use less wattage or electric power and deliver greater control and a wider range of beam spread.

Note that it is not the size of the lamp or the level of wattage that makes an impact in lighting. Lighting becomes most interesting when the size of the beam is controlled to create pools of light or emphasize certain areas or focal points in the interior. This is the advantage of incandescent lighting—such as low-voltage, some tungsten halogen, and (HID) lighting—over fluorescent lighting.

LIGHTING ECONOMY

The upward surge of electricity rates, predicted to continue, is the major factor in economizing with light. Lighting consumes less electricity than heat-producing appliances such as dryers, water heaters, dishwashers, ovens, and ranges. However, lighting does consume more power than smaller appliances. Ways that lighting can be more effectively and economically used are listed in chart 5.4.

WIRING PLANS

The planning of lighting systems requires training, experience, and thinking through what lighting must accomplish in an interior. Interior designers are often actively involved in this process. A wiring or lighting plan is a part of the working drawings. The wiring plan indicates where outlets, switches, and wall and ceiling light fixtures will be located.

Switches and Outlets

Light switches can be placed in one, two, or even three locations. Switches should easily be accessible at the doorway on the open side so that lights can be turned on at the doorway. Careful thought should be given to the type and placement of switches, according to the needs of the users. If, for example, the user is an aged or infirm person, then a "rocker switch" may be easier to operate than a standard flip switch.

Dimmer switches are knob switches that are pushed to turn on the light and rotated to increase or decrease the level of illumination or brightness. Dimmers are effective for incandescent lighting. (Only one kind of fluorescent light can be dimmed, that is the rapid-start lamp, which requires a specialized dimmer.) Dimmers make it possible to create levels of interest and different moods in the interior. Automatic sensor dimmers are used to turn on interior lights automatically to supplement natural daylight to a proportionate, preprogrammed level.

Switched outlets are plugs that are activated by switches. This allows for lamps, lighting as art, or decorative lights (such as Christmas decorations) to be turned on at the flip of a switch—the light is plugged in and turned on at the source but controlled at the switch. Switched outlets contribute convenience and safety to the interior and its occupants. If, for example, a portable table luminaire is the only or desired source of light in the room, it can be turned on at the door. This will eliminate the necessity of first turning on general lighting to reach the portable light, then returning to turn off the general lighting. It also reduces the danger of walking across a dark room. In addition, the inconvenience of fumbling over holiday packages, decorations, or tree to reach Christmas lights—or walking outside to turn on exterior lights—can be removed through switched outlets.

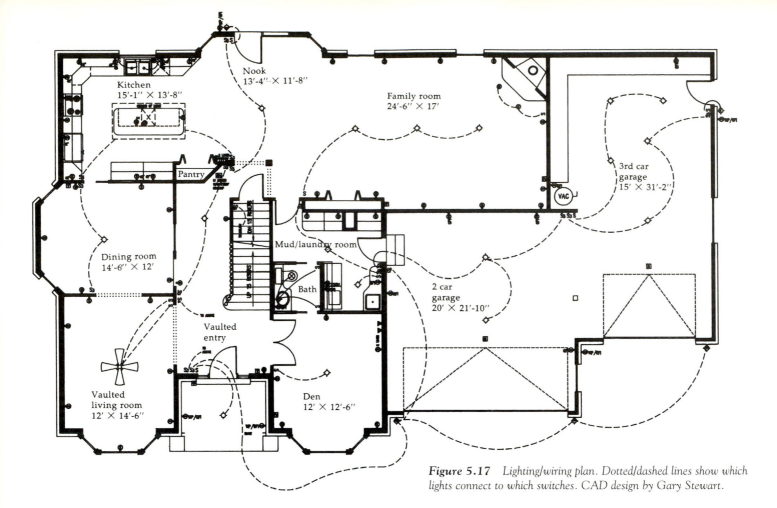

Figure 5.17 *Lighting/wiring plan. Dotted/dashed lines show which lights connect to which switches. CAD design by Gary Stewart.*

According to state and local building codes, outlets must be located from six to twelve feet along the wall for portable luminaires (floor, table, and wall lamps). The frequent placement of outlets minimizes the need for extension cords and precludes plugging too many lights or appliances into one outlet. Therefore, the building code helps ensure safety against tripping and falling and against fire from overloading a circuit and outlet. Stretching cords tight can also increase danger of damage, loose connections, and possibly tenuous circumstances where the luminaire is placed too close to the edge of a surface and could easily fall off, break, and perhaps even burst into flames.

Convenience is another major reason for including frequent outlets: it is easy to place the luminaire, appliance, or piece of equipment where it is needed. Vertical placement is an important part of planning outlets and switches for the sake of convenience. For example, a table-height outlet may be desirable for units such as entertainment components or computers. Appliances for kitchens, workrooms, or hobby areas need outlets above counter height. Outlets should have a *grounding receiver* (three-prong plug outlet) as standard in all areas for high-electric use lights, appliances, and components. *Outlet strips*—casings with spaced outlets that are prewired or portable—are useful in home workbenches, home offices, and kitchens.

The exact placement of switches and outlets can be determined when the building has been framed. It is common for the client and/or interior designer to meet the electrician at the

Lighting symbols for wiring plans

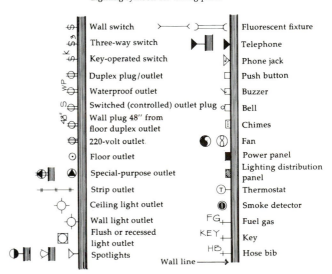

Figure 5.18 *Lighting symbols for wiring plans.*

site and mark the exact location of fixtures, outlets, and switches. There may be a need to adjust placement because of the heat ducts. Before mechanical systems are installed, it is wise to plan where the luminaires, outlets, and switches will be needed.

The planning of lighting systems in nonresidential complexes and high-rise buildings entails technical studies of lighting needs, electrical code requirements, and restrictions.

CHART 5.5   INDIRECT LIGHTING

Indirect lighting is placing a light behind a built-in or portable feature. Types of indirect lighting placed behind deflectors include the following.

CORNICE LIGHTING	VALANCE LIGHTING	BRACKET LIGHTING (UP AND DOWN)	BRACKET LIGHTING (UP ONLY)
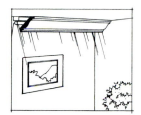	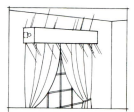	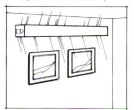	
A light behind a board mounted into the ceiling washes light down onto the wall.	A light used over the top of windows washes both the ceiling and the window treatment.	Valance lighting mounted lower on the wall washes the upper (and perhaps lower) wall with light.	A light placed just below the ceiling has the board or deflector beneath it.

SOFFIT LIGHTING	SOFFIT LIGHTING (IN A BATH)	BASE OR TOE-MOLD LIGHTING	TOE-KICK OR RISER LIGHTING
		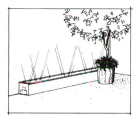	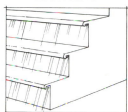
A light built into the soffit shines downward from the top of the cabinet overhead.	Soffit lighting provides even illumination for personal grooming.	A strip of light is placed against the floor where a deflector directs the light upward or perhaps downward, giving the effect of theatrical usher lights.	Lighting under the toe-kick area of cabinets or stairs. These can also take the form of usher lights.

LUMINAIRES, OR LIGHTING FIXTURES

Luminaires, sometimes called lighting fixtures, fall into two broad categories: *architectural or structural lighting* and *nonarchitectural lighting*, or *portable luminaires*. Architectural or structural luminaires are those permanently installed and planned for in the lighting or wiring plan. These include ceiling and wall fixtures that are installed to permanent wiring.

Many architectural luminaires are simple and inconspicuous. Their goal is to emphasize what they light, not call attention to themselves. Other luminaires are quite decorative and/or dramatic and can make up an important part of the design scheme.

Many styles, designs, colors, and finishes of luminaires are on the market today—painted metal, bright or antique brass, pewter, or stainless steel, for example. The glass may be clear, white, colored, or bronzed. A large portion of the appeal of lighting interiors is the charm and/or character of the luminaires. Luminaires may be found in styles to match every kind of setting and in good, poor, and mediocre design and quality. Because of the many design quality levels, the power of discrimination discussed in chapter 3 becomes paramount when selecting luminaires.

Portable luminaires (nonarchitectural lighting) are those that plug in; they (1) hang on the wall or from a ceiling hook or (2) are placed on a table or on the floor. Decorative luminaires are discussed in chapter 13, Art and Accessories.

Architectural Lighting

The categories of architectural lighting include *luminous panels*, built-in indirect lighting, *recessed* and adjustable fixtures, and *surface-mounted* and *suspended fixtures*.

Luminous Panels

Luminous panels are strips or lines of lights, usually fluorescent, over which glass or plastic translucent panels are placed. The translucent panel seems to glow, producing a soft white or colored light, according to the texture and color of the glass or plastic. It can also cause glare in some situations. Luminous panels, quite common in kitchens, are referred to as luminous ceilings.

Built-in Indirect Lighting

Refer to chart 5.5.

CHART 5.6 RECESSED AND ADJUSTABLE LIGHTING

RECESSED DOWNLIGHTS

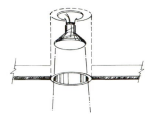

Canisters set into the ceiling cast pools
of light downward.

SURFACE-MOUNTED DOWNLIGHTS

Canisters mounted on the ceiling that hang
down. (These are used in place of recessed down-
lights where there is insufficient ceiling clearance,
or they are added later in a remodeling situation.)

EYEBALL LIGHTING

Fixtures that project an adjustable lamp from
the ceiling and throw pools of light onto the
wall are eyeball spotlights. A series of
these can form wall washers.

STRIP LIGHTING

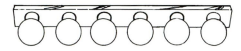

Strip or theatrical lighting is often used for personal grooming areas.

TRACK LIGHTING

Flexible ceiling-mounted fixtures that can hold spotlights or floodlights
mounted anywhere and at any position on a fixed track. (Track luminaires
come in various sizes, shapes, colors, and finishes. They are ideal for
accent lighting and wall-wash lighting.)

Recessed and Adjustable Luminaries

This category (see chart 5.6) includes various luminaires that are
set into the ceiling, called *recessed luminaires,* and those that are
adjustable. Adjustable luminaires can be recessed or surface mounted.

Surface-Mounted and Suspended Luminaires

These luminaires are clearly visible, perhaps even obvious to the
eye. Translucent covers are called *diffusers,* and serve to soften the
light. Clear or tinted glass covers may require a decorative lamp.

Suspended fixtures such as *chandeliers* or *dropped-pendant luminaires* may be dropped only a few inches from the ceiling (over a
dining or conference table), or may be suspended several feet (in
an open area such as a hotel atrium or an entrance). Sizes vary
dramatically from about six inches to several feet in diameter. The
size and placement are dependent upon the scale of the interior
and the use. In a dining area, the chandelier should be approximately thirty inches above the table. Suspended lamps, often used
in reading corners, should drop to about forty inches from the floor
or twenty inches above the seat level. These heights are, of course,
dependent on the scale of the luminaire and the ceiling height as
well as the scale and placement of the furniture.

Figure 5.19 *Recessed spotlights give soft ambient light to this quiet corner.
Lighting is planned to accentuate art and illuminate the reading area.*

Courtesy of American Lighting Association.

LIGHTING FOR THE FUTURE

In many respects, the future is here today. Lighting experts have created such amazing effects with lighting that only a few years ago it would have been impossible to believe what we almost take for granted today.

Lighting has perhaps advanced the most quickly in nonresidential settings (see the next section), but new developments in lighting control devices are already increasing energy efficiency in homes. These include:

- Electronic sensors that can turn selected lights on and off in an interior
- Various control systems that include wall-mounted, programmable control for total home or area control
- Hand-held controllers that operate on infrared frequencies to send instructions to wall receivers
- Switches that can turn lights off after preselected time periods
- Sensing devices that turn on lighting as a response to radiated heat caused by human presence and movement.[9]

Certainly lighting can make the difference in the effectiveness of the interior now; and in the future, it will do so in increasingly creative ways.

In the future, lighting organizations such as the International Association of Lighting Designers, the Designers Lighting Forum, and the Illuminating Engineering Society of North America will continue to provide state-of-the-art research and products to professionals in the design field. Communication—through printed material, conferences, seminars, and marketing—will make artistic and scientific advances readily accessible for tomorrow's interiors. For the layperson, the National Lighting Bureau publishes a variety of excellent guides on beneficial uses, cost effectiveness, and conservation. (The addresses for these organizations are found at the end of this chapter.)

Together, science and the arts have created illumination that is literally changing the shape of things to come.

NONRESIDENTIAL CONSIDERATIONS

Many of the topics discussed in this chapter are applicable to nonresidential situations as well. Here we will also discuss other considerations that apply specifically to nonresidential interiors.

Natural Daylighting

In nonresidential settings such as offices, natural daylight is often desired by employees—sometimes even considered a luxury. However, problems exist with natural daylighting (as discussed under Glare). Temperature control is another major consideration linked to daylighting. Excessive heat and cold can be the result of poor insulation or large expanses of glass.

Natural daylight almost always needs to be supplemented with artificial light; the lighting systems need careful control to maintain a healthy balance of light.

HID Lighting

HID, or high-intensity discharge, lighting is used for bright interior and exterior lighting. HID lamps establish an arc between two very close electrodes set in opposite ends of small, sealed, translucent or transparent glass tubes. The electric arc generates heat and pressure high enough to vaporize the atoms of various metallic elements inside the lamp, causing the atoms to emit large amounts of visible-range electromagnetic energy.[10]

HID lamps are used to "uplight" exteriors of large buildings and are being used more often in interiors of nonresidential buildings. They produce a greater quantity of light using less energy than an incandescent lamp. The problems being overcome in HID lighting are the noise or hum of the arc or *ballast* and the length of time to restart the lamp after a power failure.

Cold Cathode Lighting

Cold cathode lighting, or *neon lighting*, uses different gases or vapors to produce colors. Neon lighting has been an important part of exterior lighting for advertising and storefronts, but it is being increasingly used in interiors such as restaurants and retail businesses to emphasize a color scheme and add drama and excitement. Lighting specialists are often consulted to design neon lighting for interior design.

Motivational Lighting

Lighting specialists are also examining how the behavior of people can be altered or directed with *illusion lighting*. This can mean that people will be motivated to sit, walk, or face a particular direction because of the impressions given them by special lighting (particularly the manipulation of bright versus dark areas) and finishes. *Motivational lighting* can create environments where the quality, intensity, and angle of light create the appearance or disappearance of objects, walls, ceilings, and even entire rooms.[11] Lighting specialists are often called upon as consultants by interior designers to accomplish special effects in an interior. The manipulation of areas of intense brightness or darkness can affect both the mind and body, making us believe that something exists that really is not there (a wall, for example) or that something is not as close as it actually is. In addition to making us behave in a predicted manner, this can make spaces fit the needs of the people in the environment.

Safety Lighting

Safety lighting is required in public spaces where there are egress signs, such as exit signs. Other safety lighting mandated by building codes includes aisle or egress lighting and lighting for stairs and landings. (New developments in egress lighting are discussed in Lighting for the Future.)

Figure 5.20 *Neon lighting helps establish the exciting mood in this Chicago nightclub.*

Courtesy of Zakaspace.

Wiring

Nonresidential lighting plans constitute a *network of lighting* fixtures that are controlled from a central location or are automated. The interior designer need not visit the site to determine exact location, since nonresidential lighting placement is firmly established by the architectural plans. However, special needs and considerations can be met through the collaboration of the designer and the electrical engineer. The designer determines the needs and specifies, through calculations, which lamps and levels of power are required. The engineer will work with the specifications and then often oversee the actual installation of wiring components.

Wiring in newer nonresidential settings such as business offices is often carried not only in the wall but in the floor or ceiling. Prewired office systems that contain outlets for business equipment and lighting can be hooked into the architectural wiring in the wall, ceiling, or floor. Where additional electric plugs are required, outlet strips (a casing of spaced outlets) are commonly installed after the building is completed.

Lighting Economy

In nonresidential interiors, lighting is a major monthly expense, and because of the tremendous amount of electricity used, nonresidential buildings are limited by law to the amount of electricity consumed per square foot. These limitations are roughly one-tenth of what they were before the energy crunch of the 1970s. The cost and the consumption limits of lighting do, therefore, constitute a legitimate reason for controlling lighting use while maintaining effectiveness.

In addition to the lighting economy suggestions in the main body of the chapter, there are other ways to control energy consumption and costs in nonresidential lighting. One is the addition of central programmable monitoring systems that will automatically turn lights off and on in various parts of a building when required. Another is the increased usage of sensing devices (see Lighting for the Future) that monitor light usage, turning it on and off according to time, daylight levels, or whether people are moving in the room.

Fluorescent luminaires in the ceiling can be retrofitted with reflective materials that deliver the same lumens with half the number of lamps. For example, a luminaire that ordinarily contains four 60-watt fluorescent lamps will produce the same light with only two 60-watt lamps after retrofitting. In this way, energy consumption can be cut in half, greatly reducing the cost of electricity.

Electric costs can also be reduced by retrofitting incandescent luminaires with adaptable compact fluorescent (CF) lighting that delivers the same lumens or brightness with far fewer watts. These lamp bulbs connect to ballasts fitted into adapters that screw into incandescent fixtures, cutting costs immediately by up to 80 percent and producing a longer life span. For example, PL-type fluorescent lamps that use 7 or 9 watts can replace 150-watt incandescent lighting. The PL-type lamp is a small, low-wattage fluorescent twin tube with a prong base that fits into the adapter containing a ballast.

Figure 5.21 *At the IBM showroom in Dallas, pairs of recessed spotlights illuminate computer hardware. Indirect fluorescent bracket lighting provides an ambient light.*
© 1985 Norman McGrath.

New laws are being passed in many states that limit the amount of electricity a building can consume. This, in turn, limits the number, placement, and usage of lights in nonresidential interiors. Some feel that this will limit the creativity of lighting designers. However, we are already seeing advances in economical lighting. Look for new products and innovative ways lighting can be functional, beautiful—even dazzling—and still use less electricity.

Lighting for the Future

Motivational and illusion lighting may play key roles in nonresidential design in the future, as they are beginning to today. We will likely see more motivational lighting in public spaces such as banks, offices, and medical facilities. We will see remarkable lighting effects in museums, theaters, and all types of staged events. The laser show has become a standard attraction in discotheques and planetariums and is now making its way into homes as well.

A notable development is the introduction and marketing of LEDs (light-emitting diodes), which are solid-state lamps without filaments whose life expectancy projections range from seven hundred thousand to over five million hours (eighty to 570 years). LEDs have application in emergency exits or in situations where lights burn out or are shaken loose due to vibration (such as in airports, in railway stations, in industrial plants, and over doorways). Egress exit signs can also be made of etched acrylic plates that eliminate the necessity of breakable glass.

Other developments will continue to become important, such as sensing devices and central computerized monitoring systems.

New developments are being marketed that reduce office glare by improving light dispersion at the work surface where the user can control the levels of illumination. Tilting fixtures are available to adjust the direction of light and control glare at workstations.

Lower maintenance through retrofitted longer life lamp bulbs and fluorescent lamps is another trend for the present and future.

Fluorescent luminaire fixtures are now available that screw into existing fixtures, as previously discussed.

Remote-control devices are being developed and marketed that send instructions for reprogramming back to a central unit or that control lights from hallways, for example. Dimming controls can, likewise, be computer controlled.

New products such as oak-wrapped strips for fluorescent ceiling boxes and unbreakable diffuser lenses for luminous ceilings continue to augment aesthetics. In addition, exciting new designs are continually emerging in the lighting-as-art field and as decorative luminaire fixtures. Lighting design is a viable field for a design professional because of the continual demand for new products and designs in the marketplace.[12]

ENVIRONMENTAL CONSIDERATIONS

The chief environmental concern in lighting is the consumption of energy. Chart 5.4 lists several ways to reduce energy consumption. These suggestions can be summarized in two points:

1. Select fixtures and lamps that are more energy efficient. Examples include the new generation of compact fluorescent lamps and incandescent lamps with lower wattage and longer life.

2. Use less electricity. This can be done by utilizing occupancy monitors or sensors, which are devices that switch lights on and off by sensing movement and lack of it. This may save up to 30 percent in energy consumption.[13] We can also plan space to take advantage of natural daylight, dim lights when possible, and supplement with task lighting where work takes place.

LIGHTING ASSOCIATIONS

American Home Lighting Institute (AHLI)
435 North Michigan Avenue
Chicago, IL 60611

Designer's Lighting Forum (DLF)
Contact: Illumineering Engineering Society of North America for information on local chapters
Illumineering Engineering Society of North America (IESNA)
345 East 47th Street
New York, NY 10017

International Association of Lighting Designers (IALD)
c/o Wheel Gersztof Associates
30 West 22nd Street
New York, NY 10010

National Lighting Bureau (NLB)
2101 L Street NW
Washington, DC 20037

NOTES

1. Fran Kellogg Smith, "Light as Art, Today and Tomorrow," *ASID Report* XII, no. 3 (Summer 1986):8–9.

2. General Electric, *Light and Color* (Cleveland: General Electric Lighting Business Group, 1981), 21.

3. "Homework," *Home Magazine* (Boulder, Colo.) (March 1992):84.

4. General Electric, *Light and Color,* 21.

5. David Finn and Michael Ouelette, "Technics Focus—Compact Fluorescent Lamps: What You Should Know," *Progressive Architecture* (August 1992), 89–92.

6. Robert N. Moreines, M.D., *Light Up Your Blues: A Guide to Overcoming Seasonal Depression and Fatigue.* (New York: Berkley Books, 1989), 90–100.

7. James L. Nuckolls, "Glare Free Workstation," *Interiors* (August 1982): 74–75.

8. "Design Criteria for Interior Lighting Spaces" (New York: Illuminating Engineering Society of North America, 1980), 6.

9. Kellogg Smith, "Light as Art, Today and Tomorrow," 8–9.

10. General Electric, *Light and Color,* 21.

11. Kellogg Smith, "Light as Art, Today and Tomorrow," 8–9.

12. "Refections/New Products/Applications," *Energy User News Magazine* (November 1987): 8–22.

13. Judith Nasatir, "National Audubon Society," *Interior Design* (August 1991): 98.

SPACE PLANNING

SPACE PLANNING AND THE DESIGN PROCESS

The design process, discussed in chapter 1, forms the basis for planning space and cannot be separated from it. The gathering of data, which results in a design direction or program, lays the foundation for planning the space. The program also identifies goals to be accomplished in the space—the creation of a sense of place (being surrounded with a feeling of belonging to the space). The architect or designer *allocates spaces* (assigns square footage and placement to rooms or areas) by following the design process. The process of design entails making many decisions through careful consideration of the factors that make *space planning* possible.

The factors that must be considered in intelligent space planning include:

- Function and zoning
- Size and shape of the space
- Site, orientation, and climate
- Cubic and square footage
- Economy
- Stretching space
- Traffic patterns
- Storage
- Permanent fixtures (kitchen and bath spaces)
- Special needs for the elderly or handicapped
- Emotion and psychology
- Utilization of the principles and elements of design

These factors, together with the user's needs, influence the decisions on how to plan and best utilize the space.

As these considerations are reviewed and satisfied, the floor plan evolves from a conceptual bubble diagram to a finished plan. Figure 6.1 illustrates this process with a floor plan that has evolved from the bubble diagram stage through three refinements to the finished floor plan. This floor plan is ready to be blueprinted with the addition of all necessary schedules and diagrams to instruct the general contractors and subcontractors as to the construction and installation of structural components. Chapter 14 deals with the processes and systems of building.

FUNCTION AND ZONING

Functional analysis is perhaps the most important of the space allotment criteria. *Function* means the intended use of the space; it can graphically be illustrated as *zones*, as seen in figure 6.1(A). In most homes there are typically four zones: *social zones* (*formal* or *informal areas*); *work zones* (kitchen, office, laundry, sewing, hobby, or other task-oriented rooms); *private zones* (bedrooms, retreat areas, bathrooms); and *storage* zones (cabinets and closets). These zones may be large or small and may be repeated as necessary to meet the needs of the program.

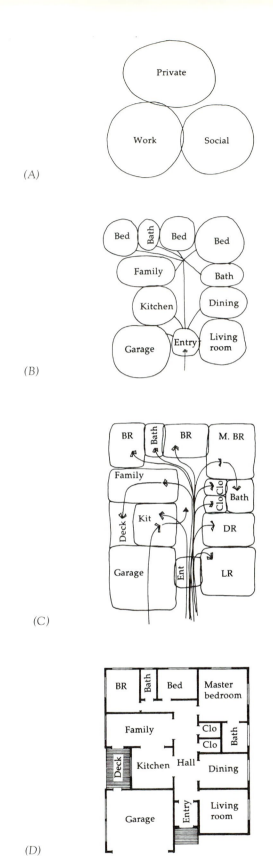

Figure 6.1 *Four phases of schematics or graphics in the evolution of the floor plan. (A) The general zones—private, work, and social. (B) Divisions within these zones for specific rooms and their relationship to one another. (C) The size and shape of the rooms and the traffic patterns. (D) The floor plan where doorways, windows, and walls are clearly defined.*

Interrelating Functions

Zones within the home are located near or overlap other zones because of an *interrelationship of functions*. Typical is the placement of the formal living zone adjacent to the formal dining; the kitchen close to the service and dining areas; the bedrooms grouped around a shared bathroom. Part of the space-planning process includes a list of what areas or functions the user wishes to interrelate; there is great latitude for individual space planning in the design of custom homes. For example, a particular user may request a home office adjacent to the master bedroom, while another person may want a home office near the front door or near the kitchen. Some people prefer the family room open to the kitchen and informal dining, whereas others specify the informal social zone separate and away from the kitchen.

When functions interrelate, or smoothly flow from one zone or area to another, and when the interior design is unique and sophisticated, we experience fine quality design. A skill worth developing is the ability to recognize what functions are being served by the design. It is then possible to evaluate how well the zoned areas interrelate and whether that relationship is smooth and effective.

DIAGRAMMING AND FLOOR PLANS

Diagramming is the process of placing a two- or three-dimensional representation of the proposed space on paper. The *graphics* evolve by refining the schematics (drawings and allocation of space) to finally become a finished *floor plan*. This process is represented in figure 6.1. The floor plan becomes the main element of the *blueprints* or *working drawings* discussed in chapter 14. The evolution of diagramming takes place as follows:

- *Bubble planning*—the placement of zones on paper according to function.

- Size and shape determination—the allocation of square footage and cubic footage and the shape of rooms and areas.

- *Refinement*—this step could take up to several *overlays*, the laying of tracing paper over the previous graphic to tighten and refine the sketch.

- *Perspective sketches* and *renderings*—three-dimensional pencil, pen-and-ink, or full-color representations of the proposed space or how a portion of the interior will appear upon completion. Drawing perspective sketches and renderings is a skill required of interior designers; perspective *sketches* are a tool for the designer in the planning process as much as for the client to visualize spaces and furnishings.

- Floor plans—the finished product that indicates specific and exact placement of walls and systems within the home (see chapter 14). Floor plans are drawn to scale (usually one-fourth inch equals one foot) and consist of symbols that make the plan understandable to the general contractor and subcontractors (see chapter 16). Floor plans are designed and produced by an architect, competent interior designer, or draftsperson. While on paper, changes can be discussed and made with little effort and expense; once the construction has begun, every change requires sizable effort and cost.

Measurement of Space: Cubic and Square Footage

Three-dimensional space (the space we walk through) is measured in *cubic feet*. Cubic footage is determined by multiplying the room width by its length and then by its height. Rooms with a typical eight-foot ceiling will contain fewer cubic feet than rooms with higher ceilings. Greater cubic footage suggests the possibility of vaulted (high, angled) ceilings and interesting vertical shapes with the accompanying illusion of greater square footage or floor space.

(A)

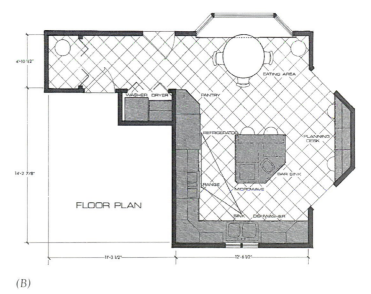

(B)

Figure 6.2 (A) Rendering and (B) floor plan layout by Michael B. Laido, CKD (certified kitchen designer) of Laido Designs, Franklin Lakes, N.J., that won first place in the 1987 CKD Excellence in Kitchen Design Competition sponsored by Maytag, Wilsonart, and Home Magazine.

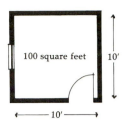
(A)

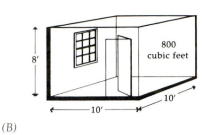
(B)

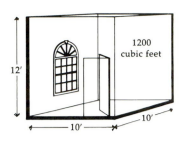
(C)

Figure 6.3 *Calculation of square footage and cubic footage. (A) Square footage is derived by multiplying the width of a room by its length. The ten feet by ten feet yields 100 square feet. (B) Cubic footage is the width multiplied by the length and then by the height of the room. The 100 square feet multiplied by eight-foot walls yields 800 cubic feet. (C) The same room with a twelve-foot ceiling contains more cubic footage and will cost more in both material and labor, even though the square footage remains the same.*

Two-dimensional space (floor area) is measured in *square footage*, which equals the length of the room or building multiplied by its width. Square footage may be the determining factor of the building size based on an estimated *cost per square foot* (see Economy later in this chapter). Square footage may also be limited by the size and building restrictions of the lot or location. In neighborhoods of newly constructed homes, there may also be a minimum acceptable square footage requirement. This may be part of the restrictive covenants, or standard rules for building sizes and materials, established by the developer or community residents to ensure a consistent level of quality and price range in the neighborhood's homes.

During the design process, part of the research phase is to ascertain the minimum square footage required for each task or area within the building. A breakdown is often based on a percentage for each general area. In homes, a general rule of thumb is that 80 percent of the space is allotted for living space, 10 percent for halls, and 10 percent for storage.

Another factor in determining square footage may be the number of people who will occupy the space. Psychological studies have repeatedly demonstrated that *overcrowding* can lead to serious emotional consequences as well as physical limitations and discomfort. It should be noted, however, that the number of square feet allotted per person will vary according to society. Whereas in Hong Kong sixty feet per person is considered adequate, in the United States four hundred to five hundred square feet per person is generally considered the minimum for comfortable living standards. In America, therefore, a family of six would ideally have three thousand square feet of living space.

Shaping the Space

The shape of the interior space has horizontal and vertical components. Although a rectangular room is certainly the easiest to build and the simplest to decorate, it can also be the most boring architecturally. Rooms with angled or curved walls, with vaulted or curved ceilings, with half walls or transparent walls, or even with cutout sections between rooms can add interest and visual expansion of the actual dimensions of the room. Altering room shapes has been a boon to new smaller homes and to the remodeling of older ones, as the alternatives give the impression of greater space and provide architectural interest where none may otherwise have existed.

The shape of interior spaces can also affect the exterior shape and dimensions of the home; this, too, must be taken into careful consideration when designing custom housing. From the interior living standpoint, it is ideal to first determine the spacial arrangements and shapes within the floor plan, then let the exterior shape be determined by the sizes and shapes of the interior spaces. However, the desired style or proportions of the exterior will often limit or restrict the interior shapes or sizes. Realistically, some compromise is often necessary. A room may need to be altered in dimension or size to make the exterior more pleasing, or the placement of doors and windows in the rooms may be dictated by their fenestration, or arrangement, from the exterior.

Site, Orientation, and Climate

The shape of the space may also be dictated by the limitations or special considerations of the building site. The architect will look carefully at the direction of the prevailing breezes in both summer and winter, the slope of the lot, any natural vegetation, the location and types of nearby buildings, and property values of surrounding architecture. Also considered will be the orientation, or direction the site faces, so that solar aspects and fenestration can intelligently be incorporated to the advantage of the home. The orientation is also important in relation to the climate. A sunbelt home will have different planning than a New England home, for example, because the former must provide control of heat from the sun and the latter must control excessive winter cold. The needs and criteria of the climate, then, are important aspects of planning a home.

Figure 6.4 *Angles and vertical height make the shape of this sunroom space interesting.*
© *Ted Spiegel.*

Economy

Economy is an important consideration in planning space. In most cases, new construction will have a financial limit (a maximum amount that can be spent) imposed by the client or by the lending institution. Therefore, the architect, designer, and builder, as well as the client or homeowner, need to make careful and wise decisions concerning the amount of space. This is because the actual square footage is proportional to the cost of the building or home. Total price is estimated on a cost per square foot. The cost per square foot will vary according to the location, the building materials used, the amount of skilled labor involved, and the number of luxury items incorporated.

A total building cost of $50.00 per square foot (excluding the building lot or property costs) can be calculated as follows:

1. An eight-hundred-square-foot building would cost approximately $40,000.00.

2. A twelve-hundred-square-foot building would be above $60,000.00.

3. A two-thousand-square-foot building would cost $100,000.00.

Therefore, smaller total square footage means lower building costs when building one-story or main level-only homes.

However, second-story and basement living space is less costly to construct than main-floor living space. This is because the roof and foundation can serve all levels and because plumbing and electrical systems can be centralized and fireplaces stacked. Further, room inside an attic (termed a half story) can be quite economical since the attic space would often be there anyway. With the addition of dormer windows or skylights and perhaps a steeper pitch in the roof, the attic space can become not only livable but charming because of its angles and nooks. In the case of basements, there may be need for a crawl space or, where there is a deep frost line that would require sinking a deeper foundation, this can be extended to become living space. Basements are a modest addition to the initial building cost in most cases. The attic or basement space may be framed with the home but finished at a later date, offering added living space as the need arises. Therefore, the initial cost of the home would not reflect the potential of that addition of living space in a high cost per square foot. In this way, a home with half story and basement space can be more affordable in the long run than a home of the same square footage on one level only.

Other Factors That Affect Economy in Planning Home Space

  ‣ Interest rates also affect the cost of the payments and, hence, whether or not the home or building can be afforded. Chart 6.1 lists examples for monthly payments of fixed-interest loans of $60,000, $70,000, and $80,000 at 8, 10, and 12 percent over both fifteen years and thirty years. These amounts represent only the principle and interest, however; they do not take into account escrow amounts required for taxes and insurance, which can easily add up to another $100 or $200 a month, depending on the location and value of the home and real estate. Taxes and insurance can be included in the monthly payment or, in some cases, can be paid directly to the government and insurance company by the homeowner.

  ‣ The cubic footage affects the cost. Areas with very high ceilings will be more costly to construct because of the additional building materials required.

  ‣ Simple building shapes also contribute to economy. A home or building with many jogs, angles, gables (roof points), and dormers (windows in the roof) will make the cost per square foot rise, increasing the cost of the interior space. The closer the home is to a simple box, the more economical it will be to build. Some of the most beautiful houses in history have been simple rectangles or boxes. Some may find variations in the form of jogs or angles in the floor plans more appealing.

  ‣ Long-range space planning can also be a boon to saving money in initial building or remodeling. When a space is to be finished or remodeled at a later date, structural planning or framing can accommodate those changes. For example, if a room will one day adjoin another via French doors, the framework for that doorway can be in place as the home is built, thus avoiding major remodeling. Planning in advance for additions in this way is wise and economical space planning. The exterior style should always be taken into consideration when planning additions so that the home will look as though the addition belonged there all along, not as an awkward afterthought. Living with the construction of remodeling can be a strain, but if careful space planning has taken place, the frustrations can be minimal and the results most rewarding.

  ‣ Careful planning to avoid unusable wasted space or poor traffic patterns can increase economy.

  ‣ The proper scale and proportion of rooms in relation to the interior space should be considered. This means judging the intended function of the area and planning square and cubic footage to meet the demands for that space. (Chart 6.4 lists several types of rooms/functions and typical dimensions and/or square footage for moderate rooms versus large rooms. This can be used as a guide in planning economy.)

  ‣ Economy is evident when the size of rooms allows the user to function without crowding or frustration. A space that is too small can necessitate costly expansion by remodeling.

  ‣ It can be economical to double up purposes in an area, called a *multiuse area*, and to make space appear larger than it is.

CHART 6.1 COMPARISON OF MONTHLY MORTGAGE PAYMENTS

PRINCIPLE AND INTEREST ONLY—FIXED RATES

Loan Amount—Fifteen-Year Loan	8%	10%	12%	Loan Amount—Thirty-Year Loan	8%	10%	12%
$60,000	$573.00	$644.00	$720.00	$60,000	$440.00	$526.00	$617.00
$70,000	$669.00	$752.00	$840.00	$70,000	$514.00	$614.00	$720.00
$80,000	$765.00	$860.00	$960.00	$80,000	$587.00	$702.00	$823.00

TOTALS: WHEN THE LOAN IS PAID IN FULL, THE FOLLOWING AMOUNTS WILL HAVE BEEN PAID:

FIFTEEN-YEAR LOAN

The amount paid back will be a little more than twice the loan amount.

$60,000 at 8% ($573.00 × 180 payments) = $103,140.00

$60,000 at 10% ($644.00 × 180 payments) = $115,920.00

$60,000 at 12% ($720.00 × 180 payments) = $129,600.00

$70,000 at 8% ($669.00 × 180 payments) = $120,420.00

$70,000 at 10% ($752.00 × 180 payments) = $135,360.00

$70,000 at 12% ($840.00 × 180 payments) = $151,200.00

$80,000 at 8% ($765.00 × 180 payments) = $137,700.00

$80,000 at 10% ($860.00 × 180 payments) = $154,800.00

$80,000 at 12% ($960.00 × 180 payments) = $172,800.00

THIRTY-YEAR LOAN

The amount paid back will be roughly three times the loan amount.

NOTE: Most of the interest is paid at the beginning of the loan. By increasing the amount paid to the principal each month, the number of payments can be reduced. For example, an additional $50.00 a month applied to the principal on any of these loans can reduce the years of payment to around fourteen to eighteen years rather than thirty years. Also, paying a half-monthly payment every two weeks rather than one payment each month can reduce the life of the loan significantly by increasing the amount paid to principal, as well. This works well for people who are paid every two weeks.

$60,000 at 8% ($440.00 × 360 payments) = $158,400.00

$60,000 at 10% ($526.00 × 360 payments) = $189,360.00

$60,000 at 12% ($617.00 × 360 payments) = $222,120.00

$70,000 at 8% ($514.00 × 360 payments) = $185,000.00

$70,000 at 10% ($614.00 × 360 payments) = $221,040.00

$70,000 at 12% ($720.00 × 360 payments) = $259,200.00

$80,000 at 8% ($587.00 × 360 payments) = $211,320.00

$80,000 at 10% ($702.00 × 360 payments) = $252,720.00

$80,000 at 12% ($823.00 × 360 payments) = $296,280.00

LIVING WITH LESS SPACE

Smaller seems to be the direction of the future. This is not necessarily bad, since large spaces demand upkeep and extra furnishings and pose not only cleaning burdens but security problems as well.

Skillful and creative planning makes the best use out of the space available. This can be done in advance in the blueprint stage. Multiuse space is generally open space as large as two or three rooms. The omission of walls is a cost-saving factor, and one large space rather than cubicles of smaller spaces can give the entire interior a more spacious and luxurious feeling. A large space allows for greater flexibility in meeting current needs and in arranging furniture as the function changes over time.

In a home where the cost disallows space for every desired purpose, some rooms can serve two or more functions. For example, a little-used but desired formal dining room can double as a library; the home office or den could act as a guest room. The most dramatic multiuse area, however, is the idea of the *great room*, a term taken from medieval England when the *great hall* was the place where dining, entertaining, conversation, and sleeping all took place. Today's great room frequently includes: a kitchen; a snack bar or island for both food preparation and eating; a seating conversation area, often grouped around a fireplace, window, or other focal point; an entertainment system of television/video/stereo equipment; perhaps a sit-down eating area (in lieu of the formal dining room); and a desk for study, scheduling, and handling personal finances, which may contain space for a personal computer and filing system.

Use of this area evolved not only from rising building costs but also from today's life-style. People today are busy, often employed in or outside the home, and time is a precious commodity. Conversely, the presence of many rooms, or a duplication of formal/informal spaces, requires time spent cleaning and maintaining those spaces. Today's life-style is less formal than in the past. Whereas a formal dinner party may have been the standard through the mid-twentieth century, today even the boss is entertained comfortably in the great room (and may even enjoy pitching in and helping with the cooking!). Further, hired help today is used in a different sense. The homeowner may have someone come in to clean but will rarely employ servants to prepare meals, serve, and clean up as was commonly the case in past eras among well-to-do families. Convenience foods and equipment, such as microwave ovens and dishwashers, have simplified life-styles and reduced much of the burden of food preparation and entertaining.

Figure 6.5 *The great room: kitchen, dining room, and family room combined makes small space seem larger.*

Gordon Lonsdale, photographer.

Stretching Space

Because of smaller spaces in today's homes, it is often desirable to make spaces seem larger than they actually are. A *space-saving device* is a method of making space appear larger. Some of these devices are:

1. The use of *open plans* with few structural walls. Many a home has been remodeled to remove walls. However, a general contractor should be consulted first to determine if walls can safely be removed without posing a threat to the structural soundness of the building. In no case should load-bearing walls be removed.

2. Vertical space, accomplished with vaulted (high, angled) ceilings, 1 1/2 or two-story ceilings, or skylights.

3. Half walls that allow visual and audible communication to the upper area of an adjoining room.

4. Extensive use of glass windows, doors, and walls. In the past, glass building materials admitted too much heat and cold. Now, however, we are able to control solar gain and heat loss through new glass types, shading devices, and energy-conserving window treatments.

Once the building is complete, decorative space-saving devices can also seem to expand space. These devices include the following:

1. Light colors seem to recede, as do dull colors.

2. Smooth textures expand space more than rough textures.

3. Properly used mirrors can expand space if, for example, the mirror reflects a view out a window and not a decoratively furnished or busy, patterned area.

4. Floor-to-ceiling draperies make walls look taller, as do top treatments and strong vertical lines in the window treatments.

5. Long vertical or horizontal moldings carry the eye and expand visual space, giving the impression of greater height or width, respectively.

6. Plain, wall-to-wall floor coverings will give the impression of greater floor area, particularly in contrast to patterned or layered floor coverings.

7. Furnishings that are small scale, are lighter in color, use small or no patterns, have legs rather than upholstered skirts or solid wood to the floor, and utilize glass or other see-through materials will also help expand small spaces. A common design error is to place large, patterned upholstered pieces and large-scale wooden furniture in small spaces.

Figure 6.6 *The size of the California den designed by Noel Jeffrey, ASID, is visually doubled with ceiling-height mirrors, reflecting nineteenth-century Chinese screens used as wall panels.*

Courtesy of Noel Jeffrey, Inc.

MAKING LARGE SPACES SEEM SMALLER

Too much space can be as big a dilemma as too little space. Feelings of unfriendliness and insecurity are common in areas that are larger than human scale in height and/or horizontal space. Noises are often amplified, or they may echo or reverberate, particularly when there are large areas of hard surfaces. Communication can be difficult because of this. Another pitfall is a lack of privacy and the inability to physically or emotionally claim an area as one's own.

Space-reducing devices are largely the converse of space-saving devices. The following suggestions call for groupings and techniques to make the space become more human in scale and more friendly:

1. Furniture can be arranged into several conversation or function groupings.

2. Area rugs, such as colored and patterned Oriental or designer rugs, can define groupings.

3. Darker colors on walls, floors, and ceilings make space seem smaller, as do patterns and heavy textures.

4. Space will appear to decrease with: large-scale furniture such as upholstery with skirts, or the overstuffed variety; wood furniture that is heavy (literally); furniture that is solid right to the floor; and tall and wide pieces.

TRAFFIC PATTERNS

Traffic patterns are also referred to as circulation or traffic flow. A traffic pattern is the repeatedly used walking path from room to room or area to area. Traffic patterns are necessary and unavoidable and require careful evaluation as an important part of space planning. Traffic patterns may be drawn in lines and arrows on the diagram or floor plan, indicating where people will be walking or where objects will be moved regularly through the space. These traffic patterns should be left free and kept as direct as possible. In a home, major traffic patterns typically lead from:

-   Front door to a central circulation system that leads to all areas of the house
-   Garage to kitchen for carrying groceries
-   Garage to mudroom or closet/locker area
-   Kitchen to formal, informal, and private living areas
-   Kitchen to service areas and entry areas
-   Laundry areas to bedrooms
-   Bedrooms to bathrooms
-   Garage to hall closet or service area
-   Back door to kitchen, mudroom, or service area

Some pitfalls to avoid in arranging traffic patterns:

-   Rooms that act as hallways, where a room must be crossed to reach another room
-   Door locations that force circulation through conversation furniture groupings
-   Areas too small for furniture and circulation
-   Private areas or areas where bathroom fixtures are open to view
-   Work areas that tend to be untidy, such as the kitchen sink or laundry area

Traffic patterns must be planned for adequate width. Hallways and stairs in homes have typically been three feet to three feet six inches wide. However, a four-foot-wide corridor and stairs will more comfortably allow two-way traffic.

Another traffic-planning feature is the location of doors and the direction the doors swing. Generally, doors should be placed toward the corner of a room to avoid cutting up the wall space, and the door should swing inward against the adjoining wall. Where *swinging doors* will be a problem, *pocket doors* or sliding doors may be a good choice that will not impede traffic.

STORAGE

Storage is a precious commodity; it fills up so quickly and is difficult to empty because possessions are hard to part with. A cardinal rule is that storage should be located at the point of first or most frequent use. It has also been suggested that in order to determine real storage needs, one should list things owned and their corresponding sizes, then list where these items should be stored and what size that storage area should be. Storage zones are desirable in specific locations:

-   The kitchen should include storage for dry goods (such as a wall or walk-in pantry) and ample storage for pots and pans, small appliances, serving bowls, informal and formal plates and dishes and glasses (stemware), silverware and utensils, linens, soaps and cleansers, and cleaning appliances (brooms, mops, or vacuums) all located within convenient reach.
-   The laundry facility should have storage for extra soap, bleach, softener, and other cleaning preparations.
-   The front hall closet is for family and/or guest coats. Depending on the weather and the life-style, there may be a place for wet outerwear such as raincoats, umbrellas, or boots. It may not always be possible, however, to accommodate all the guests' coats, scarves, and gloves when a sizable group is being entertained. In this case, the outerwear might be placed in a den or on a bed.
-   Closets, lockers, a walk-in closet, or a wall of hooks near the back entrance, garage entrance, or mudroom are for winter gear (coats, boots, school bags) and individual sports gear, again depending on life-style. In the summer, such an area could double for summer sports gear: tennis, baseball, and soccer equipment and even swimming towels and gear.
-   A closet for the vacuum cleaner should be placed where it is needed. In two-story houses, a vacuum might be located in a closet on each floor.
-   Linen closets are usually located in a hall near bedrooms to hold extra sheets, pillowcases, pillows, and blankets.
-   Bathroom storage needs include paper goods, personal hygiene sundries, and extra towels.
-   Bedrooms are often shortchanged in storage. Sizable, compartmentalized closets will be appreciated.
-   Any area where a hobby is performed requires individualized storage.
-   Home offices need closets, shelves, and/or units that can hold reference books, files, paper, and other supplies. The personal computer demands certain storage items such as printer paper and disks.
-   The family room, or entertainment room will need storage for items such as cassettes, records, compact disks, and videotapes.
-   The library, often combined with a home office or another room, will need plenty of shelves and perhaps some storage with locking doors for valuable books or papers.
-   The tool shed is a place to store lawn and garden tools and equipment, and tools for use in other maintenance projects.
-   Where no tool shed or yard storage shed exists, the garage is often used for lawn and garden equipment, tools, bicycles, and a myriad of items too bulky for home storage. With careful planning, the garage that is also a storage area can be organized to avoid a cluttered appearance.

Figure 6.7 *A great room has been created in this home by opening the kitchen, dining room, and informal family room to one another. Posts and railing visually divide the areas, while the openness, cathedral window wall, and vaulted ceiling apparently increase spaciousness.*
Courtesy of Frigidaire.

SPACE PLANNING ROOMS WITH PERMANENT FIXTURES

Rooms or areas with built-in cabinetry and permanent fixtures require extra thought and planning. Permanent fixtures are a part of the floor plan and are treated as structural components that are specified by the architect or designer, built and installed by craftspeople, and ordered and installed through plumbing companies or contractors. Because the cabinets and fixtures are fixed in place, it is important to give extra attention to their planning. The kitchen, bath, and laundry room each have specific requirements. Other rooms that may have built-in cabinetry and require careful space planning might include dens or libraries, sewing rooms, and hobby areas.

Kitchens

The kitchen has rightfully been called the hub of the home, a place where most people build fond memories of watching or helping a parent or relative prepare food and where dining or visiting with friends and loved ones often takes place. The kitchen attracts people not only because it contains food to feed the body but because it sets the stage for people to interact and bond loving friendships. Perhaps this is the underlying basis for today's great room.

Because the kitchen is the center for food preparation and storage, food service and/or dining, and cleaning up after meals, it is a room where much time is spent. Although the tasks that take place in the kitchen clearly are work, today's kitchen can masterfully be planned with labor-saving appliances and cabinetry that make storage and organization pleasant and cleanup much less of a strain. Kitchens are no longer a place of drudgery; they have become an important center of the home—a fashionable setting for the host and/or hostess to do the cooking. Today even the guests are often active participants in the food preparation process—it is a social experience in itself.

Certified kitchen designers take into account all aspects of life-style when helping clients with kitchen design. For example, when two or more people are preparing meals, rules such as the standard working triangle (discussed later in this chapter) are not as applicable. Family traffic patterns and clearance dimensions must then change to avoid congestion and confusion. If there is a hierarchy in the planning, such as an assistant to the chef, then the helper will need more space between sink and refrigerator to wash and prepare vegetables, for example. Specialty or gourmet cooking may further require extra space and perhaps a separate center. If two chefs are team cooking, each preparing individual dishes, then two separate working areas are called for—two sinks, two food preparation areas, two cooking areas, and a shared refrigerator.

Kitchen Planning Trends

One trend in kitchen planning is to accommodate the growing number of latch-key children who arrive home before working parents and who help prepare food without assistance from an experienced adult. This new segment of the cooking population will have special needs such as lower placement of microwaves and dishes. Safe appliance and cabinet designs are also important. This could include locks on some cabinets and toe-kick areas that double as pull-out stepping stools.

The growing population of people aged sixty-five years and older is also demanding changes in traditional kitchen design. Safety here is an important factor to consider, as well as comfort and convenience. For those with bad backs, for example, shelving should be high enough to avoid bending. The aged and infirm also will have special needs as they maintain a longer period of independence. The kitchen must be planned for accessibility and size/height dimensions to meet individual needs. Those who will age in good health may require personalized work spaces as well as social spaces planned with or adjacent to kitchen areas.

Another major trend is toward smaller spaces due to greater population density (more people and less land), limited funds, and higher energy costs. These factors require more efficient kitchens that combine work spaces and feature added storage over tall appliances, in the toe-kick space, as shelves on door interiors, or as shelves on the backsplash. Rollout or swing-out drawers, shelves, and pantries, pullout work and dining surfaces, and the elimination of unnecessary walkways are other ways to improve efficiency in smaller spaces.

Kitchens for the future will not necessarily become ultramodern and futuristic. Rather, with the emphasis on high-tech appliances, we will see more personalizing of the kitchen—the addition of art and accessories that give identity and reveal the style and values of those who work, eat, and socialize there. As the center of the home, kitchens will not necessarily become more fancy or more stark but will become a quiet backdrop where people are the real stars.[1]

With these current and predicted trends in mind, it is quite reasonable that the kitchen should become a center of attention, commanding more money in cabinetry, plumbing fixtures, and appliances than any other area of the home. Today people want beautiful kitchens with character and style—kitchens where cooking meals of any type or origin can be an enjoyable and a creative experience.

Zones and the Working Triangle

Kitchen planning includes working arrangements in zones or work areas. The three zones that are considered the basic working triangle include:

› The refrigerator zone

› The cooking zone (range and ovens)

› The sink/cleanup zone

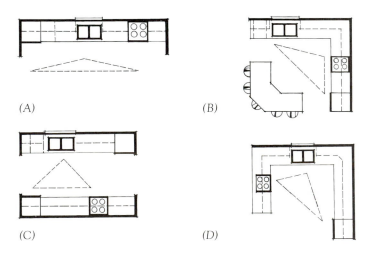

Figure 6.8 Working triangles. (A) The single-wall kitchen with refrigerator at left, stove/oven at right. (B) L-shaped kitchen with an eating bar and stove and refrigerator right of sink. (C) The galley or tunnel kitchen uses space economically but can conflict with traffic patterns. (D) The U-shaped kitchen eliminates traffic problems and provides ample counter space.

Total walking distance among these three areas should not be fewer than seven feet (too crowded—produces frustration) and not more than twenty-one feet (too spread out—leads to exhaustion). Other zones that add convenience and are considered essential to modern kitchens include any or all of the following:

- Additional food storage zones
- Various specialized food preparation zones
- A second cooking zone and/or a quick-cooking zone
- A second cleanup/sink zone
- Tableware storage zone(s)
- Serving and service storage zone
- Cleaning supplies storage zone

These zones should be planned for the convenience and consideration of the family members who cook and should be laid out logically according to individual needs. However, certain checkpoints, presented in charts 6.2 and 6.3, are fairly consistent.

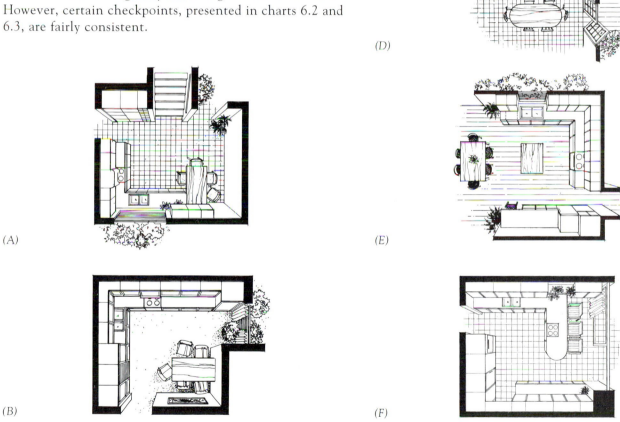

Figure 6.9 *Typical kitchen designs. (A) An L-shaped kitchen with informal dining handy at the end of the cabinetry. Kitchen is closed to other living areas; stairs to upper floor are accessed in the kitchen. (B) An L-shaped kitchen with a long countertop for food preparation and serving. Dinette is away from the preparation area. Deep floor-to-ceiling storage forms a pantry. (C) A popular U-shaped kitchen with wide eating bar beneath overhead cabinetry. Pantry, refrigerator, and kitchen desk form the wall opposite the sink. (D) A U-shaped kitchen with island eating bar that doubles as food preparation area, complete with small sink. Dining area is informal yet away from the cooking area and offers outside access through French doors. Cooktop range is separate from a built-in microwave/ conventional oven pair. (E) This U-shaped kitchen has a food preparation island and ample counter space. Long desk-countertop provides convenient serving to the dining area. (F) Easy access to the outside makes this U-shaped kitchen a pleasant environment. A long wall of cabinets provides storage.*

CHART 6.2 **CABINETRY CONSIDERATIONS FOR KITCHEN ZONE PLANNING**

FOOD STORAGE CABINETRY

Food storage can be divided into three main categories.

1. Perishables: These items require refrigeration or freezing.

2. Regularly used dry food supplies: Foods used on a daily basis such as flour (flour bin drawers with metal liners are available), baking powders, spices and supplies, boxed cereal, various pastas, rice, and legumes. These should be located in the kitchen near the zone where they will be used in food preparation or cooking. Generally, the flour and heavy supplies go in the lower cabinets and smaller supplies above. A spice rack or specially designed cabinet is desirable to keep spices organized and handy. A cabinet or cupboard specifically for boxed cereal or for items such as sugar, cornmeal, popcorn, rice, beans, and other legumes may be preferred. The shelf heights should be adjustable and the interiors must be easily cleaned.

3. Staples and canned goods: Occasionally used. These might be located in a pantry or larder—a wall of cabinets or a walk-in closet to store occasionally used or extra containers of food, utensils, serving pieces, and china. By keeping extra supplies in the pantry, the cook can save kitchen space and save trips to the store. The pantry may also be located between the kitchen and dining room as a place from which to serve food to the formal dining room. An extension of the concept of the pantry is the food storage room that is located in a cool area (such as a basement), and that stores staples, cases of food (such as canned goods), flour, cooking supplies, legumes, other items with a long shelf life (which replenish the pantry supply), and bulky cooking pots and pans. A root cellar is not often seen today, although some homes are planned to contain one. Historically, a root cellar was an underground room, often away from the house, that has stone or dirt floors and that is cool enough to keep fruits, vegetables, and even cured meats. Today a root cellar can be added within the home if the floor is left dirt and if the room is properly ventilated (since it tends to smell).

FOOD PREPARATION COUNTERTOP/CABINET-TOP AREAS

Determine the kind of food preparation that will take place and plan countertop areas accordingly. In kitchens where much food preparation takes place, a minimum of two long counters (over three feet) are required. An island or a peninsula often provides wide countertops. Where bread is frequently mixed, a large area near flour bins and cooking supplies is imperative. If vegetables are often chopped, cutting boards that are built into the countertop or that pull out near the sink will be appreciated. Some kitchens are planned with two or more cutting boards of various sizes—larger ones for mixing, smaller ones for cutting. As another example, if candymaking is a specialty, a separate area with supplies nearby and a counter of marble is ideal. The type of food preparation, then, should be the topic of careful consideration in planning the size and location of countertop or cabinet-top space. There may be a small sink for food preparation and a large sink for cleanup, often placed in an island or peninsula.

Cooking containers such as pots and pans need to be close to the range or cook top. Cupboards with sliding drawers eliminate awkward hunting situations. Vertical panels hold cooking sheets, dripper pans, muffin sheets, and other flat dishes upright and should be located near (often above or below) the oven where they are used. Cooking utensils can be located in drawers near the stove, placed in a crock, or hung on the wall. Items used every day should be most convenient.

An appliance garage consists of cabinet doors on the countertop with space behind to hide portable appliances; sliding shelves in lower cabinets can also hold appliances, and electric plugs can be installed inside these special cupboards. Cabinets can be designed with solid or glass doors (or without any doors at all) and to hold any special item.

CLEANUP CABINETRY

Cabinets need to be planned near the sink for cleaning supplies. Typically, the cabinet beneath the sink contains everyday cleaning supplies and often a trash can. A separate, taller cupboard keeps the smell away from the sink and allows for a larger trash can (trash compactors are discussed in chart 6.3). A broom closet should be planned to accommodate the equipment (brooms, mops, vacuum cleaner) and to be conveniently accessible.

Towels and washcloths should be handy to the sink. A rack for dish towels that slides into the lower cabinets is good to control clutter and to keep towels dry and more sanitary. A drawer or two should be allotted for clean kitchen linen. Drawers should be added for extra paper towels or cleaning cloths or rags, paper or plastic garbage bags, and extra disposable items such as rubber gloves or scouring pads.

TABLEWARE STORAGE CABINETRY

Cabinetry for tableware includes cupboards for plates, dishes, and stemware (cups, glasses). Lower cabinets next to the dishwasher might hold dishes for everyday use (children can then easily set the table), and upper cabinets could contain special, breakable tableware. Drawers should be planned for silverware, placemats, cloth or paper napkins, and folded tablecloths; a closet can be used for hanging tablecloths (pressed and ready for special occasions). A set of shelves for centerpieces and vases is valuable. Here the planning will proceed according to life-style and possessions.

DINING CABINETRY

Islands and peninsula eating bars are a common sight in today's kitchens. The bar may accommodate two or more stools or chairs, depending on the number of people in the household. Today the meals served at the bar generally outnumber those at a conventional table, although both a bar and a kitchen table are still considered the ideal kitchen dining arrangement. The bar is planned and built as a part of the cabinets; it may contain drawers, cupboards, or appliances on one or two sides. It may double as a desk or contain a space for a computer. It may have no cabinets and function as a cabinet-top eating surface with only bar-stool space beneath it. The bar, island, or peninsula may also be lowered so that shorter bar stools or standard chairs can be used, rather than tall bar stools.

SERVICE/STORAGE CABINETRY

Planning cabinets for table service or serving dishes also takes some thought because some dishes, platters, and utensils are used on a regular basis and others may be used only occasionally, such as on holidays or at more formal meals. Therefore, the serving pieces most often used should be accessible, and the items seldom used can go in less accessible places, such as above the oven or the refrigerator. Keep in mind that lightweight items should go overhead, and heavier items should be placed in lower cabinets to allow for ease and safety in removal. Glass or plastic dishes/lids, used for storing perishable items in the refrigerator or freezing unit, should be fairly close to the refrigerator and near a counter-top or cabinet top. Consider drawers just for lids, perhaps one for plastic and one for glass, plus a drawer or two for plastic wrap and bags, aluminum foil, and waxed paper.

It has often been said that there is never too much storage space, and although people tend to fill up whatever kitchen storage is available, it is a far better approach to plan generous storage space.

CHART 6.3 APPLIANCE PLANNING CONSIDERATIONS

REFRIGERATORS AND FREEZERS

There are many options in today's refrigerators—such as adjustable shelves, special compartments (for meat, vegetables, and dairy products), frost-free and energy-saving features, and textured doors in fashionable colors. Also available are automatic cold water and ice dispensers in the outside of the door to alleviate the need to continually open and close the door (saving energy). Keep in mind, however, that the more options, the greater the possibility of breakdown. Most refrigerators contain a freezer unit, which can be located at the top, bottom, or side (hence, side-by-side refrigerator). A second refrigerator may be desired for extra storage, and freezers are sometimes also located in the kitchen. Ordinarily a second refrigerator or large freezer will be placed in a garage, basement, or utility/storage area. Freezers come with side-hinged doors or as a chest where the lid lifts (the latter keeps cold inside rather than rushing out but is more difficult to organize and access food). The area in front of the refrigerator or freezer must allow for a minimum of three feet to open and close the door and access the food without crowding. There should be a countertop nearby for loading and unloading food.

OVENS/RANGES/COOK TOPS

Conventional ovens may be a part of a range or stove unit where the oven is below, or the unit may also have a smaller conventional or microwave oven above as well. A cook top contains cooking elements only and is placed in the countertop or cabinet top wherever it is desired—along the wall or in an island, for example.

Standard appliance sizes are listed in chart 6.5, although it should be noted that oven (and all appliance) sizes vary according to the manufacturer.

Few modern kitchens are planned without a microwave oven, which is usually placed in one of three locations: on the counter, suspended under the upper cabinets, or built into the wall. Microwaves are the least attractive placed on a counter; suspended types are smaller microwave units, and built-in units are often combined with a conventional oven (these should be able to slide out for repair). Multipurpose ovens are also available for both microwave and conventional or convection cooking. Self-cleaning or continuous self-cleaning options are also worth considering in new ovens. (Toaster ovens are discussed under portable appliances.) Ovens and ranges or cook tops can be located together or separately. The convection oven can be placed by itself in a wall away from the microwave, which may be in a quick-cooking center. Ample counter space on each side of a range is sound kitchen planning, and counter space on at least one side of an oven to place food before and after cooking while opening the door is also very important to avoid spills and burns.

DISHWASHERS

Most dishwashers are built-in units that slide under the countertop or cabinet top. Portable dishwashers are rolled to the sink and attached to the faucet and drain. Dishwashers today have cycle length and energy-saving options as well as various color and finish options. A special frame can hold wood or laminate to match the kitchen cabinets. The dishwasher should be located just to the left or right of the sink and next to the storage area for tableware.

GARBAGE DISPOSALS

The garbage disposal is a standard appliance in one side of the sink or in the center of a three-compartment sink.

TRASH COMPACTORS

Trash compactors are appliances that compress garbage and thereby eliminate frequent trips to an outside garbage can. Trash compactors are located next to the sink or virtually any place in the kitchen. For those who do not desire a trash compactor, the same space can contain a garbage container that slides or swings out.

SINKS

Many styles of sinks are available today in a variety of contemporary colors. Porcelain and stainless steel are the two most popular materials for sinks. Double sinks are common, and sinks with a third, central compartment for a garbage disposal are available. Sinks may have different-sized compartments and different depths. Smaller sinks for rinsing vegetables or alternate cleanup areas are a nice addition.

PORTABLE APPLIANCES

There are two major categories of portable appliances: appliances for food preparation and food-cooking appliances. The number of choices increases every year. When planning a kitchen, it is wise to make a list of the appliances to be used and to prioritize their location—the most frequently used will need to be most accessible, perhaps even on the countertop or cabinet top. For convenient use and elimination of clutter, plan for appliance cubbyholes or compartments on the counter. It is important to remember that portable appliances will be used only if they are convenient and accessible. If it is necessary to move bulky items out of the way and reach to the back of low or high cabinets for an appliance, it will seldom be used.

- **Portable Appliances for Food Preparation:** Blender, food processor, cabinet-top mixer, hand mixer, food mill, chopper/grinder, can opener, electric knife, knife sharpener, food slicer, pasta maker, dough roller, drink mixer, coffee grinder, juicer, plastic bag sealer, ice cream maker, weight scale, food dehydrator.

- **Portable Food-Cooking Appliances:** Microwave oven, toaster, toaster oven, coffee maker, rice cooker, crock pot, electric skillet/grill, waffle iron, popcorn popper, electric wok, warming tray, hot plate/portable range, yogurt maker, deep fryer.

Part of the kitchen-planning process is deciding which types of appliances to purchase; making selections among the many makes, styles, and options of those appliances; and making sure the cabinetry dimensions will accommodate them with precision. Chart 6.3 lists the major types or categories of appliances and surveys options and considerations in their selection and placement.

Bathrooms

The bath has come a long way since its sterile "sink/toilet/tub-in-a-cubicle" days. The bath of today is a luxurious area both in terms of square footage and fixtures. Bathtubs come in a vast selection of shapes, sizes, depths, and colors, and in plain water-holding devices or whirlpool bathtub styles. The shower is rou-tinely located in a walk-in stall, sometimes oversized, perhaps with a seat or bench built in, and even with two nozzles if desired. The health spa can be brought home in the form of a combination sauna/steam room/bathing facility that is now available as a manufactured unit measuring around twelve feet long by five feet wide by six feet high. Sinks vary from single to dual vanities to pedestal styles in sleek, sophisticated designs. The toilet, or *water closet*, takes on several stylish forms and can include a urinal. A bidet, used for personal hygiene, may be placed by a toilet. The *compartmental bathroom* generally consists of two rooms: the vanity area and the tub and toilet area. In some residential settings, the toilet is further separated by an enclosure or closet. (See chart 6.5 for minimum sizes for fixtures.)

Figure 6.10 *Even modest-sized master bedrooms can offer a beautiful and luxurious bathroom. Interior design by Kristi Palmer.*

Gordon Lonsdale, photographer.

With the popularity of physical fitness, the exercise area has become a part of many home bathroom areas. The exercise area may include one (or more) piece(s) of equipment such as the treadmill, minitrampoline, exercise bicycle, and bench press (barbells), or other strengthening and endurance units. Even a mat and a television for doing aerobics may be included.

And finally, the bathroom may include a dressing area as well as a large, walk-in closet with compartmentalized shelves, mirrors, and clothes bars for easy organization.

Master Bedrooms

The master bedroom is often space-planned as a suite, with the master bathroom an important part of the luxury of the space. The master bedroom may also include a sitting area, a fireplace or view window, and a walk-out patio or balcony. The exercise area/sauna may be a natural extension of the master bedroom.

Other rooms may connect to the master bedroom, such as a private study or office. Bedrooms or unfinished areas (such as attic space over a garage) can later be incorporated into the master suite if foresight is given to space planning. Perhaps two rooms will adjoin, such as his and hers offices or personal sitting/study/hobby rooms. A greenhouse or solarium is another lovely retreat that can connect onto a master bedroom.

Figure 6.11 *Today's master baths are often planned with separated areas for bathing and grooming and even incorporate large dressing areas and closets, exercise equipment, and whirlpool, sauna, and spa facilities. Luxury and spaciousness are bywords of contemporary master baths.*

(Both) Courtesy of the makers of Armstrong no-wax flooring.

Laundry Rooms

Because the laundry room features permanent cabinetry and stationary appliances, foresight and flexibility in planning are required. Sizes for washers and dryers are listed in chart 6.5. Cabinets should contain shelves high enough for laundry detergents, whiteners, softeners, and other frequently used products and items. Counter space for folding clothes and a closet for hanging permanent press clothing are important. The laundry room most often contains an ironing board—perhaps the built-in variety, which is excellent for saving space and keeping iron

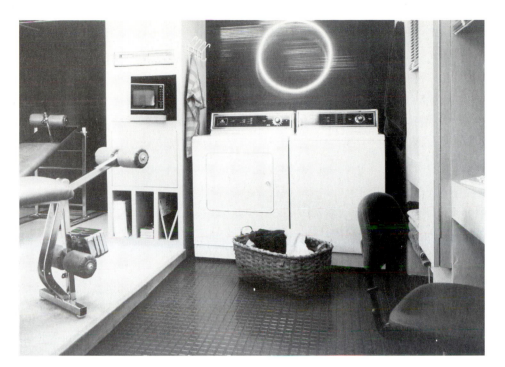

Figure 6.12 *One creative solution to laundry room design makes the laundry do double duty, as in this laundry/exercise/computer/sewing room. Note the built-in television and stereo component system with storage beneath.*

Courtesy of the Maytag Company.

and board accessible and orderly. Drawers or cabinets can hold clothes to be ironed or mended as well as mending supplies. Sewing rooms are favorite combinations with laundry facilities because the ironing board is necessary for laundry and sewing and because mending often takes place before or after laundering. Sewing cabinetry can contain work surfaces that fold or slide behind doors, keeping the clutter out of sight when no sewing is taking place. The laundry room may also double with a mudroom and may contain closets or "lockers" for coats, winter gear, or sports equipment according to the season. The laundry/utility room may hold a food freezer, and the cabinetry may be organized for tools such as hammers and nails or perhaps paint supplies. It could double as a storage room for bulky cooking appliances if the laundry room is located near the kitchen.

There are at least five options of laundry location in space planning a home.

The first, and most typical, is to locate the laundry near the kitchen. Some smaller homes have the washer and dryer in the kitchen itself, although ideally, the laundry needs to be in a place where clothes sorting can take place and where the door can be closed on the mess if necessary. Placing it near the kitchen is convenient since much of the daily household work revolves around the kitchen and only a few steps are needed to tend to the laundry in progress.

In two-story homes where the laundry is on the main floor, careful planning can locate the laundry beneath at least one bathroom and over a clothes drop, which could empty into a cabinet above the washer and dryer. It is also possible to install two or three clothes drops so that sorting takes place as clothes are being dropped: one for whites, one for dark colors and jeans, and one for bright or light colors. This concept can be extended with the idea of drawers or baskets belonging to each family member. As clothes are folded, they are put into the drawer and that individual is responsible for taking the clothes and putting them away.

A second location is in a basement. This location will keep the noise and clutter off the main floor but will necessitate climbing stairs with loads of dirty and clean laundry.

The third location is in the bedroom wing, next to the family bathroom. This location is popular in larger two-story homes and eliminates carrying laundry up and down stairs.

A fourth location is in a hallway, but this may not be good planning since the clothes have to be sorted in the hall and a mess is created in the traffic pattern.

Figure 6.13 *Louvered doors provide ventilation and conceal this compact arrangement of planning desk and stacking washer and dryer. The unit will fit in a space roughly half that needed for a conventional side-by-side washer and dryer pair.*

Courtesy of the Maytag Company.

And fifth, the bathroom may house the laundry in smaller homes. Theoretically this may be a good location since soiled clothing is often taken off there at bath time. Some conflict could easily arise between functions and users, however. Lack of space for laundry activities may also be a disadvantage.

The Home Office

The availability and affordability of equipment such as personal computers, modems, and facsimile (fax) and copy machines have made it possible for a new type of worker—the "open collar" worker who makes all or part of the living working at home. This new phenomenon calls for foresight in planning the location of the office as well as the electrical and phone hookups. It may or may not need to be adjacent to an entrance, but it should be in a place that can be closed off from the hubbub of daily home life and can, after work hours, be out of sight and out of mind.

Good lighting is essential, as is the planning of furniture placement for convenience as well as efficiency. Consideration should be given to color schemes and pattern or lack of it, and to accessorizing so that the right mood and frame of mind can be enhanced.

Studies in children's and students' bedrooms will encourage productivity and concentration, often helping them along in their school work. The space should include ample desk space for spreading out projects, areas for filing and organizing, shelving and storage space, and space for the personal computer.

Figure 6.14 *The home office is becoming increasingly important. (A) The home office of architect Myron Goldfinger and his wife, interior designer June Goldfinger. (B) Space for personal computers can be incorporated into any house plan.*

Both © Ted Spiegel.

CHART 6.4 RESIDENTIAL SPACE PLANNING FOR THE HUMAN SCALE

Room/Function	Moderate	Large Size
Entry	35 sq. ft.	over 35 sq. ft.
Hall	3 ft. wide	4 ft. wide +
Living room	13 ×15 (195 sq. ft.)	18 × 30 (540 sq. ft.)
Kitchen	8 ×12 (96 sq. ft.)	12 × 16 (192 sq. ft.)
Great room	12 ×20 (240 sq. ft.)	20 × 30 (600 sq. ft.)
Family room	13 ×18 (234 sq. ft.)	15 × 25 (375 sq. ft.)
Dining room/area	10 ×13 (130 sq. ft.)	13 × 16 (208 sq. ft.)
Bathroom	5 ×10 (50 sq. ft.)	10 × 15 (150 sq. ft.)
Bedroom	10 ×12 (120 sq. ft.)	15 × 20 (300 sq. ft.)
Two-car garage	22 ×22 (484 sq. ft.)	25 × 40 (1,000 sq. ft.)

CHART 6.5 STANDARD SIZES OF FIXTURES AND CABINET WORK

Item	Width/Length	Height	Depth	Special
Kitchen counter	as needed	36"	20–35"	28" high (disabled)
Refrigerator	28–36"	5–6'	2'6"	34–36" high
Dishwasher	24"	34"	24"	
Range	30–36"	36"	24"	
Oven	24–30"	24–30"	26"	two units make "double-oven" size
Washer	30"	36"	30"	
Dryer	30"	36"	30"	
Bathroom counter	as needed	30–34"	20"	28" high (chairbound-disabled)
Toilet	15" (seat)	28–30" (tank)	26"	
Regular bathtub	5'	16"	2'8"	
Oversize bathtub	6–7'8"	to 24"	3–4'	
Spa (sauna/steam room)	6'	8'	8'	8' wide × 16' long
Interior door	2'6"–3'	6'8"	1 3/8"	
Exterior door	3'	6'8"	1 3/8"	(Wider as needed)
Ceiling	–	–	8'	(Higher as desired)

PLANNING FOR INDEPENDENT LIVING

Many physically handicapped and aged could live at home rather than at rest homes if modifications for *independent living* were made at home. Those in wheelchairs, particularly, require modified spaces and dimensions. See chapter 2 for further information on dimensions and space planning for special populations.

EMOTION AND PSYCHOLOGY

Spaces that are planned to be emotionally appealing, beautiful, or satisfying can accomplish specific goals of the interior. This appeal can be accomplished by the shape, size, and scale of the interior or with the use of materials, colors, and textures. It can also be accomplished to an extent with furnishings. Furniture arrangement as it relates to space manipulation is discussed in chapter 7.

This element of psychological or emotional appeal is so important that it cannot be ignored in planning space. It puts people into the picture, and it is the human touch that makes architecture and interior design meaningful.

The client profile, discussed in chapter 1, will form the basis for the architect's and designer's space-planning decisions. Likewise, the homeowner should never feel hesitant to express personal preferences concerning the size, shape, and layout of the rooms being commissioned. In fact, the homeowner who doesn't speak up during the space-planning stage may experience years of unnecessary frustration because his or her needs were not made known. (The psychology of space was discussed in more detail in chapter 3, Design Principles and Elements.)

SPACE PLANNING AND THE PRINCIPLES AND ELEMENTS OF DESIGN

Effective space planning incorporates careful consideration of the principles and elements of design (discussed in chapter 3) in order to create interiors that are pleasing and effective. And since people are the most important ingredient of the space, the proportion and scale in particular should always be judged according to that of the human body. With this in mind, the space can be planned to fit the purpose. A very large or grand scale—seen in places such as cathedrals, turn-of-the century banks, or open atrium areas of hotels—is awesome compared to the human scale. But in these places, that overwhelming feeling serves a purpose—to give a different perspective or alternative to viewing space. The perspective may create a feeling of reverence, awe, contemplation, or simply relief from closed, small-scale quarters. However, the overall size or scale of the space best relates to the human frame in most interiors. Chart 6.4 indicates typical sizes for living areas in homes that have proven their effectiveness in relating to the human scale.

Other design principles and elements are readily applied in the space-planning process. Scale, proportion, balance, rhythm, emphasis, and harmony (the principles of design) are sought in order to make space functional and pleasing for many years to come. These aspects of function and pleasantness in space planning are accomplished through the manipulation of the elements of design—the delineation of space with shape or form through mass, line, pattern, texture, light, and color.

Floor Plan Symbols

Floor plan symbols are illustrated in figures 6.15 and 6.16. These include symbols for windows, doors, plumbing fixtures, appliances, walls, stairs, and mechanical equipment. (Electrical symbols are found in the previous chapter on lighting.) Keep in mind these are examples only; the number of symbols, or variations of style in executing them, are left to the discretion of the architect, draftsperson, or computer-aided design program.

A study of these symbols will increase the ability to "read" or understand the floor plans that follow.

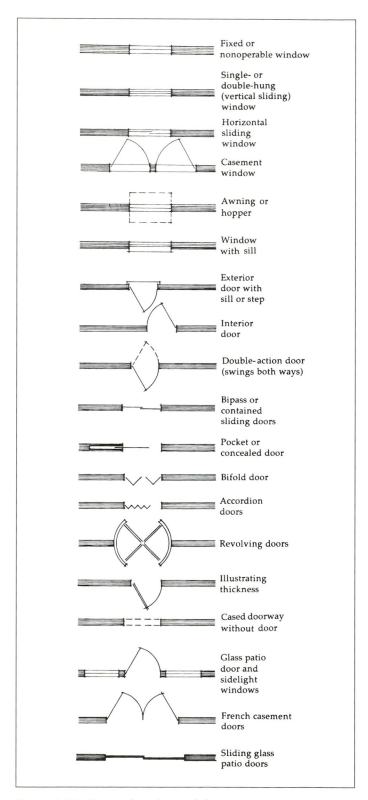

Figure 6.15 Door and window symbols.

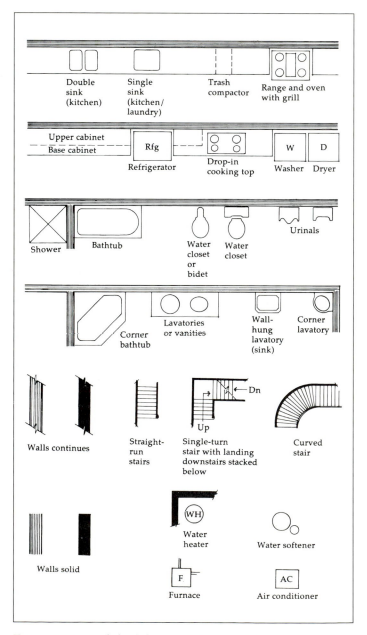

Figure 6.16 Symbols of plumbing fixtures, appliances, walls, stairs, and mechanical support equipment.

TYPES OF FLOOR PLAN DRAWINGS

There are two ways to obtain a set of blueprints for a floor plan: one is to have the plan custom drawn, and the other is to purchase a set of plans that has been mass-produced, called a stock plan. It is possible to make minor changes to a stock plan in order to customize it, and when the changes become structural or major, it usually becomes necessary to have it custom drawn, which will then cost several hundred dollars more or about the same as a custom floor plan. The specifics for each type of plan are discussed as follows.

Custom Floor Plans

Custom floor plans are produced by an architect or designer and tailored to fit the needs of a particular site and client. Although a custom plan is costly and requires some time and effort, it is the best way to get exactly what you want in a home. The danger is that when a home has many features custom designed for a particular person or life-style, it may be difficult to resell the home if the need arises.

Computer-Aided Floor Plans

Computer-aided designed (CAD), or computer-generated floor plan software, has become affordable to many professionals in the recent past. Home planners who use computers can allow architects, general contractors, and potential home owners to look over custom plans, change their minds, and change the plans much more quickly and inexpensively than hand-drawn floor plans. Although CAD-generated floor plans are slightly more costly than stock plans, they have become a standard means of producing plans for custom-seeking clients.

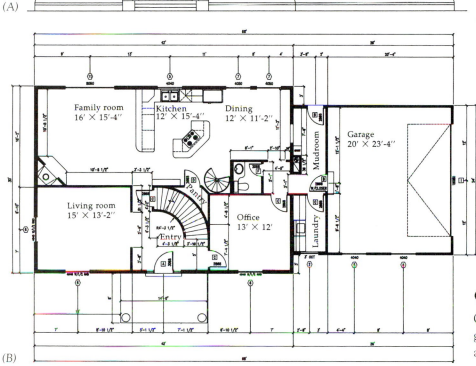

(A)

(B)

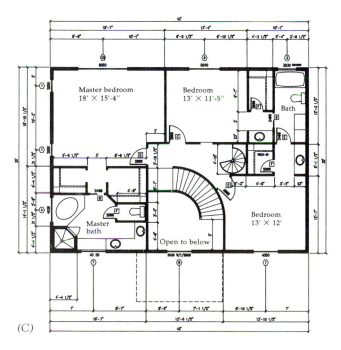

(C)

Figure 6.17 *Many designers now use the computer to create floor plans. (A) Exterior front elevation of a modest-sized computer-aided design (CAD) floor plan. (B) Main level floor plan: 1398 square feet, plus garage. (C) Upper level floor plan: 1260 square feet.*

Design by Gary Stewart.

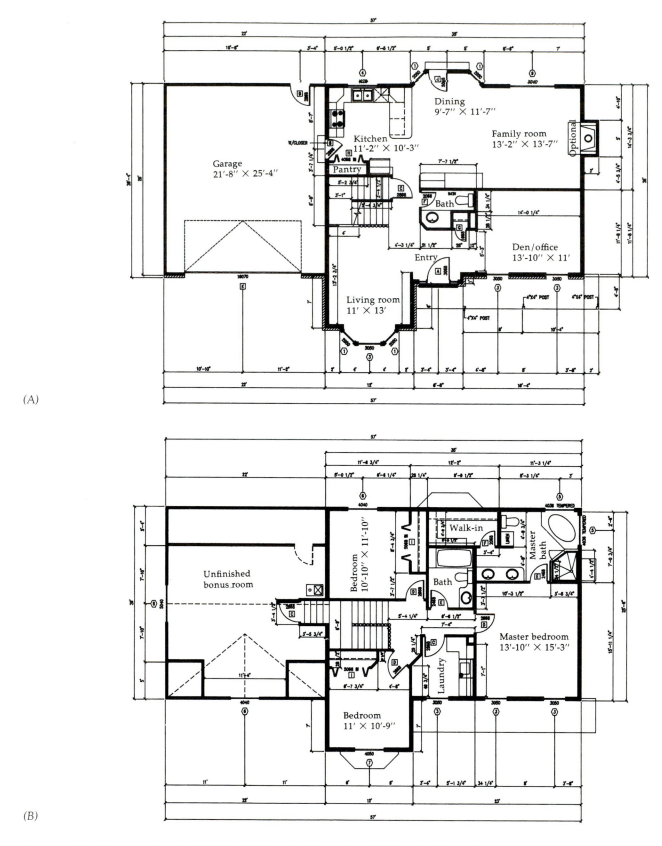

(A)

(B)

Figure 6.18 *Two-story floor plan (CAD). (A) Main level floor plan. (B) Upper level floor plan.*
Design by Gary Stewart.

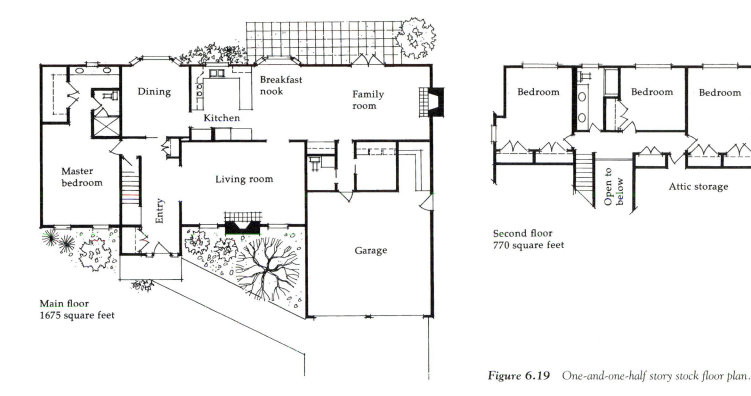

Main floor
1675 square feet

Second floor
770 square feet

Figure 6.19 *One-and-one-half story stock floor plan.*

Stock Plans

Stock plans, as seen in floor plan magazines, have been mass-produced and are usually obtained by mail order at considerably lower cost than custom floor plans. An advantage is that if another home from the same plan has already been built in the vicinity, it may be possible to walk through it for evaluation. Small alterations are possible to slightly customize the plan. Exterior building materials can also be varied in most cases. Disadvantages lie in the fact that a stock plan may be somewhat common, and it may be difficult to find a plan to exactly suit the program.

Remodeling Plans

The surge of building costs has discouraged many people who might otherwise have loved to build their own homes. These people today are often opting to remodel rather than to build from scratch. This saves the cost of new construction and allows creativity in planning for new spaces.

There are other important reasons why remodeling is a major trend. One is that an older or existing home may not have features desired by the new owners. Older homes often have smaller spaces and lack today's conveniences that we either long to have or take for granted. Remodeling may be necessary because of outdated electrical, heating, or plumbing systems. And remodeling can add much-desired spaces such as a main-floor family room, a spacious master bathroom, or a greenhouse or solarium. Lastly, remodeling may simply be a means of updating not just the floor plan but the entire look of the house—from the inside as well as the outside.

When considering a remodeling project, first sketch out your ideas, then measure spaces carefully. If you decide to tear out walls, be certain to consult a general contractor or structural engineer. It is not possible to remove load-bearing walls without replacing the support to the structure through steel or laminated beams or columns, for example. Also, the internal building systems must not be disrupted if possible. Walls that carry heating/air conditioning, major wiring, or plumbing systems may call for serious and costly rerouting.

Planning for a remodeling project should never be hurried, but it should be carefully orchestrated. Because the remodeling will disrupt family life, it should proceed smoothly according to plans that have been worked out as perfectly as possible. It is advisable to hire a general contractor if you are inexperienced, but here, too, beware. Get several references, and check them out to be certain of the quality of workmanship and reliability of the contractor. Avoid giving large sums of money in advance; rather, pay for each stage *as it is finished.* Never pay the balance until you are satisfied that the remodel has been satisfactorily accomplished and all details are complete.

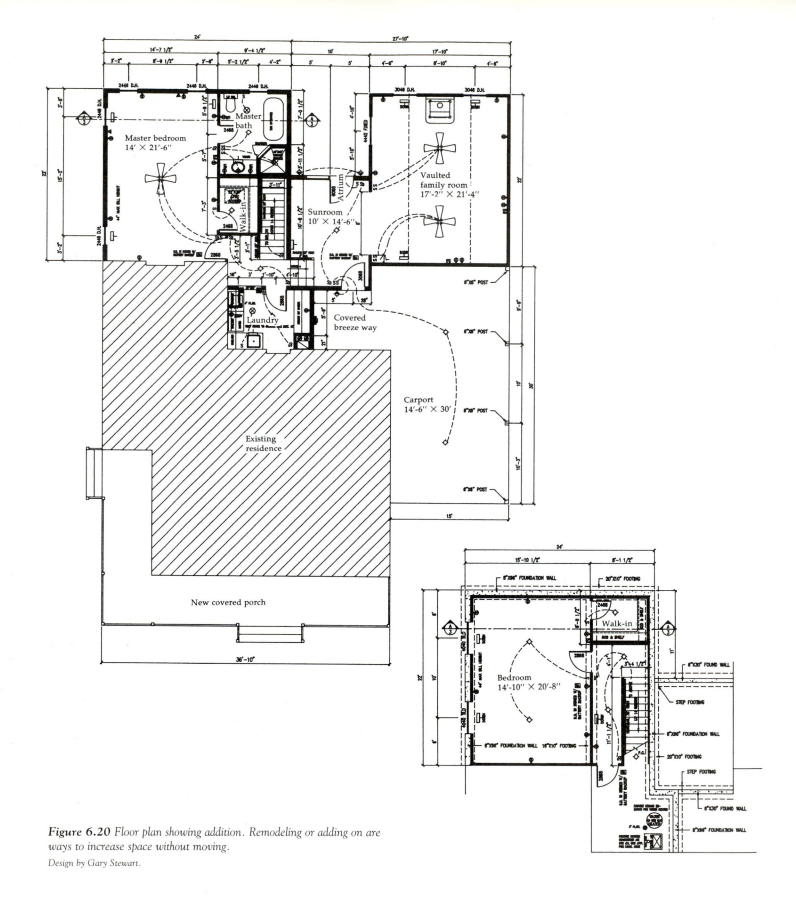

Figure 6.20 *Floor plan showing addition. Remodeling or adding on are ways to increase space without moving.*

Design by Gary Stewart.

FLOOR PLANS AND HOUSING

Floor Plan Types

There are three types of floor plans: closed, open, and combination. A *closed floor plan* is one in which most or all of the rooms are units that are opened to others only by a door, and when the door is shut, the room is completely enclosed. This gives privacy and control over sound, yet often it creates a chopped-up floor plan without flexibility.

An *open floor plan* has several areas that are open to one another without walls or with only partial walls or dividers. The cost to build may be less, and the space seems much larger than with a closed plan. There is flexibility in the use of the space. The disadvantages lie in the lack of privacy that may result and the transmission of more sound than is desirable. These floor plans may open vertically (high ceilings), horizontally (few walls), or both.

Combination (open and closed) *plans* have both open and closed areas or areas that can be opened to permit a flexible use of the space. This can be accomplished with double doors (such as a pair of pocket sliding doors, French doors, or accordion doors) and with some areas with high ceilings that open to areas such as lofts or balconies or other living space.

TYPES OF HOUSING

There are two major categories of residential housing. They are *detached* and *attached dwellings*. Within these two categories are several subcategories. Detached dwellings include the single detached family dwelling and the mobile home. The attached dwelling includes high-rise apartments and condominiums, town houses, and twin houses or multiplexes. Each subcategory has its merits and is useful for a segment of the population and for particular stages of life.

The Single Detached Dwelling

The single detached family dwelling—a home with a yard—has long been a part of the American dream. The single detached dwelling is particularly appealing because it has the greatest potential for self-expression in terms of location, style, and landscaping. It also is considered to be an investment in which funds can be retrieved by selling.

These dwellings can be prefabricated on an assembly line, designed and built as part of a *planned development* built from stock plans, or custom built. A small home has between eight-hundred and twelve-hundred square feet of living space on one or more levels. A medium-sized home contains twelve-hundred to three-thousand square feet, and a large residence is anything over three-thousand square feet. Houses of any size

or type with extra, luxurious features are considered *luxury homes*. These features might include saunas, spas, whirlpools, areas for workout and exercise equipment, greenhouse rooms, gourmet-equipped kitchens, formal dining rooms, built-in entertainment centers, central vacuum systems, stereo/intercom systems, or computerized controls for mechanical systems (lighting, heating, security). These kinds of features are most often found in *custom design* houses (designed, built, and furnished for a specific user).

Although the single detached dwelling is sought after by many, it is becoming less common because of rising building costs and less available land. In some urban areas of this country and in countries such as Japan, where crowding and land prices are such a strong factor, a detached single family dwelling is an impossible dream.

One Story and Multilevel Living

In traditional architecture, living space is assigned to predictable living areas: the main floor, the basement, the upstairs or second story, and perhaps a half story (rooms in the attic). The two-story home simplifies zoning; private living is usually upstairs. A small detached home with space on one floor (with or without a basement) is called a *rambler*. Today's architecture includes both these traditional styles and frequently divides space into *multi-level* patterns as well.

An early example still widely used today is the *split-level home*, which consists of up to four levels. This plan allows the feeling of a larger home by zoning on different levels, and the space can be economical to build as well. Split-levels consist of a ground level that contains the living/dining/kitchen areas; up half a flight of stairs is the bedroom wing; down half a flight from the ground floor is the family room wing; and down yet another half flight (beneath the ground floor) is the basement/storage/extra bedroom area. Another typical multilevel floor plan is the *split-entry home*, which essentially is a home with a raised basement. The entrance directs traffic up half a flight to the living/dining/kitchen/bedroom/bath areas and down half a flight to the family room/bedroom/bath/storage areas.

As the cost of building has skyrocketed since the 1970s, architects, interior designers, and builders have come up with ingenious solutions for cramped living by introducing new twists on multilevel living. The great room may be a step-down area; bedrooms or study may be in a loft; partial walls and vaulted ceilings give an impression of not only spaciousness but visual multilevel living space. It should be noted, however, that open areas do not screen out noise from one area to another; a lack of privacy may make this type of plan inappropriate for a household of varied ages of people.

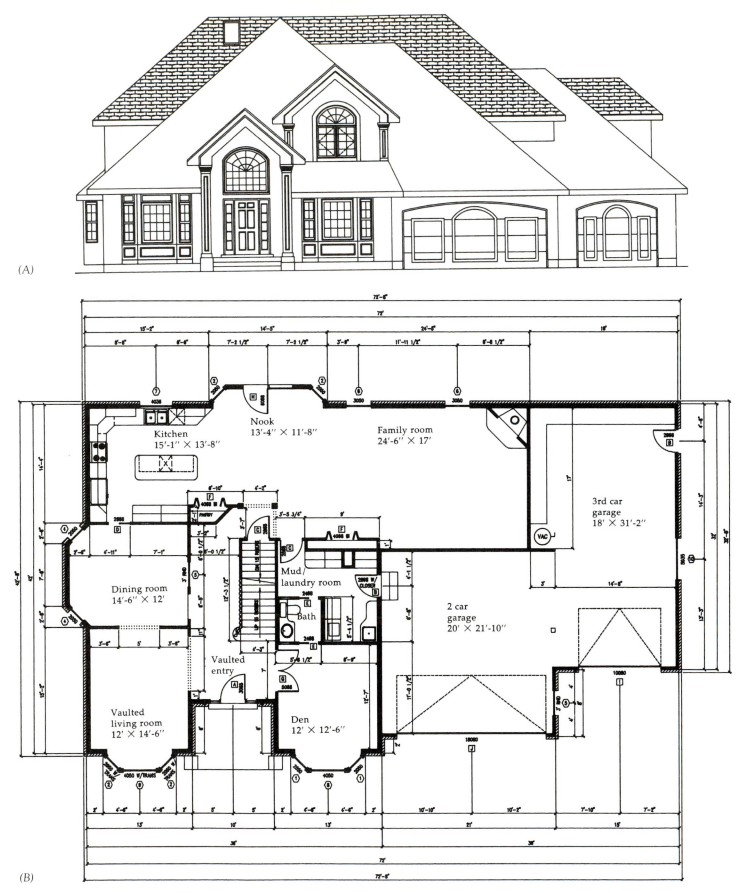

Figure 6.21 *Custom luxury home. (A) Front elevation of custom floor plan. (B) Main level floor plan. (C) Upper level floor plan.*
Custom floor plan by CAD home planner, Gary Stewart.

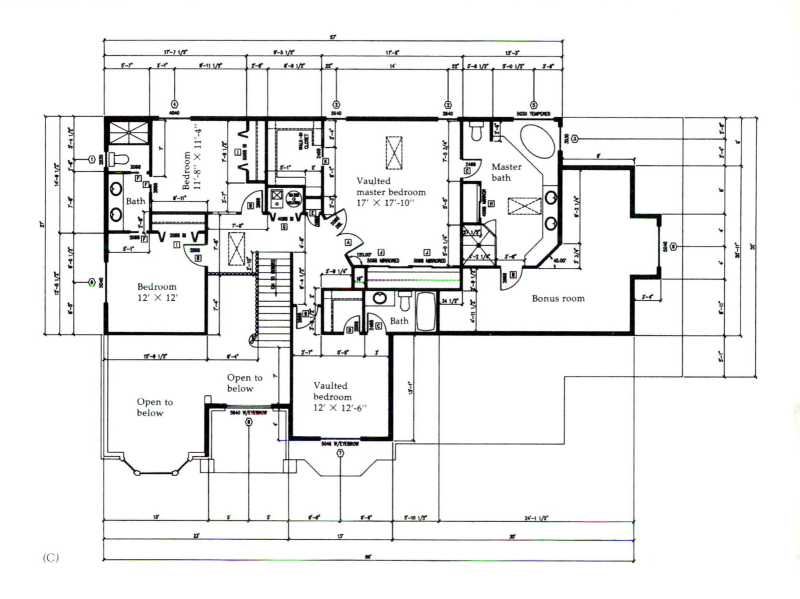

(C)

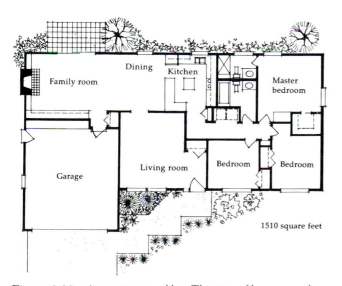

Figure 6.22 *A one-story rambler. This type of home may also have a basement.*

1510 square feet

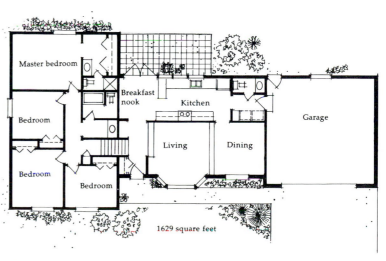

Figure 6.23 *A split-level home with living, dining, and laundry on the main floor. Up one-half flight is the bedroom wing; down one-half flight is the family room area. It may also have a basement beneath the main floor.*

1629 square feet

Figure 6.24 *A small patio home designed for a narrow building lot.*

Patio Homes

A *patio home* is a small home set on a very narrow, often shallow, building lot. These homes are economical because there are a modest number of square feet and the lot is less than full size. The homes may be two story (with the bedrooms upstairs), split level, or one level (no upstairs, and perhaps no basement). The one-story variety is especially well suited to the retirement-aged owner who doesn't want to or cannot climb stairs. They may also be appealing to the motion impaired. Patio homes are also a good choice for first or "starter" homes.

Mobile Homes

At one time the *mobile home* was commonly called a trailer. These were mobile dwellings, not unlike today's camping vehicles that could be pulled behind a car. Today the mobile home is a prefabricated residence assembled in a factory and moved to a *mobile home park,* where it usually becomes a permanent fixture. These parks vary from being cramped and ill-kept to being spacious, well-groomed, and attractive. The park may even have a clubhouse, pool, or other recreation areas shared by all the occupants of the park. The mobile home is manufactured in twelve- to fifteen-foot widths; a *double-wide mobile home* is manufactured in two sections and assembled on its pad in the mobile home park. These are often as spacious as a small house. *Single-wide mobile homes* are not as large, with small rooms and narrow hallways. Like standard houses, mobile homes are available in a wide range of prices, depending on the number and quality of features. They do, however, tend to be much less expensive than standard houses. Originally intended as temporary and movable, mobile homes are permanent housing for many people today.

Attached Dwellings

High-Rise Dwellings

High-rise buildings are multistoried structures designed to house large numbers of people in a relatively small area. They have been essentially an urban phenomenon, but they now exist in most areas of the country. High rises have been used extensively for public housing in large cities, although such projects have been mostly unsuccessful because of deterioration, lack of satisfaction, and increases in crime. Ironically, many high-rise structures house luxury units as well. Such luxury developments have all the *amenities* of the finest luxury homes, and sometimes as much space. Between these two extremes there are many moderate housing situations also contained in high-rise structures. The principal disadvantages of high-rise housing are the lack of relationship to natural green space, the inconvenience of elevators and corridors, and problems associated with getting out in an emergency.

Town Houses

Town houses and *row houses* are attached houses generally built as a single development. This type of housing creates private homes in a small amount of space. Town houses do not have large yards but may have roof gardens or small private gardens behind. Row houses from the nineteenth century were large and luxurious, but in more recent times some of these have been subdivided and broken up into separate apartments, or *flats.* Many older town houses became slum dwellings and were destroyed. Fortunately, many of those that remain are being revitalized as single homes or multiple dwellings.

Traditionally town houses were built in town right on the street, and they shared common walls with their neighbors. Today some town houses are being planned and built with jogs and setbacks so that they only share a portion of a wall with their neighbors. These are called *semidetached houses* and are often located in parklike settings or around golf courses.

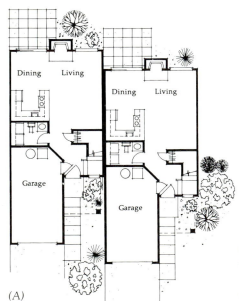

(A)

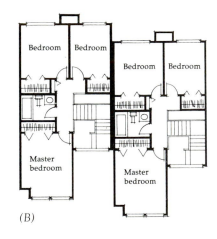

(B)

Figure 6.25 *A two-story town house, typically used for condominiums or apartments. There are approximately (A) 600 square feet on the main floor and (B) 800 square feet upstairs.*

Twin Homes and Multiplex Dwellings

Twin homes are double houses designed, like town houses, with common walls between units. They often are planned with the appearance of a single home. This double configuration is also called a *duplex*. Other examples of multiplex dwellings are the *four plex*, with four housing units, and the *eight plex*, with eight units.

NONRESIDENTIAL CONSIDERATIONS

The discipline of space planning for nonresidential spaces is far more complex than that for residential spaces. Each area—medical facilities, hospitality, business and office space, retail space, and production plants—has highly complex and specialized considerations, often based on local or state building codes. As such, an evaluation of all nonresidential space is beyond the scope of this book. However, since most of us have at least visited many or all of these spaces, it is possible to evaluate what we see as it pertains to space planning.

To this end, the following information is an extension of the space-planning principles discussed in this chapter; most of the information that applies to homes can, in some form or another, also apply to many nonresidential interiors.

Function and Zoning

Although the exact arrangement and design of spaces may vary, there still exists a certain standard of space relationships in non-residential design. This standard is seen in places such as restaurants, medical offices, and department stores.

In restaurants the specific spaces must be arranged in a logical interrelationship where the reception/waiting/payment zone or area is adjacent to the dining zones, and the serving zone overlaps the food preparation (kitchen) and storage zones.

In medical offices, the waiting rooms and reception areas must be situated so that they flow conveniently to one another and can easily be identified by the patient. Further, these areas must be conveniently located to the examination rooms, rest rooms, and payment area.

In department stores the planning of space creates the departments that carry a certain type of goods, from sports gear to clothing to children's toys. These departments are then placed near similar goods: apparel (clothing) is customarily located near the jewelry and accessories; bath and bedding linens may be near the personal and health care items (shampoo and lotion). Space planning also includes designing the right size, color, and placement of *graphics* or signage that direct customers to each department. These departments must also interrelate with stockrooms, dressing rooms, managerial offices, service counters, and cashier stations.

Figure 6.26 Restaurant space planning. Reception, waiting, and cashier areas are at the center; dining rooms extend outward. Kitchen is at the rear, with serving access to dining areas well planned.

CHART 6.6 TYPES OF OWNERSHIP

Three principle forms of ownership are private, condominium, and rental. Each type has advantages and disadvantages for certain groups of people, and for those in different stages of life.

PRIVATE OWNERSHIP

Like the single detached house, private ownership—owning one's own home—is a part of the American dream that is becoming less obtainable as the cost of housing and financing increases (see chart 6.1). Private ownership brings with it a great deal of responsibility for upkeep, maintenance, security, and care of the house and grounds. For some, this responsibility is an unwanted burden that is eliminated by other forms of ownership.

CONDOMINIUM

The word *condominium* comes from Latin and literally means "ownership with." Condominiums are complexes of any type of dwelling, from high rise to town house, that are owned privately but maintained and governed by groups of owners. These groups form homeowners' associations that use the owner's monthly fees to provide for general maintenance, security, snow removal, and care of the landscape. The homeowners' associations also establish the rules and restrictions for the condominiums. Some condominiums feature amenities such as club houses, health and fitness centers, swimming pools, tennis courts, stables, and parks—also maintained through the monthly fees. Condominiums can be geared to people with similar interests or ages such as singles, young families, and "empty-nesters" (couples whose children have left home). Condominiums are ideal for those who want to own property without all of the worries of private ownership.

RENTAL

Those who are unable to afford condominiums or private ownership will usually rent housing from a landlord who owns and maintains the rental properties such as *apartments*. Others choose to rent because renting generally carries no responsibility for maintenance or upkeep, and in some cases all or part of the cost of utilities (electricity, gas, water, sewer, and garbage) are included in the rent. Any type of housing, from detached houses to high-rise apartments to duplexes, can be rented, although costs and quality of rental units vary greatly.

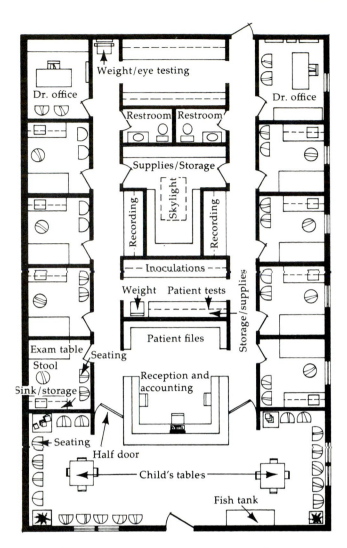

Figure 6.27 Space planning for a pediatrics clinic. Examination rooms for two doctors are symmetrically placed with the central support core, reception, files, and secretarial help shared.

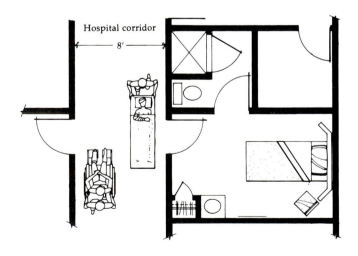

Figure 6.28 Extra wide corridors are needed in hospitals for dual passage of professionals, patients, and equipment. Private room has one bed, the life support panel anchored around the bed, and the sink and closet in the room.

Cubic and Square Footage

In nonresidential spaces, the allotment of square feet may rely on the functions to be performed. In a business office, the number of workstations may determine the square footage for one part of the office. The reception area, conference room, executive offices, library, lounge or kitchen, rest rooms, and storage are all areas that will demand specific allotments of square footage.

Traffic Patterns

The greater the volume of people or objects, the wider the traffic pattern or *corridors* will need to be. This is evident in public architecture such as hospitals and shopping centers where the traffic is heavy and corridors are wide. Local building codes must be met for corridor widths in nonresidential buildings.

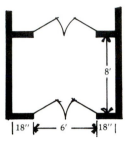

Figure 6.29
Double doors forming a vestibule, or air-lock entry, help keep cold and heat out of nonresidential buildings and homes where energy consciousness is paramount.

Two separate sets of doors are often employed in nonresidential settings as air-lock entries, or vestibules, to keep out excess cold air, rain, and snow. The vestibule area should be sizable so that foot traffic will not pile up and there is room for shelter.

Traffic patterns in nonresidential settings such as department or specialty stores can be quite complex, and architects use visible markers or guideposts to aid the users. People entering nonresidential spaces need to know three things in order for traffic to flow smoothly: (1) how to get in, (2) how to find their way around, and (3) how to get out.

Some spaces do this quite effectively. For example, in a well-planned grocery store or supermarket, the buyer must be able to find grocery carts near the entrance, locate items by checking the bright wall signs and the smaller hanging signs over spacious aisles, and then find the checkout counter with easy egress to the doors and onto the street or parking lot.

Open office planning is another example of multiuse space. Where several functions take place in one area, the furnishings or planning systems can be the delineators of space. A freestanding wall partition, desk, computer terminal desk, filing system, or shelf can be moved to accommodate changing needs, providing flexibility. Further, fewer structural walls allow for easier traffic flow, and the removal of visual obstructions makes spaces seem larger.

Space Planning for the Handicapped

State and local laws and building codes have mandated building *ingress* and *egress* (entrance and exit) accessible to occupants of wheelchairs through ramps, automated door openers, extra-wide doors, and elevators. In public rest rooms, there is generally a stall for those in wheelchairs.[2]

Psychology of Nonresidential Spaces

Space planning takes into account the effect of the space on the emotions of the people who occupy the space. Where small, closed, crowded spaces can cause frustration and even claustrophobia, large spaces can give a feeling of insecurity. Further, when people enter a building and cannot find their way around or to the exit, feelings of panic, confusion, or fear may result.

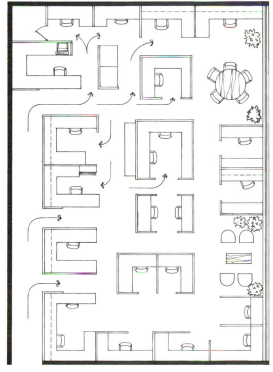

Figure 6.30 *Nonresidential space planning by architect I. M. Pei at the Pitney-Bowes Corporation in Stamford, Connecticut. (A) Open office planning using systems furniture. (B) An individual work station. (C) An open office floor plan.*

(A) and (B) © Ted Spiegel.

(C)

ENVIRONMENTAL CONSIDERATIONS

One significant way of saving natural resources is through recycling. In planning space, we must consider what materials can be recycled and where they will be collected inside a building. We are even seeing the emergence of a new type of vending machine: One line produced by Enipco of Fairfax, Virginia, produces reverse recycling vending machines that accept cans or bottles, scan them, and produce a refund/deposit. A new trend in office layouts is to plan space for larger kitchen areas where dishwashers and recycling bins can be located. Likewise, in your home, you can plan space (perhaps in the kitchen) for recycling receptacles and for sorting and temporary storage.[3] Planning space for cold-air-catching vestibules is another way you can conserve energy and reduce resource consumption.

NOTES

1. Ellen Cheever, "Trends in Kitchen Design," *ASID Report* (January 1988):8–10.

2. Einar H. Johnson, Jr., *Planning and Design Criteria to Prevent Architectural Barriers for the Aged and Physically Handicapped*, 4th revision (Salt Lake City: Utah State Building Board, n.d.), 31–37.

3. "Notes," *Interior Design* (August 1991):80.

FURNITURE ARRANGEMENT

Interior design by John Saladino. © Ted Spiegel.

Figure 7.1 *This great room is arranged for varied functions: cooking, dining, conversation, and relaxation.*
Interior design by Jane Bescherer. © Ted Spiegel.

The placement of furniture and fixtures in an interior is an extension of space planning and is directly linked to aesthetics and function. Arrangement of furniture according to aesthetic principles adds to the visual appeal of a space and may make its use more satisfying. But furnishings placed without regard for function and user needs will fall short of intended goals, and the aesthetic appeal of the design will vanish as users begin to move furniture around to make the space meet their needs. A good arrangement of furniture will be both functional and pleasing to the senses.

FUNCTION

Function is the use an environment will have and the activities that will take place there. As mentioned in chapter 1, the term life-style describes the way an individual or group lives and functions in an interior. Examining a life-style will help establish a list of functions for a space. Function will then dictate the selection and the arrangement of furniture. For example, a living room could be used to accommodate conversation, a library, musical instruments, a stereo, a television, video equipment, slides or movies, games, reading, napping, formal or informal dining, writing letters, paying bills, growing plants, displaying art, or any combination of these or other functions. The arrangement of furniture should be planned to accommodate the appropriate activities in the amount of space available. If the primary use of the living room is conversation, then it is logical that the comfortable seating pieces should be placed in groupings that facilitate communication and maximize interaction between users. If the main function of the room is television viewing, the sofas and chairs should be arranged to face the screen. Reading will require the placement of lamps near seating pieces to avoid the eyestrain caused by inadequate lighting.

Combining Functions

Often, functions will have a strong relationship to each other. For example, the conversation area previously mentioned might also accommodate informal *buffet-style dining*, and the way those two activities interface should be considered. Tables should be arranged close enough to seating for easy placement of drinks or plates, and a serving table should be conveniently located near the seating area. Tables used with seating pieces should be approximately the same height as the arm of the seating piece so that food or drink can be reached easily.

The combination of functions is an absolute necessity in small homes or apartments. Such spaces must often include both a dining table and comfortable seating in the same room. Some creative planning will not only solve the problem but will create a solution with a great deal of functional and aesthetic appeal. One such solution might include moving the sofa to the center of the room. A drop-leaf table could then be placed behind the sofa to provide dining space for one or two people. With the table pulled away from the sofa or with one leaf extended, even more diners could be accommodated. When not being used for dining, the drop-leaf table could double as a sofa table.

The consideration of function extends to every area of the home. A bedroom will naturally be used for sleeping, but it might also serve for dressing, conversation, a studio, an office, a library, an art gallery, a sewing room, or computer or stereo use. Each requires appropriate arrangement of the furniture. For example, if reading in bed is important, then a table must be placed close enough to the bedside to reach books. A lamp may be placed on the table, or some other form of lighting should be provided. Another very simple function that often takes place in a bedroom is putting on shoes and stockings. Something as obvious as a small chair or ottoman, appropriately placed in or near the dressing area, can make this simple task much more pleasant. Such considerations, though they may seem insignificant, can make life run much more smoothly.

Mechanical Functions

It is also important that furniture be arranged so as not to interfere with the mechanical functions of an interior. Heating vents and *cold air returns* should not be covered by furniture. Blocking them causes the heating, ventilation, and air-conditioning systems to function

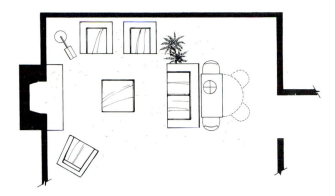

Figure 7.2 *An arrangement showing combined function.*

much less efficiently. Doors should be able to swing and open freely without interference from furniture pieces, and furniture placement should not hinder the opening and closing of windows.

Furniture designed to hold lamps or telephones should be placed near electric outlets and phone hookups for convenience and safety and to prevent tripping over cords. Unless they are custom designed and carefully planned from the beginning, most residences do not offer the kind of flexibility that allows an electric outlet in the middle of the floor. Consequently, furniture groupings will have to be "anchored" to a wall where there are electric and phone connections. Careful planning before construction or during remodeling might include floor plugs for greater flexibility in arranging furniture.

Circulation

Furniture arrangement needs to accommodate free movement or *circulation* from one space to another. Furniture should be placed to enhance that movement by allowing *traffic* to flow or by restricting and redirecting the traffic when necessary. This kind of control provides the best utilization of space because it eliminates unnecessary traffic patterns. The specific amounts of space necessary for free circulation are addressed in the next section.

Interiors have natural *traffic patterns*. These patterns can easily be seen by drawing lines on a floor plan to represent where we would most logically walk to get from one space to another—the *natural traffic pattern*. The complexity and lack of organization in the completed pattern usually shows quite clearly the need to control traffic.

We can control the flow of traffic by placing furniture at key locations so that it forces traffic to flow away from areas that should be used for seating and conversation or other functions where traffic might be disruptive. These locations can be determined by preparing a corrected plan indicating where the traffic should flow. Laying the corrected plan over the natural traffic plan will show where furniture should be placed to control the flow; for example, many homes have no entries—the front door opens directly into the living area. In this kind of plan, a sofa or other large piece of furniture could be used to divide the seating area from the door area and establish a visual

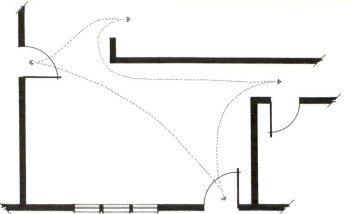

Figure 7.3 *The natural traffic pattern of this room consumes nearly half of the available space.*

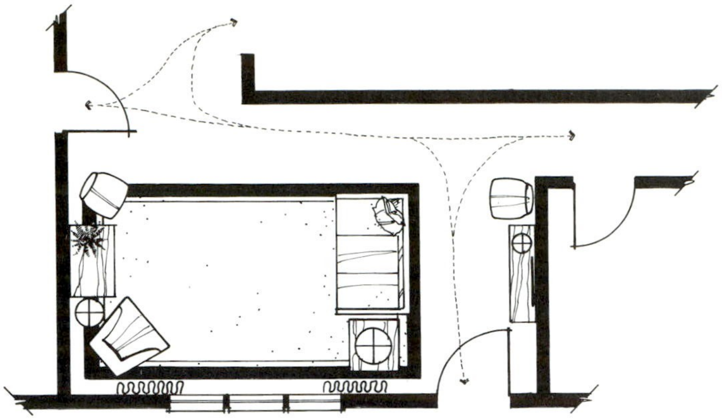

Figure 7.4 *The arrangement of furniture corrects the problem and makes the flow of traffic more efficient.*

entry that directs traffic behind the seating area instead of through it. Such placement avoids cutting the room in half with an unnecessary traffic pattern. Thus, a well-placed piece of furniture can be a simple deterrent to misdirected traffic.

HUMAN FACTORS
Anthropometry

Anthropometrics, the dimensions of the human form, are an important consideration in arranging furniture because human dimensions must be the standard of measure for interior design.

One must also consider those whose needs for circulation are different from the norm. For example, the needs of those who use wheelchairs, canes, crutches, or walkers must be addressed if they are to be able to move freely in an interior (see chapter 2).

Standard Clearances

Users without physical impairments require variable amounts of space or *clearance* to circulate comfortably within an environment:[1]

‣ Major traffic paths should be three feet or wider.

‣ Minimal clearance for traffic is one foot six inches.

‣ Seating pieces used with coffee tables need slightly over one foot of clearance between the table and the front of the seat.

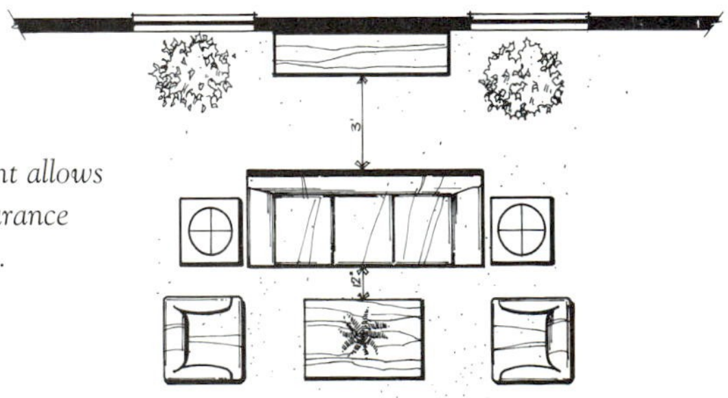

Figure 7.5
This arrangement allows three feet of clearance for major traffic.

‣ For a user to be able to extend his or her legs in front of a seating piece, about three feet of space is required, depending on the length and the degree of extension.

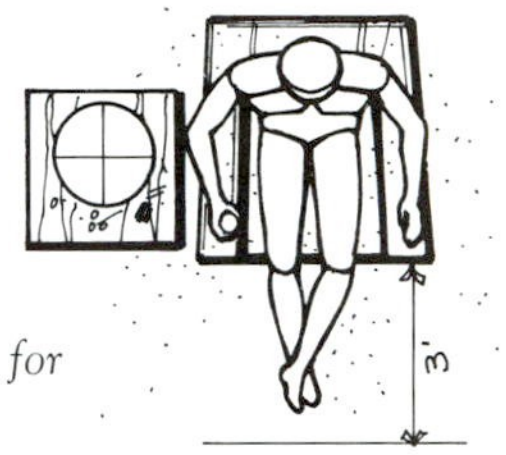

Figure 7.6 *Three feet of clearance for extending the legs.*

‣ Desks and pianos require a minimum of three feet of clearance for chairs, benches, and users.

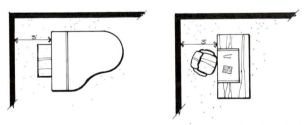

Figure 7.7 *Three feet of clearance for a piano bench and a desk chair.*

‣ Comfortable dining requires slightly more than two feet of space per user along the perimeter of the table.

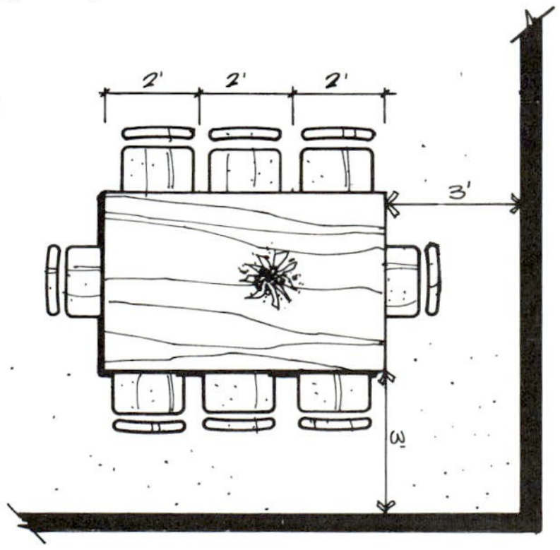

Figure 7.8 *Three feet of clearance for dining chairs.*

- In order to accommodate a seated diner and space behind for passage and serving, three feet of space should be planned.
- Getting in and out of a dining chair requires about one foot six inches of space.
- Three feet is considered good clearance between a bed and dresser.

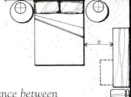

Figure 7.9 *Three feet of clearance between bed and dresser.*

- Space between two beds should be from two feet six inches to three feet.

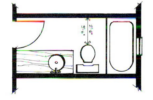

Figure 7.10 *Three feet of clearance between beds.*

- Minimal clearance to facilitate bed making is one foot six inches between the bed and the wall.
- In a bathroom, clearance of two feet six inches to three feet six inches provides adequate space for most functions.

Figure 7.11 *Standard clearance in a bathroom.*

Proxemics

Proxemics, a term coined by anthropologist Edward T. Hall, describes the way people use space and the way that use is related to culture.[2] Proxemic patterns vary in different cultures; the distances suggested here apply to Americans. Hall's study identifies four distances.

1. The space from one foot six inches to actual physical contact is considered intimate distance and is reserved for displays of affection, comfort, protection, or physical aggression.
2. Personal distance is equal to the invisible "bubble" of space with which we separate ourselves from others. Everyone has a different perception of this space, and many are made uncomfortable by those with smaller bubbles who stand too close and violate *personal space*. Personal distance usually extends from one foot six inches to four feet. In many cultures, particularly those of southern Europe, the Middle East, and South America, the personal space bubble is much smaller; people are customarily seen appropriately touching and even embracing without any threat or discomfort.

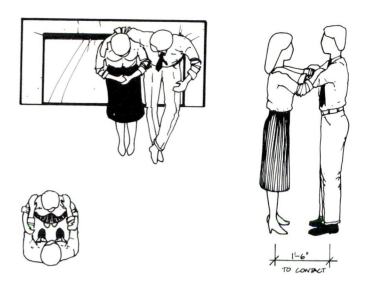

Figure 7.12 *Intimate distance—one foot six inches to contact.*

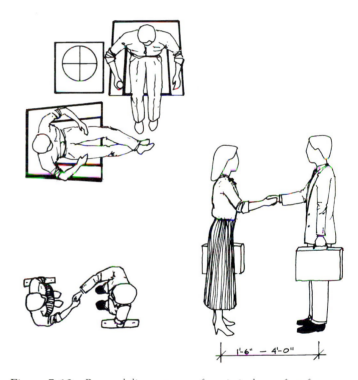

Figure 7.13 *Personal distance—one foot six inches to four feet.*

The way people normally use furniture is also affected by their perception of personal space; for example, few people choose to sit in the center of a sofa. Most people sit at one end, and most often they prop one arm on the arm rest. In this way, a sofa that can comfortably hold three people is most often occupied by only two people, since no one wants to sit in the middle. A third person sitting on an eight-foot sofa between two people leaves only about one foot between each person. This comes very close to intimate distance, leaving people who are just friends—or, worse yet, acquaintances or strangers—in the uncomfortable position of being too close. Furthermore, the middle person has no "anchor" in the form of an armrest to cling to for mental protection when that personal space is invaded.

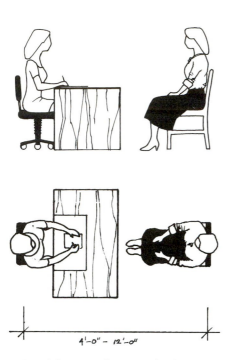

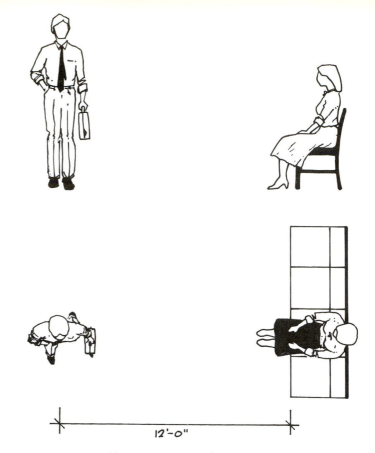

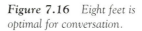

Figure 7.14 *Social distance—four to twelve feet.*

Figure 7.15 *Public distance—more than twelve feet.*

Figure 7.16 *Eight feet is optimal for conversation.*

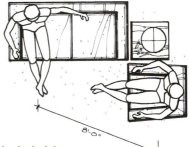

When forced into close contact, we become uncomfortable because we perceive our personal space bubble as a necessary privacy. Those who use crowded public transportation or elevators have methods of coping with the unnatural intimacy of such situations. Most will become immobile and avoid eye contact. Body contact is avoided, and when touching does occur, the tendency is to recoil quickly. Eyes are kept focused away from others; to help avoid eye contact, some may keep their eyes fixed on a book or other object.

When strangers enter an empty seating space, they tend to take seats at opposite ends, gradually filling the space but leaving a seat between themselves and others. When the only spaces left are next to a stranger, some people will choose to stand or will hesitate before taking a seat. Many would consider a person aggressive who sits next to them when there are still areas of open seating available. Under difficult circumstances, such as when airports are filled with grounded travelers, many of these notions of personal space are repressed. In such conditions, strangers may be viewed as colleagues in discomfort and the crowding perceived as more tolerable.

3. From four to twelve feet is considered social distance. At the far end of that scale, interaction tends to be more formal, and at the close end, interaction is characterized by greater involvement and less formality.

4. More than twelve feet is considered public distance. In public distance there is little personal interaction.

These distances can be helpful in planning interiors. For example, furniture groupings for conversation should be planned within the four- to twelve-foot bounds of social distance. Optimal distance for conversation is eight feet—it seems to feel neither too close nor too distant.[3]

Crowding

The effects of *crowding* on animals are well known. In crowded conditions, animals begin to suffer stress, abnormal social behavior, illness, and in some cases, death. Studies of crowding in humans have shown confusing results. Hall cites a study by Frenchman Paul Chombart de Lauwe who discovered that when the subjects of his study had less than eight to ten square meters of space per person in their residences, their social and physical pathology doubled. He also discovered that when the space grew beyond fourteen square meters per person, the problems also increased, though not as dramatically.[4]

Crowding is not strictly a function of dimensions. It also seems to be closely related to culture, personality, and the desire for involvement with other people. Those who enjoy involvement and interaction with others tolerate and, in some cases, even enjoy crowding. They find a crowded, lively environment exciting. Shops, cafés, restaurants, clubs, shopping areas, and markets are areas where one might expect to see planned crowding. The crowded environment should also provide islands of tranquility for those who enjoy less involvement or for those who need to retreat periodically. This type of person may find the *effects of crowding* (sounds, smells, and touch) overstimulating.

In our home environments, some of us enjoy being surrounded by lots of furniture, books, and art objects. Others need more visual or actual space in which to mentally expand. We must be sensitive to these differences in personality and preferences when planning furniture arrangements because the amount of furniture and its placement will affect the way we feel about our homes.

Territoriality

Territoriality is an aspect of proxemics that deals with the need to have a space of our own. This need manifests itself in many ways. For example, you may have noticed that some people select a classroom seat at the beginning of a school term and sit in the same seat each time the class meets. When someone sits in that place, they are annoyed and feel displaced. The same kind of behavior occurs in families where adults and children have determined their places at the table or in the car. Any unauthorized variation from the normal seating pattern may lead to conflict. Those who share bedrooms may find that certain parts of the room or even a certain side of a bed belongs to one person. When it is time to clean or straighten the space, things not belonging to one person may end up in a pile somewhere in the area that is perceived as the other person's territory.

Animals have the same perception of territory as humans. When pets are part of an environment, they establish a place as their own. A cat or dog often "owns" a favored chair or spot normally reserved for a human. We do the same thing. A study, a bedroom, a kitchen, a workroom, a shop, or even a comfortable chair may become personal territory to a particular person. When someone says, "Get out of my chair," or "Get out of my kitchen," they are stating that this area has become their personal territory. With time, even a tiny work space or cubicle becomes personal territory. Street vendors who use public sidewalks to conduct their business will claim a favorite spot as their personal territory. When someone intrudes, it is as if they have been deprived of their own property. These are the feelings that cause us to build fences and to consider trespassing a crime in most Western cultures.

It is important to understand this need, so that when placing furniture, space will be adequate for each person and shared areas will have space and amenities that give each user a sense of personal territory. It is interesting to note how quickly we personalize our spaces and establish territoriality. This is a natural process, and we should plan for this important human need.

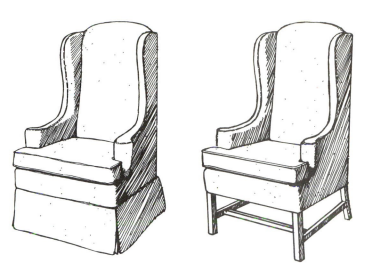

Figure 7.17 *The skirt makes the chair on the left look more massive.*

A good look at why we use our furniture the way we do—physically, emotionally, and culturally—will help us arrange the furnishings so that they will most likely be used and appreciated. We design interiors to look beautiful but, even more important, we design them so that people will feel good using them.

THE ELEMENTS AND PRINCIPLES OF DESIGN

Several of the elements and principles of design are directly applicable to the arrangement of furniture. Understanding how these important tools apply to furniture placement leads to attractive and pleasant furniture arrangements (also see chapter 3, Design Principles and Elements).

Balance, Scale, and Mass

Furniture should be arranged to provide a feeling of balance within the interior. Both balance and scale deal with mass or *visual weight* (how heavy the piece appears to be). Furniture is particularly effective in achieving equal distribution of mass because it is available in so many different sizes, shapes, materials, and colors, which are all factors that influence mass. For example, darker pieces appear heavier than lighter pieces, bold and large-scale patterns have more mass than subdued or smaller scaled patterns, heavier textures are more massive than smooth textures, and pieces the eye can penetrate are less massive than solid pieces. For this reason a glass table appears to be lighter scaled and less massive than a solid wood table, and a piece that sits up on legs has a lighter appearance than a piece that is solid or upholstered clear to the floor. Following are some guidelines for considering balance and scale in the arrangement of furniture:

- The visual weight or mass of the pieces is more important than actual dimensions in creating a well-balanced arrangement.

- Furniture can be balanced with other pieces of furniture. For example, two chairs of the same visual scale placed across from each other will be visually balanced.

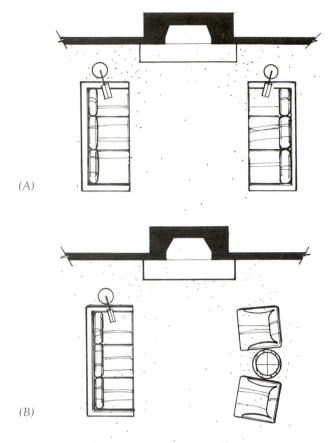

(A)

(B)

Figure 7.18 *Parallel groupings showing* (A) *symmetrical and* (B) *asymmetrical arrangements.*

- Furniture can also be used to balance *architectural elements* in an interior. For example, a sofa or love seat could be used opposite a fireplace to create balance.

- Massing furniture together may create a heavier visual scale in order to achieve balance. For example, a large-scale wing chair does not balance with a small side chair. However, if the side chair is arranged with a table and lamp, the three pieces massed together may balance the heavier wing chair.

- Groupings may be arranged in symmetrical or asymmetrical balance. For example, a pair of matching sofas facing each other in front of a fireplace creates a symmetrical grouping. If one of the sofas were replaced with a pair of chairs, the grouping would be asymmetrical but balanced nonetheless. One form of balance is not better than the other—each type has its own appeal. In a symmetrical grouping when small details such as lamps, tables, or even small *occasional chairs* are varied, the feeling will still be one of symmetry, but the grouping will have the intriguing quality of asymmetry. (An occasional chair is a small-scaled piece that sits away from the main seating area that can be drawn up on occasion when it is needed for additional seating.)

- Lighting should also be considered in planning the balance of a furniture arrangement. At night the balance of a room can be drastically altered by lighting. Artificial light will create areas of emphasis that should be balanced along with the furniture. If the lighting is well placed and the levels of light are appropriate, the balance will be maintained.

- The final judgment as to whether balance has been achieved will have to be personal, visual, and intuitive—no device exists for such measurement other than the eye.

Rhythm

The placement of furniture is an exercise in rhythm. One particularly important aspect of rhythm to consider when creating furniture arrangements is rhythm through alternation. Here are some considerations for the use of rhythm by alternation:

- An interior will be more interesting when upholstered and wooden pieces or hard and soft textures are alternated. A number of upholstered pieces without contrasting textures of wood or other hard materials to break the flow may feel monotonous.

- The alternation of textures creates contrast, an element that makes any design more pleasing.

- Alternation of rectilinear and curvilinear forms will also make the interior more appealing. The addition of rounded forms in an otherwise rectilinear design softens the impact of the straight lines and lessens any harshness such lines may have implied.

- The same subtle appeal is created when high and low forms are alternated. Particularly when seen in *elevation* (a flat, straight-on view), an arrangement of furniture is more interesting when high and low pieces are mixed in such a way that wall space is broken into interesting shapes and proportions.

- Alternation of high and low pieces away from the walls, in the open space of an environment, helps relieve monotony and can provide interest. In large spaces this principle can be employed to create interest by creating raised and lowered areas that break up the horizontal and vertical space. For example, in a very large living room, a sunken area for conversation or a fireplace is used to create interest, and in a large bedroom, a raised dais (platform) for the bed area will divide the space.

Emphasis

Emphasis deals with the creation of a focal point. A focal point is the object or area where the eye is drawn first. Furniture arrangement is an important factor in creating an area of focus within an interior. The planning of *primary* and *secondary focal points* gives the environment a sense of purpose and subtly involves and stimulates the senses as the eye moves from one area of emphasis to another. Fireplaces, windows, and other archi-

Figure 7.19 *This U-shaped grouping creates a pleasant focal point around the fireplace.*
Courtesy of Better Homes and Gardens, member of Home Furnishings Council.

tectural features are natural focal points that draw the eye naturally. Following are some guidelines for creating emphasis:

- In rooms with natural focal points, furniture can be placed to emphasize and take advantage of them. A grouping around a window or fireplace will emphasize the fine natural features of the room.

- In rooms that lack natural focal points, furniture can be placed to create groupings that take their place. For example, a case piece such as a chest or secretary could be placed against a wall with a pair of sofas placed facing each other at right angles to the case piece. The seating area would then be focused on the case piece.

- Most rooms will have just one primary focal area and other secondary or minor focal areas. In a standard-sized living room, the area around the fireplace could be the primary focal area, and the secondary focal points could be: (1) a desk with a chair and a lamp, (2) a console table with a painting or mirror and a lamp, or (3) a comfortable chair with a table and lamp for reading tucked into a corner. (4) A chest with an occasional chair could also be a secondary focal point.

- Very large spaces may require more than one primary focal area. Very large living rooms may need more than one main seating area to adequately fill the space.

- The table will be the primary focal point in a dining room, and a serving piece with a painting or mirror and side chairs could be a secondary focal point.

- The bed will generally be the primary focal point in a bedroom, and a small area with comfortable seating, tables, and lighting could be the secondary focal point.

Figure 7.20 *This very large space has two main focal groupings.*

Courtesy of Noel Jeffrey, Inc.

Line and Harmony

Whenever a piece of furniture is placed in an environment, a line is created where the piece meets the floor or where its silhouette is seen against the background. In *plan drawing* (a view drawn from above), the furniture arrangement is also a study in line. Line is a powerful tool and should be used judiciously to create harmonious furniture arrangements. Some points to consider about the harmony of line when planning furniture arrangements include the following:

> If a line is introduced into a space, it should relate harmoniously to the other existing lines. For example, a sofa or other large piece placed across the corner in a room feels awkward unless other elements repeat and enhance the diagonal line of the piece.

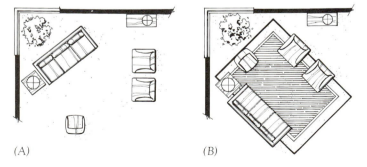

(A)   (B)

Figure 7.21 *(A) Incorrect and (B) correct placement of furniture using angles that contrast with the natural lines of the room.*

Figure 7.22 *Note the effective use of angled furniture placement in this room.*
Courtesy of Brunschwig & Fils.

- Placing large pieces at an angle often disregards the basic lines of the architecture. However, if other elements are arranged in concert with the diagonal line, the result may be very harmonious and interesting. For example, if an area rug turned on an angle is used as the format for an arrangement in a room of sufficient scale, the grouping will feel right. If the other pieces or the architectural elements in a room follow the same diagonal format and repeat and accentuate the diagonal lines, the arrangement will be pleasing.

- Chairs in a grouping placed at a slight angle tend to make the arrangement feel less formal and rigid because they soften the solid feeling of a rectilinear composition.

Form and Space

The forms in a furniture arrangement are the individual pieces of furniture. The space is the empty area between the furniture pieces. The design of space is as important as the furniture forms themselves. Furniture arrangement is a two- and three-dimensional study in space and form and should be planned with sensitivity to *negative space*. Seen in plan, the arrangement should make interesting use of space, and seen in elevation, the furniture placement should also break the wall space into interesting forms. Art and accessories hung on the wall must be treated as part of the composition. Consider the following when arranging furniture and hanging accessories:

- Negative space needs to be interesting; avoid arrangements with the furniture "holding hands" in dance-hall fashion—around the perimeter of the room. This type of arrangement is often safe but without the interest it could have if some of the furniture were drawn into the room instead of being placed flat against the wall.

- Large pieces of furniture pushed tightly into corners are not as pleasing as pieces placed leaving some negative space. This is true in both plan and elevation—the piece needs breathing room to separate it from the corner or some negative space to separate it from a doorway or window.

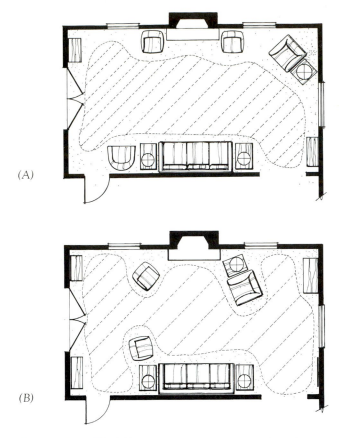

(A)

(B)

Figure 7.23 The (A) negative space in a grouping is made more interesting (B) by pulling pieces away from the wall.

- A desk that is placed perpendicular to a wall or actually moved out into the room may be more interesting than one that is pushed flat facing the wall. Turned perpendicularly, it extends into the negative space and changes the shape of the space, making it more interesting.

Figure 7.24 A desk placed at a right angle to the wall makes a functional and an interesting composition.

- The placement of furniture and accessories against the wall should be planned as an extension of the furniture arrangement. The furniture and architectural openings (windows and doors), seen in elevation, become part of the *wall composition. Accessories* (see also chapter 13, Art and Accessories) such as art pieces, collections, and hangings should be placed so they also become part of the composition.

- In many instances the accessories can be used to complete the composition and finish the balancing process. There are no rules governing the hanging of pictures and other accessories, only the consideration of form, negative space, and balance.

(A)

(B)

Figure 7.25 In (A) the paintings are hung too high. In (B) the paintings relate better to the furniture.

- When hanging more than one piece in a grouping, it is important to lay the pieces out on a table or on the floor just as we intend to hang them. By doing this, we can evaluate the composition and see how the pieces relate to each other and how the proportion of the negative spaces between the pieces relates to the pieces themselves.

- Accessories must be considered in relationship to the furniture with which they share a wall. Art pieces should not be hung so high above the furniture that the relationship between the pieces is lost.

- The scale of the accessory should relate well to the scale of the furniture with which it will be placed. If the scale of a piece is too small, several smaller pieces could be massed to create a grouping of appropriate scale and mass for the furniture. For example, a mirror or painting can be massed together with a chest or table to balance a higher case piece on the opposite side of a fireplace.

- On walls without furniture or architectural openings, the accessory pieces could be massed in groupings or hung gallery fashion. Hanging pictures gallery fashion requires that the pieces be placed in a row at eye level with appropriate spacing between each piece. If the pieces are all close to the same size, an imaginary line could be traced along the wall to mark the top or bottom edge of the pictures. If this seems too rigid, then an imaginary line could be used instead to mark the center of each picture.

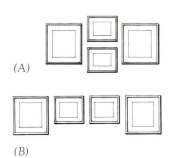

(A)

(B)

Figure 7.26 Two ways of hanging art pieces: (A) in a grouping, and (B) gallery style.

- The height of hangings should relate to other pieces in the room as well as to the composition of all the other walls. With training and practice the eye will sense when the arrangement is correct.

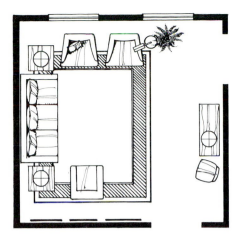

Figure 7.27 *This illustrates a possible solution for furniture arrangement in a square room.*

Proportion

Every space has its own shape and proportions. Some spaces are long and narrow, some are square, and others are well-proportioned rectangles. In a large-scale interior, the proportions will be less apparent and consequently of less concern when arranging furniture. In most environments, however, the proportions of a room should be carefully considered when placing furniture. Furniture arrangements can be planned to make best use of awkward spaces, and in some cases, the proportions of a space can visually be altered by a good furniture arrangement. The following considerations may be helpful:

- Rectangular rooms, if not too narrow, are the most flexible and easy to arrange.

- A square room is more difficult but could be arranged with a rectangular grouping as a primary focal point on one side, with open space along the opposite side for secondary focal points. An area rug could be used to help define the primary focal point.

- If the square room is large enough, an area rug could also be used to create a central focal point with a square or rectangular grouping placed in the center of the room. This would require careful planning of floor plugs or the use of recessed or other ceiling lighting.

- Long, narrow spaces can be challenging. The best way to handle this type of space is by dividing it into areas of function or use. For example, in long, narrow family rooms or game rooms, part of the space could be devoted to conversation and music/video. The next section of the room could be planned for a game, pool, or Ping-Pong table, or for eating space. The back of a sofa could serve as a divider between the spaces and help alter the *visual proportion* of the room.

- A narrow living room could also be divided according to use into seating area, music area, dining area, or even into more than one area for conversation and seating.

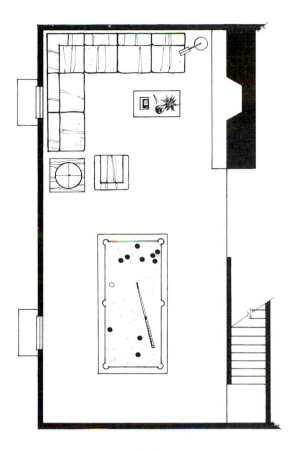

Figure 7.28 *The proportions of a long narrow room are improved by dividing the space visually according to function.*

- Long, narrow rooms do not need extra-long sofas to match the proportion of the space. The long sofa only tends to exaggerate the uncomfortable proportions. It is wiser to divide the space into smaller modules with furniture groupings.

BASIC GROUPINGS

As we carefully observe interiors, we see that most seating arrangements fit into seven basic configurations. The seven groupings can be composed of any combination of benches, ottomans, chairs, sofas, lounges, or love seats, and each grouping will be appropriate for different functions.

1. Straight-line groupings are formed by arranging furniture in continuous lines.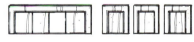

   Figure 7.29 *A straight-line grouping.*

   This configuration is the most efficient for seating the largest number of people in a space. This arrangement is used in theaters, airplanes, waiting rooms, classrooms, churches, arenas, and even in homes when they have been arranged for club meetings or other large gatherings. This type of grouping makes interaction difficult since it requires leaning forward, weaving back and forth, or craning your neck to talk with anyone except the person next to you. Its principal advantage is its ability to handle crowds.

Figure 7.30 *Pleasant use of a straight-line grouping at the Grand Hotel on Mackinac Island, Michigan.* © *Lowell Georgia/Photo Researchers, Inc.*

Figure 7.32 U-shaped groupings.

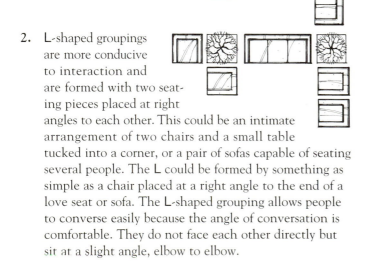

Figure 7.31
L-shaped groupings.

2. L-shaped groupings are more conducive to interaction and are formed with two seating pieces placed at right angles to each other. This could be an intimate arrangement of two chairs and a small table tucked into a corner, or a pair of sofas capable of seating several people. The L could be formed by something as simple as a chair placed at a right angle to the end of a love seat or sofa. The L-shaped grouping allows people to converse easily because the angle of conversation is comfortable. They do not face each other directly but sit at a slight angle, elbow to elbow.

3. U-shaped groupings are an extension of the L shape. They can be formed by adding a chair, sofa, love seat, or any seating piece to the L. This configuration also enables interaction and further expands the space for seating.

4. Box-shaped groupings are formed by adding seating pieces to partially close the opening of the U-shaped grouping. This is the best configuration for interaction among the largest possible group of users. Conversation pits, which are built-in seating areas designed as an integral part of the environment, are often box shaped. If built around a fire pit, the interaction is often diminished by the fire hood, which interferes with visual contact. But if the line of sight is carefully maintained, the interaction can be excellent. In more standard furniture groupings, the opening of the U will usually be closed with a chair or pair of chairs allowing sufficient room for users to enter and exit the grouping with ease.

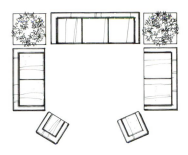

Figure 7.34   Box-shaped grouping.

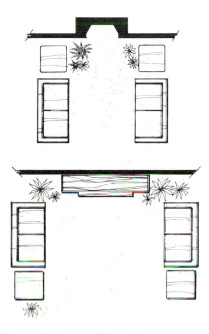

Figure 7.35   Parallel groupings.

Figure 7.33   *An inviting box-shaped grouping, ideal for conversation.*
Courtesy of Waverly.

5. Circular groupings are much like box-shaped groupings except that, as the name implies, they are arranged in circular shapes. Some modular furniture pieces and conversation pits are designed in a circular or curving fashion. These groupings, like the box-shaped groupings, are excellent for interaction because eye contact can be maintained with nearly everyone in the group. However, its unusual shape makes it unsuited to many situations.

6. Parallel groupings are an excellent arrangement for emphasizing a natural focal point or creating one where none exists. Two seating pieces are placed so they face each other at right angles to a window, fireplace, or other natural focal point. The seating pieces frame the focal point, and the users face each other for good interaction. Where no natural focal point exists, the grouping can focus on a case piece or some other object of interest.

7. Solo groupings may sound like a paradox—the ideas may not seem compatible. However, it is important to remember that single pieces placed away from main groupings of furniture generally need some form of accompaniment. For example, a reading chair at least needs a lamp and would be even better with a table to hold a book and a refreshment. The chair becomes more functional and feels more purposeful with the table and lamp. Consider also that when a single chair is placed in a particularly beautiful spot to complete a point of emphasis, it may never be occupied. Where the design may call for a chair as part of a vista—placed under a window or at the end of a hallway—people may feel "on stage" if they use it.

Figure 7.36
Solo grouping.

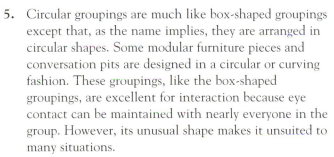

Figure 7.37 *The chair and ottoman are made more comfortable and usable with the addition of a table and lamp in this solo grouping.*
Interior design by Anthony Antine and Mark Polo. Courtesy of DuPont.

Seating pieces in some sleek, modern rooms may have no need for accompaniment. In such environments, the furniture is often treated as sculpture whose principal purpose is aesthetic. The lighting in these spaces will often be architectural and preclude the need for tables and lamps. The appeal of such designs is in their clarity and lack of embellishment; extra pieces of furniture would only detract. However, most rooms are designed with a wider range of purpose in mind and are made better by grouping pieces that extend the function of the furniture. Even a wall of books can be made more functional by placing an ottoman or occasional chair next to the bookcase for browsing.

NONRESIDENTIAL CONSIDERATIONS

The process of arranging furniture in nonresidential design is based on the same principles as residential furniture arrangement, but some of the basic considerations will be different.

Function

Many nonresidential designs will include areas of seating, dining, or sleeping that are treated in the same way they would be in a residence. However, in other cases of nonresidential design, the list of functions will not always relate to a specific person but rather to a generic need or function. For example, in an office with a receptionist, those who enter should have their attention drawn directly to the reception desk. The reception area must then be placed so that it is the first thing seen as a person enters. The designer will not ask the receptionist if a center stage position is agreeable because in this situation the function supercedes the personal preferences of a specific user.

Nonresidential Furniture Types

Nonresidential design often includes placement of fixtures that are quite unlike any furniture used in residential design. For example, in health care facilities, such as doctors' offices, clinics, and hospitals, there will be furniture specially designed for examination and procedures. The design must reflect understanding of each procedure and the relationship between different procedures so that the

Figure 7.38 *Systems furniture provides the kind of flexibility required by many businesses and institutions.*
PLACES SYSTEMS, HAWORTH INC.

fixtures and equipment can be placed for efficiency and convenience. This kind of specialized need is one of the main reasons designers develop and practice in specialty areas such as health care design, restaurant design, hotel design, and office planning. Such specialization allows a design group to stay current with the latest technology and developments in each area and with the ways to best implement these developments in a design.

Planning for Systems Furniture

Many businesses and institutions are designed with large open work spaces for many users. To make efficient use of such spaces, designers often specify *systems furniture* (discussed in chapter 8, Furniture Selection). These are prefabricated modules that can be arranged in a number of different ways to create spaces and workstations for an endless number of different needs and functions. Systems furniture provides a great deal of flexibility, but determining space and function needs for each area is an enormous undertaking. This task is made much simpler by the use of computer programs (often provided by the systems furniture manufacturer) for collecting and analyzing data on needs and functions. These programs help generate specifications for the types of modules that best meet the users' needs. The process of laying out the furniture on large-scale projects can also be simplified by the use of computer-aided design (CAD) programs for planning furniture arrangement. Such technology is a boon to the designer, particularly on projects where gathering and controlling vast amounts of information require superhuman endeavors. Those representing the manufacturer and selling the systems furniture are also available to help the designer specify the right components and plan their optimal arrangement.

Circulation

Because many of the basic problems of circulation and traffic control are the same for residential and nonresidential design, principles or solutions observed in one setting can be applied in the other. For example, many nonresidential environments are designed with open plans, where one enters directly into open areas. Spaces with open plans have a particular need for traffic control. In retail stores and restaurants, furniture and fixtures are often used to define areas for traffic. In restaurants, the placement of tables will create aisles for circulation; the patterns can be altered by rearranging the tables. In retail stores, fixtures such as clothing racks or display tables are used to create lanes for traffic. By plotting natural patterns of circulation and then determining where traffic should flow, open spaces with carefully placed furniture or fixtures can function as well as if they had actual walls or dividers to control traffic.

NOTES

1. For a complete set of anthropometric data, refer to: Julius Panero, *Anatomy for Interior Designers* (New York: Whitney Library of Design, 1981).

2. Edward T. Hall, *The Hidden Dimension* (New York: Anchor, 1969), 1.

3. Panero, *Anatomy for Interior Designers*, 19.

4. Hall, *The Hidden Dimension*, 172.

Courtesy of Noel Jeffrey, Inc.

FURNITURE SELECTION

With the development of agriculture, people stopped their no-madic wanderings and put down roots in permanent communities. In some early societies the natural spark of human creativity gave rise to the construction of furnishings that made life more comfortable and daily duties less taxing. Many discovered that life is more pleasant when there is a place to put possessions, that sitting on a stool is more comfortable than sitting on the ground, and that if one person's furnishings were nicer than another's it brought a certain amount of status and recognition. The development of furniture construction made life's activities more functional and comfortable by providing pieces on which to rest and containers for storage of clothing, food, and other possessions.

Today, furniture selection is a prime means of expressing individuality in interiors. Furniture has become an art form that can move us with its beauty, and whether or not we are conscious of it, the furniture we choose says much about our values and design sense. Because furniture often represents a sizable investment, it is particularly important that it be well chosen for its quality of design, construction, function, and comfort, as well as for its lasting good looks.

FURNITURE AS A SYMBOL

It is interesting to note how furniture became a symbol of status. During the Medieval era only the most important people had chairs; those of lesser importance used stools. The term cathedral was used to distinguish regular churches from the seat of the bishop, and in order to be a cathedral, a church had to contain the bishop's chair, or *cathedra*. This concept has been carried forth to today: when a university wants to establish a faculty position of great status, it will endow a "chair," and when a committee or department is formed, the one most responsible will be called the chair or chairperson.

During the seventeenth century, King Louis XIV of France gave patronage to the manufacture of furniture. His royal support inspired the design and construction of fabulous pieces. Those with the means spent great sums of money to acquire furnishings like the king's because they were beautiful and a source of recognition. Nicolas Fouquet, finance minister to young King Louis XIV, created such a lavish setting at Vaux-le-Vicomte, his château near Paris, that he was imprisoned and his furniture was confiscated by the king. Today we may not meet with such drastic consequences, and furniture choices can sensibly be balanced between quality, aesthetics, function, and value. However, fine furniture remains a symbol of status or taste.

DETERMINING QUALITY

In order to make the best possible selection when specifying furniture, it is important to understand relative quality and its relationship to price. Only when the quality of design, materials, and construction are in line with the price can furniture be considered a good value. Consequently, some knowledge of materials and construction is important to making wise selections.

WOODEN FURNITURE

Because wood is an excellent material for furniture construction, it has been utilized by craftspeople for thousands of years. It is a renewable resource that can be regenerated by reforestation, or planting seedlings to replace trees that have been cut down for lumber. Wood is strong yet relatively easy to cut, carve, join, finish, and refinish. Wooden pieces are easily cared for, and if well constructed and carefully maintained, they will become better looking with age and may last almost indefinitely. Beautifully finished wood appeals to our senses because of the unity and infinite variety of its grain patterns and the warmth of its colors. Wood was once part of a living organism, and even after the tree has been felled and the wood cured, worked, and finished, it still has that appealing quality of life.

Hardwood and Softwood

Woods are categorized as hardwood or softwood. *Hardwoods* such as oak, pecan, walnut, birch, maple, cherry, mahogany, and ebony come from broad-leaved deciduous trees that lose their leaves in the winter. These tend to have tighter *grains* than softwoods and consequently are stronger and harder and can be carved and worked in more detail. *Softwoods* such as pine, cedar, cypress, spruce, fir, and redwood come from conifer or cone-bearing trees. These trees do not drop their needles and grow more rapidly than hardwoods. Softwood has generally been less expensive than hardwood, making it well suited as a building material. Because it is less costly and can easily be worked without expensive, sophisticated machinery, it has been widely used by provincial craftspeople for furniture construction. Softwood has a more open grain than hardwood and, in the proper setting, adds simple warmth and character to an environment.

Other Forms of Wood

Wood in several other forms is also used for construction of furniture.

- *Plywood* is used as a substitute for solid woods and is made by *lamination*—laminating (gluing) thin sheets (*plies*) of wood or other materials, sandwich fashion, in successive layers to make a panel. When each ply is rotated a quarter turn so that the grain of each layer runs perpendicular (at a ninety-degree angle) to the layer below it, a material of great strength is created. If the grain of each layer runs in the same direction, the plywood can be bent and shaped with heat, pressure, and chemicals to create beautiful furniture designs like Eames' (see Eames' lounge chair, chapter 15).

- *Particleboard*, or *chipboard*, is made by compressing flakes of wood with resin under heat and pressure to form a solid panel. Particleboard will not warp and can be used as a base for veneers of wood or plastic laminates and can be vinyl wrapped for use in drawers.

Figure 8.1 *This case piece is representative of the expanding market in home theaters.*
Courtesy of Pennsylvania House, 137 N 10th St., Lewisburg, PA 17873.

▸ *Hardboard* is also made by compression with heat. Wood fibers are bonded together to make a strong material that is often used for drawer construction, dust panels between drawers, and backing on mirrors and case goods. Hardboard can also be used as paneling in solid colors, with simulated wood grains and textures or drilled with holes for attaching hooks and brackets.

Case Goods

Furniture pieces made without upholstery such as desks, dressers, cabinets, and chests are called *case goods* by the furniture industry. Some case goods are made of solid wood, but many pieces are made using other combinations of materials.

▸ *All-wood* construction means that the visible parts of the piece are made of wood.

▸ *Combination* indicates that more than one type of wood is used on the exposed parts of the piece.

▸ *Genuine* denotes the use of veneers of a particular wood over hardwood plywood on all the exposed parts of a piece.

▸ *Solid* refers to the use of solid pieces of a certain wood in the construction of all the external (visible) parts.

▸ *Veneer* is a thin slice of beautifully grained wood bonded to plywood or particleboard. Veneers have been used since earliest times to create pieces of great appeal and strength. Because beautiful pieces of wood are used in thin slices, handsome effects with matched grains and inlaid patterns (called *marquetry*) can be achieved with veneers. One frequently used type, *burl veneer*, comes from the scarlike growths where trees have been diseased or repeatedly pruned. This results in an irregular growth pattern that becomes a beautiful and complex grain in the finished piece of furniture.

Wood Grains

By using several cutting methods, different grain patterns can be revealed in most woods.

▸ *Plain slicing* is when the half log (*flitch*) is cut parallel to a line through the center of the log, producing a vaulted or cathedral-like grain.

▸ *Quarter slicing* indicates that the quarter log (also called a flitch) is cut so that the blade meets the grain at right angles to the growth rings, resulting in a generally straight, striped grain.

- *Rotary slicing* shaves a continuous, thin layer of wood from a log mounted to a lathe. It is as if the log were being unwound like a roll of paper. The grain produced by this method is broad, open, and bold.

Joining Methods

A well-made piece of wooden furniture is assembled by fastening pieces of lumber together in junctions or closures called *joints*. There are several ways of joining and reinforcing furniture. The most common of these are corner blocks, double-dowel joints, dovetail joints, miter joints, and mortise and tenon joints:

- *Corner blocks* are triangular pieces of wood that are glued and screwed into place at an angle. These blocks are not considered true joints but rather reinforcements. Corner blocks are used in points requiring extra strength such as points where legs join tabletops, frames for case pieces, or frames for chair and sofa seats.

- *Dowels* are a third piece of wood used to join the other two parts of the frame together. The rounded dowel is glued into holes that have been drilled into the other pieces. The quality of this type of joint relies on the strength of the dowel.

- *Dovetail* joints are used to secure drawer fronts and sides. This joint takes its name from a series of dovetail or fan-shaped notches carved into one piece and projections on the other that are carved to fit the notches.

- *Miter* joints are two pieces of wood that meet at a forty-five-degree angle. Mitered corners must be reinforced with screws, dowels, nails, or metal splines in order to be strong and functional.

- *Mortise and tenon* is an ancient method of joinery that imparts great strength. It is formed by two pieces of wood that have been carved to interlock. Into one of the pieces a square hole (mortise) is carved, and the second piece is carved with a projection (tenon) that fits into the hole. Mortise and tenon joints make secure connections for furniture frames.

Wood Finishes

Finishes are applied to wood for its protection and to enhance grain characteristics that cannot readily be seen in unfinished pieces. The first step in the finishing process is the preparation of the surface by smoothing and sanding to remove any unevenness and imperfections. The wood may then be filled with a liquid or paste *wood filler* to level the pores inherent in the natural grain. After further sanding, color may be applied to the wood.

Color is generally added in the form of *stains* mixed with water, oils, or other agents; the natural color of the wood grain can be lightened by *bleaching*. Paint can also be used to color a finish. When a paint of darker value is applied over the top of a lighter value and then wiped away, leaving highlights and shadows, the finish is called *antique finish*. When no color is added to or extracted from the wood, the finish is referred to as *natural*.

The next step in the finishing process is the application of a transparent film to protect the piece from moisture and stains. One of the oldest finishing films is *shellac*, made by dissolving the waste of the lac bug in denatured alcohol. Shellac produces a beautiful finish that, unfortunately, is not resistant to moisture, alcohol, and heat. A much stronger finish can be obtained with *varnish*. Varnish, a preparation of resinous substances dissolved in oil or alcohol, can be used on almost every surface and is very durable as well as moisture and alcohol resistant. *Polyurethane* is a synthetic resin used to give today's varnish its outstanding properties. *Lacquer* is a resin that has been dissolved in ethyl alcohol. With the addition of pigments to the lacquer, beautiful colored finishes are possible. Interestingly, lacquer is also used as a finish remover. Consequently, a sealer must be applied between stains or other finishes and the lacquer in order to keep the lacquer from softening the previous finish.

Finishes are frequently polished with mild abrasives to soften or refine the finish film. Waxes and oils are used to polish and protect finished wood surfaces; the manufacturer's instructions for specific care of wood should be followed so finishes will not be damaged.

Some furniture is *distressed* to make it appear used and worn like an *antique*. The surface of the wood is intentionally dented, scratched, and flecked with dark paint as part of the finishing process. As with any phase of the furniture manufacturing process, this can be done very well or in a poor manner. It is the care that is taken at each step, together with the quality of the materials used, that determines the value of a piece of wooden furniture.

When case goods are being purchased directly from a showroom, or even when a selection is being made from a catalog (and a comparable piece is available in the showroom), simple quality checks can be made:

- Doors and drawers should fit tightly without sticking.
- Drawers should slide easily on *glides* or ball bearings.
- Drawer interiors should be smooth and free from splinters that might snag clothing.
- Pieces should be checked for quality of joinery and presence of corner blocks.
- *Back panels* and *dust panels* should be placed between drawers.
- Sanding and finishing of unexposed surfaces should be examined for smoothness.
- *Hardware* can be examined for quality and style.
- The exterior finish can be checked for clarity and possible defects.

Figure 8.2 *Steel adds strength and durability to this outdoor seating system.*
Courtesy of Resources Council, Inc.

- *Brass* is a gold-colored metal made from an *alloy* (combination) of zinc and copper. It is used either in solid form or as a plating for furniture and accessories.

- *Chromium*, or chrome, is used as a plating on steel furniture. It is known for its brilliant silver shine. Chromium is also used as a plating on lighting fixtures and plumbing accessories.

- *Iron* is a strong black metal that can easily be wrought (worked) to create indoor and outdoor furniture, railings, grates, grills, and accessories. It will rust so it must be protected with paint.

- *Steel* is an alloy of iron and carbon. The combination has greater hardness and strength than iron but still can easily be worked. Steel is used extensively for nonresidential furniture and fittings, office systems and furniture, as well as residential pieces. Steel furniture is usually chrome plated or painted.

- *Stainless steel* is an alloy of steel with chromium. The addition of chromium makes the steel rustproof. Stainless steel is used for furniture hardware and trim, as well as for a variety of fittings in nonresidential applications.

- Other metals such as silver, gold, pewter, bronze, copper, tin, and lead are used principally for accessories or for specific functions within the building structure.

METAL FURNITURE

Like wood, metal is an important material for furniture construction and has been used as such for thousands of years. Metal has great durability and strength and can be worked in many different ways. It can be cast into solid forms, rolled into thin sheets that can be manipulated into an infinite variety of pieces and components, and *extruded* (forced through an opening) into tubes and other shapes that can also be bent and formed into beautiful furniture pieces.

Types of Metal

Though furniture could be made from most metals, only a few are commonly used:

- *Aluminum* is used for some outdoor furniture because it is lightweight and does not rust. It is also used for window frames and can be enameled, left its natural silver color, or *anodized* a dark bronze color. (Aluminum is anodized with an electrolytic process, whereby it is subjected to a chemical solution together with an electrical charge.)

Most metals can be finished in several ways. If the unfinished metal is left exposed to the natural elements in an environment, it will tarnish or rust. This quality is sometimes exploited by the designer to create a desired effect. Copper weathers to a beautiful blue-green color and A 588 *steel* weathers to a self-protecting coat of rich reddish brown rust. Metals can be polished to a high gloss and maintained with a coat of lacquer or with continued polishing, and if a less-lustrous finish is desired, the metal can be *brushed*. Metal pieces can also be painted or plastic coated in every conceivable color.

The quality of metal pieces will depend on the care and craftsmanship used in their construction. Like a fine automobile, the components of a piece of metal furniture should fit together tightly and the finish should be smooth and free from imperfections. Metal furniture can be found in many ranges of price and quality, and because of its durability and aesthetic flexibility, it can be used in almost every environment.

Figure 8.3 *A casual grouping of wicker furniture helps create the pleasant mood of this garden room.*
Courtesy of Waverly.

OTHER FURNITURE MATERIALS

Over the years, creative designers have used every material imaginable—from animal horns to *papier-mâché*—to create furniture. Today a range of natural and synthetic materials other than wood and metal are available to those who design and manufacture furniture. The most common of these are plastic, wicker, rattan, cane, and rush.

Plastic

Plastic is a type of nonmetallic compound, produced synthetically, that can be molded and hardened for a wide range of design uses. It is a complex product that is in a constant state of development and redevelopment. Consequently, it may be difficult for the interior designer to stay abreast of new technology in this field. Fortunately, of the thousands of plastics that have been created, only a few are used for furniture and interior design. Families of plastics such as *vinyls*, *acrylics*, *polyurethanes*, and *melamines* (laminates) are the most common. Each of these families belongs to a larger group of either *thermoplastics* or *thermoset plastics:*

- Thermoplastics change their form by heating and can be damaged by too much heat. Acrylics and vinyls are thermoplastics.

- Thermoset plastics use a combination of compounds that are set by heat, so they are not easily damaged by it. Melamines are thermoset, and polyurethanes are both thermoset and thermoplastic.

Plastics today can be foamed, molded, *vacuformed*, sprayed, *calendered* (rolled), or blown in just about any weight or consistency, from spongy to rigid, to create a surprising variety of forms. This great flexibility makes plastics an ideal material for creative expression as well as function. Plastics have been maligned because they are often used to imitate natural materials or intricately designed details traditionally executed by hand. Yet when plastics are used in the context of their own potential, novel pieces of great aesthetic value are possible.

Because technology changes so rapidly, it is important for the designer to understand the specifications for a particular plastic before selecting it. Some plastics may be highly flammable, and some may give off poisonous or explosive gases if they burn. Since the designer is often liable for the health and safety of the user, understanding the performance of the material under every condition is most important. Care of plastics should be according to the manufacturer's directions.

Wicker, Rattan, Cane, and Rush

Wicker, rattan, cane, and rush are all natural materials used to make furniture or certain furniture components. These materials tend to be rather informal, although cane is used to make formal pieces as well. Following are some considerations of these materials:

- *Wicker* is not a specific material but rather the term used to identify any piece that is fashioned from small twigs or flexible strips of wood. Common wicker pieces include chairs, tables, and baskets.

- *Rattan* is made from the unbranched stem of a certain Indian palm and is used to manufacture wicker furniture. Rattan poles are flexible, can be bent into beautiful forms, can be stained, lacquered, or painted, and, unlike bamboo (which is brittle and hollow), it can be nailed or screwed.

- *Cane* is made from grasses, palm stems, or plants such as rattan or bamboo. Thin strips of these materials are woven to form a mesh that is usually fitted into the seat or back of chair frames. The mesh allows air to pass through and is strong yet has the ability to give, providing a degree of comfort. Cane has been used throughout history to create beautiful pieces of furniture; today manufacturers continue to use it on pieces of classic design.

- *Rush* is a type of long grass that is twisted to form a thin cord for weaving provincial chair seats. Rush is a strong and long-lasting material with great appeal and has been used to weave floor mats as well as chair seats. Today, rush is sometimes duplicated with strong paper cords. The paper version is nearly identical to real rush and is particularly well suited to dry climates where rush can dry out and split.

UPHOLSTERED FURNITURE

The quality of fabric-covered furniture is more difficult to assess than case goods because upholstered pieces are "blind" items; you cannot see what is inside. This means that one must rely on written specifications of a particular product as well as the information that a sales representative might furnish about the product. Because quality is important to the durability of a design, we often choose manufacturers and products with which we are most familiar and whose quality we know and trust. Understanding the construction and composition of fine upholstered goods leads to the selection of pieces of quality and value.

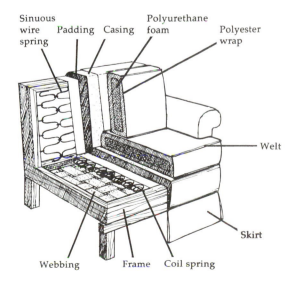

Frames

Frames for upholstered furniture are made from the same materials as case goods: wood, metal, or plastic. Wooden frames are made of hardwood since softwoods generally lack the necessary strength and may split when joined. Wooden frames should be securely joined with double dowels and glue, and the corners should be braced with blocks or metal plates and securely glued and screwed into place.

Springs

Springs are generally of two types:

1. *Coil springs* are attached to a tightly woven webbing of rubber and metal, linen, jute, or synthetic. The webbing is stretched across and attached to the bottom of the frame and serves as the base for the springs, which are then tied together at the top in at least eight places per spring.

2. *Sinuous wire* (no-sag) *springs* are fashioned from a single wire that is bent in a continuously curved zigzag and attached to the frame. This type of spring is used in chair backs or in upholstered pieces with particularly thin profiles because it requires less vertical space than traditional coil springs.

Cushioning

A layer of burlap protects and supports the padding and keeps it from working into the springs. The *padding* is a soft layer of *batting* made from a fibrous material such as cotton or polyester that covers the springs and frame and gives shape and form to the upholstered piece. A *casing* of muslin holds the padding in place and keeps the final cover from abrading the padding.

Some seating pieces are designed with *loose cushions* for reasons of aesthetics and comfort. Such cushions or pillows can be filled with foam-covered springs, down and feathers, foam, polyester fiberfill, or a combination of these materials.

Down is considered luxurious and is distinguished by its rumpled look. Because down and feathers are not resilient, such cushions require frequent plumping. Down cushions are increasingly rare due to high cost. The most common cushioning material is polyurethane foam with a wrapping of polyester batting. Polyurethane foam comes in a variety of densities and is resilient, nonallergenic, and impervious to moisture. The polyester fiberfill gives added softness and comfort to the cushion and has the quality of resilience missing in down fill. *Reversible cushions* can help extend the life of an upholstered piece because the cushions can be turned. Lower quality furniture typically has solid foam or *laminated* (sandwiched) *foam*, where the thinner outer layers are less dense and resilient than the thicker middle layer, giving some of the feeling of more costly polyester-wrapped foam.

Coverings

Coverings have a major impact on the aesthetics of upholstered furniture. Identical pieces covered in dissimilar covers will have very different finished appearances. Because the cover is such a visible part of the piece, it will often be a major factor in the selection process.

Figure 8.4 *The upholstery process showing the frame, webbing, coil springs hand-tied eight ways, and sinuous wire springs (in the back).* © Ted Spiegel.

Covers are available in a wide range of materials and qualities; manufacturers use the cover quality as a means to set prices for upholstered goods. A piece may be covered in material the client has obtained through a designer or elsewhere. These goods are referred to as *C.O.M.* (customer's own material) and are shipped to the manufacturer for upholstery on the selected piece. The manufacturer also maintains a supply of fabrics in several grades of quality that can be specified and ordered from catalogs and sample books. Each sample is assigned a grade corresponding to its quality; different prices are listed for each grade of material. An upholstered piece may be covered with custom-made *slipcovers* that can be changed seasonally.

The quality of the covering is dependent upon the material and finesse used in tailoring the piece. The materials used for upholstery are discussed in chapter 12, Fabric.

It is often necessary to order goods from catalogs without actually inspecting the pieces; one must rely on manufacturers who have an established reputation for quality and service. However, in some cases where pieces are available in showrooms, quality can be observed firsthand:

- Evaluate the comfort of the piece by sitting in it.

- Check for careful matching of patterns or *naps* (direction of pile).

Figure 8.5 *The buttoned upholstery on this chair is an example of tufting.*

- Look for smooth seams and straight *welts* (covered cords) without puckering.

- Verify that cushions fit properly.

- Be aware of loose or hanging threads that might indicate poor craftsmanship.

- Ensure that buttons are tight on *tufted* pieces.

- Examine quilted fabric to see that the quilting has been carefully executed.

FURNITURE TYPES

The vocabulary of furniture selection includes the names of a wide variety of types. These are not styles, but simply different kinds of pieces with varying functions that are often available in a wide range of styles. Chart 8.1 illustrates many types of furniture.

CHART 8.1 FURNITURE IDENTIFICATION

SIDE CHAIR
NO ARMS

Hitchcock, nineteenth century

SIDE CHAIR
NO ARMS

Sheraton, eighteenth century

SIDE CHAIR
NO ARMS

Chippendale, eighteenth century

OPEN ARMCHAIR
WITH ARMS

Queen Anne, eighteenth century

OPEN ARMCHAIR
BELTER DESIGNER

Rococo Revival, nineteenth century

OPEN ARMCHAIR
HOFFMAN DESIGNER

Prague chair, twentieth century

continued

CHART 8.1 FURNITURE IDENTIFICATION

FAUTEUIL
FRENCH OPEN ARM

Règence, eighteenth century

FAUTEUIL
FRENCH OPEN ARM

Rococo, eighteenth century

FAUTEUIL
FRENCH OPEN ARM

Neoclassic, eighteenth century

BERGÈRE
FRENCH CLOSED ARM

Rococo, eighteenth century

BERGÈRE
FRENCH CLOSED ARM

Neoclassic, eighteenth century

WINDSOR CHAIR
BOW BACK

American, eighteenth/nineteenth centuries

WINDSOR CHAIR
COMB BACK

American, eighteenth/nineteenth centuries

WINDSOR CHAIR
PIERCED SPLAT

English, eighteenth/nineteenth centuries

LAWSON LOUNGE CHAIR
ROLLED ARM

Contemporary

continued

CHART 8.1 FURNITURE IDENTIFICATION

ARMLESS CHAIR SLIPPER CHAIR	**OTTOMAN** UPHOLSTERED FOOTSTOOL	**SETTEE** DEACON'S BENCH
	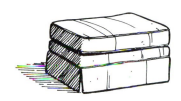	
Contemporary	Contemporary	American, eighteenth/nineteenth centuries

SETTEE DOUBLE PIERCED SPLAT	**SETTEE** BENTWOOD	**SOFA** CAMEL BACK

Chippendale, eighteenth century	Thonet, late nineteenth century	Chippendale, eighteenth century

SOFA BOW BACK	**SOFA** TUXEDO	**SOFA** LAWSON WITH ROLLED ARMS
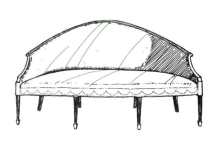		
Hepplewhite, eighteenth century	Contemporary	Contemporary

continued

CHART 8.1 FURNITURE IDENTIFICATION

SOFA
CHESTERFIELD WITH TUFTED BACK AND
ROLLED ARMS

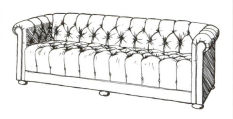

Contemporary

CHAISE LONGUE
RECLINING SOFA

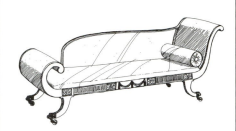

American Empire, nineteenth century

CHAISE LONGUE
PONY CHAISE

LeCorbusier, twentieth century

CHAISE LONGUE
ALSO CALLED CHAISE LOUNGE

Contemporary

WING CHAIR
UPHOLSTERED WINGS

Queen Anne, eighteenth century

WING CHAIR
UPHOLSTERED WINGS

Chippendale, eighteenth century

TUB CHAIR
ROUNDED BACK

Contemporary

CLUB CHAIR
OVERSIZED UPHOLSTERED

Contemporary, Victorian reproduction

LADDER-BACK
SAUSAGE-SHAPED TURNINGS/RUSH SEAT

American, eighteenth/nineteenth centuries

continued

CHART 8.1 FURNITURE IDENTIFICATION

LADDER-BACK
CHAISE À CAPUCINE

Country French

LADDER-BACK
PIERCED SLATS

Chippendale, eighteenth century

LADDER-BACK
ROCKER

Shaker, nineteenth century

LADDER-BACK
HILL CHAIR

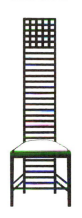

Mackintosh, twentieth century

TABLE DESK
FRENCH BUREAU PLAT

Neoclassical, eighteenth century

KNEE-HOLE DESK
SPACE FOR KNEES

Chippendale, eighteenth century

ROLLTOP DESK
TAMBOUR TOP ROLLS SHUT

American, early twentieth century

ROLLTOP DESK
FRENCH BUREAU À CYLINDRE

Rococo, eighteenth century

TALL CASE CLOCK
ALSO CALLED GRANDFATHER CLOCK

Chippendale, eighteenth century

continued

CHART 8.1 FURNITURE IDENTIFICATION

SECRETARY
DROP-FRONT DESK WITH BOOKCASE

Chippendale, eighteenth century

CHEST ON CHEST
STACKED DOUBLE CHEST

Chippendale, eighteenth century

CHEST OF DRAWERS
FRENCH COMMODE

Rococo, eighteenth century

CHEST OF DRAWERS
BLOCK FRONT

Chippendale, eighteenth century

HIGHBOY
CHEST ON RAISED LEGS

Queen Anne, eighteenth century

HIGHBOY
ALSO CALLED TALL BOY

Chippendale, eighteenth century

BREAKFRONT
FRONT BREAKS OR COMES FORWARD

Chippendale, eighteenth century

ARMOIRE
CLOSET; ALSO CALLED WARDROBE

Country French

HUTCH
OPEN CUPBOARD

American vernacular

continued

CHART 8.1 FURNITURE IDENTIFICATION

BUFFET
SERVING PIECE; ALSO CALLED
SIDEBOARD

Hepplewhite, eighteenth century

NESTING TABLES
STACK UNDERNEATH ONE ANOTHER

Hepplewhite, eighteenth century

TILT-TOP TABLE
TOP TILTS, ALSO CALLED TIP-TOP

Chippendale, eighteenth century

PEDESTAL TABLE
ALSO CALLED TRIPOD

Shaker candlestand

GATELEG TABLE
LEGS SWING OUT ON DROP LEAF

English/American vernacular

BUTTERFLY TABLE
SMALL DROP LEAF

Vernacular, seventeenth/eighteenth centuries

PEMBROKE TABLE
TEA TABLE-SIZED DROP LEAF

Hepplewhite/Sheraton, eighteenth century

TEA TABLE
SMALL, TALL TABLE

Queen Anne, eighteenth century

FLAP-TOP TABLE
TOP OPENS FOR GAMES

Duncan Phyfe, nineteenth century

continued

CHART 8.1   FURNITURE IDENTIFICATION

CONSOLE TABLE
GOES AGAINST THE WALL

American Empire, nineteenth century

CONSOLE TABLE
FRENCH

Rococo, eighteenth century

BUTLER'S TRAY TABLE
USED AS A COFFEE TABLE

Chippendale, eighteenth century

FOUR-POSTER BED
NO CANOPY

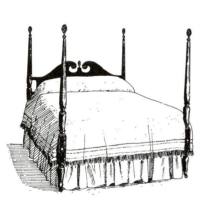

Chippendale, eighteenth century

CANOPY BED
POSTERS TOPPED WITH CANOPY

Chippendale, eighteenth century

SLEIGH BED
HEADBOARD/FOOTBOARD SAME HEIGHT

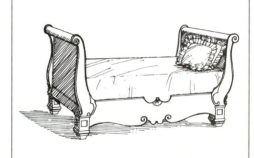

Country French

FURNITURE HARMONY

Harmonious and aesthetically pleasing combinations of furniture are the result of a selection process that may be partially intuitive but is also based on an understanding of styles, themes, and pieces that have classic quality. By studying and knowing styles from history, and by keeping abreast of innovative developments in the marketplace, we can make sound judgments about the kinds of furniture that will best suit our aesthetic needs.

Because many people find selecting furniture a difficult task, manufacturers have always made matched sets or "suites" of furniture. For example, they produce bedroom sets with dressers, nightstands, chests of drawers, headboards, armoires, and mirrors with matching details, woods, and styling. This is an easy solution for those who lack the confidence to choose, but as we know from studying the principles of design, harmony is made up of unity and variety. Matched sets are unified, but they often lack variety. The most interesting rooms have a personal mix of pieces that results in a harmonious setting that has a pleasing balance of unity and variety. Harmonious selection is often based on thematic design, which was discussed in chapter 1.

HUMAN FACTORS
Function

The first consideration in selecting individual pieces of furniture and built-in fittings and fixtures for an environment is the users and the tasks they will perform in the environment.

Figure 8.6 *A unique selection of furniture gives this interior a distinct personality.*
© *Jessie Walker Associates.*

Each environment has a certain function or group of functions for which it is designed. It is important to be familiar with all of these functions so that furniture and fittings can be designed or selected to enhance the desired function. For example, soft, deep, low seating pieces for casual television viewing and music listening are very different from the kinds of seating one might choose for work at a sewing machine or computer. Such pieces should provide proper height and back support and should be based on actual human dimensions.

Anthropometrics and Ergonomics

As discussed in chapter 7, anthropometrics are human physical dimensions including height, weight, and volume. *Ergonomics,* or, biotechnology is the study of human relationships to the furniture and products that fill our environments. These terms may seem formidable, but their application to furniture design is simple: The human form, its dimensions, and its need for movement are the bases for functional and comfortable furniture design.

The ideas of comfort and function are often linked to culture. For example, people in parts of Asia and South America learn from childhood to sit on their haunches in squatting fashion. Given the choice of a stool or a grassy spot by the roadside, these people might opt for the grass. Those from other areas of the world could certainly argue the relative comforts of sleeping in hammocks, on a Japanese futon mattress atop tatami mats, or on more conventional mattresses filled with water or coil springs. The ancient Egyptians developed sleeping arrangements with a headrest that today appears anything but comfortable.

Regardless of cultural influences, the best measure of function and comfort is the human form. Ideally furniture and fittings should be scaled to the average human form—but unfortunately, there is no such thing as an average person. Hertzberg, Daniels, and Churchill measured 132 different features of four thousand Air Force flyers and found that there were no men who fell in the average range on ten key measurements.[1] Nonetheless, most design is keyed to an average set of dimensions. These average measurements will not be optimum for everyone but will likely cause less inconvenience than if furniture, fittings, and fixtures were designed for the very short or the very tall. Personal environments can be custom designed to the dimensions of extreme individual sizes, and where possible, this should be an important goal of the design.

With all the research and developments in furniture design, it is interesting to note how little the overall form and dimensions of furniture have changed over the millenia. Today's ergonomic superchairs (see the next section) differ very little in general dimensions from the chairs used in ancient Egypt.

NONRESIDENTIAL CONSIDERATIONS

Custom Designs

Nonresidential (and residential) designs often include needs and functions that require specialized fittings and furniture that may not be available from manufacturers. Such pieces can be custom designed and built to exact specifications. For example, a restaurant design may include a long padded bench (banquette) against a wall, intended for seating with a series of tables. Such pieces must be custom designed and built for a particular set of

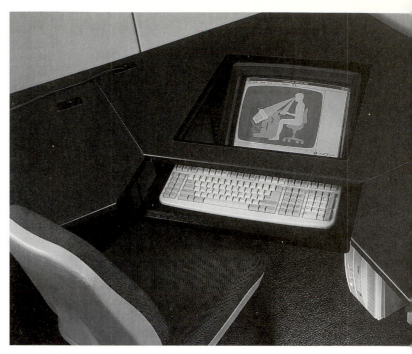

Figure 8.7 *The ergonomic placement of the computer screen encourages upright posture and eliminates normal fatigue.*
Courtesy of Nova.

dimensions—they cannot be ordered from a catalog. Custom designs help establish a distinctive look for an interior because they are one of a kind, created for a unique set of requirements.

Systems Furniture

To meet the challenge of flexibility created by complex and changing needs, product designers have developed systems furniture, manufactured in modules that can be assembled and reassembled in different configurations. The spaces created may be open, private, semiprivate, or a combination. The modules might consist of full- or partial-height panels or divider units to which coat racks, filing cabinets, bookcases, storage bins, writing surfaces, computer stations, work surfaces, drawing surfaces, and drawer units can be attached. The systems can also be integrated with freestanding furniture components. These systems contain all the wiring for task lighting, ambient lighting, telephones, computer links, and electric power. The systems designed for laboratories even provide flexible plumbing connections.

The wide acceptance of systems furniture is the result of its tremendous flexibility. The inflexibility and permanence of wall construction is eliminated by the use of modular dividers and components that define space in much the same way as conventional constructed walls. These modules also allow, with very little effort or disturbance, users to reclaim unused space or space whose designated function has changed. Because of their wide use, manufacturers find it worthwhile to invest in the aesthetic design of modular components; the result is exciting lines of systems furniture with great appeal as well as utility.

Figure 8.8 *Systems furniture provides personal workstations in an open office.*
Courtesy of Herman Miller, Inc.

Ergonomic Superchairs

In today's society many people spend the greater part of their day in work situations where they must be seated. In order to be functional, seating must offer sustained comfort. Consequently, research has led to the design of highly flexible seating pieces. These self-adjusting chairs are designed to sustain and support the human form and to accommodate the body, which is constantly shifting and changing. These chairs absorb the shock of sitting down and support the body in an upright position until the user decides to lean back. When reclining, the chair shifts to transfer body weight from the buttocks to the back, legs, and thighs. The feet remain on the floor as the user tips back, and the back of the chair flexes to provide constant support for the lumbar area. The result is sustained comfort, reduced physical strain, and less muscle fatigue in the lower back. This kind of comfort is a boon to productivity and satisfaction.

Figure 8.9 *The Ergon 2 ® chair features smooth edges that support without restricting circulation, a specially curved back that supports the lower back, and back and seat that are adjustable to height and tilt tension.*
Courtesy of Herman Miller, Inc.

ENVIRONMENTAL CONSIDERATIONS

Tropical Woods

Exotic woods such as mahogany and rosewood grow in tropical rain forests located around the equator in South America, Southeast Asia, and Africa. Tropical rain forests are being destroyed at the rate of fifty to one hundred acres per minute, or forty to fifty million acres per year. Experts say that if that kind of destruction continues unchecked, the rain forests will be gone by the middle of the next century. The use of these woods in furniture is not the principal cause of rain forest destruction; in fact, it may be part of the solution to the problem. The forests are being cut and cleared to make way for agriculture, particularly among poor displaced farmers. The soil on the cleared land cannot sustain many years of crops, however, and the farmers move deeper into the forest cutting, burning, and clearing as they go. Even if no tropical woods were used for furniture, the clearing would still go on.

If sensible programs of harvesting and replacing mature trees can be implemented, the trees will become a cash crop to be nurtured and preserved. The hope is that sensible harvesting would provide a livelihood for those who are now slashing and burning to eke out an existence.[2]

As designers/consumers we can be sympathetic of the problem by selecting wood products that are made with nontropical woods, or by specifying tropical woods that are raised or harvested under controlled environmental conditions of tree plantations or as part of sustainable harvest programs. Suppliers of such products, aware of public support, will clearly label their goods with the source of the wood.

Avoiding Waste

In a general effort to avoid wasteful use of natural resources, it is prudent to use furniture for as long as possible. For example, reupholstering furniture is preferable to discarding it and buying new. Choose pieces with classical styling that can be passed on for generations. Select quality that will last—poorly made furniture will end up in the landfill. In our consumer-oriented society, we seldom stop and think where all the goods we discard will go. The fact is they will not dematerialize, and they must go somewhere. Some manufacturers, particularly of systems furniture, are able to refurbish old lines of furniture to current standards of use and appearance. When you order furniture, specify blanket-wrapping instead of wood and cardboard packing if you can. It will save trees, landfills, and electricity.

Off Gassing

Off gassing is the term used to describe the airing-out process in which fumes from toxic substances used in the manufacture of furniture and carpet are allowed to dissipate.

To prevent toxic off gassing, specify particleboard and plywood without formaldehyde when possible. Also allow twenty-four hours after unpacking for off gassing of systems furniture panels, as you would with carpet.

NOTES

1. Ernest J. McCormick, *Human Factors Engineering* (New York: McGraw-Hill, 1970), 385–87.

2. Kathleen Pray, "Manufacturers Make a Difference," *Perspective* (Fall 1991):16–17.

© Bill Crofton/Nawrocki Stock Photo, Inc.

ARCHITECTURAL DETAIL

Architectural details are permanent features such as stairs, doors, windows, panels, moldings, trim, chimneypieces, fireplaces, and cabinetwork that make interiors distinctive. During a given historic era, certain details were popular and commonly used. The details became typical of the period, and today they are an important key to identifying rooms of a particular era. Now, as in times past, designers and builders choose details to provide an element of finish in an interior, as well as to make the design more interesting and appealing.

WALLS

In common dwellings from many periods, the wall treatment was generally the same as the building materials. For example, Medieval interiors often included a timber framework and stucco infill as a wall treatment. They might also have stone walls left plain, stuccoed with rough plaster, or simply whitewashed. Panels of wood that were joined (fitted together) and carved like furniture were used in the great churches of the Middle Ages. This type of paneling was also used in castles and manor houses as a barrier from the dampness of stone walls and as a form of decoration. This paneling, which usually reached above the level of the doors, was called a *wainscot*. The wood was framed in small vertical panels (approximately one foot by nine inches) that were carved with a motif resembling a stylized piece of folded linen called *linenfold*. Wainscoting in this style was also popular in the Medieval-style interiors of the nineteenth and twentieth centuries. These more recent wainscots were frequently finished at the top with an appealing *plate rail* (a narrow shelf used to display plates).

Figure 9.1 *Linenfold panel.*

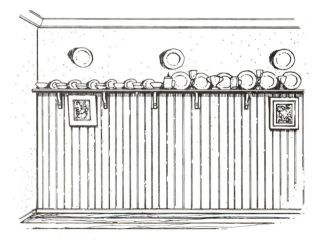

Figure 9.2 *Wainscot with plate rail.*

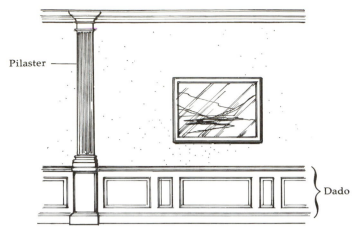

Figure 9.3 *Dado and pilaster.*

The Renaissance brought with it a return to classicism, and the designs of Rome became the basis for most wall detailing. The Roman temple was built with columns resting on a raised podium. The columns supported a complete entablature, including an architrave, frieze, and cornice. During the Renaissance the exterior details of the Roman temple were translated into interior wall details, executed in materials such as wood, plaster, and marble. The podium became the *dado* (the lower portion of a wall set apart by moldings or other treatments). The columns were applied decoratively as flat *pilasters* with appropriate bases and capitals (also treated in a flat manner), and the entablature was interpreted as a series of moldings where the wall meets the ceiling. The spaces between the pilasters were filled with molded panels that varied in size and style. During certain periods the pilasters disappeared, leaving just the simple panels. These basic classical details have been reinterpreted many times in every culture touched by the Renaissance.

Certainly, one of the most popular treatments through the years has been panels of wood. However, the influence of the International style (with its lack of historical ornament) and the rising cost of fine historic detailing have made historic paneling less common. In some historically styled homes and in certain nonresidential settings requiring a traditional feeling, paneled walls are still appropriate.

Wood Paneling

The three most common panel types are traditional, board and batten, and tongue and groove (types of wood, finishes, and joints are discussed in chapter 8, Furniture Selection):

- Traditional *paneling* is made with panels that may be flat, *beveled* (perimeter of panel is cut at an angle to meet the frame), or raised (panel projects beyond the frame). These are framed with *stiles* (vertical part of the frame) and *rails* (horizontal part of the frame). The frames are joined with mortise and tenon or dowel joints. The frame is grooved where the panel and the frame are joined, and a small space is left to allow for expansion and contraction of the panel.

Figure 9.4 *Traditional paneling adds to the historic quality of this room.*
Interior design by Gail and Stephen Huberman. © 1987 Norman McGrath.

‣ *Board and batten* is paneling made from wide vertical boards. The gap between the boards is covered with a one-inch by two-inch strip of wood called a batten. This type of paneling was used in America during the seventeenth century to cover the fireplace wall, creating what was referred to as the *palisade wall*. Reverse board and batten produces an opposite effect of boards with a wide groove between.

Figure 9.5 *Board and batten paneling.*

‣ *Tongue-and-groove* paneling consists of boards *coped* (cut to fit an adjoining piece) with a projecting tongue on one edge that matches and fits into the recessed groove on the opposite edge. The two edges of the board are generally beveled producing a V-shaped groove where the boards meet. The groove hides any irregularities in the thickness of the boards. Inexpensive plywood paneling sheets are produced to imitate the look of genuine tongue-and-groove paneling.[1]

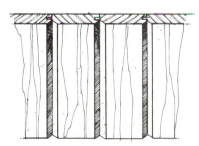

Figure 9.6 *Tongue-and-groove paneling.*

Moldings

Moldings are trims used to create decorative effects. At the same time, they may cover the unfinished ragged edges of the wall left in the construction process. Moldings are frequently made of wood that can be worked easily—most often pine and oak. Mitering the corners (cutting and fitting together the trim at a forty-five-degree angle) allows for a pleasing fit where pieces are joined. Moldings may be stained or painted. When they are painted the same color as the walls, they tend to have less visual importance. When they are painted to contrast with the walls, they become a more dynamic feature of the room. Following is a list of trim types:

- *Base* describes the molding used to finish the wall where it meets the floor. Any workable material, including rubber or plastic, could be used to make a base.

- *Baseboard* designates bases of wood. The base hides any slight irregularities in the level of the floor and keeps the wall from being scuffed by vacuums or other equipment. This trim is sometimes called a mopboard because it protects the wall during cleaning.

- *Chair rail* is a molding placed at the usual height of a chair back to protect the wall from damage. If the section below the rail is paneled, dado fashion, the trim is called a *dado cap*. The portion below the rail is sometimes called a wainscot, although wainscot is a term better used to describe a door-height section of paneling. The height of the chair rail may vary from approximately thirty to thirty-six inches.

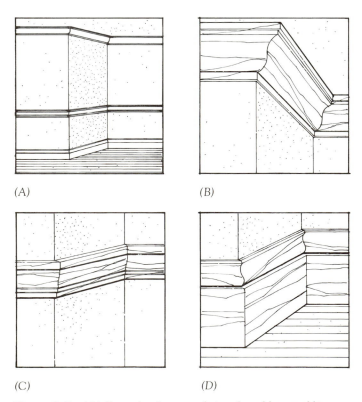

(A)

(B)

(C)

(D)

Figure 9.7 (A) *Example of crown, chair rail, and base molding. Details of* (B) *crown molding,* (C) *chair rail, and* (D) *base.*

- *Crown or bed moldings* are placed where the wall meets the ceiling to add a finishing touch to traditionally styled rooms. They are generally simple; the more complex and ornate ceiling molding is called cornice molding.

- *Cornice moldings* often include decorative ornamentation such as the acanthus leaf, egg and dart, modillions, or dentils.

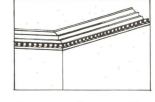

Figure 9.8 *Cornice molding.*

- *Cove molding* is rounded and makes a clean smooth transition from the ceiling to the wall. When ceilings are unusually high, a smaller molding can be attached to the wall below the cove. The ceiling, cove, and wall section can then be painted the same color, and the effect of a lowered ceiling is achieved.

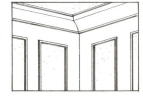

Figure 9.9 *Cove molding.*

A Note of Caution

Moldings are sometimes used to fashion frames on plain walls to give the feeling of traditional panels. This type of treatment requires particular attention to scale in order to prevent the appearance of spindly, tacked-on sticks. If this kind of treatment is done with moldings or combinations of moldings of the proper scale, and if the panels are well proportioned, the effect may be fine.[2]

DOORS

The selection of the right door is important for practical reasons. Major considerations are security against breakage and unlawful entry, upkeep with regard to climate and the amount of wear and tear it will receive, and protection against fire (burn time). Beyond these crucial safety and maintenance factors come the considerations of initial cost and upkeep cost. Upkeep considerations include painting, refinishing, ability to withstand breaking or shattering, for example. The initial cost should be balanced with the upkeep costs. When these considerations are met, aesthetics will be the determining factor in style selection.

The doorway sets the tone of the building. The scale of a large door can inspire awe and indicate the importance of the structure. The captivating doors of London, painted bright "London bus" red, cornflower blue, butter yellow, shiny black, or Georgian green, trimmed with brass hardware, are a striking counterpoint to the white stucco or somber brick of the town houses. They also provide the touch of individuality that a door demands. The doors on the interior of a house serve more common functions but are no less worthy of attention. Interior doors are framed with moldings to conceal the ragged space between the door frame and the wall. Doors are made of wood and several other materials and in several decorative styles. Wooden doors fall into two basic categories: paneled doors and flush doors. Doors are also made of metal, glass, and plastic.

- Traditional *paneled doors* of wood are made in the same manner as traditional wooden wall panels. This type of door consists of wooden stiles and rails that secure the molded panels. This traditional method is rather costly and for a few years was virtually replaced in mass building by flush doors.

Figure 9.10 *Paneled door.*

- *Flush doors,* as the name indicates, are flat with no raised or sunken panels. They are made of wood using two principal methods. The first utilizes a *solid core* of wood, also called *lumber core.* In this type of construction, a thin cross banding (veneer with a horizontal grain) is laminated (glued) to a core of wood blocks that has been framed with rails and stiles. The door is finished with a vertical-grained face veneer. The second type is *hollow core,* which is made with a stile and rail frame filled with a light-weight honeycomb of cardboard and covered with as many as three veneers of thin wood. These doors are not as strong as the lumber-core type, but because they are inexpensive, they are widely used in residential and some non-residential construction.

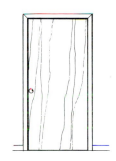
Figure 9.11 *Flush door.*

- Metal doors, once used only for areas with serious security problems, today have become quite acceptable in most settings. They are now made of steel and filled with a core of high-density polystyrene or polyurethane plastic foam, which makes them well insulated. Compared to wooden doors, metal doors are less subject to dimension changes resulting from radical temperature shifts. They can be formed in traditional paneled styles or fitted with panes of glass, and when painted, they are sometimes indistinguishable from wooden doors.

- High-strength tempered glass doors in metal frames (or unframed) are functional because they permit visibility in areas of high traffic and allow passersby to see into areas where products or services are available.

- Glass doors with metal or wooden frames make inviting entrances to patios or balconies or attractive dividers between rooms. When the glass is leaded (smaller pieces held together with lead strips), *beveled* (edges cut at an angle), or stained (colored leaded glass), it creates beautiful effects with light and can be an important decorative feature of the interior. Sliding glass doors have become less popular because they are heavy and difficult to operate. They often develop problems with their glides (sliding tracks) and are also difficult to secure.

Figure 9.12 *Sliding glass door.*

- Molded plastic doors in many designs, including the traditional paneled type, are available today. They may be embossed with a faint wood grain or perfectly smooth. When painted they have the appearance of a wooden door.

There are several other types of doors seen in today's interiors. Among the most important are pocket doors, bifold doors, accordion doors, louvered doors, French doors, Dutch doors, and Shoji screens.

- *Pocket doors* glide on a metal track from which they are suspended. When they are opened, they slide into a recessed pocket in the framing of the wall. They come as a preframed package that is installed during the framing phase of the construction process. They are particularly advantageous in areas where a door that swings open would be in the way.

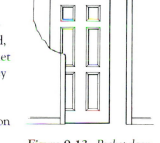
Figure 9.13 *Pocket door.*

- *Bifold* are hinged doors with two sections. One section is anchored on the side, both top and bottom, so that the doors pivot and glide freely. They are kept in place by a small wheel fixed to the top of the unan-chored section that guides the door along a metal track fixed to the top frame of the door. They stack against the *doorjamb* and project slightly into the room when open. They are also used in double configurations with four sections that stack on both sides of wider doors.

Figure 9.14 *Bifold doors.*

• *Accordion doors* are made with narrow panels of wood, metal, or plastic. They fold accordion-style on a track from which they are suspended and stack neatly in a small space. They can be manufactured as tall as sixteen feet and are used to temporarily divide large spaces.

Figure 9.16 *Accordion doors.*

• *Louvered doors* are wooden framed with angled louvers or slats like shutters. Louvered doors allow circulation of air yet still provide visual privacy. They are commonly installed on closets or other spaces where air circulation is advisable. Louvered panels are used on pocket doors, bifold doors, and standard doors.

Figure 9.17 *Louvered doors.*

• *French doors* are double doors similar to paneled doors, but the wooden frames are filled with glass rather than wooden panels. One door is often kept latched in place and the other is used for passage. New French-type doors with one permanently stationary door are frequently replacing sliding glass doors. Called *atrium*, or *patio*, *doors*, they are energy efficient and seal tightly when closed.

Figure 9.18 *French doors.*

• *Dutch doors* break horizontally in two sections so that each can open or shut separately or the two can be latched together into a single door. They may have windows in the top section. Dutch doors were originally designed to admit fresh air through the opening above and to keep out animals by closing below. In nonresidential settings, Dutch doors are used for service areas to keep out unauthorized traffic yet still allow communication or act as a service counter.[3]

Figure 9.19 *Dutch door.*

• *Shoji screens* are Japanese sliding panels made with wooden frames filled with oriental paper (or frosted glass or Plexiglas). A grid is placed on one or both sides to divide the screen into panes that resemble traditional windows. The grids can be simple rectangles or quite complex and ingenious in their design. They were used like sliding walls as dividers in the traditional Japanese house and are used today in some Western interiors for the same purpose or for a purely decorative effect (see also chapter 10, Wall, Window, Ceiling, and Treatments).

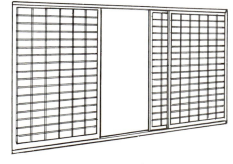

Figure 9.20 *Shoji screens.*

WINDOWS

Windows are two-way objects. Through them we look out at the world and the world looks in at us. The placement of windows is not only important to the wall composition of the interior but largely determines the fenestration (architectural arrangement of windows)—a crucial part of the style and character of the exterior. Some major considerations in the selection and placement of windows follow:

- Security. Windows are the easiest point of unlawful entry; the greater the quantity and the more accessible and poorly lit the windows are on the exterior, the greater that risk.

- Orientation and solar gain. Where solar gain is desirable, windows should be most plentiful on the south of the building, the least plentiful on the north. Limiting their number, strategically placing them, and protecting against bright sun on the east and the west orientations are imperative. Light is clearest and most steady from the north, most warm and constant on the south, clearest and brightest on the east, and most colored and hottest on the west.

- Quantity of light desired. Great quantities of light can be healthful to mind and body, yet when accompanied by heat and glare, light can be emotionally and physically unhealthful. Too much light and heat without window treatment protection can also be damaging to interior furnishings.

- The view. Windows should be planned to frame any pleasant view. The view can serve to visually expand space and bring the exterior into the interior as an extension of the design.

- Privacy. The location, the height of the wall, and the number of windows can largely determine the amount of privacy afforded the occupant. Windows high in the wall give greater privacy, as do smaller windows.

- Interior window treatments—type and budget. Windows should be covered unless there is no need for privacy, light and glare control, and energy conservation against heat and cold. Large expanses of windows make this consideration a costly one.

There are few architectural details that can compare in elegance to beautifully designed windows. The exquisite Federal-style fanlight with its delicate *tracery*, and the boldly handsome Palladian window (fig. 9.22), are treasured features of many older buildings. They represent the finest of historic architectural development. Like doors, windows are trimmed in appropriately styled moldings to complete their finished appearance.

Windows have evolved from crude openings draped with animal skins to Medieval leaded panes to large Late Renaissance windows to the glass houses of the twentieth century. Not surprisingly, glass has been an important part of that evolution. Setting the glass in place is called *glazing* and can be done with one or more sheets of glass.

- A single layer of glass is called *single glazing*.

- *Double glazing,* or *thermal pane,* is two sheets of glass sandwiched in a frame to deter heat and/or cold transfer.

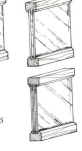

Figure 9.21 *Single, double, and triple glazing.*

- Energy efficiency can be further enhanced with the addition of a third sheet of glass to produce *triple glazing*. These are often winter *storm windows* or tinted or summer windows that act like sunglasses on the window in hot climates.

Windows that can be opened mechanically or by hand are termed *operable*. The obvious advantage to operable windows is their ability to admit fresh air. Certain types of operable windows also offer the advantage of being easy to clean because both inside and outside glass surfaces can be reached from the inside. *Fixed*, stationary, or inoperable windows are used where ventilation is unnecessary or undesirable, where the window is out of reach, or where a view is to be framed without being interrupted by a divider bar. Fixed windows are also easier to fabricate and less expensive because they have no moving parts.

Windows are made in a wide range of types. Each type is appropriate to a historic style or to a functional purpose. Following are common window types:

- Arched and round windows (fig. 9.23) have been appreciated for centuries. The *Palladian window*, previously mentioned, is an arched window with two lower sidelights framed with classical columns, pilasters, and moldings. The *fanlight* is also an elliptic arch form of the Neoclassic era. Round *porthole* windows were especially popular during the Victorian era and may be seen in some vintage houses. Hexagonal windows are six-sided variations of the rounded window. Contemporary architecture utilizes many arched and rounded windows because we still appreciate their beauty and the relief they give to the straight lines of architecture.

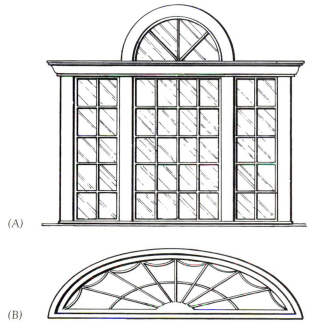

(A)

(B)

Figure 9.22 (A) *Palladian window.* (B) *Federal-style elliptic fanlight.*

Figure 9.23 *Round porthole window.*

Figure 9.24 *Awning window.*

- *Awning windows* are hinged on the top to swing outward at an angle like an awning. They may be stacked or grouped in horizontal bands along a high wall, clerestory fashion, for privacy. They may also be used as the bottom component in a sashlike window or other window arrangement. They have the advantage of being able to remain open in a rainstorm.

- *Bay and bow windows* are projecting windows. The bay is *canted* (angular) or projects straight out, and the bow is a curved projection. Bay and bow windows are attractive features on a building. They add extra space to the interior, as well as admit light. They may, however, be costly to drape because they require custom drapery rods.

- *Casement windows* are sidehinged, swinging windows. They are an important historical style popular in many countries. Double French *casement windows* are generally two panes wide and vary in height. Casement windows are also used as operable sections beside large fixed picture windows. They have great appeal because they provide maximum ventilation, and if they swing out, they keep the interior free for draperies or other window treatments. Apart from their functional aspects, casement windows are usually attractive and charming.

- The clerestory was the highest story in the Gothic church, and today, *clerestory windows* are still those that are set high in the wall. These windows may be for light only or for light and ventilation. They may be of almost any style; it is their location at the top of the wall that makes them clerestory. They provide a clear, even light that is pleasant in most interiors.

Figure 9.25 *Bay window.*

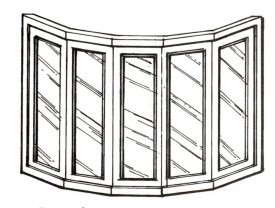

Figure 9.26 *Bow window.*

Figure 9.27 *French casement window.*

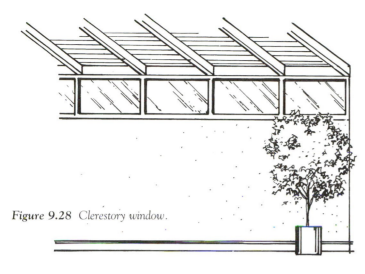

Figure 9.28 *Clerestory window.*

Figure 9.30 *Greenhouse window.*

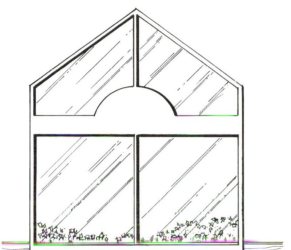

Figure 9.29 *Cathedral window.*

Figure 9.31 *Jalousie window.*

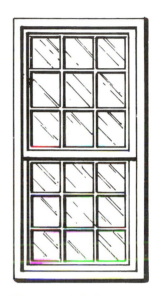

Figure 9.32 *Sash window (nine over nine).*

- *Cathedral windows* are angled, **A**-frame windows that follow the pitch of a vaulted ceiling. They embody a strong architectural quality that makes them particularly well suited to contemporary interiors. They work best in settings with pleasant views where no window coverings are necessary.

- The *greenhouse window* is a projecting glass box used to catch the sun's rays. Some may be just large enough to fill a kitchen window and others may be room sized. Like botanical greenhouses, they are ideal for plants; the room-sized version can also be a favored spot for dining and relaxing. They can also be designed as sun rooms with hot tubs, spas, or comfortable areas for conversation and relaxation.

- The *jalousie window* is made with a set of louvered slats that tilt open and closed. The principal benefit of this window is the ability to provide ventilation while restricting entrance of rain. The name is French for jealousy, and a wooden blind, slatted like the jalousie window, may have allowed jealous lovers to see in without being seen.

- The *sash window* is made with two window panels designed to slide up and down in a vertical channel of the window frame. These may be larger, single sheets of glass or divided into several smaller panes. The smaller paned windows were designated historically by the number of lights (panes) in each panel; for example, twelve over twelve indicates twelve panes in the top frame and twelve in the bottom, and six over six indicates six above and six below. A *single-hung sash* window has an operable lower window that can be raised and lowered. In the *double-hung sash* window, both sashes are operable, allowing good circulation of air. Cooler air enters through the lower opening, and warm air rises out through the top. The traditional sash window, divided into smaller panes, is a classic. Those that are well proportioned and well built add a clear note of distinction to traditionally styled houses. Because they are so popular, manufacturers have been experimenting with new methods of fabrication. Some have designed wooden grids that fit over a single pane, giving the

(A)

(B)

Figure 9.33 *The ballroom at a historic Louisiana house, Nottaway, is rich with architectural detail (A and B), including beautiful full-length, nine-over-nine sash windows.*
Both © Mathias Oppersdorf/Photo Researchers, Inc.

appearance of individual panes. The grid can easily be removed and then snapped back into the frame, making it easier to wash the windows. Others have placed metal grids between two panes of glass to create the impression of panes. The traditional framing method, with individually framed panes, is called a *true divider* system.

› A *sidelight* is a narrow window next to a door. A pair of sidelights is used to flank a door. A *transom* is a window above a door. Arched windows above a door are called fanlights. In older buildings, operable transoms were often used between rooms to improve air circulation.

› *Skylights* are custom-installed or prefabricated units mounted in the roof and ceiling to bring natural light into interiors that have no direct access to windows and would otherwise be dark. The skylight is made of glass, plastic, or Plexiglas.

Figure 9.34 *Sidelights and transom.*

Figure 9.36 *Attic window.*

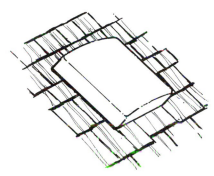

Figure 9.35 *Skylight.*

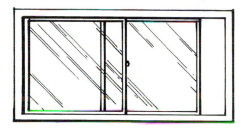

Figure 9.37 *Sliding window.*

- *Attic windows* are operable pivoting windows placed in an angled roof in lieu of dormers. They are less expensive than framing a dormer and admit more light. They are being utilized in new construction and remodeling projects where unused attic space is being transformed into living or working space.

- *Sliding windows* are technically the same as sash windows. However, the aluminum-framed windows that are used so frequently today are usually referred to as sliding rather than sash. These may slide vertically or horizontally and may also be a single operable panel of a larger window. Sliding windows may also be framed in wood or vinyl-clad wood as well as aluminum.

STAIRS

During the Middle Ages, stairs were tucked into tiny turrets (towers) or hidden between walls. In the Renaissance the stairway became more imposing, and by the eighteenth century it was often a dramatic focal point of the house. These same choices govern the design of stairs today. They may be functional and

unobtrusive or a very dramatic part of the design. Stairs often have some romantic associations, such as sliding down banisters or hiding on stairways decked with pine bows to sneak an early peek on Christmas morning. They may conjure up mental pictures of a grand entry on the night of a first date or of children watching and listening from an upstairs landing as guests arrive for a party. Stairways can be a beautiful and exciting part of an interior. Because the components from which they are assembled may be unfamiliar, they are listed, defined, and illustrated as follows:

- The *stringer* is the diagonal, notched structural piece that supports and gives form to the stair. On the completed stair, these structural stringers do not appear because they are usually covered by the treads and risers. On the finished stair, the diagonal molding on the wall next to the steps is also called a stringer.

- *Treads* are the flat, horizontal pieces on which the feet step when going up or down a stair.

- *Nosing* is the rounded edge of the tread. The nosing makes the stair less sharp and dangerous. It also prevents carpet on the stair from wearing against a sharp edge.

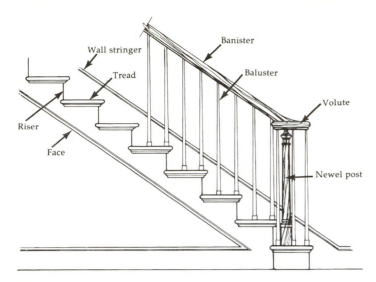

Figure 9.38 *Stairway components.*

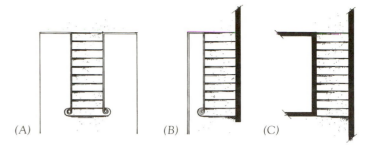

Figure 9.39 *Stair forms. (A) Open stair (no walls). (B) Semihoused stair (wall on one side). (C) Closed stair (enclosed by walls).*

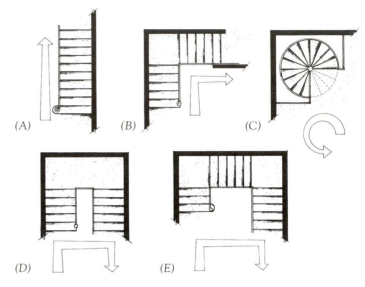

Figure 9.40 *Stair forms. (A) Straight-run stair. (B) One-turn stair (with landing). (C) Spiral staircase. (D)* U*-stair (with one landing). (E) Double-turn stair (with two landings).*

- The *riser* is the vertical member between the treads. It is the riser that acts as a toe kick as we ascend the staircase. In certain designs the riser is omitted, creating an *open riser stair*. Some people feel nervous and insecure on open riser stairs because they may not appear solid.

- The *starting step* is the first step of the stair. It is often *bullnosed* (with a rounded curve) on the open end to support a newel post.

- *Landings* are the intermediate platforms on a stair (often where they turn) or the area at the bottom and top of the stair. These are important because they allow the stair to turn and because they make the stair safer. Those who have difficulty climbing stairs are able to rest on the landing. The landing also provides exciting design possibilities—it makes a perfect place for a beautiful window.

- The *handrail* or banister is the piece that follows the pitch of the stair and is held by the hand. *Easements* are the short bends that allow for a change of direction in the handrail. A *volute* is the spiral or scroll end of the handrail that rests on the newel post. Handrails may be the traditional carved type, or they can be formed with metal pipes, tubes, flat pieces of wood or metal, or any device that is compatible with the design of the stair.

- The *baluster* is the vertical member that supports the handrail. In traditional stairways the balusters are usually turned wood. However, they could also be bent metal, square wooden pieces, or panels of glass.

- The *newel post* is a larger baluster that supports or receives the handrail at critical points of the stair, such as the starting step, the landing, and the top of the stair. The design of the newel post can be elaborate or simple. Victorian newel posts were often massive and highly decorative. The balusters, handrail, and newel posts together make a *balustrade*, or railing.

- The *stairwell* is the open space in which the stair is set. Its shape and size will vary with the design of the stair.[4]

Stairs may take several different forms. The most common forms are listed here.

- A stair whose sides are not attached to any wall is termed an *open stair*.

- A *semihoused stair* is connected to the wall on one side and open on the other.

- A stairway with walls on both sides is called a *closed or housed stair*.

- A straight stairway without any turns is said to have a *straight run*.

- A stairway that turns ninety degrees at a landing is a *one-turn stair*.

- A *double-turn stair* makes two ninety-degree turns at two separate landings.

- A U*-stair* turns 180 degrees at a single landing.

- A *spiral staircase* twists around a central axis like a corkscrew. This type of stair takes the least amount of space but is often difficult to negotiate and makes moving furniture extremely difficult.

- A *curved stairway* may be open or semihoused and is graceful and dramatic.

Figure 9.41   A charming curved staircase in a New Orleans courtyard.
© Steve Castagneto/International Stock Photo.

FIREPLACES AND CHIMNEYPIECES

The fireplace is another detail often associated with pleasant memories. The leap and flicker of constantly changing flames and the crackle of the burning wood create a mood of warmth; the memory of a chilly winter evening by a fire with family or friends is pleasant.

For thousands of years, fire was the only source of heat in buildings. During the Middle Ages, when someone discovered that a hole in the wall with a hood could siphon the smoke from a fire, the design significance of the fireplace was instantly elevated. Before that, the fire had been built in a pit in the floor and the smoke escaped through cracks or vents in the roof. The hood provided new possibilities for design. Because it was a source of warmth, the fireplace was the logical focal point in the room, and designers lavished it with attention. Through the years, the basic technology of the fireplace has changed very little. It is the design of the decorative *chimneypiece* that has changed the most. Each new period saw changes in the style of the chimneypiece that gave the fireplace the proper character for its surroundings. The projecting shelf of a chimneypiece is called a *mantel*.

Figure 9.42   This flush-face fireplace is the focal point at this historic room at Filoli.

Upholstered furniture, textiles by and photo courtesy of Brunschwig & Fils/Peter Vitale, photographer.

A fire requires fuel, heat, and oxygen. As it burns, the fire consumes oxygen, which creates a draft as more air is drawn in to feed the fire that warms the air. The fireplace works on the principle that warm air rises, drawing the smoke off as it ascends and radiating some heat into the room. The rising air creates a suction that also pulls air from the room. As the intensity of the fire dies, it begins to suck precious warm air from the room. To keep the warm air in the house from escaping, it is necessary to close the front of the fireplace with glass or metal doors.

The fireplace is made of several components.

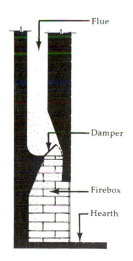

- The *hearth* is the noncombustible slab that forms the base for the fire and projects into the room to prevent embers or sparks from charring the floor.

- The *firebox* contains the fire and is built of masonry or metal on top of the hearth.

Figure 9.43
Fireplace components.

- The *surround* is the noncombustible piece that frames the opening of the firebox. It is frequently made of tile, marble, or other stone.

- The *flue* is the chimney pipe that is separated from the firebox by a movable *damper* that controls the flow of air and escape of smoke.

- *Zero-clearance fireplace units* are self-contained units with triple-insulated walls that allow placement in walls without firebrick or masonry.

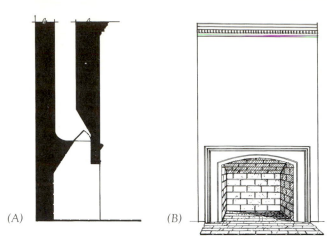

(A)   (B)

Figure 9.44 *Flush-face fireplace.* (A) *Side cutaway section view.*
(B) *Front view elevation.*

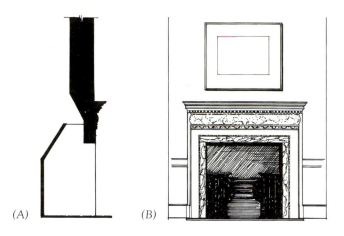

(A)   (B)

Figure 9.45 *Projecting fireplace.* (A) *Side cutaway section view.*
(B) *Front view elevation.*

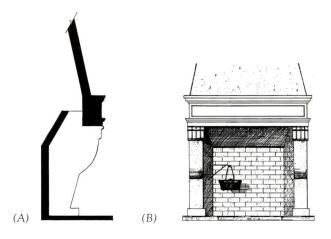

(A)   (B)

Figure 9.46 *Hooded fireplace.* (A) *Side cutaway section view.* (B)
Front view elevation.

Fireplaces can be built in any form—imagination and function are the only real restrictions. However, the most common
types are flush-face, projecting, hooded, corner, raised, freestanding, and stoves.

- The *breast* (face) of the *flush-face fireplace* is even, or flush,
  with the plane of the surrounding wall. Because the flush-
  face tends to be less decorative, it is well suited to contemporary interiors where it often consists of a surround and a
  simple molding. Several historically styled fireplaces are
  also flush-faced with or without a mantel.

- The breast of a *projecting fireplace* projects into the room,
  forming a mantel. This type is adaptable to clean contemporary versions as well as more decorative historical types.

- A *hooded fireplace* incorporates a projecting hood that
  may be formed in nearly any shape, from rounded to
  angled to boxlike. This was the first type of fireplace to
  be built during the late Middle Ages and early Renaissance. These were large-scaled, fanciful designs
  ornamented with Gothic tracery or classical columns.
  Smaller, less ornate versions were also common in
  provincial houses well after the Renaissance.

- The *corner fireplace* is located in the corner of a room; it
  may have a hood or may be built like a standard fireplace. Because they cut off the corner of a room, corner
  fireplaces often have inherent problems of balance and
  line and may present challenges in furniture placement.
  Corner fireplaces are a feature of the Southwest adobe
  houses where they form a pleasing, smooth, rounded
  extension of the walls.[5]

- Many fireplaces are designed with a *raised hearth* in front
  of the firebox. The raised hearth may be built just in front
  of the firebox or may extend the entire length of the wall.
  With a raised hearth, the firebox is elevated so it can be
  seen more easily through the furniture grouping that often
  surrounds a fireplace. The raised hearth requires less stoop-
  ing and has the added advantage of making the fireplace
  easier to fuel and clean. This type of hearth also provides a
  nice place to sit next to the warmth of the fire.

Figure 9.47 *Corner fireplace in a Southwest adobe home.*

- A *freestanding fireplace* is a metal unit or other fireplace that is placed in the room away from the wall, with the flue or chimney pipe exposed. The fireplace unit may be placed on a raised platform or may rest at floor level. The freestanding fireplace is less popular today than stoves, which are similar in concept but far more efficient.

- Until the advent of central heating, the pot-bellied stove was a standard fixture in homes, churches, schools, and stores in every part of the country. Today, in areas with cold winters, *stoves* are being used again in some homes. Stoves are generally freestanding units placed in front of a noncombustible wall with clearance between the wall and stove. Fireplaces can also be fitted with enclosed stove units called *fireplace inserts* for more efficient use of fuel and little loss of warmed house air. Some stoves and fireplace inserts are designed with forced-air systems that can heat most of a medium-sized house. These draw air from outside; the air is warmed by the stove then forced by a fan into the house, creating positive pressure. When a vent or window at the opposite end of the house is opened slightly, the warm air will be drawn to that part of the house. A fresh air intake pipe to the stove will eliminate drafts caused by combustion.

CEILINGS

Ceilings are literally the crowning glory of a room. For example, the great hammer-beam ceilings of Early Renaissance England—with their Tudor arch-shaped trusses supported on magnificently carved brackets—are awe inspiring. And the delicate-patterned plaster ceilings, designed by Robert Adam in eighteenth-century England, are still beautiful examples of the importance a ceiling design can have in a room. Today, we have a vast selection of ceiling materials and types from which to choose. Ceilings may be decorative or structural and may even serve the important function of covering, yet providing access to, mechanical systems located in the ceiling. Ceilings can provide dramatic changes in plane or space. A low cozy fireplace area can suddenly open to the main body of the room that soars to the rafters. Angled ceilings are interesting because of the variety of line and form they create. Ceilings can be formed in many ways. (The materials used to cover ceilings are discussed in chapter 10, Wall, Ceiling, and Window Treatments.) The most common types of ceilings are the plain flat, vaulted, domed, coffered, and coved (baffled and suspended ceilings are discussed later under Nonresidential Considerations).

Figure 9.49 *A barrel-vaulted ceiling in this contemporary hotel adds to the quality of space.*
Photo courtesy of Victor Huff Partnership/Karl Francetic, photographer.

- The simplest type of ceiling is flat plaster or Sheetrock. This plain treatment is ideal when the intent of the design is to emphasize other areas of the room. The flat ceiling may be embellished with textured plaster, raised patterns, moldings, or medallions, which may be painted to harmonize or contrast with the

Figure 9.48
Anaglypta.

ceiling. These are called *anaglypta*, which is the Greek word for raised ornament. Today, anaglypta patterns are frequently made of hardened plastic foam.

- A *vault* is a ceiling constructed on the principle of an arch. Therefore, a vaulted ceiling may be round (a barrel vault) or pointed like the Gothic church ceiling. In today's interiors, the tall, open, cathedral ceiling belongs to this group. Rooms with barrel-vaulted ceilings often have rounded ends with half-domed ceilings called *niches*.

- *Cathedral ceilings* are pointed with two slopes. Those with one slope are *shed* ceilings. These can be exciting because of the way they open up the space. A relatively small room with a high ceiling feels much larger than it actually is. Large spaces such as churches or buildings with tall atriums are impressive.

Figure 9.50   *This inviting retreat features a rustic beamed ceiling.*
© *Lisl Dennis.*

‣ *Domes* are bowl-shaped, rounded ceilings. When the dome covers a drum-shaped (round) room, the space is called a *rotunda*. Domes may be quite flat and dish-shaped or deep and high. Because its form is the shape of the heavens, the dome draws the eye upward and creates a feeling of expanse. In public spaces such as capitol buildings, the dome creates spaces of great dignity and grandeur. In a residence, a shallow recessed dome in an entry or dining room expands the visual space.

‣ *Beamed ceilings* frankly expose the rafters or trusses as a decorative feature of a room. They can be very simple and rough or richly carved or painted. Beams can impart a provincial or rustic feeling to an environment. The buildings of the Southwest incorporate large pine beams called *vigas* (see chapter 15, Historic Design) as structural support for the smaller cross beams, called *latillas*, which form the ceiling. Logs add a rugged feeling to cabins and ski lodges in any geographic setting. Squared, finely finished hardwood beams trimmed with molding are favored in rich traditional interiors such as

law offices, libraries, and luxury housing. Since buildings are generally no longer made of timbers, these will usually be false beams used just for their effect. Metal trusses are left exposed in some of today's designs because, like their wooden counterparts from earlier times, they have interest and strength as design forms.

‣ *Coffers* are decorative boxes constructed in the recesses between beams and cross beams. Some of the most magnificent *coffered ceilings* were built in France during the Renaissance.

Figure 9.51
Coffered ceiling.

‣ *Coved ceilings* are formed with a curved radius or straight angle where the wall meets the ceiling. This is accomplished by actually structuring the ceiling in that fashion or by the application of cove moldings. The absence of a sharp right angle has a softening effect on the room.

Figure 9.52 *This reception area shows custom cabinetry organized for efficiency.*

© 1988 Norman McGrath.

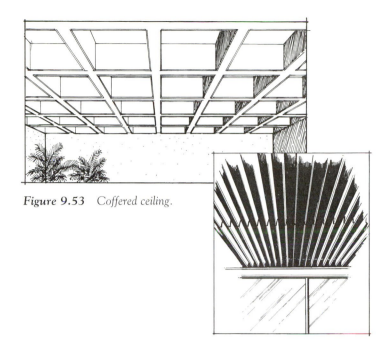

Figure 9.53 *Coffered ceiling.*

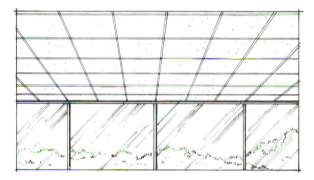

Figure 9.54 *Baffled ceiling.*

Figure 9.55 *Suspended ceiling.*

CABINETWORK

Cabinetwork, or *cabinetry,* is finished interior woodwork such as shelves and cabinets. Those who custom build freestanding and built-in units are called *finish carpenters.* Cabinetwork is manufactured in two basic ways. Cabinets can be mass-produced on an assembly line in standard sizes or crafted to custom specifications in large or small woodworking shops by skilled finish carpenters. These units are brought to the site as components and installed, fitted, and trimmed with molding.

Mass-produced cabinetwork is installed wherever standard sizes will fit the space and where a tight budget demands economy. Prefabricated units may be purchased at home improvement stores and builder supply houses.

Custom pieces are planned by the designer and executed by the *cabinetmaker* or finish carpenter; for example, custom cabinetwork is seen in living/dining rooms, kitchens, bathrooms, laundry rooms, and sewing areas of luxury homes. One area of the home where custom cabinetwork is particularly impressive is the home office, study, den, or library. Custom details make these interiors more individual, distinctive, and functional.

NONRESIDENTIAL CONSIDERATIONS

Many of the details used in residential design are the same as those in nonresidential design. However, the following details are more common to nonresidential design:

- Today, coffered ceilings are formed when concrete is poured over inverted "pans" or forms in such a way that when the concrete has set and the pans have been removed from below, a wafflelike pattern of coffers is produced. This process is called concrete slab construction.

- A *baffled ceiling* is hung with wooden or metal slats or fabric banners. These are installed in parallel or grid patterns that act as a screen for the lighting system and also serve as an acoustic treatment. The fabric banners provide an excellent opportunity to add color and texture. The wooden and metal slats also create patterns that add an interesting quality to the environment.

- *Suspended ceilings* are metal grid systems hung from the superstructure of the building with wires. The *plenum,* or space between the grid and the building structure above, contains ducts for the HVAC (heating, ventilation, and air-conditioning) system, as well as plumbing and electrical systems (see chapter 14, Building Systems). The grids are filled with acoustic panels that can be removed and replaced, allowing easy access to the equipment above the ceiling. Lighting systems, sound systems, sprinkler systems, smoke detectors, and vents for the HVAC system are often integrated with the suspended ceiling.

- Custom cabinetwork is extremely common in nonresidential design. For example, the reception desk in a hotel must be designed to fit the physical and aesthetic requirements of the project. The same is true of a nurse's station in a hospital or the cashier/host station in a restaurant. All of these kinds of pieces are custom designed and manufactured.

NOTES

1. J. Rosemary Riggs, *Materials and Components of Interior Design*, 3d ed. (Englewood Cliffs, N.J.: Prentice-Hall, 1989), 88.

2. Sherrill Whiton, *Interior Design and Decoration* (Philadelphia: Lippincott, 1974), 420–26.

3. Riggs, *Materials and Components of Interior Design*, 3d ed. (Englewood Cliffs, N.J.: Prentice-Hall, 1989), 113–16.

4. Architectual Woodwork Institute, *Architectural Woodwork Quality Standards, Guide Specifications and Quality Certification Program* (Arlington, Va.: Architectural Woodwork Institute, 1984), 77.

5. Riggs, *Materials and Components of Interior Design* (Reston, Va.: Reston, 1989), 153, 157.

WALL, CEILING, AND WINDOW TREATMENTS

© Jessie Walker.

CHART 10.1 WALL AND CEILING MATERIALS—AN OVERVIEW

MATERIALS AND CONSIDERATIONS IN THEIR SELECTION

Brick Heavy, hard, costly material, expensive to install. Lasts indefinitely and is structurally handsome. No upkeep.

Concrete Heavy, hard building blocks or cast slabs. Can be painted or left natural gray or colored before casting. Cold to the eye and touch. Moderate cost of material; can be costly to install. No upkeep unless painted.

Cork Very lightweight, flexible, sound absorbent; costly material but moderate installation. Handsome and subtle appearance. Easy upkeep.

Fabric Flexible, sound absorbent, three-dimensional; can carry out a fabric scheme by coordinating with other furnishing fabrics. Several methods and styles of applications. Can be changed at will. Cost of fabric varies from low to high; installation is moderate. Easy upkeep.

Glass Architectural glass (windows), glass block, stained glass used as transparent or translucent building materials. Can be very structural and moderately to very decorative. Costs vary from moderate to expensive.

Upkeep varies according to use and environment. *Glass tile* requires little upkeep, but cost is high as an imported item. Fiberglass is used in tub surrounds and is costly. Upkeep requires nonabrasive cleaners.

Metal Aluminum, brass, bronze, copper, stainless steel, and tin are costly to purchase and install. Effects are rich whether structural or decorative. Permanent material. Upkeep depends on finishes and location or use; most require little or no upkeep.

Paint The least expensive of the wall treatments, but it must be applied over a prepared, rigid surface such as sheetrock or wood. Color range and effects are unlimited, and paint can be reapplied at will. Paint can imitate many materials, such as marble and wood. Professional painting services are costly. Upkeep depends on the use, environment, and type of paint used.

Plaster Versatile, from very smooth to very rough (*stucco*). Can be cast into decorative anaglypta moldings and ornament to

---

WALL AND CEILING MATERIALS

Materials in use today for walls and ceilings come from a variety of sources, both natural and fabricated. Although many of the materials used on walls and ceilings can also be used on floors, there are many others that are appropriate only for walls and ceilings. Wall and ceiling materials may be hard and rigid, flexible or soft. Their weight can vary from heavy to light. Just about the only restriction for materials used on walls is the limitation of the imagination—if it can be envisioned, it can be installed. In this chapter, we will examine the materials used for walls, ceilings, and window coverings. Chart 10.1 provides an overview of the selection of materials typically used.

Making the Right Choice

It is evident from charts 10.1 and 10.2 and the information that follows that there are many selections for wall and ceiling coverings. Making the right choice can be a difficult dilemma. Some of the following guidelines may simplify the choices:

‣ Generally, hard materials will echo and reflect or amplify more sound; flexible and soft materials will absorb sound.

‣ Permanently installed materials will initially cost more but may be the least costly in the long run because they require no finishes, replacement, or upkeep. These include natural materials such as stone, wood, tile, and brick. The time frame of occupancy must also be a factor in selecting permanent materials. A long occupation can justify the costs, whereas frequent moves will not.

‣ Interiors need to be flexible for change. Shifts in the lifestyles of occupants will benefit from flexible materials that can be replaced, such as paint, wall coverings, or fabric.

‣ Pattern on the walls will lock in a style or color scheme and can be restrictive if the pattern becomes tiresome and dated before the owners are willing (due to financial or environmental concerns) to change the scheme.

‣ Upkeep is a major consideration where there is limited time for cleaning or where traffic or youngsters would tend to soil, mark, or damage the wall surfaces.

‣ Authenticity and ambience or style are factors in selecting wall materials. The reproduction of a period room or the general look or feeling or level of formality will largely dictate the actual surface and visual texture as well as the pattern. Sensitivity to the need for unity is paramount in selecting wall materials.

‣ The size of the space can be a determining factor in wall material selection. Heavy textures, large patterns, and dark or intense colors will close in spaces, making them appear smaller. Likewise, smooth or subtle textures, small patterns, and light or dull colors will visually expand the space.

‣ The purpose or function of the interior will determine the durability of wall material choices. Heavily used areas need impervious materials; little-used areas can accommodate more fragile treatments. High levels of humidity or moisture in the air or smoke and fumes or airborne oils or dirt may dictate nonabsorbent materials.

HARD OR RIGID WALL MATERIALS

Most materials that are hard or rigid will be *permanent installations* and, as such, have some common characteristics. They will usually be costly to purchase and to install and will often require little or no upkeep, depending on the finish or character of the surface. Hard or rigid materials can be very beautiful because of their inherent natural texture or pattern, and many have withstood the test of time and are considered classic wall and ceiling treatments. Examples include the rough-hewn beams, stone walls, and rough stucco walls seen in many rustic, provincial, or country settings. Smooth paneling, molding, and smooth or cast plaster have served more formal interiors throughout every period of history. Metal, smooth stone such as marble or travertine, and glass are choices for interiors where glamour, drama, or sleek sophistication is sought. Chart 10.2 presents details on each type of hard or rigid wall and ceiling materials and includes a description of the material, its applications, the required *maintenance*, special considerations, and the cost structure.[1]

document a particular period. Cost is moderate; upkeep depends on the type of paint or finish the plaster is given.

Stone Fieldstone, flagstone, *granite, marble,* and *travertine* are all heavy, costly materials that are also expensive to install. Structural or decorative effects, but all with natural beauty and little or no upkeep. Lasts indefinitely.

Cultured stone (imitation onyx and marble) is used for tub and shower surrounds and countertops or cabinet tops. Lightweight; moderate cost; requires nonabrasive cleansers.

Tile *Acoustical tile* absorbs sound. Set into a ceiling grid framework; lightweight; decorative or structural; moderate cost, no upkeep—tiles that become stained are replaced or painted.

Ceramic, quarry, Mexican, and *mosaic tile* installations are heavy and costly in terms of material and labor to install. Permanent material, they require little or no upkeep. Tile is also popular in kitchens, bathing or hot tub areas as a countertop or cabinet-top material.

Wallboard Sheetrock, masonite, wood paneling, particleboard—all come in sheet form to cover large areas and are referred to as *plasterboard* or *drywall. Sheetrock (gypsumboard)* is the most common wall and ceiling material and requires painting or wall coverings. Moderate material and installation cost. Upkeep depends on finish methods and materials.

Wall coverings A variety of paper, vinyl, or cloth products that come in rolls or bolts. Subtle and structural to very decorative patterned effects. Low to moderate cost of goods, moderate installation costs. Upkeep depends on final layer (fabric, paper, vinyl) and placement and use. Generally little or no upkeep.

Wood and Wood moldings, planks, paneling—wood is costly to purchase but modest to install. Wood has lasting beauty. It can be stained, sealed, or painted. Little or no upkeep.

Figure 10.1 *A painted brick wall forms an interesting backdrop for this contemporary bedroom.*
Courtesy of Better Homes and Gardens, member of Home Furnishings Council.

CHART 10.2 RIGID WALL AND CEILING MATERIALS

BRICK

DESCRIPTION

Clay, shale, and water mixed and shaped into solid or hollow rectangular blocks, then baked or fired to harden. Brick is colored according to the clay used (red is most typical) or the dyes added before firing. Brick used for constructing walls is typically seven to eight inches long by three to four inches wide and two to three inches thick.

APPLICATIONS

Interior and exterior walls and fireplace surrounds, vaulted or arched ceilings, residential and nonresidential.

MAINTENANCE

Low upkeep—dust or use a mild soap and water solution. Often no upkeep whatsoever is required.

SPECIAL CONSIDERATIONS

Brick can be treated with a sealant such as polyurethane that will prevent the brick from absorbing oil-based spills.

COST STRUCTURE

Moderate to high.

CORK

DESCRIPTION

The outer layer of the oak tree of the birch family that grows in the Mediterranean area. It is light in color, elastic, and very insulative. It is resilient and may be treated with a vinyl coating, making it more durable. It is sound absorbent.

APPLICATIONS

Residential and nonresidential settings where a quiet, clean surface is required.

MAINTENANCE

Dust or wipe with a damp cloth.

SPECIAL CONSIDERATIONS

Due to its insulative properties, cork should not be used where solar gain is desired. It will absorb bumps well but can be broken off and is very difficult or impossible to repair.

COST STRUCTURE

Moderate to high.

CONCRETE BLOCK AND SLAB

DESCRIPTION

Large porous bricks made of concrete with air pockets that make the material lightweight enough to handle and also make it somewhat fragile during handling. Poured slabs of concrete form walls and can be relatively smooth or very rusticated or brutalistic.

APPLICATIONS

Walls, some nonresidential ceilings.

MAINTENANCE

Little or no maintenance. Concrete block surfaces are usually painted, then treated as any porous painted surface. Concrete slabs are almost never painted but are used as a frank and structural building material.

SPECIAL CONSIDERATIONS

May be used for an exterior building material; then it must be sealed against water permeation.

COST STRUCTURE

Low to moderate, although installation or labor to install is high.

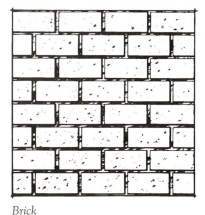

Brick

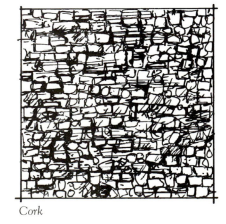

Cork

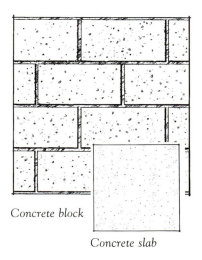

Concrete block

Concrete slab

continued

CHART 10.2 RIGID WALL AND CEILING MATERIALS *continued*

ARCHITECTURAL GLAZING

DESCRIPTION

Transparent or translucent brittle material of molten sand, potash, lime, and perhaps metal oxides for color or for reflecting and screening properties. Flawless glass is made by the float-glass process (extruded and suspended onto a flat liquid); other methods include rolled, calendered, and cast glass, which may be textured, patterned, or colored.

APPLICATIONS

Window glazing, curtain wall construction (glass walls over a steel skeleton frame), both residential and nonresidential; interior office walls and dividers.

MAINTENANCE

Transparent glass will show the dirt easily and needs occasional maintenance with a glass-cleaning solution. Professional window washers are usually employed for nonresidential installations.

SPECIAL CONSIDERATIONS

Glass for angled (skylight, greenhouse) installations must be tempered for strength (known as tempered or safety glass). Low-E (low-emission) glass screens out the harmful ultraviolet rays. *Single glazing* is one layer of glass; *double* or *twin glazing* is two layers and is more insulative. *Triple glazing* is often accomplished with an interior or exterior winter or summer storm window.

COST STRUCTURE

Moderate to moderately high.

GLASS BLOCK

DESCRIPTION

Transparent or translucent glass pressed and formed as two halves and fused together. The semihollow blocks offer light diffusion and transmission and good insulation. Designs may be imprinted on one or both sides.

APPLICATIONS

Residential and nonresidential applications where light diffusion is needed with some privacy. Glass blocks are not for use in load-bearing situations. Glass blocks may also be used in ceiling installations with artificial light behind the blocks.

MAINTENANCE

Little upkeep. If the blocks become dirty or greasy, soap and water will clean them. Polishing is not necessary.

SPECIAL CONSIDERATIONS

Variations of glass block include a fibrous glass insert that controls glare, brightness, and excessive heat gain. Solid glass blocks are also available for wall installations for greater protection against breakage and forced entry.

COST STRUCTURE

Moderately high.

FIBERGLASS

DESCRIPTION

Glass fibers spun or pressed into a lightweight, insulative mass; translucent or opaque.

APPLICATIONS

Wall panels and dividers, bathtub and shower surrounds and units. Fibrous fiberglass "wool" is an insulative material used in wall and ceiling structures. Fiberglass panels are sometimes used for corrugated ceiling panels and patio covers. Both residential and nonresidential applications.

MAINTENANCE

Fiberglass panels and pressed forms are easily scratched and need to be cleaned with a nonabrasive cleanser.

SPECIAL CONSIDERATIONS

Used where little hard use is anticipated, since it loses its shiny finish with abrasion or hard-water deposits.

COST STRUCTURE

Moderate.

Architectural glass (glazing)

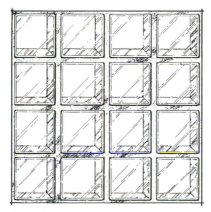

Glass block

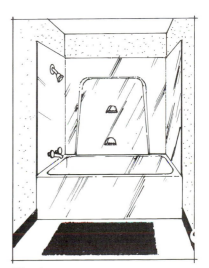

Fiberglass

continued

CHART 10.2 RIGID WALL AND CEILING MATERIALS *continued*

MIRROR

DESCRIPTION

Flawless float glass backed with a coating of silver or silver alloy. May be bronzed, grayed, antiqued (smokey), veined with gold color, or etched with a design.

APPLICATIONS

Walls and ceilings, residential and nonresidential.

MAINTENANCE

Clean with glass cleaner; polish with soft cloths or paper products.

SPECIAL CONSIDERATIONS

Mirrors will visually expand the space and may be set in place as flat, flawless panels or shaped into patterns such as tile. Mirrors may be used on folding screens or sliding closet doors.

COST STRUCTURE

Moderately high.

METAL— ALUMINUM, BRASS, BRONZE, COPPER, STAINLESS STEEL, TIN

DESCRIPTION

An extremely durable material that can be used in several forms. Sheets of aluminum, brass, bronze, copper, and stainless steel may be cut and fitted in place; strips of metal may be installed on clips. Metal panels are available, solid or perforated. Tin panels, tiles, or squares are again being produced with stamped patterns that document designs from the Victorian era.

APPLICATIONS

Walls, ceilings, and custom installations such as wrapped columns. Used occasionally in custom residences but more often in businesses, banks, hotel lobbies, and other nonresidential installations.

MAINTENANCE

Little upkeep. If surfaces should become spotted from handling, use a metal polish preparation. Painted metals can be washed with soap and water. Follow manufacturer's instructions for cleaning. Most metals are treated to be impervious to oil, dirt, and corrosion.

SPECIAL CONSIDERATIONS

Tin panels are often painted. Metals are available in shiny or brushed surfaces. Metal surfaces may be costly background finishes, but they give an exclusive and expensive look. Some metal ceiling systems are designed to be installed over existing ceilings in renovation or remodeling work, making it possible to maintain existing heating and air-conditioning ducts and wiring. Finishes (discussed in chapter 8, Furniture Selection) include anodized satin, polished, and brushed.

COST STRUCTURE

Moderately high to high.

PLASTER

DESCRIPTION

A paste mixture of lime, sand, and water that hardens as it dries. May be applied as a finish material to be smooth, textured, or rough. Stucco may be a smooth or rough consistency, depending on the fineness of the sand used. Plaster may also be cast into decorative ornaments or cornices, generally called anaglypta or anaglyphs, that can imitate hand-carved wood and be nailed or glued in place and painted or antiqued.

APPLICATIONS

Walls, exterior and interior, ceilings; anaglypta ornament, moldings. Authentic smooth plaster walls are coated over *lath* (thin strips of wood nailed to the wall studs horizontally, about three-eighths of an inch apart) or over wire mesh. Today, plaster is more often applied over plasterboard or sheetrock (see wallboard) made of gypsum or concrete block. Plaster is most often used as a finish material. It is applied as a mud to seal the *perfatape*, which conceals seams in the wallboard, or applied as rough-textured stucco. It is also sprayed on in a *texturizing* process, in various thicknesses, and sanded into the desired texture. A light application of blown plaster is usually called orange peel and is common in some residential and non-residential settings. Plain plaster applications are more common in nonresidential settings. A frothy mixture called blown acoustic plaster is sometimes used on ceilings.

MAINTENANCE

Upkeep of plaster depends on the use or abuse, since it can chip, crack, and peel. It scratches and mars easily, and smooth plaster is difficult to touch up with paint. Washability depends on the type of paint used, with oil-based paint being the most durable and scrubbable.

SPECIAL CONSIDERATIONS

Today smooth plaster walls applied over sheetrock are more costly than sprayed or textured walls. New lath-and-plaster walls are nearly nonexistent because of the labor involved.

COST STRUCTURE

Moderate.

Mirror

Metal

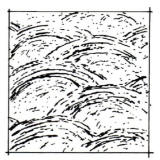

Plaster

continued

Figure 10.2 *New "scratch coat plaster" recreates the look of a centuries-old Italian villa: There are traditional paneling and painted wood moldings below and on background wall.*

© Ted Spiegel.

CHART 10.2 RIGID WALL AND CEILING MATERIALS *continued*

STONE

DESCRIPTION

Natural stone includes flagstone, granite, marble, and terrazzo, all described in this chart. In addition, other general types fit the definition of stone:

1. *Ashlar* refers to a stone that is cut into rectangular shapes so that it can be fitted together into a geometric pattern with grout.

2. *Cobblestone* (or river cobbles) are large, rounded, somewhat smooth rocks used to face walls and fireplaces in rustic settings.

3. *Fieldstone* is a rugged type of large rocks that may or may not be rounded and smooth. When laid, fieldstone has a random pattern.

4. *Sandstone* is a soft, reddish stone that is a type of fieldstone and may be cut into ashlar shape.

5. *Rubble* means rough uncut stone or stone that is not uniform.

6. *Artificial stone* is made to imitate rubble or ashlar.

Ashlar

River cobbles

Fieldstone, sandstone, or rubble

GRANITE

DESCRIPTION

A very hard crystalline rock with small amounts of feldspar, quartz, and other minerals in crystal or grain form. The size of the crystals varies from very fine to fairly coarse.

The colors vary from light to dark values and variations of gray, pink, green, brown, and black and may be combinations such as greenish or pinkish gray. May be dull or highly polished.

APPLICATIONS

Walls, countertops, fireplace surrounds. Used in both residential and nonresidential settings.

MAINTENANCE

Low upkeep; wipe with a damp cloth.

SPECIAL CONSIDERATIONS

Exact color match will need to be carefully coordinated between the designer and the quarry or supplier.

COST STRUCTURE

Very high.

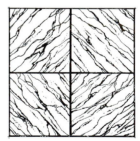

Granite

MARBLE

DESCRIPTION

A metamorphic limestone, granular or crystalline, white or colored, often with streaks. The hardest and typically the most expensive of the stones. May be cut into thin sheets or slabs. Can be polished to a high sheen. Cold to the touch. *Terrazzo* is a composite flooring of broken chips of marble set into cement and polished to a sheen. This is a practical use of marble, since up to 50 percent waste occurs from breakage at the quarry.

APPLICATIONS

Walls, fireplace surrounds, tiles for special or custom installations. Expensive look for both residential and nonresidential installations.

MAINTENANCE

Clean with warm water and infrequently with soap and water.

SPECIAL CONSIDERATIONS

The most formal of the stones; rich-looking finish material.

COST STRUCTURE

Very high.

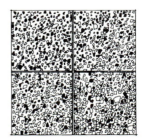

Marble

Marble terrazzo

continued

Figure 10.3 *Terrazzo marble—chips set into cement and polished—is used here for walls, counter top, and tub surround.*
Silhouette window shades by and photo courtesy of Hunter Douglas.

CHART 10.2 RIGID WALL AND CEILING MATERIALS *continued*

TRAVERTINE

DESCRIPTION

A light-colored limestone rock formed near mineral springs. Trapped gas in the stone causes holes and interesting textures that can be filled according to the intended use.

APPLICATIONS

Walls, fireplace surrounds and hearths, bathrooms. Used frequently in nonresidential settings and as accents and for custom installations in residential interiors.

MAINTENANCE

Wash when necessary with clear lukewarm water. Wash no more often than every six months with soap and water and rinse thoroughly. On vertical surfaces it needs little if any cleaning.

SPECIAL CONSIDERATIONS

Travertine is slightly less formal than marble and widely used.

COST STRUCTURE

High.

ACOUSTICAL TILE

DESCRIPTION

Acoustical tiles or panels are made from mineral fiberboard or from fabric or plastic-clad fiber, fiberglass, and even metal.

APPLICATIONS

Primarily ceilings in both residential and nonresidential settings; occasionally for walls.

MAINTENANCE

Depending on location and human contact, maintenance is usually low. Ceiling installations will not show soil easily, except around air distribution openings. Follow manufacturer's directions for cleaning. Tiles that become stained are often replaced or painted.

SPECIAL CONSIDERATIONS

Acoustical tiles may not be tiles at all but strips of insulative materials. Square, rectangular, and strip materials are usually mounted on a track or grid system, making them relatively easy to install.

COST STRUCTURE

Moderate.

CERAMIC TILE

DESCRIPTION

Fine, white clays formed into tile shape (bisque), glazed, and fired at very high temperatures. Finishes vary from shiny and smooth to painted/decal-patterned to rough. Mosaic tiles are very small tiles used to create permanent patterns and pictures on walls. Today mosaic tile comes in preset sheets, a face mount or back mount, ready to be set with grout.

APPLICATIONS

Walls, counters, backsplash areas, ceilings. Ceramic tile is used extensively in nonresidential settings because of its durability. Ceramic tile is often used in bathrooms, kitchens, and solariums or in any room in warm climates.

MAINTENANCE

Low upkeep. Dust or wipe with clear water, vinegar water, or soap and water for heavy dirt. Grout may soil and discolor. Silicone treatments will make grout less susceptible to soil. Newer developments in grout are more resistant to stains.

SPECIAL CONSIDERATIONS

Durable surface that maintains good looks indefinitely. Ceramic tile breaks, is cold and very hard.

COST STRUCTURE

Low to high—costs vary considerably in ceramic tiles. Imported tiles from France and Italy can be expensive. Labor to install is also high. However, because it is permanent, the life-cycle cost is low.

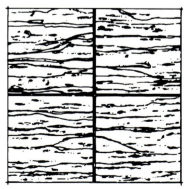

Travertine

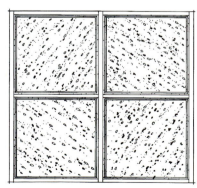

Acoustical tile

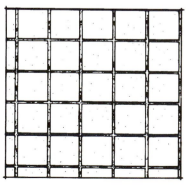

Ceramic tile

continued

Figure 10.4 *Ceramic tile on the counter and backsplash is a practical and attractive choice for kitchens.*

Courtesy of Elon, Inc.

CHART 10.2 RIGID WALL AND CEILING MATERIALS *continued*

QUARRY TILE

DESCRIPTION

Quarry tile is made of fine clay and graded shale, with color distributed through the body of the tile. Most is a *terra-cotta* rust/red, the color of the natural clay. It may be glazed but usually is left natural. Typical square or hexagonal shapes are most popular.

APPLICATIONS

Walls, counters, backsplashes, ceilings, residential and nonresidential applications, similar to ceramic tile.

MAINTENANCE

Same as for ceramic tile.

SPECIAL CONSIDERATIONS

Natural terra-cotta color gives quarry tile a timeless appeal.

COST STRUCTURE

Tile cost is low to moderate, although installation is costly.

MEXICAN TILE

DESCRIPTION

Hand-shaped clay taken from the ground and left to set before firing, reflecting imperfections of hand labor that add to their charm.

APPLICATIONS

Large squares are not often used on walls; smaller, glazed tiles are used for decorative effects on walls, countertops, backsplashes, stair risers, and doorway surround trim.

MAINTENANCE

Glazed tiles clean the same as ceramic or quarry tiles.

SPECIAL CONSIDERATIONS

Mexican tile is durable, but if not sealed it is susceptible to oily stains. The softest of all the tiles, it can be chipped or broken more easily than quarry or ceramic tile.

COST STRUCTURE

Tiles are low to moderate cost; installation is costly.

OTHER TILE MATERIALS

Many materials are available as finish wall and ceiling materials in tile form. Among them are leather, mirror, metal, carpet, glass block, brick, and stone.

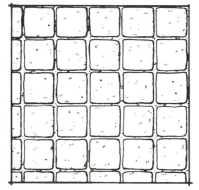

Quarry tile

Mexican tile

continued

CHART 10.2 RIGID WALL AND CEILING MATERIALS *continued*

WALLBOARD

DESCRIPTION

A general category of drywall goods including sheetrock or gypsum board (made of crushed and processed gypsum rock). It is available in sheets four feet by eight feet or four feet by twelve feet and is hung with nails or screws to wooden or metal studs. Seams are sealed with perfatape (paper) and covered with plaster mud, smoothed out to be inconspicuous. The wallboard may be left smooth or be textured. Smooth wallboard is best for wallpaper installations.

APPLICATIONS

The most common of the wall finish materials for both residential and nonresidential settings. It is a basic material that may be finished as described or overlayed with wall coverings or fabric.

MAINTENANCE

Upkeep will depend on the texture and finish given the wallboard. Paints vary in their ability to withstand repeated cleanings, as do wall coverings and fabric.

SPECIAL CONSIDERATIONS

Economical wall-covering material. It is also fragile. It will dent and scratch and can be punctured with door knobs or other hard objects thrust against it.

COST STRUCTURE

Moderate to high.

WOOD: MILLWORK TRADITIONAL PANELING

DESCRIPTION

Stock and custom-milled wood applied to walls and as cabinetry in the form of flat and raised panels, shelving, and moldings. The wood may be hardwood or softwood, plywood or solid wood.

APPLICATIONS

Walls in residential and now, to a substantial extent, in nonresidential work.

MAINTENANCE

Depends on the finish it is given. Oiled or waxed wood may need protection against moisture and will show fingerprints. Millwork is usually sealed with lacquer, acrylic, or urethane, which then is easy to clean with a mild detergent solution.

SPECIAL CONSIDERATIONS

Installation is considered to be part of the architectural detail and hence a permanent part of the building that is rarely removed unless remodeling takes place. It gives visual richness to the interior, particularly when stained rather than painted.

COST STRUCTURE

Moderate to high, depending on whether the millwork is paint grade (less costly) or stained wood (very costly).

WOOD PANELING

DESCRIPTION

Solid wood paneling comes in four- by eight-foot sheets of hardwoods. More typical, however, is high-quality veneer plywood (sandwiched) with a thin layer of hardwood (veneer) laminated to the surface. Prefinished plywood has a surface of good quality capable of being finished. *Hardboard* is made of wood fibers compressed under heat or pressure. These may have a veneer or a photo reproduction of wood applied to the surface and grooved to represent a plank wall material. They may also be formed with a surface texture to imitate carved wood panels. Tongue-and-groove strips (milled to interlock) are also used for walls as a paneling. Board and batten walls are long strips of wood with narrow strips or lath nailed or screwed over the seams.

APPLICATIONS

Walls and ceilings. The quality of the wood will determine the type of residential or nonresidential application.

MAINTENANCE

This depends on the surface of the product. Paneling may be oiled, waxed, urethaned, or treated with acrylic or other products, or it may have a plastic finish, which varies from a very thin coat to a durable, permanent finish capable of withstanding the wear of any contract installation. Wall-cleaning products are available for wood only or follow the manufacturer's instructions. Durable finishes may be washed with soap and water.

SPECIAL CONSIDERATIONS

Wood paneling ranges from a do-it-yourself project look to a very exquisite and costly appearance.

COST STRUCTURE

Moderately low to moderately high. Solid wood will cost the most.

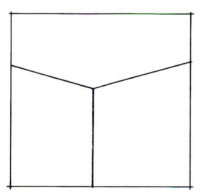

Wallboard—sheetrock or gypsum board

Traditional paneling

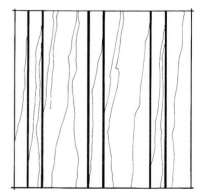

Palisade wall of board and batten

Figure 10.5 *Vertical slats of wood, painted white, give freshness and charm to this bedroom.*
© Lisl Dennis.

PAINT

Paint is used on walls and ceilings more than any other finish material. The reasons are diverse and all valid.

- Paint is a versatile material. It is flexible as a liquid and dries to a hard, protective finish with various textures and types of finish.

- Paint is an inexpensive wall finish and relatively simple and easy to apply.

- Paint offers color and texture variety and assures protection to the surface.

- Painted walls reinforce interior architecture through neutral, noncompetitive colors.

- Paint has contrast and graphic ability, providing excitement or drama.

- Paint adds richness and subtlety through low-contrast, deep, or soft colors.

- Paint can accent or draw attention to surfaces and details.

- Dark-colored paint reflects little light, which makes the surface seem to advance, and light-colored paints can visually expand spaces. These properties allow the designer to visually alter sizes and shapes.

- The chromatic and textural variety of paint allows it to imitate other materials—wood, marble or other polished stones, tortoiseshell, or fabric, for example.

- *Trompe l'oeil*, painted three-dimensional scenes that trick the eye, adds architectural interest and sometimes humor by painting scenes of architecture, accessories, or even people that are not really there.

- Skilled professional painters can produce texture and pattern, contrast and camouflage; they can create imitations of nearly any type of material. Professional painting is not inexpensive, although the cost to paint faux (false or imitation) marble, for example, is far less than surfacing with real marble.[2]

Figure 10.6 *Painted "trompe l'oeil" scenes transform the walls of this California laundry room into an ocean view.*
Courtesy of Amy Weiss Design.

Painting Guidelines and Cautions

Because paint varies in versatility and ease of application, it must be used with great discretion. Reckless abandon in painting can only bring about sloppy, haphazard work and probably garish results as well. Careful planning and preparation are imperative to achieve truly beautiful results.

Some guidelines and cautions for using paint include the following:

‣ Paint is sometimes assumed to have the power to cover and renew surfaces that have blemishes and flaws. This assumption is often met with disappointment if the surface has not first been properly prepared. Old paint that is cracked, bubbled, flaked, or peeling must be removed or sanded. Wallpaper must be removed. Cracks, holes, and damaged areas must be patched and sanded smooth. The surface must be clean and free from dust and sanding particles. A smooth surface will help assure a flawless finish and has a great deal to do with the success of a painted wall or ceiling.

‣ Before selecting paint colors, textures, or patterns, carefully evaluate the room itself. Look at the dimensions, the moldings, the architectural assets and defects. Evaluate the number of windows, the direction they face, and the amount of light admitted. Remember, any room can become quite handsome with intelligent planning.

‣ Select a color scheme by painting a small wall, portions of the wall, or a paper that can be taped to the wall. Small paint chips provided by the paint store will often look different and usually darker compared to an entire wall painted that hue. Larger swatches on the wall will allow a judgment of the color during different times of the day and under different types and directions of light.

‣ Consider *glazing* (transparent paints) for unique light-revealing effects or any of the texturizing techniques presented later in this chapter. Experiment with different color combinations; for example, a light color with two or more colors glazed over it.

CHART 10.3   TYPES OF PAINTS

The selections in paint are sometimes confusing to both the designer and the layperson. It is helpful to understand the types and characteristics of each type of paint so that the best selection can be made. It is also wise to describe the project to painting contractors or retail paint store specialists who can recommend a suitable product.

Acrylic paint is a synthetic resin water-based paint. It is odorless, quick-drying, durable, and easy to use. It cleans up with soap and water and is moderately priced.

Alkyds and alkyd enamels are resins, oil modified, that dry faster and harder than oil paints. Alkyd enamels produce a glossy surface. Alkyds are moderately priced, are easy to work with, and have very good coverage and color range. Cleanup is with solvents or paint thinners.

Artist's paint are paints—oil or acrylic—that come in small bottles or tubes and can be thinned with mineral spirits or water, respectively, and used as glazing for transparent color overlay painting techniques.

Enamel paints are oil-based or sometimes water-based paints that usually come in gloss or semigloss (may have flattening agents added for a matte finish). These paints are used most often for their hard, glossy, smooth finish.

Epoxy paints come already mixed or have hardeners mixed in at the site. Epoxies can be used to paint metal and water-holding surfaces such as bathtubs and swimming pools.

Fillers and sealers are used prior to staining or painting. Fillers are putty or stick-putty materials that fill in holes or cracks. Sealers are liquid preparations that make a smoother surface.

Finishes refer to the relative shine (see chart 10.4). Finishes also consist of a separate group of liquid sealants used on cabinetry and furniture, including shellac, lacquer, polyurethanes, and acrylics.

Flame-retardant paints retard the spread of flames or the toxic fumes and smoke given off by burning paints. Most specifications for new or remodeled nonresidential buildings will require paints to meet a Class A flame spread, the lowest possible.

Latex paint is the least costly of the paints. Latex paints vary in their quality and durability. They are easy to apply and dry quickly, reducing recoating time. They have an excellent color range and are fairly durable but must be protected from freezing temperatures. They are not as scrubbable as alkyds but do have the ability to breathe, allowing moisture to escape. Cleanup is with soap and water.

Oil-based paints were for a number of years considered the best paint to buy. They were thought to be the most durable, were the most expensive, had the strongest odor, and took the longest to dry. Cleanup of oil-based paints is with paint thinner or solvent. These paints have largely been replaced with alkyds, and they may eventually be off the market due to environmental concerns.

Primers are liquid sealers applied to some surfaces before the paint. It fills in small pores and helps the paint become more durable.

Solvents are liquids that dissolve resins, gums, or oils and are used to thin or clean up oils, alkyds, and oil-based enamels.

Stains are thin liquids that are used to color woods by penetrating the porous surface. Stains come in water base, oil base, varnish, and wax.

- In rooms where the painted walls and ceilings (or floors) become important architectural or decorative backgrounds, it is important to not overfurnish the room and thereby destroy the effects of the paint by competing with backgrounds or by changing the apparent proportions of the room.

- Select textures and patterns that are appropriate for the room setting and the surface.

- Consider orientation and climate when selecting the hue for painted walls. For example, a lively yellow may be warm and comforting in a cool room with a north exposure or in a cooler climate, whereas that same color would visually and psychologically bake the inhabitants of an interior with a broad, southern exposure or in a hot season or climate.

- Evaluate what contrast in the paint will do to the room. High-value contrast (very light hues against very dark hues) will accentuate and draw attention to that contrast. This can be dramatically effective where the contrast is in large planes and busy if the contrast is, say, around every door and window or painted as graphic stripes on the walls. On the other hand, low-value contrast (light values next to medium ones or medium values near dark values) can provide depth and richness.[3]

- Consider the psychological effect of the color. The way people feel about color is often based on experiences and

CHART 10.4   PAINT FINISHES

There are several lusters or finishes in paint. The luster can be selected for a desired result or effect.

Flat, or matte, paint reflects very little sheen. It is appropriate for walls and ceilings to give a soft, velvetlike texture. Flat paints are the least washable of the lusters. Flat paints are available in enamel, often called *eggshell enamel*, which gives a matte finish and is more washable.

Satin or eggshell paint has a small amount of light-reflecting quality, so it hides fingerprints better and is more washable.

Semigloss paint has some sheen that hides marks and is a more washable paint than flat or satin. It also contrasts nicely with either flat or gloss paints.

High-gloss, or gloss enamel, paint is the shiniest of the paint lusters and the most durable and scrubbable. Its reflecting qualities, however, will show every flaw on a surface that has not been properly prepared for painting.

Texturizing paint also comes in various textures. While the majority of the paints used are smooth, there are some thicker paints available that can be applied to give the effect of stucco or of suede. These texturizing paints will absorb more sound as well.

prejudices of the past. Certainly color preferences and prejudices should be discovered in the design program research. Recall that warm colors are lively and welcoming. Cool colors are calm, providing a restful, restrained environment.

Figure 10.7 *Painted (A) real and (B) faux columns. Contrast colors, faux marbeling, and ceiling cloud effects add architectural interest.*
Courtesy of National Paint and Coatings Association.

CHART 10.5   PAINT-TEXTURIZING TECHNIQUES

Visual texturizing can be achieved in many ways; just about any effect the design calls for can be accomplished by a skilled painter.[4]

Smooth textures are achieved by using one of the four most common methods of applying paint with a brush, roller, pad, and spray mechanism. These techniques may produce an even surface appropriate in many period settings and modern interiors where woodwork and architectural detail are not important. They also make appropriate backgrounds for the broken and textured paint techniques presented in this chart.

1. **Brush painting** is used for corners, small, hard-to-reach areas, and detail work such as window grids and moldings.
2. **Roller painting** is very useful for large areas such as walls and ceilings. Small rollers are handy for narrow areas. A different sleeve should be used for each color. Rollers do spatter somewhat, and the roller should never be too full of paint.
3. **Pad painting** is useful for smaller areas and will not spatter. Pads cover evenly and are easy to work with.
4. **Spray painting** takes on two forms. Airless spraying uses fluid pressure and undiluted paint—it gives a better coverage but uses more paint. Air compression spray guns use diluted paint with less-complete coverage. Spraying is common in new buildings, both residential and nonresidential. It is fast and economical. It should be followed with a roller to even out the paint.

Antiquing means to make a surface look old, to soften and blur slightly in imitation of the mellow patina that naturally accompanies the aging process. Techniques frequently used in antiquing include color washing, glazing, spattering, and dragging.

Color washing is a technique of applying a coat of thinned, sometimes translucent paint over a white or colored background. It is versatile, attractive, and easy to use, giving effects from rugged texture (over rough walls) to shimmering translucence (over smooth walls).

Dragging and combing are techniques that produce fine lines and may be used in wood graining. Dragging or coasting a dry brush over a wet glaze reveals a base color and can imitate fine fabric yarns. Combing uses any hard comblike tool. Dragging and combing can be done in straight lines, curving lines, or fan shapes. Cross-hatching by combing can produce a fabric burlaplike texture; by dragging with a brush, a variety of interesting crosshatch textures are possible.

Glazing is a technique where transparent colors are overlaid in sequence, thereby producing various gradations of color.

Marbling is the technique of imitating polished marble stone and can be done by artisans with a high degree of skill and artistic sense where the marbled surface cannot be distinguished from the real stone, or it can simply be a mottled whirling, moving flow painted onto the surface.

Outlining means painting contrasting colors or white values on architectural molding.

Picking out means highlighting features on molding, such as dentil trim or carved bas-relief.

Porphyry is a granitelike texture achieved by crisscross brushing, then stippling, spattering, and finally *cissing* (dropping mineral spirits on the splatters to dilute and make shadows of the spatters).

Ragging and rag rolling are the basis for marbling where the wet paint or glaze is partially removed by dabbing with a rag or rolling the paint off with a rolled rag.

Shading is the technique of blending color values from light to dark across a wall or ceiling.

Spattering is achieved by filling a brush and flipping the paint onto the base color to produce uneven spots or spatters. Lighter or darker colors can be used, with lighter or darker base colors. Spattering can vary from tiny irregular dots to large globs of paint, and the spacing can be very close or sparsely spattered on an open ground.

Smooshing is a slightly marbled effect achieved by applying a plastic dropcloth to a wall of wet paint, rubbing the hands over the plastic, then peeling off the plastic.

Sponging (or paint applied with sponges) produces a broken, splotchy effect. Larger sponge pores will produce a more coarse-looking texture and a larger splotch than finer sponges. Sponging can yield rich-looking walls and ceilings, somewhat akin to granite when more than two colors of very carefully coordinated paint of two or more shades of one hue are used. Oil-based paints will look more crisp; latex paint will look softer.

Stippling is similar to sponging but uses a stippling brush to dab on a colored glaze or paint, revealing some of the base color. The result is finer than sponging.

Wood graining is done by brushing on a glaze and drawing wood grains and lines with an artist's brush. Techniques vary according to the type of wood being imitated. When well done, wood graining can be very beautiful.

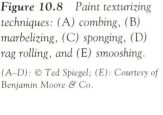

Figure 10.8 *Paint texturizing techniques: (A) combing, (B) marbelizing, (C) sponging, (D) rag rolling, and (E) smooshing.*

(A–D): © Ted Spiegel; (E): Courtesy of Benjamin Moore & Co.

WALL COVERINGS

Wall coverings—including wallpaper, vinyl and textile wall coverings, and fabric—provide tremendous variety in pattern, color, texture, sound absorption, and flexibility. Walls and ceilings benefit from the many wall coverings that add visual and architectural interest. The reasons for utilizing wall coverings include the following:

- Colors, patterns, and textures of wall coverings are unlimited.
- Wall coverings can imitate natural materials such as stone, wood, brick, or tile at a fraction of the cost of those materials.
- Costs vary, but they can be modest. Installation can be done professionally or by the layperson.

- Three-dimensional fabric wall coverings absorb sound and give a sense of quiet or peace to the interior.
- Wall coverings can cover badly cracked walls or old paint; they can even camouflage architectural flaws or defects.
- Fabric installed on the wall can coordinate with an ensemble—fabric used in other areas of the interior. Likewise, many wall covering companies offer companion fabrics to match wallpapers.
- Wall coverings can provide instant decor—they can add charm, beauty, and character to interiors.
- Fabric wall coverings can be installed flat, pleated, shirred, draped, or folded (see chart 10.8), thereby allowing creativity in the way the fabric pattern, color, or texture is utilized.

Figure 10.9 *Wallpaper adds character to otherwise plain walls.* (A) *Contemporary flamestitch wallpaper pattern.* (B-D) *Three papers and companion fabrics or borders from Mary Gilliatt's Edwardian Garden collection.*
(A) *Courtesy of Schumacher.* (B, C, D) *Courtesy of Sandpiper Studios, a division of Design Directions.*

Wall Covering Guidelines and Cautions

Wall coverings are more popular today than ever before. They are so extensively used as instant decorating that there must be some inquiry into the appropriateness of great quantities of wall coverings. In this respect, some guidelines and cautions are listed for careful consideration:

- Select wall coverings that are compatible with the style of furnishings and with the architecture of the building. Formal Baroque or Renaissance designs in a modern building are not only out of character, they may insult the integrity of both the wall covering and the architecture.

- Choose the pattern with great discrimination. Consider how long a pattern will stay stylish and aesthetically appealing. There are a great number of bright, loud, or busy patterns available today. A general rule is that the more dramatic or flamboyant the pattern, the more quickly it will become tiresome.

- Limit the number of patterns in an interior and coordinate them to provide harmony from one area to another. Patterns that differ in style or color will be discordant, and if two or more clashing wall coverings can be viewed from any one vantage point, the effect can be disastrous.

- Obvious patterns on the ceiling can visually lower the ceiling and can be psychologically disturbing.

- Patterns that clash with fabrics in the interior are poor choices. Keep in mind how often the furnishings may be changed or replaced.

- Many textured wall coverings are lovely and sophisticated, and their subtle qualities establish pleasing transitions from one room or area to another. However, some textures are cheap imitations such as plastic grass cloth. Or they are so brightly colored that they cannot be considered good design.

Figure 10.10 *An ivy-like pattern with a stripe below gives cheerful charm to this dining room.*
© *Jessie Walker.*

- Installation is a key factor in how nice a wall covering looks. The work of professional wall covering installers will look far superior to a careless do-it-yourself job.

Prepackaged wall coverings have several terms in common that are useful in selecting and ordering wall coverings. These terms, listed in chart 10.6, are helpful in determining the type and quantity of wall coverings.

CHART 10.6 WALL COVERING TERMS

Single rolls contain thirty to thirty-six square feet, or about twenty-eight feet long by twenty-seven inches wide. When calculating wall covering quantity, figure a single roll will cover twenty-five to thirty square feet, which allows for waste. In Europe, there are twenty-eight feet per single roll of wall coverings. Wallpapers are priced as single rolls and may be purchased by the single roll. It is abbreviated S/R.

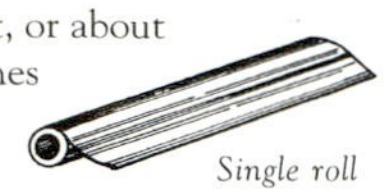

Single roll

Double roll is the equivalent of and priced as two single rolls rolled into one—it usually contains about seventy-two square feet. It saves waste and is therefore more economical.

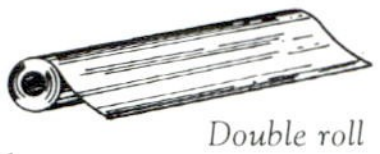

Double roll

Triple roll is priced as and equals the footage of three single rolls in one length, about 108 square feet, and is the most economical use of the paper.

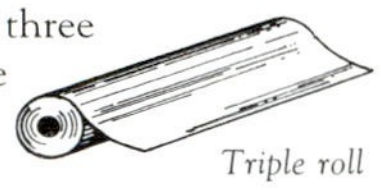

Triple roll

Dye lot is a single run of colors or a single production. The dye lot shades may vary. If it becomes necessary to reorder, always specify the dye lot number (included on a piece of paper with the roll) or send in a swatch of the paper. It is not always possible to obtain the same dye lot, so it is best to be generous when ordering.

Border is a narrow or wide band of wallpaper used to trim and accent. Borders are usually packaged in single "spools" of fifteen feet (five yards).

Pattern repeat comes in two directions. A vertical pattern repeat is the complete motif or pattern from the top of one length to the top of the next. A large pattern repeat is more wasteful, since a complete pattern repeat must begin at the top of each length. A horizontal pattern repeat means that the pattern can be matched straight across or drop-matched by lowering the next length of paper.

Peelable wall covering means the top layer of the wallpaper will peel off, leaving a substrate (lining) material that can be papered over again.

Prepasted wall covering means the paper has a dry coating of paste and will only need to be moistened to apply.

Pretrimmed wall covering means ready to hang. Hand-printed wallpapers have a selvage (border) with separate printed information, including blocks of color used in the paper. This must be trimmed off before the paper is hung. Pretrimmed papers have the selvage cut off. *Semitrimmed* has only one side of the selvage trimmed so that the selvage left on is under an overlap or is trimmed off at the site.

Scrubbable denotes a wall covering that can withstand repeated wet cleaning. Most vinyl wall coverings are scrubbable.

Sizing is a thin liquid painted onto the wall surface that reduces the amount of paste absorbed by the wallpaper. It also gives the surface "tooth," or enough abrasiveness to stick well, and it seals the surface so alkali cannot penetrate into the wallpaper.

Strippable is a term applied to papers that can be stripped off the wall completely without scraping or steaming.

Washable means the paper can be cleaned gently with a little soap and water.

CHART 10.7 TYPES OF WALL COVERINGS

Coordinating or companion fabrics are now available with many wall coverings. This is a convenient, although not inexpensive, way to coordinate fabric installations with wall coverings.

Cork wall coverings use cork, which is a natural resilient material cut into very thin layers with a paper backing.

Embossed wall coverings are those that are calendered to produce a three-dimensional, raised pattern. *Anaglypta wall coverings* are embossed to resemble sculptured plaster, hammered copper, or hand-tooled leather.

Fabric or textile wall coverings are fabrics laminated to a paper backing and sold in rolls or bolts. The most common fabric wall coverings are linen, jute, and wool. They give a rich natural-textured look and are very appropriate for both residential and nonresidential interiors.

Fabric-backed wall coverings are used for heavy-face papers or vinyl to give strength to the installation. Most nonresidential wall coverings and heavy vinyl residential wall coverings are fabric-backed.

Flocked wallpapers use *flocking*, which is a process of gluing tiny fibers in a pattern to the surface of the paper. It is a decorative effect, in imitation of cut velvet.

Foil/mylar wall coverings have a shiny, highly reflective quality. They may be patterned or flocked.

Grass cloth is made of dried grasses that are left natural or dyed a color and woven into a textile with fine cotton threads (a more refined product) or other grasses (coarser looking).

Leather is a luxurious and quieting wall covering. Leather squares or *leather tiles*, the tanned hide of cattle and swine, are dyed brown or other colors and possibly embossed with patterns.

Murals are printed scenic wallpapers that come in panels. They have traditionally been scenes of romantic or faraway places, sometimes ruins of ancient civilizations.

Paper wallcoverings are the most common wallcoverings. They may be coated with vinyl (explained below). They are easy to hang and come in an infinite variety of patterns and colors.

Vinyl wall coverings come in several types, from light to heavy weight. They are: *vinyl-protected wall coverings*, in which a thin layer of vinyl is applied over wallpaper to make it more washable and durable; *vinyl latex*, paper impregnated with vinyl and applied to a fabric or paper backing; and *coated fabric*, coated or laminated before the pattern is applied, and usually afterwards as well. Vinyl wall coverings are the heaviest of the wall coverings, the most scrubbable and strippable, and possibly even reusable. Vinyl wall coverings are more difficult to hang because of their weight. They may imitate wood, leather, tile, marble, or any other hard material.

Figure 10.11 *Wallcovering adds dignity to this dining room.*
© *Jessie Walker.*

Figure 10.12 *Fabric on the wall, here wrapped as blocks or upholstered, absorbs noise and increases comfort.*

Courtesy of DuPont "Teflon" soil and stain repellent.

CHART 10.8 METHODS OF INSTALLING WALL FABRIC

Covered frame method is a good technique for temporary installations. A lath frame (one-inch by two-inch wooden strips), is laid on the back of the fabric, then the fabric is pulled tightly over the frame and stapled. The result is a blind wooden frame with top and sides covered with fabric. This can be mounted or hung on protruding nails as panels and may not cover the entire wall. Smaller fabric-framed panels may be accessory items.

Direct pasteup uses fabrics that come prepared for installation as a wall covering with a paper or foam backing, or the installer may apply a spray backing or iron on a stiffening fabric backing. Sometimes the preparation or paste causes the fabric grain to slip, making it difficult to match patterns horizontally. A skilled professional is an asset in direct fabric pasteup. A less-permanent method is to sponge liquid laundry starch onto the wall or dip the fabric in it. The fabric will stick to the wall until it is remoistened and pulled off.

Hook-and-loop fasteners may be used to install fabric where the fabric needs to be taken down frequently for cleaning. The best known brand of hook-and-loop fasteners is Velcro. One-half of the tape, square, or circle fasteners is sewn or glued to the fabric, and the companion part is applied to the wall.

Lath method uses wood lath strips nailed to the wall perimeter, then the fabric is stapled, glued, or fastened with hook-and-loop tape. This saves the effort of preparing badly damaged walls or stiffening the fabric for direct pasteup.

Panel-track method can use several brands of metal or plastic tracks that are on the market for the professional, usually nonresidential installation of fabric on the wall; these include office systems furniture, a flexible wall where fabrics can be changed when necessary.

Stapling with a staple gun is a fast, easy method of applying fabric to the wall. The staples are usually covered with trim such as welt or gimp or braid or with wood or plastic molding.

Strapping tape method is a very inexpensive and easy method. Simply roll lengths of strapping tape into circles and apply to the wall, then press the fabric in place. High humidity or certain paint surfaces may make this method unsatisfactory, however.

Upholstered walls mean that there is a layer of batting applied first to the wall in the form of polyester or cotton batting or foam. The fabric is then stapled over the padding, and a trim is placed on top. This gives extra sound absorption and insulation values.

Fabric-Covered Walls

Fabric installed or upholstered onto a wall or ceiling has many advantages. It is the most *flexible wall covering,* as it can be applied flat, gathered (shirred), pleated, or folded. Fabrics can change their character with the different methods of installation. A patterned fabric laid flat looks quite different than one which is shirred, pleated, or folded. Installations can be quite temporary, permanent, or semi-permanent.

Fabrics are highly insulative against both noise and temperature extremes. They offer visual comfort as well as physical softness. Perhaps most important is the ability to use the same material on other installations, such as upholstered furniture, bedspreads, and accessory items.

Fabrics used on the wall may be subject to soiling and may discolor or stain when spot cleaned, making upkeep difficult. Fabrics should not be used in heavy traffic areas where people, particularly children, tend to touch the wall frequently.

CEILING TREATMENTS

All of the materials discussed thus far in this chapter may be applied to ceilings. However, the most common of the ceiling treatments will be drywall, plaster, glass and other glazing materials, metal, and wall coverings or fabric. Keep in mind that ceilings may need to be visually lowered or heightened and that patterns, dark or bright colors, or texture will lower the height. Smooth surfaces or light, pale, or dull colors will visually raise the height. Horizontal bands or beams will visually lower a ceiling, whereas angled ceilings with beams or bands that carry the eye upward will increase the visual height. Fabric is sometimes upholstered on a ceiling or draped in sunburst or tentlike fashion, which not only can absorb sound but can create a cozy atmosphere. Fabric panels or acoustical panels (see chart 10.2) absorb sound and are appropriate in many settings. Textured acoustical plaster also absorbs sound, although it is extremely difficult to paint over—it catches dust and collects soil from ceiling-mounted ducts. Ceilings are frequently given a textured finish before painting to cover blemishes and reduce upkeep. Chapter 9, Architectural Detail, discusses and illustrates different architectural ceilings.

WINDOW TREATMENTS

Because of consumer demands for beauty, privacy, energy conservation, comfort, and cost efficiency, today's window treatments have so many options that an exhaustive discussion would fill volumes. Consequently, the most significant are discussed here. Interior designers and retailers alike strive to keep abreast of the continuing technical advances in window coverings.

Window treatments are generally divided into two categories—soft and hard. *Soft window treatments* include curtains, draperies, fabric shades, and top treatments; *hard window coverings* include a wide array of art glass, horizontal and vertical slat blinds, screens, shades, and shutters. These treatments are presented in charts 10.9 through 10.15. Recent trends have favored layered treatments—of two or more fabric treatments or of practical and durable hard treatment (a blind, shutter, screen, or shade) layered over with a soft fabric treatment of curtain, drapery, shade, or top treatment.

Window Treatment Considerations

Many factors go into making a wise choice for a window covering. These include aesthetic coordination, privacy, energy consciousness, light control, and operational control.

Aesthetic Coordination

Aesthetic coordination is the careful selection of window treatments to not only look beautiful but to blend with and support the interior and exterior design and architecture.

Aesthetic coordination also requires sensitivity to good proportion. It helps to judge proportion by sketching the window treatment to scale. Window treatments that are top heavy, too wide, overdone or—on the other hand, too skimpy—

can throw off the proportions of the entire room. This is because the window itself is an important architectural feature that will inevitably draw attention because of the light and view. If the window treatment is aesthetically disturbing, the interior will seem incomplete and lacking in harmony, no matter how handsome other furnishings are.

Privacy

Privacy protects valuable belongings against burglary. If it can be seen, it can be stolen. Privacy also gives a psychological sense of well-being to many people and makes a space more useable after dark.

During the day a sheer, semisheer, or casement fabric curtain, drapery, or shade will provide privacy. A pleated fabric shade, horizontal or vertical blind, partially opened shutter, woven wood, bamboo shade, roller shade, and translucent and pierced or lattice screen—all give good daytime privacy.

At night, any translucent treatment will not give privacy. Treatments that have holes or slats that do not close completely (pleated shades, horizontal blinds, woven woods, shutters) will not provide total privacy either. Only opaque treatments that can be closed fully will provide complete nighttime privacy. These include opaque draperies and shades, solid vane vertical louvers, lined woven woods, and opaque pleated shades with hidden cords.

Energy Consciousness

Energy consciousness is important for two reasons: (1) the cost of heating or cooling a room can be reduced through energy-efficient treatments, and (2) the comfort of the room can be enhanced by controlling excess *heat gain* and *heat loss*.

Heat gain or *solar heat gain* can be a problem not only in hot climates and in the summer but anytime heat from the sun becomes uncomfortable and begins to fade or damage interior furnishings. Treatments that control heat gain are referred to as *shading devices*. The ideal shading device is actually on the exterior, preventing the sun from hitting the glass. These devices include sunscreens; awnings; rolling, angled, or movable shutters; deciduous trees; vines; trellises; and projecting architectural elements.

Once the sun hits the glass, temperatures between the window and the interior window treatment can climb to as high as 300 degrees Fahrenheit, not only heating the room but causing damage to the window treatment, too. The most effective interior shading devices are those that can reflect a high percentage of sunlight back through the glass. Window film and metallized (fabrics and pleated shades) and light-colored treatments (hard and soft) do this best. Room-darkening treatments also effectively control heat and brightness. These include roller shades; woven woods; some shutters; horizontal and vertical blinds; and fabric curtains, draperies, and shades, particularly when lined and interlined.

Heat loss is a problem in moderate to cold climates in the winter. It takes place when heated interior air rises and travels toward the window, coming in contact with cold glass,

Figure 10.13 *A colorful balloon shade is a fitting window treatment in this lavish living room.*
Courtesy of Stark Carpet Corporation.

thereby cooling the heated air, which then drops to the floor and circulates at ankle level, causing us to feel a draft. Preventing the warm air from striking the glass is the best preventative for heat loss. Insulated fabric shades sealed on the sides and at the bottom and insulated shutters are the best treatments. Other good choices are opaque roller shades and lined, solidly woven woods and heavy lined/interlined draperies that reach to the floor, are securely attached to the walls, and have sealed top treatments. The heavier and more solid the treatment, the better it insulates. Many treatments on the market claim to be energy efficient in winter, and some are—to a degree. Any treatment is better than a bare window, and some treatments allow light and view while offering a limited amount of heat loss protection. However, the best treatments during the cold winter are heavy and opaque.

Light Control

Control of light is a major consideration in selecting window treatments. Certainly the light-controlling needs must be noted in the research phase of programming in the design process. If the room needs to be completely darkened, for example, then only certain treatments—opaque draperies, perhaps coupled with window shades—will fill that need. Light control also means heat gain control through shading devices. Light is often desirable. The undesirable aspect is not heat gain as much as control of glare (too bright, directional light), which causes irritation and fatigue. Glare control is a relatively simple need to fill, because many treatments will do a fair to an excellent job—draperies, curtains, shades (of light to medium weight), all types of vertical and horizontal blinds, pleated and translucent shades, *louvered* shutters, screens, bamboo shades, and woven woods.

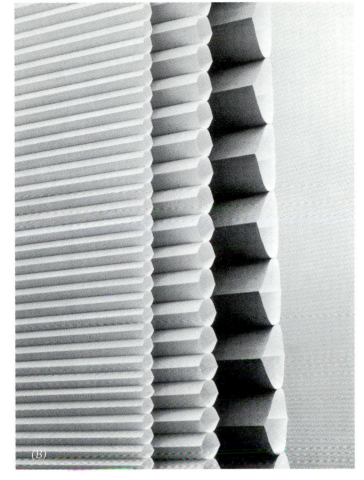

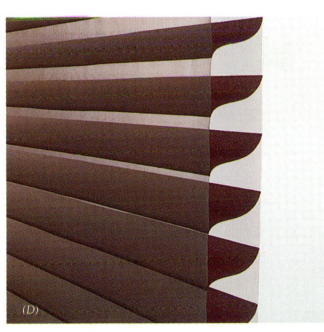

Figure 10.14 Energy conscious window coverings. (A) Soft lace draperies and swags frame these pleated shades that cut down on glare and screen light. Cellular construction or metalized backing conserves energy. Pleated shades diffuse light and conserve energy: (B) single-cell pleated shades in three sizes; (C) triple cell "honey comb" insulating shades; (D) "silhouette" shading system.

All courtesy of Hunter Douglas.

Figure 10.15 *Wood blinds control light and glare and are easy to operate. Swags and side draperies of a rich, complex fabric frame and soften the hard lines.*

Courtesy of Hunter Douglas.

Figure 10.16 *Draperies and box-pleated valance around the bed, along with the balloon shade at the window, unify the room with coordinated fabrics.*

Courtesy of Schumacher.

Within an interior, the need for light and glare control may vary according to the *orientation*, or direction the windows face. Whereas north-facing windows may need little light control, the bright east light, constant south light, or hot, piercing west light may require shading devices during particular times of the day when the sunlight comes directly through that window.

Operational Control

The selection of a window treatment should also be based on whether or not it needs to be operable, and this will largely be dictated by the needs previously discussed. Stationary treatments—tied-back draperies, ruffled curtains, top treatments, stationary screens—cannot be dropped for privacy, nor can they be removed for desirable solar gain or maximum light penetration. Ventilation may be inhibited by a treatment that is difficult to operate or that will not adequately stack out of the window area.

For many treatments on cord- or pulley-operated hardware, motorized units can operate the opening and closing of the treat-

ment. Many situations can benefit from motorized units—from hard-to-reach controls (such as solarium shades) to control by a disabled person to the convenience of automation or remote control. There are also mechanisms that can sense, by light or temperature change, when to close treatments, thus enhancing energy efficiency.

Soft Window Coverings

Fabric is used at the window more frequently than on walls because of the softness it gives to an inherently hard and poorly insulative material. Fabric at the window provides both sound and temperature insulation, visual comfort, and interest through color, texture, and perhaps pattern. In addition, light-filtering fabrics can give daytime privacy (and be layered with opaque fabrics or hard materials for nighttime privacy) and can effectively reduce or eliminate glare, which is harsh directional light. Fabrics can be installed on *traverse rods* to be drawn off the window. Fabrics also can be made into many decorative shapes, giving architectural support, authenticity, or decorative effects. There seems to be no limit to the styles and combinations of fabrics used at the window, making the window perhaps the most creative of the background material installations.

Curtains

Curtains are soft window treatments that make up a group of treatments. Curtains are often shirred, or gathered, onto a rod, making them stationary or hand operable. *Shirred curtains* may be formal or informal. Curtains can also have a variety of headings depending on the use. Chart 10.10 lists some types of curtains.

Draperies

Draperies are pleated fabric panels hung on a rod. Draperies may be opaque, casement (semiopaque), or translucent. There are many types of pleats, the most common being the French or pinch pleat. See chart 10.11.

Fabric Window Shades

Fabric shades are panels of fabric that operate top to bottom. In Great Britain they are called blinds. See chart 10.12.

Top Treatments

Top treatments are used for a number of reasons: to hide rods or pleats, to cover the area from the top of the window to the ceilings, to give a soft and finished look to the room. Top treatments may be shaped according to architectural detailing or inspired by furnishings. Fabric is often an effective medium to unite a room and carry the eye gracefully along the top of the walls. Types of top treatments are discussed in chart 10.13.

Drapery Hardware

Much of the versatility possible in soft window coverings is due to the many kinds of hardware that have been developed during this century, some of which are presented in chart 10.14. Many variations of each type are available through interior designers and window treatment specialists.

CHART 10.9   CALCULATING YARDAGE

For curtains and draperies:

1. Determine rod width (end of rod to end of rod).
2. Add on for overlaps (for traverse draperies that meet in the center) and returns (around the corner to the wall), if applicable. Twelve inches are standard for a single-hung layer, sixteen inches for a double-hung layer, and four inches for an underlayer.
3. Divide by twenty inches to determine the number of widths or cuts (a typical forty-five to forty-eight inch fabric will pleat or gather down to about twenty inches including side hems).
4. Determine the desired finished length (add six inches for puddling if desired), then add for hems, headings, and any ruffles to determine the cut length. Hems are usually four inches doubled, or eight inches. For pleated headings add eight inches. Ruffled headings will need six to twelve inches added depending on the depth of the ruffle and the width of rod. (Figure the finished length plus the rod pocket, the ruffle, and another two inches for the self-lining and hem, which is turned under.)
5. Multiply the cut length by the number of widths or cuts to find the total inches, then divide by thirty-six inches to yield the number of yards. Always round up. For pattern repeats, figure the number of complete pattern repeats needed for each cut, then multiply that number by the inches in one pattern repeat for the total inches needed per cut. There will be waste in pattern repeat fabrics because the pattern must start at the same point at the top of each cut. Yardage will be an average of 20 percent greater.
6. Costs for sewing, installation (charged by the width or foot), and the rods are additional.

For balloon shades:

1. Determine finished width, then divide by twenty inches for the number of cuts or widths.
2. Add six to eight inches for hems and headings, then add twenty inches for the pouf at the bottom.
3. Ruffle yardage is figured in widthwise or lengthwise strips, total inches of ruffle needed will be multiplied by two or three (for desired fullness), and the depth of the ruffle doubled plus one inch for self-lining. These dimensions are calculated or sketched out in scale into the width of the goods either widthwise or lengthwise.
4. Cost to sew is figured per square foot (ruffles are extra, charged per linear foot), and fabrication costs are greater if the shade is operable.
5. Installation board and cost to install are priced per linear foot. Board may be included in cost of shade fabrication.

For flat, shaped, and pleated valances:

1. Determine whether the width should run vertically in cuts or horizontally (railroaded) with no seams. Railroaded fabrics may appear a different color than the curtain or shade beneath it because of the way the light hits the weave.
2. Determine the cuts or widths (if selected) as previously determined for curtains, eliminating the overlap but figuring in returns. Multiply the cuts by doubling the finished length for self-lining, plus two to four inches for seams, or multiply by finished length plus two to four inches if lining fabric is used. Divide by thirty-six inches for yardage, then round up. Order the same quantity of lining fabric if the fabric is not to be self-lined.
3. Railroaded valances and curtains/draperies turn the width to run the lengthwise direction of the goods. Multiply the finished width by 2 1/2 (or fullness desired) and divide by thirty-six inches for yardage. For valances, figure strips this way—finished length—face only or self-lined measurement divided into the width of the goods.

For swags and cascades:

1. Determine the number of swags or festoons by sketching them in the configuration desired and determining the overlap and width of each swag. Measure for desired depth.
2. A self-lined swag up to twenty inches wide and twelve inches deep will need one to one and a half yards each; a self-lined swag up to forty inches wide and twenty-four inches deep will need three yards each.
3. Cascades and jabots need yardage equal to double their finished length. Costs to sew are determined by the workroom. To sew on ruffles or trimmings will cost extra (trimming yardage is 2 1/2 times the top of the swag); installation is per swag or cascade or per linear foot of installation board.

CHART 10.10 TYPES OF CURTAINS

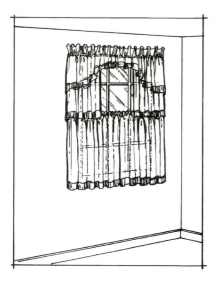

Cottage curtains are short lengths, shirred, and hung in informal style within or on the window frame. They may be tiered or layered. Café curtains cover the bottom half of the window.

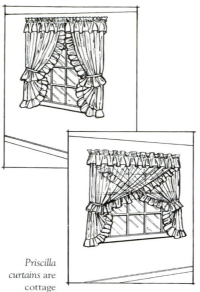

Priscilla curtains are cottage curtains that fill the window with a sheer, semi-sheer, or muslin fabric. Priscillas have a ruffle sewn on the front leading and bottom edges and on the tiebacks and have a ruffled valance. They meet in the middle or crisscross with one panel in front of the other.

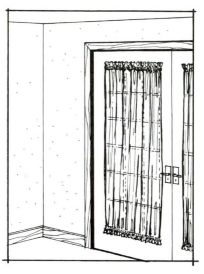

Sash curtains are sheer or semisheer fabrics shirred at the top and bottom and installed most often on casement windows and French doors so as to swing with the sash.

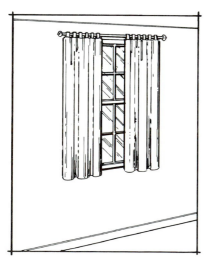

Tab curtains are flat panels with straps of fabric sewn to the top and looped over dowel rods. A simple, handsome treatment.

Bishop sleeve curtains look best as elongated graceful forms, here "puddled" on the floor.

Long or formal curtains are shirred (gathered) onto the rod and nonoperational.

CHART 10.11 TYPES OF DRAPERIES

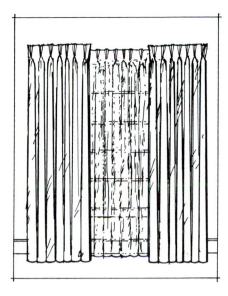

Draw draperies are installed on a traverse (cord-operated) rod and may be pulled or drawn open and closed. Privacy draperies are installed under a transparent fabric or separated tiebacks to provide nighttime privacy or insulation. Sheer draperies include transparent and translucent fabrics, often placed next to the glass and historically called glass curtains.

Side draperies are stationary panels hung to the side of windows as a treatment for softness and framing.

Tieback draperies are ideally slender stationary panels that meet in the center on narrow windows or are separated on wider windows. They are tied back with fabric bands (ties) or metal holdbacks.

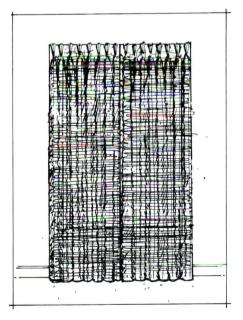

Casement draperies are draw draperies made of a woven or knit fabric with novelty yarns and a strong textural look. They are popular in nonresidential settings, such as offices, and in casual settings at home. They screen light and cut down on glare but do not provide nighttime privacy.

CHART 10.12 FABRIC WINDOW SHADES

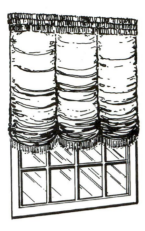

Austrian shade fabric is sewn into soft horizontal scallops and gathered vertically. Formal theaters often use Austrian shades. In homes and formal offices they are often made of sheer or semisheer fabrics, edged with fringe.

Balloon (also pouf or cloud) shades are billowy at the bottom, forming large poufs or balloons. The top may be shirred, flat-box pleated, French pleated, etc. They may be tailored or fancy with ruffles and trimmings.

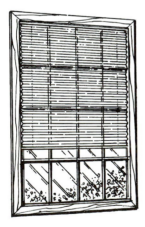

Pleated shades are factory-made products of semisheer polyester fabric, plain or printed, that fold up in accordion fashion. They may have a metallized backing for insulation against summer solar gain and winter heat loss. They may also be opaque. Also available as cellular, double-wall shades.

Roman shades are sewn in horizontal folds that raise and lower accordion style with a draw cord. They may be pleated first to give more fullness to the shade. Roman shades may also be interlined with batting, heavy lining, and moisture-barrier material to make an energy-efficient shade.

CHART 10.13 **TYPES OF TOP TREATMENTS**

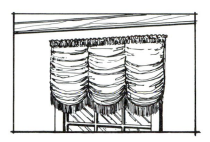

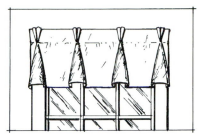

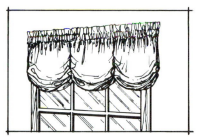

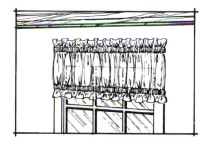

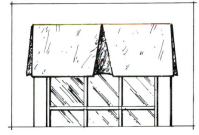

Austrian (top) *and balloon* (bottom) *valances* look like the shades previously described. Balloon or pouf valances are more casual and airy; Austrians are more formal and traditional.

Shirred (top) *and double-shirred* (bottom) *valances* are gathered on the top and on the top and bottom, respectively. Smocked valances are a variation of double shirring and tucks in a diamond-shaped pattern. Top-shirred valances may have shaped or scalloped bottoms.

Pleated valances have several different forms. They may be French or pinch pleats (top), flat-box or inverted box pleats (bottom), or variations such as rounded cartridge pleats, pleat and scallops, pencil pleats, or any number of unconventional pleats.

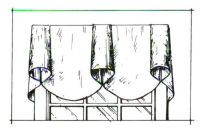

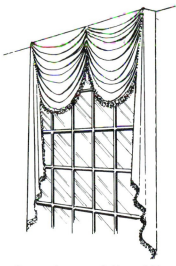

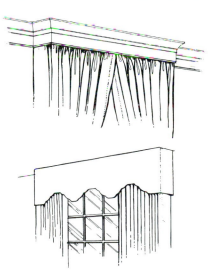

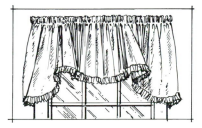

Shaped valances usually have straight tops and scalloped or shaped bottoms, although the top may also be shaped or curved. The shape might carry out a theme, document a historic period, or be a shape found in a piece of furniture—the back of a chair, for example. Fabric and lining are interlined with a stiffening material to give body to the flat fabric valance.

Swags or *festoons* are half-round fabric treatments in overlapping arrangements. Swags are the treatment perhaps most often used throughout history. Many widths, depths, and variations are possible. Cascades often frame swags and festoons. Some are placed on top and some underneath the swag.

Cornices are straight or shaped wooden top treatments. When covered with padding and fabric, they are called upholstered cornices. When cornices extend down both sides to the floor or partway, they become lambrequins or cantonnieres and may also be upholstered. These are energy efficient, since they keep warm and cool air from exchanging at the window.

CHART 10.14 TYPES OF DRAPERY HARDWARE

Conventional traverse rods are cord-operated rods with carriers to hold the drapery hooks. White is the usual color, and brown is available. Conventional traverse rods come in single-hung (for one pair of draperies), double-hung (for two sets of draperies), with a plain curtain rod underneath or a curtain/valance rod on top. They also come in one-way draw for stacking draperies to one side.

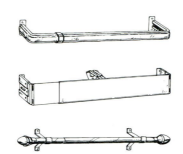

Curtain rods come in slender (one-inch) round or oval shapes or extra wide (two and one-half and four-inch) sizes. Some curtain rods are made with spring tension so no brackets are necessary on an inside frame mount. Curtain rods also come in round brass and white finishes with attached finials and may have brass rings to hold drapery hooks or clips to clip onto pleats or panels.

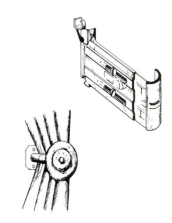

Tieback holders come in patterns such as decorative rosettes and as concealed (clear plastic placed under the drapery) holders.

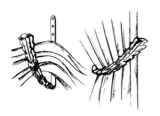

Swag holders.

Decorator rods have special carriers that look like rings but operate as traverse (cord-operated) rods. They come in wood colors, white, antique, brass, chrome, black, and specialty finishes.

Wood rods come plain and fluted, in natural or stained wood, white, and black, and they may be painted any color or covered with fabric or wallpaper. Curtains may be shirred onto wood rods, the fabric may be draped over in loose swag fashion, or the wood ring carriers may hold drapery hooks, which must be hand operated.

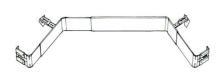

Bay and bow rods are available in nearly as many varieties as listed for conventional traverse and curtain rods. Motorized rods are for hard-to-reach draperies or large installations, or simply for the convenience of pushing a button rather than pulling on a cord or drawing a wand. Motorized systems are common in nonresidential settings. They are less common in residences.

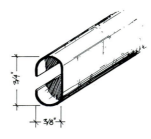

Special rodding is available to bend to any shape or angle. It is referred to as CTM (cut-to-measure) rodding.

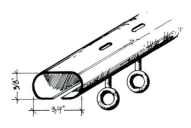

Architectural rodding comes in several varieties, and each company has patented names for their products. Nonresidential or architectural rods have sturdy ball-bearing carriers, and many of the styles are operated with a wand rather than a cord, which eliminates many problems of cord-operated rods in places such as hotels, offices, and institutions. Often nonresidential rods are for flat panels or for draperies with less fullness and simpler pleats. Components can be specified separately for any type of custom installation.

Figure 10.17 *These movable-louver shutters offer light and privacy control, plus the warmth of wood.*
Courtesy of Pinecrest, Inc.

Hard Window Treatments

Today we are at an apex of selection in window treatments. We enjoy not only historical hard materials that have endured as classics but we also have new styles and hardware that are continually being improved through keen market competition. Hard materials are generally very durable and require little maintenance. They can be clean and contemporary or very traditional, crossing boundaries in many cases. They are versatile backgrounds and are often simple statements that will coordinate with many styles of furnishings. Some can be inexpensive and offer both privacy and light control. Types of hard window treatments are discussed and illustrated in chart 10.15.

CHART 10.15 TYPES OF HARD WINDOW TREATMENTS

Stained and *art glass* gives pattern, color, and interest to the glass. Patterns and privacy level varies. Costly.

Two-inch *metal* or *wood blinds* are handsome, as well as providing light control and privacy. Moderate cost.

Miniblinds control light and glare, give relative privacy, and are sleek and inexpensive.

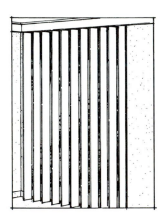

Vertical louvers are durable, can provide good light control, can offer privacy (when heavy or opaque), and can conserve energy. Moderate cost.

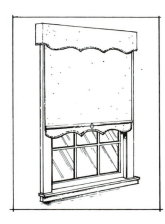

Roller shades can be translucent, or when opaque, are energy efficient. Low to moderate cost.

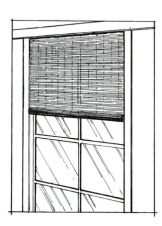

Bamboo shades give a natural look as they screen glare and diffuse light. They offer no nighttime privacy. Inexpensive.

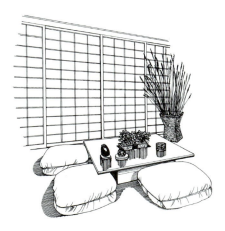

Shoji screens provide light diffusion and the serenity of old Japan. They operate by sliding on tracks. Costly.

One-inch *movable louver shutters*, shown here as double-hung, give light control, privacy, and the warmth of woods. Costly.

Plantation shutters have wide blades and have a permanent look to them. Costly.

Figure 10.18 *For centuries marble has been a preferred finish material in large public spaces, such as seen here in the Utah State Capitol building. Columns, walls, and floors are stone, a material that provides a sense of permanence and stability and one that will last through generations of heavy traffic.*
Photo by John Wang.

NONRESIDENTIAL CONSIDERATIONS

Materials for nonresidential wall, window, and ceiling materials often differ from those used in the home. These differences are threefold. Nonresidential materials generally must be:

1. More durable—they should be able to withstand harder abuse from greater traffic in less-controlled situations.

2. Less patterned and more textured in appearance—nonresidential materials are plain compared to the variety of decorative materials used in homes.

3. Flame-retardant, fire resistant or fireproof, and static- and microorganism-resistant—in order to meet state and local building codes for public safety.

Durability

Because of the durability requirement, permanent hard materials are often used in nonresidential settings. It is not uncommon to see stone (such as travertine) tile, or brick used not only on the exterior but on the interior. This allows people to touch, bump, soil, or abrade the surface without worry that the surface will be damaged. Wall covering materials are specially made to be durable for nonresidential applications. For example, vinyl and fabric wall coverings can withstand a great deal of physical abuse, and many *nonresidential wall coverings* have been tested and rated so the architect or designer can match the durability rating to the traffic classification required by code or building specification.

  ‣ Class I are decorative wall coverings.
  ‣ Class II are decorative and serviceable wall coverings. Serviceability includes colorfastness (low) and washability.

- Class III are decorative wall coverings that have good serviceability. Serviceability includes colorfastness (low to moderate), washability, scrubbability, and resistance to abrasion, breaking, crocking, and staining.

- Class IV are wall coverings that are decorative with full serviceability, including colorfastness (low to moderate), washability, scrubbability, and resistance to abrasion, breaking, crocking, staining, and tearing.

- Class V are medium commercial serviceability wall coverings that include colorfastness (very good), washability, scrubbability, and resistance to abrasion, breaking, crocking, staining, tearing, heat aging, cracking, and shrinkage.

- Class VI, full commercial serviceability wall coverings, are the same as Class V but with greater resistance to tearing.[5]

Nonresidential wall coverings are also classified as either nonmildew resistant or mildew resistant. They may also need to meet fire code restrictions, which makes the product selection somewhat different than residential wall coverings. The range of selections tends to be more textured and subtle, without the many changing designer patterns found in residential wall coverings.

Nonresidential wall coverings are often fifty-two to fifty-four inches wide and contain thirty square yards, which is more convenient and economical for large installations. However, this much weight is unwieldy and requires expert installation.[6]

Nonresidential Ceiling Treatments

There are many materials and types of treatments used in nonresidential interiors that are worth mentioning. These include acoustical ceilings in tile or larger panel sections, mounted in suspended grid systems. Ceilings are often dropped to accommodate heating, ventilation and air-conditioning systems, lighting systems, communication systems, and fire-extinguishing systems. The ceiling must allow access to these systems in case of system or component breakdown. Ceilings may consist largely of indirect lighting; they may contain soffits for lighting or accommodating the previously mentioned systems. The ceiling may be of glass, such as a solarium ceiling, in which case it must be safety glass (see chart 10.2).

Nonresidential Window Treatments

Window treatments for nonresidential interiors must be able to withstand operation from many different people who might not know how to smoothly or carefully operate them. Therefore, mechanisms are usually engineered to be as trouble free as possible. Drapery rods without pull cords are often specified. Draperies are often slid open and closed one panel at a time with a wand attached to the leading carrier. This not only prevents breakdowns that would otherwise occur in a cord-and-pulley system but discourages the handling (and soiling/damaging) of the fabric to find the cords.

Window treatment materials must be able to reduce glare for office use, a particularly important facet for those working on computer terminals (glare on the screen must be minimized or eliminated). Daytime privacy in working/nonresidential situations is also of prime importance. Therefore, hard window treatments are used frequently. Of these, the most popular are miniblinds, vertical louvers, roller shades (opaque and film), and pleated shades with metallized backings. Casement draperies—generally an open-constructed cloth—are standard in offices and situations where glare control and softness are required.

Window treatments may also be required to provide any or all of the following six energy conservation functions:

1. Allow winter solar heat gain

2. Allow daylighting all year

3. Reflect summer solar heat gain

4. "Seal" the window from the room air when mechanical heating and air-conditioning are operating

5. Insulate against heat and cold extremes

6. Allow for natural ventilation during temperate weather[7]

Nighttime privacy is a need in some installations, requiring a hard treatment that can close fully or a fabric that is lined, opaque, or a combination of hard and soft materials—such as a casement fabric over a blind or shade. Printed fabrics are sometimes used in hospitality and medical facilities. Hotels, for example, will often have coordinated or matching draperies and bedspreads; hospitals and clinics may have patterned draperies in patient rooms and sometimes as cubicle curtains. These are finished with soil- and stain-resistant treatments. Patterns are good choices where the fabric will be handled, since patterns will not readily show soil and will hide wear better than plain fabrics (unless, of course, the patterns fade from sunlight, which makes them look worn-out prematurely).

Less Pattern

Most of the materials used in nonresidential installations, however, do not include much pattern. Rather, texture is seen for nearly every surface installation. Hard materials (stone, brick, tile, concrete) often have natural patterns that read as texture and cannot be removed. Where plaster is used, it is often textured as well. Flexible wall coverings are frequently given textures that imitate natural materials such as grass cloth, leather suede, or marble. Fabric wall coverings can be amazingly durable as well as handsome. Natural linen and wool coverings are fine quality examples of beauty combined with durability. Man-made fibers can also make tough, good-looking wall covering fabrics and are often used in wall partitions or dividers in open office planning where they serve to absorb sound. Acoustical ceiling tiles, likewise, have texture and very subtle pattern, as do other ceiling panel materials—metal or fabric, for example. Textures show less soil and wear and will last longer under use and abuse than will plain fabrics. Whereas patterned fabrics and wall coverings soon become dated and the color schemes last only a few years, textured fabrics do not go out of style as quickly as do patterns. This is important in nonresidential settings where the design scheme may not be changed for many years.

Safety Codes

Safety codes are laws that ensure the safety of the occupants in public spaces. Codes routinely govern fire safety, static resistance, and protection against microorganism and bacteria growth. The architect or designer must find materials that meet either building codes or written building specifications. These materials have been tested and rated for their resistance to fire, static, and microorganisms. Most materials will have been tested in most of these areas, and the information will be written on the samples (part of product specifications) or available from the manufacturer. The documentation of these ratings is of prime importance in designer liability. Fire safety is obviously the most crucial of these standards. The material should also have been tested for smoke density and for the emission of toxic or poisonous gases while burning or smoldering. Flammability terms are presented under Nonresidential Considerations in chapter 12, Fabric.

ENVIRONMENTAL CONSIDERATIONS

Energy-conscious windows and window treatments were discussed earlier in the chapter under Energy Consciousness. Additional considerations include:

1. utilizing natural daylight to reduce energy consumption of artificial lighting and

2. remembering to close the energy-conserving treatment at night and during either very hot or very cold weather.

NOTES

1. J. Rosemary Riggs, *Materials and Components of Interior Design*, 2d ed. (Englewood Cliffs, N.J.: Prentice-Hall, 1989), pp. 5–64, 73–115.

2. Charles Hemming, *Paint Finishes* (Secaucus, N.J.: Chartwell Books, 1985), 7.

3. Ibid.

4. Ibid., 12, 53–131.

5. S.C. Reznikoff, *Specifications for Commercial Interiors: Professional Liabilities, Regulations, and Performance Criteria* (New York: Whitney Library of Design, 1979).

6. J. Rosemary Riggs, *Materials and Components of Interior Design*, 2d ed. (Englewood Cliffs, N.J.: Prentice-Hall, 1989), 85–86.

7. Reznikoff, *Specifications for Commercial Interiors*, 131.

FLOOR MATERIALS AND COVERINGS

Courtesy of Stark Carpet Corporation.

FLOORING REQUIREMENTS AND SPECIFICATIONS

When a home or new building is designed, the finish materials specified for floors are often permanent selections. The criteria that determine the choice include:

1. The durability needed and/or maintenance necessary
2. Cost of materials, installation, and maintenance in terms of time, effort, and expenses
3. Aesthetic considerations, such as establishing a particular or authentic architectural style
4. The necessity of acoustic control of noise
5. Applicable insulative and solar absorption or reflection needs
6. The fire or building codes that must be met

Floor materials are calculated and priced per square foot or square yard. Hard materials such as stone, wood, wood combined with another material, and some tiles are calculated per square foot and are costly, although they are also very durable. Sheet vinyl and carpeting are calculated per square yard and cost less than most hard materials, though they are less durable. To find the square footage, multiply the room's width by its length (in feet). Divide this figure by nine to find the square yardage (nine square feet in one square yard). Calculating yardage is a bit more complex, however, because roll goods (vinyl and carpet) must be installed all the same direction with no quarter turns. Designers and specifiers will plot roll goods to determine exact widths and cuts (vinyl is usually six feet wide; carpet twelve feet wide). Each cut (width) is multiplied by its length, then divided to determine the yardage to be ordered.

Installation costs for stone and tile are high and figured per square foot according to the charges of the installer ($3.00 or more per square foot—pr/sq/ft). Wood installation is also costly and is charged by the square foot ($2.00 or more pr/sq/ft). Wood may need professional finishing (acrylic or polyurethane), and brick may need a sealant. Carpet costs are figured per square yard and generally include pad or underlay and installation (using the tackless strip method or the direct glue-down method) at $6.00 and up.

Flooring materials are divided into three categories—hard (nonresilient), resilient, and soft. *Nonresilient flooring materials* include brick, concrete, stone, tile, and wood. *Resilient* flooring materials are asphalt tile, cork, fabric, leather, linoleum, rubber, and vinyl. Soft floor coverings include wall-to-wall carpeting and a wide selection of area rugs.

GUIDELINES FOR SELECTING HARD AND RESILIENT FLOOR MATERIALS

Hard and resilient floor materials form a substantial part of the character of an interior. The integrity of flooring is so important that it is impossible to create successful interiors if the flooring is cheap looking, a poor imitation of a natural material, or shoddy

Figure 11.1 *The slate used in this floor is a handsome, timeless material.* © *Lisl Dennis.*

design or quality. Whether the flooring is of hard or resilient materials (listed in charts 11.1 and 11.2) or is a rug or carpet (discussed later in this chapter), it will be a wise choice if it is, in itself, beautiful. We should not look at a floor covering only as a background but as a material that will provide years of satisfaction in terms of beauty, durability, and upkeep.

- The first consideration is whether the flooring material is inherently beautiful and has good design merit and integrity. It should be appealing even if there are no furnishings whatsoever in the interior.

- The material should provide a graceful and harmonious background for a variety of furnishing styles over a period of years. This means that neutralized colors, subtle textures, and a lack of definite pattern are usually desirable. The exception here is where the flooring provides drama or focus as a planned part of the interior design.

- Consider the way the material will age and how long the flooring will be in place. Hard and resilient flooring is often in place for ten to twenty years, and quality hard materials (stone, brick, tile, and wood) can last for hundreds of years, as seen in many important historic interiors.

- Consider subfloor preparation. If stone or heavy tile or brick is to be used, then the floor must be structurally strong enough to hold it. Thick floor materials will raise the floor level, as well. For thin resilient floors such as vinyl, the subfloors must be smooth and free of irregularities since these flaws will show through the finish flooring.[1]

Figure 11.2 *In this men's store, the vividly colorful tie display counterpoints a classic black and white marble flooring.*
Courtesy of Zakaspace.

- Look at the cost of the material in comparison to the number of years the flooring will last. For example, stone, brick, tile, or wood can last indefinitely, whereas vinyl, cork, and leather may have limited life spans. The total cost of the installation divided by the number of years of expected use will yield the predicted cost per year. This may, surprisingly, reveal that the more costly product is actually cheaper in the long run because it will never need replacing. This is referred to as life-cycle costing.

- Consider using materials that possess real longevity, since these not only look good for many years but they also gleam with *patina*, a mellowing of the finish as it ages and a quality often present in great interiors that have endured the test of time.

- Consider upkeep. Hard flooring materials generally require little maintenance, whereas some resilient materials may need special upkeep. A wisely selected flooring will be appropriate for the amount of soiling it will receive. Natural materials are particularly good at camouflaging

tracked-in soil. Upkeep also entails the relative ease of cleaning. For example, grooves or indentations can trap dirt, which can add to the maintenance requirements.

- Take into account the ability of the material to withstand traffic. Will the material resist wearing down, and will any finish wear off in areas of heavy traffic?

- A functional consideration is that smooth hard and resilient flooring tends to be slippery when wet unless texture is used to prevent slippage.

- Flooring for the aged and handicapped requires special considerations, such as avoiding glare, three-dimensional patterns, or abrupt pattern changes. Flooring for the wheelchair-bound must not impair the chair's smooth operation by being too rugged or by carpeting *pile* being too deep.

- Stone will withstand heavy traffic but may become scuffed or scratched. Since it is very hard, it should not be used in areas where people will be standing for long periods or where fragile items may drop and break.

Figure 11.3 *Wood flooring is available in several patterns.* (A) *Herringbone pattern wood floor.* (B) *Broad plank wood floor on the diagonal.*
Courtesy of Hartco.

HARD FLOOR MATERIALS

Hard floor materials have several advantages:

- Nonresilient materials are noted for their strength and durability.

- They are nonabsorbent and relatively impervious to soiling.

- They are easy to maintain and clean.

- They tend to be "classics," with aesthetic appeal to last indefinitely. This is particularly true of brick, stone, tile, and wood, which may be used as suitable backgrounds for many styles of interior design furnishings.

- Several varieties of these materials are available, giving the designer the flexibility to create interiors that are formal or informal, structural or decorative, textured or patterned.

- In addition, the heavy nonresilient materials such as brick, tile, stone, or concrete can serve as the structure as well as the finish materials for some floors and walls.

Disadvantages of hard floor materials include the following:

- They have a high initial cost. For example, wood is considerably more costly to purchase and install than resilient sheet vinyl. In the long run, however, wood may actually cost less than a type of vinyl that must be replaced every five or ten years.

- Special preparation is required to support floors of heavy finish materials, such as brick, tile, stone, and concrete.

- It is possible for nonresilient materials to be damaged or broken by dropping a heavy object on a tile floor, for instance.

- Hard materials tend to be cold to the touch unless heated artificially or by sunshine.

- They are nonporous, so they reflect sound and even seem to amplify noise. Because of this, hard materials are often used as backgrounds for soft materials such as area rugs.

Following is a chart of the hard flooring materials. Each type includes a description, applications (where used), maintenance guidelines, and the cost structure involved.

CHART 11.1 HARD FLOOR MATERIALS

BRICK

Description: Clay, shale, water mixed and shaped into solid or hollow rectangular blocks, then baked or fired to harden. Brick is colored according to the clay used or the dyes added before firing. Solid bricks used for paving are three-fourths to two inches thick and are referred to as "pavers."

Applications: Interior and exterior floors and patio paving, residential and nonresidential.

Maintenance: Low upkeep: sweep, dust, vacuum, damp mop, or buff.

Cost Structure: Moderate to high.

CONCRETE

Description: Portland cement, sand, gravel or rock aggregate, and water mixed and poured into forms or slabs and possibly texturized. Hardens as it sets. Naturally gray but may be colored.

Applications: Subfloors, floors may be cast or stamped into shapes. Nonresidential floors in high-rise office buildings, apartment houses, dormitories, hospitals, and retail buildings. Concrete may be both the structural element and finish material.

Maintenance: Raw concrete absorbs stains and generates dust; painted or sealed concrete is impervious to stains as long as the paint or finish remains intact. Sweep, damp mop, or hose off where possible.

Cost Structure: Moderate.

EXPOSED AGGREGATE

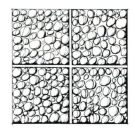

Description: Aggregate (smooth rocks or small pebbles) set or rolled into wet concrete. Part of the concrete is hosed off before it dries in order to expose the aggregate. Also called pebble tile or pebble concrete.

Applications: Interior and exterior paving or flooring where heavy traffic requires exceptional durability and where the textured look is desired. Residential and nonresidential applications.

Maintenance: When sealed with a polyurethane or other finish, exposed aggregate has very low upkeep. A brush vacuum is the easiest method of sweeping, and damp mopping may be unnecessary as it is impervious to dirt penetration.

Cost Structure: Moderate to high.

SLATE

Description: A metamorphic, finely grained, hard rock that cleaves or splits naturally into layers, making it possible to cut slabs from one-half to one inch thick. The surface may be treated in three ways: fairly rough (if it is a natural cleft or split); rubbed with sand to achieve an even plane; or honed, which produces a smooth finish and has a patina or mellow glow. Colors vary from grays to greenish or reddish grays to blacks and browns.

Applications: Slate is used as paving or flooring in both residential and nonresidential settings.

Maintenance: Low upkeep: sweep, vacuum, mild soap and water. Do not wax.

Cost Structure: Moderate to high.

TRAVERTINE

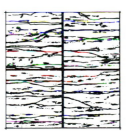

Description: A light-colored limestone rock formed near mineral springs. Trapped gas in the stone causes holes and interesting textures. When used as flooring, the holes are filled with cement or epoxy.

Applications: Floors, stair treads, fireplace hearths. Used frequently in nonresidential settings and as accents and for custom installations in residential interiors.

Maintenance: Vacuum, wash when necessary with clear lukewarm water. Wash no more often than every six months with soap and water and rinse thoroughly to prevent a slippery surface.

Cost Structure: High.

CERAMIC TILE

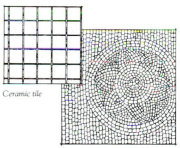

Ceramic tile

Mosaic tile

Description: Fine, white clays formed into tile shape (bisque) and fired, glazed before the first or second firing. Finishes vary from shiny and smooth to patterned to rough and matte (dull). Mosaic tiles are very small tiles that may come in preset sheets, a face mount or back mount, ready to be set with grout.

Applications: Floors; used extensively in nonresidential settings because of its durability. In residences, ceramic tile flooring is used in entryways, bathrooms, kitchens, and solariums.

Maintenance: Low upkeep: sweep, vacuum, damp mop, or soap and water for heavy dirt. Grout may soil and discolor. Silicone treatments will make grout less susceptible to soil.

Cost Structure: Low to high—costs vary considerably in ceramic tiles.

continued

CHART 11.1 HARD FLOOR MATERIALS *continued*

FLAGSTONE

Description: Flagging is a term that describes exterior or interior paving. Types of flagstone include bluestone, quartzite, sandstone, and slate. It is cut rough and left uneven in thickness. Sizes vary from one to four feet square.

Applications: Used for flooring in residential and nonresidential settings. Shape can be regular or irregular and surface will be fairly uniform.

Maintenance: Little upkeep: sweep, vacuum, or damp mop if necessary.

Cost Structure: High.

GRANITE

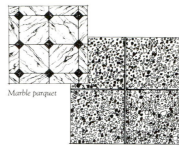

Description: A very hard crystalline rock with small amounts of feldspar, quartz, and other minerals in crystal or grain form. The size of the crystals varies from very fine to fairly coarse. The colors vary from light to dark values and variations of gray, pink, green, brown, and black and may be combinations such as greenish or pinkish gray. May be dull or highly polished.

Applications: Floors; used in high-end residential and nonresidential settings.

Maintenance: Low upkeep: sweep, vacuum, or damp mop if necessary.

Cost Structure: High.

MARBLE

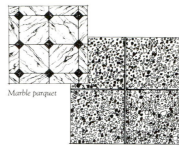

Marble parquet

Terrazzo

Description: A metamorphic limestone, granular or crystalline, white or colored, often with streaks. The hardest and typically the most expensive of the stones. May be cut into thin sheets or slabs. Can be polished to a high sheen. Cold to the touch. Terrazzo is a composite flooring of broken chips of marble set into cement and polished to a sheen. May be tiles or poured as a solid floor. This is a practical use of marble, since up to 50 percent waste occurs from breakage at the quarry.

Applications: Floors, fireplace hearths. Exclusive material for high-end residential and nonresidential installations.

Maintenance: Clean with warm water and infrequently with soap and water, taking care to rinse well, as soap residue will render the floor slippery.

Cost Structure: High.

QUARRY TILE

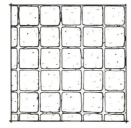

Description: Quarry tile is made of fine clay and graded shale, with color distributed through the body of the tile. Most is a terra-cotta rust/red, the color of the natural clay. It may be glazed but usually is left natural. Square or hexagonal shapes are most popular.

Applications: Flooring where a less formal, durable product is desirable.

Maintenance: Same as for ceramic tile.

Cost Structure: Low to moderate (installation is costly).

MEXICAN TILE

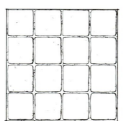

Description: Hand-shaped clay taken from the ground and left to set before firing. These tiles are a cottage-industry (families working together) product, which reflects imperfections of hand labor and adds to the charm of these tiles. They are thick and fragile, rustic and handsome. Smaller tiles may be hand painted and glazed.

Applications: Large squares are useful for flooring in both residential and nonresidential settings.

Maintenance: Porous surface should be treated with linseed oil or paste wax. Sweep, dust mop, wax, and buff. Rewax or reoil when it shows signs of wear.

Cost Structure: Low to moderate (installation is costly).

WOOD PLANKS AND PARQUET

Description: Oak, maple, cherry, or teak strips range from 1 1/2 to 2 1/4 inches wide and two to seven feet in length. Random plank widths range from three to eight inches, typically installed in three varying sizes. Strips and random plank are tongue and groove to fit snugly together. Parquet is the arrangement of strips or squares of wood preset into squares or into shapes.

Random plank

Herringbone parquet

Basketweave parquet

Basketweave/ octagonal parquet

Applications: Residential and nonresidential flooring. Solid wood may come prefinished, or may be impregnated with stain and acrylic, for a durable nonresidential surface.

Maintenance: Depends on the finish: oiled or waxed wood will need protection against moisture, require dust mopping frequently, and will need rewaxing. Two finishes used frequently today are polyurethane and acrylic. These require only sweeping, dust mopping, or vacuuming, and occasionally damp mopping with a water-vinegar solution. Hard (liquid) wax can be used on top.

Cost Structure: Moderate to high.

Figure 11.4 *"Visions Solarian" vinyl floor gives a fresh quality to this country kitchen.*

Courtesy of the makers of Armstrong no-wax flooring.

RESILIENT FLOOR MATERIALS

Resilient materials are those with some flexibility or give. These include *cork*, fabric, leather, *rubber*, and most vinyls. Like hard materials, resilient floor materials have common sets of advantages and disadvantages.

The advantages of resilient flooring are:

- ‣ Initial cost is generally lower than for hard materials.
- ‣ Resilient floor materials are warmer to the touch than nonresilient materials.
- ‣ By absorbing more sound, they produce quieter, more comforting interiors.
- ‣ They are easier on the body for standing and thereby produce less fatigue.
- ‣ Items dropped are less likely to break, and less damage is done to the floor itself because of its ability to give (resilience).

- ‣ There is a wide variety of designs or patterns, colors, and even visual textures (particularly in the vinyl flooring types).
- ‣ The maintenance is relatively low, depending on the finish and the durability of the finish.

Disadvantages of resilient flooring include the following:

- ‣ They may require more maintenance and cleaning if the surface has no protection or the no-wax surface treatment wears off (due to harsh detergents or high traffic). Damp mopping no-wax floors with water and a small amount of vinegar will clean without removing the shine.
- ‣ Resilient floors may be damaged, dented, or torn by dropping sharp objects such as kitchen knives or by dragging furniture or appliances across the surface.
- ‣ Resilient flooring is less durable than hard floor materials, making them a costly choice in the long run due to the necessity of replacement.
- ‣ If poorly installed, seams will open and become worn.

CHART 11.2 RESILIENT FLOOR MATERIALS

CORK

Description: The outer layer of the oak tree of the birch family that grows in the Mediterranean area. It is light in color, elastic, and very insulative. Resilient cork flooring is usually treated with a vinyl coating or impregnation, removing some of its resilience but making it a more durable product. It is sound absorbent.

Applications: Residential and nonresidential settings where a quiet surface is required for low or limited traffic.

Maintenance: Vinyl-cork floors may be damp mopped or buffed. They tend to show dust and footprints easily.

Cost Structure: Moderate to high.

LEATHER

Description: Squares or tiles of leather, the tanned hide of cattle and swine. Dyed brown or other colors. Embossed with patterns historically. Leather may also be cut into strips and made into shag-type area rugs.

Applications: High-end residential in small, low-traffic areas. Quiet flooring.

Maintenance: Damp mop with very mild detergent; no saddle soap.

Cost Structure: Very high.

LINOLEUM

Description: A mixture of ground cork and wood, color pigments, gums, and oxidized linseed oil poured onto a canvas or burlap backing. This smooth and washable flooring was popular for several decades but is no longer on the market. It has been completely replaced by vinyl. The term linoleum is still sometimes used out of habit to describe vinyl products.

RUBBER

Description: Tiles made of butadiene styrene rubber and synthetic materials come in two forms: a flat surface with a marbleized pattern and a raised disc or squares—a solid colored three-dimensional surface. The latter was designed to knock dirt off shoes and to provide water drainage off the surface.

Applications: Primarily nonresidential flooring.

Maintenance: Sweep or vacuum. May be washed with detergent and water. Rinsed and mopped with a water and 5 percent liquid bleach solution. Buff for shine return. New floors will require more buffing.

Cost Structure: Moderately high.

VINYL

Description: Vinyl is a shortened name for polyvinyl chloride (or PVC), a plastic solution that hardens to a solid film. Many materials may be coated with vinyl, such as cork and fabric.

VINYL COMPOSITION

Description: A blended composition of vinyl, resin, plasticizer, and coloring agents formed into sheets under pressure and heat. Sheets or tiles.

Applications: Both residential and nonresidential settings.

Maintenance: Sweep, vacuum, damp mop; detergent. May be waxed.

Cost Structure: Moderate.

SHEET VINYL

Description: Vinyl sheets come in six-, nine-, and twelve-foot widths. There are two kinds of sheet vinyl. One is a solid or *inlaid vinyl,* built up with successive layers of vinyl granules that are usually plain or patterned with a suggestion of texture. The other type, called *rotogravure* or *roto,* is a printed pattern. The surface is coated with vinyl or vinyl/urethane (a thinner layer) called the wear layer. Both types of vinyl may or may not have a cushioned backing.

Applications: Flooring, both residential and nonresidential. Nonresidential vinyls are thicker or have a thicker wear layer.

Maintenance: Most sheet vinyl is given a no-wax surface to help maintain a shiny surface. However, heavy traffic, furniture movement, and harsh detergents may remove the shine. Damp mopping with a water and vinegar solution will help keep the shine. Vinyl floors may be waxed.

Cost Structure: Moderate.

VINYL TILE

Description: Solid vinyl is composed of PVC, plasticizers, pigments or coloring agents, mineral fillers, and stabilizers. Available in solid colors, plus patterns such as marble, travertine, slate, brick, and stone. Some vinyl tiles may have a wood veneer sealed between layers.

Applications: Flooring, both residential and nonresidential.

Maintenance: Sweep, vacuum, damp mop (as for sheet vinyl) without detergents, which can dull the finish.

Cost Structure: Moderately low.

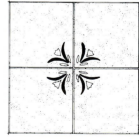

Vinyl floor

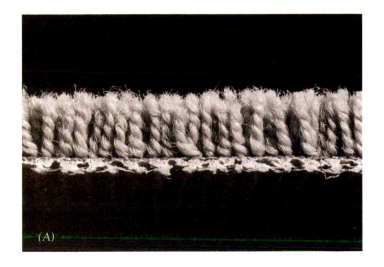

Figure 11.5 *Results from a wear test in a Hong Kong subway station, where a half-million commuters walked across it. (A) Anything Goes!™ Carpet retained resilience and surface appearance. (B) An ordinary pile with similar density and thickness, subjected to the same half-million commuters, lost its tuft twist and remained frayed and matted even after cleaning. (C) Because of its durability and easy maintenence, wall-to-wall cut pile carpet is standard in today's homes.*

(A) and (B) Photos courtesy of Shaw Industries. (C) © Jessie Walker.

SOFT FLOOR COVERINGS

Carpeting

Carpet, particularly wall-to-wall installed carpet, has become a standard item in interior design. In fact, *broadloom carpet* (twelve feet wide on average) can be used in any and every area; its use is restricted only by the aesthetic and maintenance requirements of the room. Selecting carpeting is often a difficult task; carpets are made in many fibers and in a seemingly endless array of colors, textures, and prices. However, the quality of the carpet and how well it will wear are very difficult to determine when examining the store sample. Further, the small size of most carpet samples makes it hard to visualize the effect of an entire area covered in that carpet. The following guidelines may be helpful:

- Understand which fibers are used in carpeting (chart 11.3) as well as the advantages and disadvantages of each.

- Be aware of the many carpet constructions and the selection of textures available.

- Look for well-known, national manufacturers who have a reputation for quality merchandise and who will stand behind their product in case of flaws (holes, streaks, color variations) or problems that develop after the carpet is installed (such as fading, premature crushing, or pile loss).

- It is wise to purchase carpet from local carpet dealers who are known for their business integrity, quality installation, and service (if problems arise).

- Be aware that poor quality, inexpensive carpets that appear similar to moderately priced carpets may have inferior quality yarns, less latex glue to hold the primary and secondary backing together (see Tufted Broadloom Carpets), and other compromises not immediately apparent. Ask sales personnel to recommend carpets that will stand up to the wear and traffic, and check to see if there is a written guarantee as to the quality and durability.

CHART 11.3 CARPET FIBERS COMPARISON

WOOL

Source: Wool is the fiber taken from domesticated sheep and varies from very fine to very coarse. Wool also varies in length; the shorter staple lengths are used in lesser quality—and longer staple lengths in higher quality—wool carpets. Wool may be dyed any color or left in its natural white, cream, brown, or gray hue, as are berber carpets.

Advantages: Wool has long been used for a standard of comparison as a durable carpet fiber. It is very resilient due to the overlapping scales of the staple (short-length) fiber. This resilience gives wool its long life and resistance to crushing. It takes dyes beautifully and is woven and tufted into carpets of high quality. It is traditionally used in pile for Oriental, folk, and fine designer rugs. Wool can absorb up to 25 percent of its weight without feeling damp.

Disadvantages: Wool carpets must be treated for moth resistance. When wet, wool emits a distinctive animal smell. Some people are allergic to wool. It is susceptible to *fuzzing* (fibers working loose) and *pilling* (fibers working into small balls or pills). Wool is the most costly of the carpet fibers.

Maintenance: Wool should be vacuumed regularly and spots cleaned immediately. Wool takes a long time to dry but may be wet cleaned. Professional dry-cleaning methods are recommended. Avoid scrubbing brushes that could untwist the pile or encourage pilling.

Cost Structure: High.

NYLON

Source: It is a manufactured synthetic based on the raw materials phenol, hydrogen, oxygen, and nitrogen. Nylon is heated into a solution, then extruded into long threads that may be texturized and cut into staple (short fibers) to meet requirements of the many textures found in nylon carpet.

Advantages: Nylon is the most widely used carpet fiber on the market today, accounting for over 90 percent of all carpeting sold alone or combined with other fibers. It is a flexible fiber that is used for level-loop carpets as well as cut piles, both tufted and woven, and used often for *accent* or *scatter rugs*. Nylon is strong, durable, resilient, and abrasion resistant. Nylon possesses good color retention, hides dirt, and has excellent bulk. There is a minimum of fuzzing and pilling; it is nonallergenic and mildew and insect resistant. It also has good flame resistance.

Disadvantages: First and second generation (early chemical composition) nylons were prone to static electricity, had a harsh sheen and unpleasant touch, and it took colors too vividly. However, all these weaknesses have been overcome. Fifth generation nylons now are guaranteed against stains and soiling. However, there are many qualities of nylon, and some of these problems may still exist.

Maintenance: Nylon cleans exceptionally well. It should be vacuumed regularly and spot cleaned as needed. Steam or wet cleaning is effective if the secondary backing is jute and not kept wet. Accent or scatter rugs may be machine washed and dried.

Cost Structure: Moderate.

ACRYLIC

Source: Acrylic is a synthetic fiber composed mainly of acrylonitrile, a colorless liquid that is boiled and extruded into long-chain polymers or single threads that can be texturized and cut into staple fibers and spun into a bulky yarn.

Advantages: Acrylic is the fiber that is most similar to wool. It is warm to the touch and looks similar to wool, so it is often combined with wool to lower its cost. It is soft and warm to the touch. Acrylic is often used to imitate wool berber carpet (neutral colored with natural wool color irregularities).

Disadvantages: Acrylic has low resilience, mats easily, fuzzes and pills. It has a relatively short life span compared to wool or nylon, but its life span increases dramatically when blended with either of these two fibers. Acrylic is vulnerable to oil-borne stains, which are difficult to remove.

Maintenance: Acrylic responds well to wet cleaning, but care must be taken to avoid brushing and untwisting the fibers, as the fiber will mat down and pill more easily when the fibers have been loosened. Vacuum acrylic regularly and remove spots immediately if possible, since acrylic absorbs oil-borne stains that are difficult to remove once they are set.

Cost Structure: Moderate.

MODACRYLIC

Source: Modacrylic is a synthetic long-chain polymer primarily of acrylonitrile modified by other polymers; it is, literally, a modified acrylic.

Advantages: Modacrylic is inherently flame resistant, making it a good choice to meet code or fire safety. Modacrylic is a soft, bulky fiber, historically manufactured into an imitation fur-type pile, and used for accent or scatter rugs. In broadloom carpeting it is sometimes combined with acrylic to improve flame resistance. Modacrylic dyes well, is insect and mildew resistant, and has fair abrasion resistance.

Disadvantages: The softness of modacrylic makes this fiber mat down or crush easily; hence, it is not suitable alone as a broadloom fiber. It also fuzzes and pills.

Maintenance: Accent rugs—shake or vacuum, machine or hand wash, warm. Machine dry (low setting) or line dry. Rugs of fake fur require occasional professional dry cleaning. In broadlooms, modacrylic is as cleanable as the other fibers with which it is blended.

Cost Structure: Moderate.

OLEFIN/POLYPROPYLENE

Source: Olefin and polypropylene carpets are made of ethylene or propane gas constituted into a synthetic long-chain polymer. Polypropylenes are modified olefins as propylenes are added and polymerized.

Advantages: Olefin is lightweight, inexpensive, durable, and strong. It resists fuzzing, pilling, and abrasion. Used for indoor-outdoor carpeting, nonresidential carpeting and carpet tiles. Also used for artificial turf.

Disadvantages: Olefin has a plastic feel and is not soft to the touch. Must be treated for resistance against sunlight fading and deterioration. Has low melting point. Lower qualities may crush and pill.

Maintenance: Stain and soil resistant. Vacuum regularly. Cleans well; is unaffected by moisture and most chemicals and acids. Olefin or polypropylene carpets installed outdoors (patios, around swimming pools, around nonresidential settings, and as artificial turf) may be hosed off.

Cost Structure: Low to moderate.

POLYESTER

Source: Polyester is a synthetic long-chain polymer derived from a reaction between dicarboxylic acid and dihydric alcohol.

Advantages: Polyester takes and holds dyes well. Next to acrylic, it most closely resembles wool because of its dyeability and softness to the touch. Polyester is mildew and moth resistant, nonallergenic, and nonabsorbent. It is a durable fiber that resists fuzzing and pilling. Polyester is soft and cool to the touch, an advantage in warm-weather climates.

Disadvantages: Polyester lacks the resilience and strength of nylon and must, therefore, be *heat set* to maintain yarn twist. Heat-set polyesters are good selections for most residential areas except heavy traffic lanes. Polyester lacks warmth of wool, nylon, or acrylic.

Cost Structure: Moderate to moderately high, depending on the quality of the fiber.

- Quality can be determined to an extent with hand tests. By bending back the face of a tufted carpet, the fabric into which the carpet is tufted (the primary backing) is revealed. This is called making the carpet "grin." If there is a lot of primary backing exposed, then the tufts are not close together and the carpet will be more likely to mat or crush under traffic. When the tufts are close together, the carpet will have more resilience. Also try untwisting the pile to see if it may become fuzzy, and pull at the pile to determine if the face will lose a lot of fibers.

- If it is possible, secure a sample or scrap of the carpet (or of two or three for comparison), and take it to the site where it will be installed. Lay it down to evaluate color during different times of the day and at night with artificial light, and walk on it to determine whether it will show footprints or crush easily. Drop thread or other debris on the surface and evaluate whether it will readily show soil.

- For a heavy traffic area, it is wise to select a color that is medium in value (not too light or too dark) and low in intensity (fairly dull). This will hide the inevitable shadows and soiling that accompany foot traffic. Further, patterned carpet will virtually double the life span of a carpet under heavy use because pattern can effectively hide both soil and wear.

- Look at the expected life span of the carpet as compared to its aesthetics. A vivid or demanding color may prove tiresome sooner than would a more neutralized carpet. Neutral (browns, grays) or neutralized (dulled) colors generally prove more flexible for redecorating, which typically takes place several times during the life span of a carpet.

- Select a quality padding (carpet underlay; see Installation Methods and Padding later in this chapter), and check to see that the padding delivered to the site is the one you selected.

- Keep in mind that the quality of installation may determine how the carpet looks, lays, and performs. Insist on the most highly skilled carpet installers that can be hired in your vicinity.

Understanding Carpet Fibers

Most carpets are constructed of a single fiber, such as nylon. However, there are an increasing number of carpets made of blended fibers, such as 65 percent wool and 35 percent acrylic, or 80 percent nylon and 20 percent wool or polyester. These and other blends are popular for three reasons:

1. A blend has the positive qualities of each fiber; it is durable and may be pleasing to the touch.

2. A more costly fiber can be extended with the combination of lesser expensive fibers.

3. Cross-dyeing effects can be obtained by coloring the yarn with a single dyestuff—the two different fibers take the dye differently, creating a two-tone effect.

Figure 11.6 *This carpet is woven on a twelve-foot Wilton loom. Woven patterned wool broadloom carpeting, has once again achieved status in both residential and nonresidential interiors.*
Photo courtesy of Stark Carpet Corporation.

Chart 11.3 contains a list of carpet fibers, sources, advantages and disadvantages, maintenance requirements, and cost structure. It is very important to realize that there are many quality levels of each of these fibers, both natural and synthetic. Higher quality fibers will make the carpet perform better and last longer but will also be reflected in a higher cost per square yard.

Woven Broadloom Carpet

As the name implies, broadloom carpets are wide—six, nine, or the typical twelve or thirteen feet wide—and woven or tufted by machine. The first two woven carpets originated in England and are named after the towns where they were first loomed. A *Wilton* carpet is woven on the *Jacquard* loom. It allows complex patterns to be constructed, and its hallmark is that each color in the carpet is carried as a separate *weft* beneath the face of the design. This means the carpet can be very heavy and substantial. Designs vary from Empire and Victorian large-scale designs to contemporary small-geometric patterns. Wiltons are nearly always of quality wool and are very costly. They are seen most often in exclusive areas of nonresidential interior design.

Axminster carpets are also Jacquard woven but without the extra *warps*. Only the colors needed are inserted, making complex patterns possible without great expense. Axminster carpets are of wool or nylon and are seen in many kinds of nonresidential settings such as restaurants, theaters, retail businesses, and hotels. Axminster carpets are readily adaptable to custom design, and where they are still cost prohibitive, carpeting can be printed to imitate the design.

Velvet weave carpets are also woven but without any design. They may be solid or woven of variegated yarn, usually of wool or a wool and nylon blend.

Tufted Broadloom Carpets

Tufted carpets make up the majority of carpets sold in America today. They are constructed on a loom that employs multiple needles threaded with the yarn. The carpet yarn is punched into the primary backing in a zigzag pattern. The zigzag holds the yarn more securely in case of a loose tuft that is pulled. The tufts are held securely with a *latex* coating (rubber-based glue) that holds on a secondary backing made of woven jute or polypropylene fabric. Jute stretches somewhat but will rot if kept moist. Polypropylene will not be affected by moisture, but it has very little flexibility. There are some tufted carpets that have no secondary backing, and custom hand-tufted carpets have a layer of latex to which is affixed a loosely woven scrim textile that adds some stability to the construction. *Rubber-backed tufted carpets* are tufted into a thick rubber-cushioned backing and directly glued to the surface. *Fuse-bonded carpets* (such as artificial turf) are tufted into a heavy layer of latex and are also directly glued down without padding. There are many levels of quality in the construction of tufted carpets.

Other Carpet Constructions

Knitted carpets are constructed of knitted yarns held together with a latex backing. They account for very few carpets on the market.

Needlepunch carpets are masses of fibers (rather than yarns) that are held together by an interlocking fiber-punching machine. They are inexpensive and durable and come in yardage and square tiles with or without a latex backing. They may be installed over a pad or glued down directly.

A carpet seldom seen is the *flocked carpet,* which is made by electrostatically charging nylon fibers that are blown onto a glue-covered fabric. These carpets have a short-pile velvet texture.

Carpet Textures

The texture of the carpet refers to the pile surface. This is where most of the variety of a carpet is possible. The yarns may vary in thickness, in pile height, and in level. The following textures are the most common:

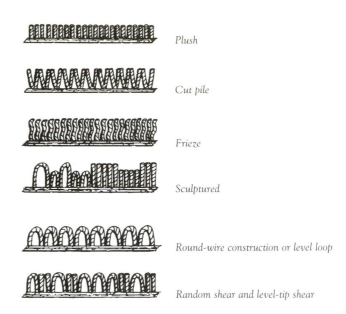

Figure 11.7 Carpet textures.

- Cut pile surfaces are tufted, then sheared to one short height. The tufting can be dense (tightly packed) or less dense with fatter yarns. Early cut piles included *plush carpet,* dense and one color. A cut pile carpet is not as dense as a plush but is resilient. A heather, or two-tone, effect is nicknamed a "trackless" because it is engineered to hide dirt and footprints. Very tightly twisted yarns are termed *frieze* cut piles; they are sturdy and durable carpets.

- *Sculptured carpets* are made of two levels of cut pile, or of a higher cut pile and a lower level loop. They may also be multihued or of several values, tufted of variegated yarn, or dyed to be colorful and form a busy pattern. Many quality levels of sculptured carpets exist, with the best design and quality found in the carpets that are only slightly variegated in color or value, so that the sculpturing is understated. This adds strength and resilience to the pile height, rather than accentuating a dramatic difference in pile height (which can easily mat down).

- *Level-loop carpets* are tufted or woven without being sheared into a cut pile. They are sometimes called *wire construction,* or *round wire tufting,* as the yarns are looped over wires for uniformity; the wires are then removed. When the wires are razor sharp, they cut the yarn to form a cut pile when removed. Variations of the level loop include the *random shear,* where some loops are woven slightly higher and then sheared off. The surface then somewhat resembles a very dense cut pile, looking more luxurious but with the strength of the loops to prevent crushing. A *level-tip shear* is the same as random shear, where the loops are the same height as the sheared loops. Another loop texture is the *multilevel-loop,* or *sculptured-loop,* or *embossed-loop pile,* where the loops are tufted at two or more levels, producing a pattern.

Installation Methods and Padding

There are basically two types of installations: direct glue-down and the pad and tackless strip method.

Direct glue-down is possible for any type of carpet; no separate cushion is used. The reasons for direct glue-down include: (1) heavy traffic, where the constant walking could cause the carpet to develop potentially dangerous ripples; (2) carpet installations where no softness is required; and (3) saving the expense of the pad, tackless strip, and labor to install two layers.

Tackless strip is a thin board with tacks embedded so that they protrude at an angle toward the wall. The strip is nailed near the wall, and the pad is stapled, nailed, or glued to the floor just inside this perimeter. The carpet is then laid over the pad and hooked over the tacks with carpet installation equipment that stretches the carpet, then pounds the tacks into the carpet.

Padding, or carpet underlay, is available in several types:

- *Sponge rubber pads* combine natural and synthetic rubber and fillers to form a flat or a waffle sponge; suitable for light to medium traffic. With heavy traffic, these pads tend to crush and lose their resiliency.

- *Foam rubber pads* are firmer flat sheets made from natural or synthetic rubbers. They are suitable for medium traffic.

- *Urethane foam* is made from synthetic polymers and is available in varying sheet thicknesses. It may be formed to be extra dense. Chopped urethane foam may be bonded (or rebonded as it is sometimes called) into sheets with additives such as paper, vinyl, fabric-backed foam, or wood chips. This factor makes bonded foam subject to many quality levels. Both urethane foam and rebonded foam are popular choices for padding.

- *Felt padding* was originally of animal hair, though *animal hair felt padding* is now rare; a *combination felt padding* made of some animal hair and some synthetic fibers is more common, and *fiber felt padding* is all synthetic. Felt padding has less resilience and is an excellent choice for Oriental rugs because too much resilience can damage the rug's backing.

Carpet Maintenance and Cleaning

The appearance and life span of a carpet often depend on the way it is maintained. Although heavy traffic will wear carpet out faster, keeping the carpet clean is a key to good looks and to increasing its life span. Soil allowed to stay on the surface of a carpet is not only unsightly; the longer it is left, the more difficult it is to remove. When dirt, grit, or sand settles to the bottom of the pile, it can abrade the yarns at the base, wear them off, and eventually destroy the carpet.

In heavy traffic areas such as hallways and rooms that contain traffic lanes, carpeting should be vacuumed every day. Areas of little traffic, such as bedrooms, usually require vacuuming only

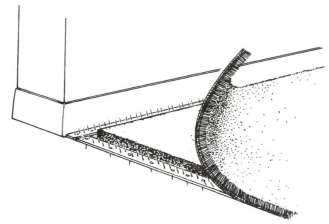

Figure 11.8 *Tackless strips are nailed next to the wall, then padding or underlay is stapled down (if subfloor is wood), and carpet backing is hooked into angled staples to anchor it securely to the floor.*

once a week. A light vacuuming is three times back and forth, and a thorough vacuuming is seven times back and forth. Repetitive vacuuming loosens and pulls the dirt from the base to the surface, then finally sucks it up into the machine.

Spots should be removed as quickly as possible and never allowed to remain on the carpet long enough to become set. Mild detergent and clear water are useful for many stains, and oil- or tar-based stains can be removed with a commercially prepared dry-cleaning solution. Carpet stores will often recommend products or sell kits for cleaning spots.

Carpets should be wet- or dry-cleaned when they become so soiled that the vacuum or spot-cleaning of the carpet can no longer keep the surface looking good. There are several methods of cleaning carpet.

- Wet cleaning is done in various ways. Steam extraction forces very hot detergent solution into the carpet, then extracts it immediately with a suction or wet vacuum. Wet cleaning can also be done by spraying a dry-cleaning chemical solution onto the carpet and then mopping the carpet with circular pads. Steam cleaning is safer in that it will not untwist the yarns. However, both methods run the risk of wetting the carpet too much, which can damage a jute primary or secondary backing, and the detergent and chemical solution may attract dirt more quickly. Rinsing the carpet with a mild vinegar and water solution will remove most of the residual detergent.

- Dry cleaning is done by sprinkling the carpet with a powdered or sawdust-like preparation and then using a rotating brush machine to work the compound into the carpet. The compound is then extracted with a vacuum. It may run the risk of leaving cleaning compound behind that will attract and hold dirt more quickly after cleaning.

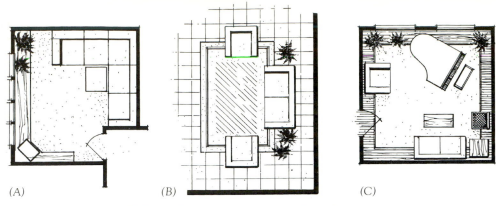

(A) (B) (C)

Figure 11.9 *Area rugs help define space. (A) Wall-to-wall carpeting is installed by direct glue-down or tackless strip and underlay or padding. (B) An area rug defines an area such as for conversation. (C) A room-sized rug is a loose rug large enough to nearly cover the room—within one foot to a few inches from the wall.*

Rug Sizes

An *area rug* defines an area, such as a conversation area. A room-size rug covers all but a few inches of floor by the walls. Wall-to-wall carpeting is installed by direct glue-down or with pad and tackless strip.

Accent rugs are generally small and made of wool or nylon. They may be tufted into a deep pile. Also included in the accent rug category are *domestic Oriental rugs,* which are machine-made Oriental rug designs woven of wool or nylon. They are durable and may be comparatively inexpensive. There are many quality levels of domestic Oriental rugs. Small decorative accent rugs are sometimes called *art rugs.*

Oriental and Area Rugs

Oriental and area rugs can give character and richness to interiors. Often a fine rug will be the basis for the decorative scheme and will seem to finish the room. *Oriental, folk, European handmade, designer,* and *natural fiber rugs* are all considered area rugs, as they generally vary from four by six feet to eighteen by twenty-four feet, defining spaces such as a conversation or dining area. Within each of these categories are several types of rugs. A basic knowledge of these will lead to a better understanding of their use in interiors.

Oriental Rugs

Oriental rugs are knotted or tied by hand by native craftspeople from Iran, Turkey, Romania, the Caucasus, Afghanistan, Pakistan, India, and China. The finest Oriental rugs originated in what was called Persia (today primarily Iran) at the height of the rug-weaving era in the fifteenth century. An Oriental rug is composed of a cotton warp, pile knots of wool or sometimes silk, and a cotton weft inserted after every two rows of knots. The design and colors are drawn on graph paper and called a cartoon. Patterns are symmetrical, often mirroring the design on all four corners. The finer the warp and knots and the greater the number of knots per square inch, the more intricate the patterns possible (finest rugs have four hundred knots or more per square inch). A fine rug can take months to weave in a rug-weaving center and years if the weaver is working alone (as with a nomadic tribe).

Figure 11.10 *This wall-to-wall broadloom carpet imitates a fine Persian Oriental rug.*

Photo courtesy of Stark Carpet Corporation.

Oriental rug weaving has for centuries been recognized as an art and skill of the highest order, which is reflected in prices of the finer rugs. Antique Oriental rugs (older than seventy-five years) are the most costly if they are in good to excellent condition. Semi-antiques are those from twenty-five to seventy-five years, and new rugs are less than twenty-five years old. Oriental rugs will often increase in value over the years despite some wear. This is true even of new rugs if they are authentic and woven in the area where they originate, called the traditional rug-weaving area. Nontraditional rug-weaving areas, such as India, have made traditional designs readily available. These rugs are not as valuable, however.

It takes an expert to evaluate and appraise a rug. It is best to shop for an Oriental rug at a reputable dealership that specializes in them.[2]

Oriental rugs are further divided into Persian, Caucasian, and Chinese rugs. *Persian rugs* have intricate curving patterns, are often floral, and have high knot counts. Persian rugs from Iran are considered the finest rugs, although there is a great variety in quality. Persian rugs are also produced in India and surrounding countries. The best-known types are the Hamadan, Hereke, Herez, Isfahan, Kashan, Kerman (Kirman), Nain, Qum, Sarouk (Saruk), Senneh, Sereband, Shiraz, Shirvan, and Tabriz.

Caucasian or Turkish rugs are generally those from the Caucasus region in the former Soviet Republic, and Turkish rugs originate in Turkey, though many are produced in Afghanistan, Pakistan, and India. These rugs are generally coarser, of brighter primary colors, and with simpler and geometric designs. Best known are the Afghan, Belouch, Bokhara, Kazak, Kurd, Qashqa'i (Kashkai), Tekke (Tekke Turkoman), and Yomut (Yamout).

Chinese rugs are woven with a deeper pile of coarse wool (fewer knots per square inch). By law, all modern Chinese rugs have the same number of knots per square inch. Designs may be traditional—with open background, central medallion, and a large-scale border, typically in cream, ming blue, gold, and/or red. They may also copy designs from Persia and France, or they may be contemporary patterns. All these will be sculptured or beveled on both sides of the design, giving a deeper, richer look and emphasizing the design.

Rugs from India have flooded the market in recent years. Since labor costs are low and skills are high, rugs of all types are produced there. By law, all wool is native, and these factors combine to make Indian rugs less valuable as investments. Persian, Turkish or Caucasian, and Chinese rugs are all made in India. Chinese rug depth and sculpturing is applied to French patterns and termed Indo-Aubusson rugs. In addition, flat folk rugs are produced in great quantity in India. Indian rugs are fine selections if investment and resale are not important to the buyer.

Folk Rugs

There are many types of folk rugs, which can be defined as any rug woven by an ethnic group or reflecting the native heritage of a country. Folk rugs are flat, reversible rugs, generally of wool. These come from India, Romania, Scandinavia, Colonial New England, South America, the southwestern United States, and pile rugs from Africa, South America, Scandinavia, and Spain. The best known of the folk rugs are the following.

Figure 11.11 *Antique rugs shown here in pale, faded colors, give charm and character to a room.* © *Ted Spiegel.*

The *dhurrie* (dhurry, durry) and *kilim rugs* have been produced for centuries in India and Romania, respectively. Indian dhurries were traditionally of cotton, so few authentic antiques exist; Romanian kilims were of wool. In both rugs, folk designs are woven with no pile. They are reversible, and they vary from dark and vivid to pale colors. Designs are often geometric but may be based on floral patterns or have only textures and no patterns. Today the designs and colors are largely dictated by European and American tastes, since the Western market has received these rugs so well.

Navajo rugs are made in the southwestern United States—Arizona and New Mexico, primarily. These flat tapestry rugs reflect native American tribe (Indian) motifs and colors—geometric, angular, simple patterns in gray, cream, white, black, brown, rust, and red. Navajo rugs can be fairly valuable as investments, although they are imitated by Mexican and Japanese laborers who produce knockoffs, which are not valuable. The types of Navajo rugs include the Chinle, Crystal, Ganado-Klagetoh (Ganado Red), Shiprock-Lukachukai (Yei and Yeibechi), the Storm Pattern, Teec Nos Pos, Two Gray Hills, and Wide Ruins.[3] Of these, the finest weave and most valuable are the Two Gray Hills rugs.

CHART 11.4 ORIENTAL AND AREA RUGS

A Persian prayer rug

Complex Persian Oriental rug. Fine rugs have over 400 hand-tied knots per square inch; more knots yield curved lines.

Caucasian or Turkish rug

Chinese rug

Romanian kilim

Scandinavian rya rug

Indian dhurrie rug

CHART 11.4   ORIENTAL AND AREA RUGS

French Savonnerie rug

French Aubusson rug

Navajo rug

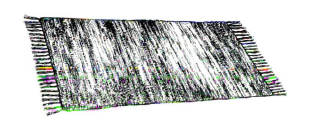

Rag rug

Portuguese needlepoint rug

Braided rug

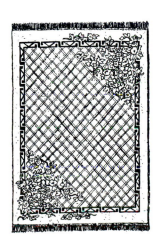

Designer rug

The *rya* and *rollikan rugs* are the best known of the Scandinavian rugs. The rya is a hand-knotted deep pile rug in abstract designs and contemporary colors. The rollikan is a flat tapestry rug that reflects the simplified, modern tastes influenced by the folk arts and flowers of Scandinavia.

Rag, braided, and *hooked rugs* are the New England colonists' contribution to folk rugs. These rugs were made of clothing that was no longer usable (rags) and turned into utilitarian floor coverings. Rag rugs are plain weave, flat rugs, originally woven on a floor or hand loom. Braided rugs are made of strips of fabric, braided and sewn into an oval or circle. Both rag and braided rugs are also manufactured by machine today. Hooked rugs are made by inserting strips of fabric into a heavy scrim or burlap backing cloth; they form simple patterns, usually floral.

Moroccan rugs are pile rugs that are geometric and vividly colored. Berber rugs may have natural colors —beiges, browns, and blacks—and perhaps some pattern. Moroccan *Rabat* rugs reflect the oriental designs, much simplified.

Central and South American rugs include those made by native craftspeople of Central and South America. Either flat tapestry or pile rugs, they most often reflect the pre-Columbian influence of native tribes (the Inca, Maya, and Aztec) in geometric patterns and bright or neutral colors similar to those used by the Navajo.

European Handmade Rugs

The best known of the European rugs are the French Savonnerie and Aubusson, the Portuguese needlepoint, and the Spanish rugs.

Savonnerie rugs have been produced at the Savonnerie factory in France for over three hundred years. These rugs are a hand-knotted pile, traditionally with deep, rich, vivid colors and large-scale patterns. The Savonnerie rugs produced there today may be of very contemporary patterns as well as the historical French motifs.

Aubusson rugs are named after the factory where they were first (but are no longer) produced. These French rugs are flat tapestry weaves, historically of Oriental rug-inspired motifs in faded or muted colors. These rugs were particularly favored during the reign of Louis XVI when light-scaled Neoclassic designs were in vogue. Today Aubusson rugs may have floral or abstract/modern patterns.

Needlepoint rugs are mainly produced in Portugal and China. Although some needlepoints are machine made, authentic needlepoints are still hand-embroidered wool on a heavy scrim. The characteristic round stitches are usually formed into lovely floral patterns. These rugs are popular because of their European flavor.

Spanish rugs are hand- or machine-woven pile rugs called Mantas. They have designs that appear three-dimensional and have subtle shadings, although the colors are bright and vivid.

Designer Rugs

Designer rugs are made to custom specifications by several companies in America. The rugs are most often hand or machine tufted of quality wool onto a canvaslike fabric, then coated with a latex to hold the stitches in place. There may be a heavy fabric sewn onto the back as a secondary backing. The value of designer rugs lies in the freedom and creativity possible. The rug may be a simplified, enlarged version of a selected textile. It may have large- or small-scale patterns and a variety of pile heights and yarn textures. The size and shape are also totally custom. In nonresidential applications, designer rugs may center around a corporate logo or carry out a specific theme. Designer rugs can be used as focal points or wall tapestries. They may be pictorial, reflecting regional histories, architecture, geology, or industry. Manufacturers have professionals who work with the designer toward the exact colors, textures, and designs for these fine rugs. And surprisingly, designer rugs are not as costly as many people think.

Natural Fiber Rugs

Natural fiber rugs include *animal skins, berber rugs, cotton rugs, floccati rugs, sisal/maize mats, tatami mats,* and *wool rugs.*

Animal skins include zebra; black, brown, and polar bear skins; and any other animal skins laid on the floor or hung on the wall. The use of animal skins has been curtailed in recent years due to conservation efforts.

Berber rugs, originally woven by the Berber tribal natives of North Africa, are made of wool that is not dyed but left in its natural color state—cream, brown, and black. The wool hues are mixed to frankly expose the natural flecks of the various colors. Berber rugs come in off-white, various beiges, darker browns, and charcoals. Berbers today are most often machine-tufted broadlooms for nonresidential and residential application. A berber area rug may be a portion of a broadloom with bound edges, cut or shaped to cover an area.

Cotton rugs are woven by hand or machine and left neutral or yarn dyed to form simple patterns and textures. Cotton rugs may be machine washable and dryable if they are small rugs, and in larger installations they absorb dirt but clean up nicely.

Floccati, or flokati, rugs originate in Greece. They are tufts of sheared goat's hair woven into a knit or woven fabric. They have a deep, luxurious pile. Floccati rugs are used in both informal and formal settings and have been favored area rugs in contemporary settings for many years. They are available in off-white and brown and are surprisingly inexpensive.

Sisal and maize mats are also available in squares or tiles, so the installations can cover small or large areas. They are not known for their comfort; sisal is particularly prickly to the touch. But these natural fibers form interesting and handsome floor textures.

Figure 11.12 *A beautiful Portuguese needlepoint rug dominates this sitting room.*

Courtesy of Stark Carpet Corporation.

Figure 11.13 *Intriguing one-point perspective is accentuated with the grid lines of the ceramic tile floor in this New York subway station. Ceramic tile can withstand years of hard nonresidential abuse and still look good.*

Italian Tile courtesy of Italian Tile Center, division Italian Trade Commission–I.C.E.

Tatami mats are traditional floor coverings for Japanese homes and are seen in contemporary Western residences as well. They are woven of dried sea grasses and edged with black fabric and are set together in geometric patterns. The thickness of tatami mats vary from about one to four inches. They offer good insulation as well as a fine appearance.

Natural wool rugs are often woven or tufted into neutral, subtly patterned area rugs. Surface textures vary from cut pile to beveled designs to level-loop construction.

NONRESIDENTIAL CONSIDERATIONS

In addition to the considerations listed in this chapter for selection of residential flooring, nonresidential flooring has further criteria and considerations.

Hard and Resilient Floorings

Hard flooring is frequently specified by interior designers for nonresidential settings. Factors that dictate this decision include the flooring budget and the traffic level or classification. A class A or I traffic rating indicates extremely heavy traffic flow. Many residential floorings such as medium-grade vinyl or tufted carpeting would wear out quickly under heavy traffic. Thus, the manufacturers of flooring produce materials that are more durable. These include solid vinyl, rubber, and particularly tile, brick, and stone. Although initially very costly, tile, brick, and stone will outwear any other flooring because they are intended to last indefinitely under even very heavy traffic. Because of their weight, the subfloor must have extra strength and support.

Another advantage of hard materials is that they will generally not show dirt or traffic-pattern shadows and will be easy to clean and maintain. Tile, brick, and stone will not be damaged unless a very hard blow is struck; then the material will need to be replaced. Rubber and solid vinyl have other advantages. In addition to their resilience and resistance to damage they are easier on the feet and are quieter than nonresilient flooring.

Figure 11.14 *Patterned carpet is a key element in this hotel lobby design. Patterned carpet can have a life span double that of a plain carpet; it hides both soil and wear.*

Photo by Andy Battenfield and Kelly Haas.

Rugs and Carpeting

Carpeting selected for nonresidential installations varies somewhat from residential settings where color, price, and durability are the criteria. Nonresidential carpets must meet some or all of the following requirements:

1. Cost of all nonresidential carpets must meet budget limitations.

2. Construction is an important criterion. In order for a nonresidential carpet to be durable, minimum requirements must be filled for *pile density,* which means the number of *tufts or stitches per square inch,* together with the distance between rows and the pile height. The more dense the tufting or the weave, the stronger the carpet is likely to be. The strength of the *tuft bind,* or how tenciously the face yarn is held onto the primary and secondary backings, is also a construction criterion. A thin layer of latex, for example, may not prevent the yarn from unraveling when pulled.

3. Weight of the face yarn will be one measure of carpet durability. Heavier *face weights* will indicate the amount of yarn used per square measure. *Finished pile weight* includes the backings as well.

4. Abrasion resistance includes the type and quality of fibers, the type, thickness, and twist tightness of the yarn, as well as the density.

5. Resilience means the carpet must have the ability to withstand light, medium, heavy, or extra heavy traffic without undue crushing or matting.

6. Appearance means the carpet will hide and release soil, resist staining and fading, fuzzing and pilling.

7. Maintenance is an important factor. Carpets that show dirt easily or are difficult to clean will have high maintenance, often an excluding factor in specification. The majority of nonresidential carpets are patterned because they show about 50 percent less wear and soiling than an unpatterned carpet.

8. Static resistance is important where delicate machinery such as computer terminals may be affected or where highly flammable materials are present.

9. Flammability resistance forms a stringent requirement in many public buildings. Testing for flammability is often conducted, and ratings are available to the client through the designer.

10. Sanitation is a requirement for carpet cleaning and maintenance in clinical and institutional facilities.[4]

ENVIRONMENTAL CONSIDERATIONS

One issue that has become prominent in nonresidential interiors is the toxins that are emitted from both the finishes applied to floor textiles and the adhesive being used. These toxins are contributors to sick building syndrome (SBS). This problem has attracted the attention of architects, *specifiers,* and interior designers who should always be aware of protecting the health and well-being of the users.

One way to reduce toxins in the interior is to allow new carpets to be unrolled outside for off gassing to take place, meaning that toxic fumes can dissipate into the air before the carpet comes indoors.

Another important issue is that discarded carpeting significantly contributes to the landfill problem. Cheap carpeting is usually poor quality and wears out too quickly. In fact, higher quality can be obtained for just a few dollars more a yard. The extended life of a better quality carpet or vinyl will not only protect against waste, it will save the cost of removal and reinstallation of another product.

The technology now exists for carpeting to be recycled into other building materials. Watch for companies that offer this recycling service. (Interestingly, recycled light bulbs are a major source for the production of ceramic floor and wall tile.)

NOTES

1. J. Rosemary Riggs, *Materials and Components of Interior Design*, 2d ed. (Englewood Cliffs, N.J.: Prentice-Hall, 1989), 22–23, 28.

2. Aram K. Jerrehian, Jr., *Oriental Rug Primer* (New York: Facts On File, 1980), 28–77, 116–76.

3. H. L. James, *Posts and Rugs: The Story of Navajo Rugs and Their Homes* (Globe, Ariz.: Southwest Parks and Monuments Association, 1976), 36–89.

4. Dianne R. Jackman and Mary K. Dixon, *The Guide to Textiles for Interior Designers* (Winnipeg: Peguis Publishers, 1983), 148–59.

© *Ted Spiegel.*

THE FABRIC INDUSTRY

Fabrics for interior design travel an interesting road from their natural or compounded raw goods state to our homes and the places where we work or visit. The fibers discussed in this chapter are woven, knitted, or extruded into goods that need an average of six finishes to become marketable.

A horizontal operation is production at only one level. The company may only produce *gray goods* or *greige* (raw, woven, untreated fabric), for example, or it may only color or finish the fabric (called *conversion*). A vertical operation is one that does several steps in the production of textiles, perhaps weaving gray goods, finishing and coloring the fabric, and selling it to regional jobbers who then buy, sample, and distribute fabrics to designers and stores. A conglomerate is a very large corporation that does all or nearly all of the steps from obtaining raw materials to producing fibers and fabrics, coloring and finishing, sampling and marketing.[1]

While some fabrics stay on the market for several years, there is an amazing turnover in current fabrics. Every six months, new fabric lines are introduced to the interior design marketplace (the spring line and the fall line), reflecting current styles, trends, favored fibers, colors, and finishes. Design inspiration is sought the world over for design trends in color, pattern, and texture.

Fabrics obtained from interior designers are purchased through a jobber (who buys "job" or dye-lot yardage) who sells cut orders to the trade. In metropolitan locations, the designer may take a client to an *open showroom* where samples of the "lines" carried by a fabric company (or fabric house) are displayed. *Showrooms* that do not allow the client to accompany the designer are termed *closed showrooms*. These wholesale fabric companies may order fabrics from converters who display their wares at fabric shows such as the New York show, attended by wholesale companies from across America. Some companies will custom design fabrics so that only they will have those fabrics; this is termed exclusive design. Fabrics imported from abroad may also be contracted by a company to carry certain fabrics with exclusive rights. What all this means is a continually evolving kaleidoscope of goods varied enough to meet any need and any situation.

FABRIC—THE CHAMPION OF VERSATILITY

Fabric is indeed three dimensional and versatile—a malleable element that can be used in more ways than any other material. Fabric softens the straight lines of the interior while complementing and establishing an interesting counterpoint to them. Fabric is used at the window as draperies and curtains, shades, top treatments, and trimmings. On furniture, fabric serves as upholstery, slipcovers, pillows, trimmings and throws (blankets or afghans). In the kitchen and bath, fabric "linens" dry and caress us as well as our precious and everyday objects. Fabrics also function as floor cloths and wall and ceiling treatments.

Because of its affordability and availability, fabric can be utilized in every room in the house. This is in itself a remarkable achievement of our civilized and modern society, for in past centuries, even nobility did not enjoy the quantity and easy care of luxurious fabrics that we take for granted today. Today we also have the ability to keep our fabrics clean, fresh, and appealing. We know how to maintain fabrics and extend their life span.

We are free to change or rotate our use of fabric—where and how it is used. If we so desire, we can change the interior design by rotating fabrics seasonally or by keeping up with current color and style trends that last only one to three years. We can replace fabrics as they wear out, as our life-styles change, or as our needs evolve.

Or we can choose durable and timelessly beautiful fabrics that will be just as appealing ten or twenty years after we bring them home. In this sense, fabric can be like a trusted old friend—a familiar face each time we walk through the door.

Figure 12.1 *Patterned fabric graciously saturates this elegant interior.*
Furniture and fabrics by and photo courtesy of Brunschwig & Fils.

Figure 12.2 Fabric humanizes. Its colors, patterns, and textures can greet us warmly each time we come home.

Fabric may be used lavishly or sparingly. However it is to be applied, the work-order form must be completed accurately for correct fabrication and installation. Since some fabrics and labor are so costly, it is crucial that interior designers be well trained to shoulder the responsibility of overseeing correct specification, fabrication, and installation.

The Human Touch

Fabric, more than any other tactile element in design, has the ability to humanize our interiors. Fabric can establish a feeling of quietude and seclusion as it absorbs the spoken word and the din of electronic equipment. Fabric can give a sense of personal space, since so often it is selected with personal preference as a prime criterion. As we return to fabric surroundings that are appealing and uplifting—fabrics that meet psychological needs— we are greeted with a sense of cordial hospitality. Seeing a familiar fabric, whether it is a handmade heirloom or a store-bought textile, gives us a sense of belonging, which is, in large measure, why we come home at all. As we freely select our fabrics and their use, we manifest to all who live in or visit our homes what values and life-styles we have chosen for ourselves.

In past centuries, smooth, elegant fabrics considered sensually appealing were the exclusive right of the wealthy. As fabrics became more readily available and as man-made fibers imitated fabrics of luxury inexpensively, the wealthy saw, to their dismay, that anyone could achieve a pseudo-elegance. Those with money and taste have often turned to a new sensual pleasure of handwoven, unique fabrics, rustic or refined. These fabrics are costly because of the complexity of the construction and finishing processes or the relative obscurity of their source. Sometimes these types of textiles are brought back from exotic travels or obtained through exclusive interior design firms to establish a look that (they hope) cannot be duplicated. In this way, fabric not only appeals to the senses, it even establishes identity and status.

Fabric does appeal to the visual, tactile, and emotional senses; it can stimulate or excite, be dramatic or theatrical, even produce a sense of intrigue and fascination. Fabric can enliven and cheer us through light, bright, or pastel colors and patterns; it can draw us to the earth with coarse, ruggedly romantic textures, patterns, and colors; and fabric can lift us above earthly cares with soothing texture, neutralized color, and subtle pattern, thereby helping us cope with today's high-stress life-styles.

Figure 12.3   *Rich yet soft colors in drapery and upholstery fabrics establish casual elegance.*
Courtesy of the International Linen Promotion Commission.

Fabric can establish seclusion and privacy by shutting out the world. (In proxemics, this is known as "territoriality.") Fabric can satisfy the deep human craving for indulgence in that which gives pleasure—which is what artistic design is all about.

Fabric Aesthetics

Often a fabric is preferred because of its beauty and emotional appeal, and this is as it should be, providing the fabric is also a durable and an appropriate selection. Three attributes— color, pattern, and texture—form the basis for personal choice. We can use these three criteria to judge the appropriate use of the fabric, whether the fabric is in itself good design, and whether combinations of fabrics are tastefully and discriminately used.

Color

Color is the most emotional and personal of fabric's attributes. It is often finding just the right color in a fabric that clinches it as the selection. Color preferences are often deep rooted and should always be respected. As mentioned in chapter 4, color affects the mental and physiological health and well-being of those who live with it. Certainly persons who suffer from depression—physiological or conditional—should not live around depressing, serious colors. Rather, they will need warm, reassuring, lighthearted, or happy colors. On the other hand, a person in a high-stress life-style needs to be soothed and calmed with fabric color, not stimulated or further excited.

For most situations, there are guidelines in selecting color for fabric coordination that will give security to both the professional and the layperson when making fabric color decisions. These guidelines are listed in chart 12.1.

CHART 12.1 FABRIC COLOR COORDINATION GUIDELINES

- Colors are typically either pure and clear or neutralized and dulled. Colors should be used together with other colors from these same families.
- Warm and cool colors can have either warm or cool undertones, produced by mixing other colors into the dye. In complementary schemes, either the warm or the cool hue should dominate.
- Consider the color of the light and how it will affect the fabric colors. Always try out fabric combinations in situ to be certain they will really coordinate under lighting conditions in that room. It may become necessary to change the quality, type, and direction of the light to coordinate and enhance the fabric color scheme.
- Look carefully at the orientation and needs of the room and its inhabitants. Is it a cold, north room that needs cheerful colors, or is it a hot south or west exposure that cries for cooling hues?
- Vary intensity or brightness within the fabric color scheme. If all the fabrics are intense, the scheme may prove unlivable, and if all colors are dull, the scheme may prove uninteresting. The law of chromatic distribution has proven its validity over the centuries of interior design: *"The largest areas are most neutralized, and as the area becomes smaller, the intensity or brightness increases proportionately."* In other words, large areas are dull and neutralized (light, medium, or dark), and only small areas are really bright. In-between objects are of in-between intensities. Certainly this law can be broken, and surprisingly wonderful color schemes can result when the designer is truly skilled and aims for a particular result.
- Be sensitive to value distribution. Light values above, medium around, and dark colors below have consistently proven pleasing. However, some schemes can be very successful as all light (high-key), all medium, or all dark (low-key) values. Some schemes even reverse the standard distribution to light below, dark above. High-value contrast (light next to dark) is stimulating and dramatic, low-value contrast (blended values) is soothing and pleasant.
- Consider what colored fabrics do to each other. Colors should enhance, support, and beautify one another, never compete or cause visual irritation.
- Avoid too many coordinated fabrics with exactly the same dyes in varying colors and patterns. Although these coordinated "designer fabrics" can be lovely, there is also pleasure derived from searching many sources and finding fabrics that do not perfectly match as much as they beautifully blend and complement. This approach takes effort and time but is inevitably worth the hunt.
- Fabric color schemes that are sensitively coordinated will feel natural and interesting, with an almost destinylike rightness. One should sense that these fabrics were somehow meant to be used together. It is, of course, the skill in the coordination that produces this effect.

CHART 12.2 GUIDELINES TO COORDINATING PATTERNED FABRIC

- Look to the source of the fabric, its period or inspiration. If it is an adaptation, does it still possess the integrity or spirit of its origination? Look at the colors of the patterns as they relate to the source. For example, a delicate Federal or Neoclassic fabric in bright yellow or brilliant orange would be out of character with the pattern itself.
- The pattern itself should be handsome, well proportioned, and livable, whether or not it is authentic.
- When bringing together more than one pattern, vary the scale of the fabrics—for example, a large pattern with a small one.
- Add appropriate support patterns and textures, such as correctly scaled stripes and geometrics with a floral pattern and, of course, plain textured fabrics.
- Consider the thematic goals of the overall look of the interior. If, for example, the fabrics are to replicate the look of English Country, then several seemingly conflicting patterns of block-printed textiles will work because they are authentic. The seemingly haphazard appearance looks lived in, hence its strong appeal. If the look is American Country, then several small-scale calico-chintz or sateen fabrics will pull off the look well. If a formal look is desired—say a Georgian or French room—then the patterns should not only support each other but should support the ambience that is the goal of the interior.

CHART 12.3 GUIDELINES FOR COORDINATING FABRIC TEXTURES

- The character of textures used together must be compatible. For example, leather is not usually compatible with refined damask or brocade but is wonderful with matelassé or tweed. Lace is not in character with dramatic modern textures, but it beautifully complements moiré or velvet.
- Harmony is a key to good texture coordination. There must be a theme or ambience, a period or style, a look that holds together and relates all fabrics in a scheme. However, there must also be variety in order to achieve harmony. For example, in a formal setting there may be velvet, damask, satin, sheer, moiré, and other different textures of the same character. In a Country French provincial setting, we may see heavy tapestry, ticking, toile de Jouy, tweed, and woven herringbone or plaid.
- The textures should be appropriate to their intended use. Fabrics as upholstery should feel comfortable. Wall fabrics should coordinate with the level of formality, and all appointments should be selected to be pleasing for their use. Refer to chart 12.4 for a comparison of fabric weights and applications or uses. Also refer to the decorative fabric glossary at the end of the chapter for definitions, weights, constructions, and finishes of fabrics by name.

Pattern

Pattern establishes the character and personality of a fabric. Pattern can firmly tie a fabric to a period—Victorian lace, Georgian Renaissance floral sprays, delicate Federal stripes, or broad, bold American Empire stripes. Period styles and their motifs or patterns look good together because they evolved around a cohesive spirit of the times predominated by one social, political, or artistic/architectural movement. This spirit or character must remain consistent in order for the patterns to coordinate and look right. Some guidelines for coordinating fabric patterns are included in chart 12.2.

Texture

To the touch and to the eye, fabrics are textural. From smooth and refined (satin, velvet, damask, brocade) to sturdy and coarse (tweed, matelassé, frieze, bouclé), fabric is aesthetically appealing because of textural relief. Relief is the way the surface reads—the peaks and valleys, highlights and shadows. This added third dimension gives depth and interest to fabric and accounts for much of its appeal. Guidelines to careful texture coordination of fabric are suggested in chart 12.3.

Figure 12.4 *Patterns and textures are skillfully arranged to create an upscale thematic Country French interior.*
Wood blinds by and photo courtesy of Hunter Douglas.

FABRIC WEIGHT AND APPLICATION

Fabric may be categorized in two ways: by weight and by specific use or application. Chart 12.4 lists four basic categories of weight and the common uses for fabrics that fall in each category. In the decorative fabrics glossary at the end of the chapter, each fabric is given a weight designation that can be cross-referenced to the information in this chart.

CHART 12.4	FABRIC WEIGHT AND APPLICATIONS
WEIGHT	**APPLICATION AND USE**
Sheer, thin, very lightweight fabrics	Bed hangings, canopies, bed curtains, window curtains, sheer curtains/draperies, window semisheer casement and contract draperies, soft top treatments, thin table coverings, wall curtains
Lightweight fabrics	Accessory items and trimmings, casements, curtains, draperies, shades, top treatments, kitchen linens, lamp shades, supported bedspreads, table cloths
Medium-weight fabrics	Bedspreads, pillows and accessories, bath linens, slipcovers, supported upholstery, wall and partition upholstery, window treatments—draperies, heavier curtains, shades, stiff top treatments
Heavyweight fabrics	Bedspreads (tapestrylike), floor cloths, wall upholstery, wall hangings and tapestries, upholstery

Figure 12.5 *Evoking a luxury of the past, today's textiles, such as this bed linen ensemble of 100 percent cotton, require little care and create great visual interest.*

Courtesy of Cotton Incorporated.

Performance and Durability

Other important criteria for selecting residential fabrics include:

- Cost limitations, both initially and for upkeep. Some low-end fabrics as well as some costly fabrics may need more frequent cleaning, thereby increasing cost. Look at the fabric's ability to hide soil and still look great. Check the cleanability of the fabric based on fiber content, construction, and durability of finishes.

- The durability of the fabric. Some fabrics will wear out faster because of the fiber, the yarn, and the construction. Some fabrics will first wear out aesthetically, because the colors, patterns, and textures date too quickly or because of functional weaknesses. These weaknesses may include fuzzing (tiny fibers working to the surface), pilling (fibers working into balls or pills), fading, *crocking* (color rubbing off), or the lack of serviceability (cleanability).

FIBERS

A knowledge of fibers is essential to both interior designers and consumers. This is because fibers do vary in strength, dimensional stability, and a host of other criteria. When selecting fibers, a close look should be given to the level of expectation for the given installation. No one fiber can do everything and meet every need. For this reason, fibers may be blended, either in the viscose-solution stage (man-made fibers) or the raw-fiber stage (natural fibers). In addition, threads may be spun together to make intimate blends, or two or more fibers can be used in fabrics—one as a base and the other(s) as pile, or as one direction of yarns (the warp or the weft). The reasons for blending fibers are threefold:

1. To extend a costly fiber with one that is less expensive

2. To strengthen a weaker fiber with a stronger fiber

3. To give different characteristics such as bulk, texture, and different color reactions to one dye

Fibers are of two general types: natural and man-made. *Natural fibers* come from two sources: cellulose and protein. *Cellulosic fibers* are derived from plants—from the fruit, such as cotton, or from plant leaves, stems, or stalks, called *bast fibers*, such as *linen* (from flax), *jute,* ramie (China grass or linen), sisal, coir (coconut), piña (pineapple), maize (corn), Oriental grasses, and other, less-common fibers.

Protein fibers come from animals (wool of sheep, hair of goats, camels, horses, rabbits, and other animals) and insects (silk from the silkworm caterpillar). *Sericulture* is the tedious process of producing silk under cultivation.

Man-made fiber also consists of two basic categories: *cellulosic* and *noncellulosic* or *synthetic. Rayon* and acetate come from cellulose—cotton linters or wood chips—to which various chemicals are added. Noncellulosic or synthetic fibers—*nylon,* acrylic, *polyester, saran, olefin, vinyl,* and many others not frequently used in interior design—begin with organic compounds such as petroleum, natural gas, coal, air, and water. Man-made *generic* fibers are produced by hundreds of companies, over four hundred worldwide, who manufacture them for specific end uses. These companies issue *trademarks or trade names* to identify their fibers.

An independent fiber category is natural/mineral fibers that must be processed in ways similar to man-made fibers. These include asbestos, rubber, and metal.

All man-made fibers are formed in much the same way. The compound is made into liquid or viscose form, then forced through holes in a shower head-like orifice called a *spinnerette*. The size and shape of the openings can build in certain fiber characteristics. Variety in the yarns comes through *texturizing* the *filaments,* through types of yarn formations, and through the tension and direction of the yarn twists. In addition, generic fibers may be combined in the viscose stage, making blended fibers that can be engineered to meet specific needs.

Chart 12.6 lists the source of the most commonly used interior design fibers, their natural types or man-made trademarks, positive and negative characteristics, uses in residential and nonresidential settings, the care and cleaning of each fiber, its relative cost structure, and its flammability rating.

CHART 12.5 MAN-MADE FIBER PRODUCTION

Ingredients for the man-made cellulosic fibers rayon and acetate.

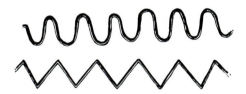

Ingredients for the noncellulosic or synthetic fibers nylon, acrylic, modacrylic, polyester, vinyl, and others.

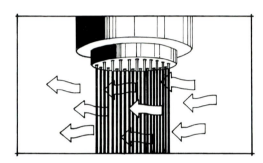

The spinnerette extrudes liquid that solidifies into filaments.

Filaments can be crimped or given texture before spinning into thread or yarn.

CHART 12.6 FIBER COMPARISON CHART

NATURAL CELLULOSIC FIBERS

Cotton boll

The Cotton Council and Cotton Incorporated logo

COTTON

Sources: Fruit of the cotton plant, a member of the mallow family. Needs extended sunlight and a long growing season.

Types: Short, long, extra long, carded, combed, mercerized. Egyptian and Sea Island are the finest cotton fibers.

Positive Characteristics: Versatile, dyes and prints well; good *hand*, dimensionally stable; absorbent fiber.

Negative Characteristics: Wrinkles, fades, shrinks unless mercerized and preshrunk. Mildews if kept moist. Eventually rots from sunlight exposure. Low abrasion resistance.

Residential Uses: Draperies, walls, upholstery and padding, slipcovers, bed and bath linens, trimmings, accessories, rugs.

Nonresidential Uses: With a flame-resistant finish, used for draperies, upholstery, and accessory items.

Care and Cleaning: Washable or dry-cleanable. Washing removes more finishes, dry cleaning recommended. May require ironing. Remove spots with mild detergent.

Cost Structure: Depending on grade, varies from low to moderately high.

Flammability: Burns readily; flammable. Must be chemically treated for flame resistance.

Flax

International Linen Promotion Commission logo

LINEN

Source: Fibers within the stalks of the flax plant; a bast fiber. Grown well in moist, moderate climates such as Great Britain and the low European countries.

Types: Tow linen (short *staple*), demiline, line linen (long staple). Ramie or China grass is a bast fiber with some similarities to linen.

Positive Characteristics: Crisp, strong fiber. Appealing natural texture in tow linens. Dyes well, maintains good appearance. Absorbent. Line linens are smooth, lustrous. Durable.

Negative Characteristics: Brittle, stiff, inflexible; sun fades; short fibers have low abrasion resistance. Stains are difficult to remove. Permanently creases.

Residential Uses: Upholstery, slipcovers, drapery, semisheer casements, wall coverings, fine table linens (line linen), kitchen linens.

Nonresidential Uses: When treated for flame resistance, wall coverings, casement draperies, upholstery blends.

Care and Cleaning: Dry-clean. Table and kitchen linens may be washed in hot water and machine dried. Ironing is required for table linens.

Cost Structure: Depending on fiber length and finishes, medium to moderately high.

Flammability: Flammable, burns readily. Must be treated for flame retardance in nonresidential settings. Paper-backed, adhered linen wall coverings are inherently flame resistant, receiving a class A rating.

JUTE

Sources: Fibers within the stalks of the jute plant; a bast fiber.

Types: Burlap, gunnysack cloth.

Positive Characteristics: Dyes bright colors, inexpensive, strong when dry.

Negative Characteristics: Will rot if kept damp, fades, is brittle.

Residential Uses: Crafts, carpet backing, wall covering. Draperies and curtain blends.

Nonresidential Uses: Carpet backing.

Care and Cleaning: Hand wash, dry thoroughly. Dry cleaning recommended.

Cost Structure: Low.

Flammability: Burns readily; flammable.

NATURAL PROTEIN FIBERS

Wool comes from sheep

The "Wool Mark" logo

WOOL

Sources: Wool of sheep; hair of goats and camels.

Types: Virgin—100 percent new wool; worsted—longer staple; woolen—short-, medium-staple fibers. Mohair: Angora goat hair.

Positive Characteristics: Great resilience, dyes well, durable, flame resistant. Appealing hand. Dimensionally stable. High absorbency.

Negative Characteristics: Some wools are scratchy, and some people are allergic to wool. Susceptible to moths. No resistance to alkalis. Low tensile strength.

Residential Uses: Upholstery; draperies; casements; wall coverings; broadloom carpets; area, designer, folk, and Oriental rugs.

Nonresidential Uses: Upholstery, carpeting, rugs (designer, folk, Oriental), wall upholstery accessory items, draperies.

Care and Cleaning: Dry-clean or clean by professional wet method.

Cost Structure: Moderate to very high.

Flammability: Flame resistant; slow to ignite, self-extinguishes when flame is removed.

Bombyx mori moth

Bombyx mori moth eggs

The silkworm (caterpillar)

Moth escapes to lay more eggs

Cocoon filaments twisted to form silk threads

SILK

Source: Filament of domesticated or wild silkworm cocoons.

Types: Cultivated, reeled—Bombyx mori produced by sericulture. Wild (raw)—off-white tussah silk with slubs from A. myllita and A. perny moth species.

Positive Characteristics: Lustrous, smooth to slubby, dry hand, excellent *drapability*. Strong when dry. Dimensionally stable. Resists organic acids. Not harmed by wetting.

Negative Characteristics: Subject to sunlight deterioration as well as soil and moisture decomposition. Low resistance to alkalis. May be eaten by carpet beetles.

Residential Uses: Draperies (must be lined), trimmings, upholstery, wall hangings and coverings, fine Oriental rugs. Accessories—pillows, scrolls, embroidered art fabric.

Nonresidential Uses: Draperies, fine trimmings, luxury upholstery.

Care and Cleaning: Dry cleaning recommended. Some silks are washable.

Cost Structure: Moderately high to very high.

Flammability: Burns slowly. Self-extinguishes when flame is removed.

LEATHER

Sources: Hides or skins of cattle or swine.

Types: Full, top grain, split leather. Sueded, buffed, embossed, glazed. Analine, pigment dyed.

Positive Characteristics: Extremely durable. Wears well and long. Resists fading, tearing, stretching, cracking.

Negative Characteristics: Quality varies according to hide, tanning, and company branding. Susceptible to marks, holes, and tears.

Residential Uses: Upholstery, desk tops, book bindings. Rarely for floor tiles, wall coverings, and area rugs.

Nonresidential Uses: Upholstery, desk tops, book bindings. Executive situations—floor coverings and wall coverings.

Care and Cleaning: Mild soap and water; no saddle soap.

Cost Structure: High.

Flammability: Flame resistant/fire retardant. Emits no toxic fumes.

continued

CHART 12.6 FIBER COMPARISON CHART *continued*

MAN-MADE CELLULOSIC FIBERS

The Man-Made Fibers Industry logo

RAYON

Source: Regenerated cellulosic from wood chips and cotton linters.

Trade Names: *Avril, Coloray, Colorspun, Enkrome,* Jet-spun, *Zantrel, Bemberg, Cordura,* XL, *Fibro,* Beau-Grip.

Positive Characteristics: Imitates silk in luster, drapability. Good solvent, insect resistance.

Negative Characteristics: Low abrasion resistance, susceptible to sun, low moisture resistance; will mildew.

Residential Uses: Draperies (should be lined), trimmings, bedspreads, upholstery, slipcovers, scatter rugs.

Nonresidential Uses: As blends, some draperies and upholstery fabrics.

Care and Cleaning: Dry-clean.

Cost Structure: Low to medium.

Flammability: Flammable—ignites readily; melts before burning.

ACETATE

Source: Reconstituted cellulosic, wood chips, cotton linters, and acetic acid.

Trade Names: Airloft, *Celanese, Chromspun, Estron,* Acele, *Celaperm, Lanese, Loftura.*

Positive Characteristics: A silklike sheen and hand. Stable fiber, low absorbency; good solvent resistance.

Negative Characteristics: Low resistance to abrasion, acids. Susceptible to sunlight deterioration. Mildew; will discolor. Weakens with age.

Residential Uses: Bedspreads, draperies (should be lined), curtains, fiberfill, mattress ticking, lining, slipcovers, upholstery.

Nonresidential Uses: As blends, some draperies.

Care and Cleaning: Dry-clean. Some acetates are washable.

Cost Structure: Low to medium.

Flammability: Flammable—ignites readily; melts before burning.

MAN-MADE NONCELLULOSIC/SYNTHETICS

NYLON

Source: Amide linkages attached to two aramid rings.

Trade Names: Anso, Antron, *Cadon, Caprolan, Cumuloft,* Nomex, *Perlon, Quiana, Cantrese,* Courtaulds, *Cordura,* Ultron, X-Static, *Zefran, Zeflon.*

Positive Characteristics: Strong, stable, durable, resilient, versatile. Sheer to thick. Not affected by water, moisture, insects, microorganisms, aging. Resists alkalis, acids, solvents.

Negative Characteristics: Conducts static electricity; sheen, harsh hand; low sunlight resistance.

Residential Uses: Bedspreads, carpets, mattress pads, scatter rugs, slipcovers, upholstery, wall coverings.

Nonresidential Uses: Carpets, curtains, upholstery, wall coverings.

Care and Cleaning: Dry-clean or wet-clean.

Cost Structure: Low to medium.

Flammability: Some flame resistant; melts before burning; self-extinguishes when flame is removed.

ACRYLIC

Source: Over 85 percent acrylonitrile units, synthetic long-chain polymer.

Trade Names: Acrilan, *Bi-loft, Creslan, Dolan, Dralon,* Fina, *Leacril, Orlon, Zefran.*

Positive Characteristics: Excellent resilience. Soft wool-like texture, hand, and appearance; dyes well. Resists alkalis, acids, solvents, mildew, insects, and aging.

Negative Characteristics: Oleophilic—holds oil-borne stains; variable strength and stability; may fuzz and pill.

Residential Uses: Carpets, upholstery blends, curtains, draperies.

Nonresidential Uses: Carpets, wall coverings.

Care and Cleaning: Dry cleaning recommended.

Cost Structure: Low to medium.

Flammability: Flammable; melts, then burns slowly.

MODACRYLIC

Source: From 35 to 85 percent acrylonitrile units, long-chain polymer.

Trade Names: Acrilan, *Dynel, Kanekalon, Elura, Sef, Verel.*

Positive Characteristics: Soft, buoyant, good hand, drapability, texture. Resists water, aging, insects, alkalis, acids.

Negative Characteristics: Restricted application, low abrasion resistance; heat sensitive; moderate strength.

Residential Uses: Casement draperies, fake fur blends, upholstery.

Nonresidential Uses: Casement curtains, draperies, walls.

Care and Cleaning: Dry cleaning recommended.

Cost Structure: Medium.

Flammability: Flame resistant; burns only with flame source; self-extinguishes when flame is removed.

POLYESTER

Source: Synthetic polymer ester of substituted aromatic carboxylic acid.

Trade Names: Alvin, *Blue C, Caprolan, Dacron, Encron,* Fortrel, *Hollofil, Kodel, Lanese, Quintess, Shantura,* Spectran, *Strialine, Tergal, Terylene, Textura,* Trevira, *Twistloc, Vycron, Zefran.*

Positive Characteristics: Resists sunlight fading and deterioration, mildew, insects; dimensionally stable; good strength. Soft hand, dyes well, resembles wool appearance. Water, heat, aging have no effect.

Negative Characteristics: Susceptible to abrasion, low resilience, oleophilic (holds oil-borne stains), pills.

Residential Uses: Sheer curtains, draperies, wall fabric, upholstery, slipcovers, carpets, awnings, fiberfill battings.

Nonresidential Uses: Curtains and draperies, wall fabric, upholstery.

Care and Cleaning: Wash or dry-clean.

Cost Structure: Low to medium.

Flammability: Flammable; will burn with flame source; self-extinguishes when flame is removed. Easily flame-retardant treated.

OLEFIN

Source: Long-chain polymer of ethylene, propylene, or other olefin units.

Trade Names: *Durel, Herculon, Marvess, Polybloom,* Polypropylene, *Vectra, Patlon, Fibralon.*

Positive Characteristics: Durable, economical, good resilience. Oily stains easily removed with water and detergent. Resists acids, alkalis.

Negative Characteristics: Low melting point, susceptible to sunlight and heat deterioration, oily, rough texture.

Residential Uses: Awnings, carpets—face and backing, upholstery, floor mats.

Nonresidential Uses: Indoor-outdoor carpeting, upholstery, carpet backing, artificial turf.

Care and Cleaning: Dry-clean or wet-clean.

Cost Structure: Low to medium.

Flammability: Flammable; burns slowly. Melts and burns when flame is removed.

VINYON/VINYL

Source: Vinyl chloride, long-grain polymer.

Trade Names: Naugahyde, Valcren, Vinyon, PVC, Phovyl, Eibranyl, HH, Leayl, Teylron, Thermoyyl, *Cordelan.*

Positive Characteristics: Imitates leather; many colors/textures.

Negative Characteristics: Splits; holes difficult to repair.

Residential Uses: Artificial leather upholstery, wall coverings.

Nonresidential Uses: Artificial leather upholstery, wall coverings.

Care and Cleaning: Mild soap and water solvents for ink removal.

Cost Structure: Low to medium.

Flammability: Melts, self-extinguishes.

NOTE

Other fibers—such as saran, spandex, fiberglass, latex, and metallic—have limited use in interiors and are therefore not included in this chart.

FABRIC MAINTENANCE

In addition to the points in chart 12.6, there are some general guidelines in chart 12.7 that, when followed, maintain the appearance and long life of fabric.

FABRIC CONSTRUCTION

Fibers are made into fabric in a variety of ways; textiles may be woven or *nonwoven*, *knitted* or *needle constructed*, *layered* or *compounded*, and *extruded*.

The majority of fabrics are still woven on looms, which vary from simple, hand-operated instruments to sophisticated, computer-controlled elaborate machinery. Weaving is the interlacing of lengthwise continuous *warp yarns* that are strung on the loom with crosswise *filling* or *weft yarns* to form a fabric. The order of interlacing determines the type of weave. There are five basic types of weaves accomplished on looms: *plain*, *twill*, *satin*, *Jacquard*, and *pile*. A fabric may be composed of a single weave, variations of a single weave, or a *combination* of weaves.

CHART 12.7 FABRIC MAINTENANCE GUIDELINES

- Regularly vacuum upholstery and window treatments as well as floor textiles. This will prevent soil from becoming embedded in upholstery fabrics and prevent dust from combining with humidity and air impurities to become sticky grime on window coverings.

- Remove spots promptly with a dry-cleaning solution, very mild detergent (1 teaspoon detergent per quart lukewarm water), or a weak water and vinegar solution, depending on the fiber and finish. Always blot the excess, lifting it out rather than rubbing it in.

- Vacuuming and spotting can preclude major cleaning. This is desirable for a number of reasons:

  1. Repeated cleaning can weaken fibers.
  2. Cleaning solutions can remove finishes and fade colors.
  3. Repeated cleaning can take body out of fabric, causing it to hang limply or lose shape.
  4. Cleaning involves cost, time, and effort.

- When selecting professional cleaners, inquire as to method and guarantee. Seek personal recommendation for quality work.

Figure 12.6 *Plain weave fabric/Oxford plaid.*

CHART 12.8 FABRIC CONSTRUCTION

WOVEN
THE PLAIN WEAVE

Plain weave: The plain weave is formed by interlacing yarns one over, one under (1/1) in regular sequence. Variety is introduced through different-sized yarns or by varying the plain weave.

Plain weave

Basket weave: *Basket weaves* are equal, two over two or three over three.

Plain basket weave

Oxford weave: The *oxford weave* variation floats two fine warp threads over and under one heavier weft thread.

Plain oxford weave

Leno weave: Another variation is the *leno weave* in which the warp threads form an hourglass twist.

The dobby attachment weaves in small geometric one-color figures. A host of fabrics are plain weaves, including chintz, broadcloth, ninon, batiste, and tweed, for example.

Plain leno weave

THE TWILL WEAVE

Twill weave: The warp-face twill weave is made of an interlacing pattern that floats one warp thread over two or three weft threads, then under one, called a weft tiedown. This order produces a diagonal *wale*. Steep wales result when two low-pitch wales float over

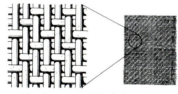

The twill weave, identified by the diagonal wale, is often used for sturdy fabric.

three. *Novelty twills* are formed by reversing or altering the order of interlacing, such as the herringbone (a zigzag chevron pattern) and the houndstooth (a four-pointed star, or a square with a tooth projecting from each side). Twills can be incorporated into complex Jacquard-woven patterns, as well. Duck and serge, as well as houndstooth and chevron, are twill fabrics.

Satin weave: The satin weave floats one warp yarn over four or more weft yarns, then is tied down with one thread (4/1, 5/1, 6/1, 7/1, or 8/1). The order of interlacing is staggered so the result is a smooth face with no wales. Many satin-weave fabrics are woven in very fine threads that increase the luster of the cloth. Satin weaves are also used intensively in cotton decorator fabrics. Satin weaves that float weft or filler yarns on the face of the goods are termed *horizontal satins*, *satines*, or *warp sateens*. In addition, satin weaves often form the background for damask and brocade.

The warp sateen is used for many printed cotton fabrics.

The satin weave produces a lustrous, smooth face.

Jacquard weave: Early in the eighteenth century, a Frenchman named Joseph Marie Jacquard invented a loom attachment that became known as the Jacquard loom. It resembled the early computers in that hole-punched cards were used, strung in sequence high above the loom. As the wires carried each card into position above the loom, the holes would allow some of the threads to raise and would keep others in position. Thus, large, complex patterns were woven at a fraction of the cost of handwoven fabrics. This loom today takes a long time to thread and set up, but then large runs of fabric can be produced at relatively little expense and time. Jacquard fabrics include matelassé damask, brocade, brocatelle, and figured velvets.

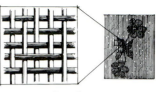

Jacquard weave

Pile weave: The pile weave inserts supplementary warp or weft threads into the fabric as it is woven. The extra threads may be looped or cut pile. Examples are velvets, corduroys, and *terry cloths*.

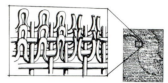

Cut and uncut pile weave

NONWOVEN TEXTILES
NEEDLE-CONSTRUCTED FABRICS

These are fiber mats, webs, or extruded (flowed on, then solidified) textiles used for fabric backings or for upholstery, wall, and carpet padding. Also, an increasing number of fabrics today are needle constructed through the processes of knitting, *tufting*, and interlocking. Knitted fabrics comprise the majority in constructions such as single and double knits and rachel or warp knits for casement draperies. Arnache and malimo needle machines use multiple needles to chain stitch or interlock threads onto a cloth as it is formed. Lace is also a needle-constructed fabric.

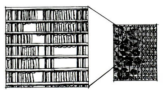

Lace construction

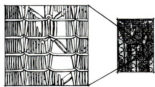

Malimo and arnache

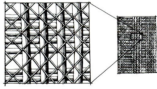

Rachel knits

LAYERED OR COMPOUNDED FABRICS

As the name layered implies, this group of fabric constructions takes more than one production step to complete. Examples of layered or compounded fabrics include *embroidery*: hand, crewel, and schiffli (machine embroidery). Appliqué, the layering of additional fabrics by gluing and/or stitching, is also a compound cloth. Tufting is yet another example and is the method by which the vast majority of carpets are constructed today. Tufting punches yarns into a base fabric. In carpet, the tufted yarn is held in place with a layer of latex adhesive, then adhered to a secondary backing of jute or polypropylene. (See chapter 11.) Early American chenille bedspreads are another example of tufted fabrics.

Figure 12.7 *Twill weave fabrics—houndstooth check and Tartan plaid.*

Figure 12.8 *Satin weave adds to the richness of these Jacquard and striped pattern fabrics.*

Figure 12.9 *The Jacquard weave produces complex woven patterns.*

Figure 12.10 *Needle-constructed Scottish lace.*
Courtesy of Lee Jofa.

Figure 12.11 *Fine embroidered table linens are an example of layered or compounded fabrics.*
Courtesy of the International Linen Promotion Commission.

FINISHES

Finishing is the process of converting textiles from their raw or gray goods (greige) state (dingy gray without pattern, color, or textural interest) into an identifiable fabric for interior design. *Finishes* can be broken into two main categories: *finishing* and *coloring*. Both of these processes take place at a variety of times. For example, the fabric may receive prefinishing steps, then be dyed, and further finished for aesthetics and/or durability. Or, the cloth may be dyed first, then treated with finishes later. Most fabric goes through an average of six different finishing steps or processes before it is ready to market.

Many fabrics are *prefinished*, such as *preshrinking* or *heat setting*. A common prefinish is *mercerizing*, which subjects cotton or linen to caustic soda. This increases the fiber's ability to absorb dye and increases luster, causing the yarn to become rounder and more consistent.

Finishes may be *durable*—able to withstand repeated cleaning—or *nondurable or soluble*—which will be removed with cleaning and will need to be reapplied.

Coloring

Coloring of fabric takes place in two general ways: by *dyeing* and by *printing*. Chart 12.9 lists terms that are used to help us understand the materials and processes used in the coloring of fabric.

Standard Finishes

Standard finishes are also called *chemical*, *wet*, or *functional finishes*. Their purpose is to improve the performance of the fabric or its resistance to environmental factors. Standard finishes may be durable or nondurable.

Examples of standard finishes are *antistatic*, *wrinkle-resistant*, *flame-retardant*, *mothproofing*, *soil-release*, and *soil-* and *water-repellent* finishes.

Decorative Finishes

Decorative finishes also may be durable or nondurable. These are also termed *mechanical* or *surface treatment finishes*. They may determine the decorative identity of the fabric, such as chintz (done by *durable press calendering*—flattening and shining with hot heavy rollers). Other decorative finishes may brighten, deluster, soften, add texture, or press or engrave designs to the surface of the fabric.

CHART 12.9 FABRIC DYEING AND PRINTING

Dyestuff: A water-soluble coloring matter that is mixed with water and chemicals to make a liquid solution or dye bath.

Pigment: A nonsoluble coloring agent that is held onto the surface of fabrics with resin binders. It looks more like paint, and white is typically printed as a pigment.

Stock dyeing: Dyeing natural fibers before they are spun into yarn.

Solution or dope dyeing: Adding dyestuff to the man-made fiber solution before extrusion.

Yarn dyeing: Dyeing the yarn by the skein, by the package, on a beam, or through space dyeing (different colors of the skein, package, or beam).

Piece dyeing: Dyeing a full length of woven fabric (forty-five to 150 yards long). Types of dyeing include beck, jig, padding, pressure jet, union dyeing, and cross dyeing.

Dye lot: When a new dye bath is constituted, several pieces are dyed at once. The new solution may vary slightly from previous batches of the same color, so may not perfectly **match** other dye lots.

Affinity: The attraction of certain chemical compositions to certain fibers. Chemical affinities must be carefully matched.

Cross dyeing: Two fibers of different affinities dyed in the same bath, accepting the dye in different ways.

Hand printing: Techniques that print fabric through hand-only labor, including batik and tie-dye.

Batik: A hand-printing process wherein areas of the cloth not to be colored are covered with a specially prepared wax. The waxed cloth is immersed in a dye bath, then the wax is removed. Other layers of wax and differing colors of dye create interesting patterns.

Tie-dye: A hand resist-method of coloring wherein strings or knots are tied around or in the fabric that is dyed, and abstract patterns emerge.

Block printing: Carved wooden or linoleum blocks are inked, then stamped onto a cloth to create block prints. Large florals in many colors on fine cotton and linen fabrics are classically traditional English patterns, where block printing originated.

Silk-screen printing: A stencil technique using a thin fabric with a film painted or transferred. Ink is **squeegeed** across, penetrating where the film is absent. A new screen is needed for each color.

Flatbed screen printing: A semiautomated silk-screen process wherein the screens are automatically raised and lowered.

Rotary screen printing: A fully automatic silk-screen process wherein the screens are wrapped around circular drums that rotate the ink onto fabric that moves beneath the rotary screens.

Roller printing: A mechanical printing method employing a large engraved metal cylinder, which is continuously inked as fabric moves around it.

Resist or reserve printing: A mechanized process in which a pattern is printed with a chemical paste that resists the dye. The background is colored and the design is light and neutralized.

Discharge printing: Removes the dyed color in patterned areas and replaces it with another color.

Heat-transfer printing: Decals are dispersed-transferred from waxed paper to the cloth under heat and pressure.

Air-brush printing: Use of hand-operated mechanical pressure ink jet guns that spray dye over a stencil.

Etch or burn-out printing: Prints a design with a chemical that dissolves one of the two or more fibers in a fabric to leave some areas more sheer and the nonprinted areas more opaque. Typical is burning out cotton in a cotton/polyester semisheer.

Colorfast: Resistance to fading.

Figure 12.12 *Printed cotton fabrics are a key element in this interior.*
© Jessie Walker.

CHART 12.10   CRITERIA FOR NONRESIDENTIAL FABRIC SPECIFICATIONS

- **Cost:** Nonresidential installations typically have a strict budget.
- **Durability:** The ability of a fabric to exist for a long time without significant deterioration. Durability includes:
  1. Abrasion resistance—The fabric's ability to withstand friction, rubbing, or grinding. Tests are conducted to rate abrasion resistance.
  2. Colorfastness—Resistance to both sun fading and fading from cleaning. Fabrics can be tested and rated for colorfastness.
  3. Resistance to crocking—Crocking is the rubbing off of color onto another fabric or onto the skin.
  4. Strength or tenacity—The actual or physical strength of the fiber. The strength of a fabric is based also on the way the yarns are spun and plied, the closeness of the weave, and the thickness of the fabric.
- **Dimensional stability:** The ability of a fabric to maintain its original size and shape dimensions. This includes:
  1. Resistance to sagging—Elongation or sagging may occur in fabrics that absorb moisture (hydrophilic fibers) when humidity is high or the fabric is wet-cleaned.
  2. Resistance to hiking—Hiking up or shrinkage can occur when humidity drops or fabrics dry out. The lack of dimensional stability in hung fabrics through sagging and hiking is called the yo-yo effect—the bottom hem becomes quite uneven.
- **Resilience:** The fabric's ability to return to its original shape after stretching or elongation. In upholstered fabrics, dimensional stability also includes resilience, or the ability to bounce back to its original shape. Resilience is the result of two qualities:
  1. Flexibility—Stretching and rebounding.
  2. Strength or tenacity—A fabric lacking strength, which tears easily, is termed tender.
- **Resistance to static electricity:** An important consideration where static electricity buildup may affect delicate instruments, such as computers, or where they may be a source of fire ignition.
- **Resistance to insects and microorganisms:** Necessary to prevent fabric disintegration and the spread of disease, particularly in hospitals and institutions.
- **Flammability resistance:** Fibers in nonresidential settings must meet the rigid fire code. Fabrics are tested for flammability, smoke density, and toxicity.
  1. Flammable or inflammable—Fabrics that catch fire easily or are highly combustible, such as cotton, linen, rayon, and acetate.
  2. Flame resistant—Natural fibers (wool, silk) that do not ignite easily, are slow-burning, and will often self-extinguish.
  3. Fire retardant—Man-made fibers that are flame resistant (not easily combustible, slow burning, may self-extinguish). These are modacrylic, saran, polyvinyl chloride, nomex, and novoloid. Fire-retardant fabrics may be flammable natural fibers (cotton, linen, rayon, and acetate) that have been given chemical finishes to inhibit their flammability. These treatments are termed flame-retardant finishes.
  4. Non-flammable or flameproof—Fibers that will melt but will not burn are asbestos, metal, and fiberglass.
- **Flame-retardant finishes:** These are chemical applications that enhance a fabric's ability to withstand or resist combustion. Most flame retardants provide one of the following degrees of durability:
  1. Nondurable—A water-soluble compound that is removed with wet cleaning, requiring reapplication.
  2. Semi-durable—A compound that will resist wet-cleaning but not dry-cleaning solutions.
  3. Durable—Treatments that will withstand repeated dry cleaning and are permanent, lasting the lifetime of the fabric.[2]

NONRESIDENTIAL CONSIDERATIONS

Fabrics installed in nonresidential buildings must meet minimum requirements for durability, colorfastness, and fire safety. These minimum acceptable standards are written as specifications by an architect or interior designer. The interior designer then selects fabrics that meet the specifications or requirements listed in chart 12.10.

ENVIRONMENTAL CONSIDERATIONS

There are two main considerations in fabric usage. The first is the potentially high turnover or replacement factor. Although using new fabrics can keep an interior up to date and in style, it is important not to waste used fabric. Recycling is a simple matter: take draperies, bedspreads, tablecloths, and linens to a charity or second-hand store. Other options include giving them away, selling them, or using them as cleaning rags.

The second, more complex, factor has to do with the toxins that are emitted from textiles due to the finishes applied. Although written data are available upon request from the fabric manufacturer, the consumer rarely asks for it. The problem is complicated in "sealed" nonresidential buildings with inadequate air circulation.

In the home, keep in mind that fresh air and adequate ventilation are essential to a healthy interior environment.

antique satin
A lightweight drapery fabric in a sateen or horizontal satin weave with slubs that imitate spun shantung silk. Most antique satins are one color, though the warp and weft yarns may be dyed different colors to produce iridescence; may also be printed. Suitable for bedspread fabric if quilted.

armure
Medium-weight fabric in one color with small woven repetitive dobby figures. Plain-weave ribbed background cloth.

arnache
Needle-constructed lightweight casement cloth. Weft threads are inserted just ahead of the multiple-needle lockstitch knitting.

batik
A lightweight to medium-weight hand-printed textile. Certain areas are waxed, then the fabric is dyed. For two or more colors, each preceding wax layer is removed, and wax is reapplied in a different pattern. A crinkled pattern is achieved by crumpling the fabric and cracking the wax. Primitive or ethnic batik patterns from Indonesia and Africa are reproduced by mechanical silk screen or roller printing.

batiste
A thin, semisheer curtain/drapery fabric.

bengaline
A medium-weight horizontal or weft-ribbed fabric produced with fine warp and plied or grouped filling yarns. Strong and refined cloth.

bird's-eye
A lightweight to medium-weight fabric with small dobby woven all-over diamond patterns in one color. Originally a toweling/linen fabric, cotton is used most often.

bouclé
Medium-weight to heavyweight knitted or woven cloth. Looped bouclé novelty yarns give a tightly curled, bumpy surface texture to the fabric.

bouclé marquisette
Fine leno-weave sheer marquisette with bouclé weft or filler yarns. Originally glass curtains of nylon; today of polyester and used as lightweight casement fabric.

broadcloth
Lightweight cotton plain taffeta weave with fine horizontal ribs. Yarn twist or tightness is slightly irregular. Also a finely napped twill weave wool in various weights.

brocade
Medium-weight formal Jacquard weave with supplemental warp or weft woven into the fabric to give an embroidered, often colorful, design. Background weave is often satin. Threads not tied down are carried as "floats" on the back of the fabric. Cut floats make broché brocade.

brocatelle
Medium-weight Jacquard fabric with slightly heavier and puffier surface than damask. Fine cloth with two sets of warp and weft.

buchram, buckram, or crinoline
Lightweight fabric, in width three, four, or five inches, stiffened and used as drapery heading interfacing. Plain weave or nonwoven web of cotton, linen, jute, or synthetic fiber.

burlap
Medium-weight jute fabric in plain, loose weave; also called gunnysack cloth. Coarse texture, solid colors. Natural and synthetic fibers imitate jute burlap.

burn-out
A method of printing designs into semisheer or lightweight casement cloths. Usually a cotton polyester base fabric printed with an acid design that eats or dissolves the cotton. Edges around the burn-out area are often printed with pigment ink to seal edges. Also used to produce eyelet holes. Also called etch printing.

calico
Lightweight cotton or cotton/polyester fabric similar to broadcloth. Usually printed in small country-style multicolored floral patterns.

cambric
Semisheer to lightweight plain weave cotton or linen fabric, often printed. May be finished dull and soft or stiff with a sheen. Also called handkerchief linen.

canvas
Versatile medium-weight to heavyweight cotton fabric in plain or twill weave. May be dyed any color and has many uses such as upholstery, shades, and awnings.

casement
Lightweight to medium-weight casual drapery fabric. Plain or combination weave or needle-constructed fabric. Interesting texture, color, and pattern through dyed novelty yarns and weave variations. May be semisheer, translucent, or opaque.

chambray
Lightweight cotton or blend fabric in plain, balanced weave. Yarns are slightly slubbed in both directions. Usually white warp and colored weft or filling.

chenille
Medium-weight to heavyweight fabric with chenille yarns that are fuzzy and resemble soft pipe cleaners. Velour textures are common.

chevron
Regular and repeated zigzag pattern, also called herringbone, formed by reversing the twill weave. Fabric is of natural and/or synthetic fibers. Medium weight to heavyweight.

chiffon
Sheer, very lightweight ninon or voile drapery fabric. Also a soft finish given to a fabric, such as chiffon velvet.

chintz
Lightweight fine cotton or cotton/polyester plain weave fabric. Solid colors or floral or exotic prints. Most often sized or glazed—hence, glazed chintz. It is a multipurpose fabric.

corduroy
Medium-weight to heavyweight pile weave cotton or cotton blend fabric. Lengthwise cords or wales are named according to width:

    pinwale corduroy—narrow wales

    wide wale corduroy—large wales

crepe
A fine yarn that is twisted so tightly that it gives a pebbly or crinkled surface in woven fabrics. Crepe may be plain or satin weave and includes the following types:

    canton crepe—heavy fabric with ribs

    chiffon crepe—soft finish thin crepe

    crepe-de-chine—sheer, very thin, limp crepe

    crepon crepe—heavy crosswise ribs

    faille crepe—fine horizontal ribs

    flat crepe—smooth, fine surface

    plissé crepe—puckered or crinkled surface

cretonne
Medium-weight unglazed printed cotton fabric slightly heavier than chintz. Versatile decorative fabric similar to toile.

crewel embroidery
Medium-weight compound fabric. Base cloth is basket weave of cotton, linen, or wool, with hand or machine embroidery of worsted wool. Patterns are meandering vine and floral motifs based on English interpretations of the Eastern Indian tree-of-life motifs.

crinoline
Same as buchram.

damask
Medium-weight Jacquard fabric with reversible pattern, historically a large floral or Renaissance design. Contemporary damasks are medium weight in a variety of designs; multiple-use fabric.

denim
Medium-weight sturdy twill cotton or cotton/polyester cloth. Navy colored denim is jeans fabric, cream or white denim is drill.

dimity
Thin, very lightweight semisheer fabric in plain weave with a crisp finish. Vertical warp spaced ribs or cords are formed with heavier or piled threads. Checks may also be woven in. One color or contrasting thread may form the ribs, cords, or checks.

dotted swiss
Plain or leno weave swiss is sheer curtain fabric, within tiny embroidered or flocked dots or squares in spaced sequence.

double cloth
Same as matelassé.

duck
Durable medium-weight cotton fabric in oxford weave similar to canvas. Different-sized weft threads and the addition of colored stripes may vary the appearance.

embroidery
A thread or set of threads sewn onto a fabric for surface ornamentation. Types include:

    piece work—embroidery done by hand

    crewel embroidery—tree-of-life motifs originating in India done by hand-guided machine using a looped crewel stitch

    schiffli embroidery—decorative machine embroidery for mass production

eyelet
Lightweight cotton, cotton/polyester, or other blend, plain weave fabric with schiffli-embroidered designs and small burn-out or etched dots that are part of the design. The fabric is usually a solid white, cream, or pastel color with matching or accenting embroidery. Also comes in smaller widths—usually five, seven, eleven, and fourteen inches—with scalloped borders.

faille
A lightweight, finely woven fabric generally of cotton, silk, acetate, rayon, or blends, with horizontal or weft ribs that are slightly heavier and flatter than taffeta. When these ribs are pressed or calendered in a water-mark design, faille becomes moiré.

felt
A nonwoven fabric made of wool and perhaps hair and cotton fibers compressed with moisture, heat, and agitation. Felt comes in many weights, from craft felts to heavy hat and interlining felts.

flamestitch
A pattern originally from the Early English Renaissance that represents the flames of a fire and is loosely a chevron design. Flamestitch patterns are multicolored and may be embroidered, woven, or printed on various weight cloths.

flannel
Any fabric that is woven and then brushed to achieve a soft nap. Types include:

    cotton flannel, flannelette—lightweight, thin fabric used for flannel sheets

    outing flannel—medium weight, suitable for upholstery; pilling may be a problem

    french flannel—fine plain weave flannel

    melton flannel—heavyweight cotton and/or wool dense plain weave; used for interlining and stiffening as a support fabric

    suede flannel—two-sided nap, trimmed and pressed

foam back
Loose adjective for a latex or other synthetic coating laminated, flowed, or sprayed onto the back of drapery and upholstery fabrics to increase energy efficiency and/or dimensional stability.

frieze or frisé
Heavyweight, sturdy nylon upholstery fabric with a looped pile. May be a Jacquard weave to achieve a sculptural or ribbed effect. Types include:

    grospoint—frieze in even or staggered rows with large loops; may also be Jacquard woven

    petit point—very small loops; resembles fine hand needlepoint

gabardine
Steep-pitched twill fabric woven of natural or synthetic yarns; lightweight to medium weight. Surface has obvious diagonal ribs that are tightly woven of fine, lustrous yarns.

gauze
Very thin (sheer or semisheer) loosely woven fabric used for curtains and draperies.

gimp
Narrow braid trimming in many designs for drapery and upholstery. Also term for metallic cording.

grenadine
Thin, sheer leno weave curtain fabric. May be flocked or swivel lappet embroidered with small dots or designs.

grosgrain
Narrow trimming ribbon or textile with round, even, heavy ribs in the weft or horizontal direction.

herringbone
Originally a medium-weight wool fabric. Pattern is a novelty or complex twill that is a regular zigzag pattern. Named after the spinal structure of the herring fish. May also be woven or printed on lightweight, medium-weight, and heavyweight fabrics and in a variety of natural or synthetic fibers.

homespun
Coarse, lightweight wool, linen, or cotton fabric from Early American hand-spun and handwoven plain weave textiles. Today in nearly any fiber, a textile that imitates this look. May be natural colors with flecks of vegetable matter. May also be simple stripes or checks.

hopsacking
Similar to plain homespun yet less sturdy. Usually woven in a loose, semiopen basket weave and given a soft finish. Lightweight casement fabric.

houndstooth
Medium-weight to heavyweight fabric with woven twill pattern in contrasting color that resembles squares with projecting toothlike corners called four-pointed twill stars. Originally a coarse provincial wool fabric, now in a variety of fibers and may be woven in finer yarns.

interfacing
A lightweight, stiffened woven or nonwoven fabric that is usually placed between decorative and lining fabric to give body and firmness. White or solid colors.

interlining
A thick, lofty woven or nonwoven textile of natural or synthetic fibers used to insulate against noise or heat and/or cold. May be a polyester batt or lambs' wool batt, for example.

Jacquard
Any textile woven on the Jacquard loom, which permits large designs to be machine woven. Used for both cloth and carpeting, Jacquard fabrics are brocade, brocatelle, matelassé, lampas, tapestry, and moquette velvet.

jersey
Single vertical knit fabric that includes tricot and some stretch knits. Fabric is usually lightweight, though some upholstery stretch jersey fabrics are medium weight.

khaki
Multipurpose twill or plain weave fabric of a greenish, dusty, earthy beige. Lightweight to medium-weight cotton or blend fibers.

knit
Knit fabrics are produced on multiple-needle knitting machines and include:

> rachel, raschel knit—warp knit casement fabrics
>
> single or jersey—lightweight knit with weft ribs used for fabrics such as tricot
>
> double knit—heavier knit textiles
>
> stretch knits—elastomeric threads for stretch upholstery
>
> knit terry cloth—knit toweling

lace
A lightweight machine- or handmade, needle-constructed fabric of natural or synthetic yarns. Open, floral, or geometric patterns sometimes on a net background, lace is typically used for curtains, draperies, and table settings. Geometric lace for contrast settings is sometimes termed architectural lace.

lampas
Medium-weight Jacquard fabric with a plain or satin background and figures of contrasting colors in both the warp and weft in ribbed, plain, or twill weave.

lappet
Swivel or discontinuous (no floats carried on back) embroidery accomplished with an attachment to the plain or dobby loom.

lawn
Fine, thin fabric that is the base cloth for batiste, organdy, and printed sheer fabrics. Usually cotton, linen, rayon, or blends.

leno
A variation of the plain weave in which pairs of warp threads are twisted in hourglass fashion as they interlock weft threads to give strength and texture. Used in thin, very lightweight, marquisette sheers as well as lightweight casement fabrics.

lining
A lightweight support fabric (cotton, synthetic fibers, or blends) in plain or sateen weave sewn onto or used as separate backing for the decorative fabrics.

malimo
Casement, contemporary fabric where groups of weft yarns are chain stitched together in clear monofilament thread with multiple needles. Groups of warp threads may also be laid and stitched into the top of the weft groups.

marquisette
A thin, sheer curtain or drapery cloth of natural or synthetic fibers in a leno weave. Slightly heavier than ninon or grenadine.

matelassé
A heavyweight textile in Jacquard weave of two sets of warps and wefts. Background surface appears puffy or cushioned since the sets of threads are woven together only where the pattern is. Also called double cloth or pocket weave.

moiré
Lightweight to medium-weight faille fabric embossed with a watermark moiré pattern. A versatile fabric.

muslin
Thin cotton cloth of a plain balanced weave similar to lawn, but stiffer. Muslin forms the base for several cotton fabrics. May be natural (bleached or unbleached), dyed, or printed. Also lower thread-count bed sheets.

mylar
Trade name of the DuPont Corporation for a clear or metallized extruded material. Used in flat sheets such as reflective wallpaper backgrounds or cut into ribbons, texturized, and woven to achieve a novelty-textured fabric.

needlepoint
Heavy upholstery-weight textile of tight hand-stitched wool yarn on art canvas net. Types include:

> petit point—finer needlepoint using very tiny stitches
>
> grospoint—coarser, larger embroidered stitches

net
Historically made by hand as a base for lace, now a machine, needle, and open construction, thin textile with a background of square, diamond, hexagonal, or irregularly shaped mesh.

ninon
Very fine sheer drapery and curtain fabric in pair warp thread plain weave variation. Usually of polyester in varying widths up to 118 inches seamless. It has excellent drapability, crisp body, and a lustrous appearance. Sometimes called French voile, triple voile, or tergal voile.

organdy
Plain weave sheer curtain and drapery cloth of natural or synthetic fibers (originally cotton), which is given a stiff, very crisp finish. A semisheer organdy is called semiorgandy.

ottoman
Natural or man-made fibers woven in a medium-weight to heavyweight fabric with broad, round weft threads that produce a horizontal rib. Fine warp threads completely cover the large-, even-, or alternate-sized filling yarns.

oxford cloth
A lightweight cotton or cotton/polyester fabric in an oxford variation of the plain weave: pairs of warp threads are grouped together and carried over and under a heavier filling yarn. Often used as a base cloth for decorative prints and may be woven with slightly heavier yarns to produce a medium-weight fabric. Oxford cloth is traditionally a finely woven shirting cloth.

paisley
A pattern printed onto natural or synthetic, lightweight or medium-weight fabrics. The curved pear, leaf, or water drop shape originated in India but is named for a city in Scotland where woolen paisley shawls have been produced for centuries.

pellon
Stiffening interfacing fabric that is a trademark of the Pellon Corporation.

percale
Lightweight plain weave cotton or cotton/polyester fabric in a fine yarn and high thread count. Finely woven bed sheets are generally percale. Percale is finished to a variety of lusters from soft to stiff, or given a textured plissé finish.

pile fabric
Medium-weight to heavyweight fabric with an extra set of warp or weft threads that are woven or knitted into the fabric to produce a deep surface texture. Examples include velvets, terry cloths, friezes, and corduroys.

piqué
Lightweight to medium-weight versatile cloth in a plain weave variation, which inserts raised cords, stripes, or geometric patterns. The rib or cord usually runs lengthwise in the face of the goods. Types include:

> bird's-eye—lightweight diaper cloth, small geometric three-dimensional weave
>
> goose-eye—larger bird's-eye with diamond-shape pattern in relief, lightweight
>
> dimity—thin, semisheer fabric with lengthwise ribs of heavier threads
>
> ribcord or pinwale—medium-weight fabric with lengthwise ribs often used for bedspreads and draperies
>
> embossed piqué—design pressed or calendered into face of fabric
>
> waffle piqué—three-dimensional square patterns

plaid
Lightweight, medium-weight, or heavyweight yarn dyed, woven, or printed with a design consisting of stripes in both warp and weft directions that cross at intervals to form different colors in square or rectangular patterns. Plaids may be plain or twill weave. Variations include:

> tartans—Scottish clan plaids
>
> plaidback—reversible plaid

plissé
A sheer, thin, or lightweight fabric given a blistered or puckered surface through chemical treatments.

polished cotton
Lightweight to medium-weight plain or sateen weave cotton fabric with smooth, lustrous yarns. Sateen weave is also called glosheen. Unglazed chintz may be classified as polished cotton.

poplin
Lightweight to medium-weight fabric with pronounced horizontal ribs. Weft threads are heavier than warp. Often a base cloth for many decorative print fabrics.

quilted fabric
Any fabric that is lined and usually interlined with a lofty batt, then hand or machine stitched through so that stitches show both front and back. Pinsonic quilting is often used for mass-produced bedspreads, where layers are fused together with ultrasound heat in a predetermined pattern.

rachel, raschel knit
Also called warp-knit casements, a lightweight drapery fabric where knitted warps form the body of the fabric.

rep, repp
A horizontally or vertically ribbed fabric in plain weave with heavier threads in one direction. Durable medium to heavy fabric with many applications. High-quality reps are often of wool.

sailcloth
Same as duck, sometimes heavier.

sateen
A horizontal satin lightweight to medium-weight fabric. Used for linings and printed decorator fabric in natural or man-made fibers.

satin
A basic type of weave where warp threads float over four to eight weft threads, then are interlaced or tied down with one weft thread. Fine thread yields a smooth, lustrous surface. Lightweight to medium weight. Types include:

> antique satin—horizontal slubs to imitate silk shantung
>
> lining satin—lightweight drapery lining fabric
>
> ribbed satin—resembles faille or calendered into satin moiré
>
> satin damask—background satin with Jacquard pattern— lighter weight known as ticking satin
>
> upholstery satin—heavier weight satins, may be the base cloth for Jacquard weaves

schiffli
Any fabric with machine-embroidered designs, other than dotted swiss, eyelet, and swivel or lappet embroidery. Threads may be one color or variegated. Embroidered on fabric from very sheer to very heavyweight and in simple to complex patterns.

scrim
Very thin plain weave cloth with loose construction. Types include:

> theater scrim—sheer, curtain-weight, softer, more drapable
>
> upholstery scrim—woven or nonwoven web dust cover fabric for the bottom of upholstered pieces.

seersucker
Lightweight to medium-weight cotton or cotton blend plain weave fabric. Crinkled or puckered surface usually in spaced stripes or plaids, permanently woven. Occasionally induced through chemicals that produce more permanent puckers than plissé.

serge
Lightweight to medium-weight fabric in natural or synthetic fibers (originally silk) in durable, crisply finished twill weave.

shade cloth
Plain or plain weave variation, such as canvas, poplin, or oxford. Medium weight to lightweight, it is stiffened to become roller shade fabric. Also called holland cloth.

shantung
Originally a spun silk fabric with slubs that formed interesting and exotic textures. Shantung today is a lightweight fabric of natural or synthetic fibers. Fabrics that imitate shantung are antique satin (sateen weave rayon/acetate) and antique taffeta (plain weave).

sheer
A translucent or transparent thin, very lightweight curtain or drapery fabric. Examples include ninon, chiffon, grenadine, marquisette, swiss, and voile.

strié
Also called jaspé, meaning shadow stripes, a sateen or satin weave with colored warp threads that produce a finely blended vertical stripe. Lightweight to medium-weight multipurpose fabric in natural or synthetic fibers or blends.

suedecloth
A lightweight to medium-weight synthetic knit or woven textile with brushed nap that imitates genuine suede.

swiss
A very thin, semisheer curtain fabric of plain weave. It is a crisply finished fabric and may be embellished with woven or flocked dots or figures. Originally of cotton, today it is often polyester. Also called swiss muslin.

taffeta
A plain, balanced weave in lightweight fabric of natural or man-made fibers. Weft threads are slightly larger, creating a fine horizontal rib. Types include:

> moiré taffeta—calendered as moiré—pressed ribs make the classic water mark pattern
>
> faille taffeta—heavier ribbed taffeta
>
> antique taffeta—horizontal slubs, a reversible fabric
>
> paper taffeta—very crisp finish, often woven in plaid patterns

tapestry
A plain weave technique used to produce heavy, complex, handwoven European pictorial tapestries. These are now most often Jacquard weave fabrics with multiple warps and wefts and are very heavy fabric. Tapestry techniques are also used for handmade flat, reversible folk rugs and further apply to a large category of fabric and nonfabric wall hangings or textiles. Tufted wall hangings may also be referred to as tapestries.

terry
Medium-weight pile weave used for absorbent cotton terry cloth toweling. Loops may be cut for a plush or velour surface texture or left uncut as loops.

ticking
Originally a twill navy blue and cream vertically woven striped fabric used to make ticks (mattress and pillow casings). Today a woven or printed stripe, in one color on cream or white. Multi-use fabric. Mattress ticking may also be a satin damask fabric, called damask ticking or ticking damask.

toile
A fabric of cotton or linen similar to muslin or percale in plain or sometimes twill weave. It is similar to a heavier unglazed chintz. Toiles are typically roller or screen printed in one color: navy, cranberry, or black on a cream background. Types include:

> toile de Jouy—eighteenth- and nineteenth-century rural scenes and people; originating in Jouy, France
>
> federal toile—American federal buildings and eagles
>
> country toile—contemporary provincial floral patterns

tricot
Nylon jersey knit that has a weft-only stretch. Lightweight, limp fabric.

tufted fabric
A pile fabric that is formed by tufting a yarn into a woven background. Early American tufted bedspreads are one example. Some upholstery fabrics and all tufted carpets utilized this method. The fabric may be tufted with a small hand-held tufting gun or on a large machine that utilizes multiple needles, tufting entire sections in rapid sequence.

tweed
Heavy upholstery-weight textile in plain balanced or variation weave or (originally) twill weave variation. Plain and twill weaves may also be combined. Made first of wool in Scotland, today's tweeds may be of wool, nylon, or a combination of natural and man-made fibers in solid colors, a heathered effect, or plaid.

union cloth
A coarse, medium-weight cloth that is approximately 50 percent cotton, 50 percent linen. Yarns are calendered or flattened somewhat. Union cloth may be dyed one color or printed and often resembles a very coarse chintz. Versatile fabric with many uses.

velour
A heavy pile fabric with a soft, velvetlike texture that includes some velvets and all plush-pile surface cloths, as velour terry.

velvet
Woven pile fabric with a soft yet sturdy face. May be of one or more fibers, including cotton, linen, wool, silk, rayon, acrylic, and nylon. Types include:

  antique velvet—streaks pressed or woven in: slubs on woven back, or slight strié effect

  brocaded—etch-printed or burn-out pattern, often exposing the woven background

  chiffon velvet—thick, soft surface finish velvet

  crushed velvet—varies from light to heavy crushing of pile

  electrostatic velvet—flocked, rather than woven pile, usually bold color and pattern

  embossed velvet—bas-relief roller calendering to produce pressed-in pattern

  moquette velvet—exposed ground with floral historic patterns of cut and uncut looped pile in Jacquard weave

  panne velvet—pile lays flat, pressed in one direction

  plush velvet—deeper pile, sometimes crushed

  upholstery velvet—deep thick pile and sturdy back

  velveteen—short, cotton-faced pile and back

  printed velveteen—roller or screen printed, typically in floral or geometric patterns

vinyl
Extruded polyvinyl chloride (vinyon) synthetic fabric flowed onto a woven, knitted, or nonwoven base cloth. Medium-weight to heavyweight upholstery fabric, which is also called imitation leather or artificial leather.

voile
Sheer, transparent fabric in plain weave with tightly twisted yarns. Often has a stiff finish. May have novelty effects such as piqué stripes, printed patterns or stripes, or woven with nubby yarns for novelty voile.

NOTES

1. Dianne R. Jackman and Mary K. Dixon, *The Guide to Textiles for Interior Designers* (Winnipeg: Peguis Publishers, 1983), 13–14.

2. S. C. Reznikoff, *Specifications for Commercial Interiors: Professional Liabilities, Regulations, and Performance Criteria* (New York: Whitney Library of Design, 1979), 154.

CHAPTER 13

ART AND ACCESSORIES

© Lisl Dennis.

Great art is a means of expression and a type of spiritual communion between artist and viewer. Art has been an integral part of interiors since the time when prehistoric artists painted the walls and ceilings of caves. Art includes a wide variety of forms such as paintings, sculpture, drawings, and prints. These kinds of pieces add great distinction and individuality to interiors because their selection represents personal taste and experience.

The decorative arts include designs such as furniture, porcelain, textiles and weavings, glass, and tableware. These kinds of pieces may be functional or purely decorative. Some are embellished to make them more appealing and better suited to their setting, while others are simple designs that clearly reflect their purpose. Either way, decorative art pieces can add beauty and function to an interior.

Our world is also filled with natural objects of great beauty. When plants, fish, rocks and shells, and other bits of nature are brought into the interior, they provide a dimension of life that can not be created in any other way. When they are combined in an individual way with pieces of art and decorative art, they provide the finishing touches—the frosting on the cake—that make interiors so interesting and personal.

FINE ART

The *fine arts* are concerned with the creation of two- and three-dimensional works of art, designed as expressions of beauty and faith or as a statement of the personal meaning or feeling of the artist. The great *masters* are those throughout the ages who have excelled in the creation of art and whose work has passed the test of time to become what we call *classics*. Every era has its masters, and these men and women were often aware of each other and the work produced by each artist. This mutual awareness often produced similarities in philosophy, technique, subject matter, or other areas of influence. Art historians have classified the work of the masters into *schools* according to these similarities and influences. Many of the masters were equally comfortable drawing with a pencil, painting with a brush, or working sculpture with their hands. The fine arts include *sculpture, painting, mosaic, drawing,* and *printmaking*.

Sculpture

Sculpture is a three-dimensional art form created by carving or assembling stone; working clay, wood, or other materials; or casting or assembling metal. Sculpture may represent the human form, animal forms, or other forms from nature in a realistic, conventionalized, or abstract fashion.

Bas-relief is French for low relief. It is a type of sculpture carved or cast in a flat manner where the design is slightly raised from the background to create a three-dimensional effect. Bas-relief is often seen in friezes (sculptural panels or bands) used on exteriors, in interiors, and even on furniture and small decorative objects.

Painting

Painting is a one-of-a-kind, two-dimensional art form created with colored *pigments* and a number of different *vehicles* (substances that give the pigment form and body). The paint can be thinned with different *media* and manipulated by pouring, dripping, splashing, or applying with brushes, sponges, or *palette knives* to many different surfaces such as plaster, wood, canvas and other textiles, paper, glass, or any material or surface capable of holding the paint.

- *Oil paint* is colored pigment mixed with linseed oil or varnish and thinned with turpentine. Oil painting is very versatile because the color application can be thick or thin, opaque or transparent. Oils tend to be one of the most permanent types of painting, which may account for their popularity with collectors.

- *Watercolor* is colored pigment mixed with *gum arabic* and thinned with water. The pigments are slightly transparent. Because the water used as a medium dries quickly, the artist must work rapidly to complete the painting. This technique imparts a fresh, underworked quality to the finished piece.

- *Acrylic* can duplicate the appearance of oils and watercolors. It is made of plastic and can be mixed with several kinds of media or thinned with water. Its appearance can be opaque or transparent. The untrained eye may find it difficult to distinguish acrylics from the older, more traditional oils and watercolors. Many artists enjoy the versatility provided by a single medium capable of so many different effects.

- *Tempera*, one of the oldest painting techniques, is pigment mixed with egg and thinned with water. It is somewhat transparent but more opaque than watercolor. Budding artists at kindergarten easels often use a form of tempera to create their bright, fresh, uninhibited paintings, and tempera poster paints are frequently used to create banners and posters. However, the tempera used by fine artists is much more refined than poster paint. Fine tempera is often called *gouache*.

- *Fresco* is Italian for fresh and is a combination of pigment and limewater applied with brushes to fresh, damp plaster. When it dries, the pigment and plaster become unified. The artist must work quickly, and plaster is applied only as far as the artist can work before it dries. Frescoes were often used to decorate the ceiling and walls of Renaissance buildings and reflect the glory of that age.

Mosaic

Mosaic is an important medium for creating two-dimensional art made of *tesserae* (small pieces of marble, tile, or colored glass) fitted together to form a pattern. The design is held in place with plaster or cement. The Romans used mosaics to decorate their floors, and artists in the Byzantine empire took the art of mosaic to a high level of perfection. The interiors of Byzantine churches shimmer with scintillating mosaic designs of great beauty.

Figure 13.1 *An interesting contemporary painting is an important part of this focal grouping.*
© Jessie Walker.

ten. Generally, the smaller the number of prints produced, the greater the value. Several screens, plates, or blocks representing different parts of the design can be utilized to create multicolored prints. When using more than one run of color, each plate, screen, or block must be carefully registered (aligned) to produce a clear and even print.

- A woodcut or wood *block print* is made by carving a design into the flat surface of a piece of wood. The background is cut away, leaving the pattern standing out in relief. The block is then inked and printed to create a negative or reverse pattern on the paper. A wood engraving is executed in the same way, except that the pattern is carved into the harder end grain of the wood, which usually results in a finer and more precise design.

- A linoleum-block print is made by cutting a pattern into a piece of heavy gauge linoleum. The process is similar to the woodcut process except that the design will have less detail in the form because of the softness of the linoleum. Woodcut, wood engraving, and linoleum-block printing are all forms of *relief printing* because the portion of the pattern that receives the ink and does the printing stands out in relief.

- *Engravings* are prints made from a metal plate that has lines hand engraved (scratched) with a tool called a burin. These lines make small impressions or grooves in the plate. The plate is covered with ink and then wiped clean, leaving ink only in the grooves. The plate and paper are pressed together so that the ink is transferred from the grooves in a negative impression onto the paper.

- *Etchings* are made by covering a metal plate with an acid-resistant substance such as wax. The artist uses a needle to draw through the wax. The plate is immersed in an acid bath that bites or etches the design into the metal wherever the wax has been scratched away. After the plate is etched and the remaining wax removed, the plate is used to print in the same manner as an engraving. Because wax is less difficult to cut than a metal plate, etching designs tend to be less rigid than engravings. Engravings and etchings are forms of *intaglio* where printing is done with the ink in the plate's recesses.

Drawing

Drawings are also one-of-a-kind, two-dimensional art forms produced with pencil, pen and ink, charcoal, chalk, crayon, or grease pencil on paper or other surfaces. Drawing is considered a fundamental skill for artists. Drawings are produced as finished works and also as preliminary studies in the development of paintings, sculpture, and other art. The work of the masters often includes a large body of drawings that were used as studies for later work and that stand by themselves as treasured art pieces.

Printmaking

Printmaking is a method of mass-producing two-dimensional fine art. Prints are produced in limited editions by the artist who prepares a screen, plate, block, or stone and then makes a numbered set of prints. The artist signs and numbers the prints that are of acceptable quality. The numbers read as a fraction and indicate how many copies were made and the order in which they were printed. For example, 8/10 would indicate that a particular print was the eighth print out of a total of

- *Lithographs* are produced on the principle that water and grease repel each other. The artist creates a design on a limestone block or metal plate with a grease pencil or with a brush and tusche (a waxy liquid). The block or plate is then chemically treated to attract ink to the greasy design and water (which repels the ink) to the untouched portions of the stone or plate. The stone or plate is then charged (wetted) with water and ink and pressed together with the paper to create a negative image.

- *Serigraph or silk screen* is a printmaking process that utilizes a fine screen of silk or other fiber and stencils cut to create a positive, direct (not reversed) image. The stencils are applied to the screen and ink is squeegeed across the pattern, forcing a thin layer of ink onto the surface being printed through the open areas of fabric where there is no stencil.[1]

- *Rubbings* are not a true form of printmaking, though they are often framed and used in much the same way as prints. Rubbings are made by placing a sheet of paper over a flat metal or stone plaque—such as a grave marker or an architectural detail that has a rather flat bas-relief or a raised pattern. The paper is then rubbed with a crayon or chalk to create a direct image of the pattern beneath. The quality of the piece is determined by the care and skill of the person doing the rubbing.

- *Reproductions* are copies of the artist's work and are an important educational tool. Without them, those unable to visit the world's museums would find it difficult to study the history of art. Reproductions may be scaled from postcard size to full poster size or larger. Color quality of reproductions may also vary. For example, colors that were red in the original may appear violet in the reproduction. Once the original piece of art is complete, the quality control of the reproduction is generally out of the artist's hands; the quality of reproductions ranges from excellent to poor. Reproductions of great art are a viable means of bringing quality art into the interior.

- *Graphic art* includes posters designed to publicize athletic contests, concerts, plays, shows of artists' works, and other cultural events. These are often worthy of display on the merits of their fine design and, in time, may become very valuable. Posters are an important resource for those who love art but are unable to afford paintings and other art forms. Unfortunately, many poster designs have no

Figure 13.2 *Framed pieces of graphic art, many of which were originally used as book illustrations, make this room unlike any other.*
© Langdon Clay.

aesthetic value, and it is essential that purchasers be knowledgeable and selective. Maps, botanical drawings, architectural drawings, fashion illustrations, book illustrations, and even some mechanical or architectural drawings may also have value as graphic art.

Obtaining Fine Art

Art can be found at many locations in a vast range of prices. The works of the great masters are generally sold for enormous sums at auction houses like Christie's or Sotheby's in London and New York. Some less well-known but important pieces are sold by art and antique dealers who operate retail shops and galleries. Contemporary artists are usually represented by galleries and dealers who act as agents for the artist. Galleries may specialize in a certain type of art such as historic, oriental, or Western. Art-minded communities and organizations often sponsor art festivals where artists informally display and sell their work. Some businesses and corporations sponsor art shows or display artists' works that may be purchased.

Those who have less to spend on art pieces should know that art teachers and artists who need to finance travels and studies will often sell their work at relatively reasonable prices, and artists frequently will barter services for art. Schools of art may have shows of student work, much of which is for sale. Because they have not usually established a reputation, students tend to sell their work at lower prices.

Economical graphic art posters can be purchased—sometimes obtained without charge—directly from museum shops or from organizations sponsoring the event being publicized in the poster. Old posters, prints, and maps can frequently be found at flea markets or bookshops. When collecting art, one should be prepared to pay fair market prices, though the price is less important than the quality and appeal of a piece.

Print shops specialize in graphic designs from museums, galleries, shows, and other cultural events. In addition, this type of shop will often have fine photography in poster format and reproductions of the masters' works in varying sizes of posters. It is important to be discriminating and choose pieces of fine quality and lasting value, because good design is uplifting and becomes more meaningful with the passage of time.

Obtaining art for our homes is certainly a matter of personal taste, but the more we learn about art, the greater our level of enjoyment and appreciation. The design of a home is a reflection of personal style, and the art chosen for such settings should also be a statement of discrimination and taste. Unfortunately, many of us are underexposed to quality art. Designers or consultants could be used to help us make wise selections, but the most pleasing and personal collections belong to those who put forth the effort to become knowledgeable about art and its history. Not everything that is advertised as original art is worthy of collection. Knowledge, training, and exposure are the only means to ensure wise selection. Following are some important guidelines to help develop the confidence to choose fine-quality art:

- Do not be intimidated by a blank wall—it may have more appeal than a piece of poor art. Take the time and steps necessary to develop confidence in your ability to choose.

- Those who are seriously interested in collecting art will study its history. This can be done formally or informally with classes or independent study. Study of art history builds a sincere appreciation and understanding of art and those who created it.

- Taking art classes and attempting to actually create works of art add profound depth to our appreciation of art and help build the ability to see quality.

- Visiting museums of fine art to observe firsthand the works of the great masters and contemporary artists sharpens the ability to discriminate. It provides the kind of exposure that enables us to detect the difference between real art and the poor quality pieces we see advertised as "original oil paintings."

- Like anything of real value, it takes time and effort to build an understanding and appreciation of art. It is a lifelong pursuit and an important part of the process of developing the ability to discriminate (discussed in chapter 3, Design Principles and Elements). It is a goal worth the effort, however, because of the satisfaction that fine art provides.

Preparing Art for Display

When purchasing a piece of art, it may be necessary to select a *frame, mat* board (heavy flat paper frame), or some other means of display that will show the piece to the best advantage and add to its quality and character. Frames are available in unassembled kits or are ready-made from art shops, from paint stores, and even by mail. In some places there may be hobby shops or specialty shops where customers can cut mats and make and assemble their own frames. However, with truly fine pieces of art, it may be worthwhile to consult a qualified framer who understands art conservation and can advise on the proper method and materials for displaying and preserving art pieces. Following are some suggestions for framing fine art:

- Generally, oil paintings are framed but left unglazed (not covered with glass). They may be framed with heavy, elaborate, period frames that often include a fabric liner to separate the painting from the frame. Contemporary oils and acrylics may be left unframed, or they may be treated with a simple, minimal frame.

- Watercolors, drawings, photographs, and prints are frequently framed behind glass with simple, narrow frames and a mat that keeps the painting from touching the glass. Clear glass is preferable to *nonglare glass* or *Plexiglas*. Nonglare glass does not allow clear color and line transmission. Plexiglas is subject to scratching and bowing. Posters can be framed like watercolors or prints but can also be mounted behind glass with no frame where the glass and backing are held together with clips. When mounting paintings, prints, graphic designs, or reproductions, it is important not to cut or *crop* the piece to make it fit a frame. Cropping destroys the value of the work.

DECORATIVE ART

The *decorative arts* include both utilitarian pieces such as mirrors, tableware, baskets, clocks, screens, lamps, books, tapestries, and rugs as well as nonutilitarian pieces like figurines or statuettes. *Objets d'art, bibelots,* and *curios* are French terms used to describe both these utilitarian and nonutilitarian objects of artistic value and beauty. Furniture, also considered a decorative art, is discussed in chapter 8, Furniture Selection.

Not all pieces created as decorative art have strict artistic value. *Kitsch* is a German term that describes bad taste and is applied to pretentious or foolish art and design. In our contemporary world we are inundated by objects of mediocre or poor design. As we develop the ability to discriminate, we can sift out the kitsch from our environment and replace it with that which is fine and uplifting. It is worth the effort to find good design because it enriches and deepens our appreciation for true beauty. Today, art has become a status symbol, and vast sums of money are often spent on questionable design. Both good and bad design can be found at every price level, and many times it costs no more to choose good design.

Mirrors

In the fourteenth century the skilled artisans of Venice discovered that a layer of *quicksilver* sandwiched between a piece of tin and a piece of glass (a process called *silvering*) created a mirror. Today, mirrors add depth, a feeling of spaciousness, and sparkle to interiors, and they can be obtained in many sizes. They can be framed to harmonize with period styles or can be used in sheets large enough to cover entire walls. However, some people may find it uncomfortable to have to look at themselves in a mirror for prolonged periods when sitting or standing. Large areas of mirror on several different walls may visually duplicate the elements of a design in a manner that creates visual confusion and makes the space seem smaller. Mirror finishes or types include clear glass, smoked glass, *Venetian glass* (veined), *beveled glass*, *leaded glass*, and *etched glass*.

Figure 13.3   *This collection of blue and white porcelain makes this interior appealing and personal.*
Courtesy of Better Homes and Gardens, member of Home Furnishings Council.

Tableware and Cookware

Tableware is the term that describes plates, cups, drinking vessels, and flatware or eating utensils. Artisans through the ages have lavished their finest creativity and the best developments of technology on the creation of beautiful and useful pieces for the table and kitchen. Materials of all kinds have been used to create tableware and cookware, and today plastics and other innovative space-age products are used alongside more traditional materials such as ceramics, glass, wood, and metal for the design of quality pieces. (These same materials are also used to create a wide variety of functional and decorative objects such as small sculpture, planters, containers, bookends, desk sets, and dressing or grooming accessories.)

Ceramics

Ceramics are made from clay that has been molded in its softened form into useful shapes, then fired or baked at high temperatures in an oven called a *kiln*. The soft clay may be molded by hand, formed in molds, or thrown on a potter's wheel run by motor or foot power. Clay mixed with water to the consistency of thick cream is called slip and is used to fill molds and for other functions in the ceramic process. *Glazes* are thin layers of glass fired onto ceramic pieces to produce a glossy surface, to add colored effects, and to make the pieces nonabsorbent and sanitary. Glazes may be dull or shiny, clear or colored, and can be used by the ceramist to create decorative effects. Following is a list of ceramic types:

- *Porcelain* is the highest grade ceramic body. It is made of fine, white clay (*kaolin*) and *feldspar* (crystalline materials) and is fired at very high temperatures that *vitrify* the clay (change it to a glasslike substance), harden the glaze, and make the piece breakage resistant. Porcelain is sometimes used in the manufacture of fine dinnerware, vases, figurines, and other decorative objects. Porcelain may be plain or decorated with colored glazes and patterns.

- *China* was the designation given by Europeans to the porcelain imported from the Orient. It contains a large percentage of animal bone ash (hence the term bone china) that produces a hard, translucent porcelain. Today, the terms china and porcelain are generally used synonymously.

- *Stoneware* is a heavy, durable, thick pottery used for less-formal dinnerware, serving and cooking pieces, as well as other art objects. Stoneware finishes may be less formal and show flecks and speckles in the clay or glaze. Stoneware finishes vary from natural browns, grays, and bluish grays to bright, lively colored patterns.

- *Earthenware* is the most coarse and inexpensive of the ceramic bodies. It is derived from red earthen clays and often finished like a common clay flower pot. It is fired at lower temperatures, making it softer and less durable. Earthenware products are sometimes referred to as terra-cotta, an Italian term that literally means cooked earth. It is commonly used for baking and serving pieces and other decorative pieces for the interior and garden.

Figure 13.4 *A good meal is made even better by a beautiful table setting.*
© *Jessie Walker.*

Glass

Glass (also discussed in chapter 10, Wall, Ceiling, and Window Treatments) is used to fashion decorative objects, dishes, serving pieces, and drinking vessels of all shapes and sizes. The quality and design of glassware ranges from inexpensive molded glass to fine lead crystal.

- Molded or *pressed glass* is a method for mass-producing glass. Molten glass is poured into forms or molds of metal or wood. The mold often leaves a seam where the molds meet. The molding process can be used to form simple and functional glass shapes or to imitate the look of cut glass.

- *Cut* or *etched glass* is decorated with patterns incised with chemicals or abrasives. The cut patterns are quite clear, and the etched designs have a frosted appearance.

- *Enameled glass* is layered with a porcelainlike finish.

- *Cased glass* is a layer of clear glass encased in a layer of colored glass.

- *Gilded glass* has a layer of silver or gold applied to its surface. Enameled, cased, and gilded glass are often engraved or cut to reveal patterns in the sparkling clear glass layer underneath.

- *Crystal* is a high-grade glass containing lead. Because of legal requirements, American lead crystal contains less lead than European lead crystal. Higher lead content makes the glass softer, allowing the glassmaker to cut more intricate designs. Fine lead crystal sparkles beautifully in the light

and rings or sings when tapped lightly with a fingernail. Crystal is used to create art objects, serving pieces, and drinking vessels. *Stemware* is the name given to formal drinking pieces with a slender pedestal and raised bowl.

Wood

Wood (also discussed in chapter 8, Furniture Selection), aside from its use in construction and sculpture, was used historically to make crude plates, utensils, and serving pieces. Today it is still used to create beautiful art objects, both carved and plain, as well as serving pieces, handles for metal utensils and cookware, spoons, and other cooking implements.

Metals and Alloys

Metals and *alloys* such as aluminum, brass, chrome, iron, steel, and stainless steel (discussed in chapter 8, Furniture Selection), together with gold, silver, pewter, bronze, and copper, are common materials used to fashion art objects, cookware, serving pieces, dinnerware, flatware (silverware), fixtures, and hardware.

- Gold, a bright, lustrous yellow, is the most precious, costly, and prestigious metal and was used historically to create dishes, flatware, drinking vessels, candle holders, and other objects of art. Because of its great expense, gold is used principally today as a plating for metal pieces or as paper-thin sheets applied to objects in a process known as *gold leaf. Gold electroplate* is a type of flatware created by the electrolytic process of layering pure gold over a silver/nickel alloy (silver plate).

- Silver is a bright, lustrous, gray-white metal used in the manufacture of objects of art and tableware. *Sterling silver* is the finest and most costly, being by law at least 92.5 percent pure silver. Sterling will tarnish and must be polished and protected from the air. It becomes more beautiful with use, developing a soft *patina* of almost invisible scratches. *Sterling II* is flatware that combines silver handles with stainless steel blades, bowls, and tines, costing about half as much as sterling silver. *Silver plate* is made of a silver/nickel alloy electroplated with pure silver. It is the most affordable type of silverware and is also used as a base for gold electroplate.

- *Stainless steel* is also used to make flatware and serving pieces. Affordable stainless steel flatware and serving pieces are readily available today. These pieces are popular because they do not tarnish or scratch easily, and they are strong, durable, and dishwasher safe. Some designs feature handles of wood or colorful plastic.

- *Pewter* is a soft, dull gray alloy of tin, copper, lead, and *antimony* used to create dishes, drinking vessels, candle holders, and other art objects. Historically pewter was considered poor man's silver. Today, though it is less costly than sterling, pewter is not inexpensive. Once considered dangerous because of its lead content, pewter is now often made without lead and is safer and easier to care for. Pewter adds character and warmth to informal, *provincial* (country) settings. Less-expensive imitations of pewter are now being made of cast aluminum.

‣ *Copper* is a bright, shiny, pinkish brown metal used principally for cookware, because of its ability to conduct heat. When copper is allowed to tarnish, it turns reddish brown then a beautiful blue-green. To maintain the original copper color and shine, it must be polished with copper paste and a soft cloth. Some copper pieces are coated with lacquer or other finishes that prevent tarnishing. These finishes must be removed if the piece is to actually be used for cooking or if a tarnished finish is desired.

‣ *Bronze* is a deep reddish brown alloy of copper and tin used primarily for sculptural pieces or plaques.

‣ Iron is cast or wrought (shaped and bent with heat) to make lighting fixtures, candle holders, and other decorative accessories. *Cast iron* is molded in its molten form to create substantial cookware and some art objects. *Wrought-iron* pieces and heavy cast pieces such as corn pone or muffin molds, skillets, and Dutch ovens are frequently used as decorative accessories in less formal, country settings.

Plastics

Plastics (also discussed in chapter 8, Furniture Selection) are used extensively to create informal tableware and other accessories for interiors. Plastic is generally less expensive than the other materials discussed in this chapter and can be used to create designs of great appeal and integrity. For example, some contemporary plastic dishes are bright, colorful, and well designed. Because they are relatively inexpensive, one can indulge in a splash of color without undue concern for the budget. Plastic is sometimes used in a lighthearted manner to imitate natural materials such as glass or metal. This is particularly true in the manufacture of disposable objects that are not meant to be taken seriously. When plastic is used to imitate natural materials in a serious manner, the design becomes questionable. For example, plastic molded to resemble carved wood or fine cut crystal might only be considered kitsch.

Baskets

Baskets are woven for function, each type or shape reflecting its specific use. Produced by almost every culture in the world, baskets incorporate beautiful patterns using materials such as wicker and willow. Because of their decorative nature, baskets make excellent additions to informal interiors, particularly when they serve a useful purpose such as a container for plants, bread, fruit, or fragrant *potpourri*.

Clocks

Today, timepieces such as *hourglasses*, *sundials*, and antique clocks are collected as objects of art. Looking at fine clocks with intricately designed cases, we appreciate the cabinetmakers and furniture designers whose creative genius made scientific instruments into functional and decorative art. The design of clocks has changed over the years. Today's *high-tech* clocks are often the work of industrial or product designers rather than furniture craftsmen, and these frank, sleek designs may be as beautiful in their own way as the handcrafted pieces of the past. Clocks may be displayed on shelves, mantels, brackets, or walls, or they may be floor clocks. Large-scale floor clocks are often referred to as grandfather clocks, and those of a slightly smaller scale are called grandmother clocks. Clocks are frequently included as a feature in appliances such as radios, microwave ovens, stoves, and VCRs. These often utilize a digital display system that indicates the hour and minutes as digits instead of using the traditional clock face.

Screens

Screens are hinged or sliding panels designed to divide and separate spaces or create areas of privacy. For centuries, the Japanese have used wooden-framed panels glazed with mulberry or rice paper called shoji or fusuma screens. In Western culture, screens have often been used to create dressing spaces. In Near-Eastern cultures screens are used as a "blind" to see out without being seen.

In today's interiors, screens are used as dividers, wall art, window treatments, and a background for furniture. Screens can be made of wood with solid panels or *louvers, lattice,* pierced wood, or wrought iron. Screens are also custom-made items that might be upholstered, covered with mirrors, painted, lacquered, papered, or treated in other interesting ways:

‣ Antique screens from Europe and America, with details appropriate to period styles, are nice additions to interiors as functional dividers or simply as objects of art.

‣ *Coromandel* are large Chinese black-lacquered folding screens, decorated with low relief, all-over patterns. They were introduced into Europe in the seventeenth century by the East India Company.

Figure 13.5
Coromandel screen.

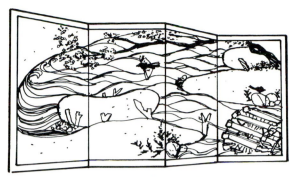

Figure 13.6   Byobu screen.

- *Byobu* are small-scaled folding Japanese screens. They are decorated with scenes painted on silk or paper and are generally used as wall hangings, on tables, or as freestanding pieces in today's interiors.

- *Shoji* or fusuma are Japanese screens made of oriental papers mounted onto a wooden frame. The frames are set into tracks or grooves as sliding panels or hinged and freestanding and used as partitions. Shoji are exterior sliding panels or window screens, and fusuma are decorative interior sliding room partitions or doors. Translucent *transoms* set above the screens add light through a grid or intricate design patterns.

- Near-Eastern screens are intricately patterned pierced wooden screens from Islamic cultures. Islamic design was taken to Spain in the eighth century by invading *Moors*. The Near-Eastern influence can also be seen today in the screens of Mexico and other countries with *Hispanic* ties. Today, many pierced wooden screens are made in India and imported to Western countries.

Decorative Lighting Fixtures

Lighting fixtures have evolved over the centuries from torches, oil- and gas-burning vessels, and candle holders into the electric fixtures we use today. (Architectural lighting and principles of lighting are discussed in chapter 5, Lighting.) Some of today's most common lighting fixtures are electric versions of historical lighting pieces. It is also common to see decorative objects such as metal *tea caddies* (antique tea containers), *ginger jars*, *cloisonné* (enameled metal) and porcelain vases, as well as figurines and other sculptural pieces, made into table lamps. Luminaire is the technical term used by lighting designers and engineers to describe table lamps, floor lamps, and ceiling- or wall-mounted lighting fixtures such as chandeliers and sconces. (The term luminaire distinguishes these lighting fixtures from the technical usage of the term lamp, which refers to a light bulb or fluorescent tube.) Following is a list of the most common *art-lighting* luminaires:

- *Table lamps* are designed to sit on the table for general lighting of a space or for reading, writing, and other specific tasks. Traditional designs usually incorporate a shade to diffuse the light.

Figure 13.7   Table lamps.

- *Floor lamps* serve the same basic purposes as table lamps but are designed to stand on the floor.

- *Torchére* is a historical term that was used to describe a candle table or candle stand. Today it describes a type of floor lamp that casts its light upward onto the ceiling.

- *Sconce* is a wall-mounted luminaire of any style that has descended from wall-mounted torches or candle holders.

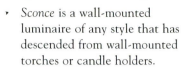

Figure 13.8   Sconces.

- *Chandelier* is a decorative, ceiling-mounted, hanging, or pendant-type luminaire. This type of fixture functions best in high-ceiling rooms and where a strong focal point is the intent of the design.

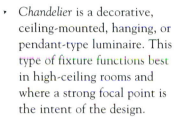

Figure 13.9   Chandeliers.

Many antique and contemporary lighting pieces are used simply as objets d'art. Candle holders made of metal, wood, and ceramic—and various styles of oil and gas lamps—are often collected and displayed because of their aesthetic appeal and not because of a need for light. Candlelight is used to create a special mood because, like firelight, it has a moving and scintillating quality that is not commonly duplicated with electric luminaires. *Neon lamp* designs created for advertising or as pieces of art are sometimes seen in today's interiors. Such pieces are far more important as decorative art than as light.

When selecting luminaires for an interior, it might be useful to consider the following applications of the elements and principles of design:

- The form of the luminaire should be pleasing and the lines should be harmonious with the other elements of the design.

- Proportions should be good. With traditional luminaires, the proportions of the base and shade should relate well to each other.

- The luminaire should be in scale with the space and with the other furnishings.

- The design should be appropriate to the function of the space.

Books

Books are not only decorative but are also appealing because of their unity of form and variety of color and texture. They may also lend a certain amount of emotional warmth to a space, because when read, they may be like old friends, associated with all kinds of memories. Second-hand hardcover books are sometimes purchased and displayed like stage props. These look attractive in settings such as restaurants and shops where the design is intended to create a homey atmosphere. In a residential setting, books purchased as props will be visually pleasing but may lack the emotional appeal of books that have been read and loved. Books stashed in attics or garages might be an untapped resource that could add a warm finishing touch to interiors.

Figure 13.10 *Collections of porcelain and books add distinction, and plants add a quality of life to this comfortable room.*
Courtesy of Better Homes and Gardens, member of Home Furnishings Council.

Walls of books make a suitable background for furniture groupings; they are a welcome addition to almost any interior. They can be carefully interspersed with objets d'art or plants to create pleasing compositions. Interesting books and magazines placed on tables for browsing make stimulating accessories. Entries, living rooms, family rooms, dining rooms, kitchens, bedrooms, and even bathrooms are all appropriate locations for books. A library or home office is becoming more practical, and a formal dining room used for meals only occasionally might double as a library or study. The table would be useful for reading or writing, and the books would make a pleasant background for occasional dining.

Textiles

Textiles serve important functional and decorative purposes as accessories. Linen, the name of the natural fiber derived from the flax plant, today is used to describe the fabric products of natural, man-made, or blends of fibers used on the dining table, the bed, and the towel rack. These items are an important part of the appearance of a completed interior and should be chosen in harmony with the other elements of the design. Fine, traditional white linens are still considered classic, but today linens also provide an opportunity to add color and pattern to appropriate settings. Because they are relatively inexpensive, linens reflect the constantly changing color and design trends. Textiles are also used in the form of rugs and carpets, *tapestries*, and other types of hangings to add warm finishing touches to interiors. The following represent some of the uses of textiles as accessories:

› Table linens include tablecloths, napkins, place mats, and runners. These are made in every possible shape and of many fibers. The man-made fibers are generally easier to care for, but the natural fibers have a fine look and feel that are difficult to duplicate. A table beautifully set with linens, tableware, and flowers chosen to create a harmonious and stimulating mood can be an important part of the pleasure of a good meal.

Figure 13.11 *Fine bed linens add to the luxurious feeling of this setting.*
Courtesy of DuPont "Teflon" soil and stain repellent.

- Bed linens are sheets, pillowcases, *pillow shams* (removable, decorative pillow covers), *dust ruffles*, bedspreads, blankets, comforters, quilts, *duvets* (nondecorative comforters) and their covers. These are available in a wide array of colors and styles. Today, bed linens are the domain of the designer and are manufactured in classic whites as well as designs compatible with every type of interior, from primitive log cabins to English Country houses to postmodern penthouses.

- Bath and kitchen linens consist mainly of towels. These are generally made of linen, cotton, or cotton terry cloth, all of which are absorbent and easy to launder. Linen (flax) cloths are particularly good for drying glassware, because they are lint free and shine glass nicely.

- Rugs and carpets are discussed with floor coverings in chapter 11, Floor Materials and Coverings. The types of rugs generally considered to be accessories are art rugs, designer rugs, and Oriental rugs, particularly when they hang on the wall.

- Tapestries and hangings were used for hundreds of years to provide actual physical warmth to the interior environment. They were used to cover the windows and walls of cold and damp castles; as bed hangings to protect from drafts, to keep in the warmth, and to provide privacy; and as table covers. Their use today is far more decorative, although they may provide a certain amount of psychological warmth because of their texture, pattern, and color. Traditional European tapestry designs are still being manufactured today, and contemporary artists are creating textile hangings with innovative methods of construction and design.

- *Fabric art* or soft sculpture are handwoven or constructed fabric or textile pieces that hang on the wall. Handmade antique or new coverlets or quilts are also used as wall hangings and table covers.

OBJECTS FROM NATURE

Plants

Caring for green and flowering plants is a satisfying and rewarding pastime. Plants add life and interest to interiors because they are continually growing and changing and because of their free-flowing and sculptural form. Each type of plant has a distinctive quality of design that makes it better suited to one style of interior than another. For example, the cactus has a strong, bristling, hard-edged quality and a dramatic sculptural form that makes it well suited to clean, structural interiors. The Boston fern is soft and feathery—characteristics that make it suitable in both traditional and contemporary environments where it adds textural variety. When selecting plants, pay close attention to the shape, texture, and suitability to the area where they are to be placed.

Plants need adequate light, proper temperatures, and careful feeding, watering, and cleaning. These needs vary according to the type of plant. Some are sturdy, whereas others are quite sensitive to environmental changes. In some interiors such as greenhouses and solariums, plant care may be the very reason for the room's existence.

Plants look healthy and well formed in floral shops or nurseries because they have been raised in greenhouses under controlled conditions. Yet when they are moved into typically overheated, overcooled, or dry human environments, they often become sickly. Living with plants from day to day, it is easy to be unaware of how bad a sickly plant might appear.

Those who have the ability to raise and maintain healthy plants are said to have a green thumb. Those who do not have green thumbs or whose interior environments are not conducive to healthy plants may need to consider alternatives. One alternative is the commercial plant service available in many places. These plant services care for greenery on a contract basis and will advise as to the type of plant that does best in a given setting. These firms may even sell or lease the plants and in some cases will offer a warranty for their product and service. Another alternative is to seek professional advice on selection and care so that a plant will thrive in its new environment.

Some plants will survive very well with artificial light, but in dark environments with dramatic lighting like certain restaurants and lounges, artificial plants may be a suitable alternative. Fortunately the quality of artificial plants is improving. Today silk leaves and blooms are combined with actual trunks and plastic stems to create fairly convincing artificial plants, trees, and flowers. Artificial plants need regular cleaning in order to continue to look their best.

Figure 13.12 *An informal display of sunflowers breathes life and color into this room.* Courtesy of Brunschwig & Fils.

Flowers and Greenery

Any time of the year, one can find growing or natural things that can be brought indoors to brighten the environment and lift the spirits. Cut flowers from the garden or florist add color and life to interiors. Arrangements can be very formal and precise, like the Japanese *ikebana* in which flowers are arranged according to strict, ancient rules of placement. Geometric bouquets purchased through florists remain popular, but bouquets of spring or summer blooms that appear to have been brought straight in from the garden and loosely arranged in an artistic way are often more pleasing because they have soft flowing lines that imitate the way flowers actually grow.

Flowers can be used as single blooms or massed in myriads of color and texture combinations. But when flowers are not available, or simply as a change of pace, other natural and growing things can be used seasonally to bring life to interiors. For

Figure 13.13 *Branches of blossoms are a beautiful seasonal alternative to plants.*
Courtesy of Brunschwig & Fils.

greenery for flower arrangements and are also very appealing in monochromatic arrangements. Dried herbs, grasses, and weeds make long-lived compositions if arranged with restraint and care. Ivy pulled from the garden is also long lasting when placed in water. With so many possibilities, there is no need to despair the lack of a green thumb. Creating arrangements of flowers and other types of plant life is a pleasing and creative activity.

Selecting the container is a delightful part of the creative process. A beautifully designed vase is a fine way to display flowers, but anything that will hold water is fair game for arrangements. Water-tight containers can often be hidden inside baskets and other porous or leaky objects to make them flower-worthy. Some of the most interesting arrangements may be created in very unusual containers. For example, an old rusty disk from a tiller could hold a fall arrangement, a wicker picnic basket could be filled with summer garden flowers, and a small copper teakettle could complement a sweet country bouquet.

Other Natural Objects

Consider this list of other objects from nature that often find their way into interior environments:

- Sea shells and rocks can be displayed as decorative accessories. Large shells can be mounted on specially designed pedestals or displayed on a table or shelf as any other art object. Small shells can be massed together in baskets, glass bowls, or any appropriate container where their beauty can be fully appreciated. Rocks can be displayed in much the same way as shells, massed together or mounted on stands. The beauty of some rocks becomes evident only after cutting and polishing, which often reveals natural designs of amazing beauty.

- Animal skins and hunting *trophies* may add an exotic or rustic quality to certain interiors. However, some people may object to such things on grounds of sensitivity, concern for conservation, or cruelty to animals. This should be a matter of careful discrimination.

- Fish can also bring life to interior environments. However, like plants, they require meticulous upkeep in order to be attractive—a dirty aquarium or sick fish are anything but appealing. As with plants, there are also services available in some areas for maintaining aquariums and fish.

OTHER ACCESSORIES

There are a number of other things in our environments that are products of rapidly developing and constantly changing technology. Appliances, computers, video systems, audio systems, and telephones are important elements of an interior. These are chosen primarily for their function, although they may be good design as well. They should be considered an important part of the design and be accommodated with sensitivity to their function and aesthetic appeal.

example, wreaths or baskets full of pine boughs and cones can be used all through the winter, not just at Christmas, to add a touch of greenery. In the early fall, branches of bright autumn leaves are cheerful, and in late fall and early winter, bowls, baskets, or sprays of hardy berries like pyracantha bring visual warmth to a cool season. Bowls or baskets full of apples, horse chestnuts, or other late fall delights are attractive and long lasting. Pumpkins, gourds, and winter squash, or piles of lemons, limes, or oranges make fine winter displays. In the spring, blossoms from fruit trees or pussy willows and corkscrew willows are interesting alternatives to flower arrangements.

In the summer there is a wonderful array of flowers available, but other growing things can be equally exciting. Fresh summer fruits and vegetables in interesting arrangements can be beautiful. Freshly cut herbs from the garden make unusual

Figure 13.14 *Here, a stack of antique boxes provides a distinctive counterpoint to the other furnishings.*
© *Jessie Walker.*

THE USE OF ACCESSORIES

Collections

Many of us enjoy collecting objects, and the collections usually say something about the background, travels, or experiences of the collector. Some collections are worthy of display and impart a personal quality to the environment. These collections might be pieces of fine art, porcelain or other ceramics, antique toys, shells, books, bottles or other glass pieces, stamps, coins, guns and swords, photographs, or any pieces of personal interest. When there is inadequate space for an entire collection, the finest pieces should be selected for display, grouped and arranged in harmony with the principles and elements of design.

The Japanese Approach to Displaying Collections

The Japanese are widely esteemed for their aesthetic sensitivity. There is much to be learned from the way they collect and display objets d'art in their traditional environments. The traditional Japanese home had a specially designated area called the *tokonoma*, which was a type of shrine for the display of one or two art objects and an arrangement of flowers (*ikebana*). These displays were changed regularly, and pieces were often chosen to honor a special guest. Objects not on display were safely stored for later use. This approach to the display of art objects is characterized by the excitement of

bringing out old and treasured pieces that have been packed away for a time and then rediscovered. These possessions become new again and are used with refreshed appreciation.

This clean or minimal philosophy is in harmony with the idea that "less is more"—a concept that has been a hallmark of the modern design movement and is still the favored approach to many designs. Such designs, stripped of all unnecessary embellishment, can be appealing

Figure 13.15
A tokonoma from the traditional Japanese house.

because they create a sense of space and freedom. Neat, well-ordered spaces devoid of mess and clutter can be peaceful and calming as well. Any object placed in this kind of environment is important because it does not compete visually with other elements of the design. Therefore, a carefully selected art piece or accessory can become a focal point in the room.

The Victorian Approach to Displaying Collections

During the Victorian era of the nineteenth century, there was a tendency to fill every available inch of space with *kickknacks*. Shelves and tables were crowded with objets d'art. When new pieces were introduced, the others were pushed a little more tightly together to make room for the new piece. Everything was on display.

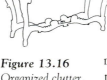

Figure 13.16
Organized clutter.

This approach, not uncommon today, is called organized clutter. Some environments may appear this way due to a lack of organization and planning, an inability to part with anything, or a desire to create a feeling of nostalgia. To others, however, each object in the space may have special significance and may add to the warmth of the environment.

Some interiors are appealing because of their clean, streamlined approach to art and accessories, while others are interesting and charming because they are filled with personal treasures. Somewhere between the extremes of Japanese and Victorian philosophies of accessory display lies comfortable and pleasing middle ground that suits an environment and provides the right balance of emotional support for the users.

Emotionally Supportive Design

Art, accessories, and furnishings have the power to provide emotional support because they are often links to esteemed people of events. This is why a piece of furniture or cherished piece or porcelain often serves as a *memento* of a person, time, or place. Those who emigrated from one country to another or who, in

Figure 13.17 *Industrial design educator Doug Stout's office provides the setting for an unusual link with his native Britain and his lifelong fascination with trains. His bookshelf displays part of his collection of British locomotives and rail cars purchased during visits to England and Scotland. They are not only visually appealing but serve as an important cultural tie with his past.*

John Wang and Doug McIntosh, photographers.

years past, moved from civilized surroundings to settle the wilderness, often carried and protected treasured objects from their past into their uncertain futures. To preserve a fragile remembrance from the past and keep it undamaged through the years is a remarkable accomplishment and source of pride. Today, these same objects are passed from one generation to another with great respect and love.

A photograph, a certificate, and *memorabilia* such as pressed flowers, a tiny christening gown, a watch or medal, and even a map can also preserve a memory and help recall an important time in one's life. Objects collected while traveling serve as reminders of exciting places and experiences. Well-designed pieces received as gifts from cherished friends may be decorative and also serve as remembrances of those people.

Drawings and crafts created by children are part of the emotional support system of a family and should be displayed with pride to encourage creativity. Such pieces often have artistic merit, and the child seeing the work on display is encouraged to

continue the creative endeavors. These pieces could be matted and displayed in a place of honor or simply taped to the refrigerator door. It is the recognition that counts.

We want to be surrounded by the things we love, whether it be in large doses or one object at a time. The clutter approach is not more correct than the minimal philosophy, merely better suited to certain interiors and individual needs. It is important to determine what kind of a balance is most pleasing to us and appropriate to our interiors, we should be careful not to discard well-loved pieces simply because we might not be completely confident of the aesthetic quality of the piece. For example, to some, a porcelain figurine might seem to be valueless kitsch. To another it might represent a cherished childhood memory, or it may have belonged to a dear friend or relative. We alone can make those determinations of value, and it is the inclusion of valued art and accessories that makes an environment emotionally supportive as well as a statement of personal experience.

Figure 13.18 (A,B) *The interior of the Salt Lake City International Airport features large-scale paintings of the ruggedly beautiful southern Utah landscape.*

Andrew Arnone and Darlene Langford, photographers.

NONRESIDENTIAL CONSIDERATIONS

Art and accessories in nonresidential interiors create a feeling of finish and add the important element of human interest to spaces that could otherwise be quite impersonal. For this reason, many nonresidential design projects have specific budgets for artwork. The decision on how to spend those budgets usually belongs to the architect, the designer, committee, or an art consultant. Sadly, sometimes the art budget is extremely limited or consumed by cost overrides in other areas. At the other end of the spectrum are the large corporations who collect art not only for its aesthetic value but for investment as well. Some of these have staff members whose sole responsibility is the acquisition of art and its dispersement to permanent collections throughout the corporation.

Many large nonresidential projects such as offices, hotels, and hospitals benefit from the use of art, though not always in permanent collections. These interiors are usually redesigned every few years, and a change in the art is often part of the new design program. Selecting pieces for this kind of design project requires extreme sensitivity, because not only must the art be purchased in large quantities but it must also be chosen for its relationship to the elements of the design, its price, and its aesthetic merit. Success in this kind of art selection is not as common as it should be, but the errors made in these situations can provide one key to understanding how to select quality art.

Fine art, regardless of price, cannot be exclusively tied to a decorative scheme by color or some other element—it must have its own aesthetic merit. If a new design program truly demands a change in the art, then the pieces being removed, if they have aesthetic merit, should still be of value in some other setting. If they have no value ten years after their initial instal-lation, then probably they had no aesthetic merit to begin with. Such pieces of decorator art or motel art will only find their way to incinerators or dusty thrift-store tables. Finding good quality prints, reproductions, or originals at the price points required by large projects may demand some effort. However, the search is worth the impact that good quality art creates in an interior design. When judging a piece of art, it might be wise to ask ourselves, What will be the value of this piece ten years from now? If it can weather the test of time, it will be well chosen. The ability to choose well comes through the process of exposure and training outlined earlier in this chapter.

Some designs such as restaurants and boutiques often require the selection of art and accessories keyed to a theme such as English Tudor or Country French. This kind of project may be like creating a stage setting, and each piece of art and every accessory will be selected because it reinforces the concept for the design. This often requires some research into the history of the decorative arts to ensure that selections are supportive and appropriate to the stated theme.

One of the most crucial aspects of a design is its relationship to the users. Designers may find it discouraging to return to a design for a post-occupancy evaluation and find that things have changed; for example, the pristine reception area has been invaded by the receptionist's personal items, and the secretary's wall is covered with postcards and pictures of the family. It is human nature to surround ourselves with things we love, and design must accommodate that tendency so that the work environment can be pleasant and supportive in every way. If a design is so clean that it forces management to create policies prohibiting personal belongings, then it has failed to meet the emotional needs of its users. It should not be difficult to provide a surface for photographs or cards and a space for personal mementos. Such considerate planning, rather than detract, will add vitality to the design.

Figure 13.19 *Accessories are the key ingredient of the interior design at the Hard Rock Café in Dallas, Texas.*
© 1987 Norman McGrath.

CHART 13.1 PLANTS FOR CLEAN AIR

POLLUTANT	SIDE EFFECTS	SOURCES	PROVEN POLLUTION FIGHTERS
BENZENE	Skin and eye irritant; may be a contributing factor to chromosomal aberrations and leukemia in humans; chronic exposure to even relatively low levels causes headaches, appetite loss, drowsiness, nervousness, psychological disturbances, anemia, bone marrow disease; carcinogenicity	Inks, oils, paints, plastics, rubber, dyes, detergents, gasoline, pharmaceuticals, tobacco smoke, synthetic fibers.	English ivy, dracena marginata, Janet Craig, warneckei, chrysanthemum, gerbera daisy, peace lily.
FORMALDEHYDE	Irritates mucous membranes of the eyes, nose, throat; can cause contact dermatitis, irritation of upper respiratory tract and eyes, and headaches; can cause asthma and is suspected of causing a rare type of throat cancer	Foam insulation, plywood, particle board, press-wood products, grocery bags, waxed papers, facial tissue, paper towels, wrinkle resisters, water repellants, fire retardants, adhesive binders in floor coverings, carpet backing, permanent-press clothing, cigarette smoke, natural gas, kerosene.	Azalea, philodendron, spider plant, golden pothos, bamboo palm, corn plant, chrysanthemum, mother-in-law's tongue.
TRICHLOROETHYLENE	Considered a potent liver carcinogen by the National Cancer Institute	Primarily used in the metal degreasing and dry cleaning industries; also in printing inks, paints, lacquers, varnishes, adhesives.	Gerbera daisy, chrysanthemum, peace lily, warneckei, dracena marginata.

From Plants for Clean Air Council.

ENVIRONMENTAL CONSIDERATIONS

It was mentioned earlier that plants add a quality of life to interiors. That is true both psychologically and physically. One of the problems associated with sick building syndrome is the dispersion of air-borne pollutants such as formaldehyde, benzene, and trichloroethylene, which are given off by such things as carpet, plywood, tobacco smoke, inks, adhesives, and a number of other sources. Plants are natural air purifiers that help remove these pollutants from the indoor air we breathe. The Plants for Clean Air Council finds that one plant will clean the air in a 100-square-foot floor space. Certain plants do a better job of eliminating specific pollutants, as chart 13.1 shows[2].

NOTES

1. Nathan Knobler, The Visual Dialogue (New York: Holt, Rinehart, and Winston, 1971), 492

2. The August 1991 issue of Interior Design is devoted to environmental considerations and has excellent information on this topic.

BUILDING SYSTEMS

Italian ceramic tile by Ceramica Nuovo D'Agostino. Courtesy of Italian Tile Center, division Italian Trade Commission–I.C.E..

BUILDING SYSTEMS

The term *building systems* refers to the ways buildings are constructed and the support systems wired, plumbed, or included during the construction or remodeling process. It is important for the interior designer or homeowner to understand these systems for two reasons:

1. To communicate with professionals (architects, general contractors, engineers, and subcontractors such as framers, plumbers, electricians, and finish carpenters) about the systems that directly affect the interior design

2. To understand what can be done physically and what is difficult to accomplish in the interior as it relates to new construction and remodeling

For example, some walls cannot be removed because they are load bearing, supporting the entire structure. Others house plumbing or wiring. Adding a communication system such as an intercom or a new central vacuum after the building is complete requires tearing off sheetrock, a wasteful and expensive proposition.

Another example is that new construction or remodeling requires support systems such as heating, air-conditioning, electrical wiring, and perhaps telephone wiring. They also require plans for structural walls and a new roof. Understanding these requirements helps us to see interior design as part of the big picture of construction. Decisions must be made during these phases in order to accomplish the desired result of the interior design plan.

For many years the study of interior design has not included building systems. Today, however, the designer and home owner are generally better informed and can benefit greatly from a basic understanding of building systems. Some of these systems, such as the construction process (including framing, plumbing, and wiring), are part of the building process. Other systems, such as solar greenhouses, can be either integral or added on. During remodeling, it is also not uncommon to remove walls to expand space, rewire, replumb, or add new systems.

Remodeling to add a new passive solar system is reflected in the chapter opening photo, in which a 1950s bungalow with a "rabbit's warren" of small rooms was transformed into a bright and easy-to-maintain open space. The original enclosed porch was removed and replaced with the greenhouse windows. The ceramic tile on the floor acts as a thermal mass to absorb heat by day and slowly release it at night. This is an example of how a sound understanding of old and new building systems is crucial to the designer's successful remodeling.

IDENTIFYING THE PROFESSIONAL ROLES

Interior design affects not only the finished space but the planning of the space and the construction of the necessary walls, units, and systems. Even if designers do not design the interior structural components, they must be able to communicate with contractors and craftspeople who build, finish, and decorate the space.

When the interior designer does specify a structural change, such as moving a wall, it may be wise to seek the expertise of the architect, general contractor, or structural engineer. By respecting and consulting the professionals in these related fields, the interior design plan can become more feasible and realistic.

The Architect

The role of the *architect* is to interview the clients, work through the programming process (chapter 1) for the building, and design the structure to be functional, structurally sound, strong, stable, and aesthetically pleasing. The interior designer/architect is one who is trained both as an architect and interior designer and who can structurally design or remodel buildings and specify all materials, finishes, and furnishings. The architect may oversee the building and receive a percentage of the total cost of construction as a fee, or the architect may be contracted to design the building and produce the blueprints that are used by a general contractor.

The Draftsman or Computer-Aided Design Planner

The plans for a new home or building are called working drawings or blueprints (discussed in the next section). Traditionally, these plans were executed by *draftsmen* or architects who drew the plans first with pencil on paper, then with ink on vellum, and then reproduced the plans into multiple sets of blueprints. Today much drafting is accomplished via computer-aided design and drafting (CADD) software by a CAD planner or draftsman. Obtaining home plans this way is faster and less expensive, since changes can be made without redrawing.

The General Contractor

The *general contractor*, who may be skilled in many areas of construction, contracts (hires out) the work to be done in each of the building phases. The general contractor will work on one of two bases: (1) a turnkey package—the finished building (according to the requirements of the itemized contract) or (2) a cost-plus basis. The turnkey package gives the client the building for a specified amount of money, with the option of adding to the building in the form of extras (items paid for by the client that are not part of the contract). The actual cost of the building may vary from the bid overruns and may be renegotiated at the finish of the building. The general contractor has the option of charging a percentage fee for the building (generally 10 percent). The cost-plus package bills the client for work done plus a percentage. With this arrangement, it may be harder to predict expenditures, and the client pays whatever the cost of the building when it is completed.

The Building Inspector

All residential and nonresidential buildings must be inspected by a city official, the *building inspector*, who has authority to halt construction if the structure does not meet codes. This is done in order to protect the health and safety of the building's occupants. Inspections are conducted periodically through the construction phase. When all items meet approval, the building inspector will authorize an occupation permit.

WORKING DRAWINGS
OR BLUEPRINTS

The working drawings, sometimes called *blueprints*, are the sets of plans that specify designs, materials, and dimensions to guide each subcontractor who works on the home or building. Working drawings include the following:

- Exterior elevations are the exterior views of each side of the building (north, south, east, and west, for example) in flat drawings (no perspective) showing the finish building materials, the location and style of doors, windows, architectural detail, roof, chimney, and other details unique to the building. Exterior elevations help us judge the building style aesthetics, or curb appeal.

- Floor plans are drawn to scale (one-quarter inch or one-eighth inch equals one foot) and show the layout of the rooms and their relationship to one another. They are used for estimating cost, for scheduling, and during the actual construction of the building.

- *Schedules* indicate how various parts of the building are to be finished. Materials and finishes for components such as doors, floors, walls, and ceilings are spelled out in figure 14.3.

- Site plans show the situation of the building on the land, legal boundaries, slope, key reference points, and possibly information on soils and vegetation. Site plans also indicate details on water, sewer, and electrical system grids (hookups).

- Foundation drawings indicate necessary details on footings, fireplace footings, anchor bolts, breaks in walls, and drains. They are used to estimate labor and materials for foundation work.

- Framing plans give projections of the building from the lowest level and up to the roof. It shows sections, key connections, and the layout of the floors and roof, with necessary information on columns, beams, and joists. Details are enlarged.

- Cross sections are vertical drawings of a slice through the interior of the building, showing the relationship and scale of the foundation, walls, beams, rooms, stairs, and other architectural elements.

- Utility plans show a building's mechanical systems: heating, ventilation, air-conditioning, plumbing (usually presented separately), electrical, and lighting plans. These plans will include layout for other systems such as fire protection, security, and communications (intercom).

- Interior elevations show types of cabinets and millwork (molding, railings) and other special interior features. They are used to obtain bids and construct the items.

- Details are enlargements of construction components where clarification or additional information is needed (for example, custom window arrangement to be framed).

Figure 14.1   *Blueprints and photos of a luxury home by architects Nadler/Philopena in Mt. Kisco, New York.*

© Ted Spiegel.

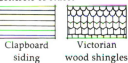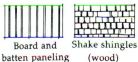

Figure 14.2   *Representation of finish building materials as indicated on the elevations—part of the blueprint plans.*

⬡A	DOOR	SCHEDULE				
CODE	NO.	W.	HT.	DESCRIPTION		NOTES
A	1	30"	6'-8"		E	W/"E" WINDOW
B	1	30"	6'8	STEEL INSUL.	E	W/ DEAD BOLT
C	1	30"	"	POCKET		
D	2	28"	"	FRENCH	S	W/ GRIDS
E	1	50"	"	"	S	"
F	1	28"	"		S	"
G	2	28"	"	STEEL INSUL.	E	W/ DEAD BLT.
H	3	26"	"		S	
J		26"	"	POCKET		
K		28"	"	"		
L	2	24"	"		P	
M		26"	"	STEEL INSUL.	E	W/CLOSER
N		160"	70"	RUF-TEX GARAGE		
O		24"	6'8"	POCKET	P	
P		40"	"	BI-FOLD	S	
Q	3	24"	"	POCKET	P	
R	3	28"	"		S	
S	1	50"	"	BI-FOLD	S	

⬡B	WINDOW	SCHEDULE			
CODE	NO.	W.	HT.	DESCRIPTION	NOTES
A	20	40"		PATIO REPLAC.	NG, NS
B	6	40"		FIXED ALUM.	" "
C	6	40"		ALUM. SLIDER	NG W/SCREEN
D	2	30"		ALUM S.H TRIPLE	W/ GRIDS
E	1	54"		ELLIPTICAL TRANSOM	W/ "A" DOOR
F	2	40"		ALUM. SLIDER	W/ GRID
G	1	40"		" "	NS, NG
H	2	30"	FIXED	PATIO. ALUM FRAME	MULLION
I	1	30"	"	ALUM. SEMI CIRCLE	"
J	1	50"		ALUM. SLIDER.	NS, NG
K	1	30"		ALUM. S.H. INSUL.	W/GRIDS
L	3	30"		" " SH TRIPLE	" "
M	2	60"		PATIO DOOR	NG, NS
N	4	30"		PATIO ALUM FRAME	2/GRIDS, 2/WD
O	1	26"		ALUM. S.H.	NG, NS
P	1	30"	FIXED	ALUM. INSUL.	
Q	2	40"		ALUM SLIDER	W/GRIDS
R	1	40"		" "	NG, NS
S	3	2/24"		SKYLIGHT DBL.	W/ DIFFUSER

LEGEND:
E – ENTRY LOCKSET   WISER   A 500
P – PRIVACY   "   "   A 300
S – STD. PASSAGE   "   "   A 100
NS– NO WINDOW SCREENS
NG– NO "   GRIDS

Figure 14.3   A door and window schedule for a 4,900-square-foot home with integral solarium.

> • Specifications are written documents that describe structural or finish materials or custom work—what is needed, where it is to be located, what quality and craftsmanship level is desired, how it is to be assembled, and any other special considerations needed for correct construction.

> • The subcontract is the agreement for specialized work performed by a person or company and specified for a building's construction or finish work. The *subcontractor* will take information from the blueprints, determine how much labor and materials are required for the job, and produce a bid or solid estimate of the job. The general contractor will usually get three or more bids and select the lowest bid, the subcontractor with the reputation for the best quality work, or the subcontractor with a reasonable bid and proven quality. The interior design package or parts of it, such as carpeting, window treatments, wall coverings, or furnishings, may also be bid in this manner.

CONSTRUCTING THE BUILDING

When construction begins, the architect or general contractor will set up a method for making everything happen at the right time. A critical path (see figure 14.8) indicates the time frame, in consecutive and overlapping order, of every step in the building and finishing process. *Scheduling* means setting up and reconfirming dates for the selected subcontractors to arrive on the site and perform their tasks. If one subcontractor fails to meet the deadline for finishing, it could disrupt the entire schedule. The next subcontractor on the critical path may not be available at a slightly later date because of other commitments. It is therefore the responsibility of the general contractor, architect, or interior designer to coordinate the schedule by frequently contacting the subcontractors and reconfirming the schedule. This responsibility may affect the work of the interior designer at the finish and/or decoration and furnishing stage. However, the smooth flow of the construction critical path is crucial to the success of the finish critical path, and in many cases, they are not separated. Large interior design firms that specialize in nonresidential work routinely work out complex and extensive critical paths that track the flow of jobs to be performed.

Figure 14.4 *Scheduling facilitates smooth progress from* (A) *construction to* (B) *finished home.*
Both © Karla Nielson.

The interior designer must understand the aspects of construction in order to effectively communicate with subcontractors, architects, engineers, and other professionals. A mutual respect and understanding between designers and these professionals will allow the designer to better discuss structural plans, architectural details, finish materials, and furnishing instructions. As a result, these aspects will be more successfully completed.

The designer has the responsibility to notify the builder of special materials or finishes that could interfere with the critical path. For example, if the designer and client change the floor-covering selection from carpeting to a wood floor, the building must be left empty for a week or longer to accommodate the floor installers and finishers. This could cause serious problems with the critical path if the designer does not notify the builder enough in advance. It is the responsibility of the architect or designer and the contractor to see that all aspects of the design are properly and correctly executed.

The jobs performed by subcontractors are explained in the following paragraphs. The list is broken into two categories: the structural building components and systems and the interior finish components.

Structural Building Components and Systems

Many kinds of *structural systems* are in use today. A few are quite common; some are unusual and rarely seen. Building methods vary according to the environment, available materials, and local building codes. The designer must become acquainted with regional building methods and variations. The system described here is *wood frame* or *wood truss system* construction, used primarily in homes and smaller nonresidential buildings.

The Foundation

After the lot has been surveyed and laid out with chalk lines, and after the hole for new construction has been excavated (dug), cement contractors set up wooden and metal frames, pour, and finish foundation footings. Footings are the strips of concrete set into the ground several inches to several feet below the excavated basement or crawl space area. Footings anchor the foundation walls and serve as a base for the weight of the building.

Foundations are the concrete block or poured concrete walls of the basement or sublevel. After the concrete forms are stripped or removed, the walls must cure for a period of time. *Cement* is a dry mixture of lime, silica, alumina, and other minerals used to bring nonadhesive materials together into a strong, cohesive unit. *Concrete* is the building material made by mixing cement and a mineral aggregate (gravel) with sufficient water to cause the cement to set into a hard mass. Before it sets, concrete is relatively easy to work and may be poured into forms to become a durable material used where strength and stability are requirements and where moisture may permeate interiors (moisture will rot a wooden structure but will not damage concrete). *Reinforced concrete* has *rebar* (strong, bendable steel bars) or wire mesh set into the wet mixture before it is dried, which gives structural strength and helps prevent cracking. *Flatwork* refers to cement for basement floors, garage floors, driveways, and walkways; it may be reinforced and poured over sand, gravel, wire mesh or rebar to minimize shifting and settling that produce cracks.

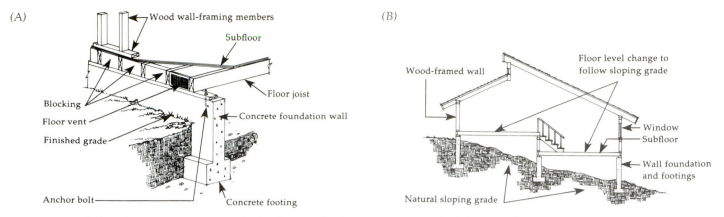

Figure 14.5 (A) *A close-up, cutaway view of a foundation wall, floor joist system, and subfloor with placement of wood wall-framing members. This illustration shows only a crawl space under the main floor—no basement. (B) A cross section showing a floor change to accommodate the natural slope of the site grade.*

Another type of foundation frequently used in frame construction is masonry block (concrete block). *Waterproofing* the foundation is done by spraying or rolling a sealant—such as a tar mixture and perhaps a sheet of heavy black plastic or tar paper—onto the foundation walls before the dirt is backfilled around it. The sealant prevents water seepage into the foundation. The foundation walls may also be insulated with styrofoam board before the backfill. *Window wells* are corrugated rounded steel or cement units that keep dirt away from a basement window. They may be open at the ground level or can be covered over with ironwork, plastic bubbles, or glass block.

Backfilling and compacting mean that some of the excavated dirt is filled into the area outside the completed footings. Compacting, coupled with wetting the excavated area, hastens the settling process so that the dirt will be prepared for the subgrade or foundation floors.

Plumbing takes place at three stages:

1. Before the foundation floor is poured, the underground plumbing brings water and sewer pipe into the sublevel and heating (natural gas lines where applicable).

2. The rough plumbing (water systems, tubs and showers, and a central vacuum) is installed and connected when the building is framed.

3. The finish plumbing is the installation of fixtures, such as sinks and toilets.

Framing, the next step, is the wood skeleton. This is a crucial step in the construction process, because the wooden frame that is set onto the foundation (called wood frame or truss construction) supports the entire building. In wood frame construction, *joists* (wood beams) are secured with *trusses* (triangular braces) and form the base for the *subfloors* (plywood or other material) and the walls. Walls are built of two-by-four studs (eight-foot lengths of lumber approximately 1 3/4 by 3 3/4 inches). Load-bearing walls carry the weight of the structure and the roof. The triangular roof truss system is made of rafters and joists. These systems are usually prefabricated to specification and called *roof trusses*. Roof trusses can also be flat.[1]

Once the walls are framed, the interior spaces are firmly established, and although it is possible to move walls after the building is framed, it is costly in terms of time, labor, and inconvenience. Framing is finished with the addition of plywood, Celotex, paperboard, styrofoam, or other exterior panel materials. These add stability to the frame, add some insulation, and provide closure.

Interior building systems are now installed, which include the *rough plumbing*, *rough electrical*, and *rough heating*. Rough plumbing is the installation of pipes that will connect water to the taps; drains from sinks, tubs, showers, and toilets; and vents for pressure balance, allowing the pipes to drain. Tubs are set at this time so the wall material can be set around them. Rough heating includes forced-air ducts and vents run from the clothes dryer hookup. Rough electrical is the wiring from the breaker box to each area of the interior where electricity will be needed for light fixtures, light switches, and electric outlets. Wiring is also installed now for intercoms, telephones, built-in stereo, and media equipment. A master panel is a luxury feature, installed at convenient locations, that can control all electric lights and major appliances.

Insulation is added at this time, in the form of batts, rigid panels, or blown (loose) insulation. A *superinsulated* structure has a deeper skeleton framework (up to fourteen inches) filled with insulation and layered with a thick *vapor barrier* plastic. Very *tight* superinsulation will require *air-exchange units* to bring necessary fresh air into the interior. Several materials can be used to deaden sound such as *sound board*, which absorbs noise and is used with sheetrock or plasterboard.

Windows are set in place and the *exterior veneer* and finish materials such as brickwork, siding, and stucco are added. The roof is finished with *tar paper*, shingles, (*shake shingles* are made of wood; *asbestos*, or fireproof, *shingles* are common) or other roofing materials such as *bartile* or metal shingles or panels.

Exterior finishing includes installing any garage doors, finishing the *soffit* (area under the eaves), the facia (the front of the eaves), *rain gutters* (channel rainfall as it drains off the roof), plastering the foundation, and any exterior painting of trim.

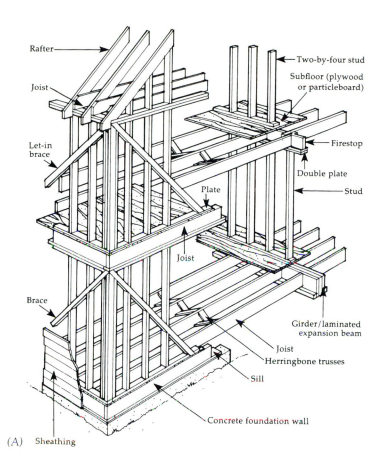

Rafter

Two-by-four stud

Subfloor (plywood or particleboard)

Joist

Firestop

Let-in brace

Double plate

Plate

Stud

Joist

Brace

Girder/laminated expansion beam

Joist

Herringbone trusses

Sill

Concrete foundation wall

(A)   Sheathing

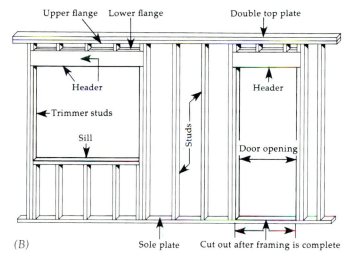

Figure 14.6   (A) *The wood-framing system. (B) A typical exterior wood-framed wall.*

Upper flange   Lower flange

Double top plate

Header

Header

Trimmer studs

Studs

Sill

Door opening

(B)

Sole plate   Cut out after framing is complete

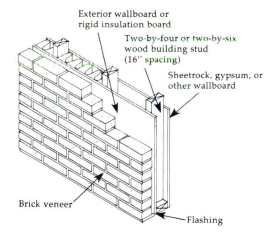

Exterior wallboard or rigid insulation board

Two-by-four or two-by-six wood building stud (16″ spacing)

Sheetrock, gypsum, or other wallboard

Brick veneer

Flashing

Insulation

Exterior sheathing

Two-by-four or two-by-six wood building studs (16″ spacing)

Sheetrock, gypsum, or other wallboard

Exterior plywood or composition board

Stucco (hand-applied)

Figure 14.7   *Exterior and interior finish components.*

Interior Finish Components

The interior finish materials and components include wall, ceiling, and floor finish materials, woodwork and cabinetry, countertops, optional wall coverings, and optional window coverings. The most common wall and ceiling material is *sheetrock*, made of pulverized gypsum rock (also called *drywall, gypsum board, plasterboard,* or *wallboard* (see chapter 10). The sheetrock is installed by nailing, screwing, or gluing horizontal or vertical panels to the wall studs and ceiling joists. To move walls after the sheetrock has been hung constitutes major remodeling and is very costly. Wallboard panels measure ten by four

or eight by four feet and are cut to fit the space. Seams are covered with *perfatape* (three-inch-wide stiff paper tape), attached and smoothed with plaster called *mud*. A smooth finish is more costly than *texturizing*, which is spraying or hand-troweling textures of plaster and then lightly sanding the wall or ceiling to a desired smoothness. Light texturizing is called orange peel, and heavy texturizing is sometimes termed brocade texture. Other finish wall materials include wallpaper, ceramic or quarry tile, wood, stone, cork, and fabric. Other ceiling materials include acoustical tile (suspended ceilings), wood, fabric, and wall coverings.

Figure 14.8 A sample critical path for building a three-thousand- to five-thousand-square-foot house.

	Week 1	Week 2	Week 3	Week 4	Week 5	Week 6	Week 7	Week 8	Week 9	Week 10	Week 11	Week 12	Week 13	Week 14	Week 15	Week 16	Week 17

Activity — Construction Days / Calendar Days

- Stake Out and Excavation
- Dig and Pour Footings
- Pour Foundation
- Utility Hook-Up
- Strip and Cure Foundation
- Sub-Grade Rough Plumbing
- Grade and Pour Basement Floor
- Backfill
- Framing and Building Erection
- Window Glazing
- Rough Plumbing
- Rough Heating
- Rough Electrical
- Roof Shingles
- Masonry/Siding, Soffit, Facia, Gutter
- Form and Pour Exterior Concrete
- Insulation
- Clean-Up
- Dry Wall (Sheetrock)
- Ceramic Tile (a. Surround); (b. Countertops)
- Install Finish Package (Woodwork)
- Interior/Exterior Painting
- Install Cabinets/Countertops/Hardware
- Finish Electrical
- Install Vinyl/Tile Flooring
- Install Wallcoverings
- Finish Plumbing
- Finish Clean-Up
- Grade Site
- Landscaping
- Paint Touch-Up
- Finish Punch List
- Install Carpet
- Finish Heating-Registers
- Clean Windows
- Install Window Treatments
- Furniture/Accessories
- Finalize Billing

The *finish package*—built-in shelves and closet systems, baseboard/door/window trim, and railings—is installed next, then painted along with the walls and ceilings. Any woodwork to be painted is also installed at this point. Doors are removed from the prehung frames, painted or stained separately, then hinged. If wood trim is to be stained, it may be installed after the general painting is done.

Railings are then installed and finished. Cabinets, countertops, and any other built-in units (prefinished) are installed, as are *window sills* of wood, marble, or tile, and tub and shower *surrounds* (cultured marble, onyx, or tile). Finish flooring is set in bathrooms and laundry areas so that the *finish plumbing* (sinks, toilets) can be installed. Finish electric work (lighting fixtures) is done before, after, or concurrently with finish flooring and plumbing.

The wallpaper is installed next. Following that, the carpet or other floors that need some protection (such as wood) are installed, and hardware (door handles and strike plates) is set in place. Appliances are installed, and window treatments may now also be installed. The last step is the delivery and arrangement of furniture and accessories.

The Critical Path and the Punch List

The *critical path* graphically illustrates the overlapping order of everything that must be accomplished in a job. The exact items will vary according to the nature of the job—whether it is new construction or remodeling. The *punch list* is a series of items that must be accomplished as the project progresses. The sample includes spaces for noting the start and finish dates.

Figure 14.8 is a sample construction/finish critical path, and figure 14.9 is a sample punch list. Both represent the types of things that are done in new construction, remodeling, and interior design, though neither is intended to address every detail of the construction/design process.

This sample critical path represents a typical time frame for a small home, which can be completed within two months. Larger homes with more features typically take from four to six months or longer to complete. Remodeling projects can take from two weeks to two years, depending on factors such as extent of demolition and reconstruction, funds available, and size of the work force. Small nonresidential buildings will take from three to eight months to build and furnish, and large nonresidential buildings require a time frame of four months to three years.

	Start Date	Finish Date		Start Date	Finish Date
Architectural plans			Windows set in place/glazed		
Turn in plans to city			Bricking/masonry exterior		
Order temporary power			Order cabinets/built-ins		
Lay out lot			Order flooring		
Order footing material			Ceiling insulation		
Order steel for footing/walls			Order finish package		
Dig hole (excavate)			Hang Sheetrock		
Order concrete for footing			Cleanup after this phase		
Deliver footing material			Order tub & shower surrounds		
Set footing			Taping & texture walls/ceiling		
Call to confirm foundation crew			Confirm painter		
Pour footing			Brick interior (fireplaces)		
Strip & stack footing material			Finish work (wood work)		
Order underground plumbing			Cleanup after this phase		
Order underground heating hook-up			Confirm cabinets/counter tops		
Caulk footing			Interior painting		
Order waterproofing of walls			Confirm tile installer		
Call for inspection of walls			Confirm flooring installers		
Order window wells			Setting of cabinets		
Water proofing of foundation			Confirm finish plumbing		
Call for inspection plumb. & heat.			Confirm heating		
Backfill house & floor			Confirm electrical		
Grading & compaction of floors			Setting of countertops		
Run water and sewer laterals			Setting of marble and tile		
Order framing material			Order garage doors		
Pour concrete floor and garage			Ceramic tile in entry		
Deliver framing material			Confirm carpet and vinyl		
Framing of house			Finish electrical		
Cleanup after this phase			Set vinyl in bathrooms		
Confirm windows/doors			Finish plumbing		
Confirm plumbing			Finish heating		
Confirm heating			Install garage doors		
Confirm electrical			Install wall coverings		
Order brick/masonry			Finish setting vinyl/carpet		
Rough heating			Install hardware		
Rough electrical			Appliances		
Run dryer/bathroom vents			Install window treatments		
Install fireplace			Finish soffit, facia, rain gutters		
Inspection of plumbing, heating, electrical			Cleanup after this phase		
			Call for final move-in inspection		
Cleanup after this phase			Set furnishings in place		

Note: the critical path and punch list are typically expanded to fit the job requirements. The punch list may consist of several sub-lists, and it may include specific items requested by a client as the job progresses.

Figure 14.9 *Sample punch list.*

Not taken into account in this sample critical path is the preliminary design process. Chapter 1, The Process of Design, outlines the method involved in gathering data and developing the design before the actual building begins. This sample critical path also does not include lead time, which is the time required to file for and obtain a building permit, to take the plans to the city and receive approval, to survey and establish the relationship of the building to the lot, and to prepare the property before the excavation begins. Lead time is also required to prequalify the client for the loan and to begin the loan processing—which can take longer to finalize than it takes to construct and finish the building.

The critical path and punch list are typically expanded to fit the job requirements. The punch list may consist of several sublists and may include specific items requested by a client as the job progresses. A punch list is also used to note unresolved problems observed during inspection tours of a project. These problems must be resolved by the contractor and subcontractors before the project is finished.

PLUMBING SYSTEMS

Plumbing is a term that indicates pipe installed within a building for carrying a volume of air or water. Plumbing typically means the water intake system, water-conditioning and/or water-heating system (including components of passive or active solar systems discussed later in this chapter), and water disposal systems—drains and sewer lines. The plumbing carried within the framework or threaded through the masonry block is termed rough plumbing. Copper pipe is generally used for water intake, and cast-iron (more costly but quieter) or plastic (PVC—polyvinyl chloride) pipe is used for sewer or waste-water disposal. Finish plumbing includes hookups to appliances (dishwashers and clothes washers) and installation of *fixtures* (sinks, toilets, urinals). Shower units and bath tubs/whirlpools are installed during the framing before the sheetrock is hung.

Plumbing is also used to facilitate *central vacuum systems* and may also be used for fresh air intake for wood-burning stoves and for furnace (heating) and central air-conditioning (cooling) units.

In nonresidential design, space will usually be allotted for a *plumbing chase* (the thick plumbing wall area) that provides access for maintenance.

(A)

(B)

(C)

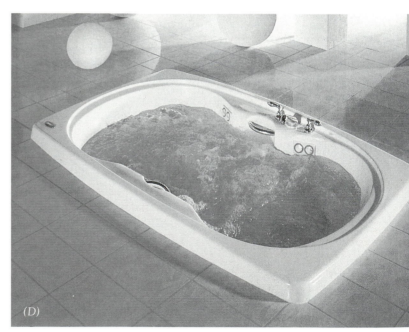
(D)

Figure 14.10   (A) *Rough plumbing is installed after the home is framed.* (B) *One-piece seamless barrier-free shower module.*
(C) *The Aventura Shower Soak*™ *connects whirlpool tub and shower.* (D) *The Sabella*™ *whirlpool bath features hydromassage.*

(A) © *Karla Nielson.* (B, C) *Courtesy of © Kohler Company.* (D) *Courtesy of Jacuzzi Whirlpool Bath.*

Figure 14.11 (A) *High-efficiency gas furnace and duct work.* (B) *Hot air is carried in duct work through the framework.* (C) *An electric baseboard unit heats this room.*

(A and B) © Karla Nielson. (C) Optix window blinds by and photo courtesy of Nanik.

HEATING, VENTILATION, AND AIR-CONDITIONING

Central heating or *space heating* of the interior is generally handled through a *furnace* and connecting hot water pipes or *duct work* or *ducts* (run through the walls, floors, and ceiling joists).

With *forced-air heating*, the furnace heats an element that in turn heats air that passes by it and is blown out. *Cold air return* vents draw air back to the furnace where it is reheated for recirculation. Warm air typically enters a room at the floor or ceiling level through *registers*. Many types and price ranges of furnaces exist, fueled by electricity, natural gas, coal, or oil. A *high-efficiency furnace* uses less fuel to heat the interior and therefore costs less to run, although these units have a higher initial purchase price. Furnaces may also be fitted with humidifying devices (*humidifiers*) that add moisture to the heated air. (Any method of heating will draw moisture out of the air, which is harmful to health, plants, and furnishings.)

Radiant heat is produced by using a furnace to heat water in a boiler. The hot water passes through pipes to a *radiator* that warms the room. This type of system is not used commonly today, but it may be found in older homes. The furnace is controlled with a *thermostat*, which can be set to maintain a specified temperature. Thermostats for small systems are often programmable to accommodate needs according to the time of day or the use of the building. Large *HVAC* (heating, ventilation, and air-conditioning) systems will be monitored and controlled by computer.

Interior furnishings must never obstruct heat registers or cold air returns. Where draperies hang to the floor, clear plastic deflectors can be placed over a vent or register that channel or direct the hot air into the room.

Room or area heating can also be handled by electric or gas-fueled *baseboard units*, radiant ceiling panels, radiators, *portable space heaters*, or *wood- or coal-burning stoves* and fireplaces or fireplace inserts. These units also must not be obstructed with furnishings that may combust, or catch on fire. Local building codes will require a *clearance*, or distance (usually about three feet), that restricts placement of combustible materials, including walls and structural components, near the heat source. An exception is for insulated *zero-clearance fireplace units*, which can be placed in combustible walls. (Space and room heating are also discussed later in the chapter under Active and Passive Solar Systems.)

Ventilation and air-conditioning are interrelated terms. *Ventilation* refers to natural breezes or air currents from opened windows and doors. The designer must be aware that window treatments and furniture placement should allow for, and not obstruct, desired natural ventilation. Ventilation may sufficiently cool the interior for most of the year, supplemented by air-conditioning only in the hottest seasons. However, hot, arid, or humid regions rely heavily on air-conditioning for livable comfort for much of the year.

Air-conditioning can be handled similarly to heating in small-scale settings: by a central system or by cooling one room at a time. A *central air-conditioning system* may be handled through the forced-air furnace unit or by a separate unit located outside or inside the building. In very humid climates, the air-conditioning unit may have a *dehumidifier*, a unit that removes excess humidity (moisture) from the air. In dry climates, an *evaporative cooling system*, or *swamp cooler*, may be less costly to run and may cool more efficiently. The evaporative or swamp cooler works by forcing air through moistened pads or filters. It is installed in a wall, window, or ceiling and connected with central duct work. With this system, windows or doors are kept ajar in the rooms where the cooled air is to be drawn.

Figure 14.12 (A) *The central air-conditioning unit cools air by refrigerating it. A dehumidifier can be added to the unit.* (B) *The evaporative or "swamp" cooler cools the air by forcing it through water-soaked pads.*
© Karla Nielson.

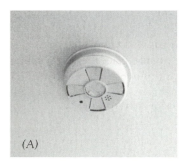

Figure 14.13 *Overhead systems.* (A) *A smoke detector sets off a shrill alarm when smoke fills the air.* (B) *A nonresidential ceiling has HVAC (heating, ventilation, and air conditioning) and a sprinkler to douse potential fires in this office.* (C) *The intercom connects voices or music to other areas in the home.* (D) *Intercom on outside of a house.*
© Karla Nielson.

The designer should be aware of the heating and cooling system and duct work in the case of remodeling or structural changes in the interior design. Walls or ceilings that carry duct work cannot easily be removed or altered. Contractors and HVAC specialists are valuable resources for the designer in this regard and should be consulted before structural changes are made.

OTHER BUILT-IN SYSTEMS

Fire Alert Systems

Fire alert systems are single or interconnected networks of *smoke detectors* and heat-sensing devices that alert the occupants of a potential fire hazard. They may emit a shrill whistle or a long or interrupted buzz or beep that will indicate danger.

Security Systems

Security systems guard against unlawful entry. They are sensing devices that take many forms. When activated they may turn on lights, set off alarms, or automatically notify security guards. Security systems can become quite elaborate, even to the point of being connected with the local police dispatcher. Security systems vary dramatically in price and options.

Communication Systems

In the home, the *intercom* system is an effective way of communicating from one area to another without raising the voice. The wiring should be installed when the home is being built, although radiolike units can be purchased and installed at a later date. The intercom can also pipe music to various rooms, and

Figure 14.14 (A) *Electrical wires are threaded through the wood framework and connected to the main breaker box. (B) Built-in entertainment systems, appliances, and electrical devices can also be controlled via the Smart House™ system, or computer software known as Home Automation™.*

(A) © Karla Nielson. (B) © 1988 Norman McGrath.

parents can listen to children in other parts of the house with the intercom. Other *communication systems* are discussed under Nonresidential Considerations.

The Smart House™ System

A new system has been developed by The Smart House Development Venture, Inc., a wholly owned operation of the National Research Center of the National Association of Home Builders (NAHB). This system is one that centrally locates the control of all the systems in a house, based on a closed loop principle for energy distribution. Small microchips are installed in each appliance and outlet, allowing the appliance to identify itself to the system. Gas systems, fire alert systems, security systems, electric appliances, and lighting—all can be controlled from a central location as well as the familiar switch. Monitor screens can be installed in several rooms, and the system can also be controlled via telephone keypad, remote control, video touch on the screen, and even by voice.

Some benefits of this new system include early fire detection, with screens showing the fire's location, which rooms are occupied, and the safest path of exit. The same information can immediately be relayed to the fire department or emergency monitoring service, and the gas service to the home can be shut off. Doors and windows can be locked and monitored from remote locations. An unauthorized entry can be relayed to the homeowner, the neighbors, or the police. A surveillance camera can also be plugged into any outlet, and the picture appears on a television plugged into any outlet.

The Smart House™ system calls for a unified cable that performs three functions: (1) power distribution, (2) control or data signal distribution, and (3) audio and video telephone signal distribution. This unified cable would replace the spaghettilike system of wires now being strung throughout the house. The system should simplify gas and electrical system construction because of ease of installation for the builder, fewer subcontractors needed, and less installation time. The result is a home that is safer, offering more convenience and peace of mind to the home owner. Costs vary from $5,000 to $10,000.[2]

Home Automation

Because of the high cost of systems such as *Smart House™*, and because so many people now own personal computers, new modestly priced *home automation* products have become available. Companies such as Home Automation Laboratories offer catalogs of add-on products that empower the homeowner to control everything in the home via the computer and telephone. As an example, you can dim/turn on/turn off any light in the house; operate the stereo, TV, hot tub, home appliances; and even open and close your draperies from nearly any point in your home or office. Home automation is possible with the use of a personal computer, software, and some standard hardware and existing personal computer technology. Some systems are voice activated, meaning that they respond to a spoken command. Others are motion sensitive, turning on lights or even barking like a dog when someone comes near. Home automation can increase home security and luxury living in any size home. Watch for developments in this exciting new area of home automation.[3]

Active and Passive Solar Systems

Many buildings today incorporate active or passive solar heating. The designer needs to understand the terms and concepts of solar energy so that the interior design may complement and augment, rather than detract from or obstruct, the system. Architectural solar systems require some investment of funds to purchase materials or to create the structure that utilizes the sun's energy for space heating and water heating. The amount spent on the system or on components is compared to the amount it would cost to purchase and run a conventional space- (furnace) or water-heating system. The *payback period* is the number of years required to save enough with the system to pay for itself. If the payback period is less than five to ten years, it is generally considered a good investment (if the occupant will stay in the home or building that long).

Active Solar Systems

An *active solar system* is made of mechanical parts that convert *incident solar radiation* (*insolation*) to thermal energy to warm air space, heat water, and even run air-conditioning units. The system consists of six basic components that may be altered as needed. These components are:

1. *Collectors* capture or collect the sun's warmth by means of panels mounted to face the sun at approximately ninety-degree angles. They may be focusing (like a magnifying glass) or nonfocusing (like a greenhouse—heating a material, which in turn heats a gas or liquid medium).

2. This thermal energy is moved by *transport,* usually via a fluid or air, from the collectors. This may require pumps, valves, and pipes for liquid transport or blowers, dampers, and ducts for hot air.

3. The transport component moves the heat to *storage,* a reservoir that stores the thermal energy. It may be simple or complex, made of water, rocks, aluminum oxide, or other materials. The storage ensures warmth at night and on cloudy days when no thermal energy is being collected.

4. *Distribution* carries the heat through pipes and ducts to the space to be heated. It usually requires larger ducts and radiating surfaces than conventional furnace systems.

5. *Auxiliary heating* is usually a central or localized system. Hooked into the solar distribution unit, the furnace is capable of taking over heating needs if the active solar system cannot produce enough heat on successive sunless days.

6. *Control,* perhaps in the form of a thermostat, is an automatic or a manual system to control heat and energy flow.

Active systems can be complex, costly, bulky, and awkward to install. Solar systems may also be subject to component breakdown, yet they generally provide 70 to 100 percent of the interior space-heating or water-heating needs. Much research is needed before selecting the system best suited for a building.

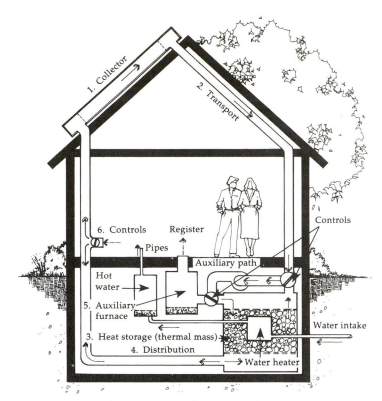

Figure 14.15 *Six components of an active solar-space or water-heating system. (1) Collectors capture the sun's warmth through panels. (2) Transport of the heat via a liquid or air. (3) Storage of the thermal energy, which may be simple or complex. (4) Distribution of the energy through ducts and/or pipes. (5) Auxiliary energy, such as a furnace, to take over heating needs. (6) Mechanical controls to gauge heat and energy flow.*

Passive Solar Systems

Passive designs share common aspects with active systems. Both collect, store, and distribute thermal solar energy for space heating and water heating. The difference is that passive designs are dependent on natural heat and cold movement. Heat is naturally transferred in three ways:

1. Radiation is the spreading of heat through space, as in the radiating heat from the sun to the earth. Heated elements that send forth warmth (fireplaces and space room heaters) are called radiant heat sources. The heat waves from the sun, called solar energy or solar gain, are long, strong electromagnetic waves. These waves are strong enough to pass through glass windows, where they refract against floors, walls, ceilings, furnishings, and people. As solar waves bounce off surfaces, some of that energy is absorbed, and the remainder becomes shorter, weaker wavelengths that cannot repenetrate the glass windows. Thus, heat is trapped and builds up inside glass-enclosed spaces, a phenomenon known as the *greenhouse effect.*

2. Conduction is the transference of heat through matter. Certain materials such as glass and metal are excellent conductors, allowing heat and cold to easily pass

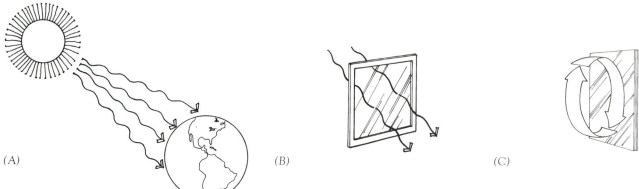

Figure 14.16 *Passive solar systems: (A) radiation, (B) conduction, and (C) convection.*

through their molecules (which is why they are most often used as cooking utensils). Glass- and metal-framed windows conduct heat and cold into the interior; metal also makes an excellent component of solar collectors used in active solar systems and passive water heaters.

3. Convection or air movement is based on *natural thermal flow* (the path of rising warm air and the subsequent falling of cool air). The greenhouse effect warms interior air, making convection work to our advantage through these natural thermal air flows.

When the passive system is augmented by mechanical devices such as pumps, fans or blowers, and duct work—or even connected to an existing furnace system—it becomes a *hybrid solar energy system*. New buildings may integrate passive solar design principles or hybrid systems into the design of the building. Existing buildings that are remodeled, or have additions, to include an active, passive, or hybrid solar system are *retro-fitted*. It is important to note that most solar systems are custom designed for the architecture and space; effectiveness will therefore vary.

Direct Gain

The simplest form of passive solar heating is *direct solar gain*, which is sunshine coming through south-facing windows. The heat is generally absorbed by a thermal mass (dense material slow to heat and cool) such as floors or walls of concrete; ceramic or quarry tiles over cement or rocks; bricks or stone; or barrels or pools of water or sand. Direct gain may allow too much heat, light, and direct sunshine to enter the interior (causing fading and damage to furnishings), and too much heat loss may occur at night. For this reason, direct gain windows may require light-filtering or shading devices and movable insulation to guard against excessive heat loss.

Indirect and Isolated Gain

Indirect and isolated passive solar gain means gathering the heat or energy separate from the occupied areas. Listed and illustrated here are some of the most commonly used passive solar systems.

› *Trombe walls* are thermal storage walls named after the French scientist who developed them. A Trombe wall system uses large areas of south-facing glass as collectors. Within a few inches of the glass, a dark-colored masonry of brick, concrete, or stone slowly conducts the collected heat to radiate warmth to the interior at night. The Trombe walls have vents at the top and bottom to utilize a natural convection loop—hot air becomes lighter and rises so that vents high in the wall bring warm air into the interior; low vents allow cooler, heavier air to return to the heat trap to be warmed.

› *Thermosiphoning* traps air in spaces in the walls and roof. The air is heated and rises to a point where it can be drawn off with fans through ducts. Fiberglass panels used in the ceilings can also admit translucent light. A thermosiphonic system is less effective than thermal mass Trombe walls but also is less costly.

› *Roof monitors* are window arrangements set high in the wall or ceiling such as clerestory windows, skylights, or cupolas (glassed-in extensions, also called sun-scoops, in the roof). Monitors admit light and solar winter heat, and they ventilate out summer heat. In the winter the lighter hot air must be circulated to the floor level and the monitors should be protected against heat loss at night.

› *Solar greenhouses* or solariums are the most popular of all indirect passive solar system options, probably because they are the easiest to retrofit and because a greenhouse sun space is a delightful, healthful, and versatile extension of interior space. They are even popular in restaurants and nonresidential settings, and in homes they can serve as living/dining space, as a hot tub or swimming pool area, or as a gardening greenhouse. A solarium works best with a thermal mass (rock or sand) surrounded by rigid insulation. Insulated glass facing within fifteen degrees of due south works best to collect sunshine. The thermal mass stores the heat in direct-gain fashion to be released through convection and reradiation in cold weather and at night. The solarium/greenhouse can be designed to close off from the interior at night and during cold, cloudy spells in order to control excessive heat gain and heat loss in the main body of the house.

CHART 14.1   SOLAR GAIN

Direct gain through windows—amplifies the heat that is absorbed by a thermal mass, such as brick, tile, or concrete.

Trombe wall—glass set very near a thermal mass wall with vents to draw the heated air into the interior and return cool air to the heating space.

Thermosiphoning wall and roof—spaces between the outer and inner wall trap heated air that is drawn off via fans and ducts or registers.

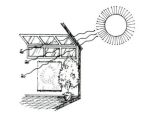

Roof monitor—window set high in the wall, such as a clerestory window, that invites sunshine and heat into the interior.

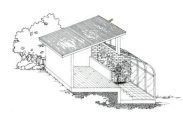

Solar greenhouse—collects passive solar heat, can provide living space, and may be closed off from the main body of the house during hot or cold spells.

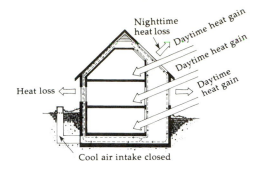

(A)

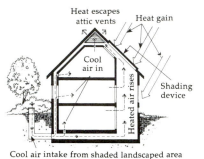

(B)

(C)

Figure 14.17 *The envelope concept combines solar gain with a convection air loop. (A) The winter heating mode. (B) The summer cooling mode. (C) Interior of envelope solarium. Mature trees provide summer shade.*
(C) © Karla Nielson.

Greenhouses can produce 10 to 50 percent of the heat for the interior, depending on the size and insulation of the building, the climate, the size and orientation of the greenhouse, and factors such as protection from prevailing winds, landscaping, movable insulation, interior air flow (an unobstructed convection loop through the house and back to the greenhouse is essential), and the design and quality of the greenhouse itself. Diagonal glass, used in many greenhouses, is the most difficult to protect against heat loss at night and excessive heat gain in the summer, making it less efficient than vertical glass.

When air is trapped in or around a home, it forms a natural insulative barrier that conserves energy. The *envelope* concept, originated by architect Lee Porter Butler, has an integral solarium on the building's south side, and vents carry the heated air through channels over the ceiling in the attic, down a double north wall, and through channels under the lower floor. The continuous air convection loop utilizes passive solar gain with or without a thermal mass.

A *berm* is an earth mass placed on the north side of a building. Southern window exposure brings in winter heat; shading devices such as trees cool in the summer.

INSULATION AND ENERGY CONSERVATION

Insulation can take several forms. It can consist of energy-efficient window coverings for the interior or exterior. Insulation also refers to standard materials used in building construction: rigid panels or sheets of insulation, batting (fluffy fiberglass rolls of insulation), and blown insulation (mainly chopped manufactured fiberglass). Strong plastic can aid insulation by forming a vapor barrier that will not allow heat or cold to penetrate by convection or air movement.

Window glazing can increase insulative values. Two or even three panes of glass, called double or triple glazing, will significantly reduce heat loss or gain. Triple glazing can be found in the form of storm windows. A tinted "summer storm window" cuts down unwanted solar gain. *Weatherstripping* around doors and windows also helps stop drafts or air infiltration. *Draft dodgers* are any material (heavy rug, fabric tube filled with sand) pushed tightly against a door to prevent cold air infiltration. Storm doors and *vestibules* (air lock entries) are other means of keeping out cold air.

The comfort of conventional and solar buildings often depends on the control of excessive heat loss or heat gain. In the winter when the heat loss occurs during overcast days and cold nights, the windows or collectors will need either *movable insulation,* such as fiberglass insulation panels on the interior or exterior, or *insulative window treatments,* such as layered fabric shades, insulating shutters, or lined and interlined draperies.

In the summer, excessive heat gain will need control through exterior or interior *shading devices.* Exterior shading devices include awnings; rolling, hinged, or angled shutters; solar screens or sunscreens; architectural projections or roof extensions; vine-covered trellises; or deciduous trees. Interior shading window treatments include metallized pleated shades, horizontal and vertical blinds, opaque roller shades, shutters, and soft window treatments such as curtains, draperies, and shades.

NONRESIDENTIAL CONSIDERATIONS

The Professionals

In nonresidential design work, the architectural team may consist of both architects and interior designers/architects, who follow project development through three stages:

1. Establish preliminary client contact, draw up a contract, make a preliminary design

2. Final review, design development, review, costing, final specifications and drawings, review

3. Construction scheduling, contracting, review, supervision/installation, project completion review

The project may entail a highly complex, computer-produced critical path, which outlines every necessary step in the given time frame.

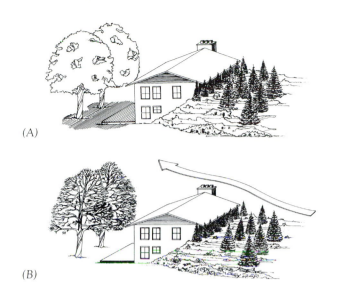

(A)

(B)

Figure 14.18 *An earth berm insulates in* (A) *summer and* (B) *winter.*

(A)

(B)

Figure 14.19 *Insulating shading devices:* (A) *pleated fabric shades and* (B) *vertical louvers.*

Both Courtesy of Del Mar Window Coverings.

CHART 14.2 STRUCTURAL SYSTEMS

In nonresidential buildings and complexes, these systems are most common are metal or concrete systems.

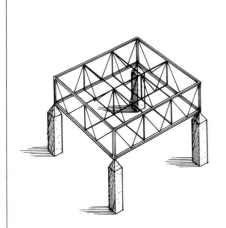

Metal or space frame is a three-dimensional truss/beam and column system assembly that creates a steel skeleton and is also called curtain wall construction. The exterior finish material can be glass or brick veneer or siding, for example.

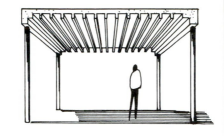

Slab system is reinforced concrete ribbed or waffle design that transfers the lateral loads to supporting end beams; slabs can span short distances and are widely used.

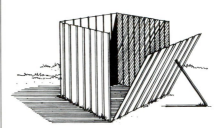

Frame system is made of a rigid steel skeleton sheathed with prefabricated rolled steel or precast concrete.

Masonry block construction consists of walls made of structurally supportive brick, such as concrete block or adobe block. Masonry block construction is commonly seen in convenience store/gas station buildings.

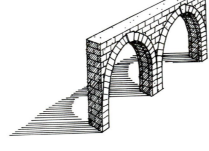

Arch systems are stone blocks cut and fitted to form a curved shape, anchored firmly in vertical supports and with a keystone to stabilize the compression and friction needed to bind the arch together. The arch system has been in existence since ancient Romans built viaducts.

Vaulted systems form an elongated arch such as seen in Medieval cathedrals. The vaulted system is used in ecclesiastical and public architecture where lofty spaces are desirable.

continued

CHART 14.2 **STRUCTURAL SYSTEMS** *continued*

Dome systems are an arch rotated about a circular plan, with a compression ring rather than a keystone that stabilizes the dome. The dome system is most often seen in rotundas of government buildings and in some churches. The dome is a soaring space inside the building and is essentially an arch system rotated around an axis.

Geodesic domes are constructed of triangular steel skeleton components filled with opaque or transparent materials. The geodesic dome was developed in the twentieth century by American architect Buckminster Fuller. Based on the strongest and most stable building shape, the triangle, this interlocking system creates lightweight and economical spaces for a variety of purposes and even for transportable buildings and shelters.

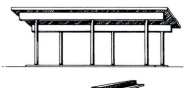

Beam systems are often seen in gas station canopies and are straight, solid structural elements of reinforced concrete, solid or laminated wood, or rolled steel section based on compressive and tensile stress. The load is laterally transmitted along the axis to the vertical support beams.

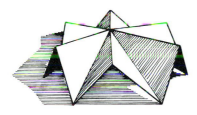

Folded plate systems are of thin, reinforced concrete in a strong, rigid geometric form.

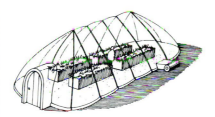

Pneumatic systems are air-inflated or air-supported lightweight, flexible membranes.

Tensile systems are fabric structures stretched over vertical posts or frames like a tent.

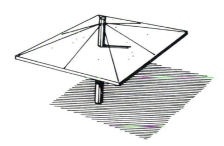

Cable systems are based on a vertical column and horizontal slab connected with flexible steel cables.

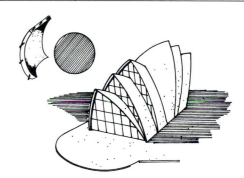

Thin shell membranes are self-supporting concrete or light-weight foam membranes over a steel-reinforcing mesh (like an eggshell) with free-form curvatures[4] as seen in the cutaway illustration.

Heating, Ventilation, and Air-Conditioning

In many large nonresidential settings, the windows are fixed or nonoperable, thus creating a mechanically *sealed environment* that eliminates natural ventilation. In large buildings and complexes, sealed environments can be effeciently controlled. HVAC systems mix warm and cool air to achieve a constant temperature. The rate of air exchange (the infusion of clean, fresh air into an environment, replacing stale air) is sometimes dictated by code.

Communication and Safety Systems

Intercom systems allow occupants to talk through wall-mounted or desk units with persons in other areas of the building. In nonresidential installations, the intercom can become rather sophisticated, including loudspeakers and two-way response without pushing buttons. Telephones also can form intercom systems. The intercom may also carry taped or radio music.

Computer networks link personal computers together or connect computer terminals, (a keyboard and monitor, or screen) with a mainframe computer (large computer processing unit). This allows workers to call up information and interface (compare or put together) information for projects and business dealings. Computer systems that network outside the immediate building are often linked by telephone systems.

Telephone systems connect workstations, sometimes with a central operator, and allow calls to be transferred, put on hold, and computer dialed, among other options. In some offices telephones can also access information from a computer.

Fire alert systems are mandatory in all nonresidential design. In large complexes, the sensing devices are connected to a central monitor. Sprinkling systems are also required to help fight fires.

ENVIRONMENTAL CONSIDERATIONS

Air quality is perhaps the most crucial of the environmental considerations in building systems. In both homes and work spaces, we can potentially be exposed to four types of air pollutants:

1. Toxins are poisonous substances that can be emitted by common building materials.

2. Carcinogens are cancer-causing substances such as tobacco smoke, airborne asbestos particles, and radon gas.

3. Ozone, which may damage lung tissue, is produced by some kinds of machinery such as laser printers (though most have filters).

4. Ions are electronically charged air particles, and they must be balanced in an interior. Negatively charged particles are healthier to breathe, but they are depleted in metal air ducts, VDT (video display terminal) screens, and plastic finishes.

These factors, and problems with HVAC listed below, contribute to Sick Building Syndrome (SBS). This refers to a building in which interior air is polluted or unhealthy.

In the 1970s architects and designers began the practice of sealing nonresidential buildings in hope of creating more evenly heated and cooled interiors. Because windows were nonoperable, air volume was continually circulated at a monitored rate to assure fresh air. Then several problems were discovered. First, the HVAC systems used a lot of electricity. The volume was reduced, resulting in less fresh air and less healthy environments. Second, the HVAC in sealed buildings can produce "moisture carry through," which propagates bacteria and fungi growth. Lowering the velocity of the air can help to minimize this problem. However, a certain number of air changes per hour (e.g., six) is necessary for adequate recirculation, filtration, and comfort.[5] Third, the duct work itself was found to emit too many positively charged ions. Consequently in some cases the fresh air intakes were improperly located (such as near a cooling tower), so contaminated air was brought in. Consequently, today the building owners and tenants are asking, "Do the windows open?"—hoping for fresh air to supplement the air brought in through duct work.

Systems should logically increase the quality of life indoors. However, with the privilege of each fixture or appliance comes a responsibility to avoid wasting resources such as water and electricity. This is a challenge each of us should take seriously as we each do our part to conserve and safeguard our natural resources.

(See also Active and Passive Solar Systems and Insulation and Energy Conservation earlier in this chapter.)

NOTES

1. John L. Feirer and Gilbert R. Hutchings, Carpentry and Building Construction (Peoria, Ill.: Chas A. Bennett Co., 1976), 343.

2. "The Smart House System," Professional Builder Magazine (December 1987): 66-82.

3. Chris Morris, "And They Called It HAL: With Home Automation You're Never Home Alone," Atlanta Business Chronicle, 14-20 August 1992, 3A, 15A.

4. "Information Design," Notes on Architecture (Los Altos, Calif.: William Kaufmann, 1982), 16-19.

5. Judith Nasatir, "National Audubon Society," Interior Design (August 1991): 99.

HISTORIC DESIGN

Lansdowne House dining room, London, eighteenth century.
© Metropolitan Museum of Art, Rogers Fund, 1932.

EARLY INFLUENCES

The design we see today is the result of centuries of influence, development, and change. It is difficult to separate innovations from the factors that shaped them. Even those trends that claim to be free from previous influence have some basis in the experience and technology of preceding generations. Some of the most significant and influential architectural designs originated in classical Greece, Imperial Rome, the Middle Ages, and the Italian Renaissance.

Greece (Fifth Century B.C.)

The Parthenon, considered one of the most beautiful buildings in the world, is the classical embodiment of ancient Greek architecture. This magnificent combination of sculpture and architecture, designed to honor the goddess Athena, rests on an outcropping of rock called the Acropolis in the capital city of Athens. The Parthenon (p.312), built during the fifth century B.C. (golden age), was partially destroyed in 1687 by a bombardment during the Turko-Venetian war. But even in its ruined state it is an inspiring sight.

The construction of the Parthenon is solid marble, generally without mortar. The triangular roof trusses were wooden and covered with terra-cotta tiles. The building, designed by Ictinus and Callicrates, is beautifully proportioned. Through minute adjustments to the curvature of the horizontal lines and by manipulation of the shape, placement, and inclination of the columns, optical illusions were created that make the Parthenon appear visually perfect.

One of the Parthenon's finest features was its sculpture, which was executed principally by a sculptor named Phidias. Much of the original sculpture was taken to England during the nineteenth century by British collector Lord Elgin. These extraordinary pieces are now housed as a collection called the Elgin Marbles in the British Museum in London.

The Parthenon shows clearly the characteristics of Greek architecture. The entire building rests on a base called the *stylobate*, which can be approached from any angle (the actual entrance was in the rear). The *columns* (supporting posts that carry the weight of the roof) form a *colonnade* (row of columns) around the exterior of the building. A *lintel*, or crosspiece, called the *architrave* rests on the *capitals* at the top of the columns. The capital is a decorative detail that helps distinguish one style or *order* of Greek architecture from another. A second set of beams rests on top of the architrave and runs the length and width of the building. On the exterior, these beams are covered with a decorative panel called the *frieze*. The architrave and frieze form the support for the triangular trusses of the roof. The trusses extend beyond the architrave and frieze and create an overhang called the *cornice*. The architrave, frieze, and cornice together form a combination of the three details known as the *entablature*. The row of roof trusses extends forward and backward to the front and rear of the building. The triangular shape of the roof forms a *pediment* (like a *gable*) at the front and rear. The pediment holds a triangular panel of sculpture called the *pediment frieze*.

The Greek Orders

At some point it was determined that certain types of entablatures were more compatible with other types of columns and capitals, and the idea of distinct styles or orders was born. The three Greek orders are *Doric*, *Ionic*, and *Corinthian*.

The simplest and apparently the oldest order is the Doric. The shafts of Doric columns are *fluted* in shallow curved sections and have no base, resting directly on the stylobate. The Doric capital consists of a square *abacus* (plate) at the top and a simple curved *echinus* (dish) below. The Doric entablature has a plain architrave and a frieze divided into *triglyphs* and *metopes*. Triglyphs are blocks divided by vertical channels, and metopes are panels placed between the triglyphs, often decorated with sculpture in low relief.

The Ionic order is a more recent development, though it appears to be related to earlier Egyptian and Near Eastern prototypes. It consists of a capital with two front-facing scroll *volutes*, whose design may have been derived from animal horns or shells. Below is a molding of *egg and dart* with a second lower molding of *bead and reel* or *anthemion* relief designs. The column itself is thinner than the Doric and is fluted with separated semicircular grooves and finished at the bottom with a molded base that rests on the stylobate. The Ionic entablature is narrower than the Doric and features an architrave that rises in three distinct planes. It has an undecorated frieze or one decorated in a continuous band of sculpture and a cornice that projects less than the Doric.

The Corinthian order was not widely used by the Greeks but was adopted by the Romans. The principal difference between the Ionic and Corinthian orders is that the Corinthian capital is shaped like an inverted bell and embellished with two rows of *acanthus leaves*. The bell shape is topped with four small volutes that support each corner of a square abacus. The Corinthian cornice may also be enriched with square *dentil* ornament.

Greek Furniture Classics

The Klismos chair is one of a group of beautiful reproductions of Greek furniture pieces taken from depictions on archaeological artifacts. The pieces, designed by *T. H. Robsjohn-Gibbings* (1905–76), are made in Greece by Saridis S. A. and are distributed in America by Gretchen Bellinger, Inc.

Figure 15.1 *The classical Greek and Roman orders:* (A) *Doric,* (B,C) *Ionic, and* (D) *Corinthian.*

(A) © Randy Masser/International Stock Photo. (B) © Brent Winebrenner/International Stock Photo. (C) © Bob Firth/International Stock Photo. (D) © Gregory Edwards/International Stock Photo.

CHART 15.1   GREEK DESIGN

CLASSICAL DETAILS

Pediment
Cornice
Frieze
Architrave
Capital
Entablature
Column
Stylobate

IONIC CAPITAL WITH
DECORATIVE DETAILS

Egg and dart
Volute
Anthemion
Bead and reel
Fluting

THE GREEK ORDERS

DORIC   IONIC   CORINTHIAN

GREEK KLISMOS
WITH SABER LEGS

THE PARTHENON
ATHENS, GREECE

Rome (200 B.C.–A.D. 400)

During the Imperial Age of Rome (beginning in the first century B.C.), Greece was annexed and absorbed into the Roman Empire. At that point, Rome began to overshadow the Greek civilization it had conquered, though the Romans never reached the level of artistic achievement attained by the Greeks. *Classical Roman* designs were magnificent and showy but never executed with the care and craftsmanship that characterized Greek design. That is probably to be expected because the far-flung Roman Empire had a massive program of building, and such meticulous care would have been impractical. The construction spread to every corner of the Empire—from Spain in the west to Asia Minor in the east and from Africa in the south to England and Germany in the north.

The Romans adapted Greek design to suit their needs, but they also brought to the style their own materials and unique engineering techniques. The Romans incorporated the *roundheaded arch* and *barrel vault* with the post and lintel, often in the same building. The perfection of the arch and vault led to the development of the dome. Bricks and concrete made from volcanic ash and lime facilitated rapid and sturdy construction. The brick and concrete were faced with a veneer of marble or plastered with stucco.

The Roman orders include the Doric, Ionic, and Corinthian styles as well as two orders developed by the Romans: the *Tuscan* and *Composite*. The Roman Doric order varies most from the Greek original. The Roman version, which incorporates a base on the column, is less massive, and the column is often left unfluted. The Roman Ionic and Corinthian orders are almost identical to the Greek, varying mostly in small details of decoration. The Tuscan order is a simplified version of the Roman Doric, without flutes or ornamental moldings. The Composite order, as the name implies, is a combination of the Corinthian and Ionic orders. Large volutes, together with a band of egg-and-dart and bead-and-reel moldings, are borrowed from the Ionic capital, and two rows of acanthus leaves are taken from the Corinthian order. The resulting design is even more decorative than the Corinthian capital.

The Roman temple was based on the design of Greek temples but differed from them in at least two important ways. First, the Roman temple was built on a raised *podium* instead of a stylobate and was approached only from the front by means of a single set of steps. Second, the interior space (*cella*) was expanded to the edge of the podium and filled the area that would otherwise form a porch at the sides and rear of the building. The exterior walls were lined with half columns that formed a continuous line with the columns of the covered porch or *portico* at the front of the building. The Maison Carrée (c. 16 B.C.), Nimes, France, is an excellent example of a small Roman temple. The Pantheon (A.D. 120) in Rome is an important example of a circular Roman temple.

The building, which was dedicated to all the gods and later consecrated as a Christian church, features a large dome (over 142 feet in diameter) that rests on a round drum-shaped cella. The round domed space is called a rotunda. The interior is lighted by an open *oculus* (circular opening at the top of the dome), 142 feet above the floor. The exterior incorporates a portico attached to the circular body of the building.

Much of what remains of Roman domestic design was first discovered in 1754 with the first excavations of *Pompeii and Herculaneum*—cities buried and preserved by the eruption of Mount Vesuvius in A.D. 79. The House of the Vettii, an example of a Pompeian house, opened into an *atrium* (a space open to the sky). The atrium contained a pool, which held rainwater collected from the roof. The rear section of the house opened into a colonnaded garden area called the *peristyle*. These houses also typically had libraries, picture galleries, kitchens, and rooms for sculpture, dining, sleeping, and conversation and reading.

The terms classical and classicism are often mentioned in conjunction with architectural design and detailing. These terms refer to the use or adaptation of Greek and Roman forms, motifs, and proportions in the designs of subsequent periods. The Roman orders and their proportions were documented and preserved in drawings by *Vitruvius*, a first-century Roman architect. Correct classical proportions are often referred to as *Vitruvian proportions*.

Color in History

Color has played an important role throughout history. Colors have reflected climate, political and social atmosphere, and trade with or exposure to other cultures. Today as we view the ruins of antiquity, we have only a glimpse into the real colors enjoyed by peoples of every era in history. These colors are useful to interior designers today as historic interiors are re-created, restored, or adaptively reused.

Color in The Ancient World

Colors of ancient Greece included stellar, slate, and mist blues; scarlet; pale violet; pale and medium malachite and olive greens; sun yellow; ivory white; marble pink; clay beige; copper brown; and charcoal. Fragments of color on the Parthenon in Athens show us that blue was dominant, with figures in realistic tints of yellow, pink, and pale blue.

The mosaics of *Byzantium* (A.D. 330–1453), the ancient Roman eastern capital, still sparkle with rich golds, blues, greens, and flesh tones. Classical Roman interiors were decorated with painted stucco and colorful mosaics, accented with rich fabrics. The brilliance and relative clarity of colors such as magenta (the imperial purple), rich gold, Pompeii red, and Roman greens, accented with black, surprised the Western world upon their discovery at Pompeii and Herculaneum.

CHART 15.2 ROMAN DESIGN

ROMAN ARCH

Keystone

MAISON CARRÉE
NIMES, FRANCE

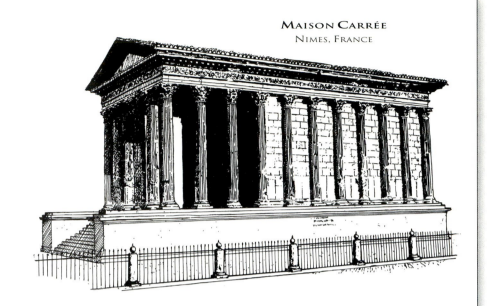

POMPEIIAN HOUSE PLAN

Peristyle

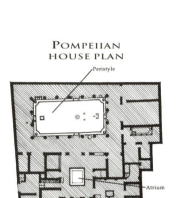

Atrium

TRIANGULAR PEDIMENT

SEGMENTAL PEDIMENT

SCROLL PEDIMENT
(BAROQUE)

PANTHEON
ROME, ITALY

THE ROMAN ORDERS

TUSCAN   COMPOSITE

The Middle Ages (800–1500)

With official acceptance of Christianity in Rome, the church in Italy began the construction of churches. These were built in a style known as *Early Christian* and were an important influence on the styles that followed. By the year 1000, all of Europe was Christian. The barbarians who repeatedly streamed out of the North to sack Rome and the rest of southern Europe had intermarried, converted to Christianity, and had in fact become Europeans. The lives of these people were inextricably tied to the church in a manner that is difficult for us to comprehend today. The church took care of every need, whether spiritual, physical, or intellectual, and in return everyone was expected to contribute money and labor to the building of churches.

Many of the Early Christian buildings had been destroyed by fire, and in the eleventh century, a new style of church with a fireproof stone ceiling became popular. These buildings used the roundheaded Roman arch and vault as forms for windows, doors, and ceilings. The French term *Romanesque*, meaning Romanlike, is the designation given to the architecture of this period. In England the same style is generally called *Norman* after William I (the Conqueror) of Normandy, who conquered England in 1066.

The *Gothic* style grew out of Romanesque around 1135; it first appeared at the church of Saint-Denis near Paris, France. The name Gothic, which has become synonymous with design from the *Medieval era*, or *Middle Ages*, was first applied by Vasari, a post-Renaissance scholar who must have decided that the style was no further advanced than that of the barbaric Goths in the sixth century. He and his contemporaries probably felt that the designers of the Renaissance had corrected the architectural drift away from the classicism of ancient Greece and Rome. With added perspective, Gothic design and architecture are today considered one of the finest achievements of all time.

Gothic architecture incorporates the *Gothic arch* (pointed arch), which led to the development of a very complex and ingenious system of vaulting that allowed the buildings to rise to great heights. These tall spaces draw the eye upward and inspire a feeling of reverence and awe. The churches, often built over the *crypt* (basement) of earlier Romanesque churches, were laid out in the shape of a *Latin cross* or *cruciform*. The main body of the church, filled by worshipers, is called the *nave*. The nave is broken by the *transepts*, which extend outward on both sides from the *crossing* (the area where the nave and transepts cross). Beyond the crossing, the main body of the church is called the *choir* (or *quire*) because the choir stalls and organ were often located there. The end of the main body that frequently houses the altar is called the *apse*. The nave is divided on each side from the *aisles* by an *arcade* (row of arches). The aisles run along the side of the nave and continue behind the choir and apse. The aisles are not as tall as the nave and extend only as high as the aisle arcade. Some churches have windows that open from the aisles to the exterior of the building, while others have small chapels that are entered from the aisles, run parallel to the nave and choir, and radiate off of the apse aisle or *ambulatory*.

The area between each opposing set of aisle arches is called a *bay*. Each bay is divided by tall *piers* (columns) that carry the weight of the ceiling, the trusses, and the roof. The *ribs* that form the framework of the ceiling spring from *brackets* carved as part of the pier and reach across the ceiling to the opposite side, creating *vaults*. As the style developed, the vaulting became increasingly more complex and ornate. In some churches, large, decorative, carved medallions, called *bosses*, are attached to the ceiling where the ribs cross.

The wall between each of the piers is open at the floor level with the arches of the aisle arcade. Above the arcade is another set of openings called the *triforium*. In some cases the triforium serves as a gallery for looking into the nave and choir. In other churches the triforium is shallow and has no room for passage. The large openings above the triforium are the *clerestory windows*. These windows, as well as the windows on the aisle, are divided into smaller sections by vertical stone dividers called *mullions*. The lower part of the windows are divided into smaller pointed windows called *lancets*. The lacelike pattern of stone above the lancets is called *tracery*. The windows are often filled with *stained glass*. Stained glass consists of pieces of plain, colored, and painted glass, fitted together with lead strips called *came* to make patterned panels of glass that are fixed to the metal framework between the mullions of the window. Light entering the windows and filling the building was symbolic of the presence of God. The quality of colored light added further to the feeling of mysticism.

The relatively slender piers support the tremendous weight of the roof and stone ceiling and have a tendency to bow outward unless they are braced. Consequently, the weight of the roof of the nave is carried outward from the wall, above the roof of the aisles, by curved horizontal braces called *flying buttresses*. These connect with tall vertical structures, called *buttresses*, built on the exterior walls of the aisle. These grow increasingly thick in steps as they reach toward the ground and carry the weight from the flying buttresses.

Each country developed characteristics that distinguished the church designs of that area. For example, elegant flying buttresses were a striking feature of many French Gothic churches. English churches often had two sets of transepts, wide fronts, and tall towers over the crossing. Italian Gothic churches were covered with elaborate patterns in contrasting colors of marble. Every area of Europe produced beautiful Gothic churches, and when one stops to consider the sacrifice, hardship, devotion, and ingenuity required to build them, they become monuments to an age of faith. Some of these beautiful buildings have been preserved, and we can enjoy them and learn about them today.[1]

CHART 15.3   MEDIEVAL DESIGN—ROMANESQUE AND GOTHIC

ROMANESQUE ARCHES

GOTHIC CHURCH INTERIOR ELEVATION

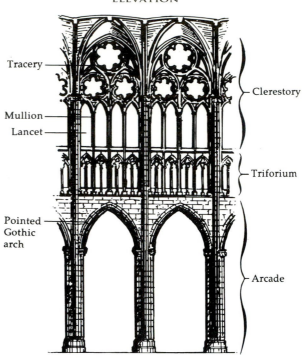

Tracery

Mullion

Lancet

Pointed Gothic arch

Clerestory

Triforium

Arcade

GOTHIC CHURCH PLAN

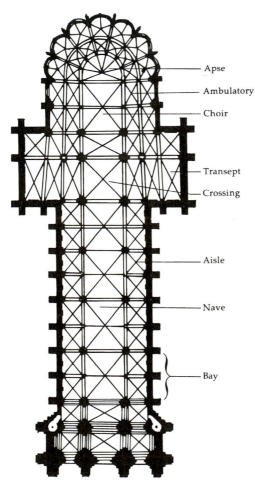

Apse

Ambulatory

Choir

Transept

Crossing

Aisle

Nave

Bay

GOTHIC CHURCH CROSS SECTION

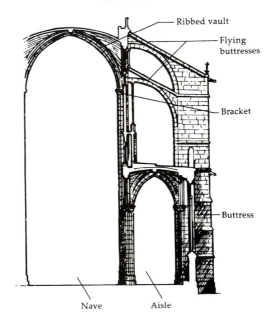

Ribbed vault

Flying buttresses

Bracket

Buttress

Nave

Aisle

Late English Medieval domestic design continued well beyond the end of the Gothic era into the seventeenth century, particularly in the homes of the common people. The common houses from the end of the Middle Ages were constructed of stone, brick, or timber. These houses had steeply pitched roofs and small *casement windows* (that swing in or out) made with *leaded glass* panes (small panes held together with lead strips, like stained glass). The *timber-framed houses* utilized two types of *infill* to form the walls between the timbers. Panels of woven sticks called *wattle* were fixed, like lath (groundwork for plastering), to the timber frame and then covered with coarse plaster known as *daub*. The second type of infill was brickwork called *nogging*. The houses often featured an overhang at each story. These may have provided additional space in cramped city settings, but their use in less crowded areas suggests that overhangs were mostly a detail of style. Roofs were frequently *thatched* with bundles of reeds attached to the roof timbers and shaved or cut into smooth rounded curves. *Slate roofs* were made of thin, flat pieces of stone fashioned into shingles. Wooden shingles were also used in some areas. These Late English Medieval common houses were the prototype for the seventeenth-century American houses.[2]

Medieval Color

Although color in castles and homes during the Medieval era was somewhat somber; the impact of color seen in the magnificent stained glass windows throughout Europe still impresses us today. Techniques used to create these colorful masterpieces were temporarily lost until research revived the production of colored stained glass during the Victorian era (1842-1910). Colors of the Middle Ages and previous periods were governed by symbolism and were not freely and creatively used.

The Renaissance (1420–1650)

The *Renaissance* began in Florence, Italy, in the fourteenth century and marked the rebirth of classical influences in architecture, art, and many other areas of human endeavor. The architectural Renaissance moved through Europe by means of *pattern books* containing drawings and descriptions published by leading architects and designers from Italy, France, and Holland. These books, along with the writings of Vitruvius, discovered in 1414, influenced architecture until the nineteenth century.

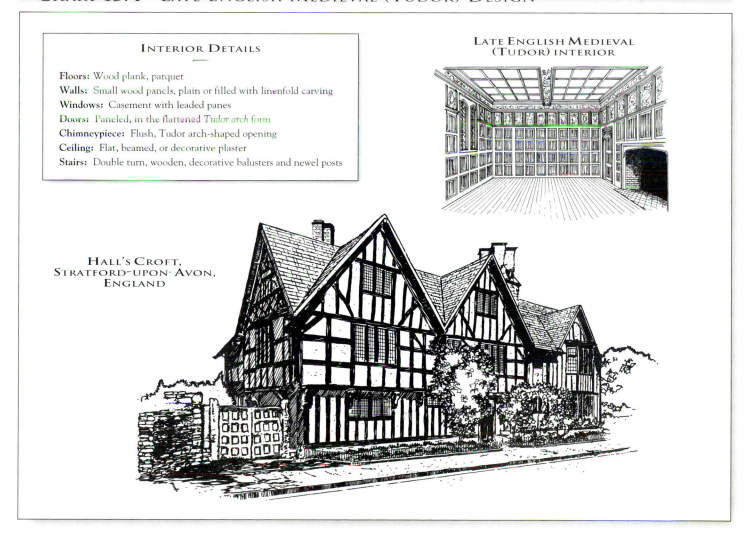

CHART 15.4   LATE ENGLISH MEDIEVAL (TUDOR) DESIGN

INTERIOR DETAILS

Floors: Wood plank, parquet
Walls: Small wood panels, plain or filled with linenfold carving
Windows: Casement with leaded panes
Doors: Paneled, in the flattened *Tudor arch* form
Chimneypiece: Flush, Tudor arch-shaped opening
Ceiling: Flat, beamed, or decorative plaster
Stairs: Double turn, wooden, decorative balusters and newel posts

LATE ENGLISH MEDIEVAL (TUDOR) INTERIOR

HALL'S CROFT, STRATFORD-UPON-AVON, ENGLAND

CHART 15.5 RENAISSANCE DESIGN

PALAZZO RUCELLAI
FLORENCE, ITALY

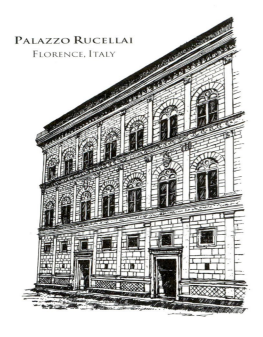

SAVONAROLA CHAIR

DANTE CHAIR

RENAISSANCE TEXTILES

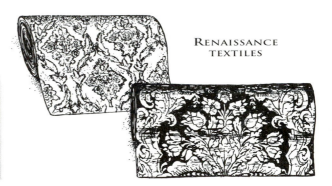

TEXTILE DESCRIPTION

Colors: Rich and vibrant reds, blues, golds, and greens predominate

Patterns: Large-scale florals, the artichoke, the pomegranate

Textures: Plain and figured velvet, tapestry, silk brocade, and damask

**VILLA ROTONDA,
ANDREA PALLADIO**
VICENZA, ITALY

The Renaissance palace was a boxlike city fortress with massive gates opening onto an open courtyard or atrium around which the house was built. The exterior of the palace was divided into three distinct stories by means of different textured stone, ranging from *rusticated* on the ground level to smooth on the third story, or by means of protruding rows (*courses*) of stone carved to form entablatures. The entablatures were visually supported by flat, false columns called *pilasters*, which progressed from the Doric order on the ground level to Ionic and Corinthian on the second and third levels. The top of the palace was finished with a very large overhanging cornice. The windows on the ground level were small and covered with iron bars. The second floor, or *piano nobile* (the noble level), and third floor had larger, well-proportioned windows. The *facade* (front face) of the building was arranged in a symmetrical fashion.

The Renaissance architect whose work had the greatest impact on English and, subsequently, American architecture was a sixteenth-century stonecutter-turned-architect named Andrea Palladio. Palladio's work, centered at Vicenza near Venice, included some public buildings but focused mainly on the design of villas for wealthy farmers. The most famous of these is the Villa Rotonda (1567). This house sits at the crest of a hill with a fine view in every direction. The basic form of the building is a plain box on a raised Roman podium. A portion of the podium extends outward on all four sides to create staircases. The four sets of steps lead up to four Roman Ionic porticoes. The house has a narrow attic story topped with a *hipped roof* of terracotta tiles that rises gently to support a low *drum* and shallow dome. The windows of the main floor are topped with triangular pediments supported by curved brackets called *modillions*. The Renaissance architects did not always try to duplicate the designs of Greece and Rome but adapted their proportions, forms, motifs, and orders to create a new and important style.[3]

Renaissance Furniture Classics

The Renaissance witnessed the development of furniture that was adapted in every country where its influence was felt—from Spain to England, and from Scotland to Germany. Some of those important pieces remain classics even today. For example, the Dante and Savonarola chairs, designed during the Renaissance, are still seen in today's interiors. These are X-frame chairs that originally were designed to fold. The Savonarola chair is made up of a series of X-shaped slats, while the Dante chair has a double X frame and usually an upholstered seat.

Renaissance Color

The Renaissance was a time of rebirth of artistic and architectural pursuits. No longer tied strictly to symbolic color, artists discovered the freedom to creatively use color. Color became a pleasing, decorative, and satisfying element for artists and patrons alike. Oil paintings reveal rich, sensuous hues such as garnet and persimmon reds, bright copper, deep cobalt blue, blue-green, medium blue, pale and deep greens, medium and deep malachite greens, rich and dull brown, marble and ivory cream and white, and metallic gold. Renaissance color elements migrated from Italy northward to Europe, notably France, Ger-

Figure 15.2 *This beautiful Philadelphia highboy shows Baroque influence in its finely carved scroll pediment, popular during the Georgian era.*
© *Ted Spiegel.*

many, the Lowlands, and England, then finally to America. In the colder climates and with more reserved attitudes, Renaissance colors tended to be more restrained.

The Period of Baroque (1580–1750)

The Baroque period is often considered the final phase of the Renaissance, and it represents the full flowering of the classical tradition reintroduced by Renaissance designers. Baroque design incorporates all of the classical elements such as columns, pediments, pilasters, entablatures, rounded arches, and domes. However, it takes on an exaggerated form in terms of scale and ornamentation. Baroque design is large scaled, bold, and even theatrical, with effects of light and shadow. Ceilings are painted with incredible realistic scenes floating in the clouds, and with angels hovering overhead. The architectural forms are taken to extremes and made to undulate and twist. The facades of the churches curve in and out, the interior spaces are rounded without corners, and columns are twisted. Hence the origin of the term "baroque," which comes from the Portuguese "barroco," or imperfect pearl with its undulating, irregular surface.

CHART 15.6 SEVENTEENTH-CENTURY ENGLISH MEDIEVAL DESIGN

THOROUGHGOOD HOUSE
BRICK CONSTRUCTION

WHITFIELD HOUSE
STONE CONSTRUCTION

CORWIN HOUSE
CLAPBOARD CONSTRUCTION

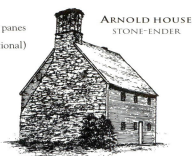

ARNOLD HOUSE
STONE-ENDER

EXTERIOR CHARACTERISTICS

- English Medieval construction—brick, stone, timber with daub and wattle or nogging, and clapboard siding
- Steeply pitched gabled roof
- Small casement windows with leaded panes
- Overhang or jetty with pendants (optional)
- Buttressed chimneys (optional)
- Columned chimneys (optional)
- Stone-ender chimneys (optional)
- Projecting entry (optional)
- Saltbox (optional)
- Gambrel roof (optional)

INFLUENCES

- Late English Medieval domestic architecture
- Early English Renaissance architecture

RESIDENTIAL EXAMPLES

- Adam Thoroughgood House (1640), Princess Anne County, Virginia
- Corwin House (c. 1675), Salem, Massachusetts
- Eleazer Arnold House (before 1676), Johnston, Rhode Island
- Henry Whitfield House (1639), Guilford, Connecticut
- Whipple House (1638), Ipswich, Massachusetts
- Bacon's Castle (c. 1665), Surrey County, Virginia
- Thomas Clemence House (1680), Johnston, Rhode Island
- Parson Capen House (1683), Topsfield, Massachusetts

NONRESIDENTIAL EXAMPLES

- St. Luke's Church (1632), Isle of Wight County, Virginia

The materials of Baroque design are rich marbles, gilded metals, and ornately painted plaster. The overall effect is impressive. The style was called "Jesuit" in France, which reflects an important function of Baroque design. Many Catholics converted to Protestantism during the Reformation, and the Jesuit order was given the mission to bring back the faithful—which they did through the coercion of the Inquisition and the enticement of the lavish Baroque style.

The Baroque style began in Italy, spread to France, and eventually made its way to Great Britain and northern Europe. As it moved north it became less exuberant, however. For example, the French found Bernini's design for the Louvre far too outlandish for their taste. However, the scale and showy quality of the style was perfectly suited to the Palace of Versailles, built for Louis XIV; it was built not so much as a home, but as a symbol of Louis's and France's power. Sir Christopher Wren, the great English designer, studied French Baroque designs and simplified them even more. The influence of the Baroque style, by the time it made its way to the American Colonies, had lost its showiness and appeared in simplified form in the beautifully refined details of the Early Georgian style.

THE ENGLISH INFLUENCE IN AMERICA

The Seventeenth-Century English Medieval Style (1608–95)

Settlers arriving in America from England in the early part of the seventeenth century quickly built crude, temporary shelters. However, as soon as conditions permitted, they constructed permanent buildings of the style they had left in England. Because these settlers were generally not from the wealthy class, they were probably unacquainted with the Renaissance style; instead, they were accustomed to Medieval construction methods and design. The result is the *Seventeenth-Century English Medieval style*.

A few of the American houses, however, showed faint traces of Renaissance design in the form of projecting doorway entries and chimneys shaped like columns. The early Renaissance houses of England were built with *columned chimneys* and ornate entries that often broke forward from the body of the house. The American versions of these details were less elaborate than the English prototypes. Bacon's Castle in Surrey County, Virginia, though

INTERIOR DETAILS

Floors: Wide wooden plank

Walls: Stucco

Windows: Small casement with leaded panes

Doors: Planks (later paneled)

Chimneypiece: Large, open, brick fireplace for warmth and cooking; large wooden mantel beam; board-and-batten palisade wall

Ceiling: Beamed

Stairs: Simple, modified, wooden, double-turn, with wooden balustrade

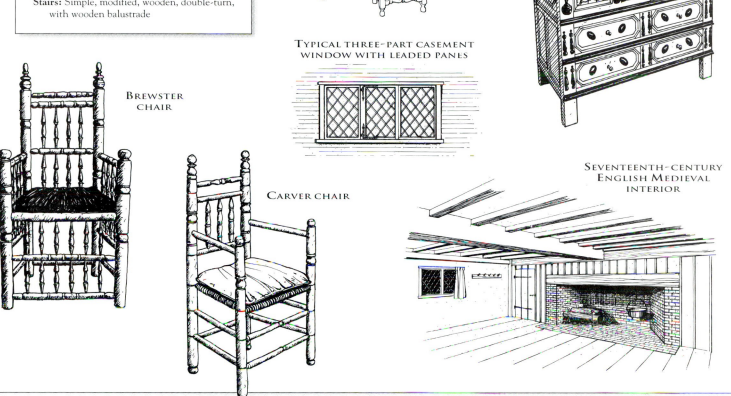

GATELEG TABLE

SUNFLOWER CHEST

TYPICAL THREE-PART CASEMENT WINDOW WITH LEADED PANES

BREWSTER CHAIR

CARVER CHAIR

SEVENTEENTH-CENTURY ENGLISH MEDIEVAL INTERIOR

essentially Medieval, was remarkable for the extent of its Renaissance design. It not only had columned chimneys and a projecting doorway, it also featured *Flemish gables* and a triangular pediment above the doorway. Dutch-inspired Flemish gables, designed with a series of steps and curves, were incorporated on some late sixteenth- and early seventeenth-century English buildings.

Seventeenth-century American houses featured varied use of materials and distinctive characteristics in each area of the country. Brick was prevalent in the South where lime to make mortar was readily available. In New England, timber houses were often covered with *clapboard*, a sheathing of hand-split oak. Houses sided with clapboard were also common in East Anglia, the English region that had been home to many of the early American settlers. In Rhode Island several houses—called *stone-enders*—were built with stone chimneys that covered the end of the building.

The Medieval characteristics of the seventeenth-century American houses were the use of stone, brick, and timber construction, daub and wattle, nogging, overhangs with decorative *pendants*, small casement windows with leaded panes, chimneys built in the shape of Gothic buttresses (*buttressed chimneys*), and steeply pitched,

gabled roofs. *Saltbox roofs*, though not necessarily Medieval, were English. The saltbox slopes to the rear from the ridge of the roof to a level below the line of the front eaves. The saltbox roof covers a lean-to addition at the back of the house. These additions were probably made in response to the need for more space. The saltbox was generally an addition made to an existing house, but by the beginning of the eighteenth century, some houses were built with saltbox roofs. The *gambrel roof*, with two different pitches on each side, was also used somewhat during the seventeenth century, but it was more popular on the vernacular houses of the eighteenth century. This type of roof, which was English, was practical because it allowed more space in the *garret* (attic).

Seventeenth-Century Furniture Classics

Seventeenth-century furniture was brought from England by settlers or made in America with rather primitive methods. The pieces are solid, sturdy, and unpretentious. Chests were important storage pieces and were frequently carved or decorated with split spindles, a method of *embellishment* also common in England. Chairs were straight and rigid with *turnings*, probably because turning was a relatively simple yet decorative way to

CHART 15.7   EARLY GEORGIAN DESIGN AND QUEEN ANNE FURNITURE

EXTERIOR CHARACTERISTICS

- Two-story rectangular block
- Built of brick, clapboard, or stone
- Symmetrical facade with five or more bays
- Hipped roof, often with dormer windows
- Tall end chimneys
- Sash windows
- Cornice with dentils or modillions
- Stringcourse (optional)
- Pediment and pilasters at doorway or windows (optional)
- Balustrade (optional)
- Cupola (optional)
- Gabled or gambrel roof (optional)
- Quoins (optional)

INFLUENCES

- Christopher Wren
- English-Baroque middle-class houses (late seventeenth century)

RESIDENTIAL EXAMPLES

- Westover (c. 1730), Charles City County, Virginia
- Governor's Palace (1706–20), Williamsburg, Virginia
- MacPhaedris-Warner House (1718–23), Portsmouth, New Hampshire
- Brafferton Indian School (1723), Williamsburg, Virginia
- The President's House (1723), Williamsburg, Virginia
- Hunter House (1746), Newport, Rhode Island
- Carter's Grove (1750), James City County, Virginia
- Wentworth-Gardner House (1760), Portsmouth, New Hampshire

NONRESIDENTIAL EXAMPLES

- Christ Church—"Old North" (1723), Boston, Massachusetts
- Trinity Church (1725–26), Newport, Rhode Island
- Independence Hall (1731), Philadelphia, Pennsylvania

WESTOVER
(BEFORE WINGS WERE ADDED)

GOVERNOR'S PALACE
WILLIAMSBURG, BALUSTRADE
AND CUPOLA

EARLY GEORGIAN
INTERIOR

---

make legs and *stretchers*. Two important examples are the Carver and Brewster chairs. The two are almost identical except that the Brewster chair has many more spindles than the Carver chair. The gateleg table with turned legs is another important piece from the period that has never really gone out of fashion.

Color in Seventeenth-Century America

Seventeenth-century colors tended to be earth colors seen in pewter, wood, and unbleached muslin, as well as in the simple homespun checks in indigo blues, yellows, and madder reds. Colors, limited as they were, tended to be dull, natural, and faded.

The Early Georgian Style (1695-1750)

The classical style began to be widely accepted in England primarily due to the work of Sir Christopher Wren. Wren was Surveyor of the King's Works (royal architect) in 1666 when the *City of London* was destroyed by fire. He was commissioned to rebuild St.

Paul's Cathedral as well as fifty-two smaller churches. His designs for churches and royal buildings were classical with some rich Baroque ornamentation. The influence of Wren extended to the building of houses as well. These medium-sized, Wren-Baroque-style houses were the prototype for American houses during the first half of the eighteenth century. Compared to the seventeenth-century Medieval houses, the *Early American* Georgian houses seemed splendid. They were, however, versions of middle-class English residences. The very large homes and palaces of the English aristocracy and royalty were not used as models for homes in the colonies.

At the beginning of the eighteenth century, Colonial America was prospering, and certain segments of society were ready for more elaborate houses. The new Wren-Baroque style of architecture was introduced in Williamsburg, Virginia, at the end of the seventeenth century. The Wren Building (1695) at William and Mary College in Williamsburg, though much less elaborate than most of Wren's English designs, is very much like his Chelsea Royal Hospital (1682) in London.

QUEEN ANNE
HIGHBOY

EARLY GEORGIAN
TEXTILES

QUEEN ANNE
WING CHAIR

QUEEN ANNE TEA
TABLE

QUEEN ANNE
ARMCHAIR

Residences in the new style began to appear in America after the beginning of the eighteenth century. The first few years of the 1700s saw the death of Queen Anne and the accession to the British throne of George I. He was succeeded by George II, George III, and George IV, who gave their name to the *Georgian* era. The new architectural style popularized by Wren in England a quarter of a century earlier is called *Early Georgian* in America.

The basic form of the Early Georgian house was a rectangular two-story box, broken by five symmetrically placed bays (sections of wall that include window and door openings). Brick was the preferred building material in the South, painted clapboard or brick were used in New England, and stone was common in the mid-Atlantic colonies. Where brick or stone were used, the first and second stories were frequently divided by a *stringcourse* or *beltcourse*. One or two Early Georgian-style houses built after 1750 include the use of *quoins* (decorative corner block details), which were more common in the Late Georgian style. Because these houses were larger, they required more than one

chimney, and the chimneys were frequently placed at opposite ends of the house. Like the English prototypes, the houses had hipped roofs, which slope from the ridge in all four directions to the eaves. The roof was often broken by dormer windows that projected to provide light for the attic story. Some builders of independent spirit ignored the English prototype and incorporated gambrel or gabled roofs into their designs. Such variations give these houses a distinctly American feeling.

Medieval details from the seventeenth century, such as casement windows with leaded panes, were replaced by *sash windows;* a door flanked with pilasters and crowned with a classical pediment took the place of the simple Medieval doorway. The pediments were the simple *triangular* type, rounded *segmental pediments* (the arch is a segment of a circle), or the more ornate, Baroque-style *scroll pediments*. On some of these buildings, pediments were also used above the windows. The rafters were extended far enough to create an overhang that was treated like a classical cornice, often with modillions or dentil trim. A few of these houses had railings or balustrades around the ridge of the roof and a windowed tower called a *cupola*. Kitchens, servants' quarters, dairies, and other types of service areas were frequently located in *outbuildings* away from the main body of the house. Some of these outbuildings were attached to the houses during the twentieth century, altering their original appearance.

Early Georgian Furniture Classics

Both the William and Mary and Queen Anne furniture styles were popular during the Early Georgian era. However, it is the *Queen Anne* style that has remained popular and is still loved and widely used today.

The Queen Anne tea table was a popular piece in eighteenth-century England and America as tea drinking became increasingly fashionable and the serving of tea a highly refined art. The tea table is characterized by its *cabriole legs* with *club feet*. Unlike the French Rococo cabriole leg, the Queen Anne cabriole leg does not continue into the line of the *apron* (face of the table just below the top) but rather makes a distinct and abrupt connection with the apron where they meet. Below the apron, the knee of the leg may be carved with a shell or other motif.

The Queen Anne *wing chair* evolved from a seventeenth-century sleeping chair; the wings provided support for a nodding head. The wing chair is upholstered and has typical Queen Anne cabriole legs, some versions with stretchers, others without.

Queen Anne chairs feature upholstered seats, round-shouldered hoop backs with a vase- or fiddle-shaped *splat*, cabriole legs generally without stretchers, and club feet. The *side chair* is armless, and the *armchair* has open arms in various forms, the most common of which is the gooseneck or shepherd's crook arm with its beautifully shaped curve.

The Queen Anne lowboy and highboy are important case pieces from the eighteenth century. The *lowboy* is a raised chest on cabriole legs, generally with two drawers or a single wide drawer and two smaller square drawers in the curved *apron* (the face of the chest just below the drawers). The *highboy* is created when a chest of four or five drawers is placed on top of the lowboy. The top of the highboy may be crowned with some type of *pediment*, but most often it will be flat with a slight cornice.

Early Georgian Color

Early Georgian colors were the Renaissance colors imported from England and France, with a preference for greens and dark dull blues; deep olive greens (examples of Colonial Williamsburg colors); and some golds, oranges, and browns reminiscent of English Medieval interiors.

The Late Georgian Style (1750–90)

The style called *Late Georgian* came to America in English pattern books. These contained drawings of houses, floor plans, and details that could be built with little or no architectural training. One of the most significant of these books was James Gibbs's *A Book of Architecture* (1728), which had reached America by 1751 at the latest. His designs had great appeal for Americans because they were conservative in scale and within their means. Also, unlike his contemporaries, Gibbs showed a strong tendency to maintain much of the richness of the Wren-Baroque design. Gibbs's book contained illustrations of homes designed with a central house or block, connected to symmetrical dependencies (outbuildings) by straight or curved passages or wings. Such dependencies created a forecourt in the Palladian manner. Gibbs also designed houses in the Wren-Baroque style—as simple self-contained rectangular houses without wings or dependencies. His designs include the use of rusticated stone, balustrades, quoins, and pilasters, details too ornate for use by other Palladian architects of his time. Gibbs often designed houses with a two-story projecting pavilion or *breakfront*.

The breakfront topped with a triangular pediment above the roofline is the most distinctive feature of the Late Georgian-style house. In most other respects, it is similar to the Early Georgian style—a rectangular box with five or more bays, hipped roof, and tall end chimneys. The hipped roof is often lower pitched than the Early Georgian roof and may, in rare cases, feature a balustrade at the eaves that hides the roof. The Late Georgian house may have a portico or a bracketed cornice, as well as pilasters and pediments at the doorway. The door may be crowned with a roundheaded *fanlight* (a rounded, over-the-door window), and the windows in the dormers may also be roundheaded. These houses may also feature a roundheaded arched window with lower rectangular windows on each side called a *Palladian window*. (They bear that name because they resemble an architectural detail used by Palladio on several of his designs.) When placed above a front door or at the end of an important room, they create an impressive focal point. The standard windows on the Late Georgian house are frequently capped with *crown* or *jack arch lintels*, which are trapezoid-shaped stone pieces with a wedge-shaped keystone. Corner trim is plain or quoined, and sometimes this style features two-story pilasters.

Late Georgian Furniture Classics

In the late Georgian period the Chippendale style was popular. This style, like the Queen Anne style, remains a favorite today.

Chippendale furniture was designed during the mid-eighteenth century by Englishman *Thomas Chippendale* (1718–99). His book of designs, *The Gentleman and Cabinet-Maker's Director* (1754), featured 160 plates with drawings of furniture pieces. Because the designs were published in book form, any skilled woodworker could build or adapt them, and as a result, their popularity soon spread throughout the British Isles and America. Chippendale's drawings showed the influence of French (Louis XV), Chinese, Gothic, and Neoclassic designs. The Chippendale chair is characterized by its upholstered seat, cabriole legs with a claw and ball feet, and a yoke-shaped back with an ornately carved splat. The backs might be carved in the form of ribbons, in Gothic tracery, in Chinese *fretwork*, or into pierced slats forming a *ladder-back*. The Chippendale cabriole legs joined the *apron* in the same manner as the Queen Anne cabriole legs. On some pieces a straight square leg known as the *Marlborough leg* was common.

Figure 15.3 *Chippendale-style chairs add sophistication to this dining room.*
© *Jessie Walker.*

The Chippendale wing chair is similar to the Queen Anne wing chair but generally has either Marlborough legs or cabriole legs with claw and ball feet, and is larger scaled.

The Chippendale *camel-back sofa* is an upholstered piece with a *serpentine*-shaped back that dips and rises from rolled arms to a hump in the center. The sofa has either cabriole legs with claw and ball feet or Marlborough legs with and without stretchers.

The *block front* is a furniture detail associated with John Goddard (1724–85) of Newport, Rhode Island. The block front, which was applied to Chippendale-style case pieces, consists of a front panel divided into three alternating vertical convex and concave sections. The inside section is concave, the two outside sections are convex, and the top of each section is finished with a carved convex or concave shell.

The Chippendale breakfront is a case piece designed in such a way that the front plane of the piece is broken (i.e., part advancing and part receding). The breakfront was commonly built as a *secretary* or a china cupboard and had an enclosed cabinet below and open shelves with glass doors above. The breakfront was also popular in succeeding periods and appears in several styles.

The Chippendale highboy, like the Queen Anne highboy, consists of a low, two-drawer chest on legs (lowboy) with an additional chest of drawers above. The chest is topped by a scroll pediment with a *finial*. In the eighteenth century, Philadelphia, Pennsylvania, was an important center for furniture manufacture. The Philadelphia highboy, with its magnificent carving, is a particularly beautiful example of the American version of the Chippendale style.

Late Georgian Color

Late Georgian colors were peach, ivory, Wedgewood blue, opal pink, and green with clean and creamy white backgrounds of English garden-printed fabrics. More intense colors such as reds, golds, and deep greens and blues were still often seen in rich imported textiles such as silks, fine cottons, linens, and in the increasingly popular Oriental rugs.

CHART 15.8 LATE GEORGIAN DESIGN AND CHIPPENDALE FURNITURE

MOUNT PLEASANT

TYRON PALACE

EXTERIOR CHARACTERISTICS

- Same basic form as the Early Georgian house
- Two-story projecting pavilion or breakfront with pediment
- Small portico over doorway (optional)
- Two-story double portico (optional)
- Building massed into symmetrical blocks and connections (optional)
- Palladian windows (optional)
- Doorways with roundheaded fanlights, bracketed cornices, or pilasters and pediments (optional)
- Corners untrimmed or trimmed with quoins or pilasters (optional)
- Crown lintels (optional)

INFLUENCES

- James Gibbs and other English Palladian architects
- English pattern books

LATE GEORGIAN INTERIOR

RESIDENTIAL EXAMPLES

- Tyron Palace (1770), New Bern, North Carolina
- Mount Pleasant (1761), Philadelphia, Pennsylvania
- Longfellow House (1750), Cambridge, Massachusetts
- Mount Airy (1758–62), Richmond County, Virginia
- Lady Pepperell House (1760), Kittery Point, Maine
- Miles-Brewton House (1765–69), Charleston, South Carolina
- Brandon (1765–70), Prince George County, Virginia
- Hammond-Harwood House (1773–74), Annapolis, Maryland

NONRESIDENTIAL EXAMPLES

- St. Michael's Church (1752–61), Charleston, South Carolina
- First Baptist Meetinghouse (1774–75), Providence, Rhode Island
- Redwood Library (1758–50), Newport, Rhode Island
- Brick Market (1761–62), Newport, Rhode Island

PALLADIAN WINDOW

Floors: Wooden plank

Walls: Large raised wooden panels, painted; also, dado with wallpaper above

Windows: Sash

Doors: Paneled, moldings with *ears* (molding breaks to form squares at corners)

Chimneypiece: Flush, with molding forming ears, and often with cornice and frieze; cornice forms mantel, over mantel with ears

Ceiling: Flat, plain or decorated with anaglypta

Stairs: Wooden U-turn, turned balusters

TEXTILE DESCRIPTION

Colors: Baroque and Rococo influence; more vivid colors—red, gold, blue, turquoise or teal, and rich coral sometimes lightened to soft peach

Patterns: Renaissance patterns still in use and strong influence of Chinese and Rococo motifs; English garden block-printed patterns

Textures: Smooth silklike textures in damask and brocade, printed cotton fabrics from slightly coarse to very refined; some velvets

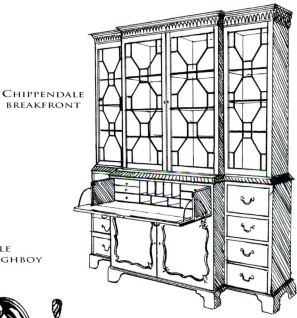

CHIPPENDALE
BREAKFRONT

CHIPPENDALE
WING CHAIR

CHIPPENDALE
PHILADELPHIA HIGHBOY

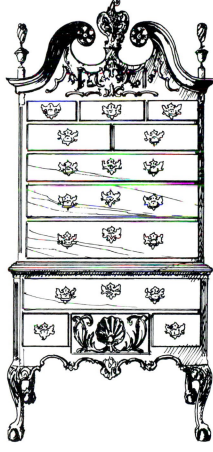

CHIPPENDALE
CAMEL-BACK SOFA

CHIPPENDALE BLOCK-
FRONT CHEST
(NEWPORT, RHODE
ISLAND)

CHIPPENDALE
LADDER-BACK CHAIR

CHINESE
CHIPPENDALE
CHAIR

LATE GEORGIAN
TEXTILES

CHIPPENDALE
SIDE CHAIR

CHIPPENDALE
TILT-TOP TABLE

Figure 15.4 *Federal-style (A) doorway with fanlight and sidelights, and (B-E) characteristic details from Boscobel.*

All © Ted Spiegel.

The Federal Style (1790–1830)

After British architect *Robert Adam* (1728–92), visited the Italian excavation sites at Pompeii and Herculaneum, he used his drawings of ancient Roman and Renaissance design to create a *Neoclassic* style. *Federal*-style houses generally are beautiful American adaptations of the Adam style from Georgian England. The typical Federal house has a symmetrical facade of five bays and, like the English prototype, usually has three stories. A few Federal houses have longer second-story windows that extend to the floor. These second-story rooms were the public spaces of the house and were given more importance with the larger windows—a concept related to the Renaissance idea of the piano nobile. The windows on the third level were usually smaller than the other two, a characteristic also typical of the English prototype. The Federal doorway was sometimes covered with a small portico similar to those designed for English *terrace houses* (row houses). The door itself was commonly topped with a roundheaded or delicate elliptical fanlight and flanked with a narrow set of windows called *sidelights*. The elliptical fan shape, discovered on the walls of Herculaneum, was possibly the most versatile and significant motif of the period. It was doubled to form ellipses known as *paterae*. These were used in every possible decorative fashion: furniture hardware, inlaid wood patterns on furniture, plaster patterns for ceilings, and elliptical room plans. The roof on the Federal house was low pitched and hipped, and it often featured a balustrade at the eaves.

The Federal period includes the work of Boston architect Charles Bullfinch, Samuel McIntire of Salem, and English transplant Benjamin Latrobe. Bullfinch's work was widely copied in the pattern books of the day and was likely the basis for much late eighteenth-century and early nineteenth-century architecture in New England. McIntire was a skilled carver as well as an architect, and his interiors and exteriors reflect the master's touch.

Federal Furniture Classics

The Hepplewhite and Sheraton style from England was fashionable during the Federal period. The Hepplewhite/Sheraton chairs are typical of the delicate Neoclassic style of the late eighteenth century. *George Hepplewhite* (d. 1786) produced a book called *The Cabinet-Maker and Upholsterer's Guide* (published posthumously in 1788), which contained furniture designs inspired by the work of Robert Adam. *Thomas Sheraton's* (1751–1806) *The Cabinet-Maker and Upholsterer's Drawing Book*, published in 1791, was filled with variations of Hepplewhite's designs. Because both men worked in the same style, it is often difficult to distinguish their designs. The distinctions are usually based on very slight differences in detail such as the direction of the curve on a drawer front or the shape of a chair back. Their chair designs featured straight square or *reeded* round, tapered legs without stretchers. The chair with the rectangular back is considered typical of the Sheraton style, and the shield- or heart-shaped back chairs are typical of Hepplewhite designs.

The Hepplewhite/Sheraton *sideboard* or *buffet* is a serving piece with drawers, raised on straight tapered legs. If the side drawers are concave, the piece is considered a Hepplewhite piece; if they are convex, it is considered a Sheraton piece.

The Hepplewhite/Sheraton *pembroke table* is a *drop-leaf occasional table* with a drawer in the apron. The top, when open, is oval in shape, and the legs are straight and tapered, without stretchers.

Federal Color

Colors during the Federal period were light and pastel. Americans were influenced by the French Neoclassical colors such as cream; powder green and pink; French lilac and turquoise; Sevres blue (a clear medium blue); Pompadour blue and DuBarry red (soft colors named after Louis XV's mistresses); and accentuated gold and silver tones. English and Americans added Robert Adam colors to the spectrum: a clear spring green called Adam green, dove gray, pale lavender, faded red, deep olive green, grayed green and blue, warm pink, and the Wedgewood jasperwear colors, which were tones of blue, warm coral pink, creamy sage or stark white—sometimes accentuated with gold leaf.

Jeffersonian Federal

Thomas Jefferson was not only an important statesman but also a fine architect, and his designs represent an important divergent style during the Federal period. Unlike the mainstream of Federal design, which was based on English prototypes, Jefferson based his work on the designs of classical Rome. In his role as statesman, Jefferson traveled to Europe where he saw remnants of Roman culture. He considered the ancient style appropriate for the new American republic and patterned his most famous nonresidential buildings after two well-known Roman temples. The Rotunda at the University of Virginia (1822–26) at Charlottesville is the American incarnation of the Pantheon in Rome, and the State House (1785–92) at Richmond, Virginia, is a larger version of the Maison Carrée in Nimes, France. His home, Monticello (1768–82), at Charlottesville, Virginia, features a prominent templelike portico that foreshadowed the ensuing Greek Revival style. The time Jefferson spent in France had a strong effect on the layout of Monticello as well as its dome—both were inspired by eighteenth-century Parisian hôtels (town houses). Jefferson's work constitutes a significant and influential departure from the typical Federal style.[4]

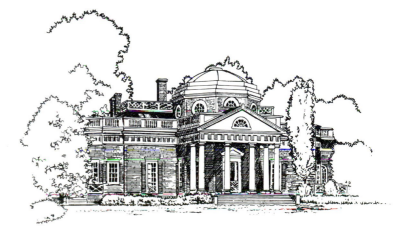

Figure 15.5 *Jefferson's Monticello, showing originality together with influence from Roman architecture.*

CHART 15.9   FEDERAL DESIGN AND HEPPLEWHITE/SHERATON FURNITURE

EXTERIOR CHARACTERISTICS

- Five-bay, three-story, box-shaped facade of brick, stucco, or clapboard
- Smaller windows on upper story
- Second-story windows to floor (optional)
- Doorway with fanlights and sidelights
- Flattened hipped roof with optional balustrade at eaves
- Classical detail from earlier periods such as the crown lintel, portico, Palladian window, stringcourse, and quoins (optional)

INFLUENCES

- Robert Adam
- English Georgian design

RESIDENTIAL EXAMPLES

- Pingree House (1804), Salem, Massachusetts; Samuel McIntire, architect
- Pierce-Nichols House (1782), Salem, Massachusetts; Samuel McIntire, architect
- Harrison Gray Otis House (1796), Boston, Massachusetts; Charles Bullfinch, architect
- Nathaniel Russell House (before 1809), Charleston, South Carolina
- Amory Ticknor House (1804), Boston, Massachusetts

NONRESIDENTIAL EXAMPLES

- State House (1795–98), Boston, Massachusetts; Charles Bullfinch, architect
- Baltimore Cathedral (1804–18), Baltimore, Maryland; Benjamin Latrobe, architect
- Lancaster Meeting House (1816–17), Lancaster, Massachusetts; Charles Bullfinch, architect
- United States Custom House (1819), Salem, Massachusetts

FEDERAL INTERIOR

FANLIGHT AND SIDELIGHTS

PINGREE HOUSE

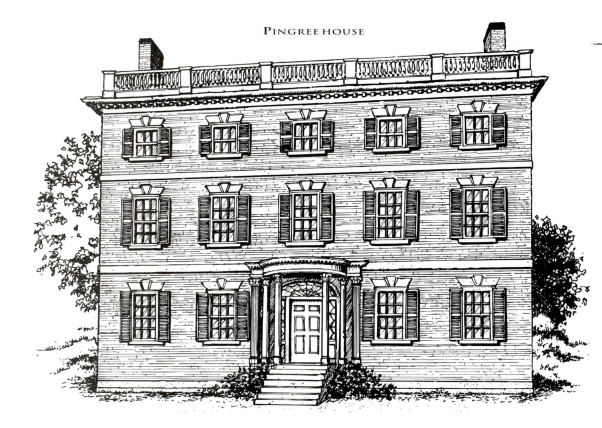

Floors: Wooden plank

Walls: Plain plaster; also dado with wallpaper above

Windows: Sash

Doors: Paneled, with fanlights used as transoms, sidelights

Chimneypiece: Projecting, classical, in the Adam style, with a raised panel in the center of the frieze

Ceiling: Plain, plaster with cornice molding

Stairs: Various configurations; wooden with turned balusters

TEXTILE DESCRIPTION

Colors: Pastel, light, creamy dull colors accented with white or a little rich color

Patterns: Fine stripes, garlands, bows, ribbons, oval shapes, classic Greek and Roman urns and motifs, tiny florals; in America also the pineapple (symbol of hospitality)

Textures: Plain satin, refined damask and brocade, plain and antique taffeta, batiste, moiré, voile, chintz (crisp cotton textures)

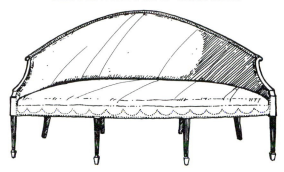

HEPPLEWHITE BOW-BACK SOFA

HEPPLEWHITE/SHERATON STYLE PEMBROKE TABLE

HEPPLEWHITE SIDEBOARD
(BUFFET)

SHERATON SQUARE-BACK CHAIR

HEPPLEWHITE SHIELD-BACK CHAIR

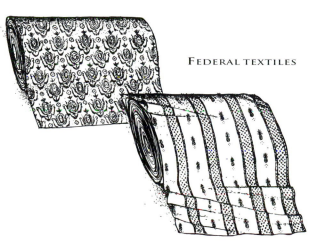

FEDERAL TEXTILES

CHART 15.10 THE VERNACULAR STYLE

CAPE COD EXTERIOR CHARACTERISTICS
- Small half house, three-quarter house, or full-sized house
- One story (some two-story versions built in Nantucket, Massachusetts)
- Gabled or rainbow roof, less steeply pitched than the Medieval houses (gambrel roofs make a Cape Ann house)
- Sash windows directly under the eaves
- Shallow eaves
- Doorway with simplified pilasters and entablature
- Shingle siding (some clapboard)

INFLUENCES
- Seventeenth-century Medieval houses
- Early Georgian houses
- New England ship carpenters

RESIDENTIAL EXAMPLES
- Kendrick House (c. 1790), Orleans, Massachusetts
- Shadrach Standish House (1730), Halifax, Massachusetts
- Hezekia Swain-Maria Mitchell House (1790), Nantucket, Massachusetts

CAPE COD COTTAGE
KENDRICK HOUSE

VERNACULAR GEORGIAN

DEACON'S BENCH

The Vernacular Tradition (Seventeenth Century–Present)

In spite of over a century of exposure to classical influences, grassroots American architecture held tenaciously to the English Medieval tradition. Generally it was only the wealthy upper class who built the classically inspired houses discussed thus far. The vast majority of people living in America built adaptations of the new styles using the sturdy Medieval house form with its gabled roof, and others remodeled existing seventeenth-century houses, adding new details to make the Medieval house more stylish and up-to-date. For example, during the Early Georgian period symmetrically placed sash windows and pilastered and pedimented doorways gave the gabled house a feeling of the new style.

During the Federal period, the addition of fanlights and sidelights at the doorway imparted a sense of belonging to the era. These hybrid houses are referred to as *vernacular*, which literally means common, and implies the houses were adapted by local builders and developed regional characteristics. It also implies a naive, unschooled approach to design quite different from that which attempted to copy faithfully the fine English

houses. Vernacular design may result from lack of exposure or resources, or it may represent a strong-willed independence or personal preference. Vernacular is not a negative term; most vernacular houses are charming and, in fact, are the most enduring type of house in America. The majority of colonial-style homes built today are vernacular versions of the Georgian- or Federal-style houses. Though vernacular is generally considered a quality rather than a style, some vernacular houses are so distinctive and well known that they have become styles.

The Cape Cod Cottage (Seventeenth Century–Present)

The dwellings characteristic of rural Cape Cod, Massachusetts, have come to typify the American small house. The Cape Cod cottage is a one-story gabled house, usually finished in shingle siding that was allowed to weather to a soft gray in the salty coastal air. In the eighteenth century, the steep Medieval-style roof was lowered and sash windows and classical doorway details were added to make the houses more in step with the times. A few houses had slightly bowed roofs, called *rainbow roofs*, attributed to shipbuilders. (This type of house with a gambrel roof

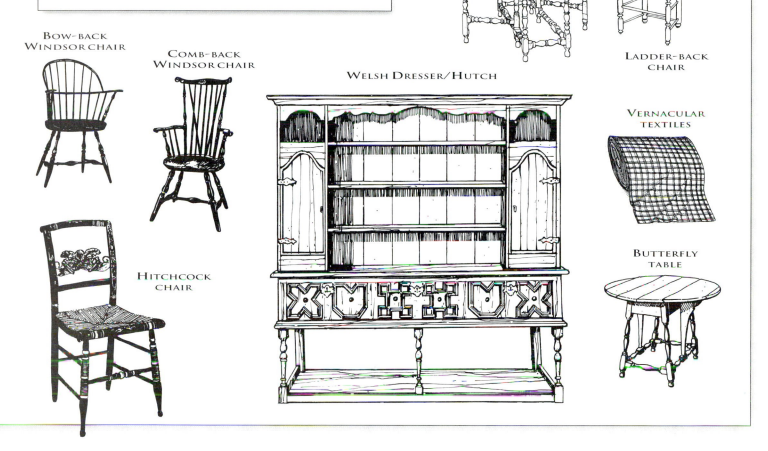

GATELEG TABLE

LADDER-BACK CHAIR

BOW-BACK WINDSOR CHAIR

COMB-BACK WINDSOR CHAIR

WELSH DRESSER/HUTCH

VERNACULAR TEXTILES

HITCHCOCK CHAIR

BUTTERFLY TABLE

Figure 15.6 *This twentieth-century adaptation of the Cape Cod house in Iowa is evidence of the consistent popularity of the style.*

is called a Cape Ann house.) The eaves of the houses are very shallow, which gives them a crisp, boxy character. The size of the houses varied: a one-room half house of three bays, a four-bay, three-quarter house with one large and one small room, or a full-sized, five-bay double house containing two full-sized rooms with the doorway in the center. The Cape Cod house has maintained its popularity since it was introduced in the seventeenth century.

Vernacular Furniture Classics

Several pieces of vernacular furniture used by the common people throughout the eighteenth and nineteenth centuries still have great appeal for today's interiors. The American *ladder-back chair* is an important piece based on an English prototype. It has a frame made of straight members turned in a fashion that resembles a string of sausages (called sausage turnings) and joined with stretchers. The ladder-back chair would often appear in more humble homes or in the kitchens and servants' quarters of grander homes. Like some other provincial chairs, the ladder-back chair has a seat of woven rush.

The Welsh dresser or *hutch* is a side piece with cupboards, drawers, and a set of open shelves above. The hutch is descended from a sixteenth-century French kitchen cupboard and was popular in England in the seventeenth century as well as in Early America.

The American *Windsor chair,* as the name implies, is based on an English prototype. The Windsor chair is characterized by its saddle-shaped seat, turned legs with stretchers, and spindle back. The early versions were invariably painted. The most common backs are the curved bow or loop back and the comb back. Some later Windsor chairs featured legs turned to resemble bamboo. The English Windsor chair has a pierced splat and may have cabriole legs (see chart 8.1, p. 160).

The *Hitchcock chair* was designed by *Lambert Hitchcock* (1795–1852), a Connecticut designer. The chair shows the influence of Sheraton and English Regency designs and is characterized by its black painted finish, turned legs, rush or cane seat, and gold stenciled fruit and flower decoration.

The Greek Revival/American Empire Style (1820–60)

The *Greek Revival* grew out of the spirit of the times and was a natural expression of the growing independence of American culture. Greek mythology, culture, and often even the classical Greek language were part of the educational training during the early nineteenth century. Literature and art often alluded to the ancient Greeks, and the Greek war of independence from Turkey had focused the world's attention on modern Greece. The Greek style was not tied directly to English influences. In fact, the Greek Revival was the first style that was truly harmonious with the American vernacular taste for the gabled house. The gabled end of the house, when turned toward the street, became a Greek temple facade. It was adaptable enough to make it suitable for fine city dwellings as well as regional vernacular houses.

The style found acceptance everywhere in the country, but it varied so much in its interpretation that it is difficult to identify a single set of characteristics. The one characteristic that seems to be universal is the use of all or part of the Greek temple form on a one- or two-story dwelling. The most extravagant examples feature a full Doric, Ionic, Corinthian, and even Roman Tuscan colonnade with a complete entablature, and the most unassuming interpretations are those where the gabled end forms an extremely simple pedimented facade that is turned toward the street. The Greek Revival door opening was generally flanked by sidelights and headed by an oblong transom (over-the-door window). The doorway might be framed by a full portico or simply trimmed with pilasters and an entablature; pilasters were sometimes used to give definition to the facade. The basic two-story temple form might be given additional space with one-story flanking wings.

American Empire Furniture Classics

The interior and furniture styles of the Greek Revival are referred to as *American Empire* style. Much of the furniture from the American Empire era was based on French and British prototypes. The French Empire and English Regency styles date from the early nineteenth century, during the reign of Napoleon in France and George IV in England. Much of the furniture from this period was heavy, based on designs from Rome, yet some of the chairs were amazingly light and delicate—inspired by a new appreciation for the designs of classical Greece, and maintaining much of the delicacy of the previous Louis XVI and Sheraton styles. The Empire and Regency designs made their way to Northern Europe and America, where the styles are known respectively as *Biedermeier* and American Empire or *Regency.* *Duncan Phyfe* (1768–1854), a Scottish cabinetmaker who worked in New York, is famous for his delicate Regency-style furniture. His designs often incorporated the lyre or harp as a prominent motif. Until recently, only the Phyfe designs from this period had widespread popularity. However, today the heavier *French Empire* and Biedermeier styles are beginning to find wide acceptance as antiques, and their reproductions are being manufactured in larger numbers.

Empire Color

The Empire style, which was strongly influenced by French taste, was a reflection of Napoleon's campaigns and personal admiration for the classical interiors. The colors that predominated are: bright royal red and gold; emerald to olive green; majestic purple and brown; and accents of pale mauve, cream, white, or black. The bold color statements were seen particularly in upholstery, draperies, and broadloom woven (Wilton and Axminster) carpeting.

Figure 15.7 *Stanton Hall in Natchez, Mississippi, exemplifies the stately quality of the Greek Revival style.*

© David A. Taylor.

EXTERIOR CHARACTERISTICS

- Bold forms with an emphasis on strength rather than delicacy
- Greek temple form with pediment (gabled end) oriented toward the front
- Porticoes and colonnades with two-story Greek columns
- Some use of Roman Tuscan columns
- Exterior finish of stone, brick, wooden siding, or stucco
- Sash windows
- Door openings flanked with sidelights and headed with oblong transoms, or flanked with pilasters and crowned with an entablature

INFLUENCES

- Previous classical styles
- The architecture of classical Greece and Rome
- Some French influence

RESIDENTIAL EXAMPLES

- Andalusia (1836), Bucks County, Pennsylvania
- Joseph Bowers House (1825), Northampton, Massachusetts
- Russell House (1828–30), Middletown, Connecticut (now Honors College, Wesleyan University)
- Shadows-on-the-Teche (1830), New Iberia, Louisiana
- James Lanier House (1844), Madison, Indiana
- Dunlieth (1847), Natchez, Mississippi
- Alonzo Olds House (1848), Rushton, Michigan

NONRESIDENTIAL EXAMPLES

- Philadelphia Water Works (1819), Philadelphia, Pennsylvania
- Girard College (1833), Philadelphia, Pennsylvania
- Second Bank of the United States (1924), Philadelphia, Pennsylvania
- Quincy Market (1825), Boston, Massachusetts
- Hibernian Hall (1835), Charleston, South Carolina
- Congregational Church (1838), Madison, Connecticut

SHADOWS-ON-THE-TECHE

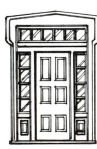

DOORWAY WITH TRANSOM

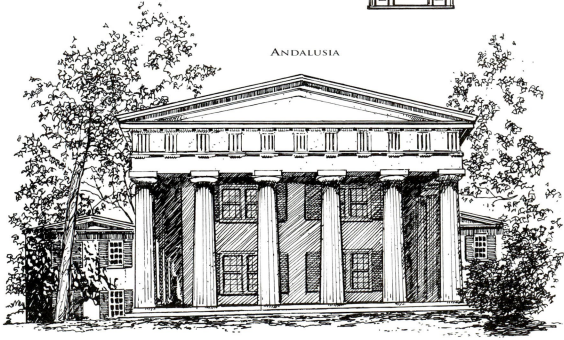

ANDALUSIA

INTERIOR DETAILS

Floors: Wooden plank, patterned broadloom carpet

Walls: Plain plaster or chair rail

Windows: Sash or French doors

Doors: Paneled, heavy molding; wooden transom with cornice

Chimneypiece: Projecting, classical, black marble, or faux painted

Ceiling: Plain with crown or cornice molding, anaglypta

Stairs: Several configurations; curved was popular; wooden with turned balusters

TEXTILE DESCRIPTION

Colors: French-inspired color schemes included rich vivid red, gold, deep green, brown, and royal purple; these were also used in America and were sometimes softened to pale mauve, spun honey, dull greens and browns, and dull gray-violet

Patterns: Plain satin background with isolated small motifs such as the laurel wreath, the star or snowflake, honeybee, or classical urns; also the griffin, festooning, both broad and blended satin stripes

Textures: Plain satin, antique taffeta and silk textures, various sheer and semisheer fabrics

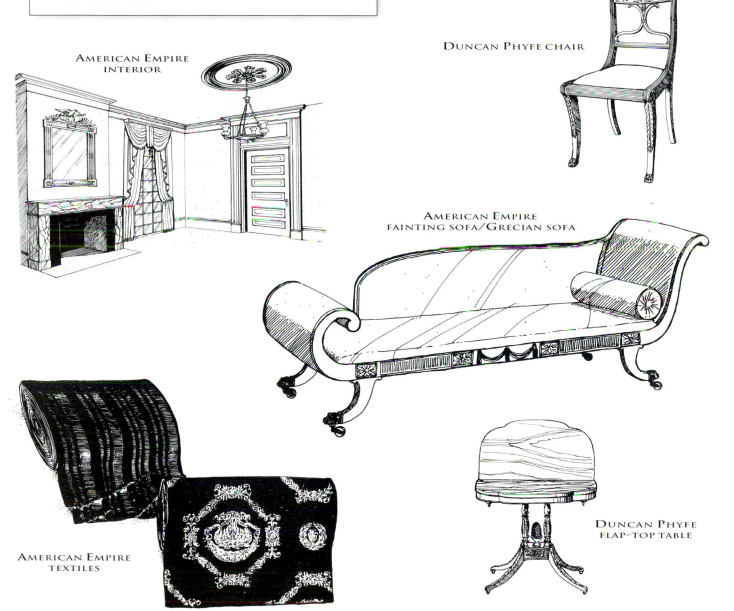

AMERICAN EMPIRE
CONSOLE TABLE

DUNCAN PHYFE CHAIR

AMERICAN EMPIRE
INTERIOR

AMERICAN EMPIRE
FAINTING SOFA/GRECIAN SOFA

AMERICAN EMPIRE
TEXTILES

DUNCAN PHYFE
FLAP-TOP TABLE

The Victorian Age in America (1837–1901)

The *Victorian era* in America corresponds to the reign of Queen Victoria of England from 1837 to 1901, though the architectural styles attached to her name extended beyond the turn of the century and coexisted with the radical new architectural developments of the Modern era. This coexistence was less than peaceful and may account for the scorn that, until recently, was heaped upon Victorian design.

Victorian architecture is not a single style but a succession and *eclectic* mixing of styles. Some of the styles have their roots in the philosophies of the nineteenth century. For example, the Gothic Revival was fired by the notion that pagan buildings (Greek and Roman) were not fit for Christian living—the only suitable style for Christians was the Gothic. However, those who adopted the styles were likely less concerned with philosophy than with aesthetics.

The nineteenth century saw the full bloom of the Industrial Revolution and a rapid succession of advancements that radically changed the way people lived. The fireplace and stove were replaced by central heating. Gas lighting and, eventually, electric lighting took the place of oil lamps and candles. Indoor plumbing made the outhouse and water pump things of the past. The modern life-style with its many conveniences, often taken for granted today, was developed by the Victorians.

The advancement of technology also paved the way for migration from the farm to the city, where industry was creating a growing middle class and a new wealthy class. This rapid change in society seemed to trigger a proliferation of decorative styles and treatments that have become the hallmark of Victorian design. As each new Victorian style developed, elements of former styles were retained and adapted to create an eclectic design patchwork that signaled the end of classical dominance. Each new variation in style was historical in nature but lacked the authenticity of the original styles upon which they were based. They were re-creations of a distant and romantic past by craftsmen in possession of the new technology of the Industrial Revolution. The most important of these styles were the Gothic Revival, Italianate, Egyptian Revival, Oriental, Mansard, Stick, Shingle, and Queen Anne styles.

Victorian Furniture Classics

Because the Industrial Revolution spawned a large furniture industry, many new pieces and styles emerged during the nineteenth century. Foremost among the styles were the Gothic Revival advocated by Englishman *Charles Eastlake* (1793–1865), the Rococo Revival, and the Renaissance Revival.

Eastlake wrote a book called *Hints on Household Taste* that discussed furniture of good taste based on Medieval and Japanese influences. He was opposed to the rapid changes in style and the machine construction so common during the Victorian

Figure 15.8 *Two examples of Victorian taste for lavish design:* (A) *Italianate style and* (B) *(opposite) Queen Anne style.*
(A) © *Guy Gillette/Photo Researchers, Inc.* (B) © *Bob Firth/International Stock Photo.*

era. The calls of Eastlake and others for a return to the simple handcraftsmanship of the Middle Ages did little to stem the tide of mass production, but it did heighten the taste for Gothic design.

The Rococo Revival was based on eighteenth-century French Rococo designs and featured a fantastic array of curved lines in both wooden and upholstered pieces. *John Henry Belter* (d. 1865) created heavily carved pieces of furniture from laminated rosewood, and his name is often associated with the Rococo Revival style.

The Renaissance Revival was influenced in part by the writings of Eastlake. A return to clean, straight lines was seen as an Eastlake principle, and many of the rectilinear designs actually came to be known as the Eastlake style. Renaissance Revival pieces also bear a strong resemblance to Louis XVI furniture. This style is also characterized by the use of a segmental pediment form in many pieces.

(B)

Victorian Color

The Victorian era was an age of richly furnished eclecticism. This era is often referred to as the mauve decades, supporting colors such as deep, old-looking red and faded rose red or mauve, wine and dark violet, taupe, and black. Also seen were sage, dark olive, clear green, dark and creamy gold, tobacco brown, rust, and accents of royal blue, bright red and magenta in traditionally designed textile patterns. From the turn of the century through the 1930s, many pure revivals were seen and colors were often documented to the era of the revival.

CHART 15.12   VICTORIAN DESIGN

GOTHIC REVIVAL

ITALIANATE STYLE

GOTHIC REVIVAL EXTERIOR CHARACTERISTICS

- Steeply pitched gables (sometimes combined with low-hipped roof)
- Parapets or battlements (low walls on the roof) that are crenellated (notched)
- Towers, spires, and finials on the roof
- Stone construction (finer houses only)
- Vertical wooden siding of board and batten (these wooden houses are called Carpenter's Gothic)
- Lacy wooden version of Gothic tracery called gingerbread used to decorate eaves and porches
- Pointed Gothic and flattened Tudor arches used for window, door, and veranda framing
- Leaded pane windows

RESIDENTIAL EXAMPLES

- Lyndhurst (1838), Tarrytown, New York; Alexander Jackson Davis, architect
- Greystone (c. 1859), Pevely, Missouri
- Town Office Building (1847), Cazenovia, New York; Andrew Jackson Downing, architect

NONRESIDENTIAL EXAMPLES

- St. Patrick's Cathedral (1858–79), New York, New York; James Renwick, architect
- Brooklyn Bridge (1869–83), New York, New York
- Baptist Church (1878), North Salem, New York
- Calvary Presbyterian Church (1883), Portland, Oregon

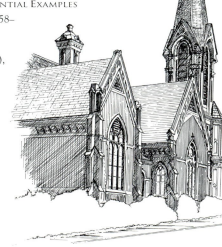

ITALIANATE EXTERIOR CHARACTERISTICS

- Also called Italian and Tuscan, inspired by Italian country houses and Prince Albert's design of Osborne House in England
- Low-pitched hipped or gabled roof
- Wide overhanging cornices with large brackets
- Square tower with a low pitched roof (optional)
- Belvedere (lookout with windows in tower)
- Roundheaded windows (optional)
- Ornate versions of classical details such as modillions and pediments
- Often used for New York brownstone and other city row houses

RESIDENTIAL EXAMPLES

- David Mayer Farmhouse (1867), Lancaster, Pennsylvania
- Edward King House (1845), Newport, Rhode Island
- Mills-Stebbins House (1849–51), Springfield, Massachusetts
- Morse-Libby House (1859), Portland, Maine

NONRESIDENTIAL EXAMPLES

- Haughwout Building (1857), New York, New York (cast-iron facade)
- Sanger-Peper Building (1874), St. Louis, Missouri (cast-iron facade)

GOTHIC REVIVAL, CALVARY PRESBYTERIAN CHURCH

EGYPTIAN REVIVAL, WHALER'S CHURCH

ORIENTAL REVIVAL, LONGWOOD

EGYPTIAN REVIVAL EXTERIOR CHARACTERISTICS

- Not philosophically suited for residential design but was considered appropriate for cemetery gates, tombs, and mausoleums (perhaps because of the Egyptian preoccupation with the afterlife and preparation for death)
- Also used for prisons and churches
- Featured sloping walls with wide cornices

NONRESIDENTIAL EXAMPLES

- Whaler's Church (1844), Sag Harbor, New York
- Gates, Grove St. Cemetery (1848), New Haven, Connecticut

MANSARD STYLE

ORIENTAL EXTERIOR CHARACTERISTICS

- Also called Moorish or Persian, inspired by Islamic design
- Pointed and horseshoe Moorish arches used for doorways, windows, and porches
- Bulbous onion domes used to crown towers or belvederes

RESIDENTIAL EXAMPLES

- Longwood (1860), Natchez, Mississippi
- Olana (1870–72), near Hudson, New York

NONRESIDENTIAL EXAMPLES

- Wise Temple (1866), Cincinnati, Ohio

MANSARD EXTERIOR CHARACTERISTICS

- Also called Second Empire and influenced by nineteenth-century French design
- Also called General Grant Style because it was popular during the presidency of Ulysses S. Grant
- Mansard roof crested with a low, wrought-iron railing
- Dormer windows that rest on or break through the line of the eaves
- Quoins (optional)

RESIDENTIAL EXAMPLES

- Governor's Mansion (1871), Jefferson City, Missouri
- John DeKoven House (1874), Chicago, Illinois
- Governor's Mansion (1878), Sacramento, California
- Iolani Palace (1882), Honolulu, Hawaii

NONRESIDENTIAL EXAMPLES

- City Hall (1872–1901), Philadelphia, Pennsylvania
- Grand Union Hotel (1872), Saratoga Springs, New York
- McKinley High School (1872), Lincoln, Nebraska
- Hill County Courthouse (1890), Hillsboro, Texas

continued

CHART 15.12 VICTORIAN DESIGN *continued*

STICK STYLE,
GRISWOLD HOUSE

QUEEN ANNE
STYLE

STICK EXTERIOR CHARACTERISTICS

- Victorian version of Late English Medieval house
- Steep gables
- Stickwork patterning applied to represent vertical, diagonal, and horizontal timber construction
- Jetties or overhangs

RESIDENTIAL EXAMPLES

- Griswold House (1862–63), Newport, Rhode Island
- Emlen Physick House (1879), Cape May, New Jersey

SHINGLE EXTERIOR CHARACTERISTICS

- Inspired by colonial seaside dwellings like the Cape Cod, Cape Ann, and Nantucket houses; appeared first as resort houses on the eastern seaboard
- Covered with shingles
- Small paned windows

RESIDENTIAL EXAMPLES

- Kragsyde (1884), Manchester-by-the Sea, Massachusetts
- Dr. John Bryant House (1880), Cohasset, Massachusetts; Henry Hobson Richardson, architect
- William Low House (1887), Bristol, Rhode Island; McKim, Mead, and White, architects
- Frank Lloyd Wright House (1889), Oak Park, Illinois; Frank Lloyd Wright, architect

QUEEN ANNE EXTERIOR CHARACTERISTICS

- Features a variety of decoration and surface embellishments such as stone, rounded fish-scale shingles, clapboard, stickwork, lathwork, turned balusters, and fretwork
- Strong horizontal lines or bands
- Combination of gabled and steep-hipped rooflines
- Turret (towers) often rounded with round pointed roofs
- Rounded gazebos—part of the veranda
- Moon gate arch—part of the veranda (optional)
- Some use of stained glass

RESIDENTIAL EXAMPLES

- Miss Parks House (1876), Cape May, New Jersey
- Glenmont (1880), West Orange, New Jersey
- Haas-Lilienthal House (1886), San Francisco, California

NONRESIDENTIAL EXAMPLES

- Hotel del Coronado (1888), Coronado, California

SHINGLE STYLE,
KRAGSYDE

INTERIOR DETAILS

Floors: Wood plank

Walls: Plain plaster with wallpaper

Windows: Sash—large panes of glass

Doors: Paneled; some sliding pocket doors

Chimneypiece: Projecting carved marble, with a roundheaded arched opening

Ceiling: Mass-produced crown moldings, anaglypta patterns, and chandelier medallions of plaster

Stairs: Various configurations, straight run favored; wooden with turned balusters and elaborate newel posts

TEXTILE DESCRIPTION

Colors: Called the mauve decades—due to the many varieties of dull, somber reds; also deeper values of green, blue, violet, and gold; backgrounds were often off-white or black

Patterns: Copied and adapted, stylized and combined from many sources including Gothic, Egyptian, Byzantine, Oriental, Neoclassic, Rococo, Renaissance, with plenty of large- and small-scale floral and lacy patterns

Textures: Velvets of every description, woven Jacquard fabrics from very smooth to very heavy, cotton prints, lace, and heavy trimming

VICTORIAN INTERIOR

VICTORIAN BELTER/ROCOCO REVIVAL TABLE

VICTORIAN BELTER/ROCOCO REVIVAL ARMCHAIR

VICTORIAN RENAISSANCE REVIVAL SIDE CHAIR

VICTORIAN GOTHIC REVIVAL SIDE CHAIR

VICTORIAN RENAISSANCE REVIVAL CABINET

VICTORIAN TEXTILES

Figure 15.9 *Exquisite Shaker craftsmanship.*
© Ted Spiegel.

OTHER INFLUENCES IN AMERICA

The Shaker Influence

In contrast to contemporary Victorian designs, Shaker furniture was particularly simple. The *Shakers* were a nineteenth-century religious group whose beliefs included the design of furniture free from excessive decoration. The Shaker chair has straight legs with straight stretchers and straight uprights with simply formed slats or a woven back. Like the woven backs, the seats are generally webbed with cotton tapes. The uprights and arms might be finished with simple finials, and the top rail was sometimes designed to accommodate a folded blanket.

The Shaker candlestand is a small *tripod pedestal table* of beautiful proportions and delicate lines. Like other Shaker pieces, it is remarkable because of the purity of its design and its suitability in contemporary environments.

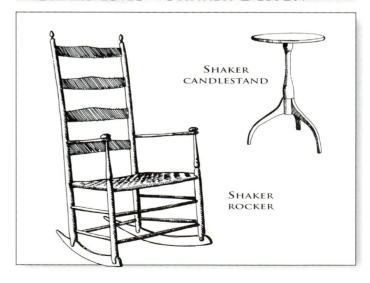

CHART 15.13 SHAKER DESIGN

SHAKER CANDLESTAND

SHAKER ROCKER

CHART 15.14 GERMAN/PENNSYLVANIA DUTCH DESIGN

EXTERIOR CHARACTERISTICS

- Large, simple, rectangular construction
- Built of roughly finished fieldstone or brick
- Transoms over front door
- Sash windows
- Gabled or gambrel roof
- A narrow, overhanging rooflike projection between the first and second stories, called a *pent roof* (optional)
- *Cantilevered* (unsupported) triangular portico (optional)

RESIDENTIAL EXAMPLES

- Troxell-Steckel House (1756), Egypt, Pennsylvania
- Thompson-Neely House (1710), Washington Crossing, Pennsylvania
- Georg Mueller House (1752), Milbach, Pennsylvania

NONRESIDENTIAL EXAMPLES

- Washington's Headquarters (1758), Valley Forge State Park, Pennsylvania
- Trout Hall (1770), Allentown, Pennsylvania

PENNSYLVANIA DUTCH
TROXELL-STECKEL HOUSE

PENNSYLVANIA DUTCH
MARRIAGE CHEST

The Swedish Influence

Seventeenth-century Scandinavian settlers introduced the house type for which America is most famous—the log cabin. The log house was a typical Scandinavian rural architectural form adapted by eighteenth- and nineteenth-century settlers of many origins. As Americans pushed the country's borders westward, the log cabin made a strong and quick shelter.

Closer to our own time, the simple dwelling has been adapted for the construction of rustic cabins and resort hotels, such as Old Faithful Inn (1904) at Yellowstone National Park.

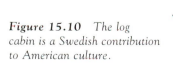

Figure 15.10 The log cabin is a Swedish contribution to American culture.

The German Influence

The German settlers in Pennsylvania used the plentiful local gray and brown fieldstone to build houses that varied only slightly from the mainstream of American English architecture. The Germans or Deutsch were mistakenly called Pennsylvania Dutch, a designation that has endured.

The Pennsylvania Dutch have long been noted for their arts and crafts. The marriage chest, used to hold a young woman's dowry, was often painted in an artistic and decorative manner and is a good example of the Pennsylvania Dutch style.

The Dutch Influence

Nothing remains of the seventeenth-century Dutch buildings in New York City (originally New Amsterdam), and of all the Dutch houses in America, the most distinctive type may not even be Dutch. Historians differ as to whether the so-called Dutch house, with the bell-shaped gambrel roof and flaring eaves, was

CHART 15.15 DUTCH DESIGN

CHART 15.16 FRENCH DESIGN

EXTERIOR CHARACTERISTICS
- Houses of stone, brick, or clapboard
- Gambrel roof with a line that breaks near the ridge
- Flaring eaves that give the roof a bell shape
- Sash windows and doors typical of mainstream English/American design

RESIDENTIAL EXAMPLES
- Dyckman House (1783), New York, New York
- Zabriskie-Von Steuben House (1752), Hackensack, New Jersey
- Richard Vreeland House (1786), Leonia, New Jersey
- Jacobus Demarest House (1719), Bergen County, New Jersey

**DUTCH DESIGN
DYCKMAN HOUSE**

EXTERIOR CHARACTERISTICS
- Galerie
- French doors
- French windows
- Bonnet roof, sometimes with dormer windows
- Frequently built over a raised basement

RESIDENTIAL EXAMPLES:
- Madame John's Legacy (c. 1727), New Orleans, Louisiana
- La Veuve-Dodier House (1766), St. Louis, Missouri
- The Fortier-Keller House (1801), St. Charles Parish, Louisiana
- Le Pretre Mansion (1836), New Orleans, Louisiana

**FRENCH DESIGN
MADAME JOHN'S LEGACY**

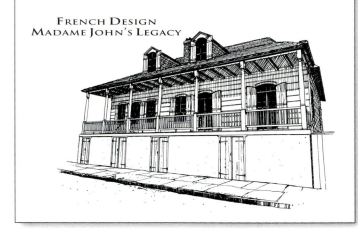

an American or Flemish development. Regardless of its origins, the house type has come to be known as Dutch Colonial. Unlike the Dutch, who were merchants, the Flemish settlers were generally farmers and built fine farmhouses.

The French Influence

The architectural characteristics of the houses of French settlers along the southern part of the Mississippi River were distinctive but not all were strongly tied to the architecture of France. Instead they represented an adaptability to the warm and wet climate and water-logged terrain of that region.

The stucco-covered houses with steeply pitched hipped roofs built by Norman French settlers were soon fitted with an encircling porch called a *galerie*. The roof was extended at a lower pitch to cover the galerie, forming a *bonnet roof* ideally suited to protect from rain and heat. French doors and casement windows opened onto the galerie and allowed the air to move freely through the house. The galerie with French windows and doors was also an important feature that persisted in the design of Greek Revival and Victorian houses of the area. These French details imparted a quality of elegance that is still associated with southern culture. Low piers raised some French houses above the dampness. Some houses were built above a raised basement—it was used as a service area and also offered protection from flooding or dampness in areas with high water tables.

The French town houses of New Orleans were built around galeried garden courtyards. During the Victorian era, with the advent of cast iron, galeries were also added to the front of the houses. These galeries of lacelike cast iron, though found elsewhere, are a symbol of New Orleans and add a touch of character that makes that city particularly charming.

The influence of France is not limited to the Mississippi basin. Many Americans of all ancestries have loved French style. French design has always been considered sophisticated and the court styles of Louis XV, Louis XVI, and today the Empire style have been widely accepted. Design from the provinces of France is a less formal but nonetheless sophisticated version of French taste loved by Americans to this day.

French Furniture Classics

The French pieces so widely used and accepted today come principally from the Rococo period of Louis XV (as well as the transitional Règence period that preceded it), the Neoclassical Louis XVI period, and the provincial countryside of France. The French Règence *fauteuil* is an open armchair from the period of *French Règence* (1715–23), between the reigns of Louis XIV and Louis XV. The piece is characterized by the use of cane for the back and seat, cabriole legs, and stretchers between the legs.

CHART 15.17 FRENCH ROCOCO/LOUIS XV DESIGN

INTERIOR DETAILS

Floors: Parquet

Walls: Large, rectangular, painted wooden panels, often with carved or painted asymmetrical, curvilinear designs; French paneling is called *boiserie*

Windows: Long French casement or French doors

Doors: Paneled, double doors

Chimneypiece: Projecting, ornate carved marble, curvilinear opening

Ceiling: Flat, plain, cove molding

Stairs: Stone U-stair, with ornate wrought-iron balustrade

TEXTILE DESCRIPTION

Colors: Colors were soft and feminine—turquoise, rose, warm creamy yellow, pale sage green

Patterns: Shells were quite popular, along with ribbons, scrolls, loveknots, country folk in country scenes, and Chinese chinoiserie motifs—pagodas, architecture, nature scenes, fretwork, and Chinese people in native dress

Textures: Fabrics were very refined and smooth—taffeta, chiffon, damask, brocade, velvet, lampas, batiste

FRENCH ROCOCO
INTERIOR

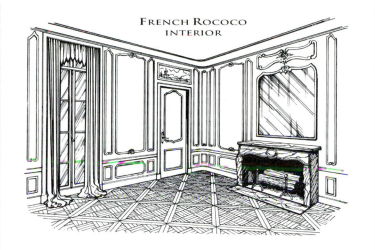

ROCOCO BERGÉRE
(UPHOLSTERED ARMCHAIR)

RÉGENCE (PRE-ROCOCO)
FAUTEUIL
(OPEN ARMCHAIR)

ROCOCO
CONSOLE TABLE

ROCOCO
BUREAU-Á-CYLINDRE
(ROLLTOP DESK)

ROCOCO COMMODE
(LOW CHEST OF DRAWERS)

ROCOCO FAUTEUIL
(OPEN ARMCHAIR)

ROCOCO TEXTILES

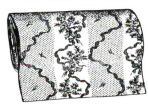

CHART 15.18 FRENCH NEOCLASSICAL/LOUIS XVI DESIGN

INTERIOR DETAILS

Floors: Parquet wood

Walls: Large, rectilinear, painted wooden panels

Windows: Tall French casement or French windows

Doors: Paneled, double doors

Chimneypiece: Projecting, carved marble, rectilinear with corner-block designs

Ceiling: Flat, plain, with decorative cornice

Stairs: Stone U-stair, with wrought-iron balustrade

TEXTILE DESCRIPTION

Colors: Pastel, light, creamy dull colors accented with white or a little rich color

Patterns: Fine stripes, garlands, bows, ribbons, oval shapes, classic Greek and Roman urns and motifs, tiny florals

Textures: Plain satin, refined damask and brocade, plain and antique taffeta, batiste, moiré, voile

FRENCH NEOCLASSICAL INTERIOR

FRENCH NEOCLASSICAL BERGÉRE
(UPHOLSTERED ARMCHAIR)

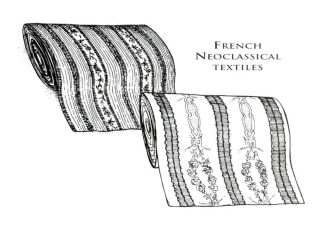

FRENCH NEOCLASSICAL TEXTILES

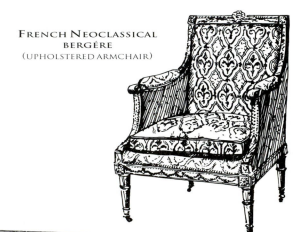

FRENCH NEOCLASSICAL FAUTEUIL
(OPEN ARMCHAIR)

FRENCH NEOCLASSICAL BUREAU PLAT
(WRITING TABLE)

Figure 15.11 *Country French charm is seen in the ladderback chair and the neoclassically inspired bed.*
Courtesy of Laura Ashley.

The Louis XV fauteuil is an open armchair from the *Rococo* (1723–74) or *Louis XV period*. The lines of the chair are curvilinear, it has no stretchers, and it has an upholstered seat and back. The line of the cabriole leg continues without a break into the line of the apron.

The Louis XVI fauteuil is an open armchair from the French Neoclassic (1774–93) or *Louis XVI period*. The piece is characterized by the rectilinear lines of classical design. The chair back is generally either oval or rectangular, and the straight tapered legs have no stretchers.

The French *bergère* is an upholstered armchair with fully upholstered sides. The fauteuil has an open space between the armrest and the seat, but on the bergère that space is filled with cushioning and fabric.

The chaise á capucine or fauteuil á la bonne femme is a ladder-back chair with a rush seat from the provinces of France. Provincial designs were influenced by court styles, so the chair may feature straight or curved lines, depending on the influence. Most of the fine reproductions feature curved back slats and legs.

The Country French *armoire* is a large carved wardrobe used for storage. Like the fauteuil á la bonne femme, the design of the armoire was influenced by the designs at court and may show asymmetrical elements common to the Rococo style or the rectilinear qualities of Louis XVI designs.

CHART 15.19 COUNTRY FRENCH DESIGN

INTERIOR DETAILS

Floors: Wooden plank, terra cotta tile

Walls: Stucco or papered

Windows: French casement

Doors: French doors

Chimneypiece: Simple version of Renaissance hooded fireplace; also, carved natural wood version of Rococo chimneypiece with curved opening

Ceiling: Plain or beamed

Stairs: Various configurations of wooden stairway with plain balusters

TEXTILE DESCRIPTION

Colors: In the Provinces, the colors were deep and somber—royal blue, cranberry red, goldenrod yellow, rich avocado green, accents of black; printed textiles sport light, lively florals

Patterns: Shells were quite popular, along with ribbons, scroll, love knots, country folk in country scenes, and Chinese chinoiserie motifs—pagodas, architecture, nature scenes, fretwork, and Chinese people in native dress

Textures: Fabrics included tapestry, printed toile de Jouy, floral fabrics, sturdy twill ticking, and woven tweeds such as houndstooth and herringbone

COUNTRY FRENCH
INTERIOR

COUNTRY
FRENCH
TEXTILE

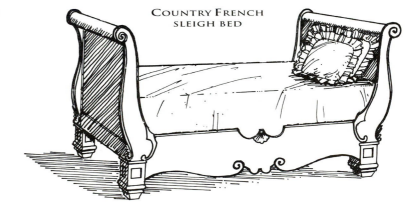

COUNTRY FRENCH
SLEIGH BED

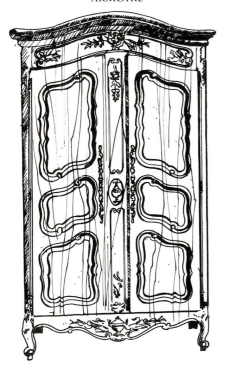

COUNTRY FRENCH
ARMOIRE

COUNTRY FRENCH
LADDER-BACK
CHAIR

COUNTRY FRENCH
PANETIÉRE
(BREAD KEEPER)

The Spanish Influence

The earliest Spanish settlement in America was at St. Augustine, Florida, predating English settlement in Virginia by nearly fifty years. However, due to lack of colonization, frequent destruction and rebuilding, and repeated English inhabitation, no significant influences of these original Spanish settlements remain.

Spanish Missions

The Spanish also controlled the area along the southwestern border of the United States, from present-day Texas to California. Traces of Spanish influence can be seen throughout that region, particularly in the design of missions and churches. These were vernacular designs incorporating Spanish detailing contributed by the missionary-priests, together with the local materials and construction methods employed by the indigenous Indians.

Some examples of remaining Spanish-style missions include:

· San José y San Miguel de Aguayo (1768–78), San Antonio, Texas
· San Xavier del Bac (1783–97), near Tucson, Arizona
· San Carlos de Borromeo (1797), Carmel, California

Southwest Adobe Style

In New Mexico, the Southwest Adobe style has endured. Colonists of European extraction arrived in New Mexico early in the seventeenth century and began building houses using the same methods employed by the local Pueblo Indians. The Indian dwellings, or *pueblos*, were communal structures of *adobe*

Figure 15.12 *San Carlos de Borromeo in Carmel, California, is considered one of the jewels of the California Spanish missions.*

(clay bricks) several stories high. The Indians reached the upper stories by means of ladders. The thick adobe bricks are natural insulators in a climate that is hot in the summer and cold in the winter. Adobes are made by forming clay (bonded with straw) in wooden frames about 1 1/2 feet long, and drying the bricks in the sun. Adobe "melts" in the rain and is stuccoed with clay and straw to slow deterioration. The mud imparts a grayish-brown to pink color that varies according to the clay used.

Figure 15.13 *The informal adobe building style of New Mexico is nicely adapted to the local terrain, where sagebrush, rabbitbrush, western cedars, and cottonwood trees abound.*

Photo by Markus Fant.

CHART 15.20 SOUTHWEST ADOBE DESIGN

EXTERIOR CHARACTERISTICS

- Thick, irregular, adobe walls with rounded corners
- Mud-colored stucco finish on exterior walls
- Deep-set windows and doors
- Vigas (log beams) protrude through the walls
- Flat roofs
- Portal (porch) with wooden post and lintels decorated with carved double corbels called zapatas

RESIDENTIAL EXAMPLES

- Palace of the Governors (c. 1610—restored to its nineteenth-century appearance), Santa Fe, New Mexico
- Casa San Ysidro (eighteenth century), Corrales, New Mexico
- Filipe Delgado House (c. 1872), Santa Fe, New Mexico

NONRESIDENTIAL EXAMPLES

- San Francisco de Asis (c. 1772), Rancho de Taos, New Mexico
- Mission Church (c. 1710), Santa Ana Pueblo, New Mexico

SOUTHWEST ADOBE INTERIOR

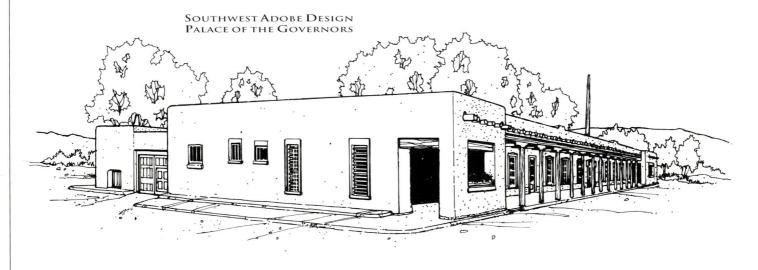

**SOUTHWEST ADOBE DESIGN
PALACE OF THE GOVERNORS**

The irregular walls support the large log roof beams, known as *vigas*, which are not cut to size but protrude through the walls. These make a convenient place to dry chilies and hang other objects. The beams are covered with thin sticks called *latillas* that are laid across the vigas in parallel fashion or herringbone patterns and form the ceiling of the structure as well as the base for the roofing material. Originally the roof was made of sod or packed earth and required constant repairs (today they are made of more durable materials). The early pueblos had no windows, but during the eighteenth century, the settlers began to incorporate paned windows deeply set into the thick adobe walls.

The first settlers' houses were built, Spanish style, around an open courtyard. The house served as a fortress, opened to the interior with no exterior windows, and was entered through a sturdy wooden gate. As the threat of attack lessened with the years, the house took on a friendlier aspect, opening to the front, which often includes a covered porch or *portal*. The porch is supported by sturdy posts capped with a carved double *corbel* or bracket called a *zapata*, and topped with lintels. When brick became available, it was used to form a row of trim along the top of the adobe walls. The trim, called *pretil*, is a protection for the weaker adobe and is characteristic of the *Territorial style* frequently seen in Santa Fe. It is a vernacular version of classical design and may feature dentil trim, simple pediments above the windows, and square painted columns in imitation of the Greek Revival.

Special ordinances in Santa Fe and Taos, New Mexico, permit building only in the Adobe (or Territorial) style, giving both those cities a unique architectural continuity found in few other places.

INTERIOR DETAILS

Floors: Wood plank or tile

Walls: Stucco

Windows: Casement

Doors: Plank or paneled

Chimneypiece: Irregular, rounded, stuccoed adobe, corner fireplace with a round, arched opening

Ceiling: Vigas and latillas

Stairs: Early versions generally one story; contemporary versions incorporate various configurations and styles

TEXTILE DESCRIPTION

Colors: Authentic Spanish colors are either dramatic and bold red, gold, and black (all used sparingly as accents) or dull, sun-drenched, very livable colors. The dull pastel colors have influenced Western trends of recent years. The influence from Latin America gives accent colors of brilliant blue-green, chartreuse, vivid violet, and sunshine yellow

Patterns: Geometric patterns based on American Indian motifs, stripes

Textures: Heavy, coarse matelassé, tweed, homespun textures, leather

TERRITORIAL STYLE

Pretil

ZAPATAS

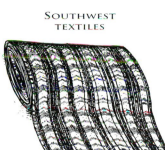

SOUTHWEST TEXTILES

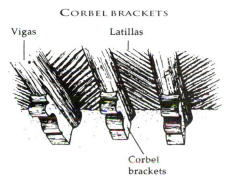

CORBEL BRACKETS

Vigas

Latillas

Corbel brackets

The California Ranch House

The early California ranch houses (c. 1820), like the Southwest Adobe houses, were flat-roofed structures built of adobe. However, the flat roof soon gave way to the low-pitched, gabled, red tile roof, which was more practical in a rainier climate. Because there was less need for protection, the house was generally not enclosed with a walled court but open and rambling with a covered porch running the length of the house. The original houses do not exist in numbers sufficient to warrant listing their characteristics. Their significance lies in the fact that they are thought to be the precursor of the twentieth-century rambler or ranch-style house found in many parts of the country. These builder/developer houses, so well suited to the informal California life-style, soon found acceptance in other parts of the country. Many of the newer versions have been adapted to the point where any similarity to the originals is purely coincidental, however.

Monterey Design

The Monterey house is a California vernacular style representative of the mainstream American English influence, local influence, and the ingenuity of its first builder. Thomas Larkin, a merchant from Boston, was the United States Consul to California when Monterey was the colonial capital. The two-story house he built in Monterey was made of adobe but built with a Georgian central hall floor plan, paned windows, and a low, hipped, shingled roof. Larkin designed the roof to cover a second-story balcony and a porch that surrounded the house like the French galerie (Larkin likely arrived at the design independent of French influence). The Larkin house was the prototype for several other houses and nonresidential buildings in the vicinity, and today the style, built throughout California and the West, is called Monterey.[5]

CHART 15.21 MONTEREY DESIGN

EXTERIOR CHARACTERISTICS

- Two stories
- Hipped or gabled roof of tile or shingles
- Second-story balcony, cantilevered or supported with posts
- Sash windows
- Generally stucco covered

RESIDENTIAL EXAMPLES

- Thomas Larkin House (1835–37), Monterey, California
- Los Ceritos Ranch House (1884), Long Beach, California

NONRESIDENTIAL EXAMPLES

- Thomas Larkin House (1835–37), Monterey, California (also used as a store)
- Old Customs House (1827), Monterey, California

MONTEREY DESIGN
LARKIN HOUSE

The Beaux Arts Influence (1881–1945)

Beaux Arts is not a style. Rather, it is the influence on the training of an architect, either direct or indirect, of *L'Ecole des Beaux Arts* in Paris, France. At the beginning of the 1880s, in the midst of Victorian eclecticism and informality, Richard Morris Hunt, the first American architect trained at L'Ecole des Beaux Arts, designed a home for the Vanderbilt family in New York that was elegant, refined, and historically correct. Thus, America was launched on a new sea of historical influence in architecture. The training at L'Ecole des Beaux Arts focused on historical design in its most minute details. This type of training, which became the standard for American architectural schools, pro-duced designers who were capable of creating the magnificent palaces and châteaus demanded by the new rich, as well as accurately styled smaller homes for those of less means.

By the early years of the 1900s, most American architects were being trained in the historical Beaux Arts tradition, and its influence was felt in most areas of the country. Much of the traditional, historical architecture of the Tudor, French, Dutch, Georgian, Federal, Greek Revival, Spanish, and Colonial styles, in the pre-World War II neighborhoods of the country, show the Beaux Arts influence. Row houses or town houses also came from the drawing boards of Beaux Arts architects. Without understanding this significant influence, it is difficult to account for much of the period-style architecture that surrounds us.

CHART 15.22 BEAUX ARTS INFLUENCE

EXTERIOR CHARACTERISTICS

- Vary according to the intended style of the building

RESIDENTIAL EXAMPLES

- Biltmore (1890–95), Asheville, North Carolina; Richard Morris Hunt, architect—French Renaissance
- The Breakers (1892–95), Newport, Rhode Island; Richard Morris Hunt, architect—Italian Renaissance
- Marble House (1892), Newport, Rhode Island; Richard Morris Hunt, architect—French Neoclassical
- Hearst Castle (1919–47), San Simeon, California; Julia Morgan, architect—Spanish Renaissance
- Benjamin Winchell House (1922), Fieldston, New York; Dwight James Baum, architect—Dutch Colonial
- Conkey House (1934), Santa Fe, New Mexico—Southwest Adobe

NONRESIDENTIAL EXAMPLES

- Boston Public Library (1895), Boston, Massachusetts; McKim, Mead, and White, architects—Italian Renaissance
- Union Station (1907), Washington, D.C.; Daniel H. Burnham, architect—Classical
- County Courthouse (1920), Santa Barbara, California; William Mooser, architect—Spanish
- Woolworth Building (1913), New York, New York; Cass Gilbert, architect—Gothic Skyscraper
- Palace of Fine Arts (1915), San Francisco, California; Bernard Maybeck, architect—Classical
- Grauman's Chinese Theater (1927), Los Angeles, California; Meyer and Holler, architects—Chinese
- Savoy Plaza Hotel (1928), New York, New York; McKim, Mead, and White, architects—Classical French Château Skyscraper

BEAUX ARTS INFLUENCE, LATE MEDIEVAL (TUDOR) STYLE

FRENCH RENAISSANCE STYLE BEAUX ARTS INFLUENCE, BILTMORE

CHART 15.23 EARLY MODERN FURNITURE CLASSICS

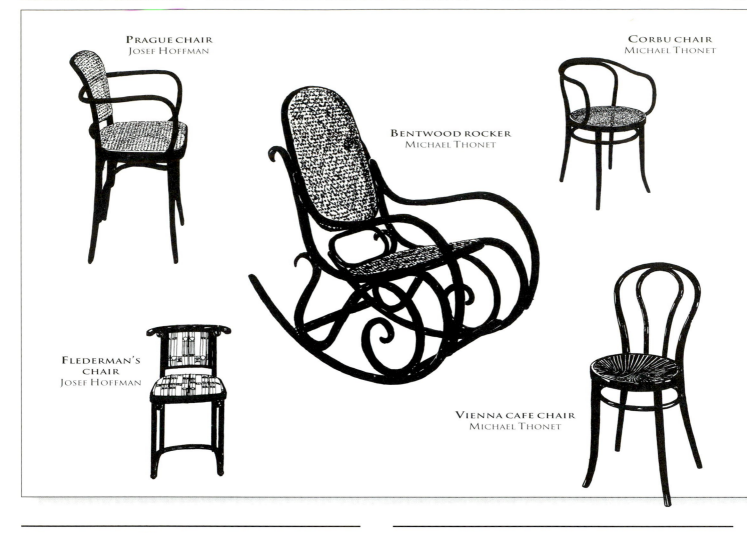

PRAGUE CHAIR
JOSEF HOFFMAN

CORBU CHAIR
MICHAEL THONET

BENTWOOD ROCKER
MICHAEL THONET

FLEDERMAN'S
CHAIR
JOSEF HOFFMAN

VIENNA CAFE CHAIR
MICHAEL THONET

MODERN DESIGN (1885–PRESENT)

It was the Victorians and their technological developments that laid the groundwork for modern architecture. Use of reinforced concrete, structural steel, plate glass, plumbing, and central heating were nineteenth-century developments. The Victorians had also experimented with novel floor plans, as well as new types of architectural massing. We often tend to think of the changes that gave birth to modern architecture as radical. In reality, it is sometimes difficult to know exactly where modern architecture begins. The technology for change was in place. All that was necessary to produce a new style was a break from the cyclical pattern of repeating historical styles. That break is usually attributed to Chicago architect *Louis Sullivan* (1856–1924) and his protégé, *Frank Lloyd Wright* (1869–1959).

Both men were familiar with historical architectural types, and their break from these styles did not happen suddenly. The new modern style grew almost imperceptibly out of experimentation with historical designs. Once the full potential of the new technology was obvious, there was no stopping the rapid development of new architectural forms.

EARLY MODERN DEVELOPMENTS

Arts and Crafts (1860s–1920s)

Other important elements in the development of modern design were philosophical. The *Arts and Crafts movement* during the second half of the nineteenth century in England was the brainchild of designers such as *William Morris* (1834–96) and Charles Eastlake. The Arts and Crafts movement rejected machine construction and advocated simple handcraftsmanship. This philosophy had great impact on many who were considered the pioneers of modern design such as the Green Brothers and even Frank Lloyd Wright.

Art Nouveau (1890–1910)

Art Nouveau was a new style that emerged at the turn of the century in France, Belgium, Austria (where it was called Jugendstil), and Scotland. Its exponents attempted to create designs unrelated to any previous style. Art Nouveau drew inspiration from nature and incorporated vines and flowers, often in extremely sinuous and twisted form, as well as animal forms such as lizards and peacocks.

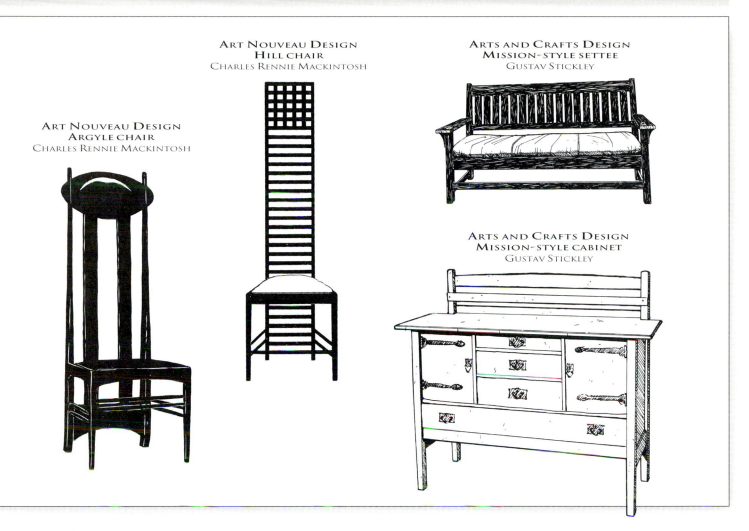

ART NOUVEAU DESIGN
ARGYLE CHAIR
CHARLES RENNIE MACKINTOSH

ART NOUVEAU DESIGN
HILL CHAIR
CHARLES RENNIE MACKINTOSH

ARTS AND CRAFTS DESIGN
MISSION-STYLE SETTEE
GUSTAV STICKLEY

ARTS AND CRAFTS DESIGN
MISSION-STYLE CABINET
GUSTAV STICKLEY

Early Modern Furniture Classics

The Vienna café chair, corbu chair, and *bentwood* rocker are pieces designed by the German craftsman Michael Thonet (1796–1871) and manufactured in Austria during the last half of the nineteenth century. Thonet invented a bentwood process for bending wood that gives these pieces their beautiful curvilinear design and eliminates the need for complex joinery. Today these chairs are manufactured by Thonet.

The Prague chair, a bentwood and cane piece arranged in a square composition, was designed at the turn of the century by *Josef Hoffmann* (1870–1956), a member of the *Vienna Secession* and founding member of its offshoot, the *Wiener Werkstäte* (Vienna Workshop).

The Fledermaus chair, with its distinctively shaped back and ball pendants, is Hoffmann's 1905 design. The Fledermaus and Prague chairs are also available from Thonet.

The Hill chair and Argyle chair are striking perpendicular Art Nouveau pieces created by *Charles Rennie Mackintosh* (1868–1928). They are constructed of black ebony with padded seats and are distinguished by a high back treatment. The Hill chair, considered an extraordinary design for the period, was particularly influential with the Secessionists in Vienna.

The Arts and Crafts movement in America includes the furniture designs of *Gustav Stickley* (1848–1942). His rectilinear oak furniture was solid with straight slats in the arms and backs; the seats were usually leather. Stickley's version of Arts and Crafts furniture, also called *Mission style*, enjoyed great acceptance when it was introduced and has recently seen a large resurgence in popularity.

THE SKYSCRAPER (1857–PRESENT)

The skyscraper is a New York and Chicago phenomenon. It was in Chicago that the metal skeleton, which is the basis for skyscrapers, was developed. However, previous innovations also contributed. The installation of the first practical passenger elevator in New York's Haughwout Building in 1857 paved the way for the tall buildings that steel would make possible. The Brooklyn Bridge (1883) had shown that steel could carry far heavier loads than iron. In that same year, William Le Baron Jenney planned the eleven-story Home Insurance Building using a skeleton framework of steel. This building demonstrated that skyscrapers could reach incredible heights without the support of thick walls. The walls could be as thin as glass; the weight of the building was carried on the steel skeleton.

The master of the skyscraper was Chicago architect Louis Sullivan. To Sullivan is attributed the famous philosophy that "form follows function." He designed a number of important skyscrapers (some with partner Dankmar Adler) and started a building trend that has not yet ceased and has left its mark on almost every corner of the globe.[6]

Examples of early skyscrapers include:

- The Auditorium Building (1889), Chicago, Illinois; Adler and Sullivan, architects
- The Wainwright Building (1891), St. Louis, Missouri; Louis Sullivan, architect
- Monadnock Building (1892), Chicago, Illinois; Burnham and Root, architects
- Reliance Building (1895), Chicago, Illinois; Daniel H. Burnham, architect
- The Guaranty Building (1895), Buffalo, New York; Adler and Sullivan, architects
- Carson Pirie Scott & Co. (1904), Chicago, Illinois; Louis Sullivan, architect

PRINCIPAL DIRECTIONS IN MODERN ARCHITECTURE

Organic Architecture (1908–Present)

In 1908 with the design of the Robie House in Chicago, Illinois, Frank Lloyd Wright was able to create a building devoid of historical precedent. The house was low and spread outward from the central chimney, creating a profile that was in harmony with the prairies of the great Midwest. Wright called it organic because it seemed to grow out of its surroundings.

In Pasadena, California, also in 1908, architect brothers Charles and Henry Greene designed a house with far-reaching implications. The Gamble House, with its shingle exterior, low roof, wide overhang, and long low profile, is a Western variation on the organic theme. Bernard Maybeck, a northern California architect, was well schooled in the Beaux Arts tradition but was also disposed to experimentation with new forms. His wooden designs in the San Francisco Bay area are also

CHART 15.24 ORGANIC DESIGN

CHARACTERISTICS
- Materials that harmonize with nature
- Architectural forms in harmony with the setting
- Well-established relationship from the inside of the house to the outdoors
- Flexible floor plan

RESIDENTIAL EXAMPLES
- Robie House (1908), Chicago, Illinois; Frank Lloyd Wright, architect
- David B. Gamble House (1908), Pasadena, California; Greene and Greene, architects
- Taliesein West (1938), Paradise Valley, Arizona; Frank Lloyd Wright, architect

NONRESIDENTIAL EXAMPLE
- Church of Christ Science (1912), Berkley, California; Bernard Maybeck, architect

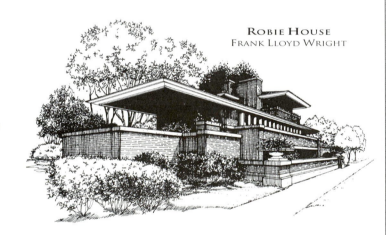

ROBIE HOUSE
FRANK LLOYD WRIGHT

GAMBLE HOUSE
GREENE BROTHERS

(B)

(A)

Figure 15.14 *Frank Lloyd Wright designs. (A) The extensive use of stone reinforces the organic concept of this design. (B) Falling Water grows out of its setting in a dramatic way.*

(A) © 1989 Norman McGrath. (B) © Sergio Penchansky/Photo Researchers, Inc.

significant examples of the organic architectural trend. These California architects spawned a new house type that became popular across the entire country. Adaptations of the California bungalow, with its low roof and wide-front veranda, are classics of low-cost housing.

Many contemporary houses share the philosophical legacy of modern organic architecture. Though they may differ from the early modern houses in line and form, designs that make frank use of natural materials such as wood and stone and that appear to have grown from their setting are in the spirit of Wright's organic architecture. Houses with soaring vertical shed roofs may seem distant cousins to the very horizontal Robie House. However, in the context of mountains, woods, or even coastal dunes, that design, too, is organic.

Figure 15.15 *Philip Johnson designs.* (A) *This glass house captures the spirit of the International style.* (B) *Classics of International style furniture are in harmony with this Johnson house.*

Both © 1988 Norman McGrath.

The International Style (1932–Present)

The *International style*, as the name implies, crossed international borders and drew inspiration from several European schools of thought. From the thinking of the *De Stijl* movement in Holland, the *Bauhaus* in Germany, and *Le Corbusier* in France came the principles that dominated and gave form to the International style.

Though isolated examples existed before, the new style was introduced into the mainstream of American design in 1932 by Philip Johnson and Henry-Russell Hitchcock when they organized the first exhibit of modern architecture at the Museum of Modern Art in New York City and published a book called *The International Style*. The definition of the new style advanced by these men rapidly gained acceptance and established a formula or framework in which less-imaginative architects could design. The style gained further momentum when many leaders of the International Movement immigrated to America during World War II. Walter Gropius, *Ludwig Mies van der Rohe* (1886–1969), and *Marcel Breuer* (1902–81), all associated at one time with the Bauhaus, became teachers of the new style in the United States.

In some ways, the International style is the antithesis of Wright's organic style. The organic style harmonizes with its setting, while the International style stands out in clear contrast. The materials of the International style are bold and hard edged: concrete, structural steel, glass, and stark, white stucco. The architectural approach is minimalist, not adding any unnecessary embellishment, and the plan is open and unencumbered. This architecture is not as "forgiving" as the organic or historical designs; there is little place for the wear and tear of human use and the gentle softening that comes with time. In order to appear pleasing, these clean pure designs must be impeccably maintained. Because of its stark cleanliness, the style has not lent itself to the charming vernacular versions of previous styles.

Figure 15.16 The Brno chairs add to the classic quality of this contemporary interior.

Italian Tile, courtesy of Italian Tile Center, division Italian Trade Commission — I.C.E.

After the years of historical eclecticism, the International movement was like a breath of fresh air. There is a purity and cool elegance to this approach that is beautiful and refreshing, but trends never continue unaltered. It is noteworthy that one of the International style's first American proponents, architect Philip Johnson, has moved away from strict adherence to its principles to embrace allusions to classical pediments and Gothic spires.[7]

International Furniture Classics

The Wassily lounge chair (1925), the world's first bent tubular steel chair, was designed by Marcel Breuer, one of the foremost designers of the Bauhaus in Germany. The Bauhaus school of art, architecture, and design attracted some of the world's finest designers from 1919 to 1933. The chair was named for *Wassily Kandinsky* (1886–1944), an important artist and Bauhaus faculty member. Breuer was one of the first of many designers to take advantage of the possibilities of this versatile combination of materials.

The Cesca chair is another bent tubular steel design by Breuer. The Cesca chair has a wood-framed seat and back of cane mounted on a cantilevered frame. The cantilever design has no back legs and was a remarkable breakthrough made possible by the strength of the metal. Both the Wassily lounge and Cesca chair are manufactured by Knoll International and Thonet.

The MR chair, made of tubular steel and wicker or leather, was designed in 1926 by Ludwig Mies van der Rohe, the last director of the Bauhaus. The MR chair, like the Cesca chair, is designed on the cantilever principle.

The Barcelona collection was designed by Mies van der Rohe for his German pavilion at the Barcelona International Exhibition of 1929. The Barcelona chair and Barcelona stool are constructed on a double X frame of polished stainless steel and are meticulously upholstered in tufted leather. The Barcelona table has an X-shaped frame of polished stainless steel with a glass top.

The Brno chair is Mies van der Rohe's 1930 design for the Tugendhat House in Brno, Czech Republic. The cantilevered design has great strength and visual appeal. The Brno chair, the Barcelona collection, and the MR chair are all manufactured by Knoll International, Inc.

The Grand and Petit Confort chairs were designed in 1929 by Swiss-born French designer *Charles-Edouard Jeanneret-Gris* (1887–1965), better known as Le Corbusier. The Grand Confort has a basketlike frame of bent tubular steel with a series of leather cushions forming the seating unit. The Petit Confort is the same design in smaller scale.

The Basculant chair was designed by Le Corbusier in 1928. The chair has a frame of tubular steel with seat and back of calf skin and arm straps of leather.

The Pony Chaise, designed by Le Corbusier in 1928, is an adjustable *chaise longue* with a frame of chromium-plated tubular steel, a base of matte-textured steel, and pony skin or leather upholstery. These three Le Corbusier designs are manufactured by Atelier International.

CHART 15.25 INTERNATIONAL STYLE

EXTERIOR CHARACTERISTICS

- Open plan
- Simple, logical, rectilinear structural forms
- Generally flat roofed
- Asymmetrical
- Large areas of glass (often arranged horizontally)
- Use of concrete, stucco, and metal
- Long, uninterrupted white wall planes
- Contrasts with setting

INTERNATIONAL STYLE
PHILIP JOHNSON

RESIDENTIAL EXAMPLES

- Walter Gropius House (1937), Lincoln, Massachusetts; Walter Gropius and Marcel Breuer, architects
- Glass House (1949), New Caanan, Connecticut; Philip Johnson, architect
- Edgar J. Kaufmann House, Fallingwater (1936), Bear Run, Pennsylvania; Frank Lloyd Wright, architect
- Lovell Beach House (1926), Newport Beach, California; Rudolph Schindler, architect
- Lovell-Health House (1927), Los Angeles, California; Richard Neutra, architect
- Farnsworth House (designed 1946, built 1950), Plano, Illinois; Ludwig Mies van der Rohe, architect

NONRESIDENTIAL EXAMPLES

- 860–80 Lake Shore Drive (1952), Chicago, Illinois; Ludwig Mies van der Rohe, architect
- Lever House (1952), New York, New York; Skidmore, Owings, and Merrill, architects
- Crown Hall (1956), I. I. T., Chicago, Illinois; Ludwig Mies van der Rohe, architect
- General Motors Technical Center (1956), Warren, Michigan; Eero Saarinen and Associates, architects
- Seagram Building (1958), New York, New York; Ludwig Mies van der Rohe and Philip Johnson, architects

INTERNATIONAL STYLE
WALTER GROPIUS

INTERNATIONAL STYLE
INTERIOR

MODERN TEXTILES

BARCELONA CHAIR
LUDWIG MIES VAN DER ROHE

MR CHAIR
LUDWIG MIES VAN DER ROHE

CESCA CHAIR
MARCEL BREUER

PONY CHAISE
LE CORBUSIER

BRNO CHAIR
LUDWIG MIES VAN DER ROHE

GRAND CONFORT
LE CORBUSIER

BASCULANT CHAIR
LE CORBUSIER

WASSILY LOUNGE
MARCEL BREUER

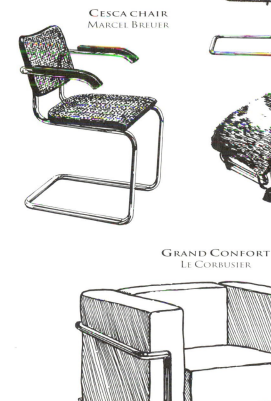

Art Deco (1918–45)

Art Deco was a compromise between the fascination with ornamentation of the Beaux Arts tradition and the stark cleanliness of the International style. Art Deco was "slick" modern but at the same time highly ornate and decorative. It was possible for the Art Deco designer to have the best of both worlds. The style represents an extraordinarily rich development in decorative motifs inspired by nature, history, and the machine.

The Art Deco style is characterized by rigid geometric forms, zigzags, chevron patterns, stepped pyramid forms, stylized billows of clouds, and stylized human and animal forms. Preferred materials were shiny metals, smoothly cut stone or marble, and etched mirrors and glass.

As an architectural style it was used for the design of sky-scrapers, movie palaces, and even some post offices and other government buildings. The style has hundreds of vernacular applications in every corner of the country, and its influence can even be seen in unlikely places such as churches, gas stations, and grocery stores.[8]

Its residential application was principally as an interior style and was simply called modern. Examples of Art Deco nonresidential buildings include:

- Richfield Oil Building (1929), Los Angeles, California
- Chrysler Building (1930), New York, New York
- Empire State Building (1931), New York, New York
- Rockefeller Center (1931–40), New York, New York

Art Deco Color

Art Deco colors were appropriate to typically sleek forms and geometric shapes. Favorite colors were rose, mauve, silver and black, and warm yellow-greens trimmed with gold and mustard yellow. Art Deco forms and colors are frequently revived in today's interiors.

Scandinavian and Postwar Design
Scandinavian and Postwar Furniture Classics

Scandinavian and Postwar American designers made important contributions to modern furniture manufacture, exploiting new materials as well as earlier methods such as bending wood.

Armchair 406 is a 1935 cantilever design by *Alvar Aalto* (1899–1976) of Finland. The flexible bent laminated plywood frame has a seat and back of woven fabric. Armchair 406 is manufactured by ICF.

The Pedestal group was created by *Eero Saarinen* (1910–1961) in 1956 and was a significant design of a furniture collection without the traditional four legs. The single base of the table and chairs is made of aluminum, and the shell of the seating pieces is made of fiberglass. The tabletop may be marble, glass, wood, or laminate. The Pedestal group is manufactured by Knoll International.

Figure 15.17 *The Chrysler Building in New York is an Art Deco monument.*

THE chair is a classic Scandinavian design by Denmark's *Hans Wegner* (b. 1914). The 1949 piece is the epitome of fine craftsmanship featuring a beautifully joined wooden frame with a seat of cane or upholstery. THE chair is manufactured by D.S.I.

The Eames lounge chair was designed in 1956 by *Charles* (1907–78) *and Ray Eames*. The lounge was designed for comfort featuring a chair and ottoman with metal bases, bent laminated wood frames, and carefully padded leather upholstery. The lounge was a great success and, like many of the classics, has been widely copied. The original design is manufactured by Herman Miller.

CHART 15.26   SCANDINAVIAN AND POSTWAR FURNITURE CLASSICS

ARMCHAIR 406
ALVAR AALTO

THE CHAIR
HANS WEGNER

PEDESTAL CHAIR
EERO SAARINEN

EAMES LOUNGE
CHARLES AND RAY EAMES

Postwar Color

The outbreak of World War II effectively cut off America from European color influence. Many interior colors were neutral and comparatively drab during the 1940s. Designers, however, turned their attention to the optimistic and bright colors south of the border—Latin American hues that were best represented in the interiors of Hollywood movies.

During the 1950s, research that was initiated before and during World War II was utilized for interiors. Dyestuffs chemically invented and applied to synthetic fibers gave rise to bright, clear, and often gaudy colors: bright yellow, carnation and flamingo pink, Oriental blue, flower red, chartreuse, avocado and pine green, and gold. These colors were usually assigned to artwork or textiles, while backgrounds and even furniture remained monochromatic colors such as rose-beige, pale turquoise, black or white, or neutrals. Colors and design from Scandinavia were introduced during the 1950s, and for the first time in America, blues and greens were stylistically used together.

The 1960s brought more textiles and color into interiors. Man-made fibers accepted chemical dyes with great intensity and contributed to the bold, bright, even psychedelic colors characteristic of late 1960s and early 1970s. Bright colors in translucent draperies sometimes caused entire rooms to be bathed in orange, gold, or pink light, for example. Carpeting and upholstery fabrics were likewise intense, with reds, orange, shocking pink, vivid blue, and clear yellow at the forefront.

Midway into the 1970s, two major color trends developed. The first was a nature-inspired trend to neutrals and earth-toned beige. Textural interest replaced pattern and neutrals replaced color. At the same time, America was celebrating its bicentennial, and although some interiors were done in vivid American flag colors, the major color thrust came from the renewed appreciation for and pride in colors of the American heritage. America turned to its historic roots and revived and adapted traditional colors to contemporary interiors.

There was also an Oriental color influence in the 1970s that came with the normalization of American relations with mainland China. The opening of trade contributed colors such as Ming and peacock blue, jade green, chrysanthemum yellow and orange, and peony pink.

During the late 1970s and early 1980s, the Post-Modern architectural movement brought vivid, contrasting colors to interior design. By the 1980s multiple colors were used together—including the continuation of historic interior colors, sometimes freshened up with brighter intensity and varied value, and neutral schemes with bright or deep accents. Colors were influenced by grays and deep, rich, vibrant "jewel" tone colors. In addition, colors were again influenced by Europe, particularly Victorian Britain and Renaissance Italy. In the late 1980s, pastels of the earlier two decades also became more refined, clearer, and brighter. Earth tones, likewise, found depth and richness as warmed-up element, earthtone colors.

Figure 15.18 *Lloyd's Bank in London is a beautifully detailed and exciting example of High-Tech design by Richard Rogers.*

CONTEMPORARY TRENDS

Design is constantly on the move, keeping pace with changes in technology and taste. Only the passage of time will determine the true classics of today. However, it is worthwhile to study the developments taking place around us so that we can put them into context. The following represent three important contemporary trends in design.

High-Tech

High-Tech design is a celebration of technology in which all the inner mechanical workings, as well as the structural members of the building, are left frankly exposed on both the exterior and interior. High-Tech designers use elements that were obviously designed for industrial use, such as warehouse lighting and industrial shelving, as furnishings within the interior. The greatest exponents and examples of this style are British: Richard Rogers's Lloyd's Bank (1986) in London, and Norman Foster's Hong Kong and Shanghai Bank (1986) in Hong Kong.

Post-Modern

Post-Modern design grew out of a dissatisfaction with the International modern style. Some people were feeling alienated by the severity of the uniform lines and the regularity of the boxy forms associated with the International style. Post-Modernism imbued modern design with a sense of individuality and even frivolity or playfulness. The characteristic forms of Post-Modernism are updated classical elements with a decidedly modern twist.

Figure 15.19 *The Keystone House by architect Michael Graves is an excellent residential example of Post-Modern design.*

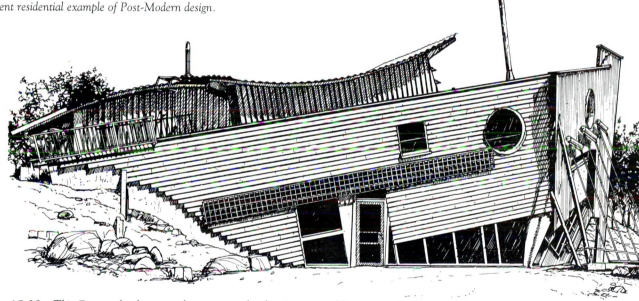

Figure 15.20 *This German kindergarten demonstrates the chaotic nature of Deconstructive design.*

Columns, pediments, domes, and arches, often in simplified or stylized form, are the elements that give individuality to Post-Modernism. Designers have also borrowed many elements of the Art Deco style such as the step-pyramid and the inverted column. The name most associated with Post-Modernism is Michael Graves, whose work for Disney World in Florida is typical of the whimsical quality of the style.

Deconstructivism

The themes that define Deconstructive design are instability, conflict, and disharmony. The materials of the style are corrugated steel, other raw metals, chain link fencing mate-

rial, and raw plywood and chipboard. The frank use of materials is similar to High Tech, but the application is more chaotic. The best description of Deconstructive design is that it appears as if someone took the design apart and didn't know how to put it back together. Some designs resemble a pile of girders and lumber with the unifying factor being the chaos and disunity. While the descriptions may sound quite grim, the actual product is often exciting. It is a style that has found appropriate application in exclusive but funky clothing stores, bistros, and night clubs. The work of Los Angeles architect Frank O. Gehry, an important proponent of the style, has received international attention.

PUTTING THINGS IN PERSPECTIVE

The styles and influences discussed in this chapter are only a part of the story. There is no style to end all styles. The development of style is an ongoing process, as one style influences another and further variations are born. New technology prompts changes in design, and often some influence of either traditional or modern design reappears.

It takes time to determine the value of a design and to put it into the context of a style. In the past, the classification of styles was done in retrospect by historians with a clear overview. But from our perspective, the design family tree has grown very bushy since the beginning of the twentieth century. We live in an information age filled with self-awareness and are often conscious of every new "ism" that appears on the scene. For the amateur, this can be confusing and discouraging. It may be comforting to realize, then, that many new developments in design, which have mushroomed along with technology, are still being sifted and judged by time.

A knowledge of the basic styles and influences listed here is a key to understanding the myriad modes that have grown out of the modern movement and the thousands of vernacular adaptations of each modern and traditional style. Understanding leads to appreciation and enrichment. We are richer because of our architectural heritage and should cherish it and preserve it for future generations to enjoy.

PRESERVATION

Preservation is often an emotion-charged subject. Preservationists and developers often disagree over whether a building should be preserved for its historic value or whether it should be removed to make way for new buildings. One problem is that it takes time to determine the historic or aesthetic value of a building. At the point where sufficient time has passed to make that determination, the building may already have disappeared. To address this problem, preservation societies have been established on both local and national levels. The National Trust for Historic Preservation is the largest of such organizations. This Trust was established in 1949 and today helps determine which buildings, neighborhoods, and historic areas should be preserved. From its headquarters in Washington. D.C., the National Trust maintains museums, assists with restoration and preservation projects, and dispenses information to any who need assistance.

Restoration is a research, partial demolition, and reconstruction process that returns a building to its original state or to some specific state during its history. *Preservation* is taking whatever steps are necessary to maintain a building in its present state or the state to which it has been restored. *Adaptive restoration* or reuse is giving new life to buildings of aesthetic or historic worth by remodeling and restoring them for new uses. One of the earliest adaptive restorations was at Ghirardelli Square in San Francisco. The old and unused Ghirardelli Chocolate factory (1915) was

Figure 15.21 *Adaptive restoration turned this building from a warehouse into an office building.*
Courtesy of Mackey Mitchell Associates, Barbara Elliott Martin photographer.

turned into a pleasant multilevel shopping center with restaurants and landscaped pedestrian areas. Adaptive reuse has spread across the country reinvigorating many old spaces that no longer serve their original purposes. This concept has been used to turn old buildings into housing, office complexes, theaters, museums, oceanariums, and many other uses.

NOTES

1. Doreen Yarwood, *The Architecture of Europe* (London: Batsford, 1974), 215–27.
2. William H. Pierson, Jr., *American Buildings and Their Architects* (Garden City, N.J.: Doubleday, 1970), 14–21.
3. Yarwood, *The Architecture of Europe*, 308–21.
4. Pierson, *American Buildings and Their Architects*, 240–85.
5. Mary Mix Foley, *The American House* (New York: Harper Colophon, 1980), 93–95.
6. Wayne Andrews, *Architecture, Ambition and Americans* (London: Collier-Macmillan, 1974), 213–20.
7. Foley, *The American House*, 241–60.
8. Carole Rifkind, *A Field Guide to American Architecture* (New York: Plume, 1980), 217–41.

THE PROFESSION

Photo by Alejandro Ruvalcaba.

THE EVOLUTION OF THE DESIGN PROFESSION

In past centuries, interiors were often executed by craftsmen who were skilled in many aspects of design. An example is Robert Adam, an eighteenth-century English designer of exteriors, interiors, and furniture. His influence was felt as far away as America. Samuel McIntire was an American architect and designer who created exteriors, interiors, furnishings, and details in the Neoclassic Federal style. During the nineteenth century, William Morris produced and designed wallpaper, furniture, tapestries, carpets, stained glass windows, and accessories in the Arts and Crafts style. Most designers of past centuries, however, were specialists, such as artists, cabinetmakers, and craftsmen, who consulted with the client on only those aspects of the design that were produced in his studio or workshop.

By the beginning of the twentieth century, many Americans had attained considerable wealth and status. Consequently, their wants and needs often extended beyond what the architect or specialized craftsman was able to provide for the interior design of homes and businesses. Thus, early in this century, people began turning to knowledgeable and charismatic men and women who acted as specifiers, coordinators, and overseers of the plans, construction, and installation of their interior furnishings. Perhaps the greatest of these society interior designers was *Elsie deWolfe* (1865–1950), whose success and credibility also helped pave the way for today's interior design profession.

In the 1950s, interior design services became affordable to, and demanded by, the general public. This was largely due to the new level of affluence, commercial development, building, and population growth of post-World War II America. Technology developed for war efforts was turned toward the domestic scene, producing a broad spectrum of affordable furnishings and man-made materials. The machine was viewed as a friend to interior design, unlike the attitude of rejection of machine-made products by proponents of the Arts and Crafts movement. The Bauhaus, a school of architecture and design in Germany between the world wars, trained designers to produce excellent design incorporating machine-age materials. Bauhaus products included the classic modern tubular steel chairs. When the school was closed, many of these talented architects, artists, and designers came to America, exerting a strong influence on design from the 1950s through today. These designers (discussed in chapter 15, Historic Design) included Mies van der Rohe, Marcel Breuer, Walter Gropius, and Wassily Kandinsky.

Designers from Scandinavia also influenced our thinking, combining machine-age materials and techniques with the timeless quality of natural materials and superb quality handcrafting in furniture, textiles, and accessories. American designers, likewise, began to design modern furnishings, based on the simple lines of the International or Bauhaus style and the Scandinavian influence. New trends in design are continually added to the spectrum of contemporary design. Postmodern designers have taken traditional elements, shapes, moldings, and architectural detail and have combined them in new, innovative, and nontraditional ways. Thus, a wealth of not only historical but also innovative new products and materials are now available for interior design.

THE DESIGN PROFESSION TODAY

The interior design profession has matured significantly from the early days of society designers. Today it is a complex and specialized discipline. The interior designer has not only skills and abilities that entail the technical and artistic training discussed in this book, but he or she also has resources and considerable knowledge of materials, furnishings, and their application. Further, the designer, in many cases, acts as director or project manager—hiring and becoming responsible for the goods and services and sometimes even the structure and systems that go into a building. Because of this, there are many professionals today who feel that the person who claims the title of interior designer should have earned that right through tests and licensing. At this writing, there are several states that do require licensing; others seem likely to follow.

Figure 16.1 *Today's interior designers deal with a variety of business procedures to accomplish a completely furnished interior.*
© *Ted Spiegel.*

Today's interior designer not only designs creative and individual interiors, but he or she also acts as a specifier, an organizer, and a *buyer* who is knowledgeable about a great number of diverse products, designs, and materials. Although the product of today's designer is the completed or finished interior, the profession has matured far beyond the era of artisans or society designers. Designers do much more than coordinate background materials and furnishings; they also must perform a variety of professional tasks requiring extensive skill and training. Therefore, the attributes and skills of today's designer are broad and diverse.

Attributes and Skills of Contemporary Designers

Successful interior designers usually have attributes such as insight into personalities and problems, enthusiasm, creativity and flexibility, keen perception, efficiency and organization, attention to detail, and a drive for continual development of creative, intellectual, and professional growth. They also need to develop many skills: business, social, artistic, visual communication, technical drawing/drafting, space-planning, research, analytical, and technical knowledge skills.

Tasks Required of Skilled Designers

The interior designer today must have skills, education, training, and experience to perform a variety of tasks:

- Preparing documents and *letters of agreement* pertaining to all contractual aspects of the interior and handling financial and business matters concerned with the design execution.

- As discussed in chapter 1, programming is the process and methods used to systematically research and define problems. Programming consists of three phases:

    1. *Research*—examining all the factors such as human factors, behaviors, needs assessments, circulation or traffic patterns, working and living relationships, and social and psychological preferences and considerations. Research also entails architectural evaluations that will meet the needs of the occupants—functions, spatial relationships and requirements, budget, mechanical systems, codes and restrictions, time frames.
    2. *Analysis*—the process of analyzing, categorizing, and assessing information, as well as establishing priorities.
    3. *Synthesis*—the written program. The program may also be referred to as the design analysis.

- Technical skills and knowledge—Designers are trained to prepare material boards, *drafting,* or technical detailed drawings. Computer skills as well are becoming increasingly important for both design and business management. Interior designers continually increase their working knowledge of construction methods, building systems, codes, architectural specifications, and safety requirements. Designers must stay abreast of innovations in materials, designs, and furnishings.

Figure 16.2 *Working drawings show placement of fixtures and furnishings in the studio of Susan Thorn, ASID, Cross River, New York.* © *Ted Spiegel.*

- Business—Designers develop skills in employee management and relations, *cost analysis* and calculations, *budgeting,* billing and collection matters, purchasing and *lines of credit,* marketing, sales, and public relations.

- Verbal and visual communication—Designers maintain continual collaborative relationships with clients, suppliers, and other professionals. They can improve productivity and increase professionalism by improving their abilities to present ideas, concepts, and contracts in written, verbal, and visual (sketches, renderings, and *technical drawings*) form.

- Design development or generating and refining the design ideas leading to a design concept.

- Space planning to organize or reorganize residential and/or nonresidential spaces.

- Working with or specifying building systems, such as heating, plumbing, air-conditioning, and all aspects of lighting. The residential designer often works with specialists in these areas.

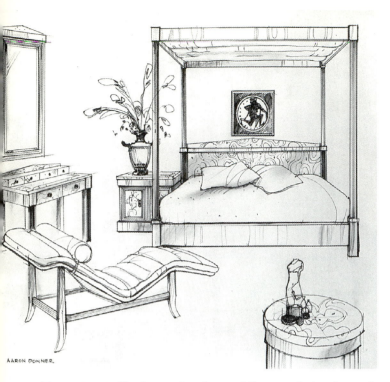 

Figure 16.3 *Sketching and rendering, skills required of professional interior designers, are means of visually communicating design concepts. Furniture designer Aaron Donner created these drawings of his furniture designs.*

• Specifying furnishings and materials that fulfill human needs and meet performance criteria such as durability, cleanability, and strength as well as function and aesthetics. This requires a thorough knowledge of all types of floor, ceiling, and wall-covering materials and textile applications as well as a knowledge of period and contemporary architecture and furnishings.

• Preparing necessary working drawings for cabinetry or interior details that can be executed by a craftsperson or subcontractor. Accurate drawings are paramount in assuring that the interiors are correctly constructed.

• Maintaining a good business relationship with many wholesalers and craftspeople and establishing contracts on behalf of the client with those who provide goods and services. The designer is generally considered liable or responsible for these goods and services.

• Oversee the installation and satisfactory completion of all contracted areas of the design project.

• Post-occupancy evaluation (POE) is the thorough evaluation of the success of the design after it is complete. The basis for evaluation is the list of requirements in the program (discussed in chapter 1). POE is a required task primarily in nonresidential design, but it is useful in residential design, as well.

The designer may also have the responsibility to educate the client in matters of function, space planning, aesthetics, color, materials, and design.

Professional Development and Continuing Education

Whereas some attributes and talents come naturally to those who become interior designers, there are many personal qualities and abilities that need to be developed or enhanced after a student completes a formal interior design education.

Through professional development, designers can keep abreast of new knowledge and technology and can increase business and communication skills. *Continuing education* courses are provided by schools, institutions, industry, professional organizations, and through on-the-job training. Another means of professional development is through POE—evaluating how effectively the design works after a period of occupancy by the users.

The following types of professional development and continuing education are available to designers.

Formal Design Education

It is a wise choice to pursue a formal education at an institution that offers an accredited and fully developed interior design program. The time spent in school gleaning from the experience of qualified teachers and learning the skills and knowledge necessary in the profession is well worth the effort.

Some who are currently practicing interior design have entered the field without formal interior design education and have spent many years apprenticing and learning the profession by working on the job. This is a slow and difficult process. Those with good design education backgrounds seem to have little difficulty finding work in design firms, corporations, industry, or any position where interior designers are needed.

Figure 16.4 On New York Designer's Saturday, at the D & D Building, designers can evaluate new products and learn insights from specialists and other successful professionals. (A) Designers take notes in a seminar entitled "Getting Published—A Professional Imperative." (B) Students and professionals learn specifics of textile design and production from China Seas president, Inger McCabe Elliot. (C) Designers examine China Seas textiles adapted for contemporary interiors from antique batik fabrics. (D) Designers at a lighting workshop at Boyd Lighting.

Figure 16.5 *The Interior Design Bookshop in New York City offers interior design publications of the history, fashion trends, and technical advances in this complex and ever-changing field.*
© Ted Spiegel.

CHART 16.1 TOPICS OF STUDY IN INTERIOR DESIGN EDUCATION PROGRAMS

- Basic and creative arts such as two- and three-dimensional design, fine and applied arts.
- Design theory, human factors and spatial composition.
- Residential and nonresidential design.
- Design for special populations (handicapped, elderly, etc.), special problems (environmental, etc.), and special purposes (historic preservation, adaptive reuse).
- Design materials (textiles, lighting, furniture, color).
- Technical knowledge such as structure and construction, building systems, energy conservation, detailing, materials, laws, building codes, and ordinances.
- Communication skills, such as verbal, written and visual presentation, drafting, and computer systems.
- Professional practice and organization and specification skills.
- History of art, architecture, interiors, furnishings, and materials.
- Research methodologies, survey, literature search, and observation.
- Computer applications: CADD

Design education is a boon in the working world. Experienced professionals in related fields can sense immediately when one who claims to be a designer knows little about the design process. A competent designer who can demonstrate depth of knowledge will command the respect of architects, contractors, suppliers, craftspeople, and clients.[1]

Educational Programs

Educational programs generally vary from two to six years of study. Additional time is needed to obtain a graduate degree. Curricula at institutions offering a certificate, diploma, or *baccalaureate degree* generally provide students with opportunities to develop their awareness, understanding, and competency in areas such as those listed in Chart 16.1.

Interior design programs are found in schools of architecture and in fine arts or home economics departments of universities and colleges and in design schools. Most schools will have an emphasis or specialty beyond minimum standards. For example, a program may specialize in presentation skills, prearchitecture, historic study and preservation, or business practices. The student should, therefore, look carefully at both curriculum and faculty to determine if the school best meets his or her needs and interests for design education. Many schools have internship options that allow students to receive academic credit for training received in professional interior design firms.

It is important to realize that design schools do not have the resources to fully prepare a student for every situation encountered by professionals. Every design project will have new circumstances, concepts, and problems to solve. From design education, one should expect to receive a fundamental working knowledge of, or expertise in, most or all of the areas previously listed. Further, a person should expect to learn principles, processes, and creative approaches to problem solving. A person

who has been trained to think and adapt will be able to handle new problems and design challenges as they arise.

Interior design programs that meet required standards are accredited by the Foundation for Interior Design Education and Research—*FIDER*. Although many programs are not yet accredited, a listing of schools with programs accredited by FIDER is available from FIDER. The National Association of Schools of Art and Design—*NASAD*—is also an accrediting body that evaluates art and design schools and those departments within colleges and universities.

NCIDQ Examination

The National Council for Interior Design Qualification—*NCIDQ*—exam is administered periodically at many locations around the country. It is now a requirement for full acceptance into several of the professional organizations listed on page 375. The two-day exam covers the candidate's knowledge of interior design and poses a creative problem that the candidate must solve. A designer who has successfully completed a baccalaureate degree and worked for the minimum two years in the field should be qualified to pass the exam. The NCIDQ exam sets a standard of excellence and competence so that professional interior designers may better serve the public.[2] In the future the NCIDQ exam may form a basis for licensing. A strong national effort to encourage states to license interior designers or at least to establish title acts is currently afoot.

Titlement and Licensing

In order to enhance the interior designer's professionalism, to assure competency and quality services, and to protect the public from the mistakes of unqualified people who label themselves "interior designers," several states have passed title or licensing acts. This means that in order to use the title "interior designer," the professional must be licensed. To obtain a license the designer usually must pass the NCIDQ exam, have a minimum number of years in the profession, and perhaps be affiliated with a professional organization. Respective requirements are established in each state.

In order to maintain that license, designers are required to earn a minimum number of continuing education units (CEUs) each year. As a general rule, one CEU is equal to ten "contact" or study hours. For example, a state that required five CEUs per year would, in effect, require fifty hours of advanced CEU training. This legislation has passed or is pending in many states in order to bring this relatively new profession up to the caliber of other titled and licensed professions such as law and architecture. Interior design is a complex, dynamic field characterized by continual technological and philosophical developments. The CEU offers a way for designers to keep abreast of changes and developments that will affect the way we live, work, and obtain services in the future.

Professional Organizations

Design organizations exist to research and make available to their members (through continuing education) new and improved design methods, information, sources, and materials. These organizations also lobby for licensing and title registration. Each organization has its own standards of excellence, various levels of association, and entrance requirements. A list follows of the organizations to which interior designers or design educators may belong. For further information, refer to the Appendix at the end of this book for these organizations' addresses.

The **American Association of Housing Educators (AAHE)** coordinates efforts and shares information with college teachers, government employees, and executives in the residential building industry. It serves to develop a better understanding of the role of housing for the well-being of the public, to increase effectiveness of housing education at all levels, to optimize quality of housing environments, and to coordinate efforts among housing authorities. It awards scholarships for its student members and those seeking postgraduate education.

The **American Society of Interior Designers (ASID)** is the oldest and best known of the design organizations. Its forerunner, *AID*, the American Institute of Interior Designers, was founded in 1931 and merged with NSID, the National Society of Interior Designers, in 1975. ASID offers a network of educational seminars, national conventions, extensive design sources, newsletters, and educational materials. ASID sponsors student chapters and activities, which range from design tours to community involvement projects. Information about the profession is frequently available from ASID upon written request.

The **Foundation for Interior Design Education and Research (FIDER)** is the body that exists to accredit postsecondary interior design schools in the United States and Canada. The agency is recognized by the United States Office of Education in Washington, DC. Its members are frequently members of other organizations, and accrediting teams are drawn from both educational and active professional careers. A list of accredited schools is available on request from FIDER.

The **Institute of Business Designers (IBD)** is the best-known organization for nonresidential designers. In order to belong to this organization, nearly all design work must fall into the nonresidential category. IBD sponsors student and professional competitions. It also provides membership for students at a reduced fee, which allows students to participate in IBD professional meetings and activities. Research in new design directions and education is made available to members of IBD.

The **Interior Designers of Canada (IDC)** is a body of professional designers who are members of various provincial associations. The purposes of IDC are to encourage excellence of interior design in the public interest in Canada, to assist educational institutions in the training of future designers, to encourage continuing education for practicing designers, to assist the provincial associations with research and common organizational information, and to uphold in practice a code of ethics and professional practice.

The **Interior Design Educators Council (IDEC)** is an affiliate of the International Federation of Interior Architects/Designers (*IFI*). IDEC was organized in 1967 with the goal of improving the quality of interior design teaching and education and, thus, raising the quality and level of professional interior design work. IDEC has a network of newsletters, various committees, and a professional journal, *The Journal of Interior Design*, which publishes findings of design research conducted by educators and professions. IDEC members join efforts to bring about positive change and improvement in design education.

The **International Federation of Interior Architects/Interior Designers (IFI)** is an international, professional body made up of institutions active in interior architecture and interior design. Headquarters are in Amsterdam, the Netherlands.

The **National Association of Schools of Art and Design (NASAD)** is an accrediting body for schools of art and design that also helps schools to meet standards of excellence in the education and training of artists and designers. In addition, NASAD has a network whereby professionals and professors can share information, keeping schools abreast of new developments and technologies in the field of art and design.

The **National Council for Interior Design Qualification (NCIDQ)** serves to identify to the public those interior designers who have met the minimum standards for professional practice by passing the NCIDQ examination. The organization tries to maintain the most advanced procedures for examination and continually reviews the examination to include expanding techniques in design development and professional knowledge. A study guide to prepare a candidate for the exam is available on request from NCIDQ.

The **International Furnishings and Design Association (IFDA)** (formerly the National Home Fashions League, NHFL) sponsors The Interior Design Society (*IDS*). IFDA is primarily aimed at retail affiliates and interior design executives who also deal with interior furnishings. IDS sponsors educational programs, seminars, and sales supports. These organizations honor and recognize outstanding work and achievement by retail and custom interior design professionals.

Figure 16.6 *At the IDCNY—the Interior Design Center, New York—in Long Island City, designers come alone or bring clientele to select furnishings that are sold only to the trade—the interior designer or architect.* © Ted Spiegel.

INTERIOR DESIGN RESOURCES

An immense number of *trade sources* exist to serve the interior design industry today. Trade sources are companies or vendors that sell goods and services to the trade (designers, architects, and specifiers) on behalf of retail clients. These goods include every element of furnishings needed in an interior. The goods and services are ordered through wholesale catalogs or through manufacturing and product representatives, or reps, or through regional showrooms, which may be closed (allowing only designers to enter and purchase) or open (allowing retail clients to accompany the designer). Craftspeople usually function independently of showrooms and sales representatives; quality craftspeople generally are in demand and have no need to market their services. Most major cities now have design *marketing centers or markets*, which are convenient clusters of trade source showrooms that serve the designer. Many craftspeople are also located near markets.[3]

Figure 16.7 *At design centers or marts, designers find a wealth of resources, such as this wall of fabric swatches by Schumacher.* © Ted Spiegel.

INTERIOR DESIGN TOOLS

Interior designers make use of a variety of tools, such as drafting instruments, presentation materials, filing systems, and a seemingly endless collection of furnishings catalogs and fabric/carpet samples, which usually demand semiannual price and/or sample updates. In addition, interior designers need to keep abreast of new technological advancements that enhance their productivity and design capabilities.

Computers in the Design Profession

Perhaps the most innovative tool available to interior designers today is the computer. Not only can client records and billings be kept and printed out on the computer, but drafting and design, computation of yardage, business and employee management and records, and correspondence also are managed by computer. Through special connections (fax, fiber optics networking, or telephone systems), items can be ordered from wholesalers and confirmed in seconds. Wholesale companies will soon make catalogs available on software disks, eliminating complete libraries of awkward books and saving the designer valuable time. The more a designer can incorporate a computer into the practice, the easier his or her job will be.

There are essentially four divisions of computers that interior designers use: the *laptop computer*, the *personal computer* (PC), the *mainframe computer*, and the *mini-mainframe computer*.

The laptop or notebook is about the size of a briefcase and consists of a keyboard, small monitor, and battery-operated computer drive unit that works off floppy disks where information can be stored and retrieved. These are valuable for travel or on-site computing.

Information can also be relayed from one *computer terminal* to another (similar to PCs) via a *computer network* system. Information can be sent to computers in other cities across the country or around the world with amazing speed via satellite or fiber optics cables.

The *software* consists of *computer programs*, available on disks, that operate the *hardware*. Software programs, written to accomplish specific tasks, are applicable for not only interior design and architecture but for nearly every profession. The types of software programs that have application in interior design include graphics and computer-aided design, word processing, business accounting, desk managing, data bases, and organizational tools. And, as mentioned previously, catalogs will soon be incorporated as software.

Graphics and Computer-Aided Design

Graphics packages or programs allow the designer to create many types of graphic designs. Some programs allow word processing and graphics to design brochures, letterheads, or complex billing sheets, for example. Perhaps the most dramatic and high-profile computer application in interior design is the innovation of software programs such as *computer-aided design (CAD)* and *computer-aided design and drafting (CADD)*. These programs produce technical drawings, drafting, and projections of proposed space. Furniture template components (two-dimensional furniture shapes) can be called up from the *data-base catalog* onto the screen to find the most suitable arrangements. Space planning can be accomplished, then interfaced with high-speed and high-resolution *plotters* (automatic drawing machines) to produce quality plans in a fraction of the time needed for mechanical drawing. CAD software enables designers to plan and experiment in full color and with a variety of textures and patterns.

CAD programs vary in scope, capabilities, and complexities. CAD programs that operate on mainframe computers can produce computer-simulated renderings (artists' conception of proposed space in perspective) and can even move the viewer through a linear-illustrated walk-through of a proposed building. PCs also can utilize programs with similar but limited capabilities. These programs, and those in the following list, are continually being refined and further developed:

> - *Word-processing programs* are designed for writing. These allow great latitude in composing, rearranging text, and working in columns, and they have the advantage of memory storage, recall, and application of documents to

Figure 16.8 *Tools of the interior design profession, as seen at the Philadelphia Daroff Design, Inc., studio.*
© *Ted Spiegel.*

A PC consists of the *computer hardware*—a keyboard, power drive computer unit, *monitor* or screen printer, and perhaps a plotter.

A mainframe computer is much larger than a PC and up to one thousand times more costly. Mainframe computers are used by very large architectural and design firms for large projects and problems. A mainframe has far greater speed and memory and is able to process data that a PC could not. However, PCs can be linked to a mainframe, allowing an entire office to access the larger, more complex machine and, thus, coordinate and synthesize large and complicated design jobs.

On the horizon is yet a new generation of computers called mini-mainframes that have more power, more disk space, and greater function capacity than a PC, yet are smaller than a mainframe—comparable in size to the PC. Mini-mainframes can work independently or in tandem with other terminals.

different clients or needs. Uses for interior design include writing programs, letters of agreement, client contracts, correspondence, *specifications,* purchase orders, and billing.

- *Business accounting* packages differ in what may be accomplished for office use. Some options include a general ledger, journals for keeping track of accounts receivable and payable, receipts, sales, purchases, and detailed records. Data or journal entries may automatically post to individual accounts. Accounting programs may produce customized or summarized reports, profit analysis, and billing.

- *Desk manager* programs or packages offer options such as keeping track of personnel schedules, activities, and payments. It may offer a day, week, or monthly calendar, a phone dialer and logger, a financial and/or statistical calculator, an editor, a note and card filer, and various graphic symbols. These can help the designer become more organized and use his or her time more efficiently.

- *Data-base programs* manage, organize, and retrieve files. Files consist of information needed for working on documents, graphics, and CAD. Data bases produce managerial spread sheets, trace inventories, and calculate interior components, such as textile yardage or office planning systems. A data base may be able to sort, summarize, and generate reports, as well as set up and produce forms.

- *Organizational tool programs* offer a variety of options, such as charts, math and graphics capabilities, and data analysis. Organizers may help establish priorities, evaluate ideas, synthesize information, and facilitate decision making. They may produce project management documents, which outline a critical path. They also report on resource interdependencies and generate all needed printed reports. An organizational program may be a tool for writing specifications, as a cross between a word- and an outline-processing program.[4]

Computer Purchase and Training

The previous list of computer programs is only a portion of the programs available today. Specific programs developed and marketed by independent companies will vary in scope, abilities, complexity, and cost. The *state of the art* continually changes, and competition makes research and marketing software programs profitable. Retail merchants and computer specialists are knowledgeable and have sources of information on current software programs.

The purchase of a computer system requires a sizable investment, but the cost depends on the complexity and capacity of the units and on how many software programs are purchased. PC hardware usually constitutes about half of the total cost; software programs, printers, and plotters require an equal investment. However, computer systems are a competitive commodity, and they tend to become more affordable with time.

Training in terms of time and payment of personnel is also costly. However, given the hours saved once training is complete, the computers will most likely be cost efficient in the long run.

Figure 16.9 *Utilizing a software program design by Steelcase, a designer is able to produce working drawings on a pen plotter directly from his CAD screen. The photo at the bottom left shows the actual furniture being utilized by the designer on the computer.*
© Ted Spiegel, courtesy of Steelcase.

Other advantages of the computer are the smooth and efficient filing of information with near-instant information retrieval, the central location of information, and the reduction of human error and oversight.

Many design schools incorporate CAD training into their programs. Some have also required or recommended basic courses in word processing, business applications, and other programs such as those previously mentioned. Programs may *interface* (use similar commands), so that a comprehensive knowledge of everything the computer can do is not necessary in order to operate a variety of programs. This makes the computer much less intimidating and makes self-training possible.

User-friendly hardware and software are relatively simple for the users to understand, making specialized training less necessary. Computer applications for design firms may be expanded as needs and skills increase, beginning with simple programs for one or two areas of application and extending to more programs or more complexity as design work expands.

CAREERS IN INTERIOR DESIGN

Interior design is a field of broad latitude in career options. Professional opportunities exist in *interior architecture* and design, in retailing, and in design-related fields.

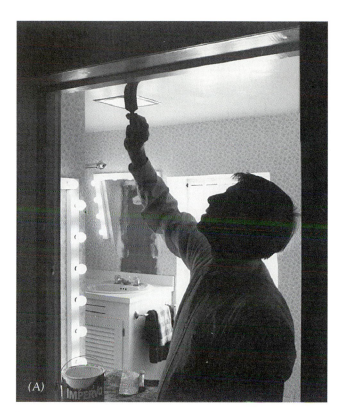

Figure 16.10 *Interior designers work closely with subcontractors, such as (A) painters and (B) electricians, to coordinate every element for an interior.* Both © Ted Spiegel.

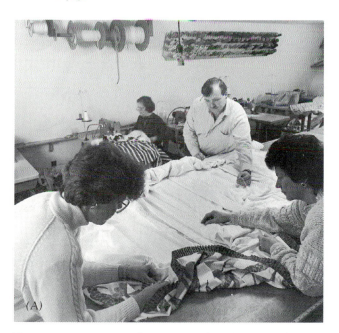

Figure 16.11 *Interior designers specify and oversee fabrication and installation of (A) window treatments and (B) carpeting and flooring materials.* Both © Ted Spiegel.

Interior Design

Interior design involves all the steps of analysis, planning, and execution of services listed at the beginning of this chapter. An interior design firm may function alone or be part of an architectural team, working in tandem on common projects or working independently within the framework of the business.

Because there is more need for interior design work than for architectural commissions of new buildings, many architectural firms have incorporated interior design departments in their firms. These interior design departments may even function independently of their architect counterparts within

Figure 16.12 *Quality craftspeople are important to successful interiors.* (A) *Upholsterers build custom furniture.* (B) *Cabinetmakers construct built-in cabinetry for kitchen, bath, or office.*

Both © Ted Spiegel.

the corporation. Thus, in some cases a design unit within the firm may win a bid to do the interior of a building that is being designed by another architectural firm.

Interior design firms may function independently of architects. Many successful firms began as a single interior designer functioning as a *sole proprietor* whose skills and expertise paved the way for more and more contracts. Hence, many such firms eventually expand into corporations where interior designers, assistant designers, draftsmen, renderers, secretaries, accountants, and resource/studio help are employed.[5]

There are two main divisions of interior design: residential design and nonresidential design. Residential design is discussed here; nonresidential design follows at the end of the chapter under Nonresidential Considerations.

Residential Interior Design

Residential firms design interiors for homes, condominiums, mobile homes, vacation houses, apartments, or any residence. Some firms handle dozens of residential interiors, while others limit their involvement to only four or five larger commissions each year. A firm may deal only with entire interiors, or it may be willing to undertake certain rooms or portions of an interior.

Retailing

Retailing is another specialty within interior design. Designers who work in the sale of goods and services to the public may specialize in window coverings, wall coverings, or hard or soft

floor coverings. Interior design services are often incorporated into quality department stores, and interior designers may be a key to the success of full-service furniture stores.

Interior Design Education

Teaching careers in colleges, design schools, and universities are open to those with proper credentials. Full-time, *tenure-track positions* offer rank advancement from instructor to assistant professor to associate professor to full professor. Advancement is based on teaching effectiveness, creative work and research, the degree held, and service to the institution and the community.[6]

Requirements for full-time tenure-track positions usually include professional experience plus a terminal degree—*master of arts* (M.A.), *master of science* (M.S.), *master of fine arts* (M.F.A.), or *doctor of philosophy* (Ph.D.). Since only a few institutions offer advanced degrees in interior design, candidates might consider related fields in which to seek terminal degrees. Possibilities might include a selection of architecture, art history, business management, CAD, education, historic preservation, humanities, psychology, or housing.

Teaching design in high schools or community colleges is another career option. High schools generally offer courses in interior design as a part of their home economics programs. Community colleges frequently offer interior design courses, and some offer vocational training or associate degrees that may emphasize design. A baccalaureate (bachelor's) degree would be the minimum requirement to teach in either of these situations, and high schools usually require a teaching certificate as well.

Figure 16.13 *Figures 16.13–16.16 Four residential interiors by designer Susan Thorn are indicative of the flexibility and resourcefulness of today's qualified interior designers. A classic French-styled living room.*
© Ted Spiegel.

Figure 16.14 *Casual and country themes are mixed here to bring warmth to a great room fashioned out of three tight, remodeled spaces.*
© Ted Spiegel.

Figure 16.15 *Modern architecture and seating contrast with a handmade credenza and richly textured accessories.*
© *Ted Spiegel.*

Figure 16.16 *This interior utilizes the collections of the client and reflects eclectic tastes.*
© *Ted Spiegel.*

Teaching part-time is also a viable career option. Designers who are active in the profession or in a related field can add immeasurably to the strength of a design program by imparting the skills and experiences gleaned from real-life situations. Many design programs rely on practicing professionals, which include interior designers, architects, *graphic artists*, rendering artists, draftsmen, lighting specialists, specialists in materials and textiles, color, CAD, and other specialists who serve as part-time instructors.

Specialized Design

Interior designers with education and work experience often become proficient and skilled in an area of specialty. A design specialist can do work that general interior designers may not be equipped to handle. Recently, the design field has witnessed the emergence of professionals specializing in lighting, CAD, and other areas.

The tendency to specialize is natural as people follow their interests and desires. But in addition, the world has become so complex and technical that it is difficult for the interior designer to have a commanding knowledge of, and expertise in, all areas of design. Certainly it is professional wisdom to call in a specialist or consultant when some aspect of a project goes beyond the designer's knowledge or experience. Specializing allows the designer to do the in-depth research to become knowledgeable about the technical aspects of one area. This knowledge, coupled with extensive experience, is required for a designer to become a specialist.

Yet another justification for design specialization is the ever-increasing risk of litigation through designer liability. Designers are becoming more responsible for the interiors they create, and for the safety and well-being of the people who inhabit or visit those interiors. If the designer, through lack of knowledge or experience, makes mistakes or is not thorough enough, the client may bring a lawsuit that can be disastrous to the designer's career. Specialization allows the designer to work only in areas where his or her knowledge and experience can help prevent mistakes and consequent litigation.

Careers in Related Fields

In addition to specialization, there are many related career options open to those with schooling and/or training in design. Some may not require any prerequisite formal education, although a considerable amount of time and effort will be necessary to succeed in a related field.

Many specialties and career options related to design are listed in chart 16.2. This list is by no means exclusive; ten years ago some of these options were unheard of, but today they are indispensable. This trend will surely continue, as designers with education, training, and the spirit of entrepreneurship continually open up new careers and specialties that will be important to interior design in the future.

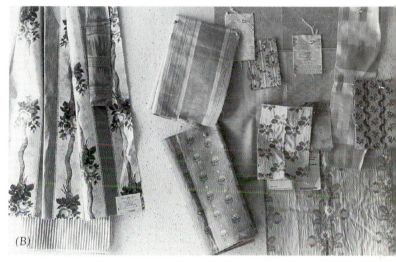

Figure 16.17 (A) *Interior designer Susan Thorn and her clients are conferring about* (B) *color schemes and fabrics for the daughter's bedroom.* Both © Ted Spiegel.

WORKING WITH A PROFESSIONAL DESIGNER

People turn to interior designers for a variety of reasons. The most important of these is the designer's knowledge of sources. An interior designer has canvassed the market, is aware of the best sources for the given circumstances, and obtains specialty goods and services in behalf of the client. Most wholesale sources will sell only through a retailer or designer; the designer who can order the items needed for a specific job is an important resource for the client. Closed showrooms will not allow retail customers to enter their premises, but clients may go into open showrooms when accompanied by their interior designer.

CHART 16.2   DESIGN SPECIALTIES AND RELATED FIELDS

- Acoustic design—planning the sound reflecting and absorbing qualities of an interior through the shape of the space and through specified finishes and materials. Theater design will incorporate acoustics.

- Adaptive reuse—the remodeling of old or historic structures to fit a purpose different from the original. A wharf warehouse, for example, could become a shopping plaza or mall; an old home could become a law, real estate, or insurance office; inner-city buildings could become luxury condominiums or co-ops. Rehabilitation or rehab is bringing any older building up to current standards where it can be inhabited.

- Amusement park design—carrying themes into every item of the park, from signs to trash cans and drinking fountains. It also deals with safety, traffic patterns, and efficiency.

- Aquarium design—for homes, offices, and aquatic parks and museums. This specialty could also include maintenance.

- Architectural space planning or floor plan design—drafting by hand or CADD.

- Art and accessory dealerships—selling fine art and/or unique accessories retail to the public or wholesale to interior designers.

- Color consultation—for marketing firms, industry, architectural or interior design firms, business corporations, government.

- Buying—for large department and furniture stores. Buyers select floor merchandise or lines (merchandise offered by particular companies) carried by the company.

- Cabinet, closet, and storage design—custom design to suit individual needs or dealerships in retail modular storage furniture.

- Communication design—working with specialized needs in offices for computer terminal stations, telecommunication conference rooms, and other areas.

- Construction/project management—overseeing the construction and acting as liaison between client and contractor. This may include hiring the architect, engineers, subcontractors, craftspeople, and consultants.

- Drafting and/or CADD.

- Design for corporate parties, charity balls, design shows, or other large gatherings where there must be organization and orchestration of many details within a given length of time.

- Design for the handicapped, aged, or infirm—including design for medical facilities, rest homes, hospices, residences, or products.

- Energy conservation—acting as consultant to architectural firms or clients to increase energy efficiency (see also solar design).

- Entertainment center design—designing the storage units for television, videocassette recorders, stereo equipment, computers, media-center rooms, and home theatre.

- Environmental safety—research into materials that will not burn or do not threaten the safety of the users or of the environment; consultation to manufacturers and architects.

- Facility management—a fast-growing field where corporations utilize a manager to plan and purchase furnishings and to coordinate and be responsible for all building repairs and maintenance. The facility may be one building or dozens of buildings in dozens of locations; the manager oversees other employees in the facilities department.

- Forensic consultation—studying a product's construction and appropriate use for manufacturing, for application, or for purposes of testifying in litigation proceedings.

- Furniture design—the design of new and innovative furnishing items such as case goods, upholstered furniture, and accessories. Furniture retail sales or rental business—residential and/or nonresidential.

- Graphic design and illustration, and signage graphics—such as creating a corporate image.

- Greenhouse and solarium design—designing spaces for healthy plants (including temperature and humidity control); also designing sun spaces for people to dine, socialize, or relax in the heated whirlpool.

- Hard-surface floor covering design—including both the actual design of the tiles or vinyl and the use/application of ceramic tiles, wood, brick, and stone on floors, walls, and ceilings (including mosaic and mural work).

- Hardware design—designing doorknobs, handles, and hinges.

- Health club/recreational facility design—buildings that house swimming pools, indoor ball courts, gyms for workout and aerobics. Safety as well as good design is important.

- Historic preservation and restoration of authentic interiors maintained as museums; also, restoring fine old buildings to their original state or an adaptation of it. Historic preservation is a growing concern in both residential and nonresidential interior design and requires thorough knowledge of specialized goods and services.

- Hospitality design—interior design for hotels, convention centers, resorts, and restaurants. A large and important area in nonresidential design.

- Industrial facilities—manufacturing plants and accompanying offices and support areas.

- In-house corporate design—design, consult with experts, and coordinate components to keep the corporate image prestigious.

- Journalism—magazine and newspaper articles on design.

- Kitchen design—planning the latest in cooking equipment and efficient food preparation and serving areas, plus accommodating a social environment. (A Certified Kitchen Designer uses CKD after his or her name.)

- Landscaping—design firms specializing in interior landscaping select, sell, rent, and maintain real and artificial plants.

- Law—handling litigation over interior design projects, working toward legislation, or serving as advisors concerning design laws, public safety, historic preservation, or a host of other design-related areas.

A designer can produce materials and finishes presentation boards, sketches, or colored renderings of the proposed finished space. These enable the client to visualize the interior and approve in advance the purchases and color schemes. Working with a designer from the outset of planning new construction can help assure better interior spatial arrangements. The designer can supervise remodeling and reconstruction of interior spaces and can custom design special items such as built-in cabinetry, wall paneling, and fireplaces. The designer has a knowledge of quality and value and can control each. He or she will know which craftspeople do the best work and will act as liaison between the worker and the client. Thus the client is then spared the frustration of dealing with many workers and subcontractors.

A designer also will be able to control a set budget and assure that services and goods stay within the limits of the budget while completing the interior.

Perhaps the most important way a designer can help is to draw upon his or her experiences with the application of the elements and principles of design. Since furnishing an interior can be a costly expenditure, a designer can see to it that aesthetic mistakes are not made and that the product is not only beautiful but fully supportive of the user's needs.

- Law office design—incorporating specialized needs, equipment, and personnel with an image.
- Library design—meeting needs of different kinds and locations (such as law libraries) and all the inherent equipment and space planning.
- Lighting design—a twofold career option: designing lighting plans and specialty lighting needs for interiors; and designing the lighting fixtures or luminaires.
- Management—in design firms, in industry, or in design-related business, or as facilities managers.
- Marketing—consultants to wholesale and retail firms and to exporters/importers of design goods.
- Medical facilities—interior design for hospitals, clinics, and other medical care facilities.
- Model home design—renting or selling furnishings to model homes. Similar to residential design but without having to deal with a user who will live there. Luxury models for condominiums, flats, or co-ops incorporate expensive and luxurious design.
- Museum design—planning spaces; meeting specialized needs for display design, background materials, specialized lighting, humidity control, and traffic flow. Curatorship—directors of museums or archives are yet another career option.
- Office design—a specialty in nonresidential design ranging from small offices to high-rise buildings. Professional offices, such as those for doctors and dentists, are another office specialty.
- Plumbing fixture design—designing sinks, lavatories, bath tubs and saunas, toilets and bidets, and faucets.
- *Product design*—new and innovative furnishing items such as furniture and accessories.
- Product evaluation—consulting with and recommending marketing strategies to companies that are introducing new designs and products.
- Publicity and public relations (PR)—establishing and/or marketing an image for corporations, company products, or other designers.
- Purchasing agent—an interior designer can act as purchaser for large companies, negotiating and overseeing correct ordering of furnishings.
- Real estate developer—interior designers often buy real estate, improve or remodel the building, and sell it at a profit. Building new nonresidential buildings and leasing them is another aspect. An interior designer-turned-developer can also arrange financing and sell homes or nonresidential buildings.
- Rendering—artists' conceptions of interior or exterior design.
- Restaurant design—a specialty in the interior design of restaurants, cafeterias, bars, and fast-food services.
- Retail design—from individual boutiques to large department stores and from single shops to entire shopping malls, creative designers are in demand.

- Retail selling—many interior designers own, manage, or work in retail stores. Specialty shops might include accessories, selected new or antique furniture, textiles, or fine art. Interior designers themselves are often expert salespeople.
- Salon design—design of beauty and barber shops, tanning facilities, nail sculpturing, and other beauty services.
- Set design—set design is needed for television, theater, movies, and for taking photographs for furniture companies.
- Showroom designer—the interior design and space planning of permanent and seasonal showrooms of furniture, fabric, carpet, accessories. This can be done on a free-lance basis or as a permanent employee of a manufacturing firm.
- Solar design—requiring knowledge of energy efficiency, sun control, and sunlight-resistant materials. Specialists in solar interior design are needed in both residential and nonresidential design.
- Textile design for fabrics, wallpaper, or carpeting—working in-house for large conversion companies, or free-lancing and selling designs (or being paid royalties) for textile design. Custom design occasionally calls for one-of-a-kind textiles.
- Training specialists—in areas such as computers, retail sales and marketing, lighting, nonresidential specifications, or other design services.
- Transportation design—including specialties in aircraft interiors (passenger jets to corporate jets), marine design (interiors of luxury liners to private yachts), bus and train interior design, and even automobile design.
- Turnkey design—in which the designer sells the project and assumes complete responsibility to hire all consultants/subcontractors and finish the project with very little input from the client, who needs only to turn the key and walk in to a completed interior. Vacation homes are one application of this specialty.
- Window-treatment design—today so many style and mechanical options exist in window treatments that it takes expertise to know which treatments to specify. Fabric coordination with overall design and furnishings is also necessary.
- Wholesale representatives, or reps—call on design firms within a designated territory to whom they provide or sell product samples or catalogs. They order stock merchandise and provide the link between the manufacturer and retailer or designer in obtaining goods and services, providing swifter service, and troubleshooting. Reps also assist the designer in preparing specifications, selecting merchandise, preparing bids, and writing purchase orders.[7]

Designer fees vary according to the circumstance and practice of the firm. Residential interior design is usually based on retail sales or retail less a percentage. This may be combined with a design fee based on the time spent drafting, rendering, shopping, and supervising construction or installation. A designer may charge a flat consultation fee only or base design service charges on an hourly fee, freeing the clients to shop on their own and purchase from whatever source they will.

Design fees may be based on the type and extent of services completed by the designer. These services may include the following:

- Consultation with clients
- Preparation of analysis or surveys
- Preliminary budget and cost estimates of required furniture, furnishings, and equipment; preparation of renderings, color and material boards, floor, wall, ceiling, and window treatment drawings; plans for cabinetry, closets, and other built-ins
- Plans for lighting
- Preparation of maintenance manuals
- Specification services
- Supervisory services

- Consultation with third parties such as architects, engineers, and general contractors. Suggestions for graphics, uniforms, logos. Fees may be based on the phases of the job, with a flat fee determined for each service mentioned.

Compensation is generally secured in phases, at the completion of certain services, or billed monthly.

Letters of agreement are contracts drawn up by the design firm and signed by the client that become legal documents. A letter of agreement will vary somewhat between residential and nonresidential projects, but both will contain the same general information. The letter will specify who the work is for, the location of the work involved, and which specific areas are to be involved. It will outline the services to be rendered by the designer, whether purchasing is to be done by the designer on the client's behalf, and which arrangement (retail, retail less a percentage, or wholesale plus a percentage) is agreed upon. The letter will outline specific phases of the design job, the client's responsibility to third-party contractors and services, compensation arrangements, and collateral matters. Disclaimers (items and services for which the designer is not responsible) will limit the designer's liability and clarify the relationship between the designer and the client. A *retainer fee*, applicable to the design fees or the goods to be purchased, is customarily required to initiate work by the design firm.

Choosing a designer or design firm for residential work may be based on personal reference or upon the quality and appeal of the finished interiors executed by the designer or the firm. The client should always interview the designer to evaluate the potential for a good working relationship based on professionalism and rapport. The designer will become thoroughly acquainted with the preferences, needs, and wants of each user and often becomes a personal friend because of the necessity of thoroughly understanding life-style and preferences.

THE FUTURE OF INTERIOR DESIGN

It is clear that in the future there will be greater demand for designers to be knowledgeable about the complex and technical aspects of interior design. Increased litigation over design projects points to the increasing accountability of interior designers for the environments they create. Because of this, designers in the future will specialize further to gain expertise in one area of design.

As more states pass title registration acts and require licensing, qualified interior designers will enjoy increased legal recognition. This trend should further protect the public against those who are not qualified to practice in the field.

Finally, the computer promises to play a commanding role in the future of interior design, being used for coordination of research and documentation, analysis, organization, CAD, and processing of all the documents and paperwork handled by the interior designer.

NONRESIDENTIAL CONSIDERATIONS

Nonresidential work is far less personal than residential work, and the image projected by the designer usually must be creative, yet conservative and businesslike. The representative of the design firm must present soundly conceived design solutions, often to a board of directors, and indicate that the firm's business practices are likewise sound. The client may visit the design firm to evaluate the level of professionalism. The design firm may also be selected by winning a competitive bid.

Nonresidential interior design firms may do a variety of interiors, but most specialize. The areas of specialty include:

- Commercial office planning and design—incorporating space planning and office systems furnishings
- Health care and clinic facilities—hospitals, same-day surgery centers, women's care centers, medical and dental offices, geriatric centers, rest homes, and hospices
- Hospitality—hotels, resorts, and restaurants
- Model interiors—model homes, condominiums, and offices
- Retail design—everything from shops and department stores to entire retail complexes
- *Tenant improvement* of offices, or facility planning—the developer sets a budget, and designers work with tenants to select and specify materials and furnishings; the developer pays the cost, with the tenant paying for any desired upgrade in materials over the budget allowance
- Adaptive reuse of old or historic buildings—giving a building new life as retail spaces, office spaces, or residences
- *Transportation design*—airlines, buses, trains, and/or cars
- Industrial design—such as manufacturing facilities

Certain organizations such as corporations, retail stores and chains, schools and institutions, government agencies, hotel chains, airlines, and energy companies employ *in-house* (staff) *designers* who are responsible for new and on-going design projects. These organizations benefit from an in-house professional who not only has aesthetic and technical skills but who also understands the procedures and policies of the corporation itself.[8]

Responsibilities of the Nonresidential Designer

In nonresidential design, many of the tasks required of the skilled designer overlap those of the residential designer, although the way they are handled or the specific requirements will vary.

The documents and letters of agreement are standard forms that are legally binding and involve all aspects of the project. Often the financial arrangement will be a cost plus a percentage for very large installations. The designer may contract only to research and design the interior, or the designer may take the project as far as the specification of furnishings, without the responsibility of ordering goods or overseeing their installation. These varying situations are made clear in the contracts.

Figure 16.18 *The Toscana Ristoranté, planned by architect Piero Sartogo, is an example of a nonresidential specialty—hospitality design.*

The programming phase in nonresidential design is conducted in much the same way as in residential design: (1) research, (2) analysis, and (3) implementation. However, the categories of research will differ. The research will focus on working situations and ease of functional interrelationships, public traffic, and specialized needs for the project.

The development of the design and the space planning often take place on a larger scale for nonresidential design, so a single design concept may be adapted for several different areas—reception area, working area, hotel rooms, hospital rooms, and then onto specialized areas (to board rooms, conference rooms, ballrooms, or examination rooms, for example).

Nonresidential designers coordinate work with specialists who plan and install HVAC systems. They work with lighting and structural engineers and other specialists; the amount of design in these specialized areas depends on the skills and time abilities of the design firm. Whereas in some cases the designer will specify lighting, in other instances that will be handled by a specialized lighting designer.

Materials and furnishings must be specified to meet not only performance criteria and user needs but also state and local codes for safety against fire, bacterial growth, and static electricity.

The nonresidential designer spends a good deal of time preparing working drawings for interior architectural detail such as moldings, cabinetry, freestanding units, columns, and any needed furnishing items necessary for the interior design.

Nonresidential design entails purchasing furnishing items or specifying items for the client's purchasing department to order. The nonresidential designer may or may not (depending on the contract) oversee installation and be responsible for subcontractors. But often the designer functions as the project manager, so that all personnel needed to build or remodel are coordinated and hired under his or her direction—from the architect and engineers to the carpet and wall covering installers, electricians, and plumbers.

Nonresidential Design Fees

Nonresidential interior design fees are often based on a flat fee, computing in advance the projected time necessary to complete the design. The flat fee may also be based on a square foot method. When fees are based on time, the salary of each person (principal, project manager, senior, junior designers, draftsmen, secretaries) who will be involved in a project is computed or projected, and the monthly salary of each person is multiplied by the number of months spent in each phase of the design job (programming, designing, construction, installation supervision). That amount will be multiplied by three to cover wages, overhead, profit, and anticipated overtime spent on the job. Square foot method is used less often but is applicable for large spaces.

Purchasing arrangements for nonresidential furnishings are typically billed at wholesale plus 10 to 20 percent. The designer may not purchase for nonresidential jobs but may specify furnishings that are ordered by the purchasing department of the client's firm. Likewise, nonresidential clients are generally responsible to pay for third-party services such as architects, engineers, and general contractors. Billings for design goods and services are billed monthly or in prearranged installments that parallel each phase of the project.[9]

ENVIRONMENTAL CONSIDERATIONS

Professional interior designers have joined forces with architects in the "greening" of our interiors. Of great importance is the responsibility to specify building materials, furnishings, and systems (1) that will preserve diminishing natural resources or endangered materials and (2) that will not emit toxins and fumes from formaldehyde and chlorofluorocarbons.

It is often within the power of the interior designer to influence a client to accept designs that will conserve energy, conserve nature, and enhance the air quality of the building. The problem for the interior designer is to sort out—from the deluge of claims, advice, warnings, and even misinformation—how the design can be harmonious with nature. The issues are challenging and complex. Environmental considerations require more evaluation, research, and implementation to be done during the design process. However, the extra effort will pay dividends in the future as we preserve our precious resources and enhance the quality of our lives.

Most interior designers are responding to the call for preservation of the environment. As Danae Loran Willson, Director of the Pratt Center for Design Excellence (CDEP), stated, "In order to rescue the future, we will have to open ourselves to new approaches, new ways of doing business, new practices, new ethics, and new risks."[10]

Part of the responsibility is ours as well. We can both help to protect the environment and assure a healthy place to live and work for ourselves. As we purchase furnishings and perhaps work with professional interior designers and architects, we should become actively involved in the design process. Make sure products are not from "endangered" sources, and ask about the content, processes and finishes of materials, and whether toxins or fumes will be emitted. Find out what kind of energy will be consumed in your lighting, and, once your interior is complete, do your part to continue to practice sound environmental protection. These practices would include conserving energy, recycling materials, and keeping furnishings for longer periods of time through wise choices and careful maintenance. A recent suggestion that 75 percent of all Americans consider themselves "environmentalists" puts on our shoulders the responsibility to do our part in protecting our natural and interior environments.[11]

NOTES

1. Arnold Friedman, "Interior Design Education: A Hot Topic in 1986," *Journal of Interior Design Education and Research* 12, no. 2 (Fall 1986): 7.

2. "NCIDQ: National Council for Interior Design Qualifications Examination Study Guide." (New York: National Council for Interior Design Qualification, 1983), introduction.

3. Harry Siegel and Alan M. Siegel. *A Guide to Business Principles and Practices for Interior Designers* (New York: Whitney Library of Design, 1982), 133–34.

4. *MacUser: The Macintosh Resource* (South Norwalk, Conn.: MacUser Publications, February 1987), 142–66.

5. Siegel, *A Guide to Business Principles,* 19–25.

6. IDEC: The Interior Design Educators Council, "Appointment, Tenure and Promotion: A Position Paper on Criteria for Evaluation of Interior Design Faculty in Post-Secondary Institutions" (Richmond, Va.: IDEC, January 1985).

7. Mary V. Knackstedt, *Profitable Career Options for Designers* (New York: Kobro Publications, 1985), 24–46.

8. Siegel, *A Guide to Business Principles,* 39–43, 50–65, 107–115.

9. Ibid., 32–35, 98–106.

10. Institute of Business Designers, "Are Designers Responding to Environmental Needs?" *Perspectives* (Fall 1991): 14.

11. Arthur Gensler, Jr., "A View on the Environment," *Perspectives* (Fall 1991): 8.

American Association of Housing Educators
c/o Jo Ann Emmel Box 3AE, New
Mexico State University, Las Cruces,
NM 88003

American Home Lighting Institute (AHLI)
435 North Michigan Avenue, Chicago,
IL 60611

American Institute of Architects (AIA)
1735 New York Avenue, Washington,
DC 20006

The American Society of Interior Designers
(ASID) 608 Massachusetts Avenue
NE, Washington, DC 20002

Barrier Free Design Center 2075 Bayview
Avenue, Toronto, Ontario, Canada
M4N 3M5

Center for Accessible Housing North
Carolina State University, Box 8613,
Raleigh, NC 27695-8613

Color Association of the United States
(CAUS) 24 East 48th Street, New
York, NY 10016

Color Marketing Group (CMG) 4001
North Ninth Street, Suite 102,
Arlington, VA 22203

Council of Federal Interior Designers
(CFID) P.O. Box 27565, Washington,
DC 20038

Designers' Lighting Forum (DLF) (Contact
the Illumineering Engineering Society
of North America for local chapters.)
345 East 47th Street, New York,
NY 10017

Environmental Design Research Association
(EDRA) L'Enfant Plaza Station, P.O.
Box 23129, Washington, DC 20024

Foundation for Interior Design Education
and Research (FIDER) 322 Eighth
Avenue, New York, NY 10001

Illumineering Engineering Society of North
America (IESNA) 345 East 47th
Street, New York, NY 10017

The Institute of Business Designers (IBD)
341 Merchandise Mart, Chicago,
IL 60654

Interior Design Educators Council (IDEC)
14252 Culver Drive, Suite A-311,
Irvine, CA 92714

The Interior Designers of Canada (IDC)
Ontario Design Center, 260 King Street
East #506, Toronto, Canada M5A IK3
(for U.S. address, see NCIDQ)

Interior Design Society (IDS) P.O. Box
2396, Highpoint, NC 27261

International Association of Lighting
Designers (IALD) 18 East 16th Street,
Suite 208, New York, NY 10003

International Colour Authority
c/o Benjamin Dent & Co, 33 Bedford
Place, London WC1B 5JX, England

The International Federation of Interior
Architects/Designers (IFI)
Waaterlooplein 219, Postbus 19126,
NL-1000, GC Amsterdam,
Netherlands

International Furnishings and Design
Association (IFDA) 107 World Trade
Center, P.O. Box 588045, Dallas,
TX 75258

The International Society of Interior
Designers (ISID) 433 South Spring
Street, Suite 6-D, Los Angeles,
CA 90013

National Association of Schools of Art and
Design (NASAD) 11250 Roger Bacon
Drive #21, Reston, VA 22090

National Council for Interior Design
Qualification (NCIDQ) 50 Main
Street, White Plains, NY 10606-1920

National Home Builders' Association
(NHBA) 15th and M Streets NW,
Washington, DC 20005-2892

National Lighting Bureau (NLB) 2101 L
Street NW, Washington, DC 20037

Office of the Americans with Disabilities
Act Civil Rights Administration, U.S.
Dept. of Justice, P.O. Box 66118,
Washington, DC 20035-6118

ADDRESSES FOR DESIGN ASSOCIATIONS

A

A lamp   Designation for an arbitrary-shaped, standard light globe or lamp bulb.

A 588 steel   The designation given to steel that rusts only to a certain point and in doing so creates its own rustproof finish.

AAHE   The American Association of Housing Educators.

Aalto, Alvar (1899-1976)   Important Finnish designer of several modern classic furniture pieces.

abacus   The slab or pillow above the capital at the top of a column.

abrasion resistance   The ability of a fabric to resist wear from friction, rubbing, or other abrasive action.

abstract design   A type of decorative design that may be based on natural or even geometric design, stylized to the point that the source is not recognizable, and the design is therefore open to interpretation.

acanthus leaves   A representation of the lobed leaves of the acanthus plant used as a decorative motif.

accent lighting   Focusing or highlighting; sometimes called artistic lighting.

accent rugs   Small rugs, often called scatter or throw rugs, used for art accents, in areas where water may spill onto the floor (such as kitchens and bathrooms), or to catch dirt where traffic enters the interior.

accessible   Capable of entering or exiting a building or an area without obstruction.

accessories   The items in an interior used to give a quality of finish or completion such as paintings, sculpture, books, lamps, vases, flowers, and plants.

accordion door   Folding door, with small vertical panels, that stacks against itself.

acetate   A man-made fiber of reconstituted cellulose and acetic acid.

achromatic   Colors without hue, namely black, white, and gray.

acoustical tile/plaster   Wall and ceiling tiles and plaster that help control noise.

acrylic   A synthetic fiber of over 85 percent acrylonitrile units; used for the manufacture of textiles and furniture.

acrylic paint   A synthetic resin, water-based paint.

acrylic sheet   A flat plate or sheet of acrylic (a hard plastic) that can be etched to allow special effects. The most common is the exit sign.

active balance   Another term for asymmetrical balance where objects that are not alike balance each other, or like objects are placed at unequal distances from a central point. It is termed active because it requires some effort or activity of the eye to analyze or discern the balance.

active solar system   A mechanical system of solar heat collection for space and water heating.

actual density   The three-dimensional, literal mass or density of a piece of furniture.

Adam, Robert (1728-92)   The most influential of four Scottish architect/designer brothers. His English Neoclassic work was influenced by the uncovering of Pompeii and Herculaneum near Naples, Italy.

adaptive restoration   Restoring older buildings for purposes other than those for which they were constructed.

adobe   Large building brick made of clay, baked in the sun.

aesthetics   The philosophy of art and beauty. The part of art and design that is beautiful and appealing to the senses.

affinity   The chemical compatibility of fibers to dyestuffs.

afterimages   When the human eye focuses on a strong color for several seconds or minutes, then focuses on a neutral area, the complement of that color will appear in shadow form.

AID   The American Institute of Interior Designers combined in 1975 with NSID to form ASID, the American Society of Interior Designers.

air-brush printing   Dye sprayed through stencils by pressure ink jet guns.

air compression painting   Spray painting powered by an air compression machine that allows paint to be diluted for application.

air-conditioning   Cool air piped into an interior through an air-conditioning unit or through a furnace unit.

air-exchange unit   Draws fresh outside air into buildings and expels stale, used air. Necessary in a superinsulated and tight structure with few or no windows.

airless paint spraying   Mechanical spraying of nondiluted paint.

aisle   A passageway separated by an arcade, running parallel to the nave of a church.

Albers, Josef (1888-1976)   Color expert in simultaneous and successive contrast. Albers taught at the Bauhaus in Germany and at Yale University.

alkyds, alkyd enamel   Oil-modified resin paints. Alkyd enamels produce glossy surfaces.

all-wood   Wooden furniture construction where all visible parts are made of wood.

allocate space   To assign space; to determine the location and layout of rooms or areas.

alloy   A substance formed by fusing one or more metals, or a metal and nonmetal.

alternate complement   A four-color scheme of a triad with the direct complement of one of the hues.

alternation   A type of rhythm wherein two shapes alternate—one, then the other. A classic example is the egg-and-dart molding seen in chapter 15.

aluminum   A lightweight silvery metal.

ambient general lighting   Overall lighting that covers a large area, often in the form of overhead luminaires.

ambulatory   A place for walking; the aisle in a cathedral.

amenities   Facilities shared by condominium owners or available to renters in luxury apartments. These include swimming pools, tennis courts, and entertainment or athletic facilities.

American Empire (1820-60)   The interior design title of the period concurrent with the antebellum Greek Revival homes. Colors influenced by Napoleonic choices of bold, deep hues.

ampere or amp   The measurement of electrical current in a circuit.

anaglypta   Embossed wall or ceiling coverings that resemble plaster, hammered copper, or hand-tooled leather.

analogous   Colors that are next to each other on the standard color wheel or as they occur in a rainbow or prism. An analogous color scheme usually contains three to six adjacent colors.

analysis   A part of programming in which information is assessed and priorities established.

ancient Greece, the golden age (fifth century B.C.)   Era of the Parthenon and height of philosophical development and architectural excellence.

angular lines   Any straight line used in interior design that is neither horizontal nor vertical. Angular lines may be diagonal lines in one direction or even or uneven zigzag lines. Angular lines suggest movement and action.

animal hair felt pad   Moderately resilient carpet underlay of 100 percent animal hair felted into padding.

animal skin rugs   Rugs of zebra, bear, sheep, and other animal skins.

anodize   To put a protective oxide film on metal through an electrolytic process with chemicals and an electric charge.

anthemion   A symmetrical stylized Greek flower motif that radiates from a central point at the bottom of the flower.

anthropometrics   The study and comparison of human body measurements (i.e., anthropometry).

antimony   A silver-white, crystalline, metallic element used in alloys.

antique finish   A finish made to appear older by the application of a darker color over the top of a lighter finish.

antiques   Furniture made before 1840 (U.S. Customs definition).

antiquing   Making a painted surface look old with a mellow patina by color washing, glazing, spattering, and dragging techniques.

antistatic finishes   Reduce conduction or static electricity.

apartment   A home or unit housed with other units that are rented for living spaces.

apron   The face or front piece of a table just below the top, the face of a chair just below the seat, the face of a chest just below the drawers, and the front piece below the window sill.

apse   A semicircular or polygonal projection of a church.

arcade   A row of arches and supporting columns.

arch system construction   A building type in existence since antiquity; the arch is held together with a splayed keystone under compression.

architect   A professional who plans three-dimensional space and creates floor plans and blueprints.

architectural elements   The walls, floors, ceilings, windows, doors, fireplaces, cabinetry, and other fixtures or details that are built in to the interior.

architectural glazing   *See* glass.

architectural or structural lighting   Permanently installed fixtures or luminaires. The wiring must be in place in advance.

architectural rods   Nonresidential drapery and curtain rods that are usually drawn with wands or batons rather than a traverse cord and pulley.

architrave   The lintel or crosspiece in a classical entablature.

area rugs   Define a specific area, such as a conversation area.

armchair   A chair with armrests as distinguished from a side chair without arms.

armoire   The French term for a wardrobe or large movable closet.

Art Deco (1918-45)   A brief period of design between World Wars I and II that has been repeatedly revived in interior design style and color.

art glass   A general term for stained, beveled, leaded, and etched glass used as primary glazing or as hard window treatments.

art lighting   A term for luminaires or fixtures that are in themselves works of art where light is the medium of artistic expression.

Art Nouveau (1890-1910)   A style of design based on natural floral motifs and colors.

art rug   A rug with a decorative texture or pattern of such interest and quality that it can be considered a piece of art.

artificial light   Incandescent and fluorescent light. Amount and direction of artificial lighting affect color hue, value, and intensity.

artificial stone   A fabricated product that imitates natural stone and is generally used for wall facing.

artistic lighting   Another term for accent lighting.

artist's paint   Oil or acrylic paint in small bottles or tubes.

Arts and Crafts movement   A school of thought at the close of the Victorian era that espoused a return to handmade, quality furnishings rather than machine-made items.

asbestos shingles   A fireproof roofing material in several color choices laid in overlapping manner and nailed tight.

ashlar   Stone cut into rectangular shapes fitted together with grout.

ASID   The American Society of Interior Designers.

asymmetrical balance   The placement of different objects on either side of a center point where they balance each other. Also called informal balance, asymmetry requires a discerning eye and sensitivity to achieve the balance.

atrium   The open entry hall of a Roman house.

atrium door   A French-door pair with one fixed side. Also called a patio door.

attached dwellings   Residences with shared walls, such as condominiums, town houses, twin houses, and multiplexes.

attic window   Pivoting window installed in the pitched roof of an attic.

Aubusson rugs   Flat tapestry French rugs woven in both historic and contemporary colors and patterns.

Austrian shades Scalloped and gathered shades that fold up. They are full and formal looking.

Austrian valance Valance in the same style as the Austrian shade.

automatic sensor dimmer A device that automatically turns on and controls the level of artificial light to supplement natural light in order to keep the light at an even level of brightness.

auxiliary heating A backup heating method needed for solar energy systems when the sun cannot supply all the heating needs of the interior.

Avril A registered trademark of FMC Corporation for viscose rayon.

awning window A top- or bottom-hinged window that swings out.

Axminster carpet A Jacquard-woven carpet where colored yarns are inserted as needed. Used extensively in nonresidential carpeting.

B

B lamp A designation for a candelabra lamp or bulb that is a smooth, torpedo-shaped oval.

baccalaureate degree The degree granted by colleges and universities and some design schools following four to five years of general education and specific topic study.

back panel A panel used to cover the back of a case piece; often made of hardboard.

baffle A device such as a board or grid that deflects light, either to direct it or to prevent glare.

baffled ceiling Ceiling hung with panels of wood, metal, or fabric that serve as a screen.

balance The placement of objects (such as furniture or art), or architectural detail (such as windows or columns), so that they create visual equilibrium.

balanced light Light from more than one direction meant to eliminate glare and high contrast of light and dark, or unflattering or fatiguing shadows.

ballast The connecting mechanism within a fluorescent lamp.

balloon, pouf, or cloud shades Loosely gathered, full, soft, and billowy shades that pull up from the bottom.

balloon valance Valance in the same style as the balloon shade.

baluster The member that supports the handrail on a stair.

balustrade The railing formed by the newel post, balusters, and handrail.

bamboo shades Shades woven of split bamboo and a cotton warp. Also called matchstick shades.

bank of light A large, well-lit area of light.

Baroque A seventeenth- and eighteenth-century design style characterized by bold, showy, and highly decorative use of classical design elements. The feeling is often luxurious, exuberant, and unrestrained.

barrel vault An arched roof with a roundheaded arch shape.

barrier-free design Design for the handicapped that presents no physical obstacles or barriers to access and allows free movement in the environment.

bartile Quarry or clay tile (gray or red) roofing material. It is costly but never needs replacing.

bas-relief (low relief) The type of sculpture wherein the figures protrude only slightly from the background.

base Finish trim used to cover the joint where the wall meets the floor.

base lighting A light placed next to the floor behind a deflector board that directs light upward.

baseboard Base trim made of wood.

baseboard units Plugged-in or prewired units near the floor for room or area heating.

basket weave A variation of the plain weave where groups of warp and weft threads are carried as one. A balanced weave carries the same number in each direction—two over and two under ; 3/3; 4/4. An unbalanced basketweave carries uneven groups of threads over and under, such as 2/3 or 3/4.

bast fibers Natural cellulosic fibers obtained from the stems and leaves of plants. The best known are linen and jute.

batik A hand process of resist dyeing. A pattern is drawn with wax onto a cloth, then the cloth is dyed. The wax-covered portion will not be colored. The wax is removed and new wax applied to allow other areas of the pattern to be colored.

batting Polyester, cotton, wool, or other suitable fibers formed into sheets for upholstery padding.

battlement A parapet indented or crenellated along the upper line of a building.

Bauhaus A German school of art, design, and architecture that functioned from 1919-33 and espoused the integration of art and technology for the creation of good design. The Bauhaus attracted many important artists and designers and had a significant influence on the development of modern design.

bay The area between columns, piers, or buttresses.

bay or bow rods Traverse or curtain rods that are prebent to a bay or bow window shape.

bay window Projecting window in a square or canted configuration.

bead and reel A molding of alternating round bead shapes and oval or disk shapes.

beam system construction Solid beams of steel, wood, or concrete supported with a series of posts.

beamed ceiling A ceiling with exposed beams or trusses.

Beau-Grip A registered trademark of Beaunit for viscose rayon.

bed molding Same as crown molding.

beltcourse A projecting row of bricks or stone on the facade that separates one story from another; also called stringcourse.

Belter, John Henry (d. 1865) A New York furniture craftsman best known for his Rococo Revival pieces of carved laminated rosewood.

belvedere A cupola or lantern. The small square towers that rise from the roof of the Italianate buildings of the nineteenth century.

Bemberg A registered trademark of Beaunit for cuprammonium rayon.

bentwood A method of softening wood with steam and then bending it into curved forms.

berber rugs Woven or tufted wool rugs left in their natural color state—white, beige, brown, or charcoal, with flecks of light or dark neutrals.

bergère French term for an upholstered armchair with upholstered side panels between the armrest and seat.

berm A pile of earth used to create a visual or physical diversion or to add variety to a landscape.

beveled glass Thick, decorative glass with a finished edge that is mitered or beveled at less than ninety degrees.

beveled paneling Paneling with edges cut at an angle other than forty-five degrees.

Bi-loft A registered trademark of Monsanto for acrylic.

bibelot French term for a small decorative and often rare object.

Biedermeier The term used to describe the Empire style as interpreted and built by the craftsmen of northern Europe.

bifold door A door with vertical double panels that folds back against itself; frequently used for closet doors.

biotechnology The aspect of technology concerned with the application of biological and engineering data to synthetic products and environments. Also called ergonomics.

bishop sleeve curtains Drapery lengths pulled into a bloused, poufed effect.

bisymmetrical balance Also called formal or passive balance, the arrangement of like parts or objects in mirror image on each side of a central point.

bleaching A prefinishing process for natural fibers that whitens gray goods. Also the chemical lightening of the natural wood color as part of the wood finishing process.

blinds Slats or louvers held together with cords or on a pulley system. Blinds may be horizontal or vertical. Sometimes pull or pouf shades are called blinds.

block front A furniture detail used on the front section of case pieces. The block front consists of a series of three panels—the two outside panels come forward and the center panel is recessed.

block print A two-dimensional art form printed from a flat wooden or linoleum block on which the background has been carved away, leaving a raised design pattern.

block printing A hand-printing technique in which blocks (usually wood) are carved, inked with fabric dye, and pressed onto the fabric.

Blue C A registered trademark of Monsanto for polyester.

blueprints Floor plans printed in blue ink and used for construction plans.

board and batten Vertical wooden siding made of parallel boards with narrow strips of wood (battens) to cover the cracks.

boiserie French term for wood paneling.

bolection A rounded, projecting molding.

bonded (rebonded) foam Carpet underlay (padding) of chopped foam and filler materials bonded together by heat, pressure, and some adhesives.

bonnet roof A hipped roof with two pitches. The top is steeply pitched and the bottom, which covers a porch, is low pitched; used on houses of French influence.

border A strip of companion wall covering used to trim and accent. Packaged in five-yard spools.

boss A projecting ornament at the intersection of ribs in the Medieval church.

bow window A curved projecting window (in the shape of a bow).

bracket An angle-shaped support.

bracket lighting A light placed on the wall behind a bracket board that directs light upward and downward.

braided rugs Strips of fabric braided, then sewn together in ovals or circles. Originated in Colonial New England.

brainstorming Generation of ideas without stopping to judge their quality.

brass A yellowish alloy of copper and zinc.

breakfront A case piece whose front plane is broken with receding or advancing sections. Also, the projecting section of the facade on Late Georgian houses that is topped with a pediment.

breast The front of the fireplace and chimneypiece.

Breuer, Marcel (1902-81) Important designer/architect associated with the Bauhaus and known for the design of several classic chairs.

brick Clay and other additives formed into rectangles and dried in the sun or fired in a kiln oven; used for walls and floors.

brilliants Several pinpoints of light that produce a glittering effect.

broadloom carpet Woven or tufted carpet typically twelve feet wide.

bronze A deeply colored, reddish brown alloy of copper and tin used to make sculptural pieces.

brush painting Application of paint with a hand-held brush. Ideal for small areas and detail work.

brushed finish A lustrous (but not shiny) finish achieved by brushing a series of uniform scratches into metal.

bubble planning The first step of diagramming where bubbles represent zones and are placed in proximity relationships.

budgeting The facet of a design project that dictates the amount of money to be spent on various aspects of the job.

buffet See sideboard.

buffet-style dining Where guests serve themselves a meal from a table or sideboard (balancing the plate on the lap may be implied).

building inspector An official whose job is to inspect new or remodeling construction for structural soundness and safety features.

building systems Components of a building that are permanent. These include HVAC, electrical and lighting systems, and plumbing.

bulb More accurately the lamp bulb or lamp, it is the glass container that houses the filament of incandescent lighting and in fluorescent lighting contains phosphorus and gas.

bullnose A 180-degree rounded wooden edge on the starting step (also on a table or cabinet top).

burl veneer Made from scarlike wood growth or from root wood that imparts a complex, swirling grain pattern to the veneer.

business accounting software Enables computers to keep accounting records.

buttress A structure built against a wall to strengthen it.

buttressed chimney In Medieval construction, a stepped chimney built in the shape of two buttresses placed back to back.

buyer One who selects lines or companies whose furnishings are sold in furniture and department stores.

byobu Small-scaled decorative folding Japanese screens.

Byzantium (A.D. 330-1453) The eastern capital of the classical Roman Empire known for its colorful tile mosaics.

C

C lamp A cone-shaped lamp or light bulb.

C.O.M. Customer's own material—purchased by the customer from someone other than the furniture manufacturer for upholstery on a selected piece.

cabinetry Fine finish woodwork, as opposed to rough carpentry.

cabinetwork See cabinetry.

cable system construction A method of nonresidential building where a canopy is held in place with steel cables hung from a central column.

cabriole leg An S-curved leg typical of the Règence and Louis XV periods in France and the Queen Anne and Chippendale eras in England and America.

CAD See computer-aided design.

Cadon A registered trademark of Monsanto for nylon.

café curtains Curtains that cover the bottom half of a window.

calendering A finishing process of ironing under heat with a large cylinder roller. The roller may have raised patterns to imprint designs, and the fabric may also be glazed with a resin, then calendered to produce a high sheen or other special finishes.

came The lead strips used to secure the pieces of glass in leaded or stained glass windows.

camel-back sofa A sofa with a serpentine back that rises to a hump in the center.

cane Thin strips of rattan or bamboo used to weave mesh for chair seats and chair backs.

canister A luminaire shaped like a can that contains a lamp at the top or the bottom.

canted Beveled or tilted at an angle.

cantilever A projecting or overhanging structure anchored at one end so that no outside support is required.

Cantrese A registered trademark of DuPont for nylon.

capital The decorative head of a column or pillar.

Caprolan A registered trademark of Allied Chemical for nylon and polyester.

Carpenter's Gothic The wooden, board-and-batten version of the Gothic Revival style.

cascades Zigzag-shaped panels of fabric that usually frame swags or festoons.

case goods Furniture without upholstery such as desks, chests, and dressers.

cased glass Clear glass encased in a layer of colored glass.

casement draperies A strongly textural-looking fabric in a woven or knitted construction. Screens light, cuts down on glare, and provides daytime privacy.

casement window A side-hinged window that swings in or out.

casing A layer of fabric between the padding and the actual cover in upholstery.

cast iron Iron cast in a mold.

cathedra The bishop's chair from which the term cathedral is derived.

cathedral ceiling A high, open, gabled ceiling.

cathedral window A pointed window set in the gable of a room with an open ceiling.

Caucasian or Turkish rugs Oriental rugs of a coarser weave than Persians, in geometric patterns and often vivid colors.

Celanese A registered trademark of Celanese for acetate.

Celaperm A registered trademark of Celanese for acetate.

cella Literally a cell. The interior space of a Roman temple.

cellulosic fibers A classification of natural fibers that come from plants and are made up of cellulose, cotton and linen being the most commonly used. Also a classification of man-made fibers that begin with cellulose, such as rayon and acetate.

cement A powder of silica, alumina, lime, and other materials. Mixed with water and aggregate, cement becomes concrete.

central air-conditioning Cool or temperate air controlled from a central unit and distributed through ducts and vents.

Central and South American rugs Folk rugs from natives of Central and South American countries.

central vacuum system A vacuum located in one unit with plumbed pipe and outlets where the hose is attached. The wall plate covering the outlet activates the system when it is lifted.

ceramic tile White clays fired to a point of vitrification. It comes in many sizes, shapes, colors, and patterns; a strong, hard material for walls, floors, and ceilings.

ceramics The art of modeling and baking in clay.

chair rail A molding placed on the wall at chair-back height.

chaise longue A French term that literally means long chair. It has an elongated seat designed for reclining.

chandelier A decorative, ceiling-mounted, or pendant-type luminaire consisting of several branches for candles or electric lamps.

chemical finishes *See* standard finishes.

Chevreul, M.E. (1786-1889) French chemist who was head of dyestuffs at Gobelin Tapestry Works near Paris. Chevreul researched and published theories that were forerunners to the Standard Color Wheel theory.

chimneypiece The decorative detail that covers the firebox and flue.

china Designation given by Europeans to porcelain from the Orient.

Chinese rugs Oriental rugs woven in Chinese traditional or contemporary patterns in a deep, sculptured pattern.

chipboard *See* particleboard.

Chippendale, Thomas II (1718-99) An important English cabinetmaker known for the designs published in his book, *The Gentleman and Cabinet-Maker's Director.*

choir The section of the church where the choir sings.

chroma The relative brightness or intensity of a particular hue or color. Low chroma is dull; high chroma is bright. Chroma, also called intensity, is a designation of the Munsell color system.

chromium A shiny silver metal resistant to rust.

Chromspun A registered trademark of Eastman Kodak for acetate.

circuit A wiring hookup that forms a path through which electrical current may flow.

circulation Movement from place to place within an environment.

cissing Dropping mineral spirits onto wet spattered paint to make shadows of the spatters.

City of London The one-square-mile area that encompasses what was once Roman and Medieval London.

clapboard Thin, horizontal, overlapping, exterior wooden siding.

classic A work of the highest excellence able to stand the test of time.

classical Rome (200 B.C.—A.D. 100) The Roman era of political conquest and architectural achievement. Roman design was discovered by the Western world when the excavation of Pompeii began in 1754.

clearance Space required by code or law around a combustible or heating unit (stove, fireplace, or furnace) so that nearby materials will not ignite. Also, the clear space between users and the objects they are passing.

clerestory window Window placed at the top of the wall or in the highest story of the nave or choir of a church.

cloisonné Decorative objects made by soldering metal strips into a pattern on a metal piece and filling the space between the strips with enamel.

closed floor plans Floor plans with many rooms that are totally private from other rooms, having solid walls and accessed only through a door that may also close.

closed showrooms A design-oriented store for placing orders of merchandise. They deal only with professional interior designers; clients are not allowed to enter.

closed stair A stairway with walls on both sides. Also called a housed stair.

club foot A round, pad-shaped foot on a cabriole leg.

coated fabric wall coverings Fabric layered with vinyl to become wall coverings.

cobblestone Large rounded stones such as river cobbles set into concrete and used mainly as nonresilient hard wall materials.

code A federal, state, or local ruling, law, or regulation that stipulates building safety and health requirements. Examples include nonflammable materials or fire-stops.

coffered ceiling A ceiling formed with recessed boxes or coffers.

coil spring A cylindrically shaped spring used for upholstery cushioning.

cold air returns Ducts used in forced-air heating systems to return cooled air to the heat source for warming.

cold cathode lighting The term for all colors of neon lighting.

collectors Units to capture the sun's energy or heat for active and passive solar heating.

Colonial America (1640-1770) The period prior to the Revolutionary War that included Medieval and Early and Late Georgian interiors.

colonnade A row of columns, often forming a corridor.

color An element of design, color is pigment in paint or part of the visible spectrum of light that enables us to see hues. It incorporates the study of hue, value, and intensity as well as color schemes, color application, and color psychology.

color group moods Groups of color that produce emotional response, such as light and bright colors producing feelings of spontaneity and happiness.

color harmony The selection and arrangement of colors to be pleasing to the eye and to the senses.

color washing Applying a coat of thinned, sometimes translucent, paint over a white or colored ground.

Coloray A registered trademark of Courtaulds for viscose rayon.

colored incandescent lighting Accomplished with colored glass lamps or by colored screens or filters placed over a white light.

colorfast The ability of a dyed or printed fabric to resist color loss from cleaning, light fading, or atmospheric impurities.

coloring A general term for the dyeing and printing of textiles.

Colorspun A registered trademark of American Viscose for viscose rayon.

column A tall upright supporting shaft.

columned chimney A chimney formed in the shape of one or more columns.

combination Wooden furniture construction with more than one type of wood in the exposed parts of the piece.

combination felt padding Carpet underlay felt pad of some animal hair and some synthetic fiber.

combination floor plans A floor plan with areas that are open and other rooms that are closed.

combination weave A fabric employing more than one type of weave; for example, plain and twill weaves seen side by side in a fabric.

combustion lighting Candlelight and firelight.

communication systems Intercom, computer network, and telephone systems that connect people within the building or beyond the building.

compact fluorescent (CF) lamps Small, fluorescent lamps that consume one-fifth of the power and can last up to thirteen times longer than incandescent. May connect to an incandescent fixture.

compartmental bathroom A bathroom in which the separate functions are housed in small rooms that open to each other.

complementary colors Colors that are in opposite position on the color wheel. Complementary colors have the greatest contrast of all the color combinations, each making the other more vivid. Types of complementary combinations include direct, split, triadic, double, tetrad, and alternate complements.

Composite A Roman architectural capital style composed of volutes from the Ionic order and acanthus leaves from the Corinthian order.

compounded fabrics *See* layered fabrics.

computer hardware The components of a computer system: the keyboard, monitor, computer power drive, printer, and plotter. It can also include larger mainframe computers.

computer network Connective cables that allow computer terminals within an office or design firm to access the same information.

computer programs The software, or disks, that operate the computer hardware. Programs are instructions, information, and data bases that allow the machine to operate specific functions. These include graphics, CAD, word processing, and so on.

computer terminal A keyboard and monitor that are connected to a mainframe. Also, a personal computer that can be connected to other computer terminals via a computer network system.

computer-aided design (and drafting) CAD (CADD) Computer software that enables the designer to draw, draft, arrange furnishing components, and compose simulated perspectives of a proposed interior space.

concept An idea for the solution to a problem.

conceptual drawings Drawings that show the concept or idea for a design.

concrete A mixture of sand, water, and portland cement that dries to a hard material; used for floors and walls, footings, foundations, and exterior flatwork.

condominium An individually owned home in a complex. The owner pays a monthly or yearly charge to maintain common landscaping and recreation and/or fitness facilities.

continuing education Skills, training, and knowledge gleaned by the professional interior designer through seminars and networks sponsored by professional organizations, institutions, and corporations.

contrast The difference that exists between two colors, values, or shapes. A large difference is termed sharp contrast, high contrast, or vivid contrast; small differences are termed low contrast. Contrast makes individual objects more meaningful.

control The monitoring unit or thermostat needed for a furnace or an active solar heating system.

conventional design A type of decorative design taken from nature and adapted, stylized, or conventionalized. The pattern is still recognizable as the nature object (flowers, for example) but is not reproduced in its naturalistic state.

conventional traverse rods Drapery rods with a cord-and-pulley system for operating pleated draperies.

conversation pit Seating areas designed and built in as an integral part of the environment. The name pit implies a sunken area, but this type of seating could be designed on a platform or on floor level.

cool colors Green, blue-green, blue, blue-violet, and violet.

cool white deluxe fluorescent lamps A quality, balanced spectrum lamp whose light does not appear cold and unflattering.

coordinating or companion fabric Decorative fabric printed in the same pattern or in a pattern that coordinates with the wallpaper.

cope To cut a section of paneling to fit an adjoining piece.

copper A bright, shiny, reddish brown metal used for cookware, tableware, decorative objects, and building components.

corbel *See* bracket.

Cordelan A registered trademark of the Japan company for a vinyl/vinyon fiber.

Cordura A registered trademark of DuPont for rayon and nylon.

Corinthian A Greek and Roman architectural style that features a capital decorated with acanthus leaves.

cork, cork wall coverings Lightweight, resilient bark of an oak tree belonging to the birch family that grows in the Mediterranean area. Coated with vinyl for floors, used in sheets or tiles or laminated to paper for wall coverings.

coromandel Large Chinese black-lacquered folding screens.

corner blocks Triangular blocks of wood attached at an angle across the corner of a joint for added strength.

corner fireplace A fireplace situated in the corner of a room.

cornice A wooden top treatment for draperies, frequently shaped on the bottom. Also, the projecting top section of a classical entablature. Found on the exterior under the eaves and on the ceiling where it meets the wall on the interior.

cornice lighting A lamp or line of light placed next to the ceiling with a board in front to direct the light downward.

cornice molding A more ornate form of crown molding.

corridor A passageway or hallway; usually indicates a nonresidential application.

cost analysis The proposed budget, including the design fee for a project or the economic feasibility of the design work. The result of programming research.

cost per square foot The total cost of the home or building, or the total cost of building one floor divided by the number of square feet.

cottage curtains Curtains often used in tiers or layers with ruffles around the edges.

cotton A natural cellulosic fiber obtained from the boll (fruit of the cotton plant). Cotton comes in short, medium, and long staple fibers and is an absorbent, soft, comfortable fiber. It dyes easily and is used in many printed decorative fabrics and in toweling.

cotton rugs Accent, scatter, or area rugs woven of cotton. Many are handwoven from India.

course A horizontal row of brick or masonry.

Courtaulds A registered trademark of Courtaulds for nylon.

cove molding A concave, rounded molding placed where wall and ceiling meet.

coved ceiling A ceiling with a concave, rounded radius where the ceiling meets the wall.

covered frame wall fabric method Fabric wrapped and stapled around a lath frame, then hung or affixed to a wall.

crenellation The notches or indentations in a parapet.

Creslan A registered trademark of American Cynamide for acrylic.

critical path The time frame and overlapping order of every step in the building and finishing process.

crocking   The rubbing off of excess dyestuffs onto another fabric or onto the skin.

crop   To trim or cut an art piece to fit a frame.

cross dyeing   Two fibers of different affinities dyed in the same bath; the colors will be accepted differently.

crossing   The area of a cross-shaped church where the nave and transept cross.

crowding   Where people are grouped together in tightly restricted areas.

crown lintel   *See* jack arch lintel.

crown molding   Trim placed where the wall and ceiling meet. Also called bed molding.

cruciform   Floor plan in the form or shape of a cross.

crypt   An underground vault, especially in a church, often used for burial.

crystal   A high grade of glass containing lead.

cubic feet or footage   The width multiplied by the length of a room and then by its height. The volume of space we walk through. Rooms with very high ceilings have greater cubic footage than those with lower ceilings.

Cumuloft   A registered trademark of Monsanto for nylon.

cupola   A small-domed structure rising above a roof.

curio   A rare or curious art object—a curiosity.

curtain rods   Plain or nontraverse rods of metal or wood.

curtain wall construction   *See* metal or space frame system.

curtains   A general term for fabric window treatments that are shirred or sometimes pleated but usually stationary or hand operated.

curved lines   Flowing lines, part of the elements of design. Large curves are smooth and gracious; small curves can give a feeling of activity in the interior.

curved staircase   A staircase with a curved radius.

custom design   Any design that is planned and executed according to individual specifications—not mass-produced.

custom floor plan   One that is executed by an architect or designer to meet the needs of the space—custom tailored to the design program.

cut glass   Glass incised with an abrasive to create decorative patterns.

cut length   The length of unhemmed fabric window treatments.

D

Dacron   A registered trademark of DuPont for polyester.

dado   A section of paneling that extends from the floor only as high as the chair rail.

dado cap   A molding used to finish the top of a dado.

damper   The movable piece in a fireplace that controls the airflow and escape of smoke.

data-base catalog   Information and graphic symbols programmed into a data-base software program. Useful in CAD and in business applications.

data-base programs   Software programs that manage, organize, and retrieve files used for working on documents, graphics, CAD.

daub   A coarse plaster used as infill wall finish in Medieval timber-framed buildings.

David Brewster Color theory   Another designation for the Standard Color Wheel theory.

De Stijl   An early twentieth-century Dutch aesthetic philosophical movement best represented by the work of painter Piet Mondrian.

decorative arts   Arts such as ceramics, metal work, textiles, and furniture that are suitable as decoration.

decorative design   A classification of design wherein the building, furniture piece, or object is decorated with ornamentation. Decorative design is broken into four categories: naturalistic, conventional, abstract, and geometric.

decorative finishes   A term for a group of finishes that add decorative appeal to fabrics. Examples of mechanical decorative finishes include various calendering, flocking, and napping finishes. Chemical decorative finishes include etch or burn-out printing and finishes that add brightness, softness, texture, stiffening, and delustering.

decorative luminaire   Another term for portable luminaire, consisting of plug-in, movable luminaires such as table and floor lamps. Also refers to an architectural or built-in luminaire that is decorative.

decorator rods   Metal drapery rods that are decorative with traverse cord-and-pulley workings.

dehumidifier   A unit connected to an air-conditioning unit that draws off excess humidity as a part of the cooling system.

demographics   The statistical data of a particular population.

dentil   A decorative trim of projecting rectangular blocks.

design   A term that describes a process of designing a building, furnishings, or composite interiors. Design also refers to the plan or scheme that made the end product possible in its executed form, material(s), and size.

design process   The sequence of steps in creating and executing a design project.

designer rugs   Custom-designed tufted or woven area rugs.

desk manager software   Programs with specific options for managing a business.

detached dwelling   A single home on a lot of its own.

deWolfe, Elsie (1865-1950)   The greatest and best known of the society interior designers who paved the way for the modern interior design profession.

dhurrie rugs   Originally cotton, now wool flat tapestry weave reversible rugs. Most are imported from India to meet Western demands.

diagonal lines   Angular lines that may go one (or more) directions in an interior. Diagonal lines suggest movement and action.

diagramming   The graphic process of planning space on paper.

diffusers   The glass or plastic cover over a luminaire that serves to soften the light and spread it evenly over the area.

dimensional stability   The ability of a fabric to maintain or return to its original shape.

dimmer switch   A manual or automated mechanism that controls the variable brightness of a lamp.

direct complement   Two colors that are directly across from each other on the color wheel.

direct glare   Glare from an insufficiently shielded light source directly into the line of vision.

direct glue-down   A method of laying carpeting where a layer of adhesive is applied to the floor and the carpet is laid directly on top of it, with no pad.

direct lighting   Lighting that shines directly on the desired area.

direct pasteup   Gluing fabric or wall coverings up with paste or adhesive.

direct solar gain   Heating an area through direct exposure of sunshine to the occupied space.

discharge printing   A process that removes the dyed color in patterned areas and replaces it with another color.

distressed   A finish made to appear old or antique by the intentional addition of dents, scratches, and flecks of paint during the finishing process.

distribution   Carrying air heated by active or passive solar systems to the various areas or rooms within a building.

doctor of philosophy   Ph.D., or doctorate degree; a possible requirement for full-time, tenure-track teaching positions in colleges and universities.

Dolan   A registered trademark of Hoechst for acrylic.

dome   An inverted round dish or cup-shaped ceiling.

dome system construction   An arch rotated in a circle to become a dome.

domestic Oriental rugs   Jacquard machine-woven rugs in Oriental rug designs.

Doric   Greek and Roman architectural style with fluted columns and plain capital.

dormer window   A window that projects from the attic.

double complement Two sets of direct complementary colors next to each other on the color wheel.

double glazing Filling a window opening with two layers of glass that provide insulation and increase energy efficiency at the window. Also known as twin glazing.

double roll A roll of wall covering with approximately seventy-two square feet, or double the area of a single roll.

double-hung Two layers of draperies, an overdrapery and an underlayer. Also, two sets of shutters, one installed directly above the other.

double-hung sash Sash window where both sections are operable.

double-shirred valance A valance shirred, or gathered, at the top and bottom.

double-turn stair A stair that makes two ninety-degree turns on two separate landings.

double-wide mobile home A mobile home that is fabricated into sections the size of a single-wide trailer, then fitted together to become twenty-four to thirty feet wide and twenty to forty feet long.

dovetail A series of fan-shaped joints used to connect drawer fronts and sides.

dowel A type of joint in which a third piece (the dowel) is glued into holes drilled in the two pieces being joined.

down Soft, fine feathers used as filling in some upholstered cushions.

draft dodgers A sand-filled tube of fabric or a heavy rug placed against a door to prevent cold air infiltration.

drafting The drawing by hand, machine, or computer of floor plans.

draftsman A person who drafts, draws, or produces floor plans and blueprints.

dragging and combing Production of fine paint lines with a dry brush over a wet glaze or combing with any hard comblike tool.

Dralon A registered trademark of Bayer for acrylic.

drapability The characteristic of a fabric to fall nicely into folds when draped.

draperies Pleated fabric hung with hooks on a traverse rod. Also refers to stationary side panels, tied-back fabric, and occasionally shirred panels.

draw draperies Operable panels hung on a cord or wand-operated traverse rod.

drawings One-of-a-kind, two-dimensional art forms produced with pencil, pen and ink, charcoal, chalk, crayon, or grease pencil on paper or other surfaces.

drop-leaf table A table with a fixed center section and side flaps that can be lowered or raised and held up with various types of supports. Also called occasional table.

dropped-pendant luminaires Simple, suspended luminaires dropped from the ceiling with a cord or chain.

drum A cylindrical portion of a building used as the base for a dome.

drywall Another term for wallboard, sheetrock, or plasterboard; wall material made of pulverized gypsum rock.

duct work or ducts Metal or plastic pipes that funnel heated or air-conditioned air throughout an interior.

duplex A twin home dwelling—two units sharing one roof and foundation.

durable finishes Chemical or decorative finishes that remain on the fabric through repeated cleaning.

durable press calendering A decorative mechanical finish that resin presses for durability and pattern impressions.

Durel A registered trademark of Celanese for olefin.

durry rugs *See* dhurrie rugs.

dust panel A panel, usually of hardboard, placed between drawers to keep dust and other objects from passing between levels.

dust ruffle A gathered, pleated, or tailored fabric covering that extends from the mattress of a bed to the floor.

dutch door A double door, split in half, with independent top and bottom sections.

duvet A nondecorative comforter that is covered with a removable cover.

dye lot A single run of color printing of wallpaper or fabric, using a particular batch of dye. Background and decorative design colors may vary somewhat with each new dye lot.

dyeing The process of coloring done in one of several stages: in the viscose solution (man-made fibers), as stock (natural fibers), the yarn state, or the fabric piece goods state.

dyestuff A water-soluble coloring matter used to make a dye bath solution.

Dynel A registered trademark of Union Carbide for modacrylic.

E

Eames, Charles (1907-78) and Ray An important husband-wife design team responsible for several modern classic furniture pieces.

Early American (1650-1750) A general term for American Provincial or country New England interiors.

Early Christian (A.D. 330-800) The architectural period following the official recognition of the Christian church by the Roman government.

Early Georgian (1695-1750) Architectural period that first brought the design and elegance of the English Renaissance to America.

ears Moldings on panels, door frames, or chimneypieces that break to form small molded squares or ears at the corners.

earthenware Coarse and inexpensive ceramic body used for dinnerware and accessory pieces.

easements Short bends in the handrail that allow it to change direction.

Eastlake, Charles (1793-1865) Nineteenth-century English designer and scholar who advocated the Gothic Revival style. Wrote *Hints on Household Taste*.

echinus An oval-shaped molding between the shaft and the abacus on a column.

eclectic A mixture of stylistic influences or a mixture of styles.

economy The relative cost of items as related to an allotted budget.

effects of crowding The effects of crowding are inordinate exposure to sounds, smells, and touch.

efficacy Lumens per watt is a measure of the efficacy or efficiency of the light source.

egg and dart A molding of alternating egg shapes and dart or arrowhead shapes.

eggshell enamel A hard finish semigloss paint.

egress The way out; exit.

eight plex An apartment building containing eight units.

elements of design The tactile portion of interiors that can be manipulated by the designer. These are space, shape or form, mass, line, texture, pattern, light, and color.

elevation A flat, two-dimensional drawing of a straight-on (orthographic) view of an object, an exterior facade, or an interior wall.

Elura A registered trademark of Monsanto for modacrylic.

embellishment Decoration or ornamentation added to an object or an interior.

embossed loop pile A looped pile surface carpet with high and low, or multilevel, loops; creates a random pattern.

embossed wall coverings Wallpapers with an imprinted, three-dimensional design.

embroidery The hand or machine stitching of threads or yarns to create a pattern on the surface of an otherwise completed fabric.

emphasis A principle of design that indicates attention is given to a certain area within an interior. Emphasis is also called focal point.

enamel paints Oil-based or sometimes water-based paints that are hard and glossy.

enameled glass Glass that has been encased with an opaque vitreous layer.

Encron A registered trademark of American Enka for polyester.

energy consciousness A term often associated with window treatments— covering windows to keep in winter heat and exclude summer solar gain or heat.

engravings Prints made from a hand-engraved metal plate.

Enkrome A registered trademark of American Enka for viscose rayon.

entablature A decorative architectural section made up of cornice, frieze, and architrave.

envelope A passive solar building system wherein air circulates in a double-wall construction around the house and includes a south-facing solarium.

epoxy paint Used to paint over metal or water-filled surfaces. Contains hardeners.

equilibrium A state of physical or visual balance or equality.

ergonomics *See* biotechnology.

ER lamps *See* R, ER lamps.

Estron A registered trademark of Eastman Kodak for acetate.

etch or burn-out printing A decorative chemical finish printed with acid to burn out one fiber—usually cotton in a cotton/polyester blend—to leave a sheer pattern.

etched glass Glass that has been engraved with a pattern by hand or by use of an abrasive cutting tool, a corrosive substance, or sandblasting.

etchings Prints made from metal plates that have patterns and designs chemically etched into their surface.

European handmade rugs French Savonnerie and Aubusson, Portuguese needlepoint, and Spanish rugs.

evaporative cooling system Also called swamp cooling, the system is based on air flowing through a wet pad. Useful and economical in arid climates.

execution The final phase of the design process where the design plans are implemented.

exposed aggregate Pebbles set into and protruding above a concrete base. Hard flooring and wall material.

exterior veneer The finish building material on the exterior, such as masonry (brick, stone) or siding (metal, wood, stucco).

extrude/extrusion To force out through a small opening; a method used to form tubular steel. Also, man-made fibers formed by forcing a viscose solution through a spinnerette.

eyeball A recessed spotlight that shines at an angle on a wall or object.

F

F lamp A flame-shaped, often fluted lamp for decorative fixtures such as a candelabra.

fabric art Handwoven or constructed fabric or textile pieces that hang on the wall.

fabric shades Vertically or horizontally operated shades of fabric, including roller, Roman, balloon, and Austrian shades.

fabric wall coverings Heavy wall coverings made sturdy and substantial with a fabric, rather than paper, backing. Used for vinyl and nonresidential wall coverings.

facade The front or principal face of a building.

face weight Yarn weight of carpeting per square measure. Heavier weights indicate more face or pile yarn, or greater density.

fanlight A half-circle- or half-ellipse-shaped window placed above a door or in a pediment.

fauteuil French term for an open armchair.

Federal (1790-1830) The post-revolutionary period in America.

feldspar Crystalline materials mixed with kaolin to make porcelain.

felt padding Animal and/or synthetic fibers compressed and needlepunched; used for carpet underlay to protect carpet without great resilience.

festoon Another term for swag, a half circle of fabric pleated or folded on the ends.

fiber felt padding *See* felt padding.

Fiberglass or glass fiber A synthetic mineral fiber made of spun glass used for insulation, tub enclosures, and contract draperies. (A registered trademark of Owens-Corning for glass fiber or fiberglass.)

Fibralon A registered trademark of Fibron for olefin.

Fibro A registered trademark of Courtaulds for rayon.

FIDER The Foundation for Interior Design Education and Research, which establishes standards for design education. Also a design school accrediting body.

fieldstone Any type of large, rugged rocks used for flooring or walls.

filament The continuous man-made fiber strand extruded through the spinnerette. Filaments are combined and spun into threads or yarns. Natural filaments are silk and horsehair.

fillers Preparatory materials for surfaces to be painted. Used to fill in nail holes, cracks, or other imperfections.

filling yarns The set of yarns woven crosswise into the set of long warp yarns that are threaded onto a loom. Also called weft.

Fina A registered trademark of Monsanto for acrylic.

fine arts The arts of architecture, painting, drawing, sculpture, and printmaking, as well as music, literature, drama, and dance.

finial An upward-pointing finishing ornament for pediment, post, or spire.

finish carpenter One who creates custom woodwork and cabinetry.

finish package The woodwork in an interior, including items such as built-in shelving, cabinets, case piece units, baseboard/door/window trim, and railings.

finish plumbing The installation of sinks, toilets, and faucet hardware.

finished length The length of a finished, hemmed fabric window treatment.

finished pile weight Weight in ounces per square measure of finished carpeting.

finishes These are a group of finishes that render a fabric more resistant to bacteria, static, wrinkling, flammability, insects, soil, humidity damage and increase insulative qualities. A general term for processes that do one of the following: prepare a fabric for coloring, give functional protection, dye or print a fabric, or add aesthetic or decorative effects to a fabric. Also, clear liquids used to seal and finish stained or painted surfaces.

finishing Processes or chemicals that render fabrics more durable or decorative.

fire alert system A network or single unit that senses heat or smoke, then alerts the occupants through a shrill noise.

fire retardant Certain man-made fibers such as modacrylic, saran, and PVC that resist burning but are not flame-proof.

firebox The part of the fireplace that contains the fire.

fireplace insert An enclosed stove unit that can be placed in an existing fireplace to make it more efficient.

fish-scale shingles Small shingles with round or pointed sawtooth ends used to create decorative surface effects on the nineteenth-century Queen Anne-style houses.

fixed window A window that cannot be opened.

fixture or luminaire The structural or decorative unit that holds the lamp or bulb and the electric connectors. In fluorescent and HID lighting, it also contains the ballast.

fixture Something that is fixed in place or an element or feature of a setting. Pieces other than typical furniture that are placed in the environment by the designer, such as pieces of specialized equipment, custom-designed work spaces, or counters. Plumbing fixtures are the sinks, toilets, and various bathtubs and hot tubs. Lighting fixtures are also called luminaires.

flagstone Hard, nonresilient stone that splits into sheets, used for paving and flooring.

flame resistant A term referring to fabrics such as wool, silk, nylon, olefin, and polyester that do not ignite easily, are slow-burning, and will often self-extinguish.

flame-retardant finishes   Chemical finishes that make a fabric that is constructed of a flammable fiber become resistant to fire ignition and spread. Chemical applications that render a fabric less flammable.

flame-retardant paints   Paints with additives that inhibit combustibility.

flammability resistance   Ability of background textiles to resist catching on fire and/or sustaining a flame. Nonresidential code requirement.

flammability tests   Tests that measure the rate of ignition, the rate of flame spread when the source of the fire is removed, how long the fabric continues to burn, how long it remains in a red-glow state, and the density and toxicity of the fumes. These tests are conducted to meet stringent nonresidential state and local fire codes.

flammable or inflammable   A term that refers to fabrics, such as cellulosic cotton, linen, rayon, and acetate, that easily catch on fire or are highly combustible.

flat   A British term for an apartment.

flat paint   Any type of paint that dries to a matte or nonshiny finish.

flatbed screen printing   The traditional method of stencil silk-screen printing where screens are manually or mechanically moved and paint squeegeed across by hand.

flatwork   Concrete laid flat for foundation and garage floors, sidewalks, and driveways.

Flemish gable   A gable incorporating steps, curves, or both.

flexibility   The ability of a fabric to stretch and rebound to its original shape; a necessary characteristic in upholstery fabrics.

flexible wall coverings   A general term for wall coverings that may be bent or manipulated to fit a shape or surface.

flickering light   An uneven source of light such as candlelight, firelight, or electric lamps that imitate this effect.

flitch   The half or quarter log that is cut to make lumber for furniture construction.

floccati rugs   Area rugs woven or knitted with tufts of sheared goat's hair left in its natural cream or brown color.

flocked carpet   A method of producing a carpet pile similar to velvet. Fibers are electrostatically charged, then embedded in a glue-coated fabric backing.

flocked wallpapers   Wallpapers with chopped fibers affixed to the surface in a decorative pattern.

flocking   A decorative process of adhering patterns of tiny fibers to the surface of a fabric; often seen in sheers and flocked dotted swiss fabrics.

floodlight   A reflective lamp spotlight with a wide-beam spread.

floor lamp   Luminaires designed to sit on the floor for task or general lighting.

floor plans   The two-dimensional layout of rooms. Part of the working drawings and blueprints used to construct a space.

flowing lines   These are a type of curved lines that suggest graceful continuous or growing movement.

flue   The chimney pipe above the firebox in a fireplace.

fluoresce   To glow or become fluorescent.

fluorescent light   Produced by an arc, or discharge, between two electrodes inside a glass tube filled with very low-pressure mercury vapor that produces ultraviolet (invisible) radiation in wavelengths. These activate the white phosphorus lining of the lamp, causing it to glow and converting the ultraviolet energy into visible light.

fluorescent lighting   Artificial lighting produced by charging mercury argon gas. Light is clear and relatively shadowless. Cool fluorescent lighting may produce a bluish cast.

flush door   Flat doors with no raised or sunken panels.

flush-face fireplace   A fireplace whose planes are flush with the wall in which it is built.

flute   A groove in the shaft of a column.

flying buttress   A horizontal brace that spans from the wall to a supporting abutment and receives the outward thrust of the wall.

foam rubber pads   Carpet underlay of foam rubber.

focal point   Also known as emphasis or center of interest, a focal point draws the eye to an area or object and holds the interest of the viewer. Architectural focal points include picture windows and fireplaces.

foil/mylar wall coverings   A mirrorlike shiny or reflective background.

folded plate system construction   A building system of thin reinforced concrete in a folded, zigzag roof pattern.

folk rugs   Flat tapestry rugs handmade by an ethnic group in native design and color.

footcandles   A measurement of the amount of direct light hitting a surface.

footlamberts   A measurement of the amount of light reflected off a surface.

forced-air heating   A conventional furnace-powered heating system in which the hot air is blown through ducts and enters rooms through registers.

form   The three-dimensional shape of an object.

formal areas   The spaces in residential design where structured visiting, dining, and entertaining take place away from kitchen and other work spaces.

formal balance   Another term for symmetrical, bisymmetrical, or passive balance.

Fortrel   A registered trademark of Celanese for polyester.

foundation   The cement footings and basement walls that support the building.

four plex   A four-unit apartment building.

frame   A case or border made to enclose a picture.

framing or framework   The wooden or metal skeleton structure used for the majority of buildings today.

freestanding fireplace   A self-contained fireplace unit that is away from the wall.

French door   Double casement-type door that opens in or out.

French Empire (1804-20)   The period during the time of Napoleon in France.

French Règence (1715-23)   The period between the reigns of Louis XIV and Louis XV in France.

fresco   A painting made on fresh wet plaster with pigment and lime water.

fretwork   Patterns of flat interlocking bands or trelliswork.

frieze   A tightly twisted cut pile carpet. Also, the section of the entablature above the architrave and below the cornice. Also, a horizontal band of sculpture or painting.

full spectrum lighting   Light that contains all color wavelengths.

function   A normal or characteristic action or some duty required in work. Used here to refer to anything that takes place within a given environment.

functional finishes   *See* standard finishes.

furnace   The mechanism that heats air or water by electricity, natural gas, coal, or oil and either blows the heated air through ducts or pumps hot water to radiators.

fuse-bonded carpet   Carpet yarns directly tufted into a liquid rubber or latex backing that solidifies to hold in the tufts.

fuzzing   The working loose of fibers to the surface of the textile.

G

G lamp   A spherical or globe-shaped bulb.

gable   The triangular end of a house formed by the pitched roof.

galerie   A covered porch on the houses of French influence.

gambrel roof   A roof line with a double pitch, flatter at the top and steeper at the bottom like a red barn.

garret   Same as attic.

gazebo   A small, open garden house.

general contractor   A builder who is licensed to construct or oversee construction of all building phases.

general lighting   *See* ambient lighting.

generic A general type of man-made fiber that is significantly different from other fibers and thereby has been granted a name, such as nylon, by the Federal Trade Commission. Within each generic group are up to dozens of trademarks or trade names produced by various chemical companies.

genuine Wooden furniture construction with veneers of a particular wood, over hardwood plywood, on all the exposed parts of a piece.

geodesic dome system construction A building system enclosing spaces with curved, triangular steel truss work. The interior structure must be independent of the dome.

geometric design A classification of decorative design based on geometric shapes: circles, squares, rectangles, and triangles.

Georgian A term used to describe design during the period while George I through George IV ruled England.

gilded glass Glass that has been encased in a layer of gold.

ginger jar A bulbous oriental ceramic pot and lid, designed to hold ginger.

gingerbread The decorative trim used on Victorian buildings.

glare Strong, steady, daylight or artificial light that can cause irritation, fatigue, and heat buildup.

glare-free Lamps that have silvered lining.

glass A hard, brittle material of molten silica sand and soda or potash, lime, and possibly metal oxides. Clear, transparent, or colored; used for window glazing, mirrors, walls.

glass, architectural glazing Glass used to fill window openings; term usually refers to nonresidential installations.

glass block Semihollow blocks of translucent glass primarily for non-load-bearing walls.

glass curtains A historic term for sheers shirred onto a curtain rod and placed next to the glass.

glass tile Vitrified tiles of dense glass composition. Imported from France.

glaze A colored or transparent liquid applied to clay objects that hardens and becomes glasslike when baked at high temperatures.

glazing The process of filling an opening with glass. Also, transparent paint colors overlayed in sequence, producing various gradations of color in a painting.

glide The mechanism on the bottom or sides of a drawer upon which it slides.

gloss enamel Hard, oil-based paint that dries to a shine or gloss.

gold electroplate A process for creating gold-plated silverware.

gold leaf Extremely thin sheets of gold used in gilding.

golden age *See* ancient Greece.

golden mean A pleasing line of division that is placed between one-half and one-third of the height or length of an object, such as tieback draperies or a chair rail.

golden section A theory of pleasing proportions based on the sequence 2:3:5:8:13:21, ad inf., where a portion or section of a line relates best to its neighbors in measurements of these or equivalent increments.

Gothic (A.D. 1150-1550) A period and style in western Europe characterized by pointed arches and steep roofs.

Gothic arch A pointed arch that is the principal form in Gothic architecture.

gouache Any water-soluble, opaque watercolor. Often used as a synonym for tempera.

gradation A type of rhythm wherein sizes of shapes graduate from large to small or small to large. Also seen in varying color values from dark to light or light to dark.

grain The markings and textures in a piece of wood created by the arrangement of the fibers.

granite A very hard crystalline rock used for floors and walls.

graphic art Artwork such as posters, fashion illustrations, and book illustrations created primarily for commercial purposes but having aesthetic merit.

graphic artist A designer who specializes in two-dimensional signage, graphics, type, and design motifs or logos.

graphics The visual signs in a retail space that direct customers to departments or to certain goods. Also, the term used for putting on paper the stages of space planning from bubble diagrams to the finished floor plans.

grass cloth Woven grasses laminated to a paper backing and used as wall covering.

gray goods or greige Woven fabrics in their natural fiber state before bleaching and prefinishes. Pieces of bolt length may not be gray but a dingy off-white.

grazing or graze Light shining at a very steep angle that emphasizes the texture of the surface.

great hall The large, multipurpose area in the English Medieval house.

great room An open area in contemporary homes that combines the living room, family room, dining room, and perhaps the kitchen, office, and/or library.

Greek Revival (1820-60) Architectural style that contained American Empire interiors.

greenhouse effect Phenomenon in which captured solar heat from long sun rays penetrates glass, and bounces off materials and furnishings, and becomes shorter, weaker, and unable to repenetrate the glass.

greenhouse window Projecting glass box for growing plants.

grounding receiver The third hole in an electric outlet required for fixtures and appliances that consume a lot of power to be connected into the circuit and to prevent electric shock.

gum arabic A sticky substance from gum trees that is soluble in water and hardens when exposed to air, used as a vehicle for watercolor.

gypsum board *See* wallboard.

H

hand The relative softness or coarseness of a fabric; the way it feels to the touch.

hand printing Processes such as batik, tie-dye, block printing, and hand silk-screen and stencil printing.

handrail The rail for grasping while ascending a stair.

hard window coverings Art glass, blinds, screens, shades, and shutters.

hardboard Compressed wood fibers formed into panels with embossed designs or a wood/plastic laminated surface.

hardware The metal fittings on furniture such as drawer pulls and keyhole covers. Also, the components that make up a computer: the keyboard, the computer power drive unit, the monitor or screen, the printer, and the plotter.

hardwood Tough, heavy timber of compact texture taken from trees with broad, flat leaves such as oak and walnut.

harmony A congruous combination of parts into a pleasing whole; the result of unity and variety balanced together in an orderly, agreeable arrangement.

hearth The slab that forms the base of a fireplace and extends into the room.

heat gain Solar heat that penetrates the interior through glass; desirable in winter and undesirable in summer.

heat loss The interior heat lost in winter back through glass to the outside. To prevent heat loss, movable insulation or insulative window treatments are employed.

heat setting The setting in of permanent creases or folds in polymer fabrics by heating the fold to the point of polymer flow (beginning to melt), then rapidly cooling the fabric.

heat-transfer printing Decals that are dispersed-transferred from waxed paper to a cloth under heat and pressure.

Hepplewhite, George (d. 1786) An important English furniture designer who produced a series of drawings published as *The Cabinet-Maker and Upholsterer's Guide*.

Herculon A registered trademark of Hercules for olefin.

HID (high-intensity discharge)
lighting HID lamps establish an arc between two very close electrodes set in opposite ends of small, sealed, translucent or transparent glass tubes. The electric arc generates heat and pressure high enough to vaporize the atoms of various metallic elements inside the lamp, causing the atoms to emit large amounts of visible-range electromagnetic energy.

high contrast The difference between small areas of light and the dark area surrounding it.

high key All colors in an interior that are light or high in value.

high rise A building containing several levels or floors of apartments, condominiums, or offices.

high tech A product of high technology.

high values Light variations of a hue; a hue with various amounts of white added.

highboy A tall four- or five-drawer chest mounted on a dressing table (lowboy). Also known as a tallboy.

high-contrast values A wide division of color value in an interior—very light colors contrasted with very dark colors.

high-efficiency furnace A furnace that uses less energy and delivers a higher output. The unit costs more initially.

high-gloss paint Any paint that dries to a very shiny finish.

hiking up The shrinking of a fabric that has absorbed moisture, then dried.

hipped roof A roof without a gabled end that slopes in four directions.

Hispanic Having to do with Spain or Portugal.

Hitchcock, Lambert (1795-1852) An American furniture designer known best for his Hitchcock chair with its black painted finish, stenciling, rush or cane seat, and delicate lines.

Hitchcock chair *See* Hitchcock, Lambert.

Hoffmann, Josef (1870-1956) Member of the Vienna Secession and founding member of the Wiener Werkstäte. He is best known for his design of the Prague chair and Fledermaus chair.

Hollofil A registered trademark of DuPont for polyester.

hollow-core door A veneered door with a hollow core filled with cardboard honeycomb.

hologram A three-dimensional image projected by splitting a laser beam.

home automation Central control of all energy-using fixtures and devices.

hooded fireplace A fireplace with a projecting hood to catch the smoke.

hook-and-loop fasteners A two-part fastening system of nylon loops on one tape and a fuzzy nylon surface on another that stick together and can be pulled apart. The best-known brand is Velcro.

hooked rugs A traditional method of making decorative rugs of strips of fabric, punched through a jutelike backing with a special hook.

horizontal lines Horizontal lines serve to visually widen or lengthen an interior and, when dominant, produce feelings of relaxation and repose.

horizontal satin *See* sateen.

hourglass A piece for telling time with two globes of glass connected by a narrow neck that allows a quantity of sand to pass during a specified time.

housed stair A stair attached to walls on both sides. Also called a closed stair.

hue Another word for color, as the hue red. An important designation in the Munsell color system.

humidifier An attachment to a furnace that adds moisture or humidity to the air. (Heating interior air strips it of moisture.)

hutch A side piece with cupboards and drawers and a set of open shelves above; also called a Welsh dresser.

HVAC Heating, ventilation, and air-conditioning. In nonresidential architecture, it is the system that maintains an even temperature (around 72 degrees Fahrenheit) and circulates fresh air through the interior.

hybrid solar energy system A passive solar system augmented with fans, ducts, blowers, or other mechanical devices.

hydrophilic A fiber that readily absorbs moisture, such as natural and man-made cellulosics and natural protein fibers.

I

IBD The Institute of Business Designers.

IDC The Interior Designers of Canada.

IDEC The Interior Design Educators Council.

IDS The Interior Design Society.

IFDA The International Furnishings and Design Association (formerly the National Home Fashions League).

IFI The International Federation of Interior Architects/Designers.

ikebana Traditional Japanese method of arranging flowers according to strict rules of placement.

illusion lighting The artistic science of creating illusion through specialty lighting.

incandescent lighting Light produced by heating fine metal filament until it glows. Warm incandescent lighting produces a yellowish cast to colors.

incident solar radiation The energy collected from the sun to power active solar panels/systems. Also called insolation.

independent living Elderly or handicapped persons who are able to live at home and care for themselves because the space is planned to accommodate their needs.

indirect and isolated passive solar gain Solar gain from a source other than the occupied space. Examples include greenhouses or solariums that can be closed off from the living or nonresidential space.

indirect lighting Produced by throwing light against a wall, floor, or ceiling to light a general area.

infill Materials used to fill the space between the timber frame of a building.

informal areas Areas for relaxed, spontaneous living, and entertaining.

informal balance Also known as asymmetrical, optical, or occult balance, it is the state of equilibrium reached through the arrangement of unlike objects or parts on each side of a central point.

ingress The entrance to a building.

in-house designer An interior designer who is a salaried staff member of a large organization; responsible for the interior design or facilities management of new and existing buildings owned by that organization.

inlaid vinyl Flooring in which successive layers of vinyl granules are built up to suggest texture.

insolation *See* incident solar radiation.

insulation A material such as fiberglass that prevents heat transfer. Commonly used in batts (fiber blanket rolls), rigid panels, styrofoam beads, or other materials.

insulative window treatments Any window covering that deters heat loss and solar gain.

intaglio Printing from plates where the design is recessed below the surface of the plate. Those recesses hold the ink.

intensity The relative pureness or brightness of a color, as opposed to the dullness or neutralization of that hue. Also called chroma.

intercom An electrical system that allows people to communicate within a building; also carries taped or radio music heard through speakers.

interface Interdependency of design phases that must be accomplished simultaneously or consecutively. Also, a computer term in which different terminals can access the same information through a central mainframe computer or a networking system.

interior architecture The nonresidential aspect of interior design that may entail remodeling and work with building systems.

interior building systems The systems that are a part of the interior: plumbing, HVAC, electrical.

intermediate hues Six hues on the standard color wheel that are produced by mixing a primary and secondary color. They are yellow-orange, red-orange, red-violet, blue-violet, blue-green, and yellow-green. Also known as tertiary hues.

International style An early twentieth-century design style based on concepts developed simultaneously in several international locations, including the Bauhaus in Germany. The style is simple, clean, functional, and modern in spirit.

interrelationship of functions The way areas work together or depend on one another to function effectively.

Ionic Greek and Roman architectural style with scroll-shaped capital.

iron A heavy black metal.

Itten, Johannes (1888-1967) A colorist who taught at the Bauhaus in Germany and at Yale University. He authored several books, including *The Art of Color* and *The Elements of Color*.

J

jack arch lintel A trapezoidal lintel with a wedge-shaped keystone used as decoration above windows. Also called a crown lintel.

Jacquard A loom attachment named after its French inventor that allows complex patterns to be woven in rapid succession. Jacquard fabrics include brocade and brocatelle, damask, lampas, matelassé, and patterned velvets.

jalousie window A louvered glass window.

Jeanneret-Gris, Charles-Edouard (1887-1965) Important architect/designer better known as Le Corbusier. Designer of several modern classic furniture pieces.

joint A closure, such as the mortise and tenon, where two pieces of wood are fastened together in furniture construction.

joists The heavy beams that support the floor and rafters.

Journal of Interior Design The scholarly, refereed journal of the Interior Design Educators Council.

jute A cellulosic bast fiber obtained from the inner stalks of the jute plant and grown in India. Its main interior use is as carpet backing.

juxtaposition Placement of colors next to each other.

K

Kandinsky, Wassily (1886-1944) A Russian artist associated with the Bauhaus.

Kanekalon A registered trademark of Kanekafuchi for modacrylic.

kaolin A claylike substance used in making porcelain. The name comes from Kaoling, a mountain in China where kaolin was first mined.

keystone The stone at the top of an arch that is angled on the sides, stabilizing compression and friction.

kilim rugs Flat tapestry folk rugs that originated in Romania.

kiln An oven capable of controlled high temperatures used for baking clay objects.

kitsch A German term that describes bad taste and is applied to pretentious or foolish art.

knickknack A small ornamental article.

knitted carpet A sturdy pile carpet that is constructed by knitting with multiple needles.

knitted fabrics Needle-constructed interlocking fabrics such as single and double knits, laces, rachel warp knits, arnache and malimo fabrics. Knitted fabrics offer speed of construction, variety in patterns, and lacy effects, and either stretch or dimensional stability characteristics.

Kodel A registered trademark of Eastman Kodak for polyester.

L

L'Ecole des Beaux Arts A school of art, design, and architecture in Paris, France, noted for its emphasis on historical studies.

lacquer A type of varnish made from shellac or gum resins dissolved in ethyl alcohol or other quick-drying solvents.

ladder-back chair A chair back with a number of horizontal slats like a ladder.

laminated foam One or more densities of polyurethane foam laminated together to form a single pad.

lamination The process of building up in layers or attaching a single ply as with plywood, foam, or plastic laminates.

lamp The technical term for light bulb.

lancet A narrow, pointed arch window.

landings The platforms of a stair where it begins, ends, or turns.

Lanese A registered trademark of Celanese for acetate and polyester.

laser A device containing a crystal, gas, or other suitable substance in which atoms, when stimulated by focused light waves, amplify and concentrate these waves, then emit them in a very intense, narrow beam.

Late Georgian (1750-90) The American period that utilized English Georgian design and Chippendale furniture.

latex A rubber-based synthetic polymer extruded or sprayed on as a coating or backing to hold woven fabrics or tufted carpets stable.

latex paint A water-based paint that is easy to apply and cleans up with soap and water when still wet.

lath Thin strips of wood laid parallel and nailed onto building studs. Historic method of plastering walls is to apply it over lath.

lathwork Grids or panels made with strips of lath, used as screens, trellises, or decorative trim on verandas.

latillas Sticks laid across the vigas to form the ceiling of the Southwest Adobe houses.

Latin cross The Western Christian cross with a tail longer than the top and arms.

lattice A panel consisting of metal or wooden strips that are interlaced or crossed to form a grid with regular spaces.

law of chromatic distribution A rule governing the distribution of color intensity or brightness. The most neutralized colors are used in the largest areas, and the smaller the size or area, the brighter or more intense the chroma proportionately becomes.

layered or compounded fabrics A group of fabric constructions that require more than one step to complete. Examples include embroidery, appliqué, and tufting.

Le Corbusier *See* Jeanneret-Gris, Charles-Edouard.

leaded glass Glass windows made of small pieces held together with lead caming to form a pattern.

leather The tanned hide of cattle or swine, largely used for upholstery. Leather is strong, is comfortable, and has a long life span.

leather tiles Actual pieces of leather cut into shapes and applied as wall or floor tiles. Resilient semi-permanent material.

leno weave A variation of the plain weave that has warp thread in hourglass twists where the weft or filling threads are woven in.

letter of agreement The legal contractual arrangement between the design firm and the client that spells out responsibilities and services of both parties.

level-loop carpet Woven or tufted carpet with an uncut pile of even loops; used in both residential and nonresidential interiors.

level-tip shear carpet Woven or tufted carpet with some loops higher than others. Surface has a smooth, velvetlike texture.

life-style The way an individual or group lives.

light An element of design that is broken into two types: natural (sunlight) and artificial.

light pipe An acrylic pipe that conducts light along its corridor. The light source can be sunlight or artificial light.

lighting as art Use of light as a medium to create artistic effects.

lighting plan   The portion of the working drawings or blueprints that shows where the lights, switches, and outlets are to be placed in a building and how they are connected to one another and to the circuit-breaker box. Also called the wiring plan.

line   The deliberate connection of two points as seen in planes and outlines of shapes. An element of design.

line of credit   The total cost of merchandise that may be purchased by a designer on credit on behalf of the designer's clients.

line or outline lighting   Lighting the perimeter of an object to give emphasis or even lighting.

linen   The best known of the cellulosic bast fibers, obtained from the inner stalks of the flax plant. Linen is strong and absorbent and varies from a coarse jutelike texture to fine table damask linen textures.

linenfold   A medieval panel motif resembling folded linen.

linoleum   A soft resilient flooring of ground wood and cork, gum, color pigments, and oxidized linseed oil. No longer produced.

lintel   A horizontal crosspiece over a door or a window or between two columns.

lithographs   Prints made from a stone or metal plate to which the pattern or design has been applied with a special grease pencil or wax.

Loftura   A registered trademark of Eastman Kodak for acetate.

long, formal curtains   Having a shirred or tabbed heading, these long curtains can be hand operable or stationary.

long-life bulb   An incandescent bulb that lasts from 2,500 to 3,500 hours.

loose cushions   Pillows that are part of an upholstered piece but left unattached in the upholstery process.

Louis XV period (1723-74)   The period during the reign of King Louis XV of France. Also known as the Rococo period and characterized by ornate, curvilinear, asymmetrical design.

Louis XVI period (1774-93)   The period during the reign of King Louis XVI of France. Also known as the French Neoclassic period and characterized by rectilinear, classically inspired design.

louvered door   Door with louvered panels.

louvers   Horizontal slats in a shutter, screen, or window, sloped downward (or movable) to control light and air passage.

low contrast   The difference between colors whose values (lightness vs. darkness) are very close—such as all light colors or all dark colors.

low key   A color scheme in a variety of dark values.

low value   Hues that have been darkened.

lowboy   A low chest of drawers raised on legs, used as a dressing or serving table. With the addition of a tall chest, it becomes a highboy.

low-contrast values   Values near each other, such as dark and medium values or medium and light values, for example.

low-voltage lamps   Bulbs that consume little energy.

lumber-core door   Same as solid-core door.

lumens   A measurement of the amount of light flow.

luminaire   A lighting fixture.

luminous ceiling   Incandescent or fluorescent lights around which a box is framed and finished, with the cover over the lights made of translucent glass or plastic.

luminous panels   Fluorescent or incandescent lights set into a wall or floor and covered with translucent glass or plastic.

luxury homes   Spacious or luxurious homes with high-quality detail, cabinet work, and furnishings.

M

Mackintosh, Charles Rennie (1868-1928)   Scottish designer/ architect, influential with the Vienna Secessionists and designer of the Hill chair.

mainframe computer   A large computer into which smaller computer terminals or personal computers can be accessed. Mainframes can handle complex data, problems, and CAD with speed and accuracy.

maintenance   The labor required to maintain a material—tasks such as sweeping, vacuuming, dusting, mopping, scrubbing, or waxing.

man-made fibers   Chemically derived and extruded from a viscose solution.

mansard roof   A hipped roof with two pitches. The bottom pitch is very steep and the top pitch flatter, so it is usually not seen from the ground.

mantel   The projecting shelf of a chimneypiece.

marble   A very hard stone cut into slabs and polished for floor and wall materials. Smooth and formal, white or colored with streaks of color.

marbling   Imitating polished marble stone with paint.

markets, marketing centers   Convenient clusters of trade sources that market goods and services wholesale to interior designers.

Marlborough leg   A straight, square furniture leg with a square foot.

marquetry   Patterns created by laminating contrasting pieces of thin wood (and other materials) into a veneered surface.

Marvess   A registered trademark of Phillips for olefin.

masonry block construction   Walls or foundations of cinder block or concrete block without any wooden framework.

mass   An element of design that denotes density or visual weight within an object. Heavier mass or density will often make an object appear larger than one that has little mass or empty space within its shape.

massing   Gathering or forming into a mass. The pulling of objects into a group so that together they have more visual weight or importance than they do separately.

master of arts degree (M.A.)   A degree that may be considered a terminal degree in interior design education.

master of fine arts degree (M.F.A.)   A degree that may be considered a terminal degree in interior design education. M.F.A. degrees require a fine arts skill and showing of work. It is considered the design education equivalent of a doctor of philosophy (Ph.D.) degree.

master of science degree (M.S.)   A degree that may be considered a terminal degree in interior design education.

masters   Those whose art has passed the test of time to become classic.

mat   A border of mat board or other material, used as a frame or part of the frame of a picture.

match   The same color from one dye lot to another.

materials and finishes boards   Boards used to show pieces of the materials and finishes that have been selected for a design.

matte paint   Any paint that dries to a flat, nonshiny finish.

mechanical finishes   A classification of decorative finishes that include calendering, napping, and flocking. Also called surface treatment finishes.

media   The substances used to dilute paint—water for watercolor and turpentine for oil paint. Also the means or methods an artist uses to produce a work.

Medieval era (A.D. 800-1500)   The Middle Ages or Medieval era in Europe was a time of poverty for the masses but in architecture was a period of great cathedral building and colorful stained glass windows.

melamine   A synthetic compound used to make plastic laminates.

mementos   Remembrances or souvenirs of a person, a place, or an event.

memorabilia   Things and events worthy of remembrance.

mercerization   A process of treating natural cellulosic fibers (cotton and linen), with caustic soda to enlarge and make the fibers more uniform, increase the luster, and better accept and hold dyes.

metal Aluminum, tin, brass, stainless steel, and other chemical compounds that are formed into strips, tiles, or sheets for use as wall, ceiling, and furniture materials.

metal blinds Originally known as venetian blinds, metal blinds provide the look of two-inch wood blinds at less cost and with less stacking space required.

metal or space frame system Strong, lightweight steel skeleton framework based on the forms of geometry.

metameric shift Colors appearing different under different lighting due to the spectral energy distribution in the materials.

metamerism The effect of light on color that causes a color to appear differently in different types of light.

metope The space between the triglyphs on the frieze of the Doric entablature.

Mexican tile Clay tile fired at low temperatures. Natural terra-cotta color or hand-painted in bright colors, glazed and unfired.

Middle Ages *See* Medieval era.

Mies van der Rohe, Ludwig (1886-1969) An important architect/designer associated with the Bauhaus. Designer of several modern classic furniture pieces.

millwork Stock- and custom-milled woodwork in the form of cabinetry, shelving, panels, and molding.

miniblinds One-inch wide, concave metal slats held together with nylon cord. Slats or louvers are adjustable and are excellent for light and glare control.

mini-mainframe computer A computer about the size of a personal computer but with greater capacity and power somewhat similar to a mainframe computer.

mirror Glass with the back coated with silver or a silver amalgam (compound) to give the surface a reflecting quality; used on walls, ceilings.

Mission style Style that features oak furniture of rectilinear design; popular in the late nineteenth and early twentieth centuries. Gustav Stickley was a great exponent of the style, which is named for and resembles handmade furniture from the early California Spanish missions.

miter To cut at a forty-five-degree angle. A joint where two diagonally cut pieces meet at right angles and are nailed or screwed together.

mobile home A house trailer for temporary or permanent housing.

mobile home park An area where only mobile homes are placed.

modacrylic A synthetic long-chain polymer fiber consisting of 35 to 85 percent acrylonitrile units. It is a soft, buoyant fabric that is inherently flame resistant and used extensively for nonresidential draperies where fire codes must be met.

modillion A projecting decorated bracket; also called a console.

monitor The computer hardware screen component.

monochromatic A color scheme using one color in any of its varieties, plus some white and black.

mood lighting Low-level lighting that creates an ambience or mood that is cozy or inviting.

Moor A Moslem of mixed Berber (North-African) and Arab ancestry.

Moroccan rugs Handmade pile rugs from North Africa that have geometric patterns and are coarsely woven.

Morris, William (1834-96) A designer of the Arts and Crafts movement who produced wall-paper, furniture, tapestries, carpets, stained glass windows, and accessories.

mortise and tenon A joint that utilizes a square hole carved in one of the pieces being joined and a projection that fits the hole in the other.

mosaic Small pieces of glass or stone fitted together and held in place with cement to create a pattern or design. Often used for floor, ceiling, or wall decorations.

mosaic tile Small tiles fitted together with grout to form a pattern in floors, walls, and countertops.

mothproofing A finish that renders a fabric, especially wool, unpalatable to moths and other destructive insects.

motivational lighting A lighting specialty that utilizes brightness, dullness, and darkness to motivate people to behave in a certain manner. It utilizes principles of psychology as well.

motorized rods Drapery rods that are electronically operable. Used for large or hard-to-reach installations.

movable insulation Interior or exterior insulation that protects against excessive heat loss or solar gain.

movable louver shutters Wooden shutters with slats or blades that can be adjusted.

mullion A vertical dividing piece in an opening, especially a window.

multilevel living Housing that contains one or more changes of planes in addition to the main floor: an upstairs, downstairs, or step-down or step-up areas.

multilevel-loop pile carpet A looped pile carpet with various levels woven or tufted to create texture or a pattern.

multiuse areas Rooms or areas with more than one purpose or function.

Munsell, Albert H. (1858-1918) American colorist whose system, based on hue, value, and chroma notation, is widely used in design.

Munsell theory Based on three attributes—hue, value, and chroma—where exact color matching is possible through a notation system.

murals Wallpapers hung in sequence to depict a scene. Also, a large-scale wall painting.

N

nap The fuzzy surface of a fabric formed by short hairs or fibers.

NASAD The National Association of Schools of Art and Design.

natural A wood finish without any added color or stain.

natural fiber rugs Animal skins, berber rugs, cotton rugs, floccati rugs, sisal/maize mats, and wool rugs.

natural fibers Come from either cellulosic sources (cotton, linen, jute), or protein fibers (silk, wool, leather) which are derived from natural sources.

natural light Sunlight.

natural saturation point The amount of naturally occurring white or black value in a pure hue according to the Munsell system for color notation.

natural thermal flow The movement of heated air up and/or toward cold air and the consequent dropping of cool air.

natural traffic pattern The pattern of movement users will follow in an environment if their circulation is not hampered or obstructed.

naturalistic design A classification of decorative design that is a copy or representation of something in nature. It is realistic decoration or ornamentation.

Navajo rugs Handwoven flat tapestry rugs in earth-tone neutral colors and geometric patterns. Woven in the southwestern United States by members of the Navajo tribe.

nave The main section of the church where the worshipers stand or sit.

NCIDQ The National Council for Interior Design Qualification.

NCIDQ examination An examination administered to interior designers after a minimum of two years of professional work experience. Must be passed for full acceptance into several of the professional design organizations.

needle-constructed fabrics Fabrics made or decorated with automated sets of needles, including knits, laces, some casements, and schiffli embroidery.

needlepoint rugs Hand or machine rugs, most often from China or Portugal, with small stitches of wool yarn on an art canvas background.

needlepunched carpet Carpeting constructed of fibers held together by needlepunching or interlocking the fibers by meshing together with barbed needles. Used primarily in indoor-outdoor and nonresidential applications.

negative space The area between the forms in a two- or three-dimensional design. Empty or void space not filled in with furnishings, accessories, or mass.

Neoclassic (1790-1830) The period in America influenced by the excavations of Pompeii.

neon lamp A thin glass tube containing a gaseous element (neon) that glows when charged with electricity. The tubes can be bent into any shape for artistic or advertising purposes.

neon lighting The red spectrum of cold cathode lighting formed with neon gas.

network of lighting Interconnected wiring of lights indicated on the lighting or wiring plan in nonresidential buildings.

neutralized colors Any hue that is dulled or grayed or lessened in brightness or intensity.

neutrals Black, white, and gray. Brown is a hue, derived from orange, but it is often referred to as a neutral, as are beige, tan, and the colored spectrum of off-whites.

newel post An upright that receives and supports the handrail at critical points on a stair.

niche The rounded, half-domed end of a room, or a similar recess in a wall.

nogging Brickwork used as infill between timber framing.

Nomex A registered trademark of DuPont for nylon.

nonarchitectural lighting Portable luminaires.

noncellulosic fibers The range of synthetically composed man-made fibers that begin as chemicals and organic substances other than cellulose. Also known as synthetic fibers.

nondurable or soluble finishes These are fabric finishes that are removed with repeated washing or dry cleaning.

nonglare glass Clear glass with a faintly textured surface that does not reflect light.

nonresidential design Interior design work where the client is not a residential occupant.

nonresidential wall coverings Wall coverings that meet standards or codes for durability, fire safety, and low maintenance. Wider and in longer rolls than residential wall coverings.

nonresilient flooring materials A category of materials that are hard and have no give or resilience.

nonwoven textiles A group of fabrics such as felt, webbing, and films that are processed into fabrics without going through the yarn stage.

Norman The name given to the Romanesque architectural style in England.

nosing The rounded edge of a tread.

novelty twill A twill weave that changes direction to create a pattern such as herringbone.

nylon A long-chain synthetic polymer fiber that consists of amides linked to aramide ring molecules. Nylon is a versatile, durable fiber used extensively for carpeting and upholstery.

O

objets d'art French term for any object of artistic worth.

occasional chair A chair kept away from the main seating area that can be pulled up and used occasionally, as needed.

occasional table A small table that can be moved and used for any purpose as needed.

occult balance Another word for asymmetrical, informal, active, or optical balance. The balance is not the same on each side but is achieved through arranging until the composition "feels right" and is therefore somewhat mysterious.

oculus Literally an eye. The opening in the dome of the Pantheon.

oil paint Colored pigment mixed with linseed oil or varnish and thinned with turpentine.

oil-based paints Paints that must be thinned and cleaned up with solvents or paint thinners. Durable, scrubbable finish. Requires a long drying time and has a strong odor.

olefin A synthetic long-chain polymer fiber consisting largely of ethylene or propylene. Olefin is durable and economical. Used for carpet face and backing and for upholstery.

one-turn stair A stair that turns ninety degrees at a landing.

onion dome A bulb or onion-shaped dome of Near-Eastern origin.

open floor plan A concept in interior and architectural planning where areas are left open, without wall divisions. The open areas can be used in a flexible manner to accommodate varying functions.

open office planning A large office space in which workstations are divided only by systems furniture and other furnishings.

open riser stair A stairway that is open because it has no risers.

open showroom A wholesale trade source that allows clients to accompany the designer into the showroom.

open stair A stair not attached to the wall.

operable window Window that can be opened.

opposition A form of rhythm (a principle of design) wherein right angles meet.

optical balance Also known as asymmetrical, informal, active, or occult balance. The balance is judged by the eye, or the optical senses.

optical density The appearance of a pattern or item as heavy or dense or filled in, and therefore judged as heavy mass.

orders The styles of Greek and Roman architecture.

ordinary incandescent lamps Incandescent bulbs that last from 750 to 2,500 hours.

organizational tool programs Software that analyzes, organizes, and synthesizes information. Used for writing specifications, critical paths, and word processing.

Oriental rugs Hand-knotted (handwoven) pile rugs from the Near and Far East woven in complex floral or geometric patterns. Used for area, art, and accent rugs and wall hangings. May be very valuable.

orientation The direction (N, S, E, W) windows face in a room. The natural daylighting of the different orientations each has a unique effect on colors.

Orlon A registered trademark of DuPont for acrylic.

Ostwald theory A system for analyzing color based on the color and the amount of white or black added to the hue.

Ostwald, Wilhelm (1853-1932) A physicist who won the 1909 Nobel Prize for chemistry and who turned his research to color, producing the well-known book *The Color Primer*.

ottoman Today, an oversized upholstered footstool. Sometimes called a hassock.

outbuildings Buildings situated away from a house used historically for kitchens, dairies, carriages, or servants' quarters.

outlet strips Prewired or plugged-in casings that contain several outlets in a row.

outlining Painting contrasting colors or white values on architectural molding.

overcrowding An excessive number of people working or living within a given space.

overlay A sheet of velum or tracing paper placed over a rough design to improve and refine it.

oxford weave Variation of plain weave in which two fine warp threads are interlaced with one heavier weft thread.

P

pad painting The application of paint with a flat fibrous pad.

padding A general term for carpet underlay or the cushioning layer covering the springs in upholstery.

paint A liquid oil-, water-, resin-, alkyd-, acrylic-, or epoxy-based material that is applied by spraying, brushing, rolling, or pad painting. Dries to a flat, semigloss, gloss, or high-gloss finish.

painting A one-of-a-kind, two-dimensional art form created with color pigments and a number of different substances (vehicles) that give the paint form and body.

palette knife A small, usually flexible knife used to mix paint on the artist's paint tray (palette) or to apply paint to the surface being painted.

Palette theory Another name for the Standard Color Wheel theory.

palisade wall   A paneled fireplace wall formed of boards and battens.

Palladian window   An arched window flanked on each side by lower sidelights.

paneled door   A traditional door formed with stiles, rails, and panels.

panel-track wall fabric installation   Metal tracks available for installing fabric on the wall. Used most often in nonresidential settings.

paneling   Sheets of wood used for wall and ceiling finish materials. May be solid wood or veneered (sandwiched).

paper wall covering   Paper front and back; no vinyl coating.

papier-mâché   A material used for the construction of furniture and accessories made from paper pulp and glue. During the nineteenth century these pieces were often painted black and inlaid with mother-of-pearl.

PAR lamp   Reflective parabolic aluminized reflector lamp with heavy, protective glass and a focused beam. Silvering is used to establish the beam spread and the reflective quality.

parapet   A low wall on the edge of a roof, bridge, or terrace.

parquet   The decorative, geometric arrangement of short lengths of wood plank for floors and sometimes walls.

particleboard   A solid panel formed by compressing flakes of wood with resin under heat and pressure.

passive balance   Another term for symmetrical or formal balance where items are identical on each side of a central point, and therefore no judgment of the composition is needed.

paterae   Oval (or round) shapes used as ornament, often decorated with rosettes.

patina   A finish that comes with use and time to wood and metal.

patio door   *See* atrium door.

patio home   A small home set on a narrow, shallow building lot.

Patlon   A registered trademark of Amaco for olefin.

pattern   An element of design; the arrangement of shapes and perhaps value (light and dark contrast) or relief (high and low areas) brought together to make a random or predictable design.

pattern book   Books of patterns for houses, furniture, and architectural detail published for general use.

pattern repeat   Wall covering or fabric pattern measurement from the top of one pattern to the top of the next, or from one pattern to another horizontally.

payback period   The number of years that a purchase (such as a solar energy system) takes to pay for itself.

pediment   A decorative design detail that originated with the triangular section of the Greek trussed roof. The pediment was adapted from a triangle into a rounded segmental pediment, a broken pediment, which is open at the top, and an ornate scroll pediment. Pediments are used for furniture and architectural embellishment.

pediment frieze   The sculptural design within the pediment.

peelable wall covering   Wall covering that can be peeled away from a substrate (backing or lining), which is suitable to be repapered.

pembroke table   An occasional table with drop leaves and a drawer in the apron.

pendants   Decorative downward projections used to embellish architectural and furniture designs.

pent roof   A narrow, overhanging rooflike structure above the first story on Pennsylvania German houses.

perfatape   A wide paper tape applied to sheetrock seams with plasterboard compound or mud.

perimeter lighting   Lighting around the outside of a room or an area. Perimeter lighting visually expands space.

peristyle   A continuous row of columns around a building. Also used to designate the colonnaded garden area at the rear of the Roman house.

Perlon   A registered trademark of Bayer for nylon.

permanent installations   Structural or finish materials that are not likely to be replaced due to their cost or difficulty to install or remove.

Persian rugs   The finest of the Oriental rugs, traditionally from Persia (today Iran). High knot count, complex, usually floral patterns.

personal computer   A small computer for home or small-business use.

personal space   The invisible "bubble" of space that surrounds us and that we consider to be our own.

perspective sketch   A three-dimensional sketch or rendering of an interior space drawn in perspective with vanishing points.

pewter   A soft, dull-gray alloy of tin, copper, lead, and antimony used to make tableware.

Phyfe, Duncan (1768-1854)   A New York furniture builder, originally from Scotland, known for his Regency-style pieces.

piano nobile   The principal floor of a building; usually a raised first floor.

picking out   Highlighting features on molding, such as dentil trim or carved bas-relief, with paint.

piece dyeing   Coloring a length of fabric after it is woven into cloth.

pier   Same as a column but without its details and proportions.

pigment   A nonsoluble coloring matter that is held onto the surface of the fabric with a resin binder. A compound that is the coloring agent for paint, ink, crayons, and chalk.

pilaster   A flat, false, decorative column.

pile   The surface of a carpeting that has depth. Rounded loops are called uncut pile, while cut loops are called cut pile.

pile density   Closeness of stitches (woven) or tufts of a carpet. Greater or tighter density yields a more durable product.

pile weave   A weave that utilizes a third set of threads that form a depth or a pile in the surface. Types of pile weave include velvet, terry cloth, and corduroy.

pilling   Tendency of fibers to work into small balls or pills.

pillow sham   A removable decorative pillowcase.

PL lamp   Compact twin fluorescent bulb.

plain slicing   A method used to cut a log parallel to a line through its center—produces a vaulted or cathedral-like grain.

plain weave   The interlacing of threads or yarns in a one-over, one-under sequence.

plan drawing   A flat, two-dimensional, scaled drawing of an environment as seen from above.

plane of light   A bank of light; a well-lit area.

planned development   A tract of land that is developed into housing of a specific style, size, price range, and type (attached dwellings, single detached dwellings, luxury dwellings).

plantation shutters   Louvered shutters with wide blades. Used in the South during colonial days as screens to encourage ventilation during the hot months.

plaster   A thick, pasty mixture of sand, water, and lime used for smooth or rough wall and ceiling textures.

plasterboard   Another name for drywall, sheetrock, or gypsum board, plasterboard is a wall material made of pulverized gypsum rock and commonly used as a wall finish material.

plastics   Synthetically produced, nonmetallic compounds that can be molded, hardened, and used for manufacture of various products.

plate rail   A narrow shelf for displaying plates.

pleated shades   Factory-manufactured polyester fabric shades permanently heat set into one-inch pleats. May be metallized on the reverse for energy efficiency.

pleated valances   A fabric top treatment that is given fullness through pleating.

plenum   The space between the suspended ceiling grid and the ceiling. This space often contains mechanical systems.

Plexiglas   A highly transparent, lightweight, thermoplastic acrylic resin made into sheets like glass. Unlike glass, it is not easily broken.

plies   Thin layers of wood laminated together to make plywood.

plotter   A computer mechanical drawing printer that can produce drafting, two- and three-dimensional illustrations, and perspectives.

plumbing   The systems that carry water, sewage, or central vacuums.

plumbing chase   A thick wall containing plumbing.

plush carpet   A tufted carpet with a dense, short, even pile in solid colors. Originally intended to imitate the pile of an Oriental rug.

plywood   A product made of thin sheets of wood glued together in layers.

pneumatic system construction   Air-inflated or air-supported structures.

pocket door   A door that slides into a pocket recessed in the wall.

podium   The base on which Roman buildings are built.

point or pinpoint lighting   Spotlighting a tiny area for emphasis or a glitter effect.

Polybloom   A registered trademark of Chevron for olefin.

polyester   A synthetic long-chain polymer fiber of polymer ester. A durable, dimensionally stable fiber that is highly versatile. Most sheer and semisheer fabrics are of polyester. Used for residential carpeting and scatter rugs and for wall covering fabrics that are often used in nonresidential interiors.

Polypropylene   A modified olefin fiber used for artificial turf, tufted indoor-outdoor carpeting, and nonwoven (needlepunched) carpets and tiles. Also used for a primary and secondary backing for some carpeting. A registered trademark of Thiokol for olefin.

polyurethane   A synthetic resin used to make foam for cushions and as a base for varnish.

Pompeii and Herculaneum (destroyed A.D. 79, excavation began 1754)   Sister cities on the Bay of Naples (Southern Italy) that contained prosperous classical Roman architecture, preserved by the ashes and lava mud flow of Mount Vesuvius. Archaeological excavations resulted in the introduction of the Neoclassic or Classic Revival style in Europe and America.

pool of light   A circle of light thrown by a downlighter or spotlight.

porcelain   The highest grade of ceramic. Made of fine white clay.

porphyry   A granitelike texture achieved by crisscross brushing, then stippling, spattering, and finally cissing paint. Also a type of stone.

portable computer   A keyboard, monitor, and drive unit that folds into the size of a briefcase.

portable luminaires   Nonarchitectural lighting such as table and floor lamps or plug-in wall lights.

portable space heaters   Small units that produce heat for a small area or a room. Types include electric and propane heaters; they vary in their size, output, electricity consumption, and safety.

portal   The porch on a Southwest Adobe house.

portico   A classical porch formed by a roof with supporting columns.

positive space   Space filled in with a two- or three-dimensional form or shape.

post-occupancy evaluation (POE)   The formal process of looking at a design once it is in use to see how well it is functioning.

potpourri   French term for the mixture of dried flower petals used to perfume a room.

Prang theory   Another name for the Standard Color Wheel theory.

prefinishes   Processes that prepare a fabric for coloring, decorative, or functional finishes. Prefinishes include scouring, preshrinking, bleaching, mercerizing, and sizing.

prepasted wall coverings   Wall coverings with a dry paste or adhesive preapplied to the back which is moistened, then pasted to the wall or ceiling.

preservation   Maintaining a building in its present state or the state to which it has been restored.

preshrinking   A prefinish process of subjecting a cloth to wet or dry heat to cause it to shrink and stabilize before further finishing or coloring.

pressed glass   Decorative glass formed in molds.

pretil   A row of brick trim used to cap the adobe walls of the Territorial-style Southwest Adobe houses.

pretrimmed wall coverings   Wall coverings with selvages trimmed off at the factory.

primary focal point   The main point of emphasis in an environment. The object, area, or grouping that first catches the eye.

primary hues   Red, yellow, and blue, as based on the Standard Color Wheel theory.

primers   Liquid preparations that seal the surface and prepare it for paint application.

principles of design   Scale, proportion, balance, rhythm, emphasis, and harmony (unity and variety).

printing   Applying color to a finished cloth by hand (batik, tie-dye, stencil) or mechanical processes (automated silk screen, roller, transfer).

printmaking   A method of mass-producing two-dimensional art pieces by various means. *See also* block prints, engravings, etchings, lithographs, and serigraphs.

priscilla curtains   Sheer, semisheer, or muslin curtains with ruffles on all edges, on the ties, and as a valance; they meet at the center or crisscross; a colonial style.

privacy draperies   A white, an off-white, or perhaps a colored fabric installed on a traverse rod next to the window to be drawn closed at night for privacy.

private zones   Areas within a home that dictate privacy—the bedroom and the bathroom, for example.

problem statement   A short declaration that identifies a design project according to purpose, location, and those for whom the design is being created.

product design   The design of furniture, accessories, or other components that are marketed in the design field.

profile   An outline of user characteristics, habits, background, and design preferences that helps determine the direction a design should take.

program   Everything that happens or must be accomplished in an interior. It also is the written document that describes what will take place in an interior.

programming   The research phase of the design.

progression   A type of rhythm (a principle of design) wherein shapes repeat in diminishing or escalating sizes or where colors graduate from light to dark. Also called rhythm by gradation.

projecting fireplace   A fireplace that projects beyond the wall plane to which it is mounted.

proportion   The relationship of parts to a whole in terms of size, detail, or ornamentation. Good proportion is pleasing and functional.

protein fibers   Natural fibers or fabrics whose source is animal based: wool, silk, leather.

provincial   Rustic; local; from the provinces or countryside.

proxemics   The way people use space and the way that use is related to culture.

PS lamp   A pear-shaped incandescent lamp, often with a long neck.

pueblo   Communal dwelling of the Pueblo Indians.

punch list   A checklist of items to be completed before final building inspection and occupation.

Q

quarry tile   Rust-colored tiles that are fired at lower temperatures than ceramic tiles and valued for their natural terra-cotta coloration. Typically square or hexagonal shapes.

quarter slicing   A method used to cut logs where the blade meets the grain at right angles to the growth rings, resulting in a straight, striped grain.

Queen Anne (1702-14)   Name given to the period design style during the reign of Queen Anne of England.

Quiana A registered trademark of DuPont for nylon.

quicksilver An alloy of mercury and tin used for mirror backing.

Quintess A registered trademark of Phillips for polyester.

quire Alternate British spelling for choir. *See* choir.

quoin Projecting or contrasting brick or stone laid at the corner angle of a building.

R

R, ER lamps Lamps with a built-in, reflective surface.

R-20, R-30, R-40 Indicate the degree of beam spread in reflector lamps.

Rabat rugs Moroccan rugs in a deep, hand-knotted pile with simplified Oriental designs.

radial balance A type of balance that is seen in the same way as radiation from a central point.

radiant heat Electrical conduit or water (steam) heat plumbing in ceilings, floors, or walls that radiates heat.

radiation A type of rhythm (a principle of design) illustrated by elements radiating out in nearly every direction from a central point, such as spokes of a wheel or concentric circles.

radiators Wall or baseboard units that contain steam heat or another heated fluid medium, permanent or portable.

rag rug A plain weave rug woven with strips of fabric, historically rags or recycled clothing.

ragging and rag-rolling Wet paint or glaze is partially removed by dabbing with a rag or rolling the paint off with a rolled rag.

rail The horizontal section of a frame for a panel or door frame.

rain gutter The metal gutter and downspouts that channel rain and snow runoff from the eaves down the side of the building to the ground.

rainbow roof A curved, gabled roof, attributed to ships' carpenters, used on some Cape Cod houses.

raised hearth A hearth built on a platform or cantilevered in front of a raised fireplace.

rambler A one-story detached home with or without a basement. The social, work, and private zones are located on the main floor.

random-shear carpet texture *See* level-tip shear.

rapid-start fluorescent lamps Eliminate flickering as the gases quickly activate the phosphorus in the light. May also be controlled with a dimmer switch.

rattan A climbing palm with slender, tough stems used to make wicker.

rayon A regenerated cellulosic man-made fiber that imitates the luster of silk at a lower cost. Primarily used for drapery and upholstery.

rebar Bendable steel bars set into concrete for reinforcement and to deter cracking.

rebonded foam *See* bonded (rebonded) foam.

recessed adjustable lighting Architectural luminaires that are fixed into the ceiling. The lamps can be adjusted to the desired angle.

recessed downlight A canister that fits into the ceiling and casts pools of light downward.

recessed luminaires A general term for luminaires that fit into the ceilings where the light is noticeable but the fixture is not.

reeding Rows of parallel convex beads or moldings used to embellish a column or leg. If the piece is grooved with concave moldings, it is fluted.

refinement or refining The process of placing overlays of tracing paper to improve a space plan design.

reflecting glare A shiny object causing a distraction in a task area.

refraction The bending of a ray of heat, light, or sound.

Regency The period or style of English architecture that paralleled American Greek Revival. *See* American Empire.

registers (heat registers) The metal grill that covers the duct opening of the HVAC system.

reinforced concrete Concrete set with rebar or metal mesh to deter cracking and to give strength.

relief printing Printing from a pattern that stands out in relief, as is done with a block print.

Renaissance The great rebirth of classical art and learning during the fourteenth, fifteenth, and sixteenth centuries.

rendering An artist's conception or perspective of a finished building exterior or interior, usually done in full color.

repetition A type of rhythm (a principle of design) wherein shapes, forms, lines, or colors are repeated in a congruous manner.

reproductions Printed copies of an artist's work.

research Examining all factors that influence a design.

resilience The ability of a fabric or flooring to return to its original shape.

resilient A material with some give or ability to bounce back.

resist or reserve printing Coating the fabric with a chemical paste that resists the dye, then dyeing the fabric. The area not printed receives the color.

restoration A research, demolition, and reconstruction process to bring a building back to a specific state of its history.

retainer fee A deposit given to the designer upon the client's signature on the letter of agreement that retains or hires the services of the designer.

retrofitting Adding active or solar systems to an existing building.

reverberation Echoing of sound waves.

reversible cushions Loose cushions that can be turned to avoid excessive soiling and wear.

rhythm A principle of design seen in an interior as a visual flowing pattern or regular recurrence. The path the eye follows. Types of rhythm include repetition, alternation, progression or gradation, transition, opposition or contrast, and radiation.

rib A projecting band on a ceiling or vault.

riser The vertical member of a stair between two treads.

Robsjohn-Gibbings, T.H. (1905-76) Designer of a group of Greek furniture reproductions, including the Klismos chair.

Rococo *See* Louis XV period.

roller painting Paint application with a roller—a sleeve of soft fibrous pile fabric that can hold and release the paint evenly. Faster than brush painting. It tends to spatter but is very useful for large areas such as walls and ceilings.

roller printing A fabric printing method whereby dye is applied to raised figures on a cylinder, then stamped or transferred to fabric as it rolls over the cylinder.

roller shade Flat fabric or plastic material on a roller rod, which is operated with a spring or pulley mechanism.

rollikan rug A flat tapestry folk rug from Scandinavia that often incorporates simplified floral patterns and stripes.

Roman shade A fabric shade that folds up from the bottom accordion style. May be interlined for energy efficiency.

Romanesque (A.D. 800-1150) The Medieval architectural period based on Roman design.

roof monitors Clerestory windows, skylights, and cupola windows that catch heat from the sun and allow ventilation for excess summer heat.

roof trusses A joist and rafter system that forms the triangular construction of a roof.

rotary screen printing A mechanized silk-screen process where the screens are wrapped around a circular drum that rotates the ink onto the fabric moving beneath the rotary screens. It is a fast and efficient process.

rotary slicing A method of shaving a continuous layer of wood from a log that has been mounted on a lathe, producing a broad, open grain.

rotogravure or roto A printed pattern overlaid with layers of vinyl for sheet flooring.

rotunda A round, domed room.

rough electrical The wiring installed when the building is framed.

rough heating   The installation of furnace and duct work system when the building is framed.

rough plumbing   The installation of pipes to carry water and sewage and central vacuum.

round wire tufting/weaving   Carpet construction technique that yields even, round loops.

roundheaded arch   An arch formed in a perfect half circle, not flattened. A Roman or keystone arch.

row house   Another term for town house.

rubber   A natural or synthetic composition that yields a resilient, solid or marble-patterned flooring.

rubber-backed tufted carpet   Carpeting tufted into a foam rubber backing that serves as a pad or underlay. Direct glue-down installation.

rubbings   Designs made by placing a sheet of paper over any object with a flat, raised pattern and rubbing it with a special crayon.

rubble   Stone or rocks set or installed to produce an uneven, random surface.

rush   A grasslike marsh plant used to weave chair seats and floor mats.

rusticated   Rough-surfaced masonry or stone.

rya rugs   Deep pile shaglike rugs handknotted with abstract, contemporary patterns from Scandinavia.

S

Saarinen, Eero (1910-61)   Architect/designer, creator of the pedestal furniture group.

safety lighting   Lighting required by code or building ordinances to protect the health and safety of the public. Examples include exit signs, aisle lighting, and lighting for stairs and landings.

sagging   Irregular elongation or stretching of a drapery fabric due to increased humidity or moisture in the air.

saltbox roof   A gabled roof with one slope longer and lower than the other.

sandstone   A granular stone that may be used as floor or wall materials, laid at random or in a rectangular, ashlar pattern.

saran   A synthetic long-chain polymer of vinylidene chloride. Saran is fire retardant and used alone or in fabric blends.

sash curtains   Sheer or semisheer fabric shirred (gathered) onto a rod at the top and bottom of the window frame.

sash window   A double window (one panel above, one below), that is opened by raising or lowering one of the panels that slides up and down in its frame.

sateen, satinet, or horizontal satin   A satin weave where the weft or filler threads float over five to eight warp threads, then are tied down under one in an irregular manner that produces a smooth surface.

satin or eggshell paint   A paint that dries to a finish slightly less shiny than semigloss but more lustrous than flat.

satin weave   A smooth, often lustrous fabric weave where warp threads float over five to eight weft or filling threads, then are tied down under one. There are no ridges or wales.

Savonnerie rug   A hand-knotted pile rug from France, originally woven at the Savonnerie Tapestry Works and patronized by King Louis XIV. Historic and contemporary patterns.

scale   A principle of design that evaluates the relative size and visual weight of objects. Classifications of scale include small or light, medium, large or heavy, and grand (extra large).

scatter rugs   Small rugs (sometimes called throw or accent rugs), often with a tufted cut pile, used in residential areas where water is likely to spill or where dirt is tracked in. Usually of polyester or nylon.

schedule   The chart that indicates the finish material used on floors, walls, and ceiling and lists types of doors and windows.

scheduling   Arranging for subcontractors and craftspeople who build or finish portions of a building and its interior to complete their work within a time frame.

schematics   Quick drawings used to generate or show ideas.

schools   Groups of artists with like philosophies whose work has similar characteristics.

sconce   A wall-mounted luminaire.

screens   A general term for a sliding or freestanding frame filled with wood, paper, fabric, or other materials, which may be placed in front of a window or used as a divider.

scroll pediment   A pediment with a flat bottom and two curved volutes at the top, often with a finial between the volutes.

scrubbable   Wall coverings that can be repeatedly washed with detergent solutions.

sculpture   The art of fashioning figures and forms of wood, clay, plastics, metal, or stone.

sculptured carpet   A carpet with more than one height to the pile, which gives a pattern to the whole.

sculptured-loop carpet   A multilevel-loop carpet, the same as embossed-loop carpet.

sealed environment   A building with nonoperable or fixed windows; HVAC provides warm, cool, and clean air.

sealers   A liquid used to prepare a surface for painting.

seasonal affective disorder (SAD)   A condition with symptoms of fatigue and depression affecting some people who are deprived of natural light during the long winter season.

secondary focal point   The point (or points) of emphasis in an environment that is (are) subordinate to the primary focal point because of size, location, color, or other design factors.

secondary hues   Green, orange, and violet, as based on the Standard Color Wheel theory.

secretary   A desk with drawers below and a bookcase above.

security system   A wiring system that detects unlawful entry.

Sef   A registered trademark of Monsanto for modacrylic.

segmental pediment   A pediment with a flat bottom and a curved radius at the top.

semidetached houses   A term for housing in which portions of walls and roofs are common to two or more units.

semi-durable   A fabric finish that will withstand wet, but not dry cleaning.

semigloss paint   A paint that dries to a luster between flat and shiny; it contrasts nicely with both and hides fingerprints.

semihoused stair   A stair attached to the wall on one side.

semitrimmed wall covering   Wall coverings with only one selvage trimmed off. The selvage edge is overlapped with the next strip or trimmed off at the site.

sericulture   Cultivated silk production.

serigraph   An art print made by passing ink through a fine screen that has been covered with a cut stencil to form the pattern. Also called silk screen.

serpentine   Literally, like a snake; a line that curves in and out as on a chest front or camel-back sofa.

Seventeenth-Century English Medieval style   The design style of seventeenth-century America, inspired by the late Medieval designs of England. Architecture, interiors, and furniture were all strongly influenced by English prototypes.

shades   *See* roller shade.

shading   Blending painted color values from light to dark across a wall or ceiling.

shading devices   Interior or exterior window coverings that deter solar gain from penetrating the interior.

shake shingles   Wooden roof shingles, somewhat irregular in width, that weather to a gray color.

Shakers   A late eighteenth-century, early nineteenth-century religious sect whose beliefs included the design of furnishings devoid of excessive decoration.

Shantura   A registered trademark of Rohm and Haas for polyester.

shape   An element of design that is the contour or outline of an external surface of a form.

shaped valance   A flat fabric top treatment with a shaped or curved bottom hem. Interlined with stiffening fabric and/or batting and sometimes quilted.

shed ceiling   A ceiling with a single slope.

sheer draperies and curtains   Transparent or translucent fabric hung next to the glass. Called draperies if pleated and hung on a traverse rod, curtains if shirred or gathered onto a curtain rod.

sheet vinyl   Rolls of vinyl in widths up to twelve feet, glued down directly to a prepared surface. May have a cushioned backing, and the thickness of the vinyl surface may vary with the quality.

sheetrock   Also known as drywall, gypsum board, or plasterboard; a rigid wall material made of pulverized gypsum rock. *See* wallboard.

shellac   A finish film for wood made by dissolving the waste of the lac bug in denatured alcohol.

Sheraton, Thomas (1751-1806)   An important English furniture craftsman best known for the designs published in his book *The Cabinet-Maker and Upholsterer's Drawing Book.*

shingles   Wood, asbestos, or tile components commonly used as a finish material on angled (gable or hipped) roofs.

shirred curtains   Fabric gathered onto a rod with or without a ruffle at the top.

shirred valance   A fabric top treatment gathered onto a curtain rod.

shoji screens   Wooden frames and divider grids filled with translucent white mulberry or rice paper. Used in traditional Japanese homes and contemporary Western residential and nonresidential interiors as well.

showrooms   Wholesale businesses usually located in marketing centers where the designer may see lines of merchandise, place orders, or buy furnishings.

side chair   An armless chair without full upholstery.

side draperies   Stationary panels hung on each side of a window.

sideboard   A dining room serving piece with space for storing tableware. The French term buffet and the Italian terms credenza or credence are also used to describe this type of piece.

sidelights   Vertical, narrow windows used on each side of a door.

silk   A natural protein fiber obtained from the filament of the silk moth cocoon. Silk is lustrous, is smooth to slubby, and has a dry hand. It has long been woven into fabrics of luxury and prestige.

silk screen   *See* serigraph.

silk-screen printing   A traditional method of stencil printing, done by squeegeeing ink through stencils on sheer silk stretched on wooden screens. Originally it was a hand technique. Now flatbed printing automates the moving of fabric under the screens and the raising and lowering of the screens, and rotary screen printing further speeds the process by rotating the pattern onto the fabric with no hand labor. Silk screening accounts for a large portion of printed designs today.

silver plate   Flatware made from an alloy of silver and nickel, electroplated with pure silver.

silvering   The process of coating with silver or silverlike substances.

single glazing   Filling a window opening with one layer of glass.

single roll   One bolt of wall covering containing approximately thirty-six square feet.

single-hung sash   Sash windows in which only the bottom section is operable.

single-wide mobile home   A mobile home that is approximately twelve to fifteen feet wide and twenty to forty feet long.

sinuous wire spring   An essentially flat spring bent in a zigzag fashion used in upholstered furniture.

sisal and maize mats   Natural cellulosic fiber mats that are coarse and rough to the touch.

sizing   A thin liquid painted on a surface before hanging wall coverings. It seals against alkali, lessens the paste quantity needed, and provides some grip for the wallpaper.

sketch   A rough, quick illustration of a proposed space or a detail of the space.

skylight   An opening for light set into the roof and ceiling.

slate   A finely grained metamorphic rock used for roofing and flooring. Colors vary from grays to greenish or reddish grays to browns and blacks.

slate roof   A roof covered with thin sheets of stone, used like shingles.

sliding windows   Windows that slide horizontally.

slipcovers   Fitted covers that can be placed over the original upholstery and secured with snaps or other fasteners.

Smart House   Registered trademark of the National Home Builders' Association for home automation.

smoke detector   A fire-alarm device that sounds when triggered by excessive smoke in the air.

social zones   Areas for formal or informal social interaction.

soffit   The trim applied to the eave, or the boxed projection above cabinets or over a sink.

soffit lighting   Architectural lighting built into a soffit.

soft window treatments   Fabric treatments: curtains, draperies, shades, and top treatments.

software   Computer program that accomplishes specific tasks.

softwood   Light, easily cut wood taken from cone-bearing trees such as pine and redwood.

soil-release finish   Allows a fabric to more readily absorb water and free soil to be lifted out with mild detergent.

soil-repellent or soil-resistant finishes   These are sprayed onto the surface of a fabric, forming a temporary barrier that prevents soil from penetrating the fabric. If the soil or stain is not removed quickly, it can be forced into the fabric through tiny cracks in the finish. The soil may then be locked under the finish, making it very difficult to remove.

solar greenhouses   A greenhouse living space that is also a passive solar collector; a solarium.

solar heat gain   Heat from sunshine collected through glass walls or windows. May be absorbed, stored, and released through many of the hard background materials such as stone, tile, brick, and concrete.

sole proprietorship   An interior design business owned by one person.

solid   Wooden furniture construction with solid pieces of wood in all the external or visible parts of the piece.

solid-core door   A veneered door with a core of solid wood pieces. Also called lumber-core door.

solution or dope dyeing   The addition of dyes or coloring matter to the viscose solution in man-made fibers before they are extruded. The dyes then become colorfast and will not fade. The process is more costly than other methods of dyeing and must be done well in advance of the finished product, making solution-dyed color somewhat risky in today's market of rapidly changing color trends.

solvent   A liquid for thinning and cleaning up oil-based paints.

sound board   An insulative material in rigid form that prevents audible sounds from being heard; usually used beneath drywall.

space   An element of design consisting of a continuous expanse of distance without forms, which is divided with walls, partitions, and furnishings. Filled space is termed positive space and empty space is called negative space.

space heating   Heating the area or space where people live and work by passive or active solar means or by mechanical devices such as furnaces or space heaters.

space planning The allotment of spaces to create a workable floor plan. The organization and division of spaces into rooms or areas to meet specific needs.

space-saving device Any means of maximizing the existing space, thereby making a space seem larger.

Spanish rugs Hand-knotted pile rugs with a coarse, sparse weave. Classified with folk rugs.

spattering A method of adding texture to painted surfaces by flipping extra paint onto a surface with a filled brush.

special rodding Drapery rods that can be bent and suited to custom or special installations.

specifications The written list of materials and furnishings, itemized according to company, stock number, color, and other pertinent ordering information, and the location where the goods will be installed. Also, in nonresidential architecture, the criteria of minimum durability, cost, and safety requirements of finish materials.

specifier A type of designer whose role is limited to selecting or specifying which products or specifications will be used.

spectral energy distribution The inherent color characteristics of an object or material due to the type and amount of dyes or pigments. This can cause the object or material to appear as different colors under different kinds of light; also describes the color of the light source.

Spectran A registered trademark of Monsanto for polyester.

spinnerette The shower head-like device through which man-made fiber viscose solutions are forced to create monofilament. The size and shape of the holes in the spinnerette can be changed to give various characteristics to the fibers.

spiral staircase A corkscrew-shaped staircase.

splat The vertical wood panel in the center of a chair back.

split complement Consists of a hue and the two colors on each side of its direct complement.

split-entry home A two-level home in which the entry is located in the center, and the person entering walks upstairs to the kitchen/living/dining areas and the bedroom/bath areas, and downstairs to the family room, extra bedrooms, and storage areas.

split-level home A three- or four-level home with half flights leading from one area to the next.

sponge rubber pad Carpet underlay. The most common example of sponge rubber is waffle padding.

sponging Applying paint with sponges for texture and color overlay.

spotlight A luminaire that focuses light in one direction, casting a pool of light.

spray painting Paint application through a spray nozzle. Fast and economical for large applications. Should be followed with a roller to smooth out the paint.

square feet or footage The width multiplied by the length of a room or building. The two-dimensional floor space.

squeegee An implement with a strong, straight crosspiece edged with rubber used to spread a thin layer of ink across and through a silk screen.

stain Color mixed with water, oils, or other agents and applied to wood as part of the finishing process.

stained glass Colored and clear glass set into patterns and hung in front of windows or used as the window glazing itself.

stainless steel An alloy of steel and chromium.

stains Liquids that penetrate wood with color.

stairwell The open space filled by a stair.

Standard Color Wheel theory Based on three primary colors—red, yellow, and blue—and the variations derived by mixing these, plus black and white. Colors are arranged in a circle, with secondary and tertiary or intermediate colors placed between the primary colors.

standard finishes Applied to fabrics to enhance durability. Also known as wet, chemical, or functional finishes.

staple Short fibers that vary from approximately one-half to two inches. Staple yarns offer greater bulk, insulation, and area coverage.

stapled wall fabric Fabric attached to a wall by staples.

starting step The first step of the stair.

state of the art The current or latest technology; the newest developments.

steel A hard alloy of iron and carbon.

stemware Designation given to fine drinking glass with raised bowls, stems, and bases.

sterling II Flatware with sterling silver handles and stainless steel blades, tines, and bowls.

sterling silver Finest type of silverware; 92.5 percent pure.

Stickley, Gustav (1848-1942) Furniture designer and exponent of the Mission style.

stickwork Flat battens used on Victorian buildings to create patterns in imitation of Medieval timber framing.

stile The upright section of a frame for a panel or door frame.

stippling Similar to sponging but uses a stippling brush to dab on a colored glaze or paint, revealing some of the base color.

stock dyeing The coloring of natural fibers (particularly wool) in the raw-goods state (stock) before they are spun into yarns.

stock plans Floor plans that are mass-produced and purchased, usually by mail order, by anyone wishing to build that home.

stone Any hard rock used for flooring or wall materials.

stone-enders Seventeenth-century houses with stone-covered chimney ends, common to Rhode Island.

stoneware A heavy, durable, thick pottery used for less-formal dinnerware.

storage Space planned for keeping foodstuffs, linens, tools, clothing, and other items owned by people. It also refers to needs of a nonresidential interior to keep extra stock merchandise, office supplies, or other goods. Also, the reservoir for storing thermal energy in a solar system.

storm windows Glass or plastic removable windows that add insulation. Summer storm windows are tinted as a shading device.

stove A freestanding wood- or coal-burning heating unit.

straight lines Lines that directly connect two points; horizontal and vertical lines.

straight run A stair that makes no turns.

strapping tape method A temporary method of attaching fabric to a wall. Rolls or circles of strapping tape are affixed to the wall and to the fabric.

strength or tenacity The inherent ability of a material to withstand stress without breaking.

stretchers Crosspieces used to brace and strengthen table and chair legs.

stringcourse *See* beltcourse.

stringer The supporting member in a staircase.

strip lighting A lighting fixture in which several lamps or bulbs are aligned in a strip. Used in grooming areas around mirrors.

strippable A wall covering that can be stripped or completely removed from a wall. Applies to most vinyl wall coverings.

structural design A basic or general category of design wherein the design is intrinsic to the structure—one cannot be separated without destroying the other.

structural systems The components of new or remodeling construction that make up the structure: footings and foundation, as well as the framework (or other systems) that supports the building and to which the finish materials are applied.

stucco Rough textured plaster or cement for covering walls.

stylobate The base upon which the Greek temple rests.

subcontractor   A person who performs a single task in construction such as foundation work, framing, electrical, plumbing, HVAC, finish work (millwork or woodwork), or tile or floor laying.

subfloors   The material (usually wood) nailed to the framework on which the finish floor materials are laid.

Sullivan, Louis (1856-1924)   Called the father of American architecture, he felt that the form of a building should follow its function.

sundial   A timepiece that shows the time by a shadow cast by a pointer.

superinsulation   Extra-heavy insulation of walls, foundations, ceilings, and attic areas to conserve energy; requires thicker than conventional walls.

surface-mounted fixture   A structural or decorative luminaire that is mounted onto the ceiling.

surface treatment finishes   *See* mechanical finishes.

surround   The noncombustible material that separates the opening of a fireplace from the wall or mantel.

surrounds (tub or shower)   The tile, marble, or imitative plastic finish material used to protect the wall against water in showers and bathtub areas.

suspended ceilings   Ceilings formed of metal grids and acoustic panels, hung from the superstructure of a building.

suspended fixtures   Structural (pendant) or decorative (chandelier) luminaires hung on a cord or chain from the ceiling.

swag holders   Metal hardware that supports swagged fabric.

swags   Also called festoons. Semicircles of fabric folded at the corners to form a soft or precise curved fabric top treatment. Often finished with a cascade on each side of the swag or arrangement of swags.

swamp cooler   *See* evaporative cooling system.

swinging door (one way)   The typical side-hinged door.

symbolism   The use of historic color where each color held significance or symbolized a value.

symmetrical balance   Also called bisymmetrical, formal, or passive balance, it is mirror-image arrangement of parts or elements.

synthesis   Bringing together the research data in the programming process.

synthetic fibers   The group of fibers that do not begin as cellulose but as chemicals or other natural elements chemically altered or composed into a viscose solution and extruded through a spinnerette. This group includes nylon, acrylic, modacrylic, polyester, olefin, saran, spandex, vinyon, latex, fiberglass, and metallic fibers. Also known as noncellulosic man-made fibers.

systems furniture   Component pieces that can be chosen and assembled to create work spaces according to the needs of the user. As needs change, new components can be added and unneeded elements can be eliminated.

T

T lamp   Tubular shaped lamp or bulb.

tab curtains   Flat panel curtains with tabs or strips sewn into loops at the top, then threaded over a dowel rod.

table lamp   Luminaires designed to sit on a table for task or general lighting.

tackless strip   The thin board with recessed-head tacks or staples protruding toward the wall. The strip is nailed down and the carpet is attached over the top to hold it in place for wall-to-wall installations over padding.

tapestry   A plain or Jacquard weave of heavy decorative textiles.

tar paper   A heavy, black, waterproof paper applied to the roof before the shingles and sometimes on the outside of foundation walls.

task lighting   Bright, concentrated light for accomplishing specific tasks.

tatami mats   Woven sea grass mats in various thicknesses. A traditional Japanese floor material, they will not hold up to heavy traffic.

tea caddy   Metal container used to import tea during the eighteenth century, often decorated with oriental motifs and designs.

tea table   A small table, tall enough to accommodate serving tea from a seated position.

technical drawings   Floor plans, elevations, and detailed drawings of architectural detail, cabinetry, storage, and built-in units.

telephone system   A network of connected telephones within a building or office.

tempera   Paint made with pigment mixed with egg and thinned with water.

tempered glass   Glass toughened by heating and rapid cooling.

tenant improvement   The designer works with the client who will occupy a nonresidential space. The design work within an established budget is paid for by the developer.

tender   A state of weakness in a fabric wherein it easily can tear.

tensile system construction   A tentlike building system.

tenure-track position   A full-time college or university appointment that offers tenure, or the status of holding one's position on a permanent basis.

Tergal   A registered trademark of Rhodiaceta for polyester.

terra-cotta   An Italian term for cooked earth used to describe hard, durable reddish brown clay products, such as that used to make roof tiles.

terrace houses   Matching row houses that became popular in England during the eighteenth century.

terrazzo   Chips of marble set into concrete and polished. A hard nonresilient flooring for residential and nonresidential interiors.

Territorial style   The later, more classical version of the Southwest Adobe-style houses of New Mexico.

territoriality   Personal attachment to a certain territory or space.

terry cloth   A pile fabric with uncut loops, used for towels.

tertiary hues   *See* intermediate hues.

Terylene   A registered trademark of ICI for polyester.

tesserae   Pieces of colored glass and stone used to make mosaics.

tetrad complement   A variation of a direct complementary scheme consisting of four colors equidistant (equally spaced) on the color wheel.

Textura   A registered trademark of Hoeschst for polyester.

texture   The relative smoothness or roughness of a surface read by the eye (visual texture) or with the hand (tactile texture). Texture is produced in several ways: by material, color, line, relief, and finish.

texturizing   Adding crimp, kink, or waviness to a man-made monofilament thread or yarn to increase bulk and loftiness and to add textural interest. An uneven surface applied to drywall or sheetrock by blowing on a thin plaster mixture, then sanding it semismooth.

texturizing paint   Thick paint that can be applied to imitate stucco.

thatched roof   A roof covered with reeds or straw intended to shed water.

thematic design   Interior design based on a theme, such as traditional, country, or ethnic.

thermal pane   A type of double glazing in which two layers of glass are produced with a pocket of air for insulation.

thermoplastics   Plastics that change their form by heating.

thermoset plastics   Plastic compounds that are hardened by heat.

thermosiphoning   A passive solar system of collecting heat through spaces in the walls or roof, then drawing the heat into ducts and forcing it into the interior through fans and registers.

thermostat   A device that controls the furnace or air-conditioning by maintaining a preset temperature.

thin shell membrane construction   A self-supporting membrane of reinforced (mesh) concrete or sprayed foam.

Thonet, Michael (1796-1871)   A German craftsman best known for his bentwood furniture designs.

tieback draperies Panels of pleated or shirred fabric tied back at a soft curve and held with ties (strips of fabric), or cords, or metal holdbacks.

tieback holders Concealed hardware to hold the ties or decorative metal rosettes that hold the draperies in the tieback position.

tie-dye A hand process for coloring fabric where a fabric is folded into various shapes, then tied in spots with string and immersed in a dye bath. Where the folds and tied portions are thick, the dye will not penetrate, creating interesting abstract patterns.

tiered curtains Short curtains layered to overlap vertically.

tight An interior that is sealed or that has few or no windows for natural ventilation; requires HVAC system or air-exchange units for fresh air.

tile A flat, geometrically shaped wall and floor finish material of kiln-baked clay.

timber frame A frame of heavy timbers used as the structure system for a building.

toe-kick or riser lighting Lighting in the toe-kick area beneath a counter, or on the stair riser just beneath the tread.

toe-mold lighting Lighting under the toe-kick area of stairs or cabinets.

tokonoma A small alcove with a low, raised platform reserved for display of aesthetic and sacred objects in the traditional Japanese home.

tone A general term for a neutralized, grayed, or toned-down hue.

tongue and groove Strips of wood milled to fit together and interlock with a filet and a groove.

top treatments Any fabric used as a short covering at the top or above a window or window treatment.

torchére In history a tall candlestand. Today a floor lamp that casts light upward onto the ceiling.

town house Another term for a dwelling that is narrow, one or two room(s) wide, and two or three stories high. It shares walls with one or two similar town houses, and one roof spans all the units.

tracery A term used to describe the lacelike ornamentation in stone or woodwork of Gothic design, often seen in windows.

track lighting A track that holds and connects several adjustable spotlights.

trade sources Wholesale companies that market goods and services to the trade or the interior design profession.

trademarks or trade names Names given by chemical companies to a generic fiber that identifies it as their product. Trademarks are registered with the Federal Trade Commission and may be accompanied by a small TM following the name.

traffic Movement of users through an area or along a route.

traffic pattern The pattern created by tracing the movement of a user through an area or along a route.

transepts The part of a cross-shaped church that extends at right angles to the nave. (The arms of the cross.)

transition A type of rhythm that leads the eye without interruption from one point or area to another.

transom A window over a door.

transport Moving the sun's heat through a liquid medium to the storage area in an active solar system unit.

transportation design A facet of nonresidential design: airlines, buses, trains, and automobiles.

traverse rods Rods equipped with cords and pulleys to draw draperies opened and closed.

travertine A light-colored limestone used for nonresilient floors and hard wall materials.

tread The portion of the stair that is stepped on.

triadic complement Three colors equidistant (equally spaced) on the color wheel, such as red, yellow, and blue.

triangular pediment A pediment in the shape of a triangle.

triforium A gallery above the arches of the arcade in the nave of a church.

triglyphs The three decorative vertical grooves on the frieze of the Doric entablature.

triple glazing Three layers of window glass for insulation.

triple roll A roll or bolt of wall covering containing approximately 108 square feet, or three times the area of a single roll.

tripod pedestal table A three-legged table; the legs converge to form a single pedestal.

Trombe walls A passive solar system of glass (that collects and amplifies heat) placed in front of a dark masonry wall (that absorbs and slowly releases the heat into the interior).

trompe l'oeil "Trick the eye." Painted surfaces or wall covering in realistic three-dimensional scenes.

trophies Mounted fish, animals, animal heads, and skins.

true divider Windows glazed with individual panes, rather than snap-in grids.

trusses Triangular reinforcing in wood or metal that distributes the load effectively. A framework for supporting a roof.

Tudor arch A flattened Gothic arch popular in the Tudor era.

tuft bind A measurement indicating the strength of the latex layer that holds tufts of carpet yarns in place.

tufted carpets The method by which most carpeting is produced for both residential and nonresidential interiors. Multiple needles threaded with yarn are simultaneously punched into a loosely woven primary backing. The tufts are held in place with a layer of latex, then adhered to a secondary backing of jute or polypropylene.

tufting A needle construction technique of inserting yarns into a woven or knitted fabric to create a pile. Examples include many cut pile carpets and traditional patterned chenille bedspreads. Also, tying back fabric and padding in such a way as to create a patterned, pillowed surface in upholstery (also a type of carpet construction).

tufts or stitches per square inch A measurement indicating the density of the tufts or woven stitches in carpeting.

tungsten filament Another name for incandescent lighting.

tungsten halogen lamp Lamp in which the filament is surrounded with halogen gas that reacts with the tungsten, producing a bright light.

turnings Decorative spindles formed by turning a piece of wood on a lathe and cutting designs into the wood with a sharp knife or chisel as the piece spins.

Tuscan A simplified version of the Roman Doric style without fluting on the column.

twill weave The interlacing of yarns in a sequence such as three over, one under, which creates a distinct diagonal rib or wale. A novelty twill may reverse, creating fabrics such as herringbone or houndstooth.

twin glazing *See* double glazing.

twin home A dwelling that may adjoin only one other dwelling. A semi-detached house.

Twistloc A registered trademark of Monsanto for polyester.

U

U-stair A stair that makes a 180-degree turn at a single landing.

Ultron A registered trademark of Monsanto for nylon.

undertones The addition of a small amount of one hue to another, rendering the latter slightly warm or cool.

unity A component of harmony (an element of design) that provides a change or relief from sameness in an interior through differences in the design and furnishing elements.

universal design Design that meets the needs of all users, without drawing attention to those with disabilities.

upholstered cornice A wooden top treatment that is padded, then covered with a decorative top treatment.

upholstered walls Padded, then fabric-covered walls.

uplighters or uplighting   Canisters, spotlights, or floodlights that cast light upward to the wall or ceiling.

urethane foam   Synthetic foam used for carpet and upholstery padding.

user   Anyone who will use a completed design.

user friendly   Computer hardware and software that are relatively uncomplicated and easy to operate.

V

vacuforming   A process of forming plastic in a mold in which all the air is drawn out to form a vacuum that forces the plastic around the mold.

valance lighting   A light over the top of a window placed behind a board that directs light both upward and downward.

value   The relative lightness or darkness of a hue according to the amount of white or black inherent in or added to the hue.

value contrast   Hues or neutrals that differ in value. High-value contrast is seen when light and dark values are used together; low-value contrast refers to similar hues or neutral values.

value distribution   The placement of differing values in an interior to create a balanced and pleasing effect.

vapor barrier   A heavy-gauge plastic applied to walls or insulative window treatments to prevent moisture and air penetration.

variety   A subelement of harmony made possible through repetition or similarity of objects or elements in an interior.

varnish   A finish film for wood made by dissolving resinous substances in oil or alcohol.

vault   A ceiling constructed on the principle of an arch. An arched roof.

vaulted system construction   A tunnel-like arch system of building.

Vectra   A registered trademark of Vectra for olefin.

vehicle   In painting, the binding agent that holds the particles of pigment together and creates the film that adheres to the surface being painted.

veiling glare   The reflecting of a light source from a shiny surface into the line of vision.

velvet weave carpet   A cut-pile woven carpet with no design. Colors are solid or utilize variegated yarns.

veneer   A thin ply of beautifully grained wood laminated to plywood or solid woods.

Venetian glass   Delicate and fine glassware made at or near Venice, Italy. A term used to describe glass mirrors with an antique or veined appearance.

ventilation   Natural fresh air through windows or through a central HVAC unit that circulates clean air through a building.

veranda   A long covered porch along the front and/or side of a building.

Verel   A registered trademark of Eastman Kodak for modacrylic.

vernacular   Design executed by local craftspeople, reflecting a regional, naive, or unschooled quality.

vertical lines   Up-and-down lines that lift the eye, and give dignity and formality to interiors.

vertical louvers   Movable louvered blinds with vertical, rather than horizontal, slats.

vestibule   An air-lock entry consisting of two doors and a compartment-like room that prevents excessive heat or cold from entering the building.

Victorian Era (1837-1901)   The English and American era that coincided with the reign of Queen Victoria. It paralleled the Industrial Revolution, during which time many styles were seen. Victorian design is characterized by revivals of nearly every previous historical style, together with rapid technological development.

Vienna Secession   A group of young Viennese artists and craftsmen including Otto Wagner, Josef Hoffmann, and Joseph Maria Olbrich who broke away from the mainstream of traditional art and design around 1897. The group eventually evolved into a more formal workshop—the Wiener Werkstäte headed by Josef Hoffmann.

viga   A large pole beam used to support the roof of Southwest Adobe houses.

vinyl   Polymerized vinyl (ethylene), essentially a plastic compound, extruded into sheets for floor and as wall coverings; also a coating for wall coverings and fabrics.

vinyl composition   A resilient hard flooring of vinyl and other compounds.

vinyl latex wall coverings   Wall coverings that are vinyl through to the backing, which is usually a fabric. They are usually very durable, heavy, and scrubbable.

vinyl-protected wall coverings   Wall coverings, usually paper, with a coating of vinyl, which makes the covering washable.

vinyl tile   Extruded vinyl sheets cut into square tiles.

vinyl wall coverings   Any wall covering with a vinyl surface, including vinyl-protected, vinyl latex, and coated fabric wall coverings.

vinyon   A synthetic vinyl chloride long-chain polymer generally extruded in sheet form, and often imitating leather, suede, or nearly any surface texture. Often called vinyl or PVC (polyvinyl chloride).

visual proportion   The way a proportion might appear regardless of actual dimensions or proportions.

visual weight   The weight or scale an object appears to have, regardless of actual weight.

vitrify   To change into a glasslike ceramic by high heat.

Vitruvian proportions   Correct classical proportions as recorded by Vitruvius.

Vitruvius   A first-century Roman architect and writer responsible for standardizing classical architectural forms.

volts or voltage   The measurement of power that comes through the power line.

volute   A spiral or scroll.

Vycron   A registered trademark of Beaunit for polyester.

W

wainscot   Medieval wooden paneling that may or may not reach to the ceiling.

wale   A pronounced rib or raised cord that may run vertically with the warp, horizontally with the filling threads or weft, or diagonally as in a twill weave.

wall composition   The arrangement of furniture, architectural openings, and accessories against a wall.

wall coverings   Paper, fabric, or vinyl rolls or bolts prepared for gluing onto the wall.

wall washer   A general term for a series of lights that wash a wall. These may be recessed adjustable lights or eyeball spotlights, for example.

wallboard   A term for rigid wall materials installed in sheets or boards: sheetrock (gypsum board), masonite, paneling. Also called drywall.

warm colors   The hues on the color wheel generally considered to produce feelings of warmth. They are red-violet, red, red-orange, orange, yellow-orange, yellow, and yellow-green.

warm white deluxe fluorescent lamp   Contains a warm light spectrum similar to incandescent lighting.

warp threads or yarns   The lengthwise or vertical fabric yarns that are threaded onto the loom and form the basis for woven cloth.

wash   A soft plane of light from spotlights or track lighting.

washable   A wallpaper term meaning that the paper can be gently cleaned with a little soap and water.

water closet   A toilet.

watercolor   Paint made with gum arabic and thinned with water. Also a painting created with this type of paint.

waterproofing   Coating the building's foundation with a tar mixture or with tar paper.

water-repellent finish   A functional, wet, or standard finish that allows the fabric to shed or repel moisture and stain due to condensation or excessive humidity.

watt or wattage   A unit of electric power equal to the power of one ampere (amp) as compared to one volt.

wattle A panel of woven sticks used as infill for timber framing or as fencing material.

weatherstripping Thin strips of insulation, usually with a sticky side, that insulate around windows and doors to prevent cold air infiltration.

weft threads or yarns Inserted into the opened shed of warp threads to create a woven fabric. Also called filling yarns.

Wegner, Hans (b. 1914) Important Danish furniture craftsman, designer of several modern classic pieces.

welt A fabric-covered piping cord sewn between two pieces of the covering in upholstery.

wet finishes *See* standard finishes.

wicker Furniture, baskets, or other objects woven from twigs.

Wiener Werkstäte *See* Vienna Secession.

Wilton Broadloom loop-pile carpeting woven on a Jacquard loom. All colors used in the carpeting are carried beneath the carpet face, creating a thick, heavy carpet.

windbreak Trees, hedges, or fences that provide protection from wind.

window sill The horizontal ridge or shelf beneath the glass, usually within the frame.

window wells The corrugated metal or concrete form that keeps dirt away from basement windows.

Windsor chair Originally an English chair with cabriole legs and a shaped splat. The Windsor chair became common during the eighteenth century in America and featured a carved seat, spindle back, and turned legs.

wing chair An upholstered easy chair with a high back and wings on each side for resting the head.

wire construction *See* round wire tufting/weaving.

wiring plan The portion of the blueprints or working drawings that indicate placement of all electric wiring, fixtures, switched outlets, and connections. Also called the lighting plan.

wood blinds Thin flat slats of wood made into miniblinds. They take more stacking space and are more costly than metal miniblinds.

wood filler A paste or liquid used in the wood-finishing process to fill the natural pores of the wood and create a smooth surface.

wood frame or wood truss system The conventional system of framing a building with wood studs, joists, rafters, and beams, reinforced with the herringbone (zigzag) truss system between joists.

wood graining Brushing on a glaze and drawing wood grains and lines with an artist's brush.

wood molding Narrow strips of concave and/or convex wood molding. May also be plastic.

wood- or coal-burning stove A self-contained stove, usually of cast-iron, that burns wood or coal for space heating.

wood plank Flooring of strips of wood. Planks may be laid in even width strips or random plank (three different widths).

wood rods Curtain and drapery rods of solid wood, often fluted.

wool Natural protein staple fibers taken from the fleece of sheep and the hairs of goats. Wool—absorbent, resilient, and flame resistant—is woven and knitted into high-quality textiles for both residential and nonresidential use. Used for carpeting, Oriental and folk rugs, wall coverings, and some window covering fabrics.

wool rugs A term for natural fiber rugs or carpeting left in its undyed state. The most common is the berber rug.

word-processing programs Software programs that offer options in text writing.

work zones Areas for tasks such as food preparation, office work.

working drawings The final mechanical drawings that are used to obtain bids and construct a design.

Wren, Sir Christopher (1632-1723) One of England's most important and influential architects, responsible for building London's City churches after the great fire of 1666.

Wright, Frank Lloyd (1869-1959) A great American architect who believed that a building should relate to its setting. He designed the complete building, including interiors and furniture.

wrinkle-resistant finish Treating a fabric with a functional finish process so it does not easily wrinkle.

wrought iron Iron that is welded and forged into different shapes.

Y

yarn dyeing Coloring yarn before it is woven or knitted into a fabric.

yo-yo effect Uneven high and low areas along the bottom hemline of a draped fabric due to alternating humidity absorption and drying.

Z

zapata Carved decorative corbel on the porch of the Southwest Adobe house.

Zeflon A registered trademark of Dow Badische for nylon.

Zefran A registered trademark of Dow Badische for nylon, acrylic, and polyester.

zero-clearance fireplace unit A fireplace unit that can be set into combustible walls with no clearance.

zigzag lines Lines that reverse upon themselves in a regular order, such as a herringbone pattern, or in an irregular order, such as a flame pattern.

zones Areas that have similar functions or purposes, such as work zones, social zones, private zones, and storage zones.

CHAPTER 1
The Process of Design

Brill, Michael. *"Better Interior Design through Post-Occupancy Evaluation." ASID Report* 12, no. 4: 13–16.

Curran, June. *Profile Your Life-Style.* Los Altos: Brooks, 1979.

Faulkner, Sarah. *Planning a Home.* New York: Holt, Rinehart and Winston, 1979.

Preiser, Wolfgang. *Post-Occupancy Evaluation.* New York: Van Nostrand Reinhold, 1988.

Reznikoff, S. C. *Specifications for Commercial Interiors, Professional Liabilities, Regulations, and Performance Criteria.* New York: Whitney Library of Design, 1979.

CHAPTER 2
Design for Special Populations

Abrams, A. Jay, and Margaret Ann Abrams. *The First Whole Rehab Catalog: A Comprehensive Guide to Products and Services for the Physically Disadvantaged.* Whitehall, Va.: Betterway, 1990.

Barrier Free Environments, Inc. *The Accessible Housing Design File.* New York: Van Nostrand Reinhold, 1991.

Bush-Brown, Albert, and Dianne Davis. *Hospital Design for Healthcare and Senior Communities.* New York: Van Nostrand Reinhold, 1992.

Design for Aging: An Architect's Guide. Washington, D.C.: The AIA Press, 1985.

Evan Terry Associates, P.C. *The Americans with Disabilities Act Facilities Compliance Workbook.* New York: John Wiley and Sons, Inc., 1992.

Interior Design 63 (August 1992). Newton, Mass.: Cahners Publishing.

Malkin, Jain. *Hospital Interior Architecture: Creating Healing Environments for Special Patient Populations.* New York: Van Nostrand Reinhold, 1992.

Montuori, Don, ed. *Americans with Disabilities Act: ADA Compliance Guide.* Washington, D.C.: Thompson Publishing Group, 1992.

Perry, Lawrence G., AIA, ed. *ADA Compliance Guidebook: A Checklist for Your Building.* Washington, D.C.: Building Owners and Managers Association, 1991.

Raschko, B. B. *Housing Interiors for the Disabled and Elderly.* New York: Van Nostrand Reinhold, 1982.

Sorenson, Robert James. *Design for Accessibility.* New York: McGraw-Hill, 1979.

Steinfeld, E. *Barrier-Free Design for the Elderly and the Disabled.* Syracuse, N.Y.: Syracuse University, 1975.

Tillman, Peggy, and Barry Tillman. *Human Factors Essentials: An Ergonomics Guide For Designers, Engineers, Scientists, and Managers.* New York: McGraw-Hill, 1991.

Woodson, Wesley E., Barry Tillman, and Peggy Tillman. *Human Factors Design Workbook.* 2d ed. New York: McGraw-Hill, 1992.

CHAPTER 3
Design Principles and Elements

Albers, Anni. *On Designing.* Middletown, Conn.: Wesleyan University Press, 1971.

Allen, Phyllis. *Beginnings of Interior Environment.* Minneapolis: Burgess Publishing Company, 1985.

Anderson, Donald M. *Elements of Design.* New York: Holt, Rinehart and Winston, 1961.

Ashley, Laura. *The Laura Ashley Book of Home Decorating.* London: Octopus Books, Ltd., 1985.

Bellinger, Louise, and Thomas Broman. *Design: Sources and Resources.* New York: Van Nostrand Reinhold, 1965.

Bevlin, Marjory. *Design Through Discovery.* New York: Holt, Rinehart and Winston, 1977.

Bloomer, Carolyn M. *Principles of Visual Perception.* New York: Van Nostrand Reinhold, 1976.

Bothwell, Dorr, and Marlys Frey. *Notan: The Dark-Light Principle of Design.* New York: Van Nostrand Reinhold, 1976.

Carpenter, James M. *Visual Art: A Critical Introduction.* New York: Harcourt Brace Jovanovich, 1982.

Cheatham, Frank, Jane Cheatham, and Sheryl Haler. *Design Concepts and Applications.* Englewood Cliffs, N.J.: Prentice-Hall, 1983.

Collier, Graham. *Form, Space, and Vision.* Englewood Cliffs, N.J.: Prentice-Hall, 1972.

De Lucio-Meyer, J. *Visual Aesthetics.* New York: Harper and Row, 1974.

De Sausmarez, Maurice. *Basic Design.* New York: Van Nostrand Reinhold, 1964.

Evans, Helen Marie, and Carla Davis Dumesnil. *An Invitation to Design.* New York: Macmillan, 1982.

Faulkner, Ray, and Edwin Zeigfeld. *Art Today.* New York: Holt, Rinehart and Winston, 1969.

Faulkner, Ray, LuAnn Nisson, and Sarah Faulkner. *Inside Today's Home.* New York: CBS College Publishing, 1986.

Gombrich, E. H. *Art and Illusion: A Study in the Psychology of Pictorial Representation.* Princeton, N.J.: Princeton University Press, 1961.

Grillo, Paul. *Form, Function, and Design.* New York: Dover, 1975.

Hale, Nathan Cabot. *Abstraction in Art and Nature.* New York: Watson-Guptill Publications, 1972.

Hambridge, Jay. *Practical Applications of Dynamic Symmetry.* New York: Davin, 1965.

Harlan, Calvin. *Vision and Invention: A Course in Art Fundamentals.* Englewood Cliffs, N.J.: Prentice-Hall, 1970.

Held, Richard, ed. *Image, Object, and Illusion, Readings from Scientific American.* San Francisco: Freeman.

Hicks, David. *On Living—With Taste.* London: Leslie Frewin, 1968.

Hicks, David. *Living with Design.* London: William Morrow and Company, 1979.

Itten, Johannes. *Design and Form.* New York: Litton Educational Publishing, 1975.

Kepes, Gyorgy. *Language of Vision.* Chicago: Paul Theobald, 1969.

Lauer David. *Design Basics.* New York: Holt, Rinehart and Winston, 1979.

Lowry, Bales. *The Visual Experience.* Englewood Cliffs, N.J.: Prentice-Hall, 1975.

Maier, Manfred. *Basic Principles of Design.* New York: Van Nostrand Reinhold, 1977.

McHarg, Ian. *Design with Nature.* New York: Doubleday, 1971.

McKim, Robert H. *Thinking Visually.* Belmost, Calif.: Lifetime Learning Publications, 1980.

Ocvirk, Otto G., et al. *Art Fundamentals, Theory and Practice.* Dubuque, Iowa: Wm. C. Brown Publishers, 1975.

Pile, John F. *Design Purpose, Form, and Meaning.* New York: W.W. Norton and Company, 1979.

Pile, John F. *Interior Design.* Englewood Cliffs, N.J.: Prentice-Hall; New York: Harry N. Abrams, 1988.

Pye, David. *The Nature of Design.* New York: Van Nostrand Reinhold, 1964.

Renner, Paul. *Color, Order, and Harmony.* New York: Van Nostrand Reinhold, 1965.

Scott, Robert Gillam. *Design Fundamentals.* New York: McGraw-Hill, 1951.

Stoops, Jack, and Jerry Samuelson. *Design Dialogue.* Worcester, Mass.: Davis Publications, 1983.

Strache, Wolf. *Forms and Patterns in Nature.* New York: Pantheon, 1973.

Weismann, Donald I. *The Visual Arts as Human Experience.* Englewood Cliffs, N.J.: Prentice-Hall, 1970.

Whiton, Sherrill. *Interior Design and Decoration.* New York: Lippincott, 1976.

Wong, Wucius. *Principles of Two-Dimensional Design.* New York: Van Nostrand Reinhold, 1972.

Young, Frank. *Visual Studies: A Foundation for Artists and Designers.* Englewood Cliffs, N.J.: Prentice-Hall, 1985.

CHAPTER 4
Color

Albers, Josef. *Interaction of Color.* New Haven: Yale University Press, 1963.

Ball, Victoria Kloss. *The Art of Interior Design.* New York: John Wiley and Sons, 1982.

Birren, Faber. *Creative Color.* New York: Van Nostrand Reinhold, 1961.

Color for Interiors: Historical and Modern. New York: Whitney Library of Design, 1965.

Principles of Color. New York: Van Nostrand Reinhold, 1969. *Color and the Human Response.* New York: Van Nostrand Reinhold, 1978.

Light, Color and Environment. New York: Van Nostrand Reinhold, 1982.

Evans, Ralph M. *An Introduction to Color.* New York: John Wiley and Sons, 1959.

Fabri, Ralph. *Color: A Complete Guide for Artists.* New York: Watson, Guptill, 1967.

Friedman, Arnold, John F. Pile, and Forrest Wilson. *Interior Design: An Introduction to Architectural Interiors.* New York: American Elsevier, 1970.

Color Fundamentals. New York: McGraw-Hill, 1952.

Gerstner, Karl. *The Spirit of Colors.* Cambridge, Mass.: The MIT Press, 1981.

Graves, Maitland. *The Art of Color and Design.* New York: McGraw-Hill, 1951.

Guptill, Arthur L. *Color Manual for Artists.* New York: Van Nostrand Reinhold, 1962.

Itten, Johannes. *The Art of Color: The Subjective Experience and Objective Rationale of Color.* New York: Van Nostrand Reinhold, 1961.

The Elements of Color. New York: Van Nostrand Reinhold, 1970.

Klien, Dan. *All Color Book of Art Deco.* New York: Cresent Books, n.d.

Kueppers, Harald. *The Basic Law of Color Theory.* New York: Barron's, 1980.

Luscher, Dr. Max. *The Luscher Color Test.* New York: Simon and Schuster Pocket Books, 1969.

Munsell, A. H. *A Color Notation.* Baltimore: Munsell Color, 1981.

Ocvirk, Otto G., et al. *Art Fundamentals Theory and Practice.* Dubuque, Iowa: Wm. C. Brown Publishers, 1981.

Ostwald, Wilhelm. *The Color Primer.* New York: Van Nostrand Reinhold, 1969.

Sharpe, Deborah T. *The Psychology of Color and Design.* Chicago: Nelson-Hall, 1974.

Sidelinger, Stephen J. *Color Manual.* Englewood Cliffs, N.J.: Prentice-Hall, 1985.

Thiel, Philip. *Visual Awareness and Design.* Seattle: University of Washington Press, 1981.

Venity, Enid. *Color Observed.* New York: Van Nostrand Reinhold, 1980.

Warren, Geoffrey. *All Color Book of Art Nouveau.* London: Octopus Books, 1972.

CHAPTER 5
Lighting

American Society of Interior Designers. *"Lighting Vertical Surfaces."* ASID Industry Foundation Bulletin, New York: American Society of Interior Designers, n.d.

DeBoer, J. B., and D. Fischer. *Interior Lighting.* Antwerp: Philips Technical Library, 1981.

Egan, David M. *Concepts in Architectural Lighting.* New York: McGraw-Hill, 1983.

Erhardt, Louis. *Radiation, Light and Illumination.* Camarillo, Calif.: Camarillo Reproduction Center, 1977.

Evans, Benjamin H. *Daylight in Architecture.* New York: McGraw-Hill, 1981.

Flynn, John E., and Samuel M. Mills. *Architectural Lighting Graphics.* New York: Reinhold, 1962.

Gebert, Kenneth L. *National Electrical Code Blueprint Reading.* Alsip: American Technical Publishers, 1977.

Gilliat, Mary, and Douglas Baker. *Lighting Your Home: A Practical Guide.* New York: Pantheon, 1979.

Grosslight, Jane. *Light, Light, Light.* Tallahassee: Durwood, 1990.

Helms, Ronald N. *Illumination Engineering for Energy Efficient Luminous Environments.* Englewood Cliffs, N.J.: Prentice-Hall, 1980.

Hopkinson, R. G., and J. D. Kay. *The Lighting of Buildings.* London: Faber and Faber, 1972.

Horn, Richard. "Task Lighting: Useful Hints for Lighting Up the Written Word." *Residential Interiors* (August 1980): 54–57, 90.

Illuminating Engineering Society of North America. *Design Criteria for Lighting Interior Living Spaces*. New York: Illuminating Engineering Society of North America, 1980.

Jankowski, Wanda. *The Best of Lighting Design*. New York: PBC International, 1987.

Kaufmann, John E. *IES Lighting Handbook Reference Volume*. New York: Illuminating Engineering Society of North America, 1981.

Kilpatrick, David. *Light and Lighting*. Kent: Focal, 1984.

General Electric. *Light and Color*. Cleveland: General Electric Company Lighting Business Group, 1981.

"Lighting Your Life: A Home Lighting Guide" Chicago: American Home Lighting Institute, n.d.

Lightolier Incorporated. *Lessons in Lighting*. New Jersey: Lightolier Incorporated, 1982.

Marstellar, John. *"A Philosophy of Light."* *Interior Design* (March 1987): 78–80.

Merrill, John J., W. Kenneth Hamblin, and James M. Thorne. *Physical Science Fundamentals*. Minneapolis: Burgess Publishing Company, 1972.

Moreines, Robert, M.D. *Light Up Your Blues: A Guide to Overcoming Seasonal Depression and Fatigue*. New York: Berkley Books, 1989.

National Lighting Bureau. *Getting the Most from Your Lighting Dollar*. Washington, D.C.: National Lighting Bureau, 1982.

Nuckolls, James L. *Interior Lighting for Environmental Designers*. New York: John Wiley and Sons, 1983.

General Electric. *Office Lighting*. Cleveland: General Electric Company Lighting Business Group, 1976.

Phillips, Derek. *Lighting in Architectural Design*. London: McGraw-Hill, 1964.

Rhiner, James L. *The Language of Lighting*. Elk Grove Village: McGraw-Edison, 1983.

Rooney, William R., ed. *Practical Guide to Home Lighting*. New York: Van Nostrand Reinhold, 1980.

Shemitz, Sylvan R. *"Designing with Light."* *Interior Design* (March 1983): 284–97.

Smith, Fran Kellogg, and Fred J. Bertolone. *Bringing Interiors to Light*. New York: Whitney Library of Design, 1986.

Westinghouse Electric Corporation. *Westinghouse Lighting Handbook*. Bloomfield: Westinghouse, 1981.

Wilson, David Winfield. *The Control of Light, part 2. Interior Design* (January 1985): 292–97; *The Control of Light, part 4. Interior Design* (May 1985): 286–91.

Zimmerman, Maureen Williams. *Home Lighting*. Menlo Park, Calif.: Lane Publishing Company, 1982.

Chapter 6
Space Planning

American National Standard, *Specifications for Making Buildings and Facilities Accessible to and Usable by Physically Handicapped People*. New York: American National Standards Institute, 1980. (Available from ANSI, 1430 Broadway, New York, New York, 10018.)

Bennet, Corwin. *Spaces for People*. Englewood Cliffs, N.J.: Prentice-Hall, 1977.

Curran, June. *Drawing Home Plans*. New York: McGraw-Hill, 1979.

Davern, Jeanne M. *Places for People: Hotels, Motels, Restaurants, Bars, Clubs, Community Recreation Facilities, Camps, Parks, Plazas, and Playgrounds*. New York: McGraw-Hill, 1976.

Deasy, C. M., FAIA. *Designing Places for People: A Handbook on Human Behavior for Architects, Designers, and Facility Managers*. New York: Whitney Library of Design, 1985.

Diffrient, Niels. *Human Scale 1/2/3*. Cambridge, Mass.: MIT Press, 1974.

Faulkner, Ray, LuAnn Nissen, and Sarah Faulkner. *Inside Today's Home*. New York: Holt, Rinehart and Winston, 1986.

Friedman, Arnold, John F. Pile, and Forrest Wilson. *Interior Design: An Introduction to Architectural Interiors*. New York: American Elsevier Co., 1982.

Hall, Edward T. *Hidden Dimension*. Garden City: Doubleday, 1966.

Hanks, Kurt, Larry Belliston, and Dave Edwards. *Design Yourself!* Los Altos, Calif.: William Kaufmann, 1977.

Harkness, S., and J. Groom. *Building without Barriers for the Disabled*. New York: Whitney Library of Design, 1976.

Information Design, Inc. *Notes on Interior Design*. Los Altos, Calif.: William Kauffmann, 1981.

Johnson, Einar H., Jr., *Planning and Design Criteria to Prevent Architectural Barriers for the Aged and Physically Handicapped*. 4th rev. Salt Lake City: Utah State Building Board, n.d.

Klaber, Eugene Henry. *Housing Design*. New York: Reinhold, 1954.

Packard, Robert T., AIA. *Architectural Graphic Standards*. 7th ed. New York: John Wiley and Sons, 1981.

Panero, Julius. *Anatomy for Interior Designers*. 3d ed. New York: Whitney Library of Design, 1962.

Panero, Julius, and Martin Zelnik. *Human Dimensions and Interior Space*. New York: Whitney Library of Design, Watson-Guptill, 1979.

Pile, John F. *Open Office Planning: A Handbook for Interior Designers and Architects*. New York: John Wiley and Sons, 1978.

Pratt Institute. *An Investigation of the Small House*. New York: Pratt Institute of Architecture, n.d.

Ramsey, Charles George, and Harold Reeve Sleeper. *Architectural Graphic Standards*. 7th ed. New York: John Wiley and Sons, 1979.

Reznikoff, S. C. *Interior Graphic and Design Standards*. New York: Whitney Library of Design, 1986.

Wakita, Dr. Osamu A., and Richard M. Linde. *The Professional Practice of Architectural Working Drawings*. New York: John Wiley and Sons, 1984.

Chapter 7
Furniture Arrangement

Better Homes and Gardens New Decorating Book. Des Moines: Meredith, 1981.

Curran, June. *Profile Your Life-Style*. Los Altos, Calif.: Brooks, 1979.

Dreyfuss, Henry. *The Measure of Man: Human Factors in Design*. New York: Whitney Library of Design, 1967.

Faulkner, Sarah. *Planning a Home*. New York: Holt, Rinehart and Winston, 1979.

Gilliatt, Mary. *The Decorating Book*. New York: Pantheon, 1981.

Hall, Edward T. *The Hidden Dimension*. New York: Anchor, 1969.

McCormick, Ernest J. *Human Factors Engineering*. New York: McGraw-Hill, 1970.

Panero, Julius. *Anatomy for Interior Designers*. New York: Whitney Library of Design, 1981.

Panero, Julius, and Martin Zelnik. *Human Dimension and Interior Space*. New York: Whitney Library of Design, 1981.

Reznikoff, S. C. *Specifications for Commercial Interiors*. New York: Whitney Library of Design, 1979.

St. Marie, Satenig S. *Homes Are for People*. New York: Wiley, 1973.

Chapter 8
Furniture Selection

Anne Charlish, ed. *The History of Furniture*. London: Orbis Publishing, 1976.

Better Homes and Gardens New Decorating Book. Des Moines: Meredith, 1981.

Boger, Louise Ade. *The Complete Guide to Furniture Styles*. New York: Charles Scribner's Sons, 1969.

Chippendale, Thomas. *The Gentleman and Cabinet-Maker's Director*. New York: Dover Publications, 1966.

Diffrient, Niels, Alvin R. Tilley, and Joan C. Bardagjy. *Humanscale 1/2/3*. Cambridge, Mass.: The MIT Press, 1974.

Dreyfuss, Henry. *The Measure of Man: Human Factors in Design*. New York: Whitney Library of Design, 1967.

Fitzgerald, Oscar P. *Three Centuries of American Furniture*. Englewood Cliffs, N.J.: Prentice-Hall, Inc., 1982.

Gilliatt, Mary. *The Decorating Book*. New York: Pantheon, 1981.

Hepplewhite, George. *The Cabinet-Maker and Upholsterer's Guide.* New York: Dover Publications, 1969.

Lucie-Smith, Edward. *Furniture: A Concise History.* New York: Oxford University Press, 1979.

McCormick, Ernest J. *Human Factors Engineering.* New York: McGraw-Hill, 1970.

Meadmore, Clement. *The Modern Chair.* New York: Van Nostrand Reinhold, 1979.

Murphy, Dennis Grant. *The Materials of Interior Design.* Burbank, Calif.: Stratford House, 1978.

Panero, Julius. *Anatomy for Interior Designers.* New York: Whitney Library of Design, 1962.

Panero, Julius, and Martin Zelnik. *Human Dimension and Interior Space.* New York: Whitney Library of Design, 1981.

Pegler, Martin M. *The Dictionary of Interior Design.* New York: Fairchild Publications, 1983.

Riggs, J. Rosemary. *Materials and Components of Interior Design,* 2d ed. Englewood Cliffs, N.J.: Prentice-Hall, 1989.

Sheraton, Thomas. *The Cabinet-Maker and Upholsterer's Drawing Book.* New York: Dover Publications, 1972.

Stimpson, Miriam. *Modern Furniture Classics.* New York: Whitney Library of Design, 1987.

Whiton, Sherrill. *Interior Design and Decoration.* Philadelphia: Lippincott, 1974.

CHAPTER 9
Architectural Detail

Architectural Woodwork Institute. *Architectural Woodwork Quality Standards, Guide Specifications and Quality Certification Program.* Alexandria: Architectural Woodwork Institute, 1978.

Friedman, Arnold, John F. Pile, and Forrest Wilson. *Interior Design.* New York: American Elsevier, 1970.

Ramsey, Charles George, and Harold Reeve Sleeper. *Architectural Graphic Standards.* New York: Wiley, 1981.

Reznikoff, S. C. *Interior and Design Graphic Standards.* New York: Whitney Library of Design, 1986.

Riggs, J. Rosemary. *Materials and Components of Interior Design.* Reston, Va.: Reston, 1985.

Tate, Allen, and C. Ray Smith. *Interior Design in the 20th Century.* New York: Harper and Row, 1986.

Whiton, Sherrill. *Interior Design and Decoration.* Philadelphia: Lippincott, 1974.

CHAPTER 10
Wall, Ceiling, and Window Treatments

Blandy, Thomas, and Denis Leamoreau. *All Through the House: A Guide to Home Weatherization.* New York: McGraw-Hill, 1980.

Brady, Darlene A., and William Serban. *Stained Glass: A Guide to Information Sources.* Detroit: Gale Research Co., 1980.

Burch, Monte. *Tile, Indoors and Out.* Passaic, N.J.: Creative Homeowners Press, a division of Federal Marketing Corporation, 1981.

Conran, Sir Terence. *New House Book: The Complete Guide to Home Design.* New York: Villard Books, 1985.

Fishburn, Angela. *Curtains and Window Treatments.* New York: Van Nostrand Reinhold, 1982.

Hand, Jackson. *Walls, Floors and Ceilings.* New York: Book Division, Times Mirror Magazines, 1976.

Helsel, Marjorie B., ed. *The Interior Designer's Drapery Sketchfile.* New York: Whitney Library of Design, 1969.

Hemming, Charles. *Paint Finishes.* Secaucus, N.J.: Chartwell Books, 1985.

Innes, Jocasta. *Paint Magic.* New York: Van Nostrand Reinhold, 1981.

Jackman, Dianne R., and Mary K. Dixon. *The Guide to Textiles for Interior Designers.* Winnipeg: Peguis Publishers, Ltd., 1983.

Judson, Walter W. *Introduction to Stained Glass.* Los Angeles: Nash Publishing, 1972.

Kent, Kathryn. *The Good Housekeeping Complete Guide to Traditional American Decorating.* New York: Heart Books, 1982.

Kicklighter, Clois E. *Modern Masonry.* South Highland, Ill.: Goodheart-Willow Co., 1977.

Landsmann, Leanne. *Painting and Wallpapering.* New York: Grosset and Dunlap, 1975.

Langdon, William K. *Movable Insulation.* Emmaus, Penn.: Rodale Press, 1980.

Neal, Mary. *Custom Draperies in Interior Design.* New York: Elsevier Science Publishing Co., 1982.

Nielson, Karla J. *Window Treatments.* New York: Van Nostrand Reinhold, 1990.

Percival, Bob. *The How-to-Do-It Encyclopedia of Painting and Wallcovering.* Blue Ridge Summit, Penn.: TAB Books, 1982.

Professional Drapery Institute. *How the Professional Installs Custom Draperies and Window Coverings.* Pittsburgh: Professional Drapery Institute, 1985.

Reznikoff, S. C. *Specifications for Commercial Interiors: Professional Liabilities, Regulations, and Performance Criteria.* New York: Whitney Library of Design, 1979.

Riggs, J. Rosemary. *Materials and Components of Interior Design,* 2d ed. Englewood Cliffs, N.J.: Prentice-Hall, 1989.

Schuler, Stanley. *The Floor and Ceiling Book.* New York: M. Evans and Co., 1976.

Shurcliff, William A. *Thermal Shutters and Shades.* Andover, Mass.: Brick House Publishing Co., 1980.

Sowers, Robert. *Stained Glass: An Architectural Art.* New York: Universe Books, 1965.

Time Life Books. *Paint and Wallpaper.* New York: Time Life Books, 1976.

Time Life Books. *Walls and Ceilings.* New York: Time Life Books, 1980.

CHAPTER 11
Floor Materials and Coverings

Arizona Highways Department. *Arizona Highways,* 50, no. 7 (July 1974) Phoenix: Arizona Highways Department.

Burch, Monte. *Tile, Indoors and Out.* Passaic, N.J.: Creative Homeowners Press, a division of Federal Marketing Corporation, 1981.

Eiland, Murray L. *Oriental Rugs: A Comprehensive Guide.* Boston: New York Graphic Society, 1973.

Hand, Jackson. *Walls, Floors and Ceilings.* New York: Book Division, Times Mirror Magazines, Inc., 1976.

Herbert, Janice Summers. *Oriental Rugs: The Illustrated Buyer's Guide.* New York: Macmillan, 1978.

Jacobsen, Charles W. *Checkpoints on How to Buy Oriental Rugs.* Rutland, Vt.: 1969.

James, H. L. *Posts and Rugs: The Story of Navajo Rugs and Their Homes.* Globe, Ariz.: Southwest Parks and Monuments Association, 1976.

Jerrehian, Aram K., Jr. *Oriental Rug Primer.* New York: Facts On File, 1980.

Kahlenberg, Mary H., and Anthony Berlant. *Navajo Blanket.* New York: Praeger, 1972.

Kicklighter, Clois E. *Modern Masonry.* South Highland, Ill.: Goodheart-Willow Co., 1977.

Kopp, Joel, and Kate Kopp. *American Hooked and Sewn Rugs.* New York: Dutton, 1975.

Neff, Ivan, and Carol Maggs. *Dictionary of Oriental Rugs.* London: A.D. Donker, 1977.

Petsopoulos, Yanni. *Kilims: Flat-Woven Tapestry Rugs.* New York: Rizzoli, 1977.

Reznikoff, S. C. *Specifications for Commercial Interiors: Professional Liabilities, Regulations, and Performance Criteria.* New York: Whitney Library of Design, 1979.

Riggs, J. Rosemary. *Materials and Components of Interior Design,* 2d ed. Englewood Cliffs, N.J.: Prentice-Hall, 1989.

Salter, Walter L. *Floor and Floor Maintenance*. New York: Halstead Press, 1974.

Schuler, Stanley. *The Floor and Ceiling Book*. New York: M. Evans and Co., 1976.

Schurmann, Ulrich. *Caucasian Rugs*. London: Allen and Unwin, 1964.

Time Life Books. *Paint and Wallpaper*. New York: Time Life Books, 1976.

Time Life Books. *Walls and Ceilings*. New York: Time Life Books, 1980.

CHAPTER 12
Fabric

American Fabrics Encyclopedia of Textiles. Englewood Cliffs, N.J.: Prentice-Hall, 1980.

Belgium Linen. New York: The Belgium Linen Association, n.d.

Birren, Faber. *Color for Interiors: Historical and Modern*. New York: Hill and Wang, 1963.

Clouzot, H., and F. Morris. *Painted and Printed Fabrics*. New York: Metropolitan Museum of Art, n.d.

Corbman, Bernard P. *Textiles: Fiber to Fabric*. New York: McGraw-Hill, 1983.

Cowan, Mary L., and Martha E. Jungerman. *Introduction to Textiles*. New York: Appleton-Century-Croft Educational Division, 1969.

DuBois, M. J. *Curtains and Draperies: A Survey of the Classic Periods*. New York: Viking Press, 1967.

Facts about Man-Made Fibers. New York: Celanese Fibers Marketing Co., n.d.

Farnfield, C. A., and P. J. Alvey. *Textile Terms and Definitions*. New York: State Mutual Book and Periodical Service, 1975.

Gakyu, Shobo, ed. *Japanese Interiors*. San Francisco: Japan Publication Trading Center, 1970.

Grosicki, A. *Watson's Textiles Design and Color*. London: Newness-Butterworth's, 1975.

Hall, A. J. *The Standard Handbook of Textiles*. Woburn, Mass.: Butterworth, 1980.

Hardingham, Martin. *Illustrated Dictionary of Fabrics*. New York: MacMillan, 1978.

Hoffman, Emmanuel. *Fairchild's Dictionary of Home Furnishings*. New York: Fairchild Publications, 1975.

Hollen, Norma, and Jane Saddler. *Textiles*. New York: MacMillan, 1979.

Hussey, Christopher. *English Country Houses: Early Georgian* (1955); *English Country Houses: Mid-Georgian* (1956); *English Country House: Late Georgian* (1958). London: Country Life.

Interplay: The Story of Man-Made Fibers. Washington, D.C.: Man-Made Fibers Producers Association, 1975.

Jackman, Dianne R., and Mary K. Dixon. *The Guide to Textiles for Interior Designers*. Winnipeg: Peguis Publishers, 1983.

Joseph, Marjory L. *Essentials of Textiles*. New York: Holt, Rinehart and Winston, 1980.

Klapper, Marvin. *Fabric Almanac*. New York: Fairchild Publications, 1971.

Labarthe, J. *Elements of Textiles*. New York: MacMillan, 1975.

Larsen, Jack Lenor, and Jeanne Weeks. *Fabrics for Interiors: A Guide for Architects, Designers, and Consumers*. New York: Van Nostrand Reinhold, 1975.

"Leather, The Revealing Facts." Signal Hill, Calif.: Lackawana Leather Co., n.d.

Lewis, Ernst. *Encyclopedia of Textiles*. New York: MacMillan, 1953.

Lewis, Ethel. *The Romance of Textiles*. New York: MacMillan, 1953.

Lyle, Dorothy Siegert. *Modern Textiles*. New York: John Wiley and Sons, 1983.

Man-Made Fibers Fact Book. Washington, D.C.: Man-Made Fiber Producers Association.

Moller, Sven Erik, et al. *Danish Design*. Copenhagen: Detdanske Selskab, 1974.

Performance of Textiles. New York: John Wiley and Sons, 1977.

Reznikoff, S. C. *Specifications for Commercial Interiors: Professional Liabilities, Regulations, and Performance Criteria*. New York: Whitney Library of Design, 1979.

Textile Fibers and Their Properties. Greensboro, N.C.: American Association for Textile Technology/Burlington Industries, 1977.

The Story of Cotton. Memphis: The Cotton Council, n.d.

The Story of Wool. New York: The Wool Bureau, n.d.

Tortora, Phyllis G. *Understanding Textiles*. New York: MacMillan, 1982.

Whiton, Sherrill. *Interior Design and Decoration*. Philadelphia: Lippincott, 1974.

Wilson, K. *A History of Textiles*. Boulder, Colo.: Westview Press, 1979.

Window Treatments Through the Ages. Sturgis, Mich.: Kirsch Company, 1976.

CHAPTER 13
Art and Accessories

Allen, Phyllis Sloan, and Miriam Stimpson. *Beginnings of Interior Environment*. 7th ed. New York: MacMillan, 1992.

Better Homes and Gardens New Decorating Book. Des Moines: Meredith, 1981.

Gilliatt, Mary. *The Decorating Book*. New York: Pantheon, 1981.

Gombrich, E. H. *The Story of Art*. Oxford: Phaidon, 1979.

Hicks, David. *On Living—With Taste*. London: Leslie Frewin, 1968.

Knobler, Nathan. *The Visual Dialogue*. New York: Holt, Rinehart and Winston, 1971.

CHAPTER 14
Building Systems

Anderson, Bruce. *Passive Solar Energy*. Andover, Mass.: Brick House Publishing, 1981.

Anderson, Bruce. *Solar Energy: Fundamentals in Building Design*. New York.: McGraw-Hill, n.d.

Anderson, Bruce, and Michael Riodran. *The Solar House Book*. Harrisville, N.H.: Cheshire Books, 1979.

Butler, Lee Porter. *Ekoseá Homes: Natural Energy Conserving Design*, 2d ed. San Francisco, Calif.: Ekoseá Inc., 1980.

Feirer, John L., and Gilbert R. Hutchings. *Carpentry and Building Construction*. Peoria, Ill.: Charles A. Bennett Co., 1976.

Friedmann, Arnold, John F. Pile, and Forrest Wilson. *Interior Design: An Introduction to Architectural Interiors*. New York: American Elsevier, 1970.

Garret, Wilbur E. *Energy: Facing Up to the Problem, Getting Down to Solutions*. 2d. ed. Washington, D.C.: National Geographic Society, n.d.

Hawkweed Group. *The Passive Solar House Book*. New York: Rand McNally, 1980.

Information Design Inc. *Notes on Architecture*. Los Altos, Calif.: William Kaufmann, Inc. 1982.

Jones, Robert W., and Robert D. McFarland. *The Sunspace Primer*. New York: Van Nostrand Reinhold, n.d.

Passive Solar Design Handbooks. Springfield, Va.: United States Department of Energy, 1978.

Pile, John. "The Lighting Direction for Health." *Interiors* (August 1982): 74–75.

Professional Builder Magazine (December 1987).

Ramsey, Charles George, and Harold Reeve Sleeper. *Architectural Graphic Standards*. 7th ed. New York: John Wiley and Sons, 1981.

Strombert, R. P., and S. O. Woodall. *Passive Solar Buildings: A Compilation of Data and Results*. Springfield, Va.: National Technical Information Services, 1979.

Whiton, Sherrill. *Elements of Interior Design and Decoration*. Philadelphia: Lippincott, 1974.

Wright, David, AIA. *Natural Solar Architecture: The Passive Solar Primer*. 3d ed. New York: Van Nostrand Reinhold, 1984.

CHAPTER 15
Historic Design

Andrews, Wayne. *Architecture, Ambition and Americans*. London: Collier-Macmillan, 1974.

Calloway, Stephen, and Elisabeth Cromley. *The Elements of Style*. New York: Simon and Schuster, 1991.

Cook, Olive. *The English Country House.* London: Thames and Hudson, 1974.

Foley, Mary Mix. *The American House.* New York: Harper Colophon, 1980.

Kidder-Smith, G. E. *A Pictorial History of Architecture in America.* New York: American Heritage, 1976.

Maass, John. *The Gingerbread Age.* New York: Bramhall House, 1957.

Norwich, John Julius, ed. *Great Architecture of the World.* New York: Bonanza Books, 1982.

Peel, Lucy, Polly Powell, and Alexander Garrett. *An Introduction to 20th Century Architecture.* London: Quintet Publishing, 1989.

Pierson, William H., Jr. *American Buildings and Their Architects.* Garden City, N.J.: Doubleday, 1970.

Rifkind, Carole. *A Field Guide to American Architecture.* New York: Plume, 1980.

Taschen, Benedikt. *Frank Lloyd Wright.* Scottsdale, Ariz.: Frank Lloyd Wright Foundation, 1991.

Walking, Gillian. *Upholstery Styles: A Design Sourcebook.* New York: Van Nostrand Reinhold, 1989.

Whiffen, Marcus, and Frederick Koeper. *American Architecture 1606-1976.* Cambridge, Mass.: M.I.T. Press, 1981.

Whiton, Sherrill. *Interior Design and Decoration.* Philadelphia: Lippincott, 1974.

Yarwood, Doreen. *The Architecture of Europe.* London: Batsford, 1974.

Yarwood, Doreen. *The Architecture of Britain.* London: Batsford, 1976.

CHAPTER 16
The Profession

"Appointment, Tenure and Promotion: A Position Paper on Criteria for Evaluation of Interior Design Faculty in Post-Secondary Institutions." IDEC: The Interior Design Educators Council. January, 1985.

Boll, Carl R. *Executive Jobs Unlimited.* New York: Macmillan, 1979.

Broom, H. N., and Justin G. Longenecker. *Small Business Management.* Cincinnati: South-Western Publishing Co., 1979.

Burnstein, David, and Frank Stasiowski. *Project Management for the Design Professional: A Handbook for Architects, Engineers and Interior Designers.* New York: Whitney Library of Design, 1982.

Dalton, Gene W., and Paul H. Thompson. *Novations: Strategies for Career Management.* Glenview, Ill.: Scott, Foresman and Company, 1986.

Getz, Lowell, and Frank Stasiowski. *Financial Management for the Design Professional: A Handbook for Architects, Engineers, and Interior Designers.* New York: Whitney Library of Design, 1984.

"Interior Design as a Profession." Richmond, Va.: Interior Design Educators Council, 1982.

Knackstedt, Mary V. *Profitable Career Options for Designers.* New York: Kobro Publications, 1985.

Loebelson, Andrew. *How To Profit in Contract Design.* New York: Interior Design Books, 1983.

Morgan, Jim. *Marketing for the Small Design Firm.* New York: Whitney Library of Design, 1984.

"NCIDQ: National Council for Interior Design Qualifications Examination Study Guide." New York: National Council for Interior Design Qualification, 1983.

Siegel, Harry, and Alan M. Siegel. *A Guide to Business Principles and Practices for Interior Designers.* New York: Whitney Library of Design, 1982.

Stasiowski, Frank. *Negotiating Higher Design Fees.* New York: Whitney Library of Design, 1985.